GODS OF THE EARTH

Also by Michael Jordan

ENCYCLOPEDIA OF GODS

GODS
OF THE
EARTH

MICHAEL JORDAN

BANTAM PRESS

LONDON · NEW YORK · TORONTO · SYDNEY · AUCKLAND

TRANSWORLD PUBLISHERS LTD
61-63 Uxbridge Road, London W5 5SA

TRANSWORLD PUBLISHERS (AUSTRALIA) PTY LTD
15-23 Helles Avenue, Moorebank, NSW 2170

TRANSWORLD PUBLISHERS (NZ) LTD
3 William Pickering Drive,
Albany, Auckland

Published 1992 by Bantam Press
a division of Transworld Publishers Ltd
Copyright © Michael Jordan 1992

A catalogue record for this book is available from the British Library.

ISBN 0-593-01921-0

Typeset in 11/12½ pt Meridien by
Falcon Graphic Art Ltd.
Printed in Great Britain by
Mackays of Chatham, PLC, Chatham, Kent.

Dedicated to the memory of
ALFONS BARB

In all the forests, and the soft-strewn snow
under the trees is dibbled thick with holes
and from the boughs the snow loads shuffle down;
and, in fields sloping to the south, dark plots
of grass peep out amid surrounding snow,
and widen, and the peasant's heart is glad –
so through the world was heard a dripping noise
of all things weeping to bring Balder back,
and there fell joy upon the Gods to hear.

'Balder Dead'
Matthew Arnold

CONTENTS

ACKNOWLEDGEMENTS

In the making of a book of this dimension I have called, inevitably, upon the kindness of a great many people.

The palaeolithic chapters were read and constructively criticized by the art pre-historian Dr Anne Sieveking and by the American author John Pfeiffer, both eminent in their field.

The Mesopotamian material was similarly vetted with great generosity by Dr Jeremy Black of the Oriental Institute in Oxford. The examples of iconography were checked by the eminent Dr Dominique Collon of the British Museum in London. Dr Georgina Herrman, in charge of the publication of Nimrud ivories, was also most helpful. Dr Chris Walker, the Assistant Keeper of Western Asiatic Antiquities at the British Museum and Carole Mendleson assisted greatly with locating artifacts, as did Dr A. J. Spencer, keeper of Egyptian Antiquities. Professor John Baines and Dr Richard Parkinson made valuable corrections to my sometimes sad ignorance of Egyptology.

In the difficult area of Israelite and Christian study, the finished typescript was improved greatly, with many small but important errors corrected, through the untiring attention of Harry Mowvley of the Baptist College in Bristol, and by the theologian and author David Christie-Murray. I have, incidentally, turned to the King James Authorized Version of the Bible throughout this section. It possesses a lyricism and cadence of words which I cannot find elsewhere.

I am similarly indebted to Dr Lyndon Reynolds of the University of Bristol for his thorough examination of my chapter covering the interface between Christian and non-Christian European theology and sociology.

Thanks must also go to Dr R. J. Palmer, Curator of Western

Manuscripts at the Wellcome Institute for the History of Medicine, for his help in reading medieval material, to Birthe Fraser of the Royal Danish Embassy in London, who provided enormous help in locating Nordic material, and to Steven Adams of the National Gallery, London, for his valuable expertise and assistance in selecting some illustrations.

The following libraries offered much valuable assistance: British Library, School of African and Oriental Studies, London, University College, London, George Watson, University of Bristol, the Warburg Institute, Somerset County Records. I am indebted to Professor J. B. Trapp of the Warburg Institute for his kind permission to examine the research notes of the late Dr Alfons Barb. Many others from far-flung parts of the world have contributed both in assistance with the text and with the supply of sometimes rare photographs. I owe them all sincere thanks. I must lay stress that although academics have given generously of their time to correct my factual mistakes and errors of logic or continuity, the thesis is my responsibility alone and it should not be inferred that they have necessarily endorsed or agreed with it.

In the early days of writing, Florence Minnis, chief librarian at BBC Bristol, read part of the embryo typescript and made useful criticism of literary style and content. Latterly, Victoria Huxley has made a positive and invaluable contribution which has enabled me to sharpen and polish key sections of the text and to cure a number of inadequacies.

I owe a debt to Mandy Little who has been tireless in her enthusiasm for and constructive criticism of the innumerable drafts which evolved into the finished book. Without her help and support through the downturns the ship would probably have sunk long ago.

Finally, I must turn to Dr Alfons Barb, of the University of Vienna, Eisenstadt and lately of the Warburg Institute in London, who in the years before his death in 1976 provided me with the inspiration and the encouragement to turn an idea into reality. In my recollection he was a generous and eminent scholar with a true richness of spirit. It is to the affectionate and enduring memory of an all too brief friendship and mentor that this work has been dedicated.

Foreword

On the Mendip Hills above my
home in Somerset is a forest, a place where my dog, Joe, lets off
steam persecuting rabbits and the occasional fugitive deer. It is
not an ancient woodland sculpted at random but a thoroughly
modern forest. There are none of the gnarled limbs of oak and
ash, no massive girths of beech, but ranks of pine and spruce and
larch that march insistently to the horizons with all the clean-cut
conformity of a green, sightless army.

Early on a winter's morning a little while ago, we watched a
curious drama unfold which, for an observer from another world,
would seem illogical. It marked the beginning of the journey
which was to lead to the writing of this book. Grinding its lumpy
way through the mist and chills, a lorry came to unload a gang of
men armed with chainsaws. They began, systematically, to hew
down rank upon rank of trees; not the stout thirty-year-old vet-
erans from which doors and floorboards are made but spindly
saplings. Too small to serve any material purpose, acre by acre
was being committed to a remarkable ritual.

Our collective wallet parts with more than twenty million
pounds in the space of two or three December weeks, not
to buy gifts or turkeys, sherry or plum pudding, in celebration of the Christ child's birth but to satisfy an innate need
whose roots, nineteenth-century vogues notwithstanding, are

buried with civilizations that arose and vanished long before the Christian era.

We bring into our homes, in mid-winter, an evergreen tree. We drape it with tinsel and coloured lights, and we top it with a small winged figure, and, on precisely the sixth day of the New Year, we abandon it to its fate on the rubbish heap.

The human race answers to its gods. They have lived in the hearts and minds of human beings for a span of time so enormous that the life of modern religions becomes almost ephemeral. The gods of earth and altar have been worshipped down the ages with passionate intensity. People have believed that if they reach out far enough and strongly enough to find answers about the puzzling and often frightening world in which they live, great forces exist in nature which will meet them halfway.

Modern living, and a religion of computer chips, fast food, soap opera, and a technology that threatens to deprive us of the mystery of the universe, have all but scoured away our old faiths, our early convictions, lost piece by piece down the corridors of the centuries as we have drifted from the mystic and the magical towards a reverence for more prosaic gods. Only the thinnest of memories is left, part of it clinging on through tradition, part resting in our wonderment of things that have been, but perhaps some rooting deep in the recesses of the mind to bubble up now and again and find form in odd habits and instincts.

Today I profess no particular orthodox religious convictions, yet I sense that somewhere there is a deep truth which conventional dogma has painted over.

A persistent quiet voice tells me that it would be naïve and foolish to believe less. I grew up like most of my contemporaries with, I suppose, a neatly packaged if simplistic understanding of faith. It was handed to me by my mother, my father, my school, my parish church: the accumulated wisdom of all the generations of Christianity and its traditions. Yet in many ways what I was taught is an enduring deception in an otherwise remarkably objective world, a dedicated mythology to which we willingly subscribe, and round which orthodoxy rallies with great vigour and voice.

My childhood was spent in the confident innocence that I had been born under the star of the only respectable and accountable faith, and one which would in the fullness of time grant me my salvation. I was baptized into the Church of England, and that, strengthened in my adolescence by the ritual of confirmation, was enough to guarantee *Lux Eterna* so long as I played my cards reasonably straight.

I was taught to believe that everything to do with Christianity, every little ritual, every story, owed itself exclusively if often obscurely to Christian history and purpose. Paganism was something else. It was promoted to my young mind as a disparate hotchpotch of cults whose antique members had worshipped strange sounding gods and practised even stranger rituals. Paganism was unenlightened, profane, violent, self-gratifying. It was the anathema. It was bad!

The strangely polarized distinctions still hold sway today. We are bound by our own limits of vision.

For the majority of us who extend a cursory 'nod to God' when we marry, give birth, and die, the thought that we may, on occasion, be driven by more obtuse spirits than those described by orthodox faith is a hard pill to swallow. It smacks of 'loony cults' and witchcraft. To suggest that certain compulsions deep within us, and in fact much of our Christian dogma, may stem from a belief spawned before history began is to earn a condescending smile. Yet we follow some strange impulses do we not?

Most of us need look no further than when we touch wood for luck. There are many other instances. The Pope kisses the earth beneath his feet – hard to explain in Christian terms. We dance round the maypole to celebrate the spring, but we fear to bring the blossoms of the may into our homes. Our ancestry is our 'family tree', but Christianity has systematically purged sacred trees from our memories. We still place little straw figures of corn dollies in our houses. Our churches contain memorials to an ancient faith whose meaning we no longer understand.

The dogma with which I grew up is, in certain respects, short on logic. This is particularly true when it comes to the alleged affinities of the Christian God, or rather lack of them, to the other deities and faiths of the ancient world.

The gods who have sustained mankind for thirty thousand years and more deserve their hearing. This book covers a canvas which, at times, may seem dauntingly broad, and it is perhaps worth a few lines at the outset to explain that which *Gods of the Earth* is and is not.

At the beginning of his monumental work on paganism, *The Golden Bough*, the Victorian anthropologist, Sir James Frazer commented: 'There is probably no subject in the world about which opinions differ so much as the nature of religion, and to frame a definition of it which would satisfy everyone must obviously be impossible. All that a writer can do is, first, to say clearly what he means by religion, and afterwards to employ the word consistently in that sense throughout the work.'

For Frazer religion possessed two elements. It was a theoretical belief in powers higher than mankind, and it was a practical attempt to propitiate or please them. His is the definition which still holds good for the *Oxford English Dictionary*: 'particular system of faith and worship; human recognition of superhuman controlling power and especially of a personal God or gods entitled to obedience and worship.' For me the definition is slightly altered. I have tried to draw a distinction between faith and its formal summary, creed, which are the theoretical aspects, and religion which I have taken as the implementation of creed by a society so as to achieve a purpose, be it propitiation, communion, or the unleashing of magical or, according to one's view, divine powers.

Implicit in religion is an understanding, running contrary to the laws of science, that it is possible to induce the supernatural powers which control our destiny and that of the natural world around us to alter events from those which would take place naturally. The logic which proceeds is that there exists, governing the cosmos, a conscious intelligence. Again this runs headlong into confrontation with science which rejects any such notion of consciousness.

Let me dispense with the negatives. This is no history of religion, nor an investigative discourse on paganism. *Gods of the Earth* is, if anything, a search to identify and rationalize the anthropology of faith across a substantial part of the civilized world. In its quest it never strays far from a particular thread, arguably the most universal and tenacious strand of creed, that of the mother goddess and her liaison with the sacred king. It is a strand which has affected and which continues to affect each and every one of us far more intimately than we might willingly care to admit.

I should also qualify use of the term 'God'. In places the word will define a specifically masculine character. Elsewhere, however, as in this foreword, the term 'God' is applied in a generic sense which should not be taken necessarily to announce a male deity. To a Christian theologian, God is beyond sexuality. In many non-Christian contexts, the supreme spiritual power is also perceived as a fusion of male and female principles and since this work intends, in part, to reconcile the gulf between pagan and Christian thought, it is not always appropriate to distinguish gods and goddesses.

Though the thread traces a loose chronology it cannot, of necessity, offer wholly a 'source to sink' journey. There are too many complex currents involved. It would also be tempting to draw in detailed probing of other elements of religious cult (sun worship to name one) but the canvas becomes too large and too unwieldy. These elements intrude from time to time, but only as peripheral 'actors' at the edge of the stage.

I have also been asked why, for example, North American and Oriental cultures have not been involved, nor some of the more dramatic revelations from Africa and Australia. Once again there is a danger of overplaying the story, and in any case a largely self-fuelling catchment area of religious evolution, that which is generally referred to as the 'Indo-European peoples' (excluding the Indian sub-continent), takes shape which is a law unto itself. I have set out to do that which the academic and theological worlds have conventionally avoided: to collate and compare, and in places to research the vital links between one phenomenon and another.

In recent decades the broad view has fallen from grace amongst academic circles, yet it is wholly inadequate to perceive cultural expressions, religious or secular, in short-term isolation. They are rarely the product of a single mind and time, rather they are constantly evolving things handed from one generation to the next, from vanquished to conqueror, to mould and adapt and to pass cherished or neglected to their successors. They are slow to form and even through holocaust are reluctant to die. It is, above all, the links which make the *Gods of the Earth* a compelling story.

The material is sifted from field notes, dissertations, museum relics and interviews. There has been a frustration in gathering evidence since, at any time, certain areas of history and pre-history are considered *passé* and valuable evidence may lie stagnating because its researcher leaves it unpublished in favour of work that is more in vogue. There also comes the daunting realization that too many academics have conflicting views, not only over reasons but about actual historical evidence.

Some illustrious scholars have travelled the journey though they are surprisingly few in number. At the turn of the century, James Frazer compiled his discourse and study of magic and religion, but he did so without the benefit of modern archaeology. The late Joseph Campbell produced a masterly study, *The Masks of God*, but in keeping with his loyalties as a Professor of Literature he relied, I believe, too much on mythological store at the expense of other arguably stronger evidence. The only other surviving

authority is the venerated and much respected commentator on
comparative religion in the United States, Mircea Eliade. Theirs
have often been global and more generalized investigations of
pagan beliefs.

This is a journey in time, to find the gods of the earth and
the natural world, how they came to be, and why the human
heart was kindled with so great a need of them. It is not a hunt
for proof of myths or legends but a quest after the truth about
some of the more closely guarded and, at the same time, strongest
compulsions in the history of the human race. The gods of earth
and sky took form from simple and inauspicious beginnings. The
need for them arose in the needs of every day, of living and dying.
These were needs shared by ordinary people whose hopes and
dreams were not so very different from our own.

The journey follows a trail of ideas and the links which
connect them, but it is without clear beginnings. We cannot
establish when the mind first grappled with the understanding
of an existence or force in the natural world beyond that limited
by earthly dimensions. Its beginning lies within a great time span
clouded by the absence of historical record, and in which very
little happened by way of human change or progress.

The Cross of Biblical morality to which Darwin and fellow
anthropologis..s were 'nailed' also straitjacketed the archaeological profession, and one certain result must have been that, in
the Victorian heyday of 'digging for history', countless evidence
of early culture in the Holy Land was scattered and lost in the
search for biblically accountable spoils. Exploration of the distant
past was governed by a general distrust that we descended from
any less exalted beginnings than those in the Garden of Eden. The
philosophy is neatly encapsulated by the words of the anonymous
but well-cited Victorian lady who commented: 'Let us hope that
it is not true . . . but if it is, let us pray that it will not become
generally known.'

In the last fifty years or so we have largely rid ourselves of such
well-intentioned bigotry, and new exciting arenas of exploration
and reasoning about the faiths of our earliest ancestors have
opened up. Claim and counter-claim are equally vigorous but
based less on dogma than rationale.

The journey is one which, on its way, unashamedly takes on
board a degree of conjecture. Academic rules tend to deny supposition and reject analogy but beliefs, of whichever complexion,
are in essence subjective things, and to seek proof positive of what
went on inside a person's head a thousand or ten thousand years

ago is whistling for the moon. The art is surely to take courage in exploring possibilities but to avoid drawing firm conclusions from supposition, and to accept that analogy can sometimes point out a direction only to lead one to a 'dead end'.

What emerges, with very little editorial hand from me, is a remarkable and striking, sometimes greatly moving canvas. Far from revealing a patchwork of isolated and disparate fragments, it unfolds into a grand design with a singularity of purpose and method that is often as baffling as it is provocative. That which is defined as paganism reveals no opposite polarity to orthodox religion but, within the brush strokes, the two are seen linked in inescapable embrace. The canvas is measured in both space and time. It is framed by the waters of the Atlantic Ocean, the Arctic, the Ural and Taurus Mountains and the Sahara Desert. Its base pigment is sixty thousand years old. Its freshest coat is being painted today. At the end it is still an unfinished work. There are blank spaces and parts where the brushwork is confused and muddy, but enough of the canvas is filled to reveal a formidable truth. With some astonishing parallels, whether they have lived twenty thousand years ago in the bitter, uncompromising Europe of a receding Ice Age, or five thousand years ago on the arid deserts of Mesopotamia, or a scant millennium gone on the edge of a dark and brooding northern forest, people have found faith in the same gods. They have striven for the same clouds and bowed before the same altars.

This is their story.

1

The Hunters

An awe of the huge and some-
times terrible forces of nature still finds its place in the most
worldly of souls. A mighty storm, a volcanic catharsis, a blistering relentless sun, can bring primal dismay tumbling to the fore.
We become conscious of the anger of heaven. Yet when and
where did the desire to seek out the powers which govern these
wayward immensities, crystallize in the human breast? How did
we find our gods?

The age of the great pagan cults which focused so much of their
attention on the living world seems long ago, but the beginnings
of faith in the supernatural are owed to a time infinitely more
ancient. The founding fathers who laid the blueprint for sacred
groves and Christmas trees, totems and corn dollies, the family
tree and the urge to touch wood, visions of resurrection and a
spirit world, were men whose life stakes were invested, not in
the harnessing of the soil but in wild animals. The story opens
with the prehistoric hunters of the Ice Age and beyond.

There is more in the point of departure, however, than a
creative desire to begin at the beginning. The *raison d'être* of the
ancient gods of nature is not hard to find but, once established,
the ways in which early people cried out to them, and strove to
quell their whims and calm their anger, were often obscured.
The priests of those arcane spirits hid their tracks well, and if
there is a key to understanding the founding principles of belief

amongst civilizations which left detailed records of the sale of a sack of grain yet next to nothing of their religious life, it lies not with them but with the cultural roots from which they stemmed.

The span of time during which our thoughts, beliefs and day-to-day affairs are accountable to history roughly coincides with the period in which we have lived a settled existence, and it reaches back only some five or six thousand years. But by that comparatively late date, the ground rules of creed had been drawn up. People had found an acceptable answer as to how Chaos was turned into an orderly Universe. They understood how the creator spirits once harnessed the supernatural forces and used them to affect the world for good and for ill. The greatest obstacle to identifying first stirrings of the ancient gods is that these lie beyond history in the wilderness of knowledge from whence there are no words to define them.

In 1960,[1] a remarkable discovery stretched the evidence for some kind of religion in a quantum leap of twenty-six thousand years backwards from that which had been previously accepted as the 'base line'. At Shanidar, in the highlands of northern Iraq, a cave was found to contain eight human skeletons resting in what seemed to be a burial ground. At a level twenty feet below the present-day floor, in a niche of stones, lay the remains of a man. Close by him, but interred earlier, lay two women and a small child. Had this tomb been discovered fifty years before, its occupants would have been labelled as deformed 'modern' freaks, yet radio-carbon dating confirmed that they were at least sixty thousand years old. They were Neanderthals, people who had hitherto been regarded by some authorities as: 'sub-human, shuffling, ape-like creatures of massive strength but only rudimentary psychic nature and therefore quite incapable of ceremonial care for their dead and dying.'

As in almost all caves, the floor of Shanidar was scattered with an amount of fossil pollen which had drifted in on air currents. In samples of dust removed from around and beneath the man, however, lay a fascinating and quite unexpected story. When the dust was searched microscopically, not only were there unusually large numbers of pollen grains from at least eight flowering plants but some were also in clumps. The only way this could have occurred was if flowers were brought and placed at the grave.

The story of a day in late spring or early summer sixty millennia ago begins to unfold. A young man of some importance was laid to rest amidst all the anguish of bereavement and the added fear of an almost certain death for those who had been dependent on him for food and warmth. He had been accorded special rites. He was laid on a bed of woody horsetails and around him were strewn flowers – grape hyacinths, bright yellow ragworts and groundsels, white yarrow, cornflowers, hollyhock and St Barnaby's thistle. Remarkably, the flowers all possess medicinal properties. A modern herbal *Materia Medica* will confirm that ragworts and groundsels are specified for healing of infected or inflamed wounds and that hollyhock is of value in treating fever.

Was the man the victim of ambush, or did fate decree that he himself became the prey of the hunted? Whatever brought his end, the people who buried him believed, if the evidence of the grave is to be accepted, that he would travel to some kind of afterlife. They laid him on his side, legs drawn up and head pillowed on hands, as if in sleep. Not only was he buried surrounded by flowers, there are also traces of pieces of meat with possibly weapons and other bits of paraphernalia placed beside him.

Neanderthals had thus, contrary to Victorian prejudice and Hollywood fantasy, the sensitivity and the mental agility to believe in a spiritual dimension to their lives. The death of the earthbound body was not a finality, only an illusion covering the reality of a journey from which lines of communication were still open.

The evidence of such early spirituality is still scant. The flower burial is a unique discovery, although many similar graves of Neanderthals have been found to contain pieces of animal carcasses, and some have included new, unused, weapons. No art or archaeological evidence has been unearthed which might shed light on what went on at the graveside of Shanidar IV or any of his contemporaries, and one wishes we had a better idea of how Neanderthals and their early successors viewed the world beyond their own. The implication in this hint of infant faith, however, is enormous. The realization of a spiritual dimension to life must have promoted a deep effect on thinking. An unseen but discernible world existed in tandem with that of sight, smell, touch and hearing. That inner knowledge would have opened the way to all kinds of abstract thoughts and images. No longer would things automatically have to be that which they seemed through the physical senses.

The life of people and the natural world around them must have begun to take on a whole new meaning, allowing ideas to germinate which went beyond a practical role for the animal

and plant kingdoms, into the realms of the spiritual and esoteric. It is arguable, in terms of evolution, that once the idea had
been grasped of passage after death to another world there was
a gathering of momentum. The human race was no longer driven
exclusively by a process of natural selection but, increasingly, by a
strength of will from within. The momentum was also increased,
as the last Ice Age reached its numbing peak, by the arrival on
stage of a new breed, Cro Magnon Man.

Archaeology relies for opening the doors into time on a
less clearly defined and more ambiguous fabric than the written
word. Its language of day-to-day secular life comes in the shape
of ancient earthworks, the remnants of hearths and middens,
and in utilitarian objects like tools, utensils and weapons. In the
search for faith Ice-Age burial grounds can offer only the merest
impression. At Břno in Moravia, a man was buried surrounded
by precious objects suggesting some kind of death ceremony. At
the Czechoslovakian site of Dolní Věstonice an old lady, her fragile
body laid to rest beneath great mammoth bones, cradled an arctic
fox in her hands. One of the fleetest of animals, it was perhaps
sacrificed to speed her on a journey.

The real mother tongue of primitive faith is art. It is the
more subjective creations of hand and eye which stand to give
colour and substance to the beliefs of such distant eras. Human
consciousness has been translated into paintings and drawings,
carvings and sculptures, for at least thirty millennia, perhaps
much more, and whilst there is no incontrovertible proof that art
and religion were linked in the prehistoric world, the combination
of archaeological clues and known historical evidence make it
almost inconceivable that they were not. One of the consummate
strengths of art is that it creates a permanent image of the object
of attention, a kind of immortality in a changing and ephemeral
world, and it is a fair guess that somewhere amongst the work of
the sculptors and painters, engravers and scratchers of the Ice Age,
are tangible demonstrations of some of the human spirit's earliest
'Articles of Faith'. To sort and understand these articles, however,
is to work in an academic minefield. Separating humour from
profanity, secular from non-secular, is akin to solving the pattern
of coloured dots on a paper. But here the puzzle continues in
not knowing how the brain of a primitive artist reasoned over
what his eye registered.

At the known outset, art focused on the natural world and
whilst it indulged in some subtle copying of twigs and leaves
it reflected, in the main, a passionate interest in animals. The

hunters' kingdom was a brutal wilderness without frontiers, where the plough was as unknown as a field of grain, and where the core of existence lay with the reindeer and mammoth, bison and horse. Paradoxically, survival may more often than not have lain with the gathering of leaves, seeds, nuts and berries. But if 'modern' hunting tribes are any indication, animals were not only the preferred choice, they were also imbued with status and therefore their more esoteric importance swelled out of proportion to their utilitarian value.

One of the most strident messages to come from the Ice-Age artist lies in contrasts. In his awareness of the animals living beside him, and in the fidelity with which he copied them, the work of ancient man stands in brutal conflict with the way he often copied himself. The first recognizable work of art that we have managed to trace is from a much younger era than the burial ground of Shanidar but still it is not less than thirty-four thousand years old. A sculptor took a small piece of bone and a flint scraper and, with painstaking finesse and delicacy, worked it into a model, barely 5 centimetres long, of a mammoth. The fragment, found only a few years ago at Württemburg in southern Germany, pre-dates by some four thousand years the Vogelherd collection of animal figures discovered at the ancient site of a reindeer-hunting tribe in Austria. This collection, carved exquisitely from ivory, includes sculptures of a bear, a mammoth, a lion and a horse.[2] The horse, almost heart-rendingly beautiful, gallops as urgently and as full of life as it did on the icy tundra all those millennia past. It stands as one of the supreme masterpieces of human art.

Animals were copied in contexts that went beyond viewing them solely as a source of meat. Some, like lions and bears, were rarely hunted although there are hints among the debris of sites in Yugoslavia that the hunters may have killed bears. Whether this was primarily for food and fur is unknown. Elsewhere in Europe, bears' teeth were collected for some mysterious purpose. Generally one gains the impression of a deep and spiritual interest in animals developing over a long period of time.

The Württemburg and Vogelherd figures are amongst the most ancient that we have stumbled upon, but there is a mark of experience in their execution which says that they were not the first of their kind. It is impossible to look at them and to believe that they mark the beginnings of art, or the first tangible manifestation of religion. They must therefore be a link in the chain of an evolving process that stretches back to unknown ages. Yet is there any evidence that such models in fact possessed religious strength?

Close scrutiny of the Vogelherd horse has revealed some curiosities. Like the other models, the surface of the ivory is very smooth not, it seems, from deliberate buffing but from handling over a long period of time. The surface is marred though, just behind the left shoulder. Microscopic examination has revealed that it is not an incidental scratch but a definite angled cut, significantly at a point where a *coup de grâce* could be administered in life. Was this a ritual stroke, a cut by which the model horse was 'put to death' in some long-forgotten ceremony? Other models offer similar hints but we can only speculate and, like its fellows, the Vogelherd horse must remain a beautiful enigma.

Primitive art teems with human figures to which the approach was shockingly different. These images are striking not in their realism but in distortion: bodies are reduced to sticks or distended to bloated spheres, heads shrink and disappear, faces become meaningless contours, legs fuse. Other strange aberrations sometimes are so severe that one is unsure whether one is in fact looking at a human form.

Among the contemporaries of the Vogelherd animals, emerges a man's head and torso from Břno and, perhaps the most famed of all the earliest art works, the 'Venus' of Willendorf. Both are grotesque, barely recognizable caricatures. Yet neither she, nor the Břno Man, nor a headless and legless torso from Ostrava Petřkovice, nor some strange figures with crooked faces from Dolní Věstonice, nor any of the other shadowily human forms from that distant time are crudely formed. There is, in many respects, as much sophistication about the caricaturing as in the fine animal carvings; a strong sense exists that the artist knew exactly his intent. Through some of their creations, the artists were journeying beyond mere objective replication and were proposing a second often highly subjective view of their world. Yet why should animals have been modelled in contours of familiarity whilst human figures were not?

There is no simple answer. One first has to accept a basic premiss that the gulf between our way of thinking and that of Ice-Age people is an enormous one. Their lives and outlooks were far removed from ours in a world cosseted from the rigours of environment by technology. Should, however, a twentieth-century mind retreat into the isolation of a frozen tundra where it is alone with the elements, rocks and sky, plants and animals, its perceptions begin to change. The natural world

seems, through the vulnerable and now timorous human eye, to
be part of a common frame — strong, self-sufficient, and at one
with itself. Spiritual strength is easily perceived in the immov-
ability of a mountain, a brilliant shaft of light, a blizzard 'white
out'. It manifests itself in the indomitable resilience of a bear or
an elk. These things become the physical extremities of a greater
unseen potency, of which the human intruder is not a part, but
an outside observer bound by the often claustrophobic prison of
his own physical and mental limitations. Yet as the assimilation of
this pervading spirituality such tangible and visible signs become,
on their own, inadequate because the human intellect demands
perversely that the cryptic essence of its godhead bears human
likeness. Logic fails and the mind simultaneously recoils from
confronting that inner likeness. The ultimate revelation is too
terrible, too immense. Perhaps an inner barrier lies also in that
it *is* the ultimate, and that to stand in its presence dissolves the
final enigma. To be without mystery is for the human psyche to
be without fear, and without hope. The human distortions in art
were created surely not as a joke but in fear. They were the
nearest that mankind was prepared to venture in putting form
on the hidden quintessence. But what was the purpose? How
was the art applied to belief?

A limitation to any understanding of the small models is
that there is no setting in which to place them. The city of
Bordeaux lies to the south of the confluence of two great rivers,
the Dordogne and the Garonne which flow as the Gironde to the
Atlantic Ocean. The bedrock through which they carve their passage is limestone. Water has punched, bored and wriggled its way
through this soft porous womb for millions of years, mining deep
beneath the earth, dissolving-out vast subterranean halls, only to
abandon its creations to time and seek out some other capricious
way to the sea. As the water turned elsewhere though, the huge
and awesome caverns it left behind did not remain empty. They
played host to ancient man. Their walls served as the canvas that
was to record the greatest and most astounding outpouring of art
along the misty edge of pre-history. They are the world's earliest
known art galleries, in which the hunters of the Aurignacian and
Magdalenian periods left an awesome legacy of their reverence
for the natural world.

The Great Hall of Lascaux,[3] discovered on 12 September
1940 by four boys and a fox-terrier dog, has been compared
to standing inside a giant walnut shell. Description fails because
the perspectives seem to deny any normal laws of physics and

geometry. This huge cauldron has defied all attempts to depict it in any meaningful way with a camera, and no artist's impression has ever fully captured its awesome lines.

As the eyes lift, fantasy begins. Looming crazily and majestically across the vault, their great horned heads bending down to the watcher below, stand five enormous bulls, the ancient and long extinct aurochs. They are only the first of dozens of frescoes bewitching the eye at every turn. Cattle stride into the gloom, and deer swim with their heads lifted from a glimmering pallid lake of limestone, all streaming towards the narrow split in the rock face that connects with the rest of Lascaux and its extraordinary secrets. There is a sense of constant, volatile movement among the images, their position and perspective altering magically with line of sight and changing illumination.

They stand motionless one moment, run madly the next. By flickering torchlight, the effect is startling. Some seem to be isolated and independent animal portraits, some overlap each other, and still more appear to be grouped in compositions. The walls are filled with images at one place yet quite bare a few metres away, and the watcher is left confused as to whether these empty canvases were once covered or forever shunned. The quality of limestone varies and, in some places, atmospheric conditions have eroded the paintings away. One of the great bulls is irrevocably spoiled. But there is also a sense that some of the surfaces have been avoided deliberately. At one place a sheen of calcite has seeped over the paintings to glaze them, whilst in others the pigment has been absorbed into the calcite and thus kept its brilliance. These infinitely slow processes in themselves attest to tremendous antiquity and to at least some original gaps in the canvases.

The deep heart of Lascaux is a black abyss, an 8-metre shaft. When it was discovered a large number of crude, burnt-out lamps, which the artist must have used to light his work, were found at the bottom. There were also remains of hemp strands which had formed the rope for his descent. Near to the base he had painted a remarkable scene – a tragedy, a prehistoric drama of death. A bison in its last moments stands, belly ripped open and entrails spilling to the ground. Into its body is thrust a long lance. Before it lies a man with the head of a bird, a 'Lowry' man of matchstick lines, arms flung wide. His penis is erect which, medically, might be attributable to a broken back, but may, equally, have more profound significance. Beside him stands a long pole topped by an object which looks, at first glance, like a bird. The apparatus is probably a spear-thrower. A number of examples have been discovered from the period, and the carving represented crudely in the painting is perhaps not a bird but an ibex. To the bottom left a woolly rhinoceros ambles away nonchalantly.

Lascaux is the jewel in the crown of all the Ice-Age cavern galleries in south-west Europe and the epitomy of these remarkable echoes from our distant past. The cavern paintings both stun the senses and flood the imagination. They must be full of messages which are lost to us yet which were readable at a glance by the artists and their contemporaries. There is nothing casual about them, in the sense that they are whimsical graffiti. They are deliberate, carefully planned and structured, and in many there is obvious composition. There is also evidence that many were drawn and redrawn over long periods. They were executed, not as masterpieces to be left in virginal sanctity, but as the working tools of people who felt a constant desire to paint.

Much of the controversy which has raged about the prehistoric galleries centres on the role of these extraordinary places. What did they mean to the people who created them? Were they refuges, schools, libraries, art galleries? Or were they mankind's earliest cathedrals? Step into one of these antediluvian halls and answers touch you with an almost heart-stopping blow. There is an immensity of nature. Time and inexorable force have sculpted the elemental earth into a myriad of features that are beyond the wit of man. Phantasmal beasts loom from every angle and monstrous organ pipes soar into infinite space. They defy the norms of architecture, and beneath them the human spirit is dwarfed and yet uplifted. They are places of the gods.

The logic may have been complex. From very ancient times the body of the earth has fulfilled two bafflingly different roles. It is, on the one hand, the realm of demons. On the other, it is the stable unchanging element of nature, the patient eternal womb. The atmosphere in a cavern surrounded by solid rock is uniquely placid, cocooned from the elements. It may, in part, have been that sense which lured men to such surroundings.

It would seem that certain principles were beginning to crystallize within the cradle of palaeolithic endeavour which were unconcerned with the mundane practicalities of living, and yet which may have had everything to do with the mystery of life. A poor argument is voiced that modern religion is in no way to be equated with ancient or primitive religion. It is claimed that the latter should better be described as 'sympathetic magic', a performance purely dictated by certain prescribed formulae. But it would be a brave individual who denied the prehistoric hunters a rationalized faith, and it is difficult to avoid the conclusion that they may have implemented and formalized a kind of religion in ways not far removed from those which we employ today. The principles which the evidence suggests they may have followed possess a familiar ring in the modern Church.

One demand is to hypostatize the spirit world into some kind of permanent form and substance. It is a need as true today as it was thirty thousand years ago. The Christian world perceives icons and other religious objects as a source of spiritual imma-nence, and there is reason to believe that ancient man created his sculptures and his great cavern canvases for much the same purpose. But for many cultures there have been, and still are, reservations about re-creating the human form, and these worries extend beyond the plain fear of generating numinous likenesses.

Modern primitives adopt a revealing response to certain kinds of art. Point a camera and, at the press of a button, create a like-ness of a 'Stone-Age' tribesman, and he may react very strongly. What has taken place is a dangerous magic. It has created his replica, but more importantly it has removed part of his spirit and placed it within an artefact. To the people of the Ice Age art may, under certain circumstances, have been a force no less powerful and terrifying than glimpses of eternal damnation. Great contrasts in the style of the art reinforce the message.

In secular surroundings the artists could be carefree. Art was drawn from life. Animals are vigorous and healthy and artists revelled in their delight of human figures. One of the finest examples of this art is at the small Magdelaine cave, quite different from the deep caverns, at Penne in the Tarn region of the Pyrenees. Two reclining nudes[4] repose in a style that would grace a modern gallery. The artists perhaps pandered to popular demand and preferred women as their models. This secular art can also be created three-dimensionally or in deep relief. The works were placed where people lived and no stigma, no hidden meaning or purpose, attaches to them. They are delightful with what seems an innocence of deeper meaning.

How different the art of the deep caverns! Almost all is two-dimensional. Animals are drawn with the same finesse of line and sensuality of movement evident in the Vogelherd beasts, but emotion pervades these works. The degree of unrest varies from cavern to cavern. One explorer described the animals of Lascaux to be grandiose and violent; at Font de Gaume, more at peace, gentle. Mammoth, bison and woolly rhinoceros stand still and implacable, deer run fleetingly, cattle stride.

There seems to be recognition in some galleries of an hierarchical order, and the characters often appear involved in some kind of interplay. Key animals are placed beside, and deliberately associated with, each other. Bison and horses are perhaps most strongly linked and are often announced separately from stags, ibex, predatory bears, lions and other lesser beasts. Often the animals appear as part of the drama of the hunt, but again there is no obvious preference for animals that were hunted, and lion and bear are as well represented as deer. Animals are wounded, bodies pierced, guts spilled, and yet, somehow, they lack distress. They are at peace in death.

Human figures in the caverns carry none of the realism seen in the open-air galleries. The fearful aversions are there. Very few appear in the painted caverns and none are women. The drawings are sometimes so crude that they are barely recognizable as human beings.

There are sound reasons both for the choice of two-dimensional working, and the abstraction of human figures in a ritual context. Art comes perilously close to the creation of life itself. Primitive people adopt a logic that three-dimensional art comes much closer to reality than two-dimensional painting or drawing, therefore the one is potentially more dangerous than the other. It may only need a certain magic to complete the animation and to breathe life into the image. It is a time-honoured, innate dread that is overcome only in sophisticated societies, and even then it is but thinly veiled. Such old tales as that of Don Juan and his stone guest still hold their morbid compulsion.

The logic continues, arguing that the more abstract and schematized the figure, the less realism and the less danger. The insistence on two-dimensional imagery in the caverns can only suggest that they were places where sufficient magic was generated to make realism a perilous game. The abstraction and distortion of human figures suggests that they reflect perhaps something more than mortal beings.

The purpose of the paintings was surely to gather unseen forces, some copied as they were perceived in the real world, others created from within, but brought together in places where men could commune with them more readily than in fleeting contacts on a frozen tundra. The paintings in the caverns must, one can believe, have taken up and carried the spiritual aura of the life they portrayed.

Religion also makes a timeless demand for esoterism at the core of worship. The desire seems to have persisted to 'code' the messages. The walls of some caverns are covered with cryptic signs which the artists used regularly. We call them vulviforms, tectiforms and the like, but only for want of a better understanding. Cavern art also teems with the imprints of hands. The palm was placed against a rock surface and paint was blown over it to create a 'negative'. Were these images thought to be the hands of unseen spirits? If only we knew. Were we able to unlock the code we might learn a great deal. An immediate message from the caverns is that the artists went to great lengths to hide their work from the eyes of the world at large. An aura of occultism, fed by great physical isolation from the outside world, wreathes the paintings constantly. It is very clear that no parts of the painted caverns were places of daily life. No signs of everyday living remain even at the entrances, and many things suggest that they were surrounded with some kind of taboo.

There is also evidence that the audiences may have been the subject of selectivity. A great constancy emerges in the placing of cavern art. An Ice-Age gallery was, as it is still, not for the faint-hearted. At La Mouthe[5] traces of engravings begin only after 90 metres of tunnel. At Les Combarelles[6] the viewer has to negotiate a similar length of tortuous corridor, 2 metres across at its widest, before meeting its secrets. Font-de-Gaume[7] is guarded by a concealed fissure 18 metres above the floor of the Beune valley. Faded and fragmentary figures stand to greet the viewer, in stygian dark, at the end of a long twisting corridor.

Even away from the large cavern systems such art was very private. Paintings have been found on the ceilings of tunnels only a few metres long, the access to which has been revealed as a small fissure in the ground. Wriggling along with a rock roof a hand span away from the nose one is suddenly confronted by a group of deer staring down imperturbably from above a blind cul-de-sac.

The labyrinthine wanderings are daunting enough for the modern explorer with his thermal suit, nylon ropes and electric lights. It takes imagination to appreciate what they must have meant to the prehistoric artist. Yet there is some hint that, on occasions, natural obstacles were deliberately compounded. Massive stalagmites seem to have been dragged into otherwise easier passageways. The general perversity was not haphazard. In a distinct number of caverns, compositions which arguably reflect the deepest meaning may be at the extent of the most tortuous passageways, or in the more confined spaces.

One guesses that the logic took into account the element of fear. Fear would have shadowed the people who made the pictures, and they must have recognized that fear would influence those who came to view them. The apprehension generated by such places is timeless and universal. It is a dread of becoming lost in total darkness, of drowning in a sudden rush of water, of becoming wedged in a bone-squeezing *chatière*. It is a fear of silence where the only noises are the dripping of water and sometimes the muffled roar of an unseen torrent. These things sharpen the imagination. The unseen, the otherwise unthinkable, stands very close when the world contracts to a tiny pool of flickering light. Beyond its orbit an unfamiliar world plays its charades upon the mind.

Fear may have been generated in the mind of the Ice-Age hunters on grounds no less absurd than our terrors might have seemed to them. The fundamental reasons for the dread were probably no different then as now, only the machinery has changed. Fear has always been, and continues to be, the henchman of religion. Christian fears have been of purgatory, of the day of judgement, and of the fires of hell. It is fear which draws the flock to maintain the letter of the faith.

Esoteric cult and ritual, reliant to a great extent on fear, were the 'power house' of the earliest hierarchy, the weapon by which a few held sway over the rest. In the open air, such powers would at once evaporate in the presence of familiarity.

The desire for secrecy would, conversely, generate its own natural selection, requiring those who aspired to create the art to be of high intelligence and strong character. These attributes they would need, to overcome the natural instincts and mental hurdles which would deter others from entering such places. The same obstacles must have faced those who came after as witnesses, and must have demanded the same strengths. Space in the caverns was thus apparently classified in degrees of élitism. It was a selectivity though, which was not necessarily based on age and experience, and the cavern people might almost have taken perverse delight in confounding our twentieth-century suppositions.

Amongst the most *sportif* caverns, as the French describe their arduous systems, is Tuc d'Audoubert.[8] The Begouen brothers, who discovered the system in 1912, poled a raft along the underground river Volp some 800 metres from the entrance until they reached a beach. They climbed a 9-metre chimney, crossed an upper gallery marked with the prints of cave bear, broke through a limestone barrier, made another series of tortuous ascents, crawled through frightening *chatières*. Only then were they witness to the final drama, the legacy of a sculptor dead for twenty thousand years. In an arena stood three bison moulded in clay, a fourth in preparation as a maquette. Each of the standing animals measures more than 2 metres in length.

The revelation of the sculptures is provocative enough, but Tuc d'Audoubert makes other remarkable statements. The bison are about to copulate, and they epitomize the fact that sexuality was one of the dominant features of palaeolithic art. Tuc also offers incontrovertible proof that it was a place of ritual. In the clay floor of a small side chamber are the impressions of many footprints. In a space where, at certain points, the floor level is only about a metre from the ceiling, they were made by children.

The prints fan out in six clear rows towards the mouth of the chamber. They are, however, not complete footprints. Only the pad of the heel has made contact with the clay. The brain of twentieth-century man must surely reel in wonderment. Was it a game or an ordeal? Were they happy or afraid? Why did they do it? It would seem that the children may have been emulating the hoofmarks of the bison in a dance, but we will never know the whole truth, and the enigmatic clay bison that have stood resiliently against all the passing millennia are not about to tell us. Similar precise arrangements of footprints[9] have been found in other cavern systems, including Niaux in the Pyrenees, but they are equally mysterious.

Even the bison are an anomaly. Fashioned in unbaked clay, each is a sensitive animal sculpture. Yet apart from a few small models found at Montespan and Bédeilhac, which some would argue are actually reliefs, they are the only known sculptures in the round from the deep caverns.

The caverns of Tuc d'Audoubert connect with another system, Trois Frères,[10] the resting place of three variations on the same bizarre figure known as the 'Sorcerer'. None is designed to be seen easily from an accessible spot. They are 'élite' canvases. The best known of them once stood out amongst scores of lighter engravings, as a single painting in heavy black outline. It is a creature with the body, legs and feet of a man, but beyond this human likeness is lost. The arms are cat-like ending in paws. The creature has a tail like a horse, and feline penis and testicles. Over time the image has faded and blurred, but when the cavern was first re-opened the details were copied by the famed nineteenth-century cave artist, Abbé Breuil. His reconstruction, which despite the recent scepticism of some authorities is the best we have, reveals extraordinary round staring eyes, and the ears and antlers of a stag. Clearly, in its pristine state, this was a compelling portrait. Its companion figures are variations on the theme, though the heads and upper bodies are bull-like. In all three, one is left in little doubt of the sexuality of the subject. The genital organs are prominently displayed.

The figures also stand in a curious fashion. The first is crouched forward in such a way that, if motionless, it would topple on its face. But all the figures exude a similar sense of frenetic movement. These creatures may, in fact, be dancing. Similar weird anthropomorphic figures are found in caverns across south-west Europe and many appear to be carrying out some kind of similar deliberate motion.

The great conundrum, of course, is what were they? Some argue that they represent mythical spirit creatures. Others take them to be masked priests in ceremonial costume. The American anthropologist,[11] Mircea Eliade, believes that we are seeing impersonations of the 'Lord of the Hunt'. He argues in favour of a spirit being who provides game and establishes the rules for the chase – the archetypal male protagonist of the natural world who punishes if the rules are broken and who must be entreated and appeased for the hunter to survive.

Eliade may be pushing supposition too far. In defence of the possibility, there does seem hard evidence that the religion of the Ice Age had developed to the point of perceiving and fashioning images of deities in something approaching human form. A frenetic male element of the sexual equation would shortly enter the stage in earnest, and figures like those at Trois Frères may have been his antecedents. But the most likely interpretation seems to be that a priest was dressing in the skins of animals and emulating their movements through carefully prescribed steps. Dance is a part of the age-old quintessence of ritual. Together with incantation, it formalizes the stages of the ceremony. Perhaps this is what the children of Tuc d'Audoubert were also striving to achieve, but here in Trois Frères was the archetypal shaman merging his own form and personality with that of the animal in order to commune with its powerful spiritual self.

Certain common denominators exist in the caverns which

may prove to be important. There is a constancy about the human figures. Though they are present in the context of the hunt, rarely are they seen to kill. Occasionally, they grasp at dead prey, but they are never drawn with weapons, which implies they were drawn either as witnesses or intercessors rather than as a physical part of the hunt. Nor, apart from some isolated pictures in which figures seem to be run through with spears, are they the victims of other hunters.

So what is the meaning behind the enigmatic 'death scene' at Lascaux? There may never be a definitive answer, but it is possible to speculate. That which seems most obvious (that the matchstick man, the hunter, has fallen victim to the hunted) is not necessarily the most rational interpretation. The figure seems to have a bird-like head. It may therefore represent, like other anthropomorphic images, a shaman. The bison is clearly the object of the hunt, the woolly rhino a third party threatening hunter and hunted alike. In the scenario of a real hunt, an already incapacitated animal is much easier to bring down than one in possession of its full strength. It may be that the artist has depicted the outcome of an attack on a bison by the rhino, the *coup de grâce* being administered with the spear and thrower. In which case why is the man lying on the ground?

He has been drawn with his penis deliberately erect. It will become apparent very shortly that in the earliest religions life and death, sexuality and decay embrace in an endless cycle. Priests often masturbated into the earth or against some sacred object in a ritualized renewal of life. The man may not have been injured or dead, but providing a rebirth of life in the presence of death, in the most powerful way he could conceive. In Lascaux's deep shaft we may be witnessing the very earliest thoughts of a sacred marriage – a priest offering his life juices to the spirits of the living world in an act of genesis.

The anomalies of palaeolithic art are perhaps important too, in searching for clues. Why were the caverns not used to create art before the upper palaeolithic period? Neanderthals ranged through the same area and engaged in a similar nomadic hunting life. Was it that the environment posed less of a threat to them, or that they lacked the mental and physical ability to create art of the kind seen in the deep caverns?

The answer probably lies less with skill than with need. Ice-Age art took on a very noticeable spurt roughly at the time of the glacial peak about twenty thousand years ago. The tundra supported its vast herds but, from the viewpoint of human beings trying to stay alive, the deterioration in the climate had necessitated considerable changes of lifestyle. Because for long periods the weather physically prevented hunting,[12] bands came together for the first time to engage in mass hunts. There were greater returns in dividing carcasses and storing them in permafrost 'larders' than living, day-to-day, in small isolated groups. People were thus tending to stay together in one place for longer periods, particularly during the worst of the weather. The cliff overhangs and some of the shallower caves along the river banks, which are often sited close to the deep caverns, afforded better protection than crude summer shelters and so became regular winter quarters.

A less vexing question is why the cavern art died out almost as abruptly as it began? About ten thousand years ago, it vanished from south-west Europe and the caverns seem to have been abandoned. The cause may well have been elemental. From about sixteen thousand years ago, the temperature in Europe began, at first imperceptibly, but then in a more marked series of peaks and troughs, to rise, and the environment began to alter in response. The semi-frozen tundra which had supported the vast herds thawed and retreated north. The herds followed and the source of meat dwindled until it no longer supported the hunting bands. They, too, migrated leaving only some small fishing communities. The great hunting plains of Europe were gone.

The successor to the cavern art in the loosest sense of the word,[13] the rock art of the Spanish Levant, overlapped it by about a thousand years, but it also began a tradition of almost diametric opposites. Animals are there though with a great shift of emphasis towards humans. In the painted caverns human figures account for less than 3 per cent of the subjects, whilst in the Levantine works they soar to more than 40 per cent. This school painted on open rock faces and on the walls of shallow shelters, and the works teem with life and vigour. Its art, one suspects, accommodated more secular demands.

Much palaeolithic art was engraved on pebbles and bones, and this 'portable' art reinforces the message of a deep and almost frighteningly sensitive awareness of nature, a message that is so clear in the deep caverns. Occasionally the sketches form compositions, though animals included in real scenes are as rare as they are in the caverns. Animals fleeing the chase, wounded and dying, are usually missing too, though on a series of pebbles from La Colombière creatures are struck by objects which may be arrows.

Among the compositions is a delightful study of reindeer crossing a stream with salmon leaping at their feet. One of the most famous of the bone engravings, the Montgaudier baton, bears obvious scenes of spring.[14] A salmon is chased by a pair of seals. Eels or grass snakes wriggle along and some grasses spring up in the first warmth. This exquisite landscape of a lost age even includes a minute flower bud, so tiny and delicate it can hardly be seen.

Only rare hints emerge of the plant world.[15] A bull at Lascaux, head down and lips flared, seems to be investigating greenery, and in another part of the system a horse is similarly occupied. On the smaller 'portable' pieces a bone from Les Eyzies includes the front end of a bison, with a procession of nine figures walking between trees that look like leafless alders. There are some similar winter trees on a bone fragment from the Roc de Courbet cave at Bruniquel.

The small material reinforces the delicate intimacy between the hunters and their world, but it is largely devoid of spiritual and sexual connotations. These find their place in a special kind of portable sculpture, and in the deep caverns. In the 1950s, André Leroi-Gourhan of the Collège de France proposed that the animal subjects had often been split into masculine and feminine groupings, not based on gender but on the sexual psyche of the beast – a philosophical pairing of sexual opposites. He seems to have confused twentieth-century logic with Stone-Age mentality, however. In practice the hunters lived with a real world of sexual behaviour. It showed itself before them at every turn. Why should they have wanted to draw artificial and subjective views of sexuality?

The caverns breathe out a strong masculinity which suggests that their painted galleries once oversaw an essentially male phenomenon concerned with the masculine world of the hunt. The message which rises irresistibly into focus is that some kind of religious event was played out in those dark recesses of the earth, overseen and reflected by the paintings, which determined the fate of men. The abundant sexuality is one-sided, epitomized by the frenetic figures which we have guessed to be shamans emulating the spirituality of the animals.

There comes a strong female balance but it is for the most part distinct and separate. In the search for femininity the journey must go elsewhere.

2

The Earth Mother

Almost every great culture that has bowed to the forces of Nature, and whose beliefs have been historically recorded, has placed in the limelight of its faith two antagonistic yet sexually impassioned champions. To one side of the stage is the unpredictable male god, whose beginnings were perhaps left to posterity in strange figures like the 'Sorcerer' of Trois Frères. Facing him stands a goddess in whom rests all the femaleness of the living world. She is the antithesis of the 'Sorcerer', the Lord of the Hunt, whichever title we give him, yet through this frenetic god she conceives her harvest.

She has earned many names from many people. She was Ninhursağa and Inana to the Sumerians. The Akkadians called her Ištar.* She evolved to become the goddess Aštoreth in Palestine, Athirat in Canaan and Astarte in Syria. She was Isis of ancient Egypt, the great Nerthus of the Celtic Bronze Age, and Freya of the Vikings. She is, as she always has been, the timeless and ageless essence of Mother Earth.

Steadily through pre-history, from at least thirty thousand years ago when the Willendorf 'Venus' took form, images have come to light which we believe reflect this great goddess of fertility. Her icons and portraits are always naked, often caricatured

* Where the pronunciation mark v appears above an s it is sounded as 'sh'.

with gross emphasis on breasts, belly, vulva and buttocks. Some draw on the gentle firmness of a body in the first flush of girlish puberty, others rejoice in the exaggerated ripeness of pregnancy. Some seem openly salacious, many are grotesque, others are reduced to gross distortions and, *in extremis*, to oblique and esoteric whispers of femininity.

The goddess was destined to become linked inextricably with her consort, yet in the art of the Ice Age there are no overt signs of liaison. In the fullness of time, god and goddess couple in a passionate seasonal rite of faith to usher in the spring and regenesis of life. Did they do so amongst the Ice-Age hunters? We can only guess and clutch at faint, tantalizing whispers of their intercourse. A single, tiny, engraved sliver of ivory is perhaps the only tangible echo left for us of a ritualized sexual union.

The magic of the fertility goddess does not appear in the painted caverns in any sense; a seeming paradox since all logic would point the searcher towards the womb of the earth to find signs of her passing. She is not there; instead it is a domain of the hunter, the spirits of the animals and the masculine guardians of the chase. Therein lies one of the great riddles of Ice-Age art which we must perhaps be content to live with. It seems that the Earth Mother was revered, to ensure the future generations of hunter and hunted, in different temples.

The absence of tangible trace does not deny that the Earth Mother at times entered into the deep caverns, or that a communion took place between her and the figures seen in those places. It confirms only that the Ice-Age artists chose not to record such events in a durable way. The means by which the fertility goddess was worshipped is also hidden in the mist, yet her icons match the cavern canvases as one of the outstanding phenomena of Ice-Age art. These ancient treasures perhaps record the naissance of a spirit whose place has never been matched.

One of the oldest sculptures,[1] a mere hint and a calculated guess on our part, has been found at La Ferrassie, just south of Les Eyzies, on the River Vézère. Here Neanderthals once lived, but among their successors was a sculptor who carved and abandoned a small oddly shaped piece of reindeer antler. Radio-carbon dating places the reindeer as having died not less than thirty-two thousand years ago — it was alive when the Vogelherd artist carved his animals. Barely recognizable as such, it is believed to reflect the headless, limbless torso of a pregnant woman on whose chest is scratched a series of faint enigmatic marks.

Whether this is an icon, once revered as a sacred thing,

or whether its sculptor carved it as art for art's sake, we will never know. It would be naïve to imagine a magical or religious purpose attaching to all such objects, or that all were produced as erotica. Past opinion has favoured the notion that a prehistoric man's life revolved around feeding his stomach and his libido with equal fervour. These activities probably ranked high in his list of priorities, but arguably he also saw the female form in a wider and more reflective sense than honest lust: breasts, bellies and genitals may also have been intensely evocative of the perpetuation of life.

A remarkable artistic style exists among these prehistoric female figures even though they may vary in configuration and purpose. The art of the painted caverns in France and Spain was to all intent and purpose the outpouring of a monoculture. It was created within a comparatively short time span between the end of the Aurignacian period in France (the dating differs from one region to another) about nineteen thousand years ago and of the Magdalenian some seven thousand years later. Its constancies are more easy to understand. Not so those among the female images. They are discovered across vast geographical distances, from Cantabria in northern Spain, through France and central Europe, down into Italy, and far north into Asian Siberia. This geographical dissemination is remarkable in itself, but they are also the product of a much greater time period. Though they reach their peak in the Magdalenian period, so-called because of the astonishing proliferation of figurines, they begin to emerge in the Late Mousterian period, about thirty-two thousand years before the present day, and their production outstrips the cavern paintings by many thousands of years.

Some are exquisitely sculpted, the labour of hours and days. Many are buffed with a smoothness that tells of much handling. Others have an air of crudeness that suggests they were fashioned in haste for some single purpose, and yet more can only have been intended as toys or casual whittlings. These carved images are smaller, more personal icons than the painted figures of the caverns. Many are worked from pebbles, or pieces of bone and ivory. Some clearly stood alone, but many of the tiny models bear tell-tale holes for a string to be threaded and worn round the neck. Others have handles to be held like batons.

There are other consistent traits. None have feet, and the legs are often fused together, ending in rudimentary stubs. Arms, likewise, are frail insignificant appendages. Breasts and bellies on the other hand are huge. But there is one hallmark above all, a familiar reluctance: no matter who the artist, from where he came and from which moment in time, he has shied away from creating the likeness of the human face.

The Ice-Age artists were not lacking in ability. From Bras- sempouy in the Landes region, comes a tiny exquisite sculpture in ivory, of a woman's head.[2] Just 3.5 centimetres high, it reveals great sensitivity, in the slender curve of the neck, the long braided hair, the fine youthful features. Clearly the lady of Brassempouy posed as a model, art for art's sake. Her portrait suggests no deeper purpose. Other Ice-Age images lack this innocence.

At a site in western Czechoslovakia,[3] part of the East Gravettian culture, one of the most haunting figures from all of pre-history has once more found the light of day, the 'Venus' of Dolní Věstonice. She is part of a collection of icons and is sculpted, unusually, from clay mixed with burned, powdered bone, fired into a dark bronze-coloured, rock hard and almost indestructible statuette.

She is a strange, compelling fusion of realism and abstraction. Her oddly shrugging shoulders support heavy and pendulous breasts above wide, rounded hips. There is a degree of sensuality in her voluptuousness and yet there is nothing remotely erotic about this image. One senses in the fine realism of the collar bones, and the dimpling of flesh down the back, that a living woman modelled for the artist, yet the statue is worked with a haughtiness, about the carriage of the head, the shoulders, the line of the back, which rises above mortality. Human likeness she may possess to a degree, but represent flesh-and-blood surely she does not. Always, inexorably and with chilling fascination, the eye is drawn to her face, for here all mortal reality is swept away.

Where eyes might have twinkled or gazed serenely, the art- ist has sought refuge in slits. Where a nose should have been sculpted, is only a downward, savage scar. Where lips should have breathed the air, there is no mouth. Some fearful inner strength of this creation made it far too dangerous to capture all in familiar lines. It is almost impossible to look at this caricature of a woman and to believe that it was sculpted as an Ice-Age artist's view of femininity in his day. Hers is not a face of the temporal earth.

Although she is complete in other respects, the ends of her legs are broken off. Had they been intact, however, and if she followed the style of similar figures, they probably ended in rounded stubs. She could not have stood upright on her own, and she can only have been planted in the earth or placed in a recess on an altar. She also has a curious arrangement of shallow holes on the top of her head which may possibly have held flowers or leaves.

So far, about sixty of these statuettes from the early Upper Palaeolithic have been found. Most are badly damaged or so fragmentary that it is difficult to recognize their original form. A few have survived almost intact and they all follow a closely similar blueprint.

The 'Venus' of Willendorf is carved from limestone[4] and has a coarser appearance which, to our eyes, verges on the comical. Her matronly body breathes the same abundant femaleness: small but accurately sculpted arms rest on a mountain of flesh and massively pendulous breasts fall over an obese midriff. All is supported, valiantly, by pudgy tapering legs. The head is framed by prim tightly permed curls, but the 'Venus' of Willendorf, like her counterpart, has no face.

According to radio-carbon dating, both figures are a little less than twenty-six thousand years old.

Quite the most startling of their contemporaries, is the 'Venus' of Lespugue,[5] found in 1922 in the Rideaux Cave of Lespugue. The original statuette, carved from a piece of mammoth tusk, is badly damaged on the left side, but the right side is intact and this has allowed a near-perfect reconstruction to be made. 'Lespugue' is best described as a bizarre arrangement of lozenges. She tapers to a small, featureless bubble of a head, and to legs fused into a peg, but her middle expands into spheres. Yet, in spite of being monstrously bloated in her lower torso, she is perfectly balanced.

Similar again is perhaps the best known of the Balzi-Rossi 'Venuses' from northern Italy. This tiny figure, carved from yellow steatite, possesses many of the features of the Lespugue statuette and delivers the same overall balance and clarity of line.

One of the most tantilizing puzzles surrounding these statuettes is in the extraordinary similarity of their design. One could be tempted to believe, when looking at the profiles of the 'Venuses' of Lespugue and Balzi-Rossi, with their lozenge shapes, their slender necks and forwardly inclined heads, that there was a central school of Ice-Age art.

An even more thought-provoking similarity exists between the Willendorf 'Venus' which was found in Austria and a small ivory figurine found among a collection of statuettes at Gagarino[6] in Russia. The Russian site, on the upper reaches of the River Don near Tambov, is 2,000 kilometres as the crow flies from Willendorf, yet the two icons might have been created by the same sculptor. Even small details like the pose of the fragile arms across the breasts are precisely mirrored.

The Russian figurines extend beyond Europe. The farthest flung site is at Maltà in Siberia, on the Balaia River near Lake Baikal. The same inescapable similarities emerge among these faceless Asian images whose legs end in pegs and whose torsos exude ripe, abundant femaleness. Yet Maltà is almost five thousand kilometres distant from the most southwesterly 'Venus' of Cantabria in northern Spain.

All these figures share a marvellous plasticity of form, but they lack movement. They stand still and impassive. In 1900,[7] a small broken figure was picked up near the entrance to a stone quarry at Sireuil in the Dordogne. It had been scooped up with the excavated rock and fallen from a lorry. Its style places it with the Aurignacian–Perigordian statuettes but, in reality, the Sireuil 'Venus' is subtly distinct. Because her buttocks project, and her legs are drawn up beneath her, she could not possibly have stood upright. Some suggestion has been made that she is kneeling, but what may be far more likely is that she is crouched, face down, on her hands and knees, and that she heralds a different kind of female imagery which burst on to the art world of the Magdalenian period.

Hers was to be a very familiar posture in the repertoire of the Magdalenian artists. Sculptures and engravings which capture the female form in similar pose have been left in many sites across Europe from Spain to the Balkans. Once again, there emerges an uncanny uniformity of art in primitive people amongst whom there is no clear evidence of communication through which ideas and fashions might be passed on.

Some of the best known of the images were left in a cave at Petersfels, near the Swiss–German border.[8] In Ice-Age times it lay just below the glacial barrier of the Alps. The small band of reindeer hunters who lived there carved a group of little female figures. Worked in coal, some are unbelievably delicate. The largest is less than 5 centimetres high, the others even smaller. They speak remarkable volumes for the artist. His tool would have been a small flint burin, and the fingers which held the tiny coal pieces must have been numbed by bitter cold, yet the workmanship is sensitive and finely balanced. Some are highly polished from months and years of being worn against the skin, touched and turned, shown and treasured. Others are crude as if whittled for a brief single purpose.

Some have holes bored through them and were probably threaded on string to be worn singly as pendants or grouped together. These images have come to be known as 'buttocks' figures. They have stimulated their fair share of argument and, at times, fanciful debate. Though the sense of movement is less obvious than in the dancing figures at Trois Frères, there is, however, once again, the feeling that the artists have set out to capture some very significant ritualized movement.

Magdalenian 'buttocks' images were not only sculpted. They were drawn and engraved on rock and bone.[9] Some of the most suggestive of them come from a cave at Pech-Merle, south of the Les Eyzies systems. Twenty thousand years ago an artist happened on a clay surface which was damp and soft, and he was unable to resist the temptation to draw. He worked with a stubby object, perhaps his finger. He drew pictures of mammoths and other animals. He traced out many dots and squiggles and meandering lines, the meaning of which is lost to us, and in the midst of this mass of doodling he sketched two women. Nude, they are apparently either crawling or poised on all-fours, their buttocks raised high in the air and their breasts hanging loosely. The posture is familiar.

There is strong argument that these images describe a woman in the position she would adopt for sexual intercourse. Modern convention assumes the facing 'missionary' position, but that is an apt title since it is not the conventional position for a primitive tribeswoman. Simple cultures almost always adopt a sexual posture in which the man mounts the woman from behind following the natural position of other animals.

At Enlène, in the Pyrenees, recent finds have pieced together a small stone plaque which seems to be a composition sketch with a man and a woman adopting this particular stance. The vital question is whether the engraving describes an Ice-Age ritual of mating. The argument is not without support. The earliest known historically recorded civilization in the near east, that of Sumer, practised a well-publicized and well-documented ritual of great importance, the Sacred Marriage, during which sexual intercourse between a king and a priestess seems to have taken place. Furthermore, there is slim evidence from contemporary art, which will be described later, that this intercourse may, in some contexts, have been practised in the posture hinted at amongst the Ice-Age engravings.

The evidence suggests that such rites went back far into prehistoric antiquity. The hunting ancestors of the people who engaged in the fertility rituals of Mesopotamia possessed a faith which, from the evidence of their own art, also seems to have shared many similarities with that of the Magdalenians in Europe.

What again is particularly remarkable is the extent to which the 'buttocks figures' cross cultural frontiers. Perhaps the extraordinary coincidence of their appearance in far-flung locations is that the language of sex is universal.

It is hard to believe that the European images reflect anything less than a cultic activity, not least because of the style in which they evolved. As time passed, the almost lifelike images such as those at Pech-Merle began to drift into abstraction. It is possible to trace a slow movement, over several thousand years, away from realism. Thus by the end of the Magdalenian period the artists were experimenting with extreme impressionism. Either they were recoiling from the dangers of realistic icons or they were moving towards greater élitism. Perhaps, in the same way that the cavern artists had isolated the message of their work through inaccessibility, the creators of this more mobile art were making it occult through its language: turning pictures that were understandable at a glance into idioms that could be read only by the élite few.

Various stages on the road to abstraction have been found.[10] At Fontalés, in the Dordogne, a limestone slab was engraved with 'buttocks figures', though of a more stylized form than those at Pech-Merle. Again, on a slab from Gare de Couze, a similar figure stands out from a mass of obscure scratches. Some of the most stylized of these images were scratched on to a block of stone in the cave of La Roche, at Lalinde.[11] By this stage of abstraction, they have come to be known as 'P' signs. The style has travelled a long way, in artistic terms, from that at Pech-Merle yet it is fashioned unmistakably from the same basic model. Nor is the style limited to south-west France – a rock fragment found at Hohlenstein in Bavaria bears the same familiar outline, and there is another comparison to be made in some of the figures engraved in the Addaura Cave at Monte Pellegrino, in Sicily.[12]

There has been an argument that the emphasis on buttocks is no more or less than the artists' accurate portrayals of steatopygia, the large fatty bottoms still seen in Hottentot women living in the African bush, but there is no hard evidence to support this. Amongst the East Gravettian figures from Petřkovice is a small statuette, carved from black haematite, which almost begs defiance of this notion. The torso of a young girl, it bears no hint of steatopygia. It is as sweet and gentle a figure as the eye could wish for.

The emphasis, in the 'buttocks figures', is one of action not form. Laurens van der Post recounts, coincidentally, a ritual amongst the Kalahari bush women which takes place at the time of a young girl's first menstruation. The women thrust and jiggle their behinds towards their menfolk emulating the mating movements of the eland antelope which they hold sacred.

There has been found, at Isturitz in the Basses-Pyrénées, a little composition engraved on bone in which a woman is being followed by a man. Both figures are naked and the woman has a harpoon-like tattoo on her thigh. The way in which the figures are composed is somewhat limited by the shape of the bone fragment, but it is possible that through their positions the scene may be hinting at a similar event, or at the approach to intercourse.

It was not only buttocks that became highlighted at the expense of other parts of the anatomy. So too, in other compositions, did breasts and vulvae; at first seen realistically they then moved steadily towards ever-greater stylization. The East Gravettian culture produced many forms of these.

Dolní Věstonice[13] was the resting place of an extraordinary figure, from a mould quite different from that of the 'Venus'. Some adventurous artist took a piece of mammoth ivory and whittled it into a thin rod, interrupted about a third of the way along its length by two startling lozenge-like bulges.

There are at least two ways of interpreting this remarkable sculpture. Some authorities would argue that it was designed to be ambiguous. The immediate perception is of an extremely stylized female figure in which the torso has been made rudimentary save for a pair of enormous breasts. Thus it could either be held as a baton, or stuck in the ground. If it is a fertility goddess though, it bears none of the features which seem to have been essential in the 'Venus' figurines.

There is an alternative suggestion that the bulges are not breasts but testicles, in which case the object becomes a phallus. A number of ivories with similar design have emerged from different parts of Europe. At Predmosti, in Czechoslovakia, a phallic-shaped piece has come to light engraved with a highly abstracted female form, and a whole collection of decidedly phallic pieces has been discovered at Mesine, in the Ukraine.

A different, but nevertheless reminiscent kind of stylized human figure, which was also found at Dolní Věstonice, is an ivory from which all else to suggest human form but arched thighs and a vulval slit has been taken away. Yet this figure can be viewed as a phallic rod standing erect upon two legs. It is highly buffed from long use, but there is also a hole for a string at the tip and, unless the string was removed, this inclusion would make it unusable as an object of masculinity in any practical ritual context. Was this in fact the purpose of some of these pieces?

Today, we have all but lost the precious sense, as a community, of helping our children through the confusing and often painful hurdles towards adulthood. In some primitive tribal societies, however, there still exists a deep sense of spiritual responsibility to ease their children through these hurdles. Puberty, the preparation for marriage, and the time of childbirth, are treated as profound moments in the human life span, and proper rituals are devoted to them.

Some of the female sculptures may have been personal mementoes, tokens carved with affection and given to girls to remind them of their lost childhood, or their initiation into fertility and a life from that moment on closely bound up with the men of the tribe. The phallic-shaped objects may have had a similar purpose.

In a number of tribal societies around the world, the loss of a girl's virginity at marriage is a moment of deep significance for the whole tribe. A wedding stick, an object greatly venerated, is used to break her hymen at the climax of a careful ritual. The curious and ambiguous palaeolithic pieces may very well be the enduring traces of such ceremonies.

Whatever the compulsion which drove Ice-Age art towards isolation and abstraction, the outcome can hardly have been more extreme than in the depiction of the vulva. Once again, obsession with a part of sexual anatomy showed itself in a profusion of styles and across great distances. The most common design, if we have interpreted it correctly, was a simple inverted triangle with a vertical line bisecting it, described as a vulviform. These signs are frequent on rocks and pebbles. Some small objects found at Břno provide an interesting variation on the theme. They are discs made from thin sections of mammoth tooth, each about the diameter of a fifty-pence piece and with a slit across half the width. Accounting for their true meaning may border on the realm of speculation but, generally, they are thought to be another artist's impression of a vulva.

Another variation comes from a cave at Castillo, in northern Spain. In this the vulva has become bell-shaped, and several of the designs are drawn in close relationship to a tree-like object.

Some indication of the extreme limits to which the Ice-Age artists went, in abstracting the whole female form, can be seen on a piece of bone from Abri Mège in the Dordogne.[14] Engraved into this fragment is one of the strangest of all impressions of womanhood, if indeed that is what we are looking at. We have no way to be sure. The head is minute and pin-like and the legs, in the tradition of the 'Venus' figurines, are fused together as a tapering stub. There are no arms; ribs and organs are drawn as 'cages'; and the vulva is rendered as a double-edged oval. Yet this figure, too, may have been one artist's answer to the problem of drawing his mother goddess.

The picture would not be complete without one other set of Ice-Age masterpieces, the sculpted figures found in the shelter of Laussel in the Dordogne which include the famed 'Laussel Venus'. Laussel is a shallow cave which contained five carvings of human figures. One is said to be of two people engaged in sexual inter-course; another is of a single male figure, the so-called 'Laussel Archer'; and the remaining three represent female figures. The most heralded of this trio is nude with heavy pendulous breasts and the traditional obese hips, and her featureless face is framed by thick shoulder-length hair. She is holding aloft a horn-like object in her right hand.

It has been suggested that there is close analogy to be drawn between 'Laussel' and other contemporary figures in the 'Venus' tradition. Yet she possesses anomalies which may make the link tenuous. If she is the incarnation in stone of a goddess, she is unusual in being a large-scale work in bas-relief and, apart from her vibrant fleshiness and absence of features, she bears none of the hallmarks of the more personal icons. It is possible that the figure once possessed facial features and that these were removed at a later date. The rock face which she dominated, though it is sheltered, lacks the feel of a sanctuary. In contrast, the other figures, the hunter and the sexually engaged couple, all smack of ritual.

So, was the Laussel woman a 'Venus' or merely an artist's impression of comely flesh and blood, pursued in some more secular dream? We must be satisfied with settling for another inscrutable riddle.

At the end of the day, we are faced with a great assortment of artistic 'feminalia' which crosses time bands and cultural barriers and which, very often, seems to possess a meaning far deeper than simple prurience. It would be foolhardy to read religious intent and purpose into all of the finds. Some, perhaps including the Laussel figures, may have provided no more than artistic sat-isfaction and secular entertainment, but others shout of worship through the settings in which they were found, the styles of execution, and sometimes the combination with other evidence.

The unanswered question is whether the common denominator was a universal vision of a goddess of fecundity, or the magical and spiritual essence of womanhood to create life, or indeed both these things. Between 1934 and 1936, C. G. Jung published his essays on the theory of collective unconscious[15]. Jung argued that humankind conforms to accepted patterns of civilized behaviour which only partially reflect our true nature. We tend instinctively to act in the ways expected of us, and our more genuine personalities are not so much extinguished as pushed away into the background. Jung describes the mask, behind which most of us live, as the persona. That which lies in our unconscious depths is our shadow, the hidden side of our innate nature which wants to do the things our persona suppresses.

Jung takes the argument further. Some stimuli are so deeply embedded that they become common features of the human psyche, our collective unconscious. Within the personality of every man, there rests a feminine element. Jung identifies it as the anima and asserts that there exists a corresponding animus within the psyche of a woman. He states: 'An inherited collective image of woman exists in a man's unconscious.' In her study of Jung's psychology, the analyst Frieda Fordham points out that whilst, *in extremis*, the anima generates obvious effeminacy, more usually it shows itself in traits by which an otherwise rugged and macho male may exhibit unexpected tenderness towards children or the weak, uncontrolled displays of emotion which include sentimentality or lack of rationality, and fear in a harmless situation all of which have been ascribed as aspects of femininity. These things conflict with the masculine persona and are manifestations of a separate component of the unconscious shadow breaking through the veneer.

One of the strongest images in a man's unconscious is that with which he apprehends the nature of womankind. This image is subtly distinct from the conscious impressions which a man gains by tangible contact with individual women through his life. It is generated from babyhood, when the image a young child formulates of its mother becomes embedded in the unconscious. Jung makes the point that this image is a subjective one, rather than an accurate portrait. It is moulded and coloured by the infant's anima.

Although this inner vision of femaleness takes on fine differences of shading, from culture and according to level of intellectual development, it remains essentially intact and consistent within society because it is an archetypal image of collective strength. The image presents contrasting and sometimes conflicting ideals according to circumstances: young and yet ripe; innocent and yet filled with wisdom; goddess and whore; pure and evil.

Jung goes on to point out that one of the essential functions of religion is to provide tangible expression of the unconscious archetypes. Is this an explanation for the phenomenon of the Venus figurines? All that we know for certain is that artists across Ice-Age Europe, themselves following a remarkable pattern demonstrated the world over, felt driven to extract the quintessence of femaleness in a strangely like-minded fashion. If Jung's argument is right, it would suggest that the imagery of the mother goddess extends back, not merely to the first 'awakening' of wisdom, but to eras in the development of humankind that lay far beyond. It would also go some way to explaining the disproportionate representation of female imagery, since all the evidence suggests that Ice-Age society was male dominated.

Collective unconscious thought, if it turns out to be relevant, can only represent part of the formula. The building of a religion is also heavily dependent on a logical, albeit often paradoxical, response to environmental conditions, and on the evolution, diffusion and interchange of ideas. For us, looking back into the misty void of these past millennia, this is one of the compelling fascinations. How strong were the cultural links? How far did they stretch? Could men from the Pyrenees conceivably have extended their beliefs and their artistic flair to like-minded dwellers in the Urals or in Italy?

The figures from east Europe and Asia have their own particular character, subtly different from that of the Franco-Cantabrian school. Although both became highly stylized and schematic by the close of the Magdalenian period, the eastern trend moved towards a geometric ornamentation that is, incidentally, still visible in the art of primitive Siberian tribes today, whilst that of the west followed a vogue of more schematic decoration. Above this regional split there remains, however, an astonishing universality of concept, and it is in this that the most tantalizing questions rest.

Perhaps it all comes down to the simple fact that these Ice-Age nomads had achieved comparable levels of mental agility, and that they were confronted with and influenced by not dissimilar problems. There is an argument to be considered that these challenges, coupled with some intercourse of ideas,

may merely have generated parallel solutions. Such is the tidy
objective answer that will satisfy the academic mind. On the other
hand, can we deny wondering at some common mystical empathy from within, guiding the hands of men whose spheres had
never touched, to create the same homage to a spirit unknown,
yet who had instilled each and every one of them equally with
her magic?

The phenomenon of Ice-Age art, as a whole, must be regarded
as a reflection of society's view of the real world. It is a collective
social comment as distinct from being a 'gallery' that expresses
a range of individual ideas. One should never forget that the
prehistoric hunters eked out a short precarious existence, with
a life span of perhaps twenty or thirty years, in an extremely
hostile world, its enmity measured in terms both of its other
occupants and of its climate. They lived hand-in-glove with the
landscape around them to a degree which we, in our closeted
and technologically cushioned environment, can hardly begin to
understand. Their art arguably translates and fixes their desire, in
the absence of technology, to deal with the adversities of their
world and to better their chances of survival through intercession
with the forces that control it.

The discovery and understanding of Ice-Age art is still in
comparative infancy. Only a little more than one hundred
years have elapsed since Maria, the daughter of a Cantabrian
landowner, Marcelino de Sautuola, took her place in history
as the discoverer of palaeolithic art in Spain. According to the
report of the event you turn to, she was either five, seven or
eleven years of age when she struggled from the now famous
great hall of Altamira, at Santander, crying 'Toros! Toros!' Now,
hardly a month goes by without some new discovery, and once
in a while such finds represent a quantum leap in understanding.
Until the discovery of predatory beasts in cavern art, like the head
of a lion on a crumbling rock surface at Trois Frères, the accepted
view was that the artists were interested in depicting only animals
hunted for food. Such advances are isolated though and, in the
main, prehistoric art remains a matter of conjecture.

One area which is offering exciting new possibilities of knowledge is the former USSR. Relaxing of political tensions has opened
up large areas which are proving rich in palaeolithic remains.

When the nineteenth-century explorers first rediscovered Ice-
Age art, they found it difficult to reconcile such a sophisticated
activity with people conventionally regarded as primitive. They
came to the conclusion that whilst, in general, the hunters were

culturally lacking, the abundance of food 'on the hoof' gave them ample leisure time and they used it to develop an artistic ability. The early workers, Lartet and Christy in 1864 followed by the French historian Piette and fellow authors Boule and Luquet, all agreed that Ice-Age painting, engraving and sculpture was exclusively art for art's sake.

Their argument can no longer be taken seriously. It is too heavily flawed. Whatever went on in the painted caverns, whatever mystery was carved into a faceless statuette, revolved around the very close intensely personal bond between the hunter and his natural world. That it was all some kind of leisure activity during which sculptors whittled and painters decorated walls with pictures with which to impress their neighbours or to gaze at in the firelight of long dark winter evenings, can be discounted. Those early theorists ignored a tremendous weight of evidence pointing to a religious meaning, though it was not until the turn of the century, with the publication of such major works as Edward B.Tylor's *Primitive Culture* and Sir James Frazer's *The Golden Bough*, that a religious interpretation was conceded.

Even now there are academics who will maintain fervently that no proof exists of a religious purpose to Ice-Age art, nor that the deep caverns can be described as sanctuaries. Turning devil's advocate for a moment, their argument in the purest academic sense, is correct. Whilst proof positive may be lacking, however, there is a great deal to be argued from a process of elimination.

No mundane refuge was sought in the caverns. They could have provided shelter for large numbers of people, from the worst of the winter weather. If, as carbon-14 dating suggests, most of the paintings were produced between fifteen thousand and twenty thousand years ago, the climate of southern Europe was not tempered by the balmy breezes it enjoys now. A short distance to the north the continent had been abandoned to the ice barrier, and summer temperatures would at best have risen to the cool sixties Fahrenheit. In winter they would have plunged regularly to twenty degrees below zero. So why were the caverns never inhabited?

The 'art for pleasure' argument is also dented by the mass of cryptic signs which suggest an esoterism, a code to be read and understood by a select few.

As to the purpose of the small portable art,[16] a theory arose in the 1960s when a scientific journalist turned photographer and archaeologist, Alexander Marshack, published some radical conclusions which, if correct, might undermine one of the most cogent arguments for an Ice-Age religion. Marshack argued that the hunters had a sophisticated sense of time and period, and that they could anticipate, accurately, events such as the melting of ice in the rivers, migration of animals, and flowering of plants. He found marks on many of the pieces which he alleged to be sequential and to tally with the days in different phases of the moon.

Marshack's argument seems, at first, quite cogent. Much is based, however, on distinctions visible only under the microscope, an instrument which the technology of the Ice Age had not produced. His calculations also ignore the fact that there is no way of telling if the groups of marks were made weekly or yearly, or in fact on any regular basis. It is being suggested that the scratched fragments became the crude equivalent of a calendar. But no calendar can determine the date, unless days are crossed off regularly, or a cursor is moved from an established base line. There is no hint of this on the so-called 'calendars' from the Ice Age.

Marshack's illustrations are unconvincing. The marks could mean anything, perhaps even a simple tally. Often they appear alongside pictures of animals and may well have been a count of carcasses or kills. None of the examples depicts the moon. That is not to suggest that the hunters were unaware of lunar periods, there is virtually no primitive culture which does not acknowledge the moon amongst its celestial gods. It is merely that Marshack declines to respond to the most obvious question. Only when people gain some measure of independence from their natural surroundings do calendar dates become of much use. What practical value could a calendar have been to an Ice-Age hunter who is known to have geared his movements, not to a settled pattern but to the highly variable movement of animals? Migrations coincide with the spring thaw but this is very rarely at the same date each year.

There is a more subtle and pertinent objection to Marshack's claim though. It is implicit in the idea of a calendar that seasonal events, recorded hitherto, provide a predictive yardstick for the future. But with the kind of mathematical assurance Marshack proposes, the very unpredictability of nature which was arguably the *force majeur* for the cavern art and for enacting hunting and fertility ritual, would largely evaporate.

The only firm conclusion that will satisfy the purist is that, among the hunters of the Upper Palaeolithic, were individuals who possessed an extremely sensitive eye, and who turned out a prodigious amount of creative work. Some was cryptic and vague, some was executed with the most exquisite realism.

Yet who can gaze into the haunting face of the Dolní Věstonice 'Venus' and not feel a chill of the unknown? If that is the effect she has on us today it is difficult to believe she exercised any less impact twenty-six millennia ago.

It is equally difficult to believe that the structure and placing of cavern art was not determined by its function, nor that this was other than to complement religious belief and practice. The way in which the one complemented the other remains the greatest unknown factor. Arguments have raged that Ice-Age religion was founded on totemism, ancestor worship, fertility magic, and sympathetic religious magic. If we knew how the art was utilized we might also have answers to these questions.

At the beginning, I raised the objection that Ice-Age art and culture cannot be thought of as an isolated phenomenon. It is a link in a great chain of unfolding knowledge, understanding and interpretation.

If the great outpouring of Ice-Age art was purely secular then that in itself raises some pithy questions. In Neanderthal times, human minds had taken on board the acceptance of a spirit world. At the other end of the Ice-Age culture, at some time before the earliest historical record was laid down, we have inescapable evidence that this same belief was alive and well, and was being rendered into stories and into art. How did the Ice-Age hunting clans sustain their illiterate wisdom if not through art and legend? If those who succeeded the Ice-Age cultures did not inherit the idea of translating belief into art from the Ice-Age pioneers, then are we seriously to believe that the use of art turned, suddenly, from purely secular to cultic? It seems improbable. Furthermore, what then was the purpose in making so much of Ice-Age art esoteric?

The Ice-Age artists painted a marvellous wonderment and awe of their world which we in our technological cynicism have allowed to slip away. Theirs was a richness of the human spirit whereas ours has become poor. The rediscovery of this out-pouring of human aspiration, which has survived intact down so many millennia, has made some of it intensely vulnerable. Modern air and microbes have already begun their wrecking process. Bacteria and fungi are eating away the ancient pigments; electric light is dulling colours. Lascaux cavern is closed to the public and we have to settle for a replica. It is our loss that such an exquisite legacy cannot endure the ravages of the twentieth century.

3

The Parting

Whatever influences have touched the sensibilities and instincts which we, in twentieth-century Europe, inherited from the distant past, the thread begins with the Ice-Age hunters. Our faiths, and the application of beliefs, that is our religion, have stemmed ultimately from those remarkable visionaries. They were the creators of the template about which, alas, we can now only wonder but which seems to have described a world whose nature had both common form and *alter ego*; where spirits were guardians both of the animate and the inanimate; and where shamanism, the art of wise men to intercede with the supernatural, attempted the first regulation of nature's caprices.

The paths of the hunters' descendants are many and varied though. Europeans are cosmopolitan peoples and their culture has been fashioned from a hotchpotch of notions that are an accumulated effect of those different routes of influence.

When the ice receded, from about fourteen thousand years ago onwards, the lands which had provided the rich hunting grounds, the chilly tundras, altered to dense forests. It was of course a change over many generations but, slowly, the herds moved north following the ice. The hunters were left with stark choices: they could remain and adapt their lifestyle, or they could move. So they parted. Some stayed, became fishing communities, and gradually evolved their own cultures. Some turned south

following the sun to the warmth of the Mediterranean lands and
the eastern Levant. The evidence of these latter adventurers lies
in the dry earth of Mesopotamia where heat replaced cold as the
overwhelming climatic adversary.

Others turned north following the great herds. They became,
in the fullness of time, the Celtic, Germanic and Nordic tribes
laying down cultures which, in comparative terms, were slow in
progress. Their beliefs were moulded by life on the semi-frozen
plains across which they chased animals for sustenance much as
men had done for thousands of years past.

The ongoing similarities of faith that appear in cultures which
became isolated by vast horizons and ages are amongst the most
provocative features of the story which begins to unfold. Cultures
which effectively had little or no contact after the parting of the
ways as the glaciation retreated, evolved striking harmonies of
thought and style, separated by periods perhaps as great as fifteen
thousand years.

In part, the urge of the nomadic hunters to migrate over
long distances and across cultural divides served to syncretize
evolving beliefs, yet creeds and religious devices have also grown
in astonishing kinship where cross-fertilization of ideas seems
improbable. A little, perhaps, rests in things which are beyond
rational explanation.

Arguments have been raised that many of the cultural notions
which appeared in Scandinavia and other parts of northern
Europe were brought there, at a comparatively late date, by
travellers from the south. This argument of an influx of 'modern'
influences possesses elements of truth – southern Scandinavia,
to name but one region, experienced several incursions, each of
which brought its own cultural identity.

The essential 'fires' had already burned themselves into the
human spirit though, and any similarity in the way the flames
gained brightness and strength was, at that stage of cultural
development, probably as much attributable to the effects of
environment as to the borrowing of ideas. The influence of
surroundings and climate was great and it explains at least
some of the mystery. We are all members of the same species,
no matter when in the last thirty millennia we happen to have
been born, and the evidence seems to indicate that, because of
our environment, we evolve in remarkably comparable ways.
Until we achieve independence from our natural world, it largely
governs the way we behave.

Comparing two modern tribes of hunters at a cultural level

roughly similar to that of the people living in Europe during the last glaciation, one at home in a South American jungle and the other in a frigid northern forest, one might imagine that similar kinds of awareness would prevail, but this is not the case. The hunter in the tropical rain forest tends to be nonchalant about religion. Often he has no obvious totems and no prominent ritual. Gods may be around and about but they do not bother him very much. His northern counterpart, on the other hand, takes his gods very seriously indeed. Why?

It is not so much environment that is the determining factor in itself, but rather the interaction between environment and the people living in it. Both sets of hunters may possess an accurate awareness of the natural world surrounding them, but it is one they have gained in the context of different ground rules. In the tropical jungle there is no change of the seasons. Life is a never-ending larder of plenty. All in all he has no urgent need of help or protection from the spirit world, but the hunter of the tundra or of the deep and chilly northern forests gains a different awareness of his Earth. The world seems infinitely more hostile towards him and thus he turns much more passionately to his gods.

The contrasting demands of the two environments on those who live in them also bring differences of a more practical kind. The hunter in the north develops certain skills for which his counterpart has no need and no experience. In general, primitive people living in hostile and changeable climates have a more acute awareness of surroundings and locations. Often they develop abilities in map-making, whereas few jungle-dwellers would understand the purpose of such things. The hunter questing over the endless frigid tracts must be able to predict where the herds will travel, and he must be able to orient himself. The rain-forest tribesman, because he does not have to follow his food over long distances, needs no particular awareness of where he is in the landscape.

Conversely, two situations that are climatically and scenically at odds with each other, a cold Siberian forest and a hot Mesopotamian desert, can generate similar beliefs because of the ways the two environments affect the people living in them. They generate problems which are not dissimilar. In the semi-frozen latitudes, beliefs were moulded by the lurking annual doubt of whether the long dark northern winter would ever soften into spring. Those in the south were conditioned by the uncompromising heat of the sun. Mutual anxieties were the stuff of an unconscious empathy between hunter gatherers who otherwise seem poles apart.

The migrants who turned to the north faced great limitations, partly through weather, partly climate, and partly terrain. More temperate conditions spread very gradually and, for as long as the land was covered by ice, there was no opportunity for hunting or fishing communities to establish themselves and to make progress. Hence, for millennia after the era of the cavern painters in south Europe, culture in northern latitudes remained rudimentary. It was not until about 9000 BC that the earliest evidence even of simple Stone-Age tools and weapons found its way into the icy ground of Scandinavia.[1] The earliest migrants into this virgin land hunted red deer and elk through arctic forests that were young, open and scattered with lakes, and they seem to have lived in temporary winter settlements, spending the short summers on the move.

There are strong comparisons to be drawn between the lifestyle of the first colonists of the far north and that of the Ice-Age hunters, and the people who left their scant signs in the north were drawn to demonstrate their first pangs of spirituality in ways whose likeness with those of their distant Magdalenian forebears is touchingly clear.

The Scandinavian hunters began their exploration of ways[2] in which to make tangible that which is intangible through esoteric patterns and through human and animal carvings which they scratched on antler, bone and amber pebbles. As the Stone Age began to near its close, they advanced to painting and carving larger works on rock canvases. These artworks, like their more ancient counterparts in Europe, were not 'gallery pieces' to be completed and hung for posterity. They were the working tools of another nurseling society's struggle to come to grips with the complexities of life and death in its own inclement landscape.

At first the art was crudely experimental, then vividly and often movingly realistic, but, eventually, another inescapable urge, that which drove towards abstraction, began to repeat itself. The art retains familiar diffidence about creating certain images in lifelike form. Like many of the cavern paintings, the Scandinavian works come embellished with indecipherable yet insistently important motifs – circles, spirals, triangles, chevrons, nets and lines, some decorated with barbs, some unadorned. The artists also found the same compulsive need to draw, not hands as in the caverns, but the outlines of feet. Can these indeed have been the footsteps of gods?

It has been suggested that the 'nets' represent rope cages or covered traps. One writer points out that signs are often drawn near the animals' genitals which could lure speculation away on a different chase. The straight lines may be forces residing within the animal during life, surging out of its body in the moment of death. On the other hand, they may record nothing more occult than the strict procedures over cutting up the carcass, a butchery practice closely followed as late as medieval times. There are many theories but none provide answers.

Beyond scattered fragments, little speaks for the faiths of the first pioneers in the far north. Through six thousand years of what is known as the Maglemosian culture period of the Old Stone Age, during which the climate slowly became warmer and drier and the pine forests changed to oak, small communities hunted and fished. On the strength of art evidence, material progress and spiritual aspiration were virtually unchanged. It is impossible to imagine them remaining wholly stagnant, but clearly, if there was an inheritance from the migrants of the distant Magdalenian era it was still very much a prisoner of environment.

As late as 2000 BC, in the middle neolithic period in Scandinavia, when sophisticated city states were blooming in the Near East, and when Jutland was being experimentally cultivated, huge animal silhouettes were being hacked into the bare rock faces of Norwegian fjords.

The carvings were generally created on vertical faces of granite or slate, incised with grinding tools, but more usually chipped out. At first the figures were lifelike, sometimes on a colossal scale. A whale, cruising for eternity across an exposed slab at Leiknes, measures a full 8.2 metres in length. Often, as in the cavern paintings, the animals move! Elk thunder by, whilst reindeer look nervously over their shoulders. There are no signs of weapons, but some of the later pictures bear symbols and other motifs such as the familiar lines passing through the bodies. Some of the carvings also seem to have traces of paint.

Most art has been left on exposed rocks.[3] Such caves as exist have rarely been used for religious purposes although there are isolated possibilities of one-time sanctuaries within such shelters. To the north of Trondheim, in the darkest recess of a cave, fourteen vaguely human figures, dating from the Late Stone Age, perform some forgotten ritual across the surface of the rock. Another smaller group faces them. They are painted in red ochre, each body an abstract line with a large round head and twig-like arms and legs. They are phallic and they seem to dance. In the Äland Islands, sixty fragmented and stylized statues were found in a cave, again suggesting esoteric ritual. Each has a small hole in the top of its head – reminders of the Dolní Věstonice goddess.

Generally though, the holy places of the north were under the open skies and, inevitably, they have suffered greatly from the attack of the elements. One of the objections that is raised to any link between the art of the Magdalenians and that of Scandinavia argues that the earliest migrants did not continue the tradition of rock art. But perhaps they did! The first northern artists may not have gained the expertise to gouge out their works on more enduring granite, and worked only in dyes and on soft stone.

Countless works may long since have weathered to oblivion. There must, at some time or other, have been many more paintings, but only those which are sheltered have survived. On the south-west coast of Norway, near Førberg, a life-sized painting of a cow elk has been preserved from the rain only because its artist chanced on a surface that was protected by a huge rock overhang.

The siting[4] of the stilled and weathered testimonials which have survived possesses a strong familiarity, they share remoteness and inaccessibility. They are in lonely places far away from the daily paths of human footfall. Some must have been worked with their artists suspended on wooden platforms hundreds of metres above the ground although what seems today to constitute inaccessibility is perhaps deceptive. The sea level has dropped considerably and many canvases which are now far out of reach were probably worked from the waterline. Water is not the only association which can be discerned. Very often the pictures are found in areas which are still linked with hunting. They lie beside trackways that have been used since time immemorial by migrating animals. At Møllefossan in southern Norway, elk are drawn on flat rocks close by a shallow ford used by herds crossing the river Etnar.

Too many of the carvings are placed near water to be a mere coincidence and this choice of location seems to be another bond with the Magdalenian period. Water develops an almost universal spiritual 'pull'. Many are found on slabs within sight of lakes. Near the head of the Trondheimsfjord in Norway a huge bull reindeer, supremely lifelike in his quest, treads a ledge over which tumbles a cascade of water. At Fykanvatn, reindeer, elk and bear, carved with great accuracy and feeling, tread their eternal journey through the spray of a waterfall on the very edge of the glacier. Thirty metres above the sea, on a sheer cliff at Hell in Stjørdalen, a pair of reindeer follow each other down a phantom mountain path.

As time progressed though, the old familiar trend emerged. The people of the far north could not lose their most ancient fears. The era of intensely realistic and often very beautiful art was destined to change with the approach of the Scandinavian Bronze Age. From about 1500 BC figures became smaller and the inevitable drift towards stylization crept over them.

Human figures began to appear occasionally but they, like those in the caverns, were never realistic. At Rødøy in Norway, a naked, stick-like figure in a horned headdress skis across a cliff face; perhaps this was the image of a priest or shaman. The earliest,[5] a set of tiny schematic figures, carved in bone, has been found on a bone fragment at Ryemarkgård in Sjaelland, Denmark. Clearly these were no ordinary men and there must have been a deep and powerful mystery that drove some artist to hatch their strange form into his primitive tool. Did they perhaps embue it with strength?

All are crude caricatures of things too profound to render in lifelike copy, but very often these grotesque murmurs of human form seem to indicate worship of spirit guardians of animals. On an axe made from an antler base someone has carved a heavily stylized figure. But the work contains an oddity, an error which it is difficult to believe was not deliberate. The legs each possess one joint too many, and they end in tiny, almost hoof-like feet. Here is the same imagination that generated the dancing half-man, half-animal creatures in the cavern of Trois Frères. Spirits, or shamans dressed as animals? Whatever its identity, this bizarre figure incised into the antler weapon was no idle scratching. It too perhaps provided the axe with a sanctity and an insurance in its use. It is worth noting that the fragment possesses 'tally marks' very similar to those found on small portable art in palaeolithic French sites.

The artists tended to carve new pictures on top of canvases that had been drawn during the Stone Age.[6] The evidence of one carving upon another, according to some authorities, is proof that the artists constantly re-worked the art as the 'living' tool of a religion. The argument has been questioned on the grounds that the later artists simply 'missed' noticing that which was already there, but when one studies the examples of superimposed figures it seems far more likely that they returned to age-old sanctuaries and placed their own offerings over those of earlier generations as the continuing mark of an ancient tradition.

Pictures became still more stylized, verging towards the abstract. At Bardal on Trondheimsfjord one can find Old Stone-Age portraits of elk superimposed by smaller and more vague sketches from the late Bronze Age. Human figures begin to appear increasingly, sometimes in sexual encounters. These works, predominantly Bronze Age, were being produced by hunting groups who were also experimenting with husbandry and agriculture. Farming techniques, which were to trigger the next major explosion in the advancement of religious belief, did not reach south-eastern Europe until 6000 BC and they did not begin to spead north and west with any kind of momentum until some two thousand years later. Simple farming only reached the southernmost tip of Denmark early in the third millennium. The first archaeological proof appears in west Sjaelland from about 2700 BC.

Farming seems not to have penetrated[7] across the Skagerrak and on to the Scandinavian peninsula until later still. It is significant in the search after gods because it was an advance which allowed people to free themselves from the endless daily 'grind' of searching for food. It provided surpluses which permitted specialization within a tribe. That, in turn, allowed for more elaborate social organization. On the cultural and religious front builders could be employed to erect shrines and temples; scribes could establish the art of writing; intelligentsia could devote their lives to the search for the infinite.

Cultural development across Europe sometimes appears confusing because material advances did not progress simultaneously. There was a wave of practical achievement, from the shores of the Mediterranean to the Arctic Circle, rather like the unfolding of spring. Hence, southern Europe was enjoying its Bronze Age whilst Scandinavia was still wrestling with stone tools and weapons. The wave was mirrored within the Scandinavian area. As Jutland and southern Sweden were experiencing the first herding and crop growing, the far north hunted as timelessly as ever. As with the practical march, spiritual belief had, at any one time, made varying progress.

Contrasting the two extremes across the continent, life in most of Scandinavia meant hunting and gathering for thousands of years after people in the far south, in western Asia, had turned to settled farming existence. Between these limits central Europe

represented a middle ground and during the third millennium a
social fabric developed there in which two prominent cultural
groups emerged, identified today by the kind of personal possessions they deposited in graves. Both developed more or less
simultaneously and both spread rapidly.

The Beaker People[8] earn their name from the manufacture
of large numbers of bell-shaped beakers but they also show
the first evidence of metal-working skills since they buried their
dead accompanied not only by these drinking cups but by small
metal daggers. The Battle Axe culture, which interred its more
esteemed members in circular mounds of earth or barrows, armed
themselves both in life and in death with axes that bore perforated
stone heads, but they too had advanced to the use of metal and
the dead were also provided with weapons crafted from this new
material.

The role of metal in the evolution of European beliefs is not
insignificant. It can safely be assumed that civilization began in
the near east, and that the sophistication of lifestyle brought with
it progress in thinking and (the term is used anachronistically)
philosophy. However, the more advanced cultures lacked the
mineral resources with which to make the new and vital com-
modity of bronze, and so the central European Beaker People,
who had discovered mining sites of copper and tin, developed
an extensive metal trade with the south through Asia Minor. If
one of the major routes for the spread of relgious and social ideas
has been conquest, another is commerce, and so the European
traders almost certainly picked up elements of western Asiatic
culture on their travels. They had also developed business contacts with the Scandinavian tribes who, likewise, lacked the
essential ingredients of bronze. It is not impossible, therefore,
that certain notions of art and ritual, which had originated in
the eastern Mediterranean, were carried by the metal traders to
peoples in the far north.

The cultural time-chasm which lay between south and extreme
north strikes home forcibly when one looks at contemporary relics from the ancient near east from whence farming stemmed.
In the third millennium, a high civilization was unfolding in
Mesopotamia. To its north, in the mountains, the Hittites were
developing their own ideas. On the Mediterranean seaboard,
Phrygians, Syrians and others were making parallel progress in
stark contrast with the north.

The beginnings there possess a striking familiarity though,
not only with those of the far north but of the Ice Age. Ten

thousand years ago, palaeolithic tribes of nomads were scattered in a broad arc, from the Zagros mountains of Iran, over the Taurus range in modern Turkey, and down to the Aegean Levant. The rugged uplands bounding the Fertile Crescent were covered with great swathes of oak woods. The land had been spared the worst rigours of the ice by warm damp winds from the south, it was the hunting ground of leopards and bears, and of men who wielded stone-tipped spears in a common quest for wild pig, goat, deer and gazelle. The people of these mountains were being lured towards a more settled life. But at that time, they were still hunters and gatherers and the scant remains of their art bear arresting comparison with those of palaeolithic Europe some fifteen thousand years earlier. Because of the disparity of dates there can have been no direct contact but, if the tribes in the east possessed ancestral links that stretched back far enough, technically there was no physical obstacle to cultural exchange having taken place, at some period in time, right across the axis from south-west Europe, through the Balkans and beyond.

In any event, the pioneers on the fertile crescent left, amongst their legacy, numbers of small clay figurines which bear tacit testimony to common patterns of awareness. They created animal sculptures – boars, lions, sheep, bears – crudely wrought but definitely lifelike. Their human figures, on the other hand, bear familiar hallmarks – distorted trunks that lack hands and feet, necks which taper to nothing, bodies caricatured with huge breasts and bellies, faces that are not faces. These images burned themselves into the imaginations of people searching for truths in the mountains of the Taurus, as powerfully as they did from the Pyrenees to the icy wastes of the Arctic.

One of the finest prehistoric sites of permanent habitation to emerge from the dust was Catal Hüyük on the Turkish Konya Plain.[9] Evidence was decisive that for some considerable time interest in the new lifestyle must have gone on side by side with the old. Remnants of houses, built from mud bricks, cradled amongst their debris the still intact traces of murals depicting bulls and hunted stags. Then in 1951, at an ancient village near Chemchemal some twenty miles south of Zarzi in northern Iran, Robert Braidwood of Chicago University established a specific moment, a little more than eight thousand years ago, when a tribe elected to grow rather than glean their food from the wild.

It should not be imagined that the change began at Chem-chemal, or that agriculture and husbandry came in an overnight flash of inspiration. The dawn of food production was probably

triggered by specialists developing skills within the villages over
several generations. Primitive sickles and milling stones were in
use for some time before the idea of collecting seed and resowing
it in cultivated plots caught on. Domestication of animals was
probably a haphazard business, less a need for meat which was
running around on the hoof in plenty than the age-old wish
to keep pets. The changes probably took a thousand years and
happened at different times in different places. At Hassuna in
northern Iraq are the remains of a village dating to at least 5000
BC which was already comparatively civilized growing subsistence crops and breeding cattle.

Vestiges of ancient creeds have emerged all over the near east
and around the shores of the Mediterranean. Yet within their
alien designs familiar patterns flutter in provocative harmony. On
the west bank of the river Jordan, some ten miles south of its rendezvous with the Sea of Gennesareth, is the ancient neolithic site
of Munhata.[10] From it has emerged a female figurine, arguably
the image of a mother goddess. She may have been consigned to
the hot dry earth of Palestine by worshippers who seem a million
miles removed from the hunters of Old Stone Age Europe, yet
in her distorted face and bloated body lies an almost frightening
conformity. In what deep engine of the mind did such uncanny
parallels of human thought and endeavour find their inspiration?
We may theorize but answers that provide rational explanation
elude us.

It has to be said, as with European Ice-Age art, that not
every figurine carved or moulded in the female form has to
be a goddess. Another figure discovered in Israel, the 'Venus'
of Beer-sheba, was promptly seized on when discovered, as
evidence of pagan fertility worship by the Israelites. Yet whilst
it is undoubtedly true that the Children of Israel worshipped
their 'other gods', this tiny delicate nude figurine in stone was
probably designed simply as a pleasing sculpture of a young
girl.

Very little, in fact, has been discovered from the parts of
Syrio-Palestine which came to be occupied by the Israelites.
This is no doubt attributable to the busy iconoclasts amongst
them who tried to ensure that anything hinting of idolatry was
thoroughly obliterated. The antagonism applied, presumably in
equal measure, both to statues and images which formed part
of old Hebrew tradition and to those belonging to the original
indigenous tribespeoples.

More productive ground lies northwards in the Taurus Moun-

tains of central Turkey.[11] From 1935, until the war years
interrupted progress, the Turkish Department of Antiquities
began to excavate an ancient mound known as Alaca Hüyük.
They came upon a remarkable burial place, in some respects
perhaps equalling the royal tombs at Ur. Dating from the Old
Bronze Age, it was the last resting place of a royal family, people
of great wealth, the élite of a sophisticated society.

From thirteen graves were exhumed kings, queens and their
royal court, the dust of a dynasty dead at least four-and-a-half
thousand years. Each royal personage had been interred in a
fashion which was traditional to the area, crouched inside a
sealed stone jar. These people were also sun worshippers and
every corpse was laid with great care facing towards the south.

Among the shattered remnants of one of these coffins was
the fragmentary body of a young woman. Perhaps she had been
a princess who in her brief time on earth was the darling of her
people. She was laid to rest with a gold diadem circling her hair
and with gold bracelets at her wrists. Beside her they had placed a
gold cup and other trinkets, crafted exquisitely in precious metals.
A copper model of a bull stood by, protecting her in death, and
they had laid her in a trench surrounded by blocks of stone. Across
it were placed logs hewn on their upper surfaces and finally sealed
with clay. They had sacrificed five oxen and, with reverence, to
placate her soul, they had placed the heads and the shin bones
over the logs.

In the frail skeletal bosom lay a figurine worked in silver with
breasts and shoes of gold. Its most striking feature is the head
which, like so much of early religious art, has been distorted —
here it has been worked into the bizarre shape of a hammer. This
was an arcane goddess, the product of some forgotten strand of
creed among the many which bridged the chasm between the
era of hunters in the Taurus Mountains and the new civilization
taking shape on the plains. Close by lay another hammer-headed
female figure, this one a small statuette modelled in copper. Were
these things representations of a mother goddess and, if so, why
did a goddess of fertility become linked with death? Though they
are the progeny of a much more modern and sophisticated school
than the Munhata figurine, still they were born of a pre-literate
age and no answers await us in an antique text. The silver idol
might have been a personal talisman guarding its earthly charge
on her journey; a gift from a father to his daughter, from a king
to his mistress; or perhaps this woman, dressed so finely, was a
votary priestess whose life had been in the service of the deity

she now embraced so closely in death.

In a second grave, also the resting place of a woman of high rank, lay ten copper figures but these are significantly different. They are joined in pairs with bodies that end in semi-circular discs, quaintly holding hands and reminiscent of some ancient craft of paper folding. They lay in the dust beneath the woman's chin and, from their relationship one to another, they may once have been joined in a necklace. Beside her face were three more small copper figurines that may, like the others, be images of a mother goddess.

The ways in which people buried the dead reveal certain constancies across great divides of pre-history. Certain traits which repeat themselves with uncanny regularity begin to suggest mutual themes implicit in death which may or may not be attributable to cultural borrowing.

Taking first the style of burial in the near east,[12] five hundred miles south of Alaca Hüyük in the Sinai desert, there exist at least three stages of ancient burial cairns. In the third and fourth millennia BC, these cairns were constructed from rough blocks of stone in the centre of which was a small chamber to hold the body. The graves were not casual heaps of stone. They were precisely built on prepared ground, usually with a foundation wall which had the effect of raising them up above the surrounding land. As time went on, ridges of high ground were chosen for building the cairns. Gods were often perceived to live in mountains.

Some very simple versions, dating to about 1500 BC, have been found on heights above abandoned turquoise mines where the victims of Egyptian forced labour were buried. The chambers are small, only large enough to take a body in a huddled position. The design of many of these burial places offers the distinct impression of forming a womb-like chamber in which the body is curled like a foetus. The enormously powerful link between the earth and the birth of life was irrepressible in people's minds. Did that same link also forge itself between the uterus of the living earth and the apparent extinction of life?

From as early as the third millennium, the cairns on the high places were becoming not burial mounds alone but places of cult. In northern Palestine, at Megiddo, there survives a ruined cairn,[13] measuring about 9 metres across, built of rough stones, and bearing all the appearance of an altar. Such places often became the focal point of fertility rites amongst the later peoples of Palestine and Syria, but from very early on they seem to have become inextricably linked with the worship of the mother goddess. A similar altar-like cairn at Nahariyah has the remains of a small shrine beside it, whose fragmentary lingering evidence suggests that it was dedicated to an unnamed fertility goddess. From the remains of funerary meals it must be guessed that ancestor worship and cult were inseparable and that relatives of a dead person would eat feasts at the shrine, gaining strength in the belief that the spirits of their dead lived on awaiting regenesis in the womb of the earth mother.

Drawing a comparison with neolithic northern Europe, the practice of burying the dead in stone graves began in very similar style to that of third millennium Bronze Age Turkey. The earliest tombs were cut from the earth and lined with stone slabs.[14] The body was laid inside and the grave covered with planks of wood over which turf was heaped. This simple style of interment was superseded in the third millennium by a massive monument, the megalithic dolmen, that reared impressively above the bleak skyline and heralded the dawn of a new culture in Scandinavia. Dolmens have a curious distribution pattern. One can discover them around the Mediterranean; they are in the British Isles, from where they may have first arisen; they are in Scandinavia and in northern France; yet they do not touch central Europe.

More or less all the far northern dolmens are in Denmark and part of Sweden. More than two thousand of these awesome mansions of the dead survive in Sjaelland alone, but sadly all have been ransacked long since and whatever priceless murmurs from the past they once harboured they are now extinguished.

The dolmens were erected with rough-hewn blocks of stone topped by a massive covering slab to make either a four-sided or polygonal tomb. There is usually no entrance although some have a doorway on the south or east side and even the rudiments of a passage formed by two upright slabs at the entrance. Was this shaping important? The suspicion grows that it was seen as a womb with a vaginal opening. From the mother of the earth came life, and to her unchanging embrace it returned. It is important to realize, when looking at a dolmen today, exposed to the air, that it was not built thus. The side slabs were hauled in to make the walls and these were then banked around with massive earthworks up which the roofing stone was dragged and levered into position. Only the cap remained visible. The tomb was effectively within the embrace of the earth and the entire area was surrounded by a ring of stones, marking it off as sacred ground.

From the dolmen came a different kind of tomb, the passage grave, which makes the suspicion of a symbolic link with the womb much stronger. These vast monuments, which were first built in about 2200 BC, marked the height of the megalithic culture in Scandinavia. They were communal graves in which as many as a hundred people could be interred. Like the dolmens the passage graves were constructed on a massive scale with large stone blocks. At first they were rounded chambers but later the grave was characterized by a passage of some length which led into the grave chamber. The largest of them which still survives is at Karleby near Falkoping. The passage is of more than 11 metres leading into a cavernous tomb almost half as long again. The grave remained open until full when it was sealed with turf and, like the dolmens, the sides were banked around with great ramps of earth leaving only the capping stones open to the light of day.

The people who built these places revered the spirits of their dead. Like the cairn shrines of the near east, they were habitations of spirits very much present. The tombs were not shut and barred. Each necropolis served as the gathering place of the tribe's ancestors and they were regularly the focus of great and surely very evocative ceremony. They stood witness to feasts and perhaps sacrifices. Many reveal remnants of pottery and animal bones. At Gronhøj in east Jutland seven thousand potsherds were unearthed, the remains of rows of offering vessels that had stood on either side of the entrance in a hallowed forecourt marked out by boulders.

We know little more of the rituals.[15] which became associated with the early northern necropolis but the scant evidence suggests, ever more strongly, links with the earth. Beneath certain barrows in Denmark, discolorations and indentations have been discovered which can only have been the marks of ploughshares. It may be that a ritual ploughing of the field took place, suggesting that out of death and the harrowing of the old came regenesis. Sacred fields which may have enjoyed a similar purpose persisted until Christianization in many parts of the north. In South Wales, Bronze-Age mounds containing stone burial cists have yielded traces of boughs and sheaves of barley and wheat spread on the ground which perhaps reflect similar sentiments.

With the dawn of the Scandinavian Bronze Age, in about 1600 BC, a new culture swept in once more. Battle-Axe hordes rampaged through Jutland from the south, and the megaliths went out of fashion. The new invaders reverted to single stone

cists within earth mounds. These were usually sited on high
ground. Thousands upon thousands still mould the horizons of
Danish hills and placidly line the ancient ways to the sea, and
once more there are parallels with places far away from the snows
of the north: the coffin was built of stone, lined with planks and
covered with wood in an almost carbon-copy of the cist graves of
Anatolia. The body was laid on its side with the legs tucked up as
the lure towards the foetal position of birth reaffirmed itself.

In some strange tombs in Sweden, the emphasis on a return
to the womb takes an extreme twist. The entrance is closed by
a slab through which is cut a circular hole and it seems that the
corpse was either pushed or pulled through the opening into its
resting place. Such 'vaginal' openings took a prominent place in
much later folklore but always there was the accompanying sense
of re-birth as the individual passed through the narrow aperture.

The bond between mother goddess and the closing, as well
as beginning, of mortal life was emphasized by another curious
phenomenon of prehistoric art which bridged the divide of continents.[16] In the near east at Kültepe, not far from the Alaca Hüyük
burial ground of the Hittite kings and queens, is an ancient site
dating, in its deeper levels, to about the third millennium BC.

In a grave, stone figurines were discovered which bear strong
similarity to the paired copper idols of the royal cemetery. The
statuettes also possess paired heads on slender necks which fuse,
like grotesque Siamese twins, into single disc-shaped bodies which
are covered with intricate geometric designs. Their circular and
semi-circular bodies may, in part, allude to some antique worship of the sun. Yet the most compelling feature of these
near-abstractions rests in their huge staring eyes, a strong and
persistent feature of the religious icons of Anatolia. Some of the
stone figures found at Kültepe bear heads which are reduced
to little more than eyes. The British archaeologist, Mallowan,
found similar 'eye idols' at Tell Brak in northern Mesopotamia
and clearly these reflect some forgotten theme of an all-seeing
numinous presence. Was this the mother goddess?

The staring face was present on figures found in a site near
Kültepe but made, it is believed, in the early part of the second
millennium. By this time, however, the style had changed. On
the floor of one of the houses in Kültepe lay a soapstone mould
from which would have been made a lead casting. It includes the
impression of four figures – a god, and a goddess, the small figure
of a child, and in the arms of the goddess an infant. These figures
are very much in a Mesopotamian style; they wear the tiered

head-dresses and the tasselled skirts of Mesopotamian deities and
the male figure bears an axe and a club at his shoulders. Yet the
huge eyes speak of the old culture of the mountains. And what
of the inclusion of the children? Are they the progeny of union
between mother goddess and her consort?

Kültepe has yielded up other lead figurines which bear the
obsessively staring eyes of the local tradition. Amongst them are
two separate statuettes of goddesses. In one, destroyed from the
waist down, her hands are cupped under her breasts in a pose
uncannily reminiscent of some of the Ice-Age figurines and she
wears her hair in the distinctive style that becomes identifiable
with the Egyptian goddess, Hathor. Another, nude with a prominent pubic triangle, is drawn with the same huge eyes and a
similar pose. The hands again rest beneath the breasts.

From how distantly in the muddy backwaters of time have
such themes travelled?[17] It is one of the truly fascinating questions about such imagery, because similar 'eye idols' have been
discovered in Britain and in other parts of northern Europe. The
face with staring eyes – sometimes it forms part of a stylized figure
with nude breasts – sometimes it is alone, carved on the surface
of a pot or urn.

The faces were certainly a product of the Bronze Age but did
the imagery stem from deeper levels of pre-history? Some authors
have suggested that the Scandinavians did not understand their
meaning and that they used them purely for decoration. This
seems improbable. The theme may, technically, have come from
the south, but the bronze in which the faces were frequently
moulded was extremely expensive and they were the product
of local Norse craftsmanship. The 'eye idol', the all-seeing power
of the diety, defies language barriers and becomes a universal
sign of a spiritual presence.

Thus, symbols of the mother goddess include the womb and
the staring eye, but another was poised to take its bow on
the stage: the tree.

In classical times the Greeks planted sacred groves round
the tombs of their heroes, but as early as the third or fourth
millennium, the oak and other trees on hilltops, often linked
with cemeteries, seem to have been associated with fertility
goddesses in Syrio-Palestine. These trees were the *terebinths* of
the Bible which in the St James's version of the Book of Genesis
are described as 'tree' or 'grove'.

In Bronze Age Scandinavia,[18] people were drawn to the
same mystical union. They began to bury the dead, within

their earth barrows, in oak logs split lengthwise and then hollowed out, sometimes a smaller log containing the body being inserted into an outer sarcophagus built from a larger trunk. The sleeping ones lay in these wombs of wood in their finery and on a stretched cowskin. They were covered by a woollen cloth and provided with the goods for their journey – food, jewellery and weapons.

In the later Bronze Age of the north, the practice of interring the body was slowly replaced by cremation. It began occasionally in Denmark and gradually took over from inhumation. The decision seems to have been made on the belief that through fire and smoke part, at least, of the spirit of the dead person would be returned to the gods of the sky whose role in Nordic religion was to take on an increasing importance. But the sense of the womb was retained and the ashes were placed in a stone or pottery container within the oak trunk. These seagoing peoples also buried their dead within barrows but surrounded by the raised stone outline of a ship. Death, in their eyes, involved a journey across the sea.

Separate cultures thus evolved, north and south, which demonstrate extraordinary similarities of concept and style, whether due to cultural borrowing or the development of parallel ideas. To the peoples of the north would come the great deities, Nerthus and Cernunnos, and later Othin, Thor, Freyr and Freya. Theirs was the sacred ash tree of the world, the Yggdrasil, their vehicles were the burial ships buried at such places as Oseberg and Sutton Hoo, and the sacred wagons like those found at Djebjerg, and their memorials were such exquisite tokens as the Gundestrup Bowl.

These people gave us part of our inheritance. The rest came from the south. Vestiges of cultures of tremendous antiquity, yet with a sophistication unparalleled by their contemporaries in the north have come to us through the fabled empires of Mycenae and Minos; through the classicism of Greece and Rome; through Judaism and Christianity.

In the area of the Fertile Crescent, there is argument that a slow movement began to take place some seven or eight thousand years ago out of the hills and down the river valleys towards the alluvial plains. The people may have been lured on one of the last great migrations of humanity into a new expanding world. What triggered their journey, if indeed it took place for there is no firm evidence, no one knows – perhaps there was some change in the climate, perhaps they saw the prize of one of the richest farming soils on the face of the earth.

Almost certainly the migrants came into contact with indigenous tribes of people along the banks of the rivers and, as they did so, cultures merged. They brought with them their stocks, their mythology, and their gods. They brought carvings and paintings of animals, and gross distorted female images. But the era of their culture and beliefs was coming to a close. Farming heralded the dawn of a changed lifestyle and with it came fresh aspirations, new needs, different fears. A new kind of belief was poised to evolve out of the old.

The Fertile Crescent was the most likely setting for the Garden of Eden, yet it was the land between the rivers, Mesopotamia, that was destined to oversee the birth of civilization. The biblical Ur, the world's oldest known city, was probably there. Those who claimed this huge alluvial plain now enclosed by twentieth-century Iraq were faced with daunting problems and these, more than any other single factor, changed the fabric of the old gods.

The evidence lies in the dry earth of Mesopotamia where, thousands of years before the birth of Jesus the Nazarene, there arose a civilization that first turned from the spear to the plough. It is there that the pathway in search of the gods of the earth leads.

4

The Garden of Eden

Two hundred miles across the desert, west from the modern Iraqi capital of Baghdad, before the river Euphrates abandons Syrian territory, lies the small border town of Abu Kemal. A few miles further upstream is Tell Hariri. It is a place which appears on few maps. 'Tell' is the Arabic name for a mound of ruins covered by wind-blown soil.

One day in the summer of 1933, an Arab burial party began to dig a grave to the west of the river, and they unearthed a statue. It was large, heavy and disfigured, but clearly it had once been very beautiful and, among informed circles of the French archaeological service, certainty began to grow that beneath the mound lay something of major importance. In December, the archaeologist André Parrot commenced a dig which rapidly unearthed a great deal of pottery and bricks.

Parrot had found a lost city.[1] Over several seasons he explored a palace of vast dimensions, built by the west Semitic king, Zimri-Lim, in the seventeenth century BC, roughly at the time when Hammurabi I was ruling over the First Babylonian Dynasty. The palace covered six acres and had more than one hundred and fifty rooms which included a huge library of cuneiform tablets. Parrot had discovered Mari, the largest second millennium site in western Asia. His find was dramatic enough in its own right, yet something more lay below Zimri-Lim's city. As Parrot dug deeper, shedding centuries layer by layer, he came upon a much older and more arcane place. Built at some time between the beginning of the fourth and middle of the third millennium, it comprised primitive temples to the gods.

What ghosts must have surrounded Parrot as he scratched through the dry earth in this place. Here was a world that had existed before the Pharaohs built their memorials, before the golden age of Mycenae, before fabled Helen stood on the ramparts of Troy. Here people had worshipped for perhaps a thousand years before human hand had scratched the first intelligible written word. Parrot was standing on one of the foundations of civilization. Yet a few years before this find the race of people who had built it was unknown. Their time period in our journey is a singularly compelling one because within its span lies the 'hinge' on which the thread turned from the animal-focused cults of the hunters, to the great religions of civilizations that farmed the land. The period is long, and its thread dauntingly frail. Evidence is confused, locked into tens of thousands of fragments of clay and paint, carving and sculpture, tagged, logged and abandoned to museum basements around the world.

The people who built the oldest temples[2] at Mari and other sites gradually being unearthed throughout Mesopotamia were the Sumerians. Their contemporaries in northern Europe were far behind them. Sumerian culture was the first to change from a nomadic life hunting animals to settled husbandry and crop growing. It was the linchpin of ideas which eventually found expression in Christianity and the classical paganism of Greece and Rome.

The ethnic origins of the Sumerians are unknown but almost beyond doubt they owed their beginnings to scattered and independent tribal clans. At one time it was believed that the peoples who actually triggered the evolution of Sumer arrived from somewhere in the hills of the north, mingling with the local fishing communities along the banks of the major rivers. There is no firm evidence for this migration though and an increasing number of prehistoric sites being located in northern Mesopotamia suggests that there were indigenous peoples living in that part of the world for many thousands of years.

Nonetheless, something catalysed one of the huge leaps in the progress of the human race, and history suggests that such events are often stimulated by the arrival of outsiders. Beyond doubt there was mixing with Semitic tribes from further west.

This we know because of the existence of Semitic place names and other 'foreign' elements in the Sumerian language. There is no reason to suppose that tribal migrations did not also take place from the north and there is a fascinating possibility that some elements of Mesopotamian culture stemmed from a common stock of Ice-Age hunters. The tribes which now live in the sub-Arctic regions of Asia must have migrated at some time in their past from warmer regions further south and ethnological evidence supports this. Whilst some followed the receding ice northwards, others may well have turned south across the Zagros mountains and eventually provided part of the Sumerian stock.

As the scattered Mesopotamian communities became welded together, they preserved the legacy of their culture and their beliefs in a form quite different to the paintings and sculptures of the Stone-Age artists. They inscribed wedge-shaped cuneiform characters on tens of thousands of clay tablets, and in the legends, hymns and laments which they poured out in these enigmatic and beautiful texts they preserved the details of a spirit world which was no longer generic but identifiable through names and personalities.

A mighty creator god, An, and his female principal, Ki, were the supreme forces,[3] the universal founders of the cosmos. Between them they made the heavens and the earth, once together and inseparable. They engendered Enlil, the god of the air who cleaved heaven and earth in two. An carried off heaven and the primal figure of Ki took the earth, accompanied by Enlil. To the goddess Ereškigal, perhaps the alter ego of Ki, was given the nether world. The notion of a primal creative force in an empty void of chaos, dividing and ordering it often through some cosmic catharsis, is one of those persistent quirks of human imagination which has coloured religion from the beginning.

Mankind has also been captivated by triads of deities, not so much distinct threesomes but a quintessence which manifests itself in three forms. In Mesopotamian belief the male creator god and his female identity, his anima, are extended into a trinity because Ki, with Ereškigal, is the primal twin personification of good and evil. Very often, and not only at cosmic level, a goddess is perceived as possessing a light and dark side.

The Sumerians' hunting fathers also probably bequeathed to them the germ of many other spirits. Amongst these, and including An and Enlil were seven great gods of fate. The earliest legends tell of Utu the sun god, and the moon deity, Nanna.

The Sumerians seem to have shared, in common with many

other primitive religions, the concept of a vast primeval ocean, the Abzu or 'deep', ruled by the god Enki, on which rested the terrestrial world.

Almost certainly the same notion found its way into biblical texts. The four rivers of paradise in the book of Genesis stemmed from this ocean, and it is implied that the Flood drained away into it. In several early legends this sea is plugged by a huge boulder. In the book of Revelation it wells up from beneath the new Jerusalem and flows as the great river of life. In the hearts of the Sumerian farmers though, it was sweet water which commanded most earnest attention. Their greatest fear was not of a winter that might never soften into spring, but of desolation and death under a fierce and uncompromising sun.

The lower part of Mesopotamia[4] is an intensely arid flood plain formed from millions upon millions of tonnes of rich alluvium, deposited by the twin rivers Tigris and Euphrates, which form a shifting emptiness in places many metres deep. The soil possesses tremendous fertility. It lacks only the 'Achilles' heel' of Mesopotamia, water. The summer temperature soars to 55°F in the shade and for eight months of the year the land bakes so that at the end of the dry season the rivers have dwindled to a sluggish meander. Winter swells them a little with spasmodic rain storms but they do not flood until the melting snows of late April, pouring into the head waters, turn them into mighty torrents. Thus, for the Sumerian farmers, success in the hunt was no longer the central issue. For them the deciding element of life was water. Water was provided by different deities. The fierce sudden rain that came of storm and lightning, and did little for the land, was governed by Iškur, the storm god. But the guardian of the sweet gentle rains that the Sumerians had left behind in the hills to the north was Enki.

Unlike the more precise wetting of the Nile basin, the Sumerians could not predict with any certainty the coming of the waters to the great plain of Mesopotamia, and so Enki was seen as a complex and at times almost Machiavellian character. Like other deities he filled more than one role, and he was also the celestial major-domo. Enlil, who became the national god of Sumer, made general plans but detail and execution were left to Enki. Enki thus provided a convenient escape from any difficult questions about the mysteries of nature. If something could not be readily explained, 'Enki did it'. But Enki was dear to Sumer because he was the god who filled its sacred rivers of life, the Euphrates and the Tigris.

A temple hymn[5] speaks of Enki's power with its own raw eloquence, and with it comes a reminder that certain themes in tribal philosophy become almost universal. The legends of north European and Asiatic tribes tell of water, the semen of the gods. Was this imagery handed down from the same stock that gave such vision to the Sumerians?

> After Father Enki has lifted his eye over the Euphrates
> He stands up proudly like a rampant bull.
> He lifts his penis, ejaculates,
> Fills the Tigris with sparkling water.
> The wild cow mooing for her young in the pastures,
> The scorpion infested stall.
> The Tigris surrenders to him as to a rampant bull.
> He lifts his penis, brings the bridal gifts
> Brings joy to the Tigris like a big wild bull on giving birth.
> The water he brings is sparkling water, its wine tastes sweet.

The irrigation channels[6] which the Sumerian farmers dug in an effort to combat Enki's caprices are still visible today, but such watering causes long-term problems because the river water contains salt and, no longer able to escape the raised banks of the dykes, it slowly poisons the land. It was a problem the Sumerians never cracked, it probably affected their approach to religion and finally it beat them into abandoning many of the great cities of the south.

Five places out of the seven are accounted for: An, Enlil, Utu, Nanna and Enki. The remaining thrones were taken by two goddesses whose roles are sometimes confusingly alike. One was Ninhursaĝa, the most significant Sumerian mother goddess. The seventh place was taken by Inana, and beside her even the mighty Enki was outshone. She was arguably the greatest deity ever to arise in the long and turbulent history of the Mesopotamian empires: the Queen of Heaven. To call her a 'mother goddess' would be misleading and probably inaccurate. Unlike more typical mother goddesses she took many lovers and there is no overt indication that she bore children. She was a goddess of life and love who oversaw the fecundity of the living earth, but she was hardly a figure of ripe motherhood.

The most strident question remains an enigma. Did such a personality epitomize the successor to those strange, silent figurines which go back to the distant Ice Age? Does this goddess hold somewhere in her make-up the key which confirms that the faceless and bizarre schemes of prehistoric imagination are more than grotesque parodies? All we know for certain is that Inana comes from far in the past beyond the earliest written records, and that she did not stand alone. Mesopotamia is littered with identifiable goddesses who would arguably fit the mould, such is the legacy of a fragmented tribal past. But Inana achieved a fame that took her head and shoulders above her rivals. She was not only the Sumerians' Queen of Heaven, but also in their eyes she was a spirit of the earth, living neither above nor beneath but flowing through their lives everywhere. Ki may have been *grandmère* of the cosmos but Inana was the mistress of the earth.

Such was the aristocracy of heaven. It was in the hands of these unseen but ever-present beings that the fate of Sumerians' lives were placed. Their luck depended on the whims of deities that shared almost all human activities and foibles, and who they considered, on the whole, to be capricious and unpredictable. At their bidding was a celestial horde of lesser gods watching over hills and valleys, cattle and sheep, ploughshares and cooking pots. These were spirits of time and place, and all had to be regularly appeased, fed and watered. The Sumerian's attitude towards the human soul and life beyond death seems to have been ambiguous. Unlike the king, who was also a god and returned to the gods, the person in the street was little more than a transient and subservient lump of clay, destined only for the nether world they had been born from, and to an existence without form or meaning. Sumer had grown though. Tentatively her people pushed aside the age-old phobia against representing deities in human form. They did not care for dumpy images, adorned with pendulous breasts and peg-legs. They dared to draw the spirit world in human proportions. Only in the faces of the gods and in sculpture in the round did they seem sometimes to hesitate.

Sumerian art is hard to come by. Almost all they produced has vanished. The shifting soil which provided the key to the national bread basket has engulfed cities deep beneath the ground, but while the cities lived it was also the despair of their artistic set. All is alluvial silt and small pebbles. Larger durable material for sculpture or carving could only be imported, at considerable cost, from the hills in the north. So sculptors worked in clay, which they generally failed to bake.

In consequence, few Sumerian art treasures have withstood

the ravages of time. We are left with a limited number of small
sculptures, mostly in terracotta, and were it not for one other
notable phenomenon we would have little idea of Sumer's
remarkable art. We do, however, possess a pictorial memory in
the shape of thousands upon thousands of cylinder seals. Worked
either from small pieces of stone, or more cheaply from fired clay,
these objects enjoyed the same popularity in the ancient world as
do plastic credit cards today.

The seals turn up from about 3500 BC onwards.[7] Made like
small stamps, their original purpose was to label goods in transit
with a simple design which was impressed into a soft clay seal.
In time though, the scenes became more elaborate and required
a larger surface area, so the stamp turned into a cylinder which
could be rolled across a flat clay surface. Sumer was also exploiting
the potential of the drill at about the time that the cylinders were
becoming more elaborate, and this opened the way for rendering
minute detail. The intricate works were bored out and hung on
a string, becoming a kind of personal signature for the owner.
By the middle of the third millennium, legendary and religious
scenes adorned them. But the layout and proportions of many
hint of major composition, and there is a reasonable assumption
that much was copied from larger wall canvases. The seals
became the talismans of the élite that no one could be without
and so these tiny exquisite miniatures, glyptics, are today almost
the sole surviving repository of Sumer's religious art.

Among the finest is the Great Seal of Adda, a temple scribe
who lived in the reign of Sargon the Great. The best seals were
commissioned individually, and they may serve as a rule of
thumb guide to the popularity of a legendary theme – the more
surviving copies, the greater the popularity. On Adda's seal, Inana
or Ištar as she was then known stands characteristically, centre
stage, wings spread, her shoulders bristling with weapons – she
was also, perversely, a goddess of war – atop a mountain. The
hunting god stands to her right, separated from her by a tree, and
Šamaš, the sun god, who has cut his way through the mountain
at her feet identified, as always, by a curved object not unlike a
modern pruning saw which he holds aloft. To her left, one foot
raised on the mountain, Enki is surrounded by streams of water
with leaping fish, and behind him stands his lieutenant, Isimud,
the god with two faces.

Understanding the mythology which the art describes bears
its headaches. Many of the seals include scenes and personalities
which are still meaningless. The artists did perhaps anticipate our

confusion over identifying figures less than a centimetre tall.
Gods and goddesses are invariably distinguished from mortals in
the clothes they wear – they sport massive, horned mitres and
distinctively tasselled dresses or skirts – and by small, personal,
idiosyncracies to which all the artists conformed. What we have
though, at last, is a written legacy from which we can theoretically discover the meaning of the art. One of the most intriguing
challenges now lies in marrying these scenes on the seals with
the texts on the tablets.

We do not have concrete evidence of the beginnings of Sumer's
romance with the written word. For a time after they began to
coalesce into an identifiable culture the Sumerians were, we
guess, illiterate. The journey towards literacy must have been
slow, at first probably an experiment with pictorial symbols.
The earliest known written tablets,[8] from Uruk, modern Arab
Warka, and dating to about 3400 BC, are already sophisticated
and evidence a fully developed writing system. It is, as with the
prehistoric art of Europe, a link in a chain that has already begun.
Much of the early writing was applied to daily 'dross' – matters
of economy, deeds of sale, building lists, but in the middle of
the third millennium, some seven thousand years after the
shamanistic culture of the hunters was beginning to fade, began
the age of the Sumerian *belles lettres*. Amongst the great temple
hymns, the laments and the heroic legends must be vestiges of
traditions which Sumer's people remembered from their distant
past. Unfortunately such golden anthologies of material are not
the open doors to beliefs of pre-history that one might wish them
to be and they are full of pitfalls.

Accurate translation alone is a problem in getting to grips
with the truth, but the difficulties do not end with philology.
Across an enormous time span, mythology and religion had
been sustained by word of mouth. Many of the writings bear
the hallmarks of this heritage, in the cadence of words and the
repetition of phrases. Such things are signs not of a child of
literature but of memory, and unlike the indelible evidence of
the written word man retains the liberty of changing his mind!
Furthermore when he puts 'pen to paper' it tends to be with
the product of present not past thinking. One of the functions
of legend is to perpetuate an idea, a belief, but it may only do
so until that same belief becomes dated or ostracized. This may
happen through changing politics, outside influence may affect
it through declamation, or simply it may fade through the
maturing of ideas. Then the legend usually changes so that it

remains workable within the new framework but often in the process its original purpose is put aside and forgotten. Not only in Sumer's case, but in many other developing traditions including notably that of Judaism, these complications are all part of the literary arithmetic. Not only were Sumerian traditions a heritage from fragmented and independent tribes united perhaps only by ambition and a common tongue, but the indigenous prehistoric population, the so-called Ubaid people, identified only by distinctive tools and painted pottery, were diluted and adulterated through many centuries of infiltration by Semitic nomads from the west and by other immigrant groups.

Fusion of different local traditions, syncretization, may begin to explain some of the anomalies, perhaps why a deity possesses unconnected roles or why two deities come to share a similar role. But the chequered and complex political history of Sumer also serves to make her cultural record confusing. During the so-called Early Dynastic period Sumer was fragmented into city states, ruled by kings who had taken over the collective role of the tribal elders in religious and political affairs, and who were constantly feuding with their neighbours. Their squabbles are recorded in such famous 'documents' as the Stele of the Vultures from the southern city of Lagaš, and it is because of this fragmentation that Egypt, not Sumer, lays claim to be the first true nation state.

A loose federal arrangement, marked by pre-literacy, held for four centuries and, almost certainly, tribal cantonization helped to perpetuate the separate strands of religious and cultural thinking. All was to change with the coming of Sargon the Great from the Semitic state of Akkad in the north. Sargon was poised to stamp his name indelibly on history. By 2335 BC he had turned federal Mesopotamia into an empire, the Akkadian Dynasty. Sargon was both moderate and pragmatic as an overlord. He willingly bowed to the cultural genius and economic superiority of the Sumerians, and he provided the catalyst for Sumer to become literate. On religious matters, however, his own Semitic people recognized different gods, still essentially the astral spirits of a hunting people, and Sargon felt bound to give them proper place. Thus, although the broad platform of Sumerian creed remained inviolate, names and sometimes personalities changed as their traditional identities were coerced to become more acceptable to the Akkadian regime.

The Dynasty ended in violence when a Gutian horde descended from the east. The invaders had none of the pragmatism or tolerance of Sargon and, for a hundred years, Sumerian culture was consigned to cold storage. Then a rebel general, Utu-Hegal of Uruk, biblical Erech, mustered an army routing the Gutians and paving the way for the 'Indian summer', the Third Dynasty of Ur. But Sumer was approaching her twilight. The final years of the dynasty were marked by weak and ineffectual kings with Semitic names, and this wonderful 'lost' civilization collapsed with a slowly fading breath as the Babylonians prepared to carve up Mesopotamia in the next major reshuffle of hegemonies.

Such is the outline of Sumer's history. Sumerian kings, for the most part, lived in their power bases surrounded and protected by people who believed them to be gods. It was no longer the shaman who spearheaded the religious life of the tribe but the king. Destined to return to the gods on his death he governed by divine right, living in the aura of his personal deity, the tutelary god that protected his city. Every quirk of the king's behaviour was a mark of the god, of whom he was tangible manifestation, and thus beyond criticism. If the king went to war, it was a battle between his god and the god of the enemy.

The sanctuaries of the spirits had changed too. Their citadels were carved not by nature from the living earth; they were built by the hands of men. Yet the purpose was the same – to protect the most intimate worship of the god in his house, the instrument of power, from the eyes of ordinary people. Early Sumerian sites are spoken of as temples, but they were unlike the sanctuaries of the hunters. Although the exclusive province of the king and his priests they were built as living places, to serve the daily needs not only of the gods but of their earthly retinue. Each complex had its administrative centre, its bakery, silversmith, brewery, carpentry, butcher. In its earliest design no prying eye could rest on the holy of holies, the shrine in which stood the symbol of the god but this later changed to a more open public view. Temple design began, however, like the most secret places of the deep caverns, so that the sanctuary could be seen by only the few.

The early temples were modest, and the cult place of the god was quite tiny. They developed though, first into two-stage buildings in which the sanctuary was built atop a flat plinth. One of these temples was found at the ruin of ancient Uruk, one of the oldest and most prestigious cities of the south. Another, at Uqair, bore on its walls the fragile remains of ancient frescoes. By the time of the Third Dynasty the temple had become massive. It was dominated by the great ziggurat, the ramped tower by which the Assyrians and Babylonians were to become so obsessed. It

was the stairway of the gods, the road by which they moved
between heaven and earth. The temple was a place of daily ritual
and sacrifice where meat and vegetables were offered up to the
spirits; a place of mystery, procession, dance and incantation. The
temple hierarchy controlled the economy and agriculture. There
was no freehold ownership. Every acre was leasehold and the
temple managed all that went on. The gods overshadowed the
very stuff of life.

Libraries were filled with laments on the frailties of men
and with great hymns of praise. Many must have been handed
down from generation to generation. To open their pages is to
step into a time neither barbarous nor inarticulate, but imbued
with wonder and eloquence and beauty:

> House full of brightness, clad in radiance,
> shrine of the holy Inana, adorned with the true mes.
> Zabalam, shrine of the pure mountain, shrine of the clear dawn
> It has let the word, which fills the heavens resound . . .[9]

These 'mes' were the divine powers that control the very
workings of the universe. It was with such omnipotent powers
and within a culture capable of producing immensely beautiful
and eloquent word pictures that Inana reigned as queen. Her
origin it seems was in Unug (Uruk), ruled by a succession of
power brokers who constantly overshadowed their neighbours.
Unug's patron god was An, creator of heaven, but the people
also took to their bosom the young and beautiful goddess of
love, daughter of the moon god Nanna. Beautiful and ambitious,
after a respectable period of courtship she was elevated to be
the handmaiden of the creator god, and with her ascendancy
she took a new title, Inana, Queen of Heaven. She was accorded
the rights of a great deity and she assumed control over the
natural world.

Enki and Enlil, together, created an entourage of lesser spirits
to do her bidding. Two sisters, Ašnan and Lahar, were sent to
earth to supervise grain harvests and cattle herds. In a separate
dispensation the goddess Uttu was sent to guard the other green
plants. Inana commanded them all.

This prestige was certainly true for her presence in Unug and
for many other Sumerian cities, but Inana's dominance of the
earth and its germination is, in some places, less clear cut. Was
she the prima donna of all Sumer, or does it appear so because
she happens to have held sway in those cities which have been

brought to light? There come tantalizing references to that other goddess, Ninhursağa, yet most of the places said to have had shrines in her honour have never been found. They exist only in literature, their remains lost deep in the shifting alluvial soil.

In 1903, however, part of a ziggurat was found near Bismaya, on the site of the ancient city of Adab. All that is left of the temple are the first-storey walls which now stand about a metre and a half high. Beside them was an inscription identifying the deity to whom the ziggurat was dedicated. Her name Ninhursağa means the Queen of the Mountain. She also belonged in another lost city, Keš, believed to have lain somewhere between Adab and Nippur on the banks of some old and long abandoned canal system. Only once is it mentioned on a votive inscription,[10] dedicated to the great king, Ur-Nammu, and that inscription in itself poses a puzzle of chronology:

For his lady Ninhursağa, Ur-Nammu built her beloved Keš.

Aside from the problems of whether Keš was rebuilt in the Third Dynasty, only to succumb once more, these few words say much for the warmth and affection felt for Ninhursağa. A shrine at Tell el'Ubaid bears an inscription which breathes with the same sense of great tenderness:

Ane-pada, son of Mes-ane-pada, King of Ur
Built this for his goddess, Ninhursağa.

The marvellously evocative temple hymn from Keš leaves little doubt about the measure of esteem in which she was held. Many of the kings were 'nourished by Ninhursağa's milk'. She was the gentle mother figure. There are mentions of several other titles: Nintu, the 'Queen who gives birth'; Ninmah, the 'Great Queen'; Aruru, the sister of Enlil; and 'Mama' from whence the modern childhood name stems. But it may be that these vestiges of a fragmented tribal society all eventually became synonyms for Ninhursağa herself, a name she took to commemorate the making of the earth's mountains by her son Ninurta. The pervading message is that she was a compassionate and familiar goddess. The mother of the gods, though the 'true and great lady of heaven', also implies that there were contenders to the title one of whom was surely Inana.

Inana was in a different league! The first prima donna of the spirit world for whom we have solid evidence: she who, like so many of her later counterparts, took on the conflicting roles of goddess of love and fertility, and of war:

> Arrayed in battle,
> beautiful . . . who handles the utug-weapon,
> who washes the tools in the blood of battle.
> She opens the door of battle.
> The Wise One of Heaven, Inana.[11]

And from her temple at Zabalam:

> The great dragon who speaks inimical words to the evil,
> who makes everything as clean as the whitest of things,
> who goes against the enemies' land.
> Through her the firmament is made beautiful in the evening.

Her portrait on the seal of Adda sums up her public image succinctly. The way she stands imperiously at the summit of a mountain, commanding, armoured, wings spread, is very much Inana as the Sumerians saw her. Yet her character was more complex. She was at times a schemer; she could be petulant, petty, and yet also, in her own fashion, capable of profound concern and compassion.

Inana can in no way be seen as synonymous with or a successor to Ninhursaĝa. Portraits of Inana were being made as early as the third millennium and she enjoyed her authority from a distant time in Sumer's religious tradition.

Even disguised by synonyms, Inana and Ninhursaĝa are reasonably easy to identify in literature. There is less obvious distinction in art yet, for reasons which will become clear, it is important to separate the one from the other. Neither carry, as a matter of habit, accoutrements comparable to the sun god's saw, or Enki's streams of water. Sometimes both are drawn heavily armed, though one wonders if this was not down to confusion on the part of the local seal engravers. From Sargon's time onwards, however, deities earned symbols. On occasions, these symbols came eventually to replace images of the god, perhaps once more revealing an age-old fear in the magic of realism.

Sometimes 'keys' to the symbols can be gleaned from votive inscriptions and commemorative steles, but the greatest boon to identifying who is symbolically who lies in kudurru or boundary

stones, introduced by the Kassites who ruled southern Mesopotamia after the collapse of the Third Dynasty. The stones came
to be used as proof of land ownership, and they were effectively
underwritten by a deity – abuse the real estate and the god's
wrath came down on you! The stone was engraved with both
the name of the deity and the appropriate symbol, though with
some pitfalls because the engravers were prone to include more
than one symbol for the same god and also to include symbols
for gods not mentioned in the text. Nonetheless kudurru stones
are fairly reliable points of reference.

Inana's name and 'signature' changed in the Akkadian period,
but before that her symbol was a bundle of reeds tied in three
places and with a ribbon fluttering from the top. The choice of
symbol may be explained by the fact that her home city lay close
to the edge of the southern marshes. She often rides in a reed
boat, and her temple is sometimes described as being built with
reeds:

The Lord has created an altar,
In his reed filled house that he has purified for you
He performs your rites.[12]

With the coming of Sargon, Inana became assimilated with
Ištar, the first of many name changes which this supreme goddess was to withstand. Ištar – the shining star of the heavens
– took the symbol of a star. The Akkadians brought with them,
and subtly merged, some of the trappings of an astral deity.

Ninhursağa's symbol[13] is less certain, either in what it depicts,
or in what the object implies. It is a device, drawn with minor
variations, but generally an open loop with outward spiralling
tips like a Greek omega. The kudurru stone which provides the
most decisive link came from Susa. It includes several major
Sumerian deities, and on the upper right hand of the second tier
is the omega. If all the other symbols on the stone are matched
with listed guarantors, the name remaining is Ninhursağa. The
stone also bears a slightly confusing forked lightning symbol, but
this represents the storm god.

The omega may be contemporary with the reed symbol of
Inana. Though it generally appears from early in the second
millennium, it has been found on a damaged and isolated seal
of the Early Dynastic Period, dating from about 3000 BC. What
does it mean though? That may seem an academic question but
it becomes vital to know the answer. One of the most rational

arguments is that it represents a womb, although not the organ
from the human body. Surgery or dissection may have been the
subject of taboo in Mesopotamia because knowledge of anatomy
seems particularly sketchy. It may have relied largely on inspec-
tion of the insides of warriors felled in battle, generally male, and
on probing the viscera of domestic animals.

Gynaecology[14] thus progressed from knowledge of the repro-
ductive organs of a cow or a sheep, not those of a woman. The
uterus of a hooved mammal is bicornuate, resulting from the
partial joining of two primitive chambers which once lay on the
left and right sides of the abdomen. From the single sac sprout
a pair of blunt 'horns' which run into the Fallopian tubes, thus
giving the organ its description. If such a uterus is cut in half,
the shape becomes that of the omega.

Interest in this kind of imagery to signify the fertility goddess
was already time honoured. The design of the vulva preoccupied
the Ice-Age artists, and there is strong suggestion that variations
on the uterus design were adopted elsewhere. It is arguably the
basis of the Egyptian SA symbol. The uterus, therefore, would
not be unfitting as symbol of a Sumerian fertility goddess, and
Ninhursaǧa was unquestionably associated with the cow itself.
Cattle predominate in the carvings at Tell el'Ubaid, and at a
Ninhursaǧa shrine in the Diyala region the Sumeriologist,
Delougaz, found a model of a bison, a beast probably by then
extinct but kept on in artistic memory. The omega motif largely
disappears from Akkadian art, but it emerges again on a number
of cylinder seals made in the Old Babylonian period around the
nineteenth century BC. At this point in time, when it is engraved
beside a human figure either an element of confusion or of
syncretism creeps in because the goddess often has bow cases
on her shoulders, symbols of Ištar. She also holds a leashed
lion cub – a popular animal, unfortunately, with several other
deities including Ištar.

Ninhursaǧa though, has unequivocal and significant links
with lions. The Keš temple hymn refers to the 'great mountain'
– a play on her name – and to the 'great lion . . . on the high
plain'. The main portico in her temple at Tell el'Ubaid bears a
magnificent relief of a lion hybrid and, very often, the ends of
the omega spirals are surmounted by tiny lions' heads.

The term 'mother goddess' is a comparatively modern usage
stemming only from classical times. There is no such Mesopotamian phrase. But the message which emerges from Sumer is
that two goddesses shared, on the face of it, similar roles, though

not always in the same places or at the same time. There is also an inference that, even if they were slowly drawing together as facets of the one, Ninhursağa played the more maternal role, whilst Inana displayed the temperament of the precocious mistress. Whether by circumstance or design, the glories of one were destined to survive the passage of time whilst memory of the other faded. From the end of the Third Dynasty, Ninhursağa seems largely to have disappeared, apart from her occasional appearances on Old Babylonian and Kassite carvings, though there is strong argument that she reappeared as Belet ili, in Babylon. Whether, in truth, this is a reflection on her fate is yet to be explored, but ostensibly it was Inana and her successors who stole the limelight. Inana was the heroine of the earliest legends to find their way into the written word. Here, at last, we may have messages to explain the role of those enigmatic female figures demonstrated so passionately by ancient art, and to decipher how devotion was translated into ritual.

The lines of Sumerian legends and hymns[15] shape a great seasonal festival of New Year to invoke the gods of the earth. It was held in April or May at the time of the harvest when the effects of drought could also be at their most serious under the blistering heat. Hope was for new germination that would escape the immensely destructive capacity of the Tigris flooding the plain in October. It lay in the capricious hands of Enki, and it lay with the female essence of fertility. The persona may have altered from that perceived by the hunters. Inana was very much the goddess of life in the fields, and through her essential female fruitfulness came the resurrection of the world, and it was this fecundity, this cyclical abundance locked in her womb, that the people of Mesopotamia sought to release in a supreme rite of devotion – the Sacred Marriage. This public act of passion and reverence to the mother earth, of all pagan rituals, was in the fullness of time to be the ultimate anathema for the leaders of the Children of Israel. Yet in its pure ideology it was fundamental to the faith and lives of millions.

Inana was the womb of the earth which the peasant farmer tilled. The earth was her temporal self, as was all that grew from it, and the womb must be fertilized by the semen from the skies to bring new life to the fields and orchards. Inana, the goddess, had to be sexually impregnated. The alternative was famine and desolation. It was a delightfully clear and profound metaphor. Yet the calendar could provide no comfort, no prediction. The wetting of the plain was a capricious thing. How was it to be

both ensured and survived? What magic was needed to invoke
the goddess? The answer lay, as one guesses it always had done,
in ritual. This for the Sumerians was the reason for an annual
drama which, by the time it had degenerated into the Palestinian
cult of Aštoreth, was to provide such powerful pen-fodder for
the prophets of Israel. Two people, chosen by divine right, climbed
into a ceremonial bed in full and public view, and made love. This
was no apology for a ritualized orgy. The substance of the Sacred
Marriage was a profound and glorious celebration of that which
the goddess herself celebrated in the heavens.

The Marriage was no local observance. It was a national
festival to honour the country's first lady. At least five Sumerian
accounts of it have been discovered, from widely differing times
and places. A heady mixture of sexuality and divine cult, full
of ceremonial glitter and paraphernalia, the festival must have
generated a unique electric energy.

On the eve of the New Year, a bed made of cedar and rushes
was prepared in the *gipar* house, a bower built to receive the
goddess each year, by the king in a garden of the palace. The
bed was spread with a special coverlet and fragrant oils were
sprinkled on the ground. As the climax of the night approached,
a girl chosen to fill the part of the goddess was ritually bathed
and prepared. For her, a votary priestess, there was perhaps little
thought of an ordeal by legitimized rape. In her eyes, she was to be
deflowered by a god, because her partner in the Marriage was her
king. Clearly the ceremony afforded enormous kudos to her who
briefly became Inana. She was singled out for honours. When the
city of Uruk was excavated, a necklace was found lying close to
the great Inana temple. An exquisite piece of jewellery, made of
semi-precious stones, it is inscribed:

Kubatum, the lukur-priestess of Šu-Sin.

There is a great deal in the Canticus Canticorum which bears
strong similarity to Sumerian poetry describing the Sacred Marriage, and there is some strength in the argument that the Hebrew
songs, at least in part, may owe their beginnings to Sumerian
poems written down during the Third Dynasty. Šu-Sin was one
of the sons of Šulgi and it could be that he, not Solomon, is
referred to in the opening of the biblical Canticus. Lukur is
the title which designated the Inana votary, Kubatum. Thus
four thousand years ago, on a heady New Year's eve, a young
woman became immortalized in history. She was dressed with

great ceremony and, wearing her necklace, she was led to the bower. There she lay beside her king so that the parched and dead fields of her country might bloom again.

An ancient hymn[16] celebrating the occasion bubbles with the wonderful imagery that so often flows through the lines of Sumerian poetry:

> As for me, my vulva. For me the piled-high hillock,
> Me, the maid, who will plough it for me?
> My vulva, the watered ground – for me,
> Me, the Queen, who will station the ox there?

The analogy is apt to the occasion. Following the plea comes a response which one can imagine as a great roar of exuberance:

> O Lordly Lady, the king will plough it for you,
> Dumuzi the king will plough it for you.

It is difficult not to be caught up in the magnetism which these few verses from a long dead civilization have managed to carry, undimmed, down the span of years. For these people, as for so many ancient cultures, religion was not an abstract facet of life. It was the means of life itself. It embraced every aspect of their world. It brought their gods into each breathing moment of their days.

Dumuzi is the other half of the sexual equation. He lived in a time somewhere between myth and history: an heroic age not unlike that in which the Siberian legends were set, and perhaps paralleling that of the biblical Patriarchs. He was not a great deity like Inana, yet his impact on the ancient world was incalculable, and his presence poses enormous questions, not least for the Christian faith.

According to the Sumerian 'King List',[17] the chronicle of the royal dynasties, Dumuzi actually existed and was the son of a great warrior king Lugalbanda. It is no more possible though, to qualify his life and times historically than it is to confirm the existence of Abraham or Moses. The heroic age of Sumer took place deep in its time of illiteracy, the period of proto-history, and in the early section of the 'King List' there are many inconsistencies and anomalies.

There is no real clue to why Dumuzi was singled out for the honour of being the traditional consort of the Queen of Heaven. The old texts identify several of the heroic rulers to be her divine lovers, but only Dumuzi, or Tammuz as he became for the Hebrew writer of Ezekiel, became truly legendary. According to the lists he was a native of Kua, near the city of Eridu far to the south of Uruk where, incidentally, Inana sported her own ebullient champion. The connection is thus unclear.

There exist in a number of collections around the world old Babylonian sculptures which are conventionally tagged as 'erotica'. It would be all too easy to dispose of them under this label, but some are worth a second glance. The British Museum holds filed in its basements three small terracotta models, all made some time in the second millennium. None has come from excavations which have been properly recorded, so their exact origins are vague.

One, preserved only as a fragment, has a naked couple embracing on a bed. But a similar model is complete. Measuring about 15 centimetres by 8 centimetres, there is nothing to link it positively with the Sacred Marriage, and neither the man nor the woman wear any jewellery or other identifiying features. Yet they lie together in an arrangement which is very precisely described in the legend of the Sacred Marriage.

The bed is modelled on a massive construction of four timbers lashed together and spanned, as the texts seem to require, by rushwork, and it is unlikely that the average Sumerian farmer would have risen to such luxury. It has another odd feature: the legs at the foot are shorter than at the head which suggests that it may have been designed to tilt and give a clearer view to the onlooker. The model was mass produced by filling a mould — the upper surface is fine, the underneath rough, and the legs are applied as stubs. It is very similar to examples found elsewhere including numbers of lead plaques excavated from the site of Aššur. One possibility is that they were deposited as temple votive offerings.

The third terracotta depicts a man, naked but for a bonnet, entering a woman from behind. It is very gracefully moulded, clearly depicting a ritual, and in view of the speculation about the 'buttocks images' is an intriguing find because the woman's posture is unmistakably reminiscent of that drawn in the Ice-Age art. She is wearing a girdle round her waist and a necklace, perhaps like that of Kubatum, the lukur priestess. What she is doing, additional to receiving the man, has been the subject of debate. The usual argument is that she is leaning over a tall urn and drinking through a straw. This explanation is short on reason, though it could be argued that she is taking, symbolically, the water of the sacred river, the celestial semen.

There is another possibility. There is much in Sumerian and Akkadian literature which touches on the magical plant of life. The notion persisted. Amongst letters written to the seventh-century-BC Assyrian king, Ešarhaddon, is the comment: 'We were dead dogs. The Lord, the King gave us life by means of placing the plant of life under our noses.' There are obscure references to kissing the sacred straw of the harvest in a fertility rite and it seems possible that, although other illustrations show drinkers using reed straws, the woman is smelling or kissing the holy plant as a complement to her ritual intercourse.

Most of the small sculptures are of Babylonian origin, but there is an engraving on a Sumerian cylinder seal, much older than the terracottas, which may also describe the Sacred Marriage ceremony. Carved in the Early Dynastic period, it depicts a couple on a bed, with an onlooker, a plant in an urn, and under the bed a scorpion, one of the many ancient symbols of fertility because of its habit of carrying its babies around with it.

The legend and ritual of the Sacred Marriage lay within the core of the Sumerian's belief. Its essence was the union of god and goddess and there must be some reason for believing that the ritual had travelled from deep in pre-history, perhaps first immortalized in the enigmatic crouching figurines of the Ice Age. In Mesopotamia it was destined to take several forms, but that drawn in the old hymns is probably the oldest. The male and female elements of nature, through their divine intercourse in the spring of the year, brought new life to the world. Yet somehow the logic was impaired. Dumuzi was a demi-god. Inana had made him thus. Dumuzi, the immortal consort impregnated the womb of the goddess with new life, yet for half of every year the magic of this regenesis failed.

I (Inana) cast my eye over all the people
Called Dumuzi to the godship of the land.
Dumuzi the beloved of Enlil
My mother holds him ever dear
My father exalts him.[18]

Life withered in spite of this celestial union. Death came in the desolation of the Mesopotamian summer and autumn. Plants shrivelled, cattle starved, sheep and goats became barren. There had to be an antithesis to the story of new life. It comes in a complex and, in some respects, deeply disturbing story. For many years, a certain legend was recognized in tiny disconnected pieces and only recently have the fragments been assembled into a recognizable whole. Their rebuilding has, in itself, presented an epic labour. The complete text is the product of at least twenty-eight different source tablets, and because the earliest known fragments date only from about 1750 BC even these are 'secondhand' Old Babylonian copies.

Two legends effectively are bound into a single epic:[19] Inana's Descent into the Underworld, and the Death of Dumuzi. Dressed in her emblems of power, Inana descends to challenge the forces of evil. But the mistress of the underworld, Ereškigal, perhaps Inana's dark *alter ego*, takes her captive. As Inana passes through the seven gates of the dead, she is stripped of her finery and subjugated, and at the climax of the ordeal, is brought in her nakedness, and placed on Ereškigal's throne in a grotesque parody of queenship. Before Ereškigal and the Anunnaki – the seven terrible judges of the nether world – the goddess of life is condemned. They fasten on her the gaze of death and she is hung, lifeless, from a stake. All is not lost though. Following the goddess' instructions, after three days and nights of absence, her maid Ninšubur seeks help from three of the great gods. Only Enki receives the messenger with sympathy. He wills an illness on Ereškigal, sending two strange creatures, Kalatur and Kurgarra, ostensibly to minister to her. They are instructed to flatter Ereškigal until she promises a reward. It is to be the body of the dead goddess. The two amorphous beings sprinkle the corpse with the food and water of life. Thus her resurrection begins. After three days Inana returns from the dead.

> . . . When Inana had been subjugated, the garments that
> had been removed were carried away.
> Then her sister (Ereškigal) rose from her throne
> and she (Inana) took her seat on her (sister's) throne.
> The Annunaki, the seven judges (of the netherworld)
> rendered their decision against her (Inana)
> They looked at her with the look of death
> They spoke to her with the speech of anger
> They shouted at her with the shout of guilt
> The afflicted woman was turned into a corpse
> and the corpse was hung on a hook.
> After three days and nights had passed
> her major-domo, Ninšubur
> carried out the instructions of her mistress . . .[20]

Such is the first part of the legend. But there is a sequel because Inana may not leave the underworld unless another takes her place, and the goddess is followed back to life by the galla, the demon beasts who are to return her by force unless she complies. The final choice of victim, chosen wildly in an irritated pique, is Dumuzi but, realizing the implication for the natural world, Inana is persuaded to hand out sentence with Solomonesque pragmatism. Dumuzi is to remain in the underworld for half of every year, and his sister Geštinana stays hostage for the other half.

Thus the Sumerians accounted for the death of the natural world under the blistering heat of the Mesopotamian sun. As legend provided Sumer's religion with an understanding of the miracle of nature's genesis, so legend provided the explanation for its fullest cycle – the endless alternating cycle of life and death.

The legend of the Dying and Rising God was finally on the record. When it first took root in the minds of men we do not know. Perhaps it evolved out of the agricultural pioneers on the plains, perhaps much, much earlier.

That the esoteric product of visionary and intellectual imagination now rested in the hands of a comparatively sophisticated society, clearly made it no less powerful a tool than it had been round the camp fires of the hunters. So strong was the message of the death and rebirth of the earth that it was destined to capture the imagination of civilizations long after Sumer and her treasures were buried beneath the shifting earth.

The experience of Dumuzi, the masculine, frenetic, unpredictable protagonist of the duet of life, mirrored the primal ordeal of Inana with the coming of each New Year. In the spring month of Nisan, the month of Easter, successive kings down the centuries acted out the part of Dumuzi in the earthbound festival. By Babylonian times, as Marduk, they suffered abasement at the hands of their own people, were stripped of their clothing and symbolically scourged. They endured this humiliating ordeal so that the world might flourish once more. Each in his lifetime emulated that which Dumuzi, the Sacred King of Sumer, had begun.

In spite of the huge advance of literature, putting the pieces of the Sumerian jigsaw together is still down, in no small way, to conjecture. It is also accomplished in the acceptance that Sumerian religion did not arise in isolation, its roots came from the hunters, collected, fused, adapted, moulded from the old beliefs disseminated by the shamans round their nomadic camp fires. Gods and goddesses and heroes like Dumuzi are improbable as entirely new characters on the stage. They are too well formed, too polished. The jigsaw is also down to seeking evidence, not merely of phenomena, but of the effects the phenomena created.

As to ritual in Sumer, the Sacred Marriage was probably the high spot of the year, but other seasonal dramas, including that to celebrate Dumuzi's death and rebirth, must have taken place. We have hints of festivals: 'The Month of the Feast of Šulgi', and the 'Month of Eating the Barley of Ningirsu' were part of the calendar. Only the Marriage, though, seems to have survived in the record as a detailed calendar event. We have positive written entries that two of the Third Dynasty kings practised the ceremony – Šulgi of Ur in Unug (Uruk), and Iddin-Dagan at Isin. We even have details of the lavish banquets they staged afterwards.

The fact that the Marriage seems to have been a comparatively public festival has led to the poor suggestion that ritual was being replaced by drama. On the contrary, mysticism and mystery were still very much the keys to power, for which reason the more esoteric ritual could not be recorded overtly. The Assyrians practised, as did other nations of the ancient near east, a remarkable yet never clearly described cult of tree worship. It marks the next important turning point in the trail after the earth goddess.

There is a vociferous argument that tree worship never happened in Sumer, yet the cult bore tremendous significance amongst their successors in Mesopotamia, and the odds must be that it first took root with the Sumerians. It was perhaps through such rituals, practised in the privacy of the temple sanctuaries and recorded in whispered hints, that the power of the sacred king was truly sustained.

Therein lies an intriguing story which begins with André Parrot at Tell Hariri.

5

The Day of the Sapling

We have no means of knowing when mankind first forged a mental link between trees and gods, nor is there any method of identifying where such a bond originated but, probably, since the notion is universal, there was more than one starting point. Perhaps the most important, from the viewpoint of Christian Europe, is Mesopotamia.

There are arguments that tree worship did not exist there in pre-Babylonian times, but certain evidence suggests otherwise. Sumerian art and literature seem to offer a possible mechanism which would explain not only the intimacy of the fertility goddess and her consort with trees but, ultimately, the deeper meaning of such objects as the wooden crucifix in Christian legend, and of small, apparently insignificant, habits like the urge to touch wood.

It is difficult to appreciate that the thinking of an obscure and distant civilization influenced our own twentieth-century culture, or that it should be so vitally important in the search for origins of faith. Sumer's marvellously evocative literature is still virtually unknown to all but dedicated academics. Yet what is contained in her ancient texts, with their enigmatic names and activities, is not only as central to Mesopotamian wisdom as that of Christian Rome was to western Europe, but it provides a unique code to understanding mysteries of later religions.

Amongst the many Sumerian stone carvings depicting trees

one in particular bears close examination. There came a moment
when Parrot, digging through the most ancient layers of Mari,
held in his hands a small sherd of broken pot.[1] The chlorite vessel
had been carved from a solid block of stone and the fragment now
rests, with other small pieces of the same object, in the Museum
of Damascus. They account, at a guess, for about half the height
of the vessel, and the context in which it was found suggests that
it may have served some cultic purpose from as long ago as 3000
BC. Mari was then a frontier post on one of the main trade routes
to the north, little more than a group of temples, one of which
was dedicated to Inana.

Similar vessels have been unearthed as far south as the Ara-
bian Gulf, and in the Indus valley at Mohenjo-daro. One found
at Khafaje, about a hundred miles from Ur, rests in the British
Museum. The theme drawn on each pot is individual and invariably reflects some aspect of Sumerian mythology, and though
the vessels were not made by Sumerian craftsmen the style is
altogether unique. The source was discovered just beyond the
Baluchistan border, at a remote mountainous site known as Tepe
Yahya. This place lies on the ancient trade route between Sumer
and India. Scattered around the quarry were large boulders of
crude chlorite and more than a thousand vessel fragments,
some thrown away as half-finished rejects, others apparently abandoned when the factory was overrun by some distant
marauding army. The greenish grey stone has a density and a
coldness, smooth and soapy to the touch. Just to handle such
pieces is to bridge great spaces in time.

There is some reason for believing that Parrot's pot was
commissioned at Mari. It has a particular style of guilloche
(wavy) bordering around the base which was a hallmark of
the city. The fragment includes, in its centre, and rising to the
upper broken edge, a bare tree-trunk with criss-cross patterned
bark. Beside it is a figure reaching down to touch a leafy sapling.
Parrot thought it to be a man, but it lacks some expected features
– there is no beard or distinctive dress style, and it could, equally,
be a woman. The figure wears a long striped skirt, and is either
nude to the waist or covered by a plain, close-fitting bodice.
Reaching from the ground towards the waistband, and patterned
with stripes that almost blend with the skirt, is a snake, and in
the background several goaty-looking animals are browsing on
the foliage in a garden setting.

The picture rests, like so many others, on a museum shelf,
occasionally dusted off and photographed for some book on

Mesopotamian art but remaining obstinately enigmatic. The trail in search of answers to the meaning of the picture must turn to literature.

One of the most popular sagas[2] in Babylonian times, if the extent of copying is any measure, was the vast and rambling Epic of Gilgameš, Mesopotamia's greatest legendary hero, whose exploits must have stirred the pulse of every red-blooded male. He was the 'Superman' of the ancient world. Legend had it that his father was the mighty Lugalbanda; that his mother was Ninsun, and that he succeeded Dumuzi to the throne.[3] Yet, like Dumuzi, he was a product of the heroic age and there is no historical record of Gilgameš. According to the writers, he made Uruk his capital. In a romantic way he was a tyrant, a rumbustuous and at times almost Rabelaisian character who was rumoured to be a mighty despoiler of women. He left alone neither maiden with mother, daughter with hero, or wife with husband.

A copy of the Babylonian version of the Epic was discovered, virtually complete, on tablets at Nineveh in the impressive library of the last Assyrian emperor, Aššurbanipal. It was probably collected together piecemeal from separate Sumerian originals and it is divided into twelve chapters or cantos. It is important to recognize that the Epic possesses, particularly in its later sections, an obsessive underlying theme. Beneath all his lust and vigour Gilgameš was preoccupied with a more profound quest, the search for immortality. In this sense the saga is comparable with that of the medieval European knights in their search for the Holy Grail. The twelfth and last of the cantos, however, the so-called legend of 'Gilgameš, Enkidu and the Nether World', rests uneasily with the others. In essence it tells of how Gilgameš's friend Enkidu went to the nether world in a doomed attempt to retrieve two objects belonging to Gilgameš but was lost for ever. It has always seemed lacking in sense and pointless. It has been as if the core of the story is not present and that the Babylonian scribes tagged the material on to the end of the Gilgameš Epic out of convenience.

Before the Second World War, discovery of genuine Sumerian documents was still in its infancy. Understanding of Sumerian culture was largely down to the diligence of the Babylonians who copied the original material into Semitic Akkadian. Unfortunately, because the scribes were not always slavishly loyal to the authors, the copies have their limitations. The scribes made omissions, added, and changed details, as and when it suited. So, from the early part of the twentieth century, the race was on to find and translate genuine Sumerian texts.

In 1939, five years after Parrot's discovery in northern Syria, Samuel Kramer, the world's leading decoder of cuneiform, obtained a broken prism inscribed with part of a Sumerian poem.[4] There already existed other translated fragments, from Nippur and Ur, which seemed to belong to the same work. Whilst the material clearly constituted part of a story, Kramer did not recognize it as fitting any known mythological saga but, during the war years, he searched for and found several more fragments which were identifiable as parts of the same legend, and by 1940 he had in front of him at least two hundred and fifty lines of a great and, in its entirety, unknown Sumerian epic. Part, though, he recognized as the twelfth and, hitherto, unsatisfactory canto of the Babylonian Gilgameš Epic. What Kramer had discovered was the original complete chapter of which the Babylonians had copied only the second half. The full story takes on a new and fascinating light. Far from being an epilogue, it begins as a creation prologue, an arcane 'In those days, in those distant days' tale of genesis, not uncommon in Sumerian mythology.[5] The first five or six lines establish this primal setting, thus:

After heaven moved away from earth,
After earth had been separated from heaven,
After the name of mankind had been fixed . . .

Then comes a brief account of how Enki set sail on a mission to the nether world, after which Kramer's original fragment from Ur fits in:

On that day a tree, a *halub* tree –
On the bank of the pure Euphrates it had been planted
The Euphrates was its drinking water –
Mightily the south wind plucked at its base, tore at its crown;
The Euphrates on its waters carried it off.
A lady walking in fear at the word of An,
Walking in fear at the word of Enlil,
Seized the tree in her hand and brought it to Unug:
'To pure Inana's holy garden thou shalt bring it'
The lady tended the tree with her hand, she let it stand
    at her foot.
'When at last shall I have a holy throne that I may sit
    on it?' concerning it she said;
'When at last shall I have a holy bed that I may lie on
    it?' concerning it she said.

The tree grew large but she could not use it.
At its base the snake who knows no charm had set up
    for itself a nest,
In its crown the Imdugud bird had placed its young,
In its midst Lilith had built for herself a house.
The ever shouting maid, the rejoicer of all hearts,
The pure Inana, how she weeps!

The narrative, surely more than coincidentally, describes the
illustration on the Mari vessel. The story continues:

In that manner her brother, the hero Gilgameš stood by her.
Armour weighing as much as fifty minas he fastened at
    his waist.
That which weighed as much as fifty minas,
He treated like thirty shekels.
His bronze axe, his axe of the road,
His axe of seven talents and seven minas, he seized in his hand.
At its [the tree] base he smote the snake who knows no charm;
In its crown the Imdugud bird took its young,
And brought it to the mountain;
In its midst Lilith destroyed her house,
And escaped to the desert places . . .
. . . The tree, he plucked at its base, he tore at its crown;
The sons of the city who had accompanied him cut down
    its crown
Unto the pure Inana for her throne he gives it,
For her bed he gives it.
He, its base into his pukku he makes,
Its crown into his mekku he makes.

The mood of the story changes dramatically in the final scene,
that which the Babylonians preserved, as the obscure *pukku* and
mekku fall into the Underworld and Gilgameš's closest friend and
ally, Enkidu, dies.
    It is a bad mistake to interpret anything contained in the
Gilgameš Epic as trivial.[6] This chapter is deep and profound in
its meaning. It also contains some common features of the biblical Genesis story which includes the tree and the serpent.
Embedded in the seemingly innocuous lines is some of the heart
of Sumerian belief. We are looking at subtle analogy and symbolism, an art at which the Sumerians were past masters. We have a
story which forms part of a quest, the main thrust of which is

man's eternal dream of reaching beyond mortality. Gilgameš is
the personification of the dream, Inana is the goddess who represents and personifies the essential life force of the world and
the other characters are the antagonists of life – the Imdugud is
a mischievous creature of myth, Lilith is the goddess of desolation
and destruction, whilst the snake is the universal symbol of evil
and knowledge, and the goat-like animals symbolize the ravages
of natural wcar and tear.

There exists in the legend a link between the goddess and
a tree in a section of narrative important enough, apparently, to
have survived for many hundreds of years since the same event
was carved on a vessel used in a shrine centuries earlier. It also
seems to have been recognized almost from one boundary of
Sumer to the other.

There is much more here than a Mills and Boon account
of maidenly distress and knight errant. Yet the saga is cloaked
in what seems mundane triviality. One of the keys to understanding the meaning may lie with the two objects which,
despite desperate efforts to retrieve them, Gilgameš loses irrevocably, and with the mortal loss of Enkidu, into the land of death.
Elsewhere in the Epic there are parallels. Gilgameš's quest led
him to the mythical home of Utnapištim, a shadowy personality
whose name is thought to mean 'he who has found life'. Alone
among mortals, Utnapištim had been granted immortality by
Enlil. He discouraged Gilgameš, pointing out that sleep is a
mirror which reminds constantly of death, but allowed the
man to bathe in the water of life. Weighed down with stones,
Gilgameš sank to the bottom of the primeval Abzu, the deep.
There he found the Plant of Life. For a brief while he claimed it,
but on his way back to Uruk the elixir was taken from him by the
ubiquitous snake, complex spokesman of evil and knowledge. It
ate the plant and thus achieved its third enduring characteristic,
that of endless rejuvenation.

The ancient legend of Etana of Kiš , known from Babylonian
tablets, brought a similar mystical plant into the light.[7] The sun
god instructed Etana that an eagle would satisfy his quest for the
'Plant of Birth'.

Now Etana had daily been imploring Šamaš , saying:
You have eaten, O Šamaš, the fattest parts of my sheep;
O earth, you have drunk the blood of my lambs.
I have honoured the gods and revered the departed spirits,
The sailtus have used up my incense.

The departed spirits from many sacrifices
Have used up my lambs.
O Lord, from your mouth may the commandment go forth.
Give me the Plant of Birth!
Reveal to me the Plant of Birth!
Take away the burden, establish me with a son and heir!
Šamaš opened his mouth, saying to Etana,
Follow the road, cross into the mountainland,
Discover a pit, look inside.
Therein has been cast an eagle;
He will reveal to thee the Plant of Birth . . .

In a dreamlike search Etana and the eagle fell to earth, then rose again in an attempt to meet and gain help from Ištar. As with Gilgameš's quest, Etana's also ended in tragedy and frustration. Like the Plant of Life, the Plant of Birth was taboo. Its elixir was not be be grasped by any mortal hand.

Did the *pukku* and *mekku* possess a similar strength, an intrinsic power of life, and if so why? A scant but perhaps vital clue to their identity is to be found when Gilgameš speaks of: 'My *pukku* with lustiness irresistable. My *mekku* with dance rhythm unrivalled'. Perhaps these things were a drum and drumstick – objects of great veneration among early people – the old guardians of home and hearth against the spirits of misfortune and death.

Kramer's argument was that the Babylonian scribes invented the death of Enkidu to provide a dramatic highlight for an otherwise poor tale which they wished to incorporate into the Epic. But there is an underlying complexity which suggests otherwise. The key to the legend, the subject from which all else flows, is neither Inana nor Gilgameš but the *halub* tree. The story seems to be bound up with the tree's fate.

At face value, the legend is inconsistent. At the time after the world's creation, Inana, goddess of life, found a small sapling beside the sacred river, the Euphrates. For many years she tended it and watched it grow but, to her deep distress, she found it to be harbouring forces of darkness. Inana's intention, *prima facie*, was little more inspiring than to have for herself the wood for a bed and a chair. Gilgameš claimed his 'pound of flesh' for saving her lumber, made a musical instrument, but was then devastated when it was lost to the underworld. It seems that we may have read the story wrongly; we may have placed inferences on the text, which do not exist.

The Sumerian poet made a subtle but confusing play on words.

At the beginning, when referring to the sapling, he described the south wind as having: 'plucked at its base and tore at its crown'. The same phrase was chosen, one feels deliberately, to describe Gilgameš's action, and it has been assumed to imply that he cut the tree down. Yet nowhere is such a fate explicitly revealed. A young tree has great built-in resilience to the winds, a point which would not have been lost on the Sumerian farmer. The south wind may have battered the sapling, but the agent of its fall is more likely to have been the floodwater of the Euphrates. In his notes on translation this is a point on which Kramer agrees.

The story has perhaps little to do with lumberjacking and carpentry. Behind the façade, it points to the primeval challenge of the forces of life against those of desolation and destruction. 'Throne' and 'bed' are allegorical references. The *halub* tree becomes the tangible presence of the goddess. The same powerful image of a throne, carried down to Solomon and his Mercy Seat, has persisted as one on which the invisible presence of a deity rests. The bed, too, became deeply entrenched in ritual in Babylonian times and beyond. A Babylonian text in the British Museum, part of an elegant and evocative temple hymn, includes a passage which implies that marriage bed and altar are one and the same:

> The Eanna – its habitation
> The House – it has been presented to you.
> In my enduring house, floating cloudlike
> Whose name is truly a vision sweet
> Where a fruitful bed, bedecked with lapis lazuli
> Gibil has purified for you in the shrine, the great
> For you who are best suited to queenship
> The Lord has created an altar.[8]

The hymn contains another hint of allegory with the words: '. . . from the land of the *halub* tree to the land of the cedar . . .' It is well established that Dumuzi was symbolized by the cedar tree, and since the hymn describes preparations for the Sacred Marriage, it is possible that therein lies another reference to Inana becoming embodied by the *halub*. Symbolism was playing its part in the more esoteric and more profound aspects of religion, as it had done in the past.

Gilgameš and Inana enjoyed a complicated emotional bond which at times bordered on enmity. Once, when she had been spurned by her chauvinistic champion, she sent a wild bull to terrorize his city, and he likewise treated her with a mixture of arrogance and awe. But, as already established, Gilgameš's true purpose, throughout the Epic, was the quest for eternal life. He had restored the tree to Inana and in doing so had freed it to become her *alter ego*. To own part of the tree would be to grasp, once again, at his elixir. Gilgameš was being directed to follow one of the oldest and most deeply held laws of animism – that every object in nature possesses spiritual powers conveyed by its invisible guardian.

The fourth-millennium pot fragment from Mari may be the only surviving art depicting the part of the legend in which Inana tends the tree, but there emerges from the end of the third millennium, the interpretation of another scene which proved unusually popular with seal engravers.[9] A slender tree trunk with branches and a few leaves on its upper part is bent over by a figure wearing a horned helmet, the insignia of a god or a demigod, standing with axe poised to chop away part of the foliage. Kneeling in the arch of the trunk, on one seal, is a goddess, her pose almost identical to that on the Mari carving as her hands reach towards the base. Another godly figure is half rising from the ground armed with a mace.

A second version lacks the goddess figure but includes the Akkadian star symbol of Ištar. It also includes a woman holding a ceremonial bucket. In another the goddess beneath the trunk wears a tasselled skirt, again a hallmark of divinity. In another, two figures rest beneath the tree. The missing image of the snake, or any of the other proponents of adversity in the legend may, in these later engravings, be replaced by the figure with the mace. The underworld god, Nergal, was drawn in this style, often rising from the ground.

One must assume with such a legend that the essence was enacted in ritual. Both the Epic and the carvings suggest some emphasis on the removal of the crown of the tree and in this there is an intriguing speculation.

The winter of 1985 was exceptionally harsh in Britain. Many trees died in the prolonged sub-zero temperatures and in my own garden was a young acacia which by late spring still looked particularly unhappy. As a last resort before consigning it to the bonfire, I tried an old horticultural trick of removing the crown from the main stem. Within two weeks the tree was on the mend and sprouting healthy new green growth. Nobody seems to be sure of why this drastic surgery works but nine times out of ten it is dramatically effective. For cold substitute heat and drought

that have rendered a tree sickly and dying; water it, and de-crown
it, and technically there exist the ingredients of magical rebirth. It
should be said that no botanical identity has yet been established
for the *halub* but the illustrations on the cylinder seals suggest
perhaps a willow or poplar, and with both species the excision
of the crown is an effective remedy.

There is no proof that this chapter of the Gilgameš Epic
accounts for the first restless pulses of sap in the Tree of Life,
but by Babylonian and Assyrian times it had grown into a truly
remarkable phenomenon and the only common source of inspiration was Sumer. It is probably fair to assume that the biblical
Tree stemmed in spirit from Inana's garden beside the Euphrates.

Why should trees have been singled out as the focal point
of a Mesopotamian cult? Probably through the same logic that
brought bulls to veneration. Despite its newly acquired veneer
of civilization, Mesopotamian life was still precarious and short.
It deferred to the principle of survival of the fittest and strongest.
Trees were and still are uncommon on the alluvial plains. The
great trees stood in the mountains, the dwelling places of the
gods. They were also perceived to be the largest living things in the
natural world, reaching their arms to the heavens and providing
the closest animate link between god and mortal. Those which
do spring up on the plains – date palm, willow and poplar – are
undeniably tough, and they cope with a concentration of salt
which has all other greenery withering. Thus, in Mesopotamian
eyes, the trees stood out as lone and tenacious survivors.[10] One of
the great cities of the southern marshes, Eridu, was the centre of a
tree-worshipping cult long after Sumer had collapsed, and among
the obscure Sumerian texts in the British Museum is a temple
hymn which suggests that the priests of Eridu were bowing to
the power of trees in the third millennium or earlier.

> In Eridu there is a black kiškanu-tree,
> Growing in a pure place,
> Its appearance is lapis lazuli, erected on the Apsu.
> Enki, when walking there, fills Eridu with abundance,
> In the foundation of it is the place of the underworld,
> In the resting place is the chamber of Nammu.
> In its holy temple there is a grove, casting its shadow,
> Therein no man can enter
> In the midst are Utu and Dumuzi,
> In between the river with the two mouths.[11]

The kiškanu-tree, and the 'grove' clearly have deep significance, no longer in a legendary garden setting but within the
sanctuary of a temple. There are also hints that the Tree itself
had changed. In ritual it was not necessarily destined to remain
a living plant. The phrase: 'its appearance is lapis lazuli', is echoed
in the ninth Babylonian canto of Gilgameš:

Carnelian it bears as its fruit.
Vine grapes are hanging there, sweet to look at.
Lapis lazuli the foliage is,
Fruit it bears, wonderful to behold.

By the era of the Isin kings, and probably by the Third Dynasty
of Ur or earlier, there is other evidence that the Tree was being
changed into a stylized totem, with indications that a wooden
trunk or pole was decorated with metal bands and ribbons, and
studded with precious stones.[12] The bulk of art evidence comes
later, at the time of the Middle Assyrian period, but the scant
records from the end of the Sumerian epoch leave a firm hint
that the Tree had its place in Sumer's ritual.

In Eridu, the Tree of Life was indivisible from the Water of
Life. The ancient text tells that the shrine was built on the Abzu.
This vast undergound sacred sea may have been represented by
a pool beside the shrine with its 'grove' – a term for the totem
of the tree which was to become popular with the translators
of the Old Testament. The same text also speaks of the 'river
with the two mouths', which alludes to the two sacred rivers of
Mesopotamia.

Enki is often depicted with two streams of water flowing
from him to his left and right, and one of the most famous
of all Sumerian sculptures, the icon of Gudea of Lagaš, holds
a vase from which spring these same sweet waters of life.[13]

The god king was the guardian of the sacred water, linked to
his role as Dumuzi in the Sacred Marriage. A hymn to the Isin
Dynasty king, Ur-Ninurta, entrusts him to: 'keep open the holy
mouth of the Tigris and Euphrates.' Another, to Šulgi of Ur cries:
'Shepherd Šulgi, thou possessest water, pour out water!'

The king was also 'The Gardener', the 'nukarribu', he who
alone was to guard and to tend the sacred grove. This sacred duty
goes back at least to Sargon's time. A fragment of text, relating to
Sargon's childhood, includes the line: 'Akki, the waterscooper,
placed me as his gardener. When I was a gardener, Ištar was
in love with me.' A gentle insight that spins one more thread

binding sacred grove and goddess of the earth. It may also help
to explain such obscure snippets of unlikely trysting, as when in
an episode of Gilgameš, the hero complains: 'You loved Isullanu,
your father's gardener.'

We know that a number of specific kings from later dynasties
built garden sanctuaries of a kind that would become more
precisely identified in Babylonian times. Nur-Adad, a king of
the Larsa Dynasty, immortalized his love of the Tree of Life in
a brief inscription:

Of Enki his pure and beloved dwelling he built for him,
of his ancient kiškanu-tree its place he restored for it.[14]

Evidently Eridu, Nur-Adad's city, had been subject to some
level of destruction and he had rebuilt the cult sanctuary.

Another Larsa Dynasty ruler, Sumu-ilu, left this inscription:

Unto Nin-isin . . . the fine garden
where a plant is growing, the Plant of Life, he gave.

There is a small but intriguing point about these terse words
that Nin-isin is certainly Ninhursaǧa by another name.

A king of the same dynasty, Warad-Sin, offered a similar
dedication:

The house of the Plant of Life, the holy dwelling . . .
her secure making place, her house . . .
for my life and the life of Kudur-Mabuk, the father who
begat me,
I built for her.

It is obvious that the building of the garden was a moment of
great importance in history. A date formula has been discovered
among chronicles of the First Babylonian Dynasty: 'The year in
which the Garden of the Gods was made.'

Evidence points to Eridu, the southern city of the marshes
between the mouths of the great rivers, as the most important
location of the paradise garden, despite the legendary link with
Inana's city of Unug. It is equally obvious, however, that similar
sanctuaries were constructed in many other cities, each with its
garden to house the Tree of Life, and perhaps the Marriage bower
and the Sacred Pool which came to represent the Abzu.

The art must be weighed with the writing. Cylinder seals from

as early as the end of the Early Dynastic period are engraved
with images which can be interpreted as tree worship. Gods or
priests and kings sit facing plants that range from shrubs in pots
to small trees. Heraldic animals flank sacred trees. On one seal a
pair of stags face reverentially towards a small tree which grows
centre stage. Another from a slightly later date bears a tree atop
a mountain, flanked by two bison under ritual slaughter.

Inana's symbolic link with trees is complicated by the fact
that Dumuzi was also identified by the cedar, a tree whose
phallic-shaped cones give it a strong appearance of masculinity:

> My shoulder is the cedar, my breast is the cypress,
> My . . . is the consecrated cedar,
> The cedar, the consecrated of Aššur,
> The shade of Dilmun.

The texts thus suggest that there was not one, but two sacred
trees which came to symbolize the partners of the Sacred Marriage, and that both stood adorned in the sanctuary. Dumuzi's
Tree may, in the fullness of time, have become the stone pillar
or *massebah* frequently mentioned in Old Testament texts.

Through the lines of another glorious piece of Sumerian
poetry, there drifts an image:

> Hero, whose body is shining splendour,
> who in the forest of fragrant cedars is cheered with joy,
> standing in the sanctuary of Abzu, the adorned,
> purified with the sparkling water.[15]

There is also some fairly hard literary backing for the belief that
a dead, or at least sickly tree, represented the death of the natural
world. The king sprinkled a wilting branch or potted shrub with
the Water of Life to begin the magic of resurrection, paralleling
that of Inana after her descent to the underworld.

If there are questions, they lie most thickly in the area of
interpretation of the mythology. The Descent legend provided
two distinct but interwoven themes. On the one hand it describes
the confrontation, so beloved of Mesopotamians, between good
and evil. The dark side of the cosmic forces triumphs briefly and
is then overcome. On the other hand, the fate of Dumuzi, whilst
mirroring the primordial ordeal of Inana, symbolizes the cyclical
death and rebirth of nature. Did the Mesopotamian rituals of the
Tree celebrate the revival of the goddess from her battle with

Ereškigal separately from the spring revival of her incestuous lover, or did ritual mingle the two aspects of the legend? That which persisted in tradition was a fusion of both parts of the story. The death and restoration after three days of hope for mankind was inseparable from the annual festival of spring rebirth.

The message which comes through the texts points to ceremonies of revival being directed principally towards the symbol of the dying and rising god:

A tamarisk which in the garden has no water to drink,
whose foliage on the plain sends forth no twig.
A plant which they water no more in its pot,
whose roots are torn away.
A herb which in the garden has no water to drink . . .
among the flowers of the garden he sleeps
among the flowers of the garden he is thrown.[16]

The texts have to be matched with the many illustrations of the king pouring water over a tree or branch in a pot.

The goddess of life presented the imagery of one who was barren for half of the annual cycle whilst her consort was 'sleeping'. Rites surrounding the Tree of Life, Inana's sacred tree, were perhaps seen as an act of symbolic fertilization of one whose womb was ready but needing a catalyst.

There is also an uncertainty in how the Sumerians saw the roles of Enki and Dumuzi, since both were perceived to be the inseminators of the earth. There is no suggestion that Enki was ever a celestial lover of Inana but, on occasion, he is described as the Gardener in the heavenly setting of Dilmun, the Sumerian paradise:

He brought him the cucumbers of his cultivation,
He brought him the apples in their luxuriant greatness
He brought him the grapes in their clusters.
Enki, his face turned pale, he gripped the staff.
Enki waited for Utu
In his house he cries: 'Open!'
'Thou, who art thou?'
'I am the gardener, I would give thee cucumbers, apples and grapes,
according to thy wish.'
Utu with joyful heart opened the door of the house.
Enki to Utu behaved kindly.

He gave him the cucumbers of his cultivation.
Gave him the apples in their luxuriant greatness,
Gave him the grapes in their clusters.[17]

We have to live with the dilemmas until such time as clearer
pictures emerge. Perhaps such pictures will never come. There
is, however, much which can be pieced together. Faintly, but
constantly, there comes a message from this ancient and eloquent
civilization of Sumer that she possessed two great cyclical rites,
one public and robust, a drama into the spirit of which each
and every Sumerian could join. Beside the public show there
was another, a deeper darker rite performed by the king and his
priests in the seclusion of the sanctuary. In its purpose it paralleled the Sacred Marriage, the awakening of the earth mother's
powers of regenesis by the god but it was a more profound rite
of intercourse whose strength came through allegory and cipher.

There exist weaknesses in the thread which can never be
ignored. The Mesopotamian civilizations – Sumer and those
which followed in her wake – lived through a time span which
represents only a fraction of that covered by the prehistoric hunters, but a formidable one nonetheless. History, by comparison
with today's experience, was still moving very slowly, and it
accounts for some of the striking longevity of certain themes
and ideals in the hearts of men. Mesopotamian society arose,
however, from disparate tribal origins and, notwithstanding the
cohesive influence of such 'giants' as Sargon the Great, local
cults persisted. They sustained their own peculiar traditions and
differences about gods and goddesses some of which would have
been irreconcilable one to another.

Much of Sumer's exquisite legacy was preserved in the art
and literature from the Old Babylonian period whose writers
and artists followed her footsteps. Much as it is tempting to
take this translated material as 'gospel', it offers no absolute proof
unless there are unquestionable Sumerian originals. We have no
means of evaluating how much or how little of it was tampered
with and adapted by Babylonian scribes and engravers.

Time has been gentle with all too little of Sumer's sensitive
and strangely beautiful language and art. Pursuit of wisdom
perhaps grew more in the Sumerian age than it had in the
past 60,000 years, pushed onward by a settled lifestyle and by
a new found gift, the ability to commit human thought to the
written word. It is a curious human limitation, that whilst we
can draw pictures in the mind, alter them, and elaborate them, if

we do not have language in our heads and our hearts we cannot reason about the images we create. The more words we have, the deeper can our reasoning penetrate. The Sumerian people used their boon to explore the edges of imagination and to translate these frontiers of the mind into tangible record. They used it to feed off one another, to advance their rationalization about the world. They were possessed of a great curiosity and a sense of challenge. What they left behind shouts that they shared the same richness of spirit, the same clarity of understanding about nature, that the hunters so well displayed through their own haunting and timeless art.

Sumer passed on the framework of the first written belief in the gods of the earth, fashioned we may believe from an ancestral faith. The legends and rites, festivals and hymns, which those arcane nomads handed on as their legacy may have finally achieved maturity during the Akkadian era of Sargon, but the 'book of the mind' from whence they came was infinitely older. The grand design was a child of the scattered visionary people who came to build a shining new world on the dusty plains of the two sacred rivers.

The culture of the great Third Dynasty of Ur had, by the end, come a long way from that of their hunting forefathers. They rendered to their gods a sense of humanity that their predecessors seem to have shunned, and the spirit world had probably changed almost out of recognition. Yet central figures had emerged and become indisputable personalities, and whilst we cannot know for certain that the mother and consort were descendants of those arcane deities left to us in scattered and nameless pieces of stone and clay, we must assume that they stemmed from the images of some primal faith nurtured and grown in the greyness of pre-history.

The way in which the inheritors of Sumer's gift, Kassites, Hurrians, Babylonians, Assyrians, Hittites, Amorites, and a host of others, amongst them the group of nomadic herdsmen who came to be known as the 'Children of Israel', chose to use their inheritance was in each case very different and yet the same.

6

The People Who Loved Trees

Tucked away behind the British Museum's celebrated Hall of Egyptian Sculptures is Gallery Nineteen. The indulgences of the Pharaohs lure their regular throng of London sightseers but few visit this shy appendage. Those who do tend to pause, perhaps in puzzlement, and walk on because what rests there is something of an enigma. The walls of this long, narrow hall are hung with slim, but massively wrought, carved stone panels. The shallow reliefs are in a style reminiscent of Assyrian palaces in the first millennium BC. They breathe an aura of cartoon super-heroes. Hugely muscled limbs, thin humourless lips, and cold bulging eyes, embellish figures with a chilling absence of warmth or sentiment.

It is not these dramatic figures though, to which the eye of the visitor is insistently drawn. The focus of the works is another object, a small bushy tree of bizarre construction.

The Assyrians brought tree worship to its most glittering pinnacle. That might be adequate justification to dedicate this chapter to their day in the journey, but there is also a more significant reason. The first millennium BC was a momentous epoch in the world of the ancient near east. It marked the end of the old orders and the beginning of the new, the demise of conservative doctrine and the emergence of ideas as radical as those of the ancient hunter gatherers who wandered northern

Mesopotamia and whose scant remains may still lie under the
alluvium of the south. It saw the consolidation of the Hebrews and
the changing fortunes of Israelite nationalism; through it stormed
Darius, Cyrus, Alexander and Pompey. Influences brought to bear
on the Israelites during this time not only affected their way of life
but also deeply coloured their ideology, and if it is true that Egypt
and her beliefs swayed the Patriarchs and the wandering Hebrew
pioneers, it is equally certain that Babylonia and her great rival in
Mesopotamia, Assyria, were *forces majeures* in the forging of the
religion of the Israelite kingdoms.

The popular notion is that the Babylonians were the great
thorn in the side of the prophets including Ezekiel and Jeremiah,
but this misconception came about because much of the definitive writing-down of Israelite history and religion was carried out
during the period of the Exile under neo-Babylonian rule in the
sixth century BC. It is worth bearing in mind that the First Babylonian Dynasty had gone largely unnoticed until the hegemony
created by Hammurabi I, and although at their apogee the neo-
Babylonians did control the known world, their illustriousness
was short-lived. The arguably overrated Nebuchadnezzar oversaw the destruction of Jerusalem in 587 BC but he achieved
comparatively short-term dominance over the Bible lands.

The major power and the dominant cultural influence during
the first half of the millennium lay to the north – in the Assyrian
cities of the Tigris. It was Assyrian state religion that rested hand
in reluctant hand with that of the prophets in both kingdoms, but
particularly in the northern state of Israel, for much of the period
of the Davidic line of kings. That which the Assyrians took as their
religion becomes of great significance in trying to fathom some of
the anomalies raised by the Old Testament.

To return to Gallery Nineteen, the carvings owe their discovery to an Englishman, Austen Henry Layard, who brought them
before the gaze of curious Londoners in 1849. The Assyrian city
in which they lay undisturbed for nearly three thousand years
was found only by a fortuitous turn of events.

In the mid-nineteenth century, at the beginning of the era
of Mesopotamian rediscovery, the landscape of the northern
plain was littered with *tells*, some small mounds, others huge
expanses of windblown soil forming sizeable hills.[1] Almost all
were shrouded in mystery. On the northernmost tributary of
the Tigris lies Iraq's second city, Mosul. A hundred and fifty
years ago it was a small provincial town but it has been the
modern stepping-off point for a number of major Assyrian sites.

It was a casual meeting there, in 1845, between Layard and the French consul in Mosul, Paul Emile Botta, which provided the catalyst for a momentous discovery. Layard's dream was to find the lost city of Nineveh, the fabled city first mentioned in Genesis: 'And the beginning of his [Nimrod's] kingdom was Babel, and Erech, and Accad, and Calneh, in the land of Shinar. Out of that land went forth Asshur, and builded Nineveh, and the city of Reheboth, and Calah' (Genesis 10:10). Layard's interest in Mosul was aroused by a report that, three years earlier, Botta, the amateur archaeologist, had discovered the imperial city of Dur Šarrukin at Khorsabad some way north of the town. Dur Šarrukin was the fortress capital of the eighth-century Assyrian king, Sargon II (not be to confused with the Akkadian 'Sargon the Great' who lived more than a thousand years earlier). Historical documents found at Khorsabad persuaded Layard that Nineveh lay somewhere close by.

The following year at the village of Nimrud, twenty miles south of Mosul, Layard found a huge and partly exposed mound of ruins. Believing that he had found Nineveh he rounded up a labour force and began to dig, but he unearthed a much older city, Kalakh, the Calah of Genesis.

Kalakh and the later capital of Dur-Šarrukin probably saw the zenith of Assyrian might. It reached its climax with Aššur-nasir-apli II who ascended the throne of the Assyrian empire in 884 BC. It was his city which Layard was bringing back to the light of day.

> Palace of Aššur-nasir-apli, the priest of Aššur,
> Favourite of Enlil and Ninurta, beloved of Anu and Dagan
> The weapon of the great gods, the mighty king
> King of the world, King of Assyria . . .

Thus begins the standard inscription which Layard was to find inscribed from end to end of the city. In one of the bloodiest and most tyrannical eras the world has suffered, Aššur-nasir-apli ruled the whole of Mesopotamia as far south as Babylon. The throne was darkly blood-wetted when he came to it but, even by Assyrian standards of despotism, the conquests he undertook were staggeringly brutal. There was once a fortified town in northern Mesopotamia supposedly called Kinabu. A scribe preserved Aššur-nasir-apli's victory speech for posterity: '. . . I slew six hundred with the sword, three thousand prisoners I burned in the fire. I kept no one alive as hostage. I piled their corpses as high as towers. The city king fell into my hands alive. The king I flayed and hung his skin on the wall of Damdammusa . . .'

Such was the character of a man who chose, improbably, to humble himself publicly before the sight of a quaint bushy plant. Layard was turning his spade over Aššur-nasir-apli's palace, catalogued as the 'Northwest Palace'; Aššur-nasir-apli had rebuilt the city of a distant predecessor Šalmaneser I and even by modern values he achieved a great architectural feat. The ruin of the Northwest Palace covers 10,000 square metres. At its centre is an enormous courtyard surrounded by long narrow rooms, lavishly built with the resources of a regime bulging with affluence. These state rooms were framed with cedar, cypress, mulberry, juniper and pistachio wood, and lying among the debris Layard found his panels.

The artwork of the palace presents a paradox. The visitor to Aššur-nasir-apli's court witnessed Kinabu's ordeal, in gruesome detail, in reliefs on the courtyard walls. His spirits were undoubtedly subdued already by the massive iconography: sculptures of fabulous winged bulls – the *aladlammu*, lions with human heads, other strange and terrifying hybrids, carved from blocks of awe-inspiring dimensions, loomed colossally beside doors and gates. People must have paused and marvelled, and been instantly aware of their own physical frailty. It is a forceful psychological tool utilized by more than one despot in history. Religion and mythology had abandoned their age of innocence and become, ever more closely, the bedfellows of power and politics. Religious art was, to the Assyrian élite, much more than a means of perpetuating the mechanism of mythology and rite, much more than a focus for idolatry. It had become a massive instrument of propaganda. Yet despite all of this, the visitor entering the state rooms would have been confronted by Aššur-nasir-apli's very un-warlike reverence for the object which apparently so dominated his domestic and spiritual life.

Layard found the gypseous alabaster panels lying where they had fallen when the upper walls of the state rooms collapsed. They were probably executed by local craftsmen but they have a distinctly foreign style. The workmanship bears comparison with that of bas reliefs at Sakjegözü and Carchemish in northern Syria which at the time was a vassal state. The statistics are extraordinary. The Tree motif is in nine of the rooms incorporated into at least 128 scenes. The king, wearing the royal fez and a splendid brocaded and tasselled robe, daggers thrust into his belt, is present in many but not all the carvings. A second figure, drawn more than 140 times, appears in all but two rooms, sometimes alone, sometimes with the king. It has wings and frequently wears the mitre of a god with marks along its sides suggesting the great horned head-dresses of Sumerian deities. Sometimes it is in human guise with a human visage, in others it bears the head of an eagle. Texts call it a *šedu* when it takes strictly human form, and the bird-like version seems to have been identified as an *apkallu*, an antediluvian sage. Whatever its origin it exudes the sense of being a priest playing the role of a deity. On sixty-nine occasions it holds in its right hand a tree-cone which it points, not at the king as it may appear on some reliefs, but past him at the Tree. The left hand holds a ritual bucket. The carvings give little away, but these containers were made either of metal, or more probably of plaited reeds lined with bitumen. In six carvings the figure holds a piece of plant and in one a mace. Occasionally it tends the Tree empty handed. Sometimes it turns away and points the cone at king or courtier, or even towards an open doorway.

Perhaps the most striking of all the panels is that which Layard assumed had been fixed above Aššur-nasir-apli's throne. The Tree is centre stage. Above it, as in most of the carvings, hovers the famous winged disc which the Assyrians, like so many nations, borrowed from Egypt. King and winged god are mirrored to the left and right in a confrontation style inherited from the old Sumerian model.

These carvings were the keynote of the palace decor. There are exceptions – the south wall of the throne room bore an enormous tableau of warrior prowess, and its outer façade displayed a comparable procession of tribute bearers – but they are at strident odds with the rest.

Under the hand of this man of steel, tree worship blossomed into a cult of dizzy eminence the like of which had never been equalled and which probably the world will never see again. Rulers who succeeded Aššur-nasir-apli, and who were so absolute in their power that they too ascribed to themselves the title: 'Great King of the World', went on their knees in homage to the Tree. Facsimiles of rituals by which they honoured it were carried in the pockets of princes, merchants and scribes. Traces of Aššur-nasir-apli's vision were still bubbling to the surface a thousand years on. Yet, paradoxically, in all the hundreds of texts, Sumerian, Akkadian and Babylonian, from great steles to tiny fragments of clay, there appears not a line of clear explanation. In the rituals of the Sacred Tree the gods of the earth

clung to their secrets. There are answers, but to find them means
delving deeply and minutely. They are fragmentary and intricate
parts of the thread; to begin to weave them into a coherent strand
we have to turn back a little way towards the time of Sumer and
discover some obscure connections.

In the fourteenth century BC 500 years before Assyria first
flexed her muscles on the upper Tigris, the military outpost of
Nuzi, near to modern Kirkuk and part of the ancient kingdom
of Arrapha, was laying its claim to posterity.[2] In about 1700 BC
Arrapha was absorbed into the Mitannian empire – a cultural
agglomeration bound by a common language, Hurrian. From
about 2200 BC Hurrian-speaking people were pushing steadily
further and further into Mesopotamia until, by the Third Dynasty of Ur, they had peacefully infiltrated the far south. During
Hammurabi's reign they turned north-west, finding their way
into northern Syria and Anatolia. They had thus acquired many
elements of Sumerian culture. At times Assyria was to come
under direct Hurrian rule, and from about 1400 BC Aššur
had a population including a high proportion of Hurrian-speaking
immigrants. Thus, whilst Assyria gleaned much Sumerian tradition through Old Babylon, there was a second clear line of cultural
contact between the city states of Sumer and the small emergent
state of Assyria, via the Hurrians.

When the Nuzi site was excavated in the early 1940s, an
enormous number of tablets – mostly of business records and
transactions – came to light. Many bore seal impressions, and
large collections, which seem to have been assembled over four
or five generations, came from the tiny houses of two local
merchants, Tehip-tilla and Šilwa-Tešub. Part of the interest
lies in that some of the impressions had been made with older
seals that had been in use when the town of Nuzi was known
by a more antique name of Gasur. Thus the area has yielded up
evidence of an art tradition spanning at least five hundred years
back to the early part of the second millennium.

The Tree preoccupied the seal cutters, and what they created
may provide a fascinating and even unique insight into a stylized Sumerian Tree, hinted at in poetry yet never found in any
of their authentic art. If the inference of the literature has
been interpreted correctly, the 'grove', the euphemism by which
the Tree has come to be known through the biblical writers,
was made from wood and metal adorned with precious stones
and bunting. The images drawn by the stone carvers to reflect
Aššur-nasir-apli's 'grove' are taken from no living plant; they

reflect the creation of the woodcarver and the smith. Because one of the key motives in turning from living plant to stylized totem is to allow the ingenuity of the artist free rein to move from the real world of nature to a subjective expression of the spirit within, the artists may have looked for ways of including the symbols and ciphers of the deity of the Tree within their designs.

By the time the Tree had been taken over by the Assyrians, however, the motifs had become too subtle to disentangle. The only way to reveal the meaning of Aššur-nasir-apli's design is to trace its path back. The art of Nuzi lies at a critical stage along that path.

In its most frequent form the Tree on the Nuzi seal impressions is vaguely reminiscent of a bunch of unopened flower stamens on a long pole, and it has been tagged the 'bouquet tree'. Because of the bonanza of impressions found, it is possible to trace the tenuous evolution of design from which the 'bouquet' emerged. The archive kept by Tehip-tilla was extremely large including many thousands of tablet impressions; among them were several with the 'bouquet' design, but a number of others reveal a simpler arrangement with a less recognizable plant form. On a single impression made in the time of Tehip-tilla's mother, the artist has drawn something subtly different. Instead of stamens there is what appears to be a slim chalice, and the sepals, which on the other designs surround the bouquet, have become graceful scrolls or volutes.

If it is a chalice then a logical progression begins to emerge. It originally perhaps held a small plant or a tree branch. We know from later descriptions that the 'grove' was carried, on occasions, in procession, and the use of a vase on a long pole would fit in with this notion.

The exact design of the chalice may be highly significant.[3] Away from the Nuzi collection, a number of contemporary Old Babylonian seals depict what is thought to have been a ceremonial weapon, though archaeology has failed to deliver the actual object. The weapon was symbolic; it would have been useless as a fighting tool. It looks, from the miniatures, to have consisted of a mace head both on a short baton and a long pole, and from the base of the head sprang a pair of scimitar blades which often ended in lions' heads. Theoretically, the weapon combined smashing power and cutting edge and it has been tagged the 'lion club'. Several mythological figures hold it, including various gods, bull men and, most frequently, Ištar. It

is definitely one of her weapons. Some experts believe that there
is a link between the 'lion club' and the chalice with its volutes:
Ištar's weapons of war transformed through the ingenuity of the
artist into a symbol of fertility.

There is another possibility, however. Among the Old Babylonian seals in the British Museum is one which appears, with
little doubt, to identify Ninhursağa. Standing before a hero she
has beside her the familiar omega symbol.

On another seal of the same period, rather than being suspended
in mid-air, the omega is attached to a baton, although here the
goddess wears breastplates and weapon cases, and her foot rests
on a leashed lion cub. On a third the change is complete. The
goddess stands in the same pose but the object in her left hand
no longer bears the omega. It has been changed into volutes
which now hold a slim vase. It is almost identical to that on
the seal impression from Nuzi made in the time of Tehip-tilla's
mother. Thus, the chalice design could have been based on the
omega.

Another intriguing implication of this trio lies in a trend
towards syncretizing the images of the two Sumerian goddesses,
Ninhursağa and Ištar. The breastplate and weapon cases were
attributes of Ištar, whilst the lion and the omega were generally
those of Ninhursağa. If these two fertility goddesses were made
to merge by incorporating two sets of symbolism, it could go
some way towards explaining the extraordinary design of the
Aššur-nasir-apli's Tree. That, however, involves tracing a separate strand of the thread linking forward in time from Hurrian
Nuzi, to Kalakh and her craftsmen. They created designs which
whisper of the contorted stems of lotus, yet the stubby palmettes
with which they contrived to surround the curious cat's cradle of
branches do not relate to the lotus and are actually biologically
impossible. So what are they?

Close by the Tigris lies the site of the palace of Kar-Tukulti-
Ninurta, named after the emperor who built it some four hundred
years before Kalakh. As the remains of the walls were uncovered paintings came to light which have been remarkably well
preserved. In one of a pair, two gazelles stand on the lower
branches of the Tree facing inwards in classical confrontation
pose; its companion fresco shows a hint of the extraordinary
tangle of branches familiar from Kalakh. This seems to be an
earlier design for the Tree than that which decorated Aššur-
nasir-apli's Northwest Palace, but it has several common features
including the inverted V-marks on the trunk and the palmette.

The earlier palmette has its differences though. Instead of being a fan of stubby leaves it takes on the appearance of a lobed capsule with a number of hollow chambers. Occasionally there are nine of these lobes but almost invariably the number is seven, that which predominates in the palmettes at Kalakh. Some of the Nuzi seal designs look very similar to this 'bouquet' tree. The stamens have developed knobbly rounded ends, or have become branches ending in pronounced lobes.

The number seven repeats itself, time after time, in association with the Tree. Sometimes, on Old Babylonian seals, the ends of the branches are detached and become seven globes surrounding the baton; sometimes the baton is missing and the globes are suspended in space.

Theories about the symbolic meaning of the number seven are legion. It represents the seven great spirits. It has astrological significance. It is a magical number. Beyond doubt it held great import and by the early centuries AD we have abundant literarary evidence of its popularity through such manuscripts as the *Theologoumena Arithmetica* of Jamblichus and the *De Opificio Mundi* of the Jewish Hellenic philosopher, Philon. Yet it must in some way also be peculiarly relevant to fertility goddesses.

In Milan's Biblioteca Ambrosiana rests an original 1477 manuscript by Michael Scotus, the *Liber physiognomiae*. Scotus was one of a clique of European physicians including Magnus Hundt, Wilhelm von Conches and Mundinus, holding to an archaic view that the uterus was built of seven cells, polyembryony, an idea which had been known and discussed in ancient medicine. Amongst others the second century AD neo-Pythagorean Nikomachos describes male semen ejaculating seven times during coitus, and the *Corpus Hermeticum* accredits nature herself with a seven-celled womb.

In the margin of page 96v of Scotus' manuscript is a small drawing described as '*forma matricis in muliere*' complete with notations including '*hermafrondita*', '*dextrum,*' '*sinistrum*' and so on. It possesses a similarity to the 'bouquet' models painted on the walls at Kar-Tukulti-Ninurta so striking as to be unavoidable, a similarity which extends to the impression even of the vulva at the lower margin of the Assyrian panel. Where exactly the model for Scotus' drawing came from we can only surmise but the odds must be in favour of it having travelled from the medical scholarship of the ancient near east.

Medieval physicians in Europe gained knowlege from a number

of sources – from Arab physicians, and from the classical scholars of Greece and Rome, who in turn had paid close attention
to Mesopotamian and Egyptian medicine.[4] Perhaps, even in
Mesopotamian times, the concept of a human uterus changed
from that of the bicornuate model reflected in Ninhursağa's
omega and became based on the belief in a seven-chambered
organ, arguably reflecting the seven great spirits of nature,
themselves the product of divine sperm.

If supposition is right, then the Assyrian 'bouquet' which is
also to be found in a number of Hurrian and Old Babylonian
designs, and which in turn led to the full palmette, is the cryptic
representation of a new concept of the uterus in which the symbolism of Ninhursağa became melded and blurred with that of
Ištar.

There were strong cultural links between Kar-Tukulti-Ninurta
and a number of Hurrian-dominated cities including Nuzi, and the
style of wall painting found at Kar-Tukulti-Ninurta is definitely
Hurrian. Assyria had, in practice, been subject to Mitannian rule
until shortly before the accession of Tukulti-Ninurta I when the
Assyrian hegemony was extended by his predecessor, Aššur-
uballit. So direct Hurrian influence on the styling of the Assyrian
Tree was a distinct possibility.

The search needs to widen to discover if any other clues
exist which point to a link between palmette and omega.[5]
A hundred years after Layard, another Englishman, the late
Oxford scholar M.E.L. Mallowan, retraced Layard's footsteps. In
1957 Mallowan led the British School of Archaeology excavation
of a *tell* a short distance from the Northwest Palace and, as a result,
uncovered one of the finest warehouses of Mesopotamian art.
The massive building which he dubbed 'Fort Šalmaneser' after
Aššur-nasir-apli's son, Šalmaneser III, seems to have been built
as a treasure storehouse. Šalmaneser had scoured the lands for
palace furnishings and the decor of earlier kings, presumably
thinking that it was better to assemble everything under lock and
key rather than leaving state treasures to their fate in crumbling
and abandoned palaces.

Mallowan's expedition brought this vast antique store to the
light of day, probably for the first time since it had been sacked
by the invading armies which saw to Assyria's end in the seventh
century BC. The invaders had fired the store, after looting it of
anything they considered valuable, but because they were unable
to carry anything heavy they tended to tear off the gold overlay
from furniture and trinkets. Beside the north gate two pieces of

fretwork were recovered, presumably having been seized from a table and then dropped in the mayhem. They still bear traces of gold and perhaps once adorned jewellery boxes on the dressing table of a courtier's wife.

One piece is an exquisite model, in ivory, of a cow suckling her calf against a background of columns ending in lotus flowers and buds. It demonstrates an empathy with nature that serves as a poignant contrast with the heartless warmongering image of Assyria.

The tiny sister piece, worked with great delicacy and still bearing traces of blue lacquer and gilding is typical of a design of sacred tree that has been discovered as far away as Phoenicia. Although damaged the fragment incorporates a mix of tree and lotus, with branches bearing buds at the top and older blooms lower down. Were it complete it would probably include two inward facing devotees. It is made curious, however, by the inclusion of a shallow cup spreading from the central trunk. To the casual eye the pattern is meaningless, but placed beside the omega it begins to resolve itself. The spiralled ends of Ninhursaǧa's symbol have changed into lotus buds that mimic, with uncanny accuracy, the uterine tubes with their flared 'horns'. Lower down the trunk the older blooms, each with seven stamens, take on a distinct semblance to the Nuzi models and to the Assyrian palmette. It would seem, therefore, that here the artist interwove the two concepts of the uterus.

The Assyrian artists frequently brought the palmette into their artistry in subtle ways that must have held clear meaning for them yet which we look at now in confusion. Sometimes it sprouts from the back of an animal. Was this a fertility talisman? It grows from the backs of gazelles in the Kar-Tukulti-Ninurta frescoes. Mallowan discovered an ivory cow with a palmette growing from it, unfinished and abandoned, when he reopened parts of the Northwest Palace at Kalakh.

Thus the Assyrian Tree of Life, embodiment of the goddess of life, extended its influence into the everyday fabric of life. The more formal context in which the Tree was drawn changed over the centuries in ways which may also hold significance but which, at the moment, escapes us.

Before the ninth century BC, the Tree was almost always drawn with attendant animals, though Syrian carvings with stylized trees and bull-men are known from the eighteenth century. Several of the Assyrian seals made in about the twelfth century describe what is obviously a totem flanked by animals, although one from

this period does show the Tree flanked by hybrid bird-men carrying ritual buckets. The earliest known example with a human
worshipper is a Mitannian seal roughly contemporary with the
paintings drawn on the walls at Kar-Tukulti-Ninurta. The Tree
is accompanied by a deer and a man. By the ninth century
BC, the state of the art had become very refined and the seal
workmanship is full of the most delightful and intricate detail.
Again there are small tantalizing riddles which beg explanation.
One seal impression with a group of figures echoing those on the
Kalakh throne panel has a Tree drawn as a strangely spiky affair
that has lost its palmettes. But the need for uterine symbolism
does not go unanswered because the mirror image of the king
holds a rope, seemingly suspended from the winged disc, and at
the end of the rope the artist has rendered the omega.

In Assyrian art of the Tree there is one invariable limitation
which speaks volumes.[6] The only human figure to be involved
intimately is the king. As in the ritual of ancient Sumer, it
is he who by divine right becomes the sacred guardian of the
Tree. He is the 'Gardener'. He alone may enter the shadow of
the goddess as her high priest. The winged beast, the *apkallu*,
also touches the Tree creating a strong impression that contact
with it is exclusive to king and priest playing the role of the
mythical guardian.

The cone and bucket held a very close function in the ritual,
although they came to be used in situations where the Tree was
not necessarily apparent. At the time of Layard's discovery in the
mid-nineteenth century AD a galaxy of inventive and morally
expedient explanations were being bandied about. On a more
esoteric level these included cosmic symbolism and prophylactic
magic. A more down-to-earth author was convinced that the cult
revolved around fruit picking which, incidentally, would have
required some dexterity since the fruit is always held the wrong
way round! Another believed that we are seeing the anointing
of the king with oil – improbable since the bitumen-lined basket
was a water container and oil was dispensed from stone jars.

A shrewder assessment appeared in the *Babylonian and Oriental Record* of 1889 – the ceremony involved anointing with
holy water using a cone as a sprinkler. The writer listed options
of pine, cypress, fir, cedar, and then, in deference to the fruit-
pickers' lobby, pineapple and pomegranate. His proposals did
not pass unnoticed by the Society for Biblical Archaeology who
predictably shot him down in flames the following year. His suggestions had come scandalously close to implying precedents for

Christian baptism. Their own theory, which trod a respectable path, argued ceremonial pollination of the date palm.

In fairness to these speculators they knew nothing of the Sumerian precedent, and they were hamstrung by a dedication to biblical truths which effectively suppressed objective analysis.

Looking at all the evidence of art over a period of time, some of the suggestions of the old theorists were probably not far short of the mark. Prophylactic magic is a slightly misleading term in that they were trying to encourage rather than prevent, but is perhaps essentially sound. A ceremony of allegorical fertilization is also more or less likely. The Tree would seem to be the embodiment of the goddess, and there is, incidentally, more of the symbolism of Ištar to be found in the Kalakh panels. Her astral star symbol was destined to change once more and it became a flower the design of which is incorporated into the protective archers' wrist bands worn by the worshippers. The cone, therefore, with its strongly phallic connotation, was the male element of the sexual equation. It may well have been a cedar cone since Dumuzi, we know, was closely linked with the cedar tree, and the bucket may have carried water. Here was the celestial semen being transferred to the Tree, with its symbolic uterus motifs, by the phallus of the god king.

Whether the ritual in some senses paralleled the Sacred Marriage in its purpose remains in the realms of speculation but, on evidence, it seems very likely. There is some hint that both were conducted in the same season of the year. Historical records confirm that many of the Assyrian warlords, including Aššur-nasir-apli II, took their legions away on extensive campaigns but that they were usually at home for the Mesopotamian New Year at the spring equinox.[7] If their presence was essential for the Sacred Marriage, and if the king was also required, in person, for the ritual depicted in the Kalakh carvings, the 'window' in the calendar can be substantially narrowed. Its seasonal importance is self-evident, merely by considering the implications of Aššur-nasir-apli's artistic obsession with the Tree ceremonial. If ever a despot was likely to put trifling religious indulgence to one side it was he. Yet if the Kalakh decor has any message it is that the Tree took a significant place in his life.

Aššur-nasir-apli's life and times mark him down as the mightiest warlord the world had known. He reigned for twenty-six turbulent years and at the end his son, Šalmaneser III, took over an empire infinitely stronger than that which his father

had inherited. He seems from the historical record neither to
have been deeply religious nor particularly philosophical. He
bothered little with letters, collected no library and, when he was
not letting the blood of his fellow man, spent much of his leisure
time in the field letting that of lions and other game. He was, on
the other hand, a thorough pragmatist, a man of great political
shrewdness. An inscription was found at Nimrud, composed to
mark the end of the building programme of Kalakh:

> For ten days[8] I regaled the happy peoples of all lands,
> together with the populace of Kalakh, treated them to
> wines, provided them with baths and ointments, and
> showered honours upon them, and then I sent them
> home in peace and joy.

The historical record implies, however, that peace and joy
were not hallmarks of Aššur-nasir-apli's domestic administration which, for a large part of his reign, was less than solid.
The capital cities of Assyrian despots can only have seen a scant
military presence for much of the year. That is evident from the
ease with which the enemies of the regime finally overthrew
such fortresses as Kalakh and Nineveh.[9] Certainly hints emerge
that Aššur-nasir-apli's major-domo in his absence was a weak
and ineffectual man. It would have been logical to seek some
psychological hold over the civilian population, and propaganda
may have asserted the need for the presence of the king as a vital
participant in certain key religious ceremonies. Until about 1650
BC Mesopotamian kings had been gods, in no way comparable
with a modern sovereign. By the Assyrian period they were no
longer deified in their lifetimes, but as high priests of Aššur
they were indispensable and the sense emerges that if they were
usurped, the godhead went with them.

The sensitivities of the Assyrians are probably misunderstood or overlooked. They have been cast as heartless war-
mongers, largely by Jewish and Christian propagandists keen
to distort the reality of what was a far less clear-cut position than
the books of the Bible offer. The Assyrians' overt brutality and
belligerence may not reflect national character but rather long-
term expediency. Their homeland was at the centre of perhaps the
most vital strategic crossroads in the ancient world, and between
their more headline-catching conquests they also experienced
leaner times which greatly sapped their resources. For all the
outward aggression of Assyrian rulers they were probably little

different, at heart, from any farming colonists of Mesopotamia. Their religious convictions may often have been as deep as those of the other dwellers in that capricious landscape. They may not have fully understood Sumerian tradition but they recognized its strength.

The lives of ordinary Assyrian peasants depended on the fickleness of the sacred rivers, and the rebirth of nature from the annual impact of drought. Personal security lay less in the clash of arms on some far-flung battlefield than in the fertility of the broad swathe of land sweeping gently to the east of the Tigris.

It may be that in his wisdom Aššur-nasir-apli, like others of his dynasty, set out to remind those at home that his presence in the religious life of the country was essential to their continued well-being.[10] The old Sumerian Sacred Marriage between lukur priestess and king was probably replaced by then with the festival of hašadu, a more symbolic marriage between two model images. The king was still involved though, albeit less overtly, in the deeper ritual of the Tree and the allegorical impregnation of the goddess in the strict privacy of the temple grove. One senses that the Tree ritual was the more influential and, furthermore, followed a scenario of which only the king and his immediate priests had complete knowledge.

Integral to the mysticism of these rites must have been the ideology that the king's presence was essential. It may be that without this mysticism the power of the warring and frequently absent Assyrian rulers was shaky. Whether a propaganda exercise or otherwise, Aššur-nasir-apli's approach certainly found popularity with his successors. Some way up the Khosr river, north-east of Mosul, Sargon II built his colossal memorial at Khorsabad and, notably, used the same school of art. Identical human-headed winged figures hold the cone and the bucket on either side of the city gates.

At Kalakh, Mallowan worked on a south-west palace used largely by Ešarhaddon, the emperor who reigned in the early part of the seventh century BC and who preceded the biblical Sennacherib. Like other buildings, it seems to have been ravaged by fire in the final onslaught and this palace, too, bore traces of the same deep influence. In the remains of the throne room were panels of ivory depicting the same hybrid beasts with the same accoutrements. The panels are decorated with seven-lobed palmettes. In these late works there is crudeness though, which would not have been tolerated in Aššur-nasir-apli's time. The days of glory were beginning to fade.

One more great canvas immortalizing Assyria's power was yet to unfold – Nineveh.[11] In 1849, Layard realized his life's dream. He began to dig at Küyünjik. Ironically it was a place that Botta, the amateur archaeological diplomat, had toyed with and passed over. Layard found his beloved city, the lost citadel which saw the end of the empire. Aššurbanipal built the last magnificent palace there just three centuries after Aššur-nasir-apli II had ruled the world.

Ashurbanipal, the scholar king, collected one of the finest of all Mesopotamian libraries. In common with his predecessors he ordered the execution of a series of magnificent tableaux to record his exploits in the hunt and on the battlefield. The pictures of dying lions in these reliefs are truly exquisite; they show that the craftsmen had lost none of their impressive ability to capture scenes of nature. In many of the panels the king is dressed in a long robe decorated with the most intricate embroidery. At the centre of the breast, and on the shoulders, can be found a minutely detailed facsimile of the scene which rested above Aššur-nasir-apli's throne in Kalakh.

Ashurbanipal was the last great king of Assyria. He died in 626 BC leaving an impossibly overstretched empire in the hands of weak and ineffectual rulers. In 616 BC the neo-Babylonians teamed up with the Medes and Scythians in a war of attrition against the enemy of centuries. In 612 BC they reduced Nineveh, and all the other great cities, to rubble.

Outwardly the Assyrians who had, perhaps unwittingly, conserved so much of Sumer through the Old Babylonian and the Hurrian connections, must have seemed set to rule western Asia for ever but, in truth, their castles were balanced on the flimsiest of foundations. In less than fifty years from the rape of Nineveh nothing remained but ruins consumed by hungry windblown earth and an exquisite, often haunting legacy in shattered fragments of ivory, stone and clay.

Of all the paradoxes which are Assyria perhaps the most baffling is that a nation which had slaughtered its way to conquest on a scale the world had never before witnessed loved a small and almost ludicrously quaint model tree. That single enigmatic creation, evolved from the legacy of Sumer, as much as any other figment of its epoch was to plague the fashioning of Judaism and perhaps, in time, influence the very trappings of Christianity.

7

The Sumerian Legacy

If there is a name which epitomizes Christian visions of heathendom in the ancient near east; a single epithet which conjures arcane fantasies and images of mythical splendour, which stirs a flutter in the most cynical of hearts, it is Babylon, the Gate of God.

Although abandoning some of the old traditions and adding new ones, Assyria sustained the essential fabric of Sumerian religion with faith and diligence for more than five hundred years through the hiatus between old and new Babylonian cultures. Through Babylon and other connections something of Sumer's unique magic had stirred them. Assyria was far from being the only chatelaine of the heirloom, but she was a far more loyal executor than has been credited.

Nonetheless, aside from the period of Assyrian domination, for fifteen hundred years after the demise of Sumer and until the Greeks plundered her eminence, Babylon was recognized amongst other near eastern nations as the undisputed seat of kingship, and when the Assyrian thread was severed in 612 BC, it was back into the hands of the neo-Babylonian conquerors that the safekeeping of the legacy passed. To continue the quest after the gods of the earth and the seasonal rituals that fêted them involves back-tracking to search the beginnings of the Old Babylonian hegemony as that of Sumer was fading.

Sumer arose on a sparsely inhabited desert plain owned by unsophisticated wandering tribesmen, but when she fell the 'Land of the Two Rivers' had grown up not a little. As her sun set in the nineteenth century BC there was no clean transition and there was generated a great cultural emptiness which other influences were eager to fill. Assyria was not destined to spread her wings significantly beyond her limited borders in the north for another six hundred years, but in the Mesopotamian south-east Semitic tribes, from amongst whom had come the rulers that oversaw Sumer's twilight years, were set to carve out the First Dynasty of Babylon.

Babylon has existed as a location on the map, about 170 miles south of Baghdad, for about five thousand years, but until the mid-eighteenth century BC it was hardly noticed in the annals of the ancient world, remaining weak and unprepossessing. Once in a while though, there comes one who rises above the tide of humanity, who shakes the world a little and drives it onward leaving his name etched on its changing face. Such a man was Hammurabi. For a time he swept away Babylon's anonymity.

Hammurabi took over the seat of power some time between 1848 and 1792 BC in a city that was virtually indistinguishable from a number of petty states around it.[1] For thirty years he claimed no greater battle honours than three minor campaigns and his greatest achievement at home was to set the seal on the civil administration of Babylon with his much-vaunted Code of Law. Suddenly, and apparently out of character, Hammurabi became the conquering militant. He claimed all the lands of the southern plain. He rampaged into the northern kingdom of Zimri-Lim, taking the great fortified palace at Mari. He assaulted and briefly subdued Assyria, and at the end of his reign he envisaged himself as the legatee of Sumer. He was, by his own inscription, 'King of the Four Quarters of the World'. Hammurabi gave Babylon her questionable right to be regarded as the intellectual jewel of southern Mesopotamia, a level of approbation which may not be entirely in perspective.

Had Hammurabi handed the reins to similar power brokers Babylon's continuing brilliance would be easier to comprehend, yet his successors shared none of his short-lived energy and in little more than a hundred years from Hammurabi's accession Mursilis I swept down from the Hittite power base in the Taurus mountains sacking the city. That which followed in many respects provides a *déjà vu* of the Sargonic take-over of Sumer.

In the sixteenth century BC the Persian Kassite Dynasty took over and, whilst not abandoning their own tribal gods entirely, they also revitalized much of the ancient religious tradition of Babylon and established a Babylonian nation. A significant, though comparatively short-lived, cultural link also developed in the fourteenth century BC between Babylon and Egypt, forged through marriage of respective royal families.

During the Kassite period, Tukulti-Ninurta I brought his legions from Assyria to ravage the city, razing her walls and plundering the temples. It is probable that this expedition absorbed a level of the culture, and that it was further supplemented when the Assyrians returned at the height of their expansionism, to create the 'Ninth Dynasty'. The second Babylonian dynasty proper was established by the Chaldeans arriving from the hinterland surrounding the lower reaches of the two rivers, the so-called neo-Babylonians, from amongst whose ranks was to come Nebuchadezzar II of biblical notoriety. In 614 BC Cyaxares the Mede marched into Assyria, followed by Nabopolassar, the Babylonian overlord. He and Cyaxares made the fateful treaty that two years later saw Nineveh reduced to rubble.

Such is the essence of Babylon's course through history. She was less substantial than other great empires of the ancient near east, and in many respects her rise to fame and her influence are enigmas. Nonetheless, she left her indelible stamp on the world's culture, though even in this there is a paradoxical irony. The fate of Babylon's literature rested, to no small extent, with her arch-enemy in the north. Assyria's gr at library at Nineveh was smashed, but cradled in the tomb of its wreckage lay large numbers of Babylonian tablets. The Babylonian creation myth, to name but one, is known only through Ashurbanipal's collection.

Though proper historical records did not begin in Babylon until 747 BC with the Ptolemaic canon and the Babylonian Chronicles, the Old Babylonian period of Hammurabi delivered steles, inscriptions, temple hymns, laments and poetry, of a kind that had been produced in the south of Mesopotamia since the Sargonic era in the third millennium.[2] These reveal a heavy Sumerian influence.

The hopes and the concerns which the Babylonians delivered to the gods were those of a Mesopotamian civilization whose life had been a constant struggle for survival against a perilous environment, but the literature also reveals its own peculiar pedigree. To a greater extent than Assyria, Babylonian scribes incorporated their own word-of-mouth mythology with pure Sumerian legends and identities, so that by the time of the neo-Babylonians tradition had become a heavy mingling of Sumerian and Semitic notions. The question is, just how much of what emerged in writing was a product of borrowing from Sumer, and how much was their own oral tradition?

From as early as the middle of the third millennium, Babylon described the archetypal gods of the firmament as Anum and Antum, and her creator gods dominated a host of lesser beings right down to the personal hearth gods.[3] Iš tar took undisputed place as first lady, though Enlil was removed in favour of Marduk. The urge to replace Enlil made good sense. Patron deity of the eminent city of Nippur, he had been seen very much as the national god, the Sumerian 'Britannia'. Hence Enlil's name bore far more than religious connotations, and political sensitivities dictated his removal. Marduk was not merely 'a rose by any other name' though. He possessed a Babylonian identity and a Babylonian biography, and in Babylonian legendary terms he took on the characteristics of so many other deities that to many people he was little less than creator of mankind and saviour of the cosmos. Did he originate as a king of the mythical heroic age, drawn along the lines of Dumuzi, but whose annual fate bore its own distinct hallmarks? There is no real evidence one way or the other.

The Babylonian creation account, in which Marduk plays a key role, was probably first composed during or shortly after Hammurabi's time. The legend was obviously based on the Sumerian explanation of creation but certain intrinsic elements are altered and the Babylonian story possesses an edge of raw violence not shared by that of Sumer which suggests a cruder source.

In Sumerian legend two forces, male and female, modulated chaos into creation. An and Ki were the primal beings. Ki was carried off by Enlil to fashion the matter of earth, whilst An remained in the heavens.

For the Babylonians the goddess Tiamat was the loose counterpart of Ki. She had assembled of her own genesis eleven phantasmal monsters to do battle with the great gods in a time before the world was made, and in a terrible and primordial war with Marduk who, according to Babylonian tradition, was her great-great-great grandson, she met a violent destiny. Unlike Enlil, Marduk did not carry off his ancestral *grande dame* but fought with Tiamat and killed her with an arrow. In the ever-picturesque language of Mesopotamia, he sliced her corpse in two 'like a dried flat fish' and out of her body alone he forged heaven and elemental dirt. In Babylonian eyes, creation out of chaos was thus the result, not of parting the primal heavenly couple but of dividing a female cosmic entity at the hands of a warrior hero. It is details such as these which reveal separate tribal origins and the 'foreignness' of one tradition and another, but in general Babylon took on board Sumer's framework of myth and ritual. One incidental effect of mixing traditions was that each god inherited many names, but within this kaleidoscope Babylon was true in her reverence for the cyclical death and rebirth of nature, the motive force of which was expressed through the twin spring rites of confrontation with evil, and of abasement and atonement. The great rite in the spring was the Akitu, derived from a more ancient Akkadian barley festival and which seems to have been spread over the first eleven days of Nisan, the month which was to become that of Easter in the Christian calendar. According to Babylonian descriptions the main ceremonial was preceded by five days of preparation.

On the evening of the fourth day the vast and peculiarly Baby-lonian Creation Epic was recited, possibly in the form of a drama along the lines of a medieval mystery play, and the king entered into a ritualized set-to with Tiamat. Having undergone the clas-sic confrontation battle, Marduk was imprisoned and sentenced to ordeal 'by water'. His bride was smeared with blood from his wounds. Finally the gods restored him to his people. The king, as Marduk, was therefore humiliated in a symbolic re-enactment of the legend. The fate of Marduk was, however, distinctly different from that of the older dying and reviving Akkadian god Dumuzi.

Intimate and fascinating details have survived: on the fifth day a ceremonial meal was offered, privately and behind a screen, to the statues of the god and his consort which stood on pedestals in adjacent shrines of the *cella*, the inner sanctuary of the temple.[4] The god Nabu who arrived by sacred barge was also fed. When the gods had finished their meal, the remains were sent to be consumed by the king and a bowl of water was delivered to the gods so that they could wash their fingers.

It is difficult to imagine people with the intellectual panache of the Babylonians actually thinking of a real personage consuming mouthfuls of food behind the curtains, but the notion now existed that the images of the gods possessed very human traits and human needs. They were *alive*! In the home of the craftsman who carved their images, the gods went through a curious ritual before being placed in their shrines. The mouth of the statue was washed and opened to imbue it with life. This 'opening of the mouth' ceremony was performed with great seriousness and seemingly without hint of cynicism. Food was often provided in staggering quantities. A late text from Uruk lists the following daily total: 500 kg bread; 40 sheep; 2 bulls; 1 bullock; 8 lambs; 70 birds and ducks; 4 wild boars; 3 ostrich eggs; 54 containers of beer and wine. This prodigious appetite, which must have left many deities ripe for celestial thromboses, is a capacity mirrored in far-flung religions. At a single sitting the Norse god, Thor, would regularly put away several oxen and drink mead by the gallon.

On the fifth and sixth days of Akitu the king presented himself at the temple for the climax of an atonement ritual which, in its various forms throughout the ancient near east, bears serious implications for the Christian Easter tradition and its supposed originality. The king was to abase himself, to be stripped briefly of his divinity and power and in doing so to take on the collective responsibility for the omissions of his people during the past year. Without this humiliation, the cycle of life would not continue. The king was joined, outside the sanctuary, by his high priest who removed the king's royal insignia and clothing, offering them to the god. Naked, the king was hit about the face and brought into the sanctuary to crouch before the god. He recited an admission: 'I have not failed to revere my god, I have not brought ill to my city, I have not forgotten the divine rites, I have not suffered my people ill-treatment, I have not weakened my nation's defences.' The high priest followed this public humiliation with a speech, restored the king's insignia, and hit him again. If the Sacred King wept publicly with tears of contrition for Marduk's pleasure there followed a great feast and triumphal procession. A white bull was slaughtered and the king led the god's image by the hand in procession to the Akitu house.

The Babylonian festival 'round' which has to be seen as an agglomeration of different elements from different cults included a *hašadu* marriage festival which symbolized the old Sacred Marriage, the physical consummation between the god king and his priestess bride. Records suggest that it was conducted splendidly and amidst great excitement in the *bit gipari* house of the temple field, where cultic statues probably replaced the living players. Whether an old-style Sacred Marriage between king and priestess ever happened in Babylonia we do not know.

The Assyrians and Babylonians did not endorse slaughter of men and women as any kind of routine procedure in the way that was a part of Canaanite and Hebrew ritual, but human sacrifice occasionally took place. There were, inevitably, crises in the course of kingship and under grave circumstances of national security, the king temporarily abdicated. Then a chosen substitute king and his queen, anyone from a traitor to a lunatic but usually culled from the dregs of society, reigned for up to one hundred days amidst all the trappings of kingship before suffering death. They took with them a figurine of 'all that is evil' as an offering to the underworld to expiate the state from dire consequences.

In the Babylonian scheme of things we have a subtle shift of emphasis away from Sumerian notions. Babylonian cosmogeny envisages a world wrenched from the body of Tiamat by the supremacy of Marduk. Joseph Campbell, in his profound study of mythology, believed that Babylonian thought stood midway along an evolving line.[5] It began with a *prima materia*, a supreme female presence alone in chaos, she of pure logic, that which may have evolved through pre-history. She and the creator were aspects of the one, the dynamic force through whose matriarchal labours came, self-conceived, the nativity of the spheres.

This concept of creation through solely female parthenogenesis evolved into the belief in an ordered world born of the goddess through sexual intercourse with a god or demi-god. Babylonian cosmogeny which stemmed from it opened the way to move from a mistress of creation to a creator god with masculine attributes. This, Campbell argued, is a start down the road towards the biblical god of Genesis who creates out of himself. The sexual emphasis has thus turned about.

Campbell's argument is questionable. It assumes an evolving process during which the fount of creation becomes sexually changed and that the biblical notion represents a later stage of building a patriarchal religion. Yet can it be automatically assumed? The Babylonian Tiamat may reflect little more than a localized trend which gained popularity for a time. Attempting to impose evolutionary steps on the formulation of ideas including religion, a popular vogue amongst Victorian analysts, does not always work. History would seem to suggest that the concept of an all-father from whose breath comes the ordered world and everything it embraces, is a peculiarity of very few ancient cultures, including the Israelites, and that in modern Christianity the principle is, if anything, moving towards reversal.

Another Babylonian trend is less debatable — that which pointed towards monotheism. 'Bel' who appears amongst biblical writings of the Israelites in exile became, during neo-Babylonian times, a name for Marduk. But 'Bel' also became familiar as a title of rank. It implies 'Lord', the style of addressing a god, and

Marduk was being used in the same way. Thus Nergal was the 'Marduk' of the attack, Nabu that of accounting, and Šamaš that of justice. Arguably the first infant undercurrents, if not of monotheism then at least of henotheism, were beginning to pulse. What changes of need drew people to this new vision of divinity?

Babylon, like that other great bourgeois society of the ancient world, Egypt, was beginning to free herself from day-to-day preoccupations with existence. She was gaining a new edge of sophistication which brought new horizons in understanding of the world and new kinds of dependence. Polytheism is at its most effective in meeting the spiritual demands of a society whose rigours and apprehensions stem from fundamental physical needs. Because these are diverse in character – the need for food, water, shelter, fire, procreation – a veritable army of individualistic spirits is required to deal with them. Polytheism is often a product of the old animistic creeds in which each and every object in the world possesses and is protected by its own guardian spirit.

As society transcends urgent physical vulnerability though, and assumes that the basics of life are more within its own governance, so the need for a vast heavenly pioneer corps begins to diminish. The creator godhead remains inviolate and undiminished, but the individuals of the pantheon merge closer towards being facets of the whole. Transcendence to a cultural chic breeds its own dangers though. Babylon's pursuit of wealth and sophistication, perhaps the chief explanation for her lack of military dominance outside of southern Mesopotamia for any accountable period, also provided a foundation for decadence. Hers, therefore, is arguably the first historical illustration of the pursuit of materialism and hedonism at the expense, at least in part, of pure religion. If the exiled biblical writers were any judge, the ritual of the Sacred Marriage had been largely superseded by cultic prostitution and a jolly, if cynical, street-level sexual free-for-all.

Babylon, at heart, was nonetheless a Mesopotamian culture with Mesopotamian problems and that which took shape in her ritual and mythology was the product of a shared experience. Its parallels with Sumer and Assyria are therefore comparatively easy to explain. Aside from Jungian explanations according to which religions answered the need to express an unconscious but common perception of archetypes, the peoples of the 'Land of the Two Rivers' came originally not from a common stock but from a stock with common experience; they traded extensively one with another; they developed language and writing skills which were sufficiently alike to allow easy exchanges; and above all they found mutual problems confronting them in their relationship with the natural world.

What of other peoples though, who struggled, conquered, and fell in the seedbed of the ancient near east? What of civilizations which did not share common language or need? It is to those that the journey must now turn, not only in anticipation of the future, but to fill some of the gaps which the Mesopotamian story alone cannot satisfy. The thread points towards Europe. The great civilizations of western Asia were doomed; the armies of Macedonia and Rome would grind into decay those 'colossal wrecks' around which, boundless and bare, the lone and level alluvium now indeed stretches far away. But to reach the classical empires which gathered it up, the thread had to pass through the hands of cultures which, thus far in the journey, have not received a hearing.

Late in the third millennium BC, in the far north-west of Asia Minor, in the mountain fastness of the Taurus, old Asiatic tribes of the land of Hatti came under the control of ambitious rulers known as Indo-Europeans who were then poised to move south in expansion of the new Hittite empire.[6] Below them on the western seaboard were other tribal lands with developing cultures: Phrygians, Syrians, Sidonians and others, many of which have come under the common banner of 'Canaanites'.

Within the ideologies and understandings of these peoples, the same hallmarks appear which characterize the beliefs of the Mesopotamians. Carl Jung's argument for a collective unconscious producing stereotypes that emerge from behind our 'socially acceptable' persona seems reasonable up to a point in explaining common traits. It may well have been given conscious expression in the shape of fat and motherly ladies bulging with nature's progeny, but can it be responsible for all the variations on the theme which those Ice-Age matrons heralded?

Jung contends that, in recording the dreams of his patients, he discovered certain kinds of symbolism which are extremely commonplace.[7] The mythological symbols of the mother figure have always been earth, wood and water. Creative efforts, including ritual, also follow corresponding tracks forged through some deep and innate sympathy. Primitive cultures often construct symbolic trees with steps cut into them by which the shaman can ascend towards the gods. Arguably the Mesopotamian ziggurat temple with its ramped sides was designed for the same

purpose, and Jacob's dream ladder of the biblical Book of Genesis
also provided a stairway to his god.

Beyond fairly basic symbolism it is not easy to credit Jung's
theory, yet it may provide the only explanation for common
development of beliefs and traditions in which there is no
evidence of borrowing. It is tempting to argue that all cultural
roads diverged from Sumer, but this would be too simple a vision.
Explanations have also been offered in terms of an evolutionary
progression of religion. It used to be argued that totemism always
led to animism, to gods of nature, to polytheism and so on.
These theories effectively circulated through authors like Tyler
and Frazer. There are, however, enough cases on record where
the progression has not taken place to see that it too stands as a
flawed argument. Though each may possess its elements of truth
neither, on its own, is accurate.

Within the familiar broad pattern of fertility goddesses, missing gods, confrontation battles and sacred marriages, the ethnic
traditions with which the Hittites, Canaanites and a host of other
small cultures kept faith, often read, as among the Old Babylonians, with a degree of crudeness and banality when set beside
those of Sumer.

Sumer's influence towered above the rest with the possible
exception of Egypt. Sumer's early ability to transpose her spoken
beliefs and traditions into a written record allowed her to steal the
march. She had spread her cultural net far and wide, largely the
reward of her economic success as a major trading nation, and
into the baggage of traders passed her customs, literature and art.
She became the cultural fountain at whose waters other nations
drank.

In the 1950s the Swedish theologian, Simon Mowinckel, published a thesis arguing that it is necessary 'to see each separate
religion as a unique structural whole; all the separate elements
which it contains derive their contents and meaning from the
whole . . . and not from that which they signify in another
whole.'[8] Mowinckel was using this doubtful argument to support
the Christian defence that its dogma and tradition is thoroughly
divorced from the cultures amongst which it grew. Mowinckel's
claim has been widely respected and supported amongst theologians. Yet looking at the story thus far it is difficult to find much
justification for the argument. The mechanism by which religious
beliefs come to their time of glory is surely much less clear cut.
Religions take their substance from a myriad of circumstances and
influences, both from within the essential human psyche, from

within the nursery of their foundation and from alien sources. History shows that whilst some significant elements of creed, the 'Jungian bits', are intrinsic, many more may be attributable to cultural borrowing.

Those who rally against the notion of one culture taking on board the ideologies of its neighbour point to language as an argument. Visiting traders lacked the ability to interpret the literature – the legends and laments, rituals and inscriptions – of their hosts; they failed to understand much of the foreign symbolism they saw. Soldiers of invading armies were probably even less equipped for such intellectual adventures. In respect of Egypt the argument is probably valid, but Egypt was a special case in that she represented a dominant cultural power whose written language, hieroglyphic script, was not generally understood. The same cannot be said for Sumer, much of whose literature was translated into Semitic Akkadian.

Akkadian became to south-west Asia that which Greek and Latin were to medieval Europe. The great libraries of the ancient world, not only those within Sumer's historical borders but in far-flung cities, Ugarit, Hattusas, Mari, all owned copies of Akkadian and Babylonian literature. Gilgameš and others became universal heroes.

A trenchant memento of the esteem in which Akkadian was held as a lingua franca was left to posterity by the great Persian emperor of the fifth century BC, Darius. On a cliff face at Behistun, he directed the carving of a massive epitaph to his passing, and hewn into the rock is his enduring inscription written in three languages, Elamite the local tongue, Persian and Babylonian.

Palestine, the land 'given by God' to the Children of Israel, was the major bridgehead across which religious focus passed from western Asia to Europe, and therefore the manner in which not only Israelite religion, but also that of her cultural contacts took shape becomes a sensitive issue.

Several major groups of peoples touched the Hebrew immigrants strongly with their culture. The assortment of Canaanite tribes on the western seaboard of Syrio-Palestine, and the Hittites whose expatriate colonies are frequently mentioned in the Old Testament narratives were equally influential. Both drew, directly or indirectly, on Sumer's inspiration. Canaanite and Hittite clans mixed freely with the Israelites, though it is probably also true that the Israelite newcomers wiped out many original villages as they expanded their range northwards. The religions of these groups are important not only because of close physical contact

with the Israelites but also because, although affected strongly by
Mesopotamian traditions, Canaanites and Hittites were never a
part of Mesopotamian culture and they grew in their own peculiar fashions dictated by origins and by different environmental
pressures.

The Hittite political situation was tortuous in the extreme,
involving ebb and flow of empire, innumerable comings and
goings and at least two languages. In the ancient texts, those who
found this understandably confusing lumped all as 'Hittite' which
is probably a sound compromise to follow. It will only confuse
matters to delve into political history, other than to appreciate
that from early in the second millennium, through a peak of
power roughly contemporary with Hammurabi, until 1191 BC
when they were beaten back by Philistines, the Hittites controlled
the lands as far as today's border with Lebanon, beyond which
point stood Egypt's colonial presence.

Certain elements of the Hittite pedigree are significant in terms
of religion. Before Assyrian control of the area at the beginning of
the eighth century BC, the primitive population in remote mountain valleys, the old inhabitants of the 'Kingdom of Hatti', often
physically isolated from one another, remained fragmented and
fiercely independent in their beliefs and traditions. Local shrines
and local practices, some a survival from very ancient times, thus
persisted in a way that had scarcely been possible in Mesopotamia
after the Sargonic era. Because Hittite religion existed on two
levels, that of state with its Indo-European background and its
Mesopotamian leaning, and that of the local strongly introverted
tribal groups, it offers an intriguing interplay between old and
new style faiths in a region which experienced very different
conditions from those in Mesopotamia.

In 1906, Hugo Winckler of the German Oriental Society began a
dig close to the Anatolian village of Boghazköy. He was, innocently, beginning the first modern exploration of the Hittite capital,
Hattusas, and into his hands was shortly to fall one of the great
libraries of the ancient world.

Thus far, in terms of exploration, all so-called Hittite scripts
discovered were written in hieroglyphic which, in hindsight,
was revealed to be a comparatively 'modern' style of communication.[9] The library found at Boghazköy was filled, by contrast,
with tablets written in a strange, unfamiliar style of cuneiform.
It turned out to be a much older language. When translated,
these ancient and often fragmented 'books' opened a hitherto
unknown window on history.

Hatti claimed a thousand gods![10] The figure may not be an entirely idle boast. Her archetypal Asiatic deities were joined by those of the Indo-Europeans, all were dispersed amongst isolated villages which provided them with local names, and these bulging celestial ranks were swelled still more by the arrival of Mesopotamian traditions in the pockets of Hurrians. As time went on, roles of similar deities became merged, in part, and there emerged a grand tier of universal gods whose citadel lay, not at Hattusas, but a day's journey away at a lost city which the records speak of as Arinna.

The Hurrians brought with them some familiar names: Anu and Antu, Enlil and Ea, but these deities were always regarded as 'foreign'. The more identifiably Hittite gods reigned paramount and they were concerned with particular local needs. Hatti was a kingdom, not of the desert plains, but of the mountains. Religious belief in these high and awesome places was moulded less by threat of drought than by the immensity and anger of cosmic forces, the mountain storms that generate thunder and lightning, flood and avalanche.

The sun goddess and the sun god of Arinna stood supreme at the head of the state religion. The writings speak of them in eloquent terms: 'Queen of the Land of Hatti, Queen of Heaven and Earth, Mistress of the Kings and Queens of the Land of Hatti, directing the Government of the King and Queen of Hatti.' Although their precise relationship one to another is vague, they were perhaps more business partners than lovers. The goddess's more romantic consort is usually identified as the weather god, Tešub: 'King of heaven, Lord of the Land of Hatti, God of Battle'. Tešub, because of the ever present and violent caprices of the weather, took an infinitely more sensitive place in the hearts of Hittites than did Adad, his counterpart on the Mesopotamian plain and Akkadian successor to Iškur. His consort is identified in some texts as the goddess Hebat and a prayer attributable to the seventeenth-century Hittite priestess queen, Puduhepa, places Hebat in the role of the sun-goddess of Arinna. There is much woven in her character that reminds of Ninhursaĝa. She is a comfortably matronly lady, without any warlike accoutrements, and often she is found standing on a lion. Was she drawn in these portraits from some Mesopotamian model introduced at the suggestion of the sophisticated and much-travelled Hurrians? It seems possible.

Ištar's closest Hittite contemporary was Šauška, though the role of the fertility goddess seems to have been taken by several deities in different times and circumstances. More is known of Šauška only because the fifteenth-century-BC warrior king, Hattusilis II, adopted her as his patron goddess, and at his behest she reigned over a number of cult centres across the Taurus region.

One of the key roles in the Hittite pantheon was that of Telepinu, a god of farming, and he most closely mirrors Dumuzi, though because of the fragmented situation, other deities including Tešub also, on occasion, played Telepinu's part. In Hittite tradition though, the fate of this god changes.

It is the legends and their festivals which provide the great fascination because here the evidence includes primitive elements which are distinct from those in the writings of Sumer. The saga which parallels that of the Mesopotamian 'Death of Dumuzi' is the Legend of the Missing God. The framework of the story underlines broadly Hittite religion's striking fidelity to the Mesopotamian framework, but in the detail the emphasis shifts, from death to rage. It attempts to provide answers for, and to expiate, the sudden dramatic violence of the elemental forces of the mountains. To the inhabitants of the mountains the notion of a dying and rising god of vegetation must have held no more than remote interest. So Telepinu merely went missing for a while in temper.

Such is Telepinu's anger that he puts his boots on the wrong feet and, with his rage even more cataclysmic, he takes retribution on nature. Influence of the Sumerian account creeps in with description of trees and meadows which parch and springs that run dry but, nonetheless, the emphasis is on the *anger* of the god. Hunger and starvation walk the land.

Meanwhile, the sun-god gives a feast for the thousand deities but discovers there is insufficient food to satisfy them, so Tešub sends an eagle to look for Telepinu.[11] The eagle returns after a fruitless search. In desperation, Tešub goes out to search for the missing fertility god but he too comes back empty-handed, at which point the goddess Hannahannas, one described as the 'Great Mother', suggests sending a bee to take up the search. The bee discovers Telepinu sleeping and, not knowing how to wake him, it does its best by stinging him. This piece of initiative does not improve Telepinu's frame of mind and he continues his wholesale destruction of the natural world with even greater chagrin. Eventually though the storm loses its rage, and the eagle brings the god home.

The Canaanite equal of the Legend of the Missing God makes

a pointed contrast, one which arose from the needs of a trading
nation dependent equally on the land and on her relationship
with the sea.[12] Canaan represents less an ethnic identity than
a form of culture which spread down the Mediterranean coast.
Away from the cities on the plains – Megiddo, Lachish, Jericho,
Ugarit – the Canaanite provinces were probably thinly populated
and most Canaanites were farmers, rugged and resilient, with
little political aspiration. Canaanite agriculture existed under
the same constant threat of drought, famine and pestilence that
thwarted the Mesopotamians.

Canaan reached her cultural summit between 1600 and 1200
BC, though as with so many glorious stepping stones marking the
progress of man, her seat of excellence was lost to the world for
more than three thousand years. Ugarit, the ancient city on the
north Syrian coast by modern Ras Šamra, yielded one of the
great libraries of the ancients and amongst its writings some of
the truth about Canaan has been revealed. Hitherto its traditions
and beliefs were known only through the condemnations of the
Old Testament whose commentators constantly harped on the
vexed issue of its cultic practices. They promoted the view that
not only Babylonian but Canaanite religion represented a licence
for sexual excesses. But whilst there may be some justification
for the biblical label on Babylon, Ras Šamra's evidence suggests
little of the depravity that books such as Exodus imply.

Canaan was essentially an economic bridgehead. Her principal
trade was Lebanese timber through the port of Byblos. She also
acted as the shipping agent between Egyptian traders sailing up
the coast, and both the Mesopotamians inland to the east and
the Hittite and Phrygian economies in Anatolia. She provided
the same vital trading frontier between Asia and emergent
Europe. Thus, like the Hittites, she was open to many different
influences and her culture took shape as an amalgam of ancient
local traditions, deeply infused with those of the powers
around her.

Canaan had been settled deep in prehistoric times, like the
other parts of western Asia, by nomadic tribes. Egyptian texts
found at Luxor, and written in the context of Egyptian control
of the more southerly part of the region early in the second
millennium, describe an aboriginal tribal society with spirit guardians amongst whom deities linked with later Canaanite cults are
notably missing. It is only in documents inscribed after the change
to a sedentary life of farming that the names more familiarly
associated with Canaan and her fertility rites take the stage.

The supremo of heaven, for the Canaanite farmers, was el.[13]
The heroic figure of Baal became the equal of the Dying and
Rising God, though the term 'Baal', like that of Marduk, also
signifies 'Lord'. In legend Baal, wielding weapons fashioned by
divine craftsmen, conquered chaos in the form of tyrannical but
undisciplined forces of the seas and rivers, and a splendid palace
was built to celebrate his triumph. Baal then challenged Mot, the
destructive god of drought and sterility in the fields, and in this
fateful chapter he became the spirit of dying and resurrecting life.
Before setting out on his journey, and as if with premonition, he
sired a bull calf, the enduring symbol that was to be his strength
in absence. The conflict ended, inevitably, in disaster – Baal was
killed and the world fell barren. His sister, Anat, began a search
for him reminiscent of the hunt for Telepinu. At last Anat came
upon the corpse of the dead god and buried it. She begged Mot
to restore him to the world of life without avail and, in remorseful
rage, she cleaved the underworld god and winnowed him before
Baal was revived and brought home in triumphant resurrection.
Through this epic story ancient local traditions of a people influenced as greatly by the sea and its caprices as by the vagaries of
an arid hinterland come to the fore.

A number of striking features appear in the Baal legend
which begin to suggest the rooting of other common patterns.
As in so many instances the mother goddess is drawn in the texts
as more than one personality. Her attributes are to be found in
Anat, the sister of Baal and, incidentally, a goddess of war, and in
Ašerah. The suspicion grows that the two deities are less distinct
characters than aspects of the one. In the legend of Baal and Anat,
the mistress 'face' of the fertility goddess is drawn with much to
remind of Ištar. She is young, as virile as her incestuous lover,
imperious, and decidedly bloodthirsty. She is, like her Akkadian
counterpart, a goddess both of love and hate. Anat plays the
virgin bride with whom Baal consummates nature:

He is passionate and he takes hold of her vagina,
She is passionate and takes hold of his testicles,
Baal makes love by the thousand with the virgin Anat.[14]

It is also Anat who rescues Baal's body from the Underworld;
she who exacts terrible retribution on Mot. Anat is definitely a
lady with sanguinary tastes:

Much she fights and looks, Battles and views.

Anat gluts her liver with laughter
Her heart is filled with joy
Anat's liver exults,
Her knees she plunges in the blood of soldiery
Thighs in the gore of troops.

An Egyptian stele found at the site of Beth-shean, south-west of the Sea of Galilee, cites Anat as being: 'Antit, Queen of Heaven and Mistress of all the Gods.' Often her images reveal strong Egyptian influence and Egyptian records indicate that she was adopted as a patron goddess by Rameses II. Yet icons bear hints of other traditions. They are usually naked with breasts and vulva exaggerated. Anat's other 'face' is Ašerah, the more motherly aspect of fertility. She is described as 'The Lady of the Sea' which, in a culture owing much of its prosperity to maritime trade and fishing, is appropriate. She is also the 'Creatress of the Gods', an older and more dignified personality than the lusty and vengeful Anat.

Elsewhere in the ancient near east, the fertility goddess arguably takes on a third aspect, that defined first in the character of the Sumerian Ereškigal. In Canaanite legend though, the underworld is seemingly devoid of this dark side of the female. It is Mot who rules, and the goddess is purely his adversary.

The legend of Baal and Mot which accounts in greatest detail for the battle between the two gods, contains a description of Anat's revenge on the underworld god that may at some time have become misplaced:

She seized divine Mot,
with a blade she split him,
with a sieve she winnowed him
with fire she burnt him,
with mill-stones she ground him,
in a field she scattered him;
his flesh indeed the birds ate,
his limbs indeed the sparrows consumed.[15]

The description may not seem out of place, yet it should, if following the typical line of reasoning, have been applied to the fate of the dying and rising god. In many near eastern economies where corn was a staple crop, the fertility god was a deity of the corn and his demise was pictured in terms of the reaping, winnowing and sowing of the seed. The account almost exactly parallels that in the Egyptian legend of Osiris and it is possible that the inspiration came from Egypt but was misunderstood.

Increasingly, the death of the fertility god became violent and bloody according to the ways in which the annual fate of nature was most strongly perceived. The Phrygians, in the north-east corner of the Mediterranean, followed a local cult of Attis and Kybele in which the god Attis castrated himself and bled to death, signifying the loss of virility in the natural world.

In Syrian tradition, Tammuz, whose Semitic prefix *adon* meaning 'lord' the Greeks misunderstood to be a proper name and from which they derived Adonis, was gored to death by a wild boar. The animal came to personify the god, and although in Jewish tradition the pig is taboo because it is said to be unclean, it is actually much more likely that the Israelites avoided eating pork on the grounds that the pig was sacred in Canaan.

The Syrian cult was again regional and the sense of loss of virility in nature was the parochial intention behind castration. The priests of both Attis and Adonis suffered ritual castration and regularly mutilated themselves in passionate offering of their bodies and their manhood so that the earth might gain strength from their blood and semen. Not such an antiquated concept: the red poppies which sprang up in the fields of Flanders during the First World War were seen very much as being the resurrected life-force of the men who shed their blood so freely.

Evidence from classical times points to a spring festival in Canaan which involved a moderate amount of blood-letting. The priests would gash themselves with knives and there were bizarre initiation rites involving novices standing beneath slaughtered bulls to be drenched in blood and gore. Human sacrifice certainly took place though with what regularity is open to imagination. Kings adopted a prominent symbolic role in Canaan but as to whether at times they suffered death in the rites, or whether substitutes took their place as they did in Babylonia during times of crisis and bad omen is uncertain.

Returning to the Hittite cult, rulers were not treated as gods in the mould of the Mesopotamian sacred king, but each took on the role of high priest and thus was involved in an 'annual progress' during which he and his queen visited all the cult centres and celebrated the main festivals.[16] The information about these rites is contained in a limited number of tablets but evidence for the part played by the king is very vague.

There seem to have been two rites of great significance to

the Hittites. The spring New Year festival, Purulliyas – 'of the earth' was concerned with the renewal of nature. The celebrations opened with the theme of the confrontation legend which tells of combat between the weather god Tešub and the dragon Illuyankas to bring order out of chaos, and presumably Purulliyas continued with the drama of the missing god and his return to calm the ferocity of the elements.

The festival was of sufficient national importance to over-ride more materialistic concerns. The emperor Mursilis II is on record as having returned to Hattusas in the middle of a military campaign to celebrate Purulliyas, reminiscent of warriors like Aššur-nasir-apli II who was insistent on his own presence at the Assyrian New Year festivals in Kalakh.

Rivalling Purulliyas was the festival of Andahsum. Also a New Year rite, it seems to have centred around a particular edible plant which flourished in spring. Whether the *andahsum* possessed magical properties like the plant of life so sought after by Gilgameš, and by Etana of Kiš, or whether it was merely a harbinger of spring is unknown, but an obscure document concerning the Andahsum festival sheds fascinating light on a quite different mystery. It details the ritual of 'bringing forth the Ištar instruments', and whilst there is no description of the objects, they were taken to the temple gates and passed to singers who carried them in procession. Is this a faint hint that the *pukku* and *mekku* beloved of Gilgameš were indeed musical instruments?

Whilst there are many passing references to sacred prostitutes, there are no hard descriptions of the Sacred Marriage in Hittite lands, but its existence is in no doubt. The Keret legend found at Ras Šamra describes the event in Canaan. The king, at the head of his men, marched out into the desert where he engaged in ritual battle with the forces of chaos. When darkness was vanquished, wedding presents were handed round and in an atmosphere of happy celebration the king bedded his priestess queen, his goddess of life, in the open air.

There is one extraordinary, if contentious, piece of Hittite evidence.[17] A remarkable gallery of rock carvings at Yazilikaya, two miles to the south of Boghazköy the site of Hattusas, may hold a startling memory of the marriage. Yazilikaya is a violent, cathartic eruption of rock penetrated by canyons, equal in the magnificence of its setting to the deep caverns. On one sheer face an array of converging stony figures stream incessantly and forever in onward procession. Some argue that here stand the thousand gods of Hatti. The Hittite authority Garstang believed that Yazilikaya may witness, in its great dual procession, the union of Tešub and Hebat carved to commemorate the marriage of Hattusilis III to the priestess Puduhepa. In a side gallery is a relief of a thirteenth-century-BC king, Tudhaliyas IV, in the embrace of his tutelary god. Yazilikaya is a moving testimonial to an eloquent, enigmatic, mountain civilization. The concept is too vast to be any local shrine and it includes every deity in the official state religion.

Whilst there are descriptions of images of gods, we have reliefs but no real statues in the round. These may have been made of wood or of precious metal that has rotted away or been vandalized. But there seem to have been swings of fashion between realism and abstract, and one wonders how many truly lifelike images were actually sculpted and how often a deity's presence was indicated more obtusely. The Hittites and Canaanites clearly enjoyed symbolism and they may have been more superstitious than some of their neighbours in the ancient near east, favouring a more abstracted presence in the round. The Hittites, like other nations of the near east, adopted a stele over which ceremonial oil was poured, the *huwasi*. This seems to have been a stone pillar carved with inscriptions and the image of the god, and it may have derived locally from the Mesopotamian cedarwood pole which signified Dumuzi. It is frequently linked with a second object, the *istanas*, which the texts hint at being made of carved wood and representing the mother goddess.

Canaanite shrines incorporated similar objects, described as the *massebah* and the *ašerah*.[18] Biblical texts confirm that the latter was wooden and, according to votive inscriptions found in Syrio-Palestine, was the symbol of the mother goddess. The dedication of a Phoenician from Kition is directed 'to his lady, the mother of the *ašerah*'.[19] At Ma'zub near Ptolemais, a temple portico was built 'for Aštoreth in the *aserah*'. It is likely to have been a carved totem of the Sacred Tree. Innumerable biblical references refer to it – Deuteronomy 12.3: 'And ye shall overthrow their altars, and break their pillars (*massebahs*), and burn their groves (*ašeras*) with fire; and ye shall hew down the graven images of their gods, and destroy the names of them out of that place.'

Trees are never far from reach. In Hittite legend the missing fertility god, Telepinu, was given a peace offering on his return. An evergreen tree was set up before him and decked with gifts suggesting, again, a deep respect for the Mesopotamian tradition of adorning the Sacred Tree. The skin of a sheep was hung in

the branches and the skin was stuffed with all the bounty of
nature. Into it were placed mutton fat, cattle, oxen, sheep, the
soft bleating of lambs, corn and wine, the length of days and
progeny, prosperity and abundance.

Similar links emerge from other traditions. The Phrygian god
Attis, allegedly bled to death beneath a pine tree and as late as
Greek and Roman times, a pine tree was decorated and brought
into the temple during services to mourn the passing of the god.

The Hittites shared a deep conviction in the great spiritual
powers of trees. A document, most of which has been destroyed,
contains tantalizing reference to the beginning of a ritual which
took place in some kind of sacred grove. The image or the symbol
of the god was brought out of the temple and seated in a decorated chariot: '. . . the women go in front, also the dancers and
the temple harlots go in front and they hold lighted torches . . .
and the god comes behind and they take the god down through
the Tawiniya gate to the wood. And where the god comes to the
Tarnawi house (bath house) in the wood, the priest takes Muttis
and water and goes round the Tarnawi house and the god enters
the Tarnawi house . . .'

One is tempted to find some parallel with Mesopotamian rites
of the gardener and the grove. Was the 'wood' some special place
which equated with the Mesoptamian garden shrine and with the
Canaanite 'grove'?

Another fragment emerges from a tablet found at Ras Šamra.
The Old Babylonian terracotta model which rests in the British
Museum and which depicts, enigmatically, a ritual act of intercourse with the woman bending over and apparently drinking
from a straw in an urn may have its answer in the legend of Aqhat
describing a spring sowing ritual: 'He embraced the ripening stalk
and kissed it (saying), May, Oh! May (this) ripening stalk shoot
up in the parched land.'

Within these very different landscapes whose bounty was
so near and yet often so far from the grasp of the new farmers, themes have emerged which have puzzled and fascinated
watchers of the ancient near east for more than a hundred years
since serious archaeology of the region began.

In some respects western Asia showed a primitive face. Animistic thoughts were deeply entrenched even in early agricultural
societies which theoretically had stepped beyond such notions.
Skeletons of dogs have been unearthed from the foundations
of houses, placed there to guard against evil spirits much as
cocks and chickens were interred in Britain until quite recently.

Ancient instructions tell householders how to make a model of
a dog from tallow and place it before the door of the house. An
inscription reads: 'You are a little dog from the table of the royal
pair. As, by day, you do not allow others into the courtyard, so
during the night, do not allow in the evil thing.'

Myth and ritual visibly followed remarkably constant patterns as they evolved, though myth did not always involve
ritual and, conversely, ritual could stand alone without a supporting legend. Myths also differed markedly in depth. Some
were little more than pieces of entertainment, others possessed
profound substance and implication. It seems, in general, that
lesser 'philosophical lights' desired to emulate that which they
saw in Sumer, Assyria and Babylon, and that often the results
were imperfect imitations.

The grouping of dieties into threes became increasingly significant and whether some of these triads were seen as different
facets of the goddess of fertility; mistress, mother, guardian of
the underworld, or of the interplay between consort and goddess
in the shape of life and death, the rumours from prehistoric times
that the lighting and extinguishing of life's spark do not merely
stalk one another but stand arm in arm, came still more strongly.
Genesis and nemesis were aspects of the one.

Likewise, trees in the form of stylized decorated posts emerged
both as symbols of life and fecundity and, whilst not yet the
machinery of death, they became strongly associated with the
ending of life.

The confrontation drama between good and evil, chaos and
order, became a universal explanation of origins. The seasonal
rites which followed performed two vital needs. The king, taking
the sins of his people upon himself and thus incurring personally
the displeasure of the gods, released the world from its past and
present problems through his own humiliation and through the
slaughter of a substitute, if not indeed his own death. Thus expiated, the real king and his palace were insured through protective
and purifying rituals and thrust back into a new, refreshed, potent
state of sexuality and vigour through the triumph and jubilation
of resurrection and marriage festival. Above all the message
from the ancient near east is that the king as a sacred religious
institution was fundamental whether in the once fertile plains
of southern Mesopotamia or the mountain kingdoms of Hatti.
His ritualized death and restoration in the spring lay at the core
of a nation's success or failure.

There are those who would argue passionately that what

happened in Mesopotamia during the eras of Sumer and Babylon can bear no relation or influence on the making of Christianity. The passage of time between the two cultures, they will insist, was too great. The Akitu in honour of Marduk which began as a Sumerian barley harvest rite, took place on the last known occasion in Babylon when the Persian king Cambyses 'took Bel by the hand' in 538 BC. But elsewhere in southern Mesopotamia, including ancient Uruk, Anu and Ištar were still being honoured in this great spring festival of death and regenesis less than two hundred years before the birth of Jesus the Nazarene.

8

Isis and Osiris

Four powers whose cultures
acknowledged the sacredness of the living earth closely affected
the fashioning of Judaism. Three strands, Assyria, Babylon and
Canaan have been explored; the fourth was Egypt, one of the
great rivals for command of the eastern seaboard of the Mediterranean. For important periods until the twelfth century BC, she
effectively controlled the land of Palestine and southern Syria,
but it was not only the Hebrews who felt her influence. She left
a lasting impression on the classical empires of Greece and Rome
which, in turn, put their mark on Christianity.

Egypt followed patterns of religion that are familiar and yet
strange, for she is not a part of western Asiatic culture. Egypt
is African. There was some Semitic mixing of her prehistoric
peoples but most seem to have migrated from equatorial Africa
and from Libya, and Egypt's cultural integrity gives her story of
the gods of the earth a certain bite. From the ages before the
First Dynasty arose in the fourth millennium, many figurines
and carvings have been unearthed which epitomize the hesitant styles of Egypt's earliest art. They are typical of a people
experimenting with agriculture and herding, but also hunting
in a Nile valley that was once lush from frequent rains and
grazed by hippopotamus, antelope and giraffe: the art depicts
scenes of the chase and wild animals but amongst these, once

more, one discovers an urgent attention to the mother goddess and her fullness.

There are ripe *enceinte* figures and something about them is at once shocking. The statues, fashioned in clay, are separated from the 'Venus' figurines of Europe by at least ten thousand years, by thousands of miles, and by quite alien cultural origins. Borrowing can hardly have been possible, yet the posture and design are instantly familiar. Viewed from the side, each figure has the classic pose of the buttocks images which gave rise to the P-signs in south-west France. Each goddess is moulded bending forward, with a faceless head, obvious breasts, and legs which fuse into a peg.

One other remarkable feature of the predynastic goddesses lies in the position of their arms. They are raised aloft, or more precisely since the figure is bending forward, they are curved gracefully to the front. Why were almost all created in this style and only very few with the arms resting beneath the breasts?

We are looking at a fertility goddess and at least one such deity within the recorded dynastic period was, like Ninhursaĝa, a cow goddess. Perhaps the figurines are so styled to reflect an intercourse position in which the female shaman imitated a cow's horns just as the more recent Kalahari women emulated their sacred Eland antelope. A second possibility lies in the posture's resemblance to the omega shape, in which case this could be a very early piece of symbolic art bringing the cornuate uterus design into a sacred figurine. Among the finds from the fourth millennium period and also later, are drawings of a huge celestial cow whose belly is studded with stars; and of a woman bending across the vault of heaven; and of the sun born from these female colossi to chase each day across the heavens and descend to the underworld.

The works, though, were part of Egypt's antiquity. She was poised to abandon tribalism, and to plunge into a new kind of organization, a cohesive nationalism headed by a god-king. Notwithstanding her distinct origins, Egypt shared this in common with other successful empires. In the words of Sir James Frazer: 'It is no accident that all the first great strides towards civilization have been made under despotic and theocratic governments, like those of Egypt, Babylon and Peru, where the supreme ruler claimed and received the servile allegiance of his subjects in the double character of a king and a god.'[1]

Egypt's peculiarity is that in her refining marches she achieved

single government long before Mesopotamia abandoned her fragmented city states. So how great was Egypt's influence in western
Asia and, conversely, to what extent did Mesopotamia's culture
rub off on the Pharaohs?

Egyptian religion and ritual remained fairly isolated although
a number of its features proved deeply attractive to other cultures even if they failed at times to understand what they were
borrowing. One of the general limitations against the widespread
dissemination of beliefs and the style of their expression rested in
the obscurity of the written language. Egypt began to experiment
with the art of writing during the last centuries of the fourth
millennium but despite the awe in which her social, economic
and military sophistication were held, hieroglyphic script was
vulnerable to misinterpretation, as was the complex thinking
behind Egypt's religious symbolism. The winged disc is a case
in point. The wings of the sacred falcon hovering protectively
above the head of an exalted ruler were copied in one form or
another by virtually every aspiring nation in the ancient near
east. Yet whilst revelling in its appearance and in admiration for
the country which spawned it, few foreigners understood any of
its political or religious implication. They would not have been
aware, for instance, that the falcon, the king and the god Horus
were all intimately linked in an annual renewal of coronation.

The Greeks were besotted with the organization and the
romance of Egypt and they threw themselves into a great love
affair with her symbolism and literature. The images of a mild
and sanctimonious madonna which emerged as a westernized
model of Isis, adored throughout much of classical Europe, bore
great similarity to the goddess of fertility and crops worshipped
in Egypt. Yet, in Hellenizing for domestic consumption, they frequently got it wrong! Herodotus and Plutarch set themselves up
as authorities on Egyptian tradition but stand accused, rightly, of
being all too often in a hopeless muddle with their interpretations.
Plutarch was struck deeply by the legend of Isis' ill-fated consort
Osiris and yet Plutarch's Greek translation, incidentally the only
source until very recent times of a connected narrative, shows
a slim grasp of the legend's deeper thrusts. Plutarch rendered
a version limited largely to the picture-book aspects of the action
and including some innovations of his own but ignored the more
profound train of thought.

Whilst the Greeks had some ability to interpret Egyptian
hieroglyphics, perversely the modern world did not, until a
chance discovery at Rosetta (Rashid) on the Nile Delta where,

in 1799, a basalt slab was unearthed. Inscribed and erected in 196 BC to honour Ptolemy V, the Rosetta Stone is the key to present-day understanding of Egyptian hieroglyphs. It parallels Darius' inscription at Behistun because it is inscribed in three languages: Egyptian hieroglyphic, demotic (a more modern version) and, most importantly, Greek.

In terms of external influence, probably very little of Egypt's religion came from abroad. The Egypt-watcher gains no sense of an adulteration of old tribal mythologies with later imports, and this, above all, makes Egypt's tale fascinating because, in spite of her integrity and individuality, the gods still reached down and brushed her with the unseen hand that touched other cultures. She perceived a familiar vision and arrived at familiar means of expressing it.

Egypt honoured and revered the passing of the seasons with religious festivals. There might seem, on the face of it, to be little to choose between the environments of Mesopotamia and of Egypt. Both lands are subject to extremes of heat and drought, both are crossed by major river systems which flood periodically, both are heavily dependent on water. There are, however, significant differences.

In Egypt, the Nile flood is less of an uncertainty than that of the Tigris and Euphrates. From late April until July the lands around the Nile are cracked and blasted by hot relentless winds off the desert; the land is dead awaiting the rise of the waters bringing their gift of life from the mountains of Ethiopia and from the great equatorial lakes. Towards August comes the metamorphosis and, providing that the river reaches a critical height, the plains are covered by a great turbid relief. The crops are sown as the waters recede sometime in November and are harvested in March and April. Since time immemorial the Egyptian farmers have celebrated these moments. They have honoured the goddess Isis as her tears for her broken and scattered consort Osiris swell the holy river, and as Sirius begins to rise, appropriately, in the early morning heavens to greet the dawn of a new year. They have honoured the flooding of the fields. Frazer describes an antique festival held between 6 and 16 August before cutting through the river banks, when a small earthen figure called 'the bride' was built by each dyke to symbolize the impregnation of the semen of the river into the womb of the soil. The farmers have honoured the sowing of the crops and the harvest.

An Egyptian's religion thus followed a predictable course up to a point. His perception of the cosmos mirrored doggedly that

of so many contemporarics. Heaven and earth were distilled from
the essence of a creator, unknown and unseen, his name a
hidden mystery. The Egyptian does not seem to have been wholly
enamoured of polytheism though. The word for a deity is *neter*,
but it is not a precise term equating to present-day notions of a
god among many, nor is it a term of address like *Bel* or *adon*,
rather it is something which defines a single spiritual principle.
Thus the nine great *neters* of Heliopolis – Atum, Šu, Tefnut, Geb,
Nut, Osiris, Isis, Seth and Nephthys are perhaps to be seen more
as aspects of the one. This 'upper tier' assembly which ratified all
important ceremonies was the Ennead.

Neter summarizes many diverse facets of the same presence, a
concept towards which Mesopotamian cultures may have been
drifting but to which the Egyptian pondering the universe had
become attracted much earlier. The names ascribed to each
facet often differed from one city to another, merely because
of local tradition, but effectively they were miscible. They often
duplicated each other rather than describing distinct and separate
divinities and this allowed 'personalities' to merge and exchange
roles, and to take on multiple responsibilities, with a freedom and
fluidity that was not possible in the Mesopotamian scheme of
things. Re was almost universally acclaimed as the source of light
in the heavens, the sun-god, but in different cities various deities
effectively headed the pantheon. Thus, whilst Re was the 'Creator
Sun God' of Heliopolis and Atum was 'Lord of Heliopolis', Ptah
was the counterpart at Memphis, Atum at Thebes and Thoth dominated Hermopolis. At times during Egyptian history such powerful deities were either in ascendancy or waning in popularity.

Beyond the familiar pantheon and the seasonal round of ritual,
though, the Egyptian's religious upbringing took a quite different
slant. People ventured, to an unparalleled extent, towards preoccupation with the cult of the dead and the life hereafter. Any
brief attempt to understand why religion took this course would
be glib. There are no easy answers and it probably came about
through the delicate interaction of several factors. A cultural
focus less diffuse than that of Mesopotamia may have provided
a climate which stimulated a greater pooling and evaluating of
radical ideas.

The nation's acquisition of great wealth and security for her
intellectual élite would have softened the daily demands of existence and allowed some of her people to explore the possibilities
of the infinite, to quest beyond the spiritual horizons of their
neighbours.

Whatever the reasons, the afterlife loomed large. The Egyptian was of the view that successful passage to the evergreen aeons depended on proper facilities being accorded to the life force, the *ka*. The preservation of corpses began very early in Egyptian history and it became bound up with the traditions of Osiris, the mortuary god. The earthly body had to be preserved. If the body decomposed or was otherwise destroyed, the soul or *ba* could alight on a likeness of the dead person locked into a statue or a painting, but this was strictly a second line of defence and the Egyptian went to involved, sometimes extraordinary, lengths to ensure that the body retained its vital appearance.

The mortal remains of Egypt's kings, above all, were to be preserved. These demi-gods descended from a legendary dynasty of numinous rulers and they represented an unbroken line of 'Divine Dead'. Each was an incarnation of the god Horus in life, and in death became his murdered father, Osiris. The obsession with a proper departure from life led to construction of ever more grandiose tombs for the royal deceased which by the fourth and fifth dynasties had resulted in that Egyptian landmark, the pyramid. Within the most resilient citadel that the mind of the Egyptian architect could conjure, the earthly remains were embalmed and mummified, and provided with all that they might require.

Such indulgence was dependent on wealth and influence, and it was only divine right or, for a commoner, the power of wealth which offered such protection. Much of Egypt's art too, was executed with the dead rather than the living in mind, and a great deal of her literature and inscription is, in effect, a training manual, a do-it-yourself guide to paradise. The so-called 'Book of the Dead' was the Egyptian's mortuary bible.

So who is Osiris and why has he been of such pressing interest? Amongst the first herdsmen and agriculturalists he may have begun his career as a tree spirit. In early dynastic times he was the spirit of the corn, the progenitor of crops symbolized by a pillar, perhaps an unwitting parallel of design with the Mesopotamian gilded wooden post. But from these beginnings he took on a more august mantle so that by the Eighteenth Dynasty he was a creator god whose image seems almost indistinguishable from that of Re; he was the sun as it passed through the dark realms of the underworld. Yet he became the perennial victim of nature's curse, provided with the credentials to achieve that reasoned if somewhat paradoxical governance of fertility and fatality. In certain legends he took shape as a mortal and on his violent demise he became the first mummy. He did not reign as the god of the dead from the outset but he became more and more closely linked with the ceremonial of death, and his pillar was replaced by a swathed and mummified figure drawn as a man, its face green and adorned with a long stiff beard which denoted almost all gods, and only the hands holding sceptre and flail left free.

Osiris was no dying and rising god in the sense of an Asian Dumuzi since Egypt's origins are in the African south and to the east in the Libyan desert. Osiris represented the implacable and universal belief that new life can only bloom, phoenix-like, out of the worms of the old, but in him that concept took a radical shift. Osiris rose from the corruption of nothingness to reign for ever over the paradise kingdom of the dead. It is a prickly thought that those African origins spawned a tradition that sails provocatively close to Christianity. Nor is this the only Egyptian innovation to do so. The goddess Isis raises further questions.

Isis was a much less clearly defined figure. She probably began her career as a corn goddess in prehistoric times but over the centuries she attracted more and more attributes to the extent that in some texts, though the title is typically from the classical period, she is described as 'the goddess with a thousand names'. The Greeks extended her realm still further so that she took on such diverse duties as the protection of seafarers under the title of Stella Maris. In her symbolism, there are familiar strands. Isis was represented by the cow, just as Ninhursağa had been in Sumer. In a festival which marked the peak of the dry season a gilded model of a cow was carried through the streets at night when all the houses were lamplit to illuminate a symbolic search of Isis for her lost lover.

Another deity who demands close scrutiny is Hathor, a confusingly similar Egyptian goddess of love who, in the Egyptian pantheon, parallels in some respects the relationship of Ninhursağa to Ištar, and who was also recognized as the cow goddess.

The temple of Hathor at Dendara, north of Thebes, is one of the best preserved of its kind. Features of Hathor's appearance in its paintings and sculptures bear striking similarity with a Mesopotamian object, the omega, which seems to have provided the improbable inspiration for a hairstyle! The goddess wears a wig that parallels the motif and an involuntary empathy seems to have arisen between an Egyptian fertility goddess and Ninhursağa. Both Hathor and Isis are drawn with the head or the horns of a cow holding the golden orb of the sun, another possible cross-fertilization because Osiris is sometimes seen as the sun-god during the hours of darkness. The head-dress was common regalia for Hathor. She wears it prominently in the Nineteenth-Dynasty Hall of Hypostyle in the temple of Karnak. From the same building comes a fine schist stone sarcophagus on the lid of which is an image of a late dynastic princess and votary of Amun-Re, Ankhnesneferibre. She wears, as did many Egyptian queens and ladies, a vulture head-dress but resting above it are the uterine horns and orb. On the walls at Dendara, both the Hathor wig and the horned head are depicted together in scenes where Hathor holds sistrums, the rattles used in ritual service. Both forms also seem to emerge in the design of Egyptianized gold pendants of a kind found widely distributed in such regions as Gaza.

The Egyptians apparently loaded the same kind of cryptic meaning on to the omega design as did the visionaries of Sumer and from it may have come the hieroglyphic symbol SA. Derived from a tied bunch of reeds, the object is usually held by the goddess of birth, Taweret, and a similar motif, popularly tagged the 'Isis knot', is sometimes associated with Isis. Though similar in appearance and, arguably, sentiment, the ankh which later became associated with classical European goddesses like Venus and Aphrodite bears an altogether different meaning. The hieroglyph for 'life', it has been derived, according to different authorities, from such disparate everyday objects as a sandal strap and a penis sheath.

The SA differs from the familiar omega symbol in that the 'vaginal entrance' is tied together with a broad band, and thus it may have signified a protection against the dangers of childbirth. There has existed since very ancient times a tradition amongst Egyptian women of carrying a padlock as a protective amulet during pregnancy, and occasionally the lock is substituted by a coiled piece of wire, unmistakably an omega-style uterus with the entrance closed. The uterus motif was destined to find its way on to hundreds of small classical amulet gems made of the 'blood' stone, haematite. The logic behind the symbolism seems to be that during pregnancy it is vital to 'lock in the blood' since the invariable precursor to miscarriage of a foetus is haemorrhage from the womb.

A model of a vulture, the symbol of the tutelary goddess of lower Egypt, is often worn as a head-dress by both Isis and Hathor, and the hieroglyph which signifies vulture also means 'mother'. In the Hebrew language the word for vulture is similar to 'compassion' and 'uterus'. The association may explain why the SA is sometimes drawn on Egyptian figurines with little wings sprouting from its sides, and why in some classical designs, the uterus is also drawn with wings.

The story of Osiris and Isis begins, inevitably, long before the first Egyptian toes wriggled in the Saharan sands. The saga has probably never existed as a single definitive document but allusions to it were inscribed on pyramid walls dating back to the latter part of the third millennium in the Old Kingdom, others were penned on to coffins dating from the Middle Kingdom period more than five hundred years later, and still more were found written into various sacred books and on scarabs. The basis of the story is thought to go back to predynastic times and overall it was composed across nearly five thousand years. The only 'comprehensive' version to be discovered was that of the Greek writer, Plutarch, and no one has properly verified its accuracy or been certain of its sources.[2]

Today we have several accurate translations but they form less of a comprehensive narrative than a fragmented series of sketches. The more popular version relates that Re, learning his wife Nut had been less than faithful and had consorted with the earth god, Geb, cursed her in a way that he believed would render her barren. Re vowed that she should be delivered of a child 'in no month and no year'. But Nut had also distributed her favours to Thoth, god of wisdom, and in a wager Thoth won from the moon goddess the seventieth part of each day of the Egyptian year calculated not on a proper solar cycle but on the rising of the star Sirius. Thus Egypt structured her calendar of 360 days. Out of his fragments of time Thoth made up the five days needed to round off the solar course, yet significantly these five still lay outside of the official twelve-month year and on each of the days which had escaped the curse of Re, Nut delivered a child. The firstborn was Osiris, followed by the elder Horus, Seth, Isis and Nephthys. Isis and Osiris became inseparable – goddess of fertility and consort. In the minds of the Egyptians the pair were once very much mortal living royalty who travelled the world demonstrating new-found techniques of cultivation and finally returned to Egypt to be hailed as deities.

Osiris' brother, Seth, conspired with seventy-two others towards his death. Seth, in Plutarch's version the god Typhon, hunted the lion and the elephant and pillaged the land whilst Osiris coaxed and nurtured its bounty. Seth coveted his brother's harvest and in stealth he measured Osiris' body and built a finely wrought chest. During a drunken binge Seth put up a challenge by offering the chest as a gift to anyone who would fit into it exactly. All tried but none fitted until Osiris stepped in and lay down. The lid sprang shut and what was by now a coffin was soldered with lead and hurled into the Nile. Over the years which followed Isis searched fruitlessly for her husband's body until at last she discovered the chest embedded deep in a tamarisk trunk.

Isis fled with Osiris' coffin to a cave in the distant mountains where she would be safe from Seth, and there she broke open the chest and wrought her magic over the remains of the god. She made 'light with her feathers, wind she made with her wings'.[3] She conceived Osiris' son Horus the younger. Yet the confrontation between good and evil, light and dark was never over. Seth found the body of Osiris and tore it into fourteen pieces. Thirteen he cast out over the Nile and the god's penis he threw to a crocodile so that the shade of Osiris might never more father a child. Meanwhile Isis gave birth in the safety of the papyrus swamps. Horus 'would' avenge his father. When the child grew to be a man, there began the battle of the gods which was waged from one end of Egypt to the other as Horus matched himself against Seth and against the evil that destroyed Osiris.

The conflict is also known in a confused and fragmented way from the Pyramid Texts, the earliest literary source of Egyptian mythology; in the 1980s, the American writer Normandi Ellis reworked part of the Papyrus of the scribe Nebseni into modern idiomatic prose. Whilst not rendering a true translation of its text she has conjured an evocative turbulence which may capture the original sentiment:

> Beneath the sun's wasting heat, rain fell and dried before reaching the ground. Then the earth rose up like an animal and shook itself. Hot winds blew and stirred the sand into black and red clouds. The sun was blotted from the sky. The two gods seized each other. Blind with rage and stumbling they fought with magic, with words, with clubs and knives. They fell upon each other with their hands. They wrestled about the earth in the shape of bears, in the shape of snakes, in the forms of men and wolves and wild beasts. Swords of iron battered shields of gold. Seth buggered the warrior and Horus cut off his balls. They threw vomit and shit in each other's faces. In heaven the gods wept and looked

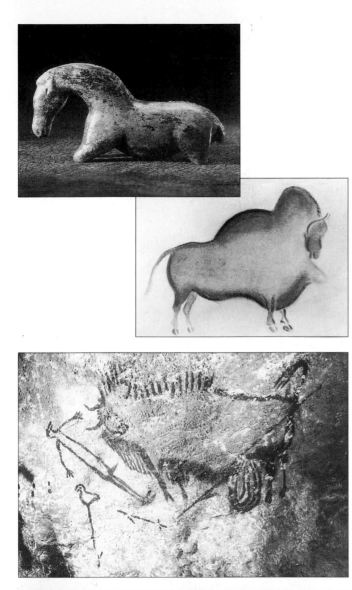

(Far left) Running horse carved in mammoth ivory. *Circa* 32000 BC. Vogelherd, Baden-Württemberg, Germany. *Institut für Ur und Frügeschichte, Tübingen Schloss (photo: Joachim Feist).*

(Near left) Bison painted on limestone. *Circa* 15000–12000 BC. Font de Gaume, SW France. *Photothèque du Musée de l'Homme, Paris.*

(Left) Death scene, painted on the wall of a vertical shaft. *Circa* 15000 BC. Lascaux, SW France. *Photothèque du Musée de l'Homme, Paris.*

(Below) Sculptures of bison, in clay, each over 2 metres in length. *Circa* 15000 BC. Tuc d'Audoubert, SW France. *Photothèque du Musée de l'Homme, Paris.*

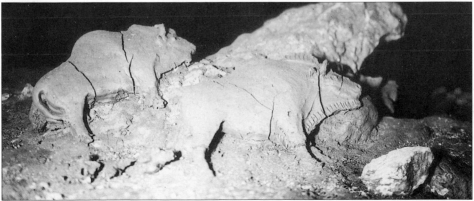

(Left) 'Sorcerer'. *Circa* 13000 BC. Trois Frères, SW France. *Photothèque du Musée de l'Homme, Paris.*

(Bottom left) 'Venus' figurine sculpted from a mixture of clay and burned powdered bone. *Circa* 24000 BC. Dolní Věstonice, Czechoslovakia. *By permission of the Moravské Museum, Břno (photo: L. Pichova).*

(Above right) 'Venus' figurine carved from mammoth ivory. *Circa* 24000 BC. Lespugue, France. *Collection du Musée de l'Homme, Paris.*

(Below) 'Venus' figurine carved from limestone. *Circa* 28000 BC. Willendorf, Austria. *Courtesy of Naturhistorisches Museum, Vienna.*

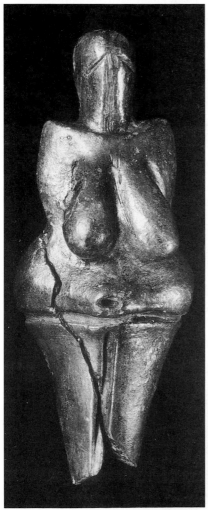

(Left) Stylized figure carved from mammoth ivory, possibly androgynous with either breasts or testicles. Dolní Věstonice, Czechoslovakia. *By permission of the Moravské Museum, Břno (photo: L. Pichova).*

(Bottom left) Stylized figure carved from mammoth ivory, suggesting arched thighs and a vulval slit. Dolní Věstonice, Czechoslovakia. *By permission of the Moravské Museum, Břno (photo: L. Pichova).*

(Below) 'Venus' bas-relief carved in a shallow shelter. *Circa* 20000 BC. Laussel, SW France. *Phototheque du Musée de l'Homme, Paris.*

(Above) Abstract figurine, carved in coal, less than 5 centimetres in height. Magdalenian Period. Petersfels, Germany. *Institut für Ur und Frügeschichte, Tübingen Schloss (photo: Joachim Feist).*

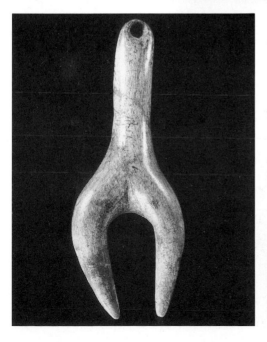

(Above) Amber animal figures sculpted from fossilized pine resin washed up along the coasts. *Circa* 8000 BC. Denmark. *By kind permission of the Nationalmuseet, Copenhagen.*

(Right) Elk incised on flat rocks near a ford on the river Etnar. The thicker outline appears to have been partially superimposed over an earlier one. *Circa* 2000 BC. Møllefossan, southern Norway. *University Museum of National Antiquities, Oslo.*

(Below) A reindeer and a whale incised on the edge of a glacier. *Circa* 2000 BC. Fykanvatn, Norway. *University Museum of National Antiquities, Oslo.*

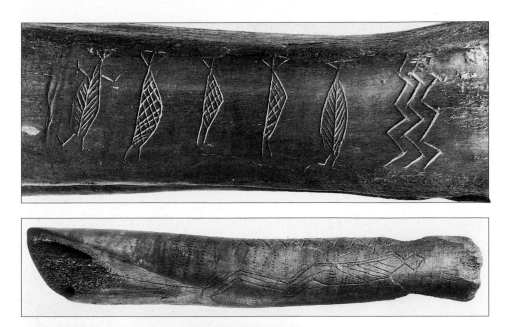

(Top) Earliest known example of human figures in Scandinavian art. Etched on a fragment of bone. Ryemarkgard, Sjaelland, Denmark. *By kind permission of the Nationalmuseet, Copenhagen.*

(Above) Figure incised on to a reindeer horn axe which also displays 'tally marks'. The legs appear to possess one joint too many for a human limb and end in tiny hooves. From the Jørdlose bog, Denmark. *By kind permission of the Nationalmuseet, Copenhagen.*

(Left) 'Venus' figurine sculpted in clay. Yarmukian Culture, Neolithic – fourth millennium BC. Horvat Minha (Munhata), Jordan Valley. *Courtesy of the collection of Israel Antiquities Authority exhibited and photographed in the Israel Museum, Jerusalem.*

(Above) Circular pre-Israelite cairn altar built of rough stone. Megiddo, Israel. *By kind permission of The Oriental Institute, the University of Chicago.*

(Right) Dolmen burial mound, partly unearthed. Megalithic. Denmark. *By kind permission of the Nationalmuseet, Copenhagen.*

(Bottom right) Interior of passage grave. *Circa 2200* BC. Denmark. *By kind permission of the Nationalmuseet, Copenhagen.*

(Above) Cist grave. *Circa* 1600 BC. Denmark. *By kind permission of the Nationalmuseet, Copenhagen.*

(Left) 'Face urns' about 11 centimetres in height, with large staring eyes. Late Neolithic. Sjaelland, Denmark. *By kind permission of the Nationalmuseet, Copenhagen.*

(Below) Seal of the scribe Adda depicting the goddess Ištar surrounded by other deities of the pantheon. *Circa* 2000 BC cylinder seal impression. *Courtesy of the Trustees of the British Museum.*

(Right) Kudurru boundary marker incised with names and symbols of Mesopotamian deities. *Courtesy of the Trustees of the British Museum.*

(Middle) The great ziggurat at Ur (Tell el Muqayyer) seen from the east during excavations 1922-4 directed by Sir Leonard Woolley. *Courtesy of the Trustees of the British Museum.*

(Bottom) Portico embellishment of the Tell el'Ubaid temple of Ninhursaĝa depicting a winged lion-hybrid and attendant animals. *Courtesy of the Trustees of the British Museum.*

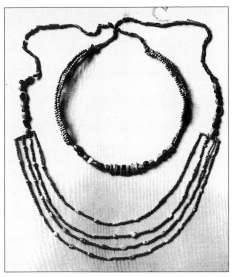

(Top left) Terracotta plaque, apparently mass produced and probably depicting the Sumerian sacred marriage ceremony. *Courtesy of the Trustees of the British Museum.*

(Top right) The necklace of the lukur-priestess Kubatum. Uruk (Warka). *Courtesy of the Deutsches Archaologisches Institut, Berlin (photo: K. Limper).*

(Left) Fragment of chlorite pot describing part of the legend of Inana and the *halub* tree and offering early evidence of tree worship in Sumer. Third millennium BC. Mari. *By kind permission of the Museum of Damascus (photo: M. Musselmany).*

(Bottom left) A bearded hero about to attack a tree with an axe. The god Nergal rises from the base and a female figure holds a ritual bucket. Late third millennium BC cylinder seal impression. *Courtesy of the Trustees of the British Museum.*

(Above) Colossi guarding one of the gates into the North-west Palace of Aššur-nasir-apli II. Ninth century BC. Nimrud, Iraq. *British School of Archaeology in Iraq.*

(Above) Relief in gypseous alabaster originally fixed above the throne of Aššur-nasir-apli II. Ninth century BC. North-west Palace, Kalakh (Nimrud, Iraq). *Courtesy of the Trustees of the British Museum.*

(Right) Relief in gypseous alabaster depicting the winged figure holding cone and attending the sacred tree. North-west Palace, Kalakh (Nimrud, Iraq). *Courtesy of the Trustees of the British Museum.*

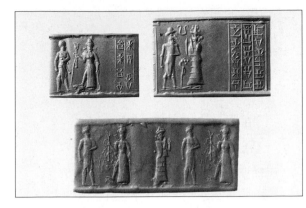

(Above left) Sequence of development from 'omega' to 'chalice' in symbolism of the sacred tree. Old Babylonian cylinder seal impressions. *Courtesy of the Trustees of the British Museum.*

(Middle left) Reproduced and partly restored wall painting of 'bouquet' tree. Kar Tukulti Ninurta (Iraq). *British Museum collection (photo: Michael Jordan).*

(Bottom left) Drawing in the gutter of an AD fourteenth-century manuscript, *Liber Physiognomiae*, depicting a seven-celled uterus reminiscent of the Mesopotamian 'bouquet' tree. *Folio 96 verso of MS L 92 Sup. Biblioteca Ambrosiana, Milan (photo: The Medieval Institute, University of Notre Dame, Illinois, USA).*

(Below) A cow suckling its calf against a tracery of lotus flowers and buds, *circa* seventh century BC. Kalakh (Nimrud, Iraq). *By permission of Lady B. Mallowan.*

(Near right) A fragment of fretted ivory, *circa* seventh century BC, bearing traces of blue lacquer and gilding. The design may include fertility symbolism. Kalakh (Nimrud, Iraq). *By permission of Lady B. Mallowan.*

(Right) Unnamed Babylonian king and subject, his divine status reinforced by the symbols of deities. *British Museum collection (photo: Michael Jordan).*

(Above left) The Ištar Gate at Babylon through which the processions of devotees of the goddess passed during the Akitu festival (half-size replica). *By kind permission of Dr Dominique Collon.*

(Above right) Image of Marduk reproduced from an engraved baton. Neo-Babylonian. *British Museum collection (photo: Michael Jordan).*

(Far left) Bronze figurine of the Hellenized Syrian goddess Astarte, 'The Goddess of Byblos', showing strong Egyptian influence in the style of headdress. Phoenician. AD first century. *Courtesy of the Trustees of the British Museum.*

(Left) Pre-dynastic clay figurine of fertility goddess. Egyptian. Fourth millennium BC. *Courtesy of the Trustees of the British Museum.*

(Above) A mummified ithyphallic Osiris impregnates Isis in the form of a falcon, watched by Isis and Horus. Sarcophagus from the Temple of Seti I. Abydos. Nineteenth Dynasty of Egypt. *Circa* 1300 BC. *Griffith Institute, Ashmolean Museum, Oxford.*

(Far left) The birth goddess Taweret in the form of a hippopotamus, holding an ankh and with her hand resting on the *SA* symbol of birth. Papyrus of Ani, Nineteenth Dynasty of Egypt. *Circa* 1250 BC. *Courtesy of the Trustees of the British Museum.*

(Left) Sistrum rattle decorated with the head of the goddess Hathor. Bronze. Egyptian (Roman Period 30 BC–AD 395). *Courtesy of the Trustees of the British Museum.*

(Bottom left) Isis suckling Horus. Bronze figurine. Probably late Dynastic Egyptian, after 600 BC. *Courtesy of the Trustees of the British Museum.*

(Top left) Carved ivory fragment depicting a stag framed by a lattice of greenery, *circa* seventh century BC. Kalakh (Nimrud, Iraq). *By kind permission of the Organization of Antiquities and Heritage, Baghdad.*

(Top right) Portico of first-century synagogue at Tell Hum (Israel) showing iconoclastic damage. *By courtesy of the Palestine Exploration Fund.*

(Above) Limestone menorah from the AD first-century synagogue at Hamat Tiberias. *Courtesy of the collection of Israel Antiquities Authority exhibited and photographed in the Israel Museum, Jerusalem.*

(Left) 'Adoration of the Golden Calf' (Nicholas Poussin, 1594–1665). *Reproduced by courtesy of the Trustees, The National Gallery, London.*

(Above) 'Image of the goddess Cybele carried into Rome' (Andrea Mantegna, 1430–1506). *Reproduced by courtesy of the Trustees, The National Gallery, London.*

(Below) Demeter, Persephone and Triptolemos on decorated vase. Classical Greek. *Courtesy of the Trustees of the British Museum.*

(Middle right) Apollo. Marble. Classical Greek. *Courtesy of the Trustees of the British Museum.*

(Right) Dionysos. Marble. Classical Greek. *Courtesy of the Trustees of the British Museum.*

(Far right) Aphrodite. Marble. Classical Greek. *Courtesy of the Trustees of the British Museum.*

away, all but Thoth who watched the bloody onslaught
for he was unafraid of truth. They might have killed each
other but for the flashing hand of truth which sometimes
parted them . . . the knives thrust into Seth came away
with Horus' blood. The eye he tore out was the eye of
god.[4]

There is, in the closing words of Ellis' interpretation of the
duel, a strident message. The eternal conflict between light and
dark, good and evil seems to have preoccupied men since the
beginning of recorded history and, if the art of earlier eras is
an indicator, the theme extends back much further in time. The
drama of confrontation is one of the first recognizable themes.
There has already come evidence that the ancient civilizations
made a firm connection between fertility and death. Inana and
Ereškigal are two Mesopotamian deities who, though a contradiction of each other, form an indissoluble pair. In Sumerian
legend Inana chose to confront the darkness within herself, and
the one is envisaged as being entwined for ever with the other.
   From the titanic battle between Horus and Seth, a forceful
drawing together of the two opposed principles, a more advanced
stage of the reasoning is seen to evolve. It is a principle in man's
understanding of himself which will prove its tenacity as the
journey goes on. The Egyptian sentiment reveals that dark and
light are not merely 'counterweights' necessary to each other,
but that each *is* the other! Horus and Seth found only mirrors of
themselves. As Horus hacked off Seth's testicles, as Seth ripped
out Horus' eye, it was not his enemy's blood which gushed out,
but his own.
   Although ancient Egyptian culture was contemporaneous with
Mesopotamia's, it took a giant step, perhaps ahead of time, in the
denouement of creed. Egyptian thought had come to terms with
the inescapable truth that human nature is a conflict of opposites
and that we live on a delicately balanced knife edge. Each of us is
a mirror of our other self. The demon is within us and everyone
fights his or her personal battle. The beast lurks as it did for Horus.
It is never truly vanquished and only truth can save us.
   Away from the never-ending battle of attrition between the
gods Osiris, the father, was not lost. The gods joined together
the broken corpse which Isis had painstakingly recovered. Its
genitals she replaced by an image, and the body was swathed
in linen bandages. Once more Isis fanned life into it with her
wings and Osiris revived to reign as god of the dead. The more

authentic texts draw a beautiful and poignant lyricism of their own:

> My mouth shall be mine that I may speak again; my legs that I may walk; and my strong arms that my enemies may fall. The doors of the sky are thrown open; the mighty Geb throws wide his jaws for me. He opens my eyes that were closed; extends my legs which were contracted. To my thighs which were swathed together Anubis gives strength; Sakhmet the goddess stretches me out. The sky will gather me up; they will make commandments for me in Memphis. My heart shall surge once more; my arms shall take strength; my legs shall take strength. I will live again; my soul and my flesh will be free to go in and out from the portals of the west.[5]

The significance of the god who descended and rose again in western Asia lay with the fate of the natural world. Egypt equalled the model but into it she forged a new dimension, the fall and resurrection of man himself. In the rebirth of Osiris to reign over the glorious kingdom of the dead lay the Egyptian's faith in paradise and eternity. The Egyptian felt no anxiety towards death because, through Osiris, a bright awakening was perceived. The 'Book of the Dead' or, more accurately, the 'Coming Forth by Day' preserved the heavenly procedure for resurrection and, by enacting the ritual which the gods had performed over Osiris' sundered parts, it was believed that an Egyptian would be able to pass beyond the grave. The instructions for the journey were posted at appropriate places where the dead would be able to follow them and it was imperative that after embalming, the body went through the exact ceremonies. The words of the Ani Papyrus provide pungent detail:

> My mouth is opened by Ptah. That which was on my mouth is loosened. Thoth comes filled and armed with magic, and the bonds of Seth which held my mouth are stripped away. Atum has cast away the bonds of Seth. My mouth is split open with the iron of Šu with which he split the mouths of the gods.[6]

The mummy was laid on its back in its granite or limestone sarcophagus and, thus prepared, its soul flew towards the Hall of the Two Truths, to make confession before Osiris who was not merely condemned to the netherworld but was assigned to be its judge. Having been weighed in the balance, the *ka* was fated to pass either to eternal life or to nothingness, a form of damnation.

Osiris' disintegrated corpse was, according to legend, buried at holy places all over Egypt hence the tombs of Osiris found in many ancient sites. His backbone rested at Busiris in the Nile Delta, but his head was interred in the royal cemetery at Abydos far down the river towards Karnak in Upper Egypt. The tomb of an obscure first-dynasty king, traditionally the resting place of the sacred relic, became to Egyptians, as Frazer puts it: 'what the Church of the Holy Sepulchre at Jerusalem is to Christians'. So great was the ethos of Abydos, so strong the influence of Osiris' mummified remains in this holy city that it became the most coveted of burial places. Perversely, very few of the rich seem to have been buried at Abydos, but many Egyptians still 'invested' heavily during their lifetime, to be carried in death to Abydos and wait there awhile in the company of their god before returning home for burial.

The ordinary man-in-the-street may have found it beyond his means to afford his dead the luxuries of grand tombs, but from the thousands of graves opened throughout the Nile valley, there is little doubt that many who passed from mortal life were taken through the rites of Osiris to rise in glorious resurrection and live with the god in eternity.

Officially, Osiris was commemorated in a confusing assortment of rites that trace back to his various responsibilities for trees, crops, fertility and death. There is an additional aberration in that because the state followed its 360-day calendar based on the first sighting of Sirius in the dawn sky, so ceremonial followed a revolving pattern rather than falling annually on the same day. Whilst the peasant in the field celebrated seed sowing at sowing time, state religion observed the equivalent rites on some quite different date!

On the basis of the Alexandrian calendar introduced in 30 BC and which Plutarch followed, he describes a passion festival mourning the death of Osiris between 13 and 16 November. At its climax, the priests went to the river carrying a gold casket representing the box in which the god was entombed alive and into which they poured sacred water with the cry that Osiris was found. The dead god was represented either by a model made of earth and grain, or by a small living boy who may also have signified Osiris' son, Horus.

The ensuing funeral was celebrated on separate dates. Inscribed on the walls of the Osiris shrine in the temple of Hathor at Dendara, its rites began with two black cows ploughing a field which was then sown by a small boy with various kinds of grain. The essential need to scatter seed on the land was perhaps at the heart of the legendary smashing and scattering of Osiris' body. According to some traditions, human sacrifice encouraged the germination of the corn. Victims were slaughtered and cremated in the fields close to one of the graves of Osiris. Their ashes were strewn with winnowing fans in a ritual re-enactment of the scattering of the pieces of the god's body.

Towards the end of the rites an image fashioned from cloth stuffed with corn was placed in a wooden coffin and lowered into the grave, but only after the one from the previous year had been removed. The method of making the image was of great importance because by the end of the season it had sprouted new shoots, bursting through the body to signal the god's resurrection.

There was also a strong interest in the symbolism of the tree instrumental in Osiris' fate. The Roman writer, Firmicus Maternus, described a ceremony in which a felled pine was hollowed out, and from the cut wood an image of the god was wrought then returned to the cavity of the trunk. Among the ruins of Dendara, within whose tumbled walls was the temple of Osiris, a coffin was discovered in which, typical of many others, the mummy of the god was depicted closely associated with a female tree figure. Traces such as these emphasize a bond between god and tree as inseparable as that of the fertility goddess and her Tree of Life in Mesopotamia.

Small, yet exquisite, details press home the reminder that once upon a time religion was no pious abstraction. It was a part of life and it shared all the laughter and the joy as well as the severity and tears of mortality. Osiris was well-endowed in physical attributes – necessarily so if he was to father the fat of Egypt's land. Portraits sometimes make it plain that whilst he might be dead, an essential area of his anatomy remained thoroughly functional in paradise. Frazer delivers a cameo sketch of village women who used to parade through the streets singing songs and carrying puppet images of Osiris. These models were articulated 'obscenely' with strings and the Egyptian ladies no doubt stimulated a degree of merriment in the inventiveness of their manipulations.

According to one isolated account contained in the classical writer Apuleius' *The Golden Ass*, Isis may have been represented in procession by a special uterus symbol. Apuleius described how, in the Isis festival, the gods appeared walking in procession. First came the jackal-headed god of embalming, Anubis. He was followed by a priest carrying the effigy of a cow on his shoulders. 'Another again carried in his blessed bosom the venerable image of the most high deity. It was not shaped like cattle, bird, or wild beast, nor even like a human being, but a clever invention of awe-inspiring novelty, the unutterable demonstration of a religion which was both sublimer in every way and to be covered in deep silence. In this manner was it fashioned from glittering gold. A small vessel most skilfully hollowed out, with well-rounded bottom, the outer surface covered with wonderful Egyptian imagery. Its mouth slightly raised, jutted out in an extended channel with a long neck. On either side was fastened a handle, far receding in wide extension. Upon this handle sat a viper, twisted into a knot and with the wrinkled swelling of its scaly head erect.'

The description, in Latin, uses words which are frequently found in anatomical descriptions of the uterus, and it fits with pictures of a uterine object which were commonly drawn on amulets.

We have comparatively scant information about the Isis festivals – a great deal more is known from the Roman world – but it would be surprising if Egypt, notwithstanding her better abilities to meet the needs of feeding her population, did not indulge in a Sacred Marriage festival in her religious calendar. The evidence has survived, though less overtly than in Mesopotamia.

The temple at Luxor bears wall paintings of such a divine ritual, and similar evidence has survived at Deir el Bahari and in the temple at Karnak. According to the texts the Pharaoh and his queen played out the earthly consummation of the eternal lovers. In these two temporal divinities, descendants of the gods of Egypt's first dynasty, rested the dramatic parallel to the sowing of the seed in the fields. The Sacred Marriage, however, was not an event staged purely in its own right. It seems to have constituted part of the festival of a lesser fertility god, Min, in the first month of the summer period, but it also involved separate harvest ceremonies and mortuary rites connected with the Osirian cult.

The final strand of the prelude to the rise of Israel falls into place. Egypt sends important messages from the past. Neither Judaism nor Christianity can claim to be the innovators of visions of judgement and resurrection to life eternal. These things are under copyright to Egypt. She also set in motion a swing of focus from goddess to god which can be measured beside the shift to a stronger patriarchal emphasis delivered by the Babylonians. That movement, it would appear, tends to coincide with the release from over-riding dependence on nature. Of infinitely greater significance though, is the transition of the kingdom and the throne of the dying and rising fertility god from the temporal to the eternal realms.

Egypt's story if anything delivers more questions than answers. Did Sumer once copy from Egypt? Did the corn growers in those deserts of the south find inspiration in Mesopotamia through some forgotten cultural exchange? Or is it all another inexplicable demonstration of human dreams innocently imitating themselves, chasing precisely the same unfathomable rainbows of the mind? These are the imponderables. Yet within the harsh landscape bounded by the fertile crescent and the Sahara, whose bounty was so near and yet often so far from the grasp of the new agriculturists, themes have emerged. Within the frame of this intricate and interwoven canvas with its personalities questing for assurances about their futures and reasons for their existence, the world took an enormous stride along a seven-thousand-year pathway. Elsewhere, across the Indus, the foundations were being laid of Vedic gods who would ultimately join with an Indo-European pantheon in Hinduism and, far to the east, other civilizations were making similar progress though their evolution was for the most part distinct and separate.

The near east stood waiting for major change. Soon the great despots of its mightiest nations would no longer be able to claim the title 'Great King of the World'. Political upheaval and garnering of knowledge through libraries of the written word were bringing changes in faith. True polytheism, the worship of large numbers of deities each responsible within a hierarchical celestial government for individual aspects of man's life, was becoming outmoded within the advancing societies of the near east and the western world. It cannot be dismissed as a misguided aberration, reflecting a profane and inarticulate era of human achievement. Polytheism was, and still is, as responsive to the needs of society as anything the human spirit has achieved, but it has always met a particular set of conditions and a particular level of ability to cope with those circumstances. It continues to satisfy the demand in many parts of the world, not least among them India. But elsewhere its final epoch, marred by corruption, came among the classical empires of Europe. If the days of the pantheon as a body were numbered, however, those of its chief protagonists were secure. The mother goddess and her consort, whether from their lofty Mesopotamian seat, 'the carnelian mountain of Dilmun', or from the great tombs on the banks of the Nile, were ready to continue their journey.[7]

The question which must now be begged is just how much influence Babylonian, Assyrian, Canaanite and Egyptian thought can claim, not only in the origin of certain spiritual concepts which found footing in the books of the Old Testament, but also in the visionary boundaries of the later Christian evangelists.

9

The God of Israel

Conventional wisdom brands the course of the journey to seek out the Gods of the Earth, thus far, as being a quest after pagan beliefs. It presumes that Judaism or, more appropriately in this context, Yhwhism has no part in the objective, nor has the Christian Movement. It relies on well-worn interpretations of paganism and argues that the religion of the 'Children of Israel' was forged afresh in the dawn of a new age of enlightenment, rising like an incandescent flame from that which went before. Yet 'pagan' is one of the most misused and misunderstood words in the English language. It is an emotive and subjective term, not one which determines an exact creed. It means unenlightened or profane, but the term is peculiarly applied, by a Church which demands allegiance to a single god, to those cultures which recognize, at least in name, many deities. The proper distinction therefore, must be between polytheism and monotheism and the evidence shows that the Yhwhists were less committed to monotheism than popular notion allows. The term 'heathen', incidentally, is less punishing and refers only to one who is not a member of a widely recognized religion.

In reality, the distinction between the Old Testament religion of the Yhwhists and other faiths is blurred. The evidence of archaeology and history are in stark conflict with what is taught at Sunday School. In the ideology supposedly determined by

Moses, Yhwhism brandished some radically new principles, but in practice it compromised itself with a metamorphosis of more familiar ones. Its final shaping was pressured by other established creeds in western Asia, and from within its own ranks.

In the early days, the mentors were Egypt and Canaan, and as time went on, though Canaanite tradition held its popularity locally, the hand of Assyria was felt over the religious orthodoxy of state and monarchy. Any argument that Israelite religion grew up uncontaminated by her neighbours is a nonsense. There is some irony in that, of the contemporary literature, the Old Testament succeeds in imparting some of the least-veiled accounts of pagan belief and practice. How much reliance can be placed on this document though?

The use of the Testament as a reliably objective source of information has to be guarded, not least because there is very little contemporary Palestinian literature against which to judge its accuracy. The Israelites left a dearth of written material to give a balanced picture of their culture and history. Apart from the fifteenth-century archive of letters, written on the tablets found at 'el Amarna, and the Qum'ran texts, the Old Testament remains sharply isolated in recording events and beliefs from a Palestinian viewpoint between the turn of the second millennium and the end of the second century BC.[1]

Israelite kingdoms such as that of Solomon may have been well organized, but Palestine did not spawn massive political organizations in the mould of Mesopotamia, Egypt and Syria, so there was little to prompt the inscribing of steles and monuments. The record was largely a matter of more personal manuscripts and it was not the fashion to write these in the cuneiform style. The Israelites found themselves in a part of western Asia dominated by Egypt and they adopted the Egyptian vogue of papyrus writing. Unfortunately, whereas in Egypt papyri have been preserved by the perpetually dry desert air, those in Palestine and Syria where it rains in winter have, with few exceptions, long since rotted away.

The Old Testament is far from being a single work of one author.[2] Its material was generated piecemeal over a long period of time. A limited amount, including a few chapters of the Book of Daniel, was written in Aramaic, the rest was predominantly in Hebrew. None of the manuscripts from which the Old Testament was copied was written until after the composition of Daniel in about 170 BC, and though some parts of the original material may have been committed to writing as early as the end of the

first millennium BC, most was penned after the Israelites were
exiled to Babylon in 587 BC. None of the originals exists. We only
possess generations of copies, which have been through many
changes, and translations which will have altered the content of
the original material still further.

Today, we have two 'sources'. The oldest, that from the
second century BC, already with a thousand years separating
it from Moses, is a Greek translation of Hebrew manuscripts.
This version, the Septuagint, so-called because allegedly seventy scribes sat down to the task of translation into Greek
and came up with identical results, was made for the Jewish
Diaspora community in Alexandria. It includes the two books
of Maccabees which originated in Jerusalem and which provide
separate accounts of historical events in the second century. The
other 'source', the definitive Old Testament in Hebrew, is based
possibly on decisions made at the Council of Jamnia in the first
century AD. There is no precise detail of why the Council met
but its agenda is thought to have included the formulation of a
canon – a final choice of which books should and should not
be included in the authorized Testament. The earliest version in
existence based on the alleged Jamnia statement is the so-called
Palestinian text inscribed by Jewish Masorete scholars in the
seventh century AD.

As a religious document, the Old Testament serves two distinct
cultural masters. It constitutes the sacred canonical writings of
Judaism, and it is the 'building block' and preface for the cult
of Christianity. It is also more than a reflection of religious belief
and practice. It has to be read as a social and political commentary, and as a book of law. The writers who have put words into
the mouths of Israelite leaders like Moses imply that they were,
with one 'hat' on, relaying the words of God, and with the other
were establishing the tenets of a social order. They were delivering condemnations of pagan practice in an atmosphere of almost
constant unrest and bickering. They tried to use verbal weapons as
a welding influence, to impress on a motley following of peasants,
who had stemmed from a stock of itinerants and mercenaries, that
they had the backing of supernatural forces which were different
from and more effective than anything else around.

In the cautionary tale of what may be assumed safely from the
texts, those whose utterances make up a significant part of what
now appears in print were prophets and priests, not scribes, and
we do not know how their statements were preserved. We can
only assume that they were committed to memory by students,

and then many years later related to writers. Thus we have to accept that the material in the books of the Old Testament has been linked together artificially and through a word-of-mouth tradition.

The context in which a particular section now finds itself may be different from that in which it was born, and therefore the function may be well and truly disguised. The accuracy may also be deeply suspect. There are great pitfalls in placing any reliance on the accuracy of word-of-mouth communication. Over a thousand-year period it is inevitable that many altering circumstances and events influenced the originals and they were finally written down under different political and religious pressures from those under which they began.

It is almost beyond doubt that the writers were highly selective over what they included and omitted from amongst oral traditions. They had certain messages which they wished to put over and they drew on material which was relevant to their needs. But it is equally clear on reading the texts that in some instances, where total elimination of 'embarrassing' evidence was not possible, they deferred to alien culture with a degree of eclecticism. Thus certain passages deliver what are clearly foreign traditions but painted in such a way as to make them appear reasonable and even generated within the framework of Israelite ideology. Curious 'cameos' intrude such as Moses' deeply suspect snake-totem, the so-called 'brasen serpent' of Numbers 21.8. The tribes must also have brought with them traditions from their nomadic past; they did not, it can be assumed, reach the promised land with a blank 'cultural sheet'. When the popularity of disavowed or alien practice was impossible to conceal, the writers merely ranted against 'abominations' and suggested that they were symptoms of 'backsliding' amongst idolatrous minorities who earned the just rewards of incurring divine wrath.

The first major section of the Old Testament, the five epic books of the Pentateuch from Genesis to Deuteronomy, span the time from Adam to the death of Moses. They sound many echoes of the Heroic Age of Mesopotamia. There is almost nothing by way of historical or archaeological evidence to confirm or deny what they contain, and probably they represent a mixture of some historical truth and a good deal of mythology accounting for cause and effect. Unless one subscribes to biblical fundamentalism Adam was a figment of imagination, and equally such heroes as Noah, Abraham and Isaac are as difficult to substantiate as Dumuzi and

Gilgameš. Did they live and die as mortals, or were they the stuff of legend?

The Pentateuch has seen a heavy editorial hand, as has much of the writing of the early 'prophetic books' – Joshua, Judges, Samuel and Kings – the so-called Deuteronomistic history. The shades of the real world have been coloured with romance, but the distortions have gone further.

Contrary to the Old Testament impressions archaeological evidence suggests that the tribes who arrived in Palestine did so from distinct and separate origins, and this ethnic separation was never forgotten.[3] There was a single consolidation for less than a century under David and Solomon, but from then on the tribes divided permanently into two nations. Judah, centred first on Hebron and later Jerusalem, was in the southern part of Palestine. To the north was Israel whose capital became first Tirzah and then Samaria and whose main religious centres were Bethel and Dan. Only once, briefly, did they feel compelled to settle differences and unite against a common foe in the form of the 'Sea Peoples', the Philistines. Otherwise, right to the end, there was enmity between them. Even their respective downfalls came quite separately. Israel fell to Assyria in 722 BC, a century and a half before the Babylonian armies sacked Jerusalem in 587 BC and ended the sovereignty of Judah.

Though the biblical writings ostensibly represent both nations' culture, they actually survived through Jerusalem. As a result, what we now read in the Old Testament has an inherent bias towards the Judaeans.

To be able to disentangle the truth behind the lines of the Old Testament requires some understanding of the origins of the peoples involved. As with the Mesopotamians, a brief dip into the Israelites' ancestry pays dividends. The tribes began coming together in a time of unrest and ethnic mixing in western Asia when the Third Dynasty of Ur was collapsing. Hurrians were scattered widely down as far as the Egyptian hinterland, and there were probably Hittite colonies established well to the south of their main borders. The so-called Hyksos hordes were causing widespread havoc. Elamites were advancing from the east, Amorites from the west, and Kassites were in southern Mesopotamia. In Babylon the future dynasties were experiencing little more than birth pangs. Waves of multinational vagrants, herdsmen, soldiers of fortune and guerrilla bands surged across the landscape seeking power and pasture. Ineffectual kingdoms rattled swords at each other and national boundaries came and went almost with the regularity of the tide.

Out of this mêlée emerged a group of nomads led allegedly by Abraham, the first identifiable biblical personality. Abraham was followed by Isaac, Jacob, the head of the tribe of Israel, and his twelve sons whose families perhaps constituted the beginnings of the Israelite nation. The name 'Hebrew' offers no racial or ethnic identity. It is a title of inauspicious borrowing from the Akkadian *habiru* – a derogatory term implying an alien, a barbarian of no fixed address. Abram, as he was first called, is less a real name than a term meaning 'high father'. One clue to his possible origin is that several of the sons of Shem, among them Serug, Nahor and Terah who was reputedly Abraham's father, are also place names along the upper Euphrates where the Amorites lived.

According to the place names mentioned in Genesis, Abraham's clansmen wandered extensively. The evidence surrounding entry into Palestine is extremely conjectural but it may have taken place towards the start of the second millennium, perhaps in company with nomadic Hurrian-speaking tribes. They probably had an eye on the unpopulated hill country to find grazing land for their flocks whilst avoiding the heavily fortified Canaanite cities. Sometime during the mid-fifteenth century BC, however, in the reigns of Amenhotep III and IV, Egyptian colonial rule began to lose support from home, and the opportunity was seized to follow the example of the Hittites in Syria and throw out the Egyptian occupation forces.

On this occasion, the rebel elements seem to have included the Habiru who had by this time become, if not a *force majeur*, certainly one to be reckoned with. Several cities of the north fell. Egyptian sources suggest that Gibeon, Mizpeh and Shiloh were overrun; others including Shechem may have acceded voluntarily. According to archaeology some major disaster beset Jericho which, although the texts do not state that Joshua attacked the city, might tie in with biblical accounts. The fall of this fortified city in about 1400 BC may have rounded off the unrest and left the first main group of tribes with a secured power base.

About two hundred years later, a separate group, mainly composed of the tribe of Levi, may have emigrated north from Egypt. Theirs was the most celebrated Exodus though not necessarily the first, because older Habiru stock were almost certainly in Egypt and emigrated from there during the Hyksos dynasty. The later group had, according to Genesis, gone to Egypt driven by famine. They stayed in the Wadi Tumilat, the 'Goshen' of the Bible. If accurate, that fact would in itself preclude the possibility of all the tribes migrating from there. The Wadi Tumilat is far too small to have supported them!

Under Rameses II, a change of policy towards aliens effectively found them doing forced labour on Egyptian public works projects, and it was only after the death of Rameses' successor, Seti II, in about 1194 BC, that the Hebrews managed to extricate themselves. Whether Moses actually led them or was a figure of legend is unknown. His name has Egyptian connotations but no Egyptian archives mention him. The Levites had to be led by someone, nonetheless, and it might just as well be Moses.

The Levite group settled the southern half of Palestine and adopted Hebron as their capital. It was their descendants who gave birth to the kingdom of Judah. The scenario, drawn in the Book of Joshua, of the Hebrews marching into Palestine as one, clasping their new-found covenant with God like a virgin child and laying waste all before them, is an over-simplified picture, however, as is the implicit suggestion that the nomadic horde of Israel waded in a constant sea of blood. The actual events of the push from the Negev desert must have been infinitely more complicated.

During the thirteenth and twelfth centuries BC, the late Bronze Age Canaanite city states were collapsing and, according to pottery remains, were taken over by aliens with a simpler lifestyle.[4] Some of these were 'Sea People', Philistines, but others must have been Hebrews. The immigrants probably lived side by side with the old inhabitants; obviously the arrangement was not without friction and bloodshed since the ultimate aim was to carve out the homeland which, by tradition, was identified to Moses by his god, but it was probably achieved by a protracted campaign of intermittent skirmishing over many years.

Archaeology and carbon dating narrow down the 'window' of time in which Jericho collapsed. If this is set beside the earliest date on which, from Egyptian dynastic records, Moses could have left Egypt, and the length of time spent traversing the Negev desert is added on, it becomes very improbable that Joshua succeeded Moses to lead the tribes into Palestine from the south. The achaeological evidence suggests that a major disturbance to the fortified walls took place earlier, at a time which would place Joshua's celebrated trumpet-blowing march during the take-over of the north. The narrative of events which has come down to us is compromised though, in favour of the Judaean side of the story.

The Israelites, as a whole, found only limited points of agreement with the pagan culture around them, but the northern nation of Israel was always less committed to Yhwhism. They shared older and closer links with the Canaanites who were established farmers and had their spiritual roots deep in the fertility religion. The two basic dogmas were, nevertheless, anathema to each other. The Israelite way of life was pastoral and their faith was undoubtedly moulded from the influences placed on them during their long time of wandering migration.

The principles of Israelite religion, which demanded loyalty to a single deity, may have seemed radical, but they were not entirely original. It comes as a surprise and something of a shock to those of us who have grown up with Sunday School religion, that they did not take on board monotheism – the belief that the supernatural forces were limited to one deity in the heavens.

Significantly, the country of the ancient near east which did subscribe to monotheism, if only briefly, was Egypt.[5] Traditionally polytheistic, Egyptians had worshipped their host of deities headed by Amun, the patron god of Thebes, who was often syncretized with the creator sun-god of Heliopolis, Re. During the time that Israelites lived amicably in Egypt, however, Amenhotep IV substituted a universal and virtually exclusive supreme god, Aten. He was, in fact, persuaded to adopt pure monotheism more for political reasons than mystical: the Theban priesthood of Amun had, for many years, been gaining influence and engaging in an increasingly rancorous conflict with the royalty. The beginnings of discord can be traced back to the reign of Tuthmosis IV. Whilst, however, the priesthood had gained considerable power it never possessed the strength to curb the will of the Pharaohs. Thus for Egypt, the supernatural forces of the heavens became narrowed, for a time, to a single god. No image of this super deity was allowed. Amenhotep's vision of him decreed that he was symbolized by the disc of the sun, its rays stretching down as human hands. Such was Amenhotep's dedication that he even changed his name to Atenakhen, meaning 'raising high the name of Aten'.

There is, of course, fierce argument whether Atenakhen influenced the tribes, but some of them were in Egypt at the time and undoubtedly the concept of Aten preceded that of Yhwh. What the Israelites actually envisaged was something less demanding than pure monotheism. In the climate of their emergent culture, they found it impossible to grasp the concept of a lone and unique power in the heavens. What they were asked to observe was henotheism, the *worship* of a single god, which only many centuries later was to lead to monotheism.

According to the texts, the god of the founding fathers was El, a name which almost certainly was not original but borrowed from the creator god of Canaan.[6] *El* is also used freely in a descriptive sense. In Genesis, *el* is linked with several other names: the writers mention *el elyon*, the 'most high god'; *el sadday*, the 'god of the mountain' from the Akkadian word *sadu* for a 'high place'. At Beer-sheba, it is *el olam*, the 'everlasting god'; and later it becomes *el betel*, thought to be an obscure derivation of the name of the Canaanite storm god. The Mesopotamians had adopted a similar qualifying epithet to address their deities, placing the symbol of Marduk in front of the name of a patron god.

Either the religious leaders wanted to syncretize, to fuse the identities of several gods from a single tribe under one name, or they were asserting that El represented the sum of the creator spirits of all the tribes. We do not know if the nomadic Hebrews had traditions of polytheism, or whether tribal groups each bowed to their own distinct god.

Where the Hebrew becomes particularly intriguing is that in the plural sense it offers two words, both of which have become bluntly translated as 'gods'. *Elohim* appears in some contexts. This is the Hebrew word applied at the beginning of Exodus 20, in the preface and notorious first commandment of the Decalogue, frequently hauled out in support of the argument for one faith, one god: 'I am Yhwh thy god, which have brought thee out of Egypt, out of the house of bondage. Thou shalt have no other gods before me.'

It is improbable that we are seeing the precise words of Moses, but the statement, even in its English translation, is explicit. It recognizes the existence of other gods, merely precluding them from worship. The Hebrew text places a qualification on this denial, however, because *elohim* implies an upper tier, of creator or tribal gods. There are several references in Exodus to a 'company' of gods at the head of which is Yhwh. Exodus 15.11: 'Who is like thee among the gods, Lord, who is like thee, glorious in holiness . . .' Here the word for gods is *elim*, however, and it comes to imply a lower tier in the pantheon, a distinction not unlike that between the seven creator gods and the lesser deities of Mesopotamia.

The writers may have been tacitly acknowledging that their god ruled over a pantheon of lesser gods with their proper place in the heavens, but that any deities of potentially equal rank were to be strictly disavowed. The distinction is far from unique. A similar selectivity existed towards the city gods of Mesopotamia. The god Nabu was the tutelary deity of the Assyrian king, Adad-nirari III, and amongst his royal inscriptions is one which reads: 'Trust thou in Nabu, and trust thou in no other god.' It was an almost universal determination to treat as unreliable other tribal or city gods, and at best to forget them altogether.

Israel, the northern state, was constantly reluctant to part with the name El but, according to tradition, Moses met with a creator god on Mount Sinai or Horeb and was told that his name was Yhwh. The roots of the Hebrew word have no clear translation. Yhwh is an enigmatic 'no-name', though traditionally it is supposed to mean 'I am who I am'. It appears regularly only in the Jerusalem Bible and elsewhere it is replaced by the title *Lord*.

Elsewhere in the Old Testament writings, the Psalms are littered with intriguing references which can only mean acceptance of many gods in the pantheon and which must, incidentally, have placed the translators in a great quandary. The St James' translation includes the term 'saints', one which does not altogether do the original Hebrew justice. 'And the heavens shall praise thy wonders, O Lord; thy faithfulness also in the congregation of the saints' (Psalm 89.5). This verse can also be translated as: '. . . thy faithfulness in the assembly of the holy ones'. It is significant because 'saints' implies mortal beings who are blessed and canonized, whilst 'holy ones' can have a broader meaning.

The translation of the next verse reads: 'For who in the heaven can be compared unto the Lord? Who among the sons of the mighty can be likened unto the Lord?' But 'sons of the mighty' is a euphemism. The Hebrew is *elim*, the lower order of gods. Coupling the two verses in context, 'saints' and 'sons of the mighty' are one and the same. All are gods. Psalm 82 also has a key verse in its opening. According to the St James' version it reads: 'God standeth in the congregation of the mighty; he judgeth among the gods' (Psalm 82.1). If this is translated very precisely though, it should read: 'Gods (*elohim*) stand in the congregation of El; he judgeth among the gods.' The implication here is that the creator god El even presides over a pantheon of other great deities.

There is also a curious and distinctive reference, in Psalm 16.3, to the 'holy ones that are in the earth'. In whatever way the psalmists imagined these lesser gods, it is certain that they did not envisage them with a pedigree that included stints of mortality in the sense either of a Dumuzi or a modern saint. There was no recognition of life after death in Israelite faith at that time, at least none of any account. They imagined a place of the dead, Sheol, that was a nothingness, a total limbo. They did not consider distinctions of soul and body, only a homogenous mortal psyche.

The book of Samuel makes tantalizing reference to similar earthbound spirits when, at Saul's command, the witch of Endor calls up the spirit of Samuel and is terrified to see 'Gods ascending out of the earth' (1 Samuel 28.8ff). This though, is the only admission throughout the books of the Old Testament written during the exile and earlier, that the dead rise again, and it is worth noting that although the 'shade' appears to the witch, he conveys nothing of use to Saul. The incident is portrayed very much as a non-event. It is not until the comparatively 'modern' book of Daniel, and in the experience of the Jewish Maccabean revolt which took place in the second century BC, that the idea of a life beyond the grave was anticipated: 'And many of them that sleep in the dust of the earth shall awake, some to everlasting life, and some to shame and everlasting contempt (Daniel 12.2).[7] There were many victims of the rebellion, and it is likely that life after death, a concept well established in Egypt and for the divine kings of other nations, managed to extend its franchise to the Israelite common man under circumstances of great bereavement.

Out of the revolt emerged a group who became the Pharisees. Life beyond death was an integral part of their understanding. Matthew includes a brief account of Jesus being quizzed by the Sadducees, who rejected the idea, over the hypothetical situation of a woman, married in her earthly life to seven brothers, all of whom suffered a short mortal existence. As one brother went to his grave, the bride was handed on to the next, a convention in practice designed to ensure offspring to a woman. The Sadducees, however, were naturally curious about whom she would be wedded to in Paradise! The Pharisees were not tempted to intrude on the debate (Matthew 22.23ff).

Isaiah includes a scant comment about immortality, but expert opinion agrees that this is also a late piece of writing from the second century BC and therefore rendered in the same climate as the book of Daniel. Isaiah 26, probably refering not to the Babylonians but the Macedonians, complains that: 'Other lords beside thee have had dominion over us . . . They are dead, they

shall not live; they are deceased, they shall not rise . . .' (Isaiah
26.13ff). The point is made clearly enough, yet five verses on
Isaiah envisages a better outcome for Yhwhists: 'Thy dead men
shall live, together with my dead body shall they arise. Awake
and sing, ye that dwell in dust; for thy dew is as the dew of
herbs, and the earth shall cast out the dead' (Isaiah 26.19).

These isolated and comparatively 'modern' passages are, however, the only instances where the books admit to the possibility
of immortality. Thus the saints of the psalmists are, on evidence,
gods born and bred!

As to what the Patriarchs believed about their gods, the
Pentateuch gives away little. It is not until Moses' time, which
marks the beginning of a protracted transition towards the
kingship of Saul, that the religion of the Israelites is more
clearly defined. They were, it is stated, being asked to make
radical departures from the religious traditions of the ages in
the near east. They were expected to place their faith in an
unknown god who judged them from the uneasy space of an
empty seat. Genesis offers no more description of El than we
have about his namesake at Ugarit. Both seem to have been
perceived in human form because they saw, heard, walked and
touched, yet they were also invisible.

Israelites were denied familiar elements of creed which for
thousands of years had given security and comfort. Their kings
were never to enjoy the divine status of Mesopotamian rulers
and neither nation enjoyed the advantages of a stable dynastic
line. Aside from occasional longer periods of rule, such as the
forty-year kingship of Jereboam II, the northern state of Israel
in particular suffered a succession of brief and ineffectual reigns.

One of the most disturbing prohibitions lay in the imposition
of the second law of the Decalogue which must have been a
bitter blow: 'Thou shalt not make unto thee any graven image,
or any likeness of anything that is in the heaven above, or that
is in the earth beneath, or that is in the water under the earth.
Thou shalt not bow down thyself to them, nor serve them: for
I the Lord thy God am a jealous god . . .' (Exodus 20.4ff). The
argument of the religious leaders must in part have been that a
god with no name and no form cannot be compromised.

Other nations enjoyed the comfort of more tangible local
patron gods and household guardians. Rarely, if at all, did they
have to invoke directly the grand creatures of the upper world.
Yet this was demanded of the Israelites and, from the beginning,
they found the imposition extremely difficult. The Pentateuch lets

slip many moments of lapse. It also admits that even the Patriarchs practised idolatry. In Genesis, Laban's daughter, Rachel, steals 'images that were her father's' (Genesis 31.19). Asking these wanderers, of meagre intellect, to place themselves in the hands of a single, invisible, creator god was a serious gamble.

It failed disastrously in Egypt and, even through the 'careful' lines of the Old Testament, it is obvious that it did not truly succeed amongst the Israelites for a long time. The texts lack a single shred of evidence that the followers of Moses and their descendants accepted anything less than the existence of other gods. It also reveals that, with few exceptions, and despite the unflagging vitriol of the priests and prophets, the Judaean and particularly the Israel kingship was marked by active worship of the old gods side by side with Yhwh. King and commoner alike knelt before 'pagan' images. Yhwhism was only generally accepted by admitting many of the elements of pagan dogma and ritual.

The writers go to considerable and sometimes bizarre lengths to disguise the attraction of pagan symbolism. There is an obscure moment in Exodus when Moses complains that his voice is carrying little weight because God remains invisible: 'And the Lord said unto him, What is that in thine hand? And he said, A rod. And he said, Cast it on the ground. And he cast it on the ground, and it became a serpent; and Moses fled before it' (Exodus 4.2 ff).

Later, in the book of Numbers, Moses is once more faced with revolt against the unseen god who has dragged the Hebrews from the comparative safety of enslavement into the 'hell hole' of Sinai: 'And the Lord said unto Moses, Make thee a fiery serpent, and set it upon a pole: and it shall come to pass, that every one that is bitten, when he looketh upon it, shall live. And Moses made a serpent of brass . . .' (Numbers 21.8 ff). At face value the object was a healing symbol, but Moses did various wonders with his magic rod and arguably the Hebrews saw it less as a snake venom antidote than as a symbol of a tribal deity. The Levites may actually have taken on a snake god, called Nahash, during their early wanderings. It was not until the reign of Hezekiah, nearly two hundred years after Solomon, that any attempt seems to have been made to remove the serpent totem: 'He removed the high places, and brake the images, and cut down the groves and brake in pieces the brasen serpent that Moses had made: for unto those days the children of Israel did burn incense to it . . .' (2 Kings 18.4).

There is also evidence of a bull deity. According to Exodus it first appeared in Sinai while Moses was absent making his Covenant at which time, in response to public demand, Aaron cast a gold calf (Exodus 32.4). The bull emerged again at the time of the split between the two nations. The explanation of the schism, in 1 Kings 11, is that all but Judah were actively worshipping pagan gods. With the exception of Judah and Benjamin ten tribes were handed over to Jeroboam, an exiled man-servant of Solomon, in an act of divine justice, and thus the northern kingdom of Israel came into being (1 Kings 11.26 ff).

According to 1 Kings 12: '. . . the king took counsel, and made two calves of gold, and said unto them, It is too much for you to go up to Jerusalem: behold thy gods O Israel, which brought thee up out of the land of Egypt. And he set the one in Bethel and the other he put in Dan' (1 Kings 12.28 ff). The notion that Jeroboam was copying an earlier act of apostasy in Sinai may, however, be a piece of distorted Judaean narrative.

There is no written evidence to hint at a bull cult in the north before 922 BC but the bull seems more likely to have been copied from popular Canaanite cult than from a distant memory of Egypt. What was Jeroboam's intention? Was he, as the narrative suggests, anxious to provide some alternative focus of Yhwhist worship for people who were prevented access to the temple in Jerusalem? It seems highly unlikely that any Yhwhist would consciously substitute an object such as the golden bull for the Ark of the Covenant. It is important to remember that the *presence* of Yhwh was not signified by the Ark but by the empty space of the Mercy Seat above it. To symbolize the Israelite god with an idol was in total contradiction of Yhwhist principles. The more probable explanation is that Jeroboam was offering the ten tribes, confirmed by the writers to be strongly swayed towards the foreign Canaanite religion, that which they wanted – a focal point of Baal worship.

There is very little to suggest that Jeroboam was a Yhwhist. He had spent much time in Solomon's court, then fled to Egypt and doubtless been influenced by traditions there. According to 1 Kings his main worry was the chance of his kingdom returning to Yhwhism (1 Kings 12.31 ff). The text also confirms that he sacrificed regularly to the bull idols and developed hill shrines.

In general, the 'backstreet' religion at local level was that of Canaan. It beckoned the willing hearts of the Israelites, and they greeted it with eagerness. The texts are so liberally peppered with references to pagan practice that the conclusion is inescapable. The die-hard prophets seem to have stood isolated in their objections.

Canaanite religion was given a boost because the Temple in Jerusalem was looked to increasingly as a central point of faith. The move reached an extreme of centralization in 621 BC after which all other shrines were banned, but before that time rank-and-file Israelites had few local places built for orthodox worship. So they looked towards the old Canaanite sanctuaries – not the Canaanite temples because almost all of these had been destroyed. They were drawn, irresistibly, to climb the hills and to set up shrines to Yhwh beside those of the pagan gods. It was this which inflamed the ire of the prophets and goaded them, not without justification, to cry 'idolatry'! These places were the core of their invective. 'For they also built them high places, and images, and groves, on every high hill, and under every green tree' (1 Kings 14.23).

Yet what exactly were the 'high places, and images, and groves'?[8] 'Image' translates *massebah*, the stone pillar; 'groves' replaces the Hebrew word *asherim*, derived from the Canaanite *ašerah* and meaning the carved and ancient wooden images which in other religions symbolized the Tree of Life and the Earth Mother. The 'high place' had long been a part of Israelite tradition. In its original form, it was the funerary cairn. Genesis tells that: '. . . Rachel died, and was buried in the way to Ephrath, which is Bethlehem. And Jacob set a pillar upon her grave . . .' (Genesis 35.19 ff). By the time the Judaean kings were being interred, however, the tomb had been separated from its commemorative pillar, and the latter became associated with high ground known as the *bamah*.

There is a series of cairns on a ridge at Malhah, near Jerusalem which, although built on the old tradition of a raised mound of stones, almost certainly never contained human remains and were erected purely as ancestral shrines. At what stage the pillar became a commemorative object on its own, in Israelite tradition, is uncertain. Jacob allegedly set up such a monument, after he dreamed of ascending a ladder to heaven, but the episode was perhaps a later embellishment. 'And he was afraid, and said, How dreadful is this place! This is none other but the house of God, and this is the gate of heaven. And Jacob rose up early in the morning, and took the stone that he had put for his pillow, and set it up for a pillar, and poured oil upon the top of it' (Genesis 28.17 ff). This was the old Hebrew version of the *massebah*. Once the Israelites began to use the *bamah* as a cultic place, however, the *massebah* shed its commemorative role. On the argument that it copied a Canaanite model, it became a stone obelisk or totem linked with rites of fertility. If the level of invective coming from the writers is any measure, the change of use for unorthodox purposes became widespread and the charity of the priesthood took a particular nosedive once the *bamah* also became openly associated with the *ašerah*.

The *ašerah*, the image of the goddess, was a cause of persistent agonizing for the early leaders of the Israelites.[9] It represented the 'unspeakable abomination'. Occasional light is shed on the popularity of this banned spirit. Elijah challenged the idolatrous Ahab to pit 450 prophets of Baal, and 400 of the *ašerah*, against Yhwh. The prophets of Baal met a notable and untimely end in the river Kishon, but the prophets of the *ašerah* are not mentioned which can only imply that they went unharmed (I Kings 18.40 ff).

Part of the problem for the Israelite priests lay in that not only *massebahs* and high places were fundamental to popular religion, but so also were sacred trees. They were known as *terebinths*, though whether they were a separate concept which came down through the ancient traditions of the nomads, or whether filched from Canaanite culture and introduced to the texts retrospectively, is a mystery. Like so much which we have misinterpreted as being borrowed and adapted to Yhwhism, however, it seems more likely that the *terebinth* was an object of tribal significance going back to very ancient times.

An oak of some importance, growing in Shechem, is referred to in Genesis: 'And they gave unto Jacob all the strange gods which were in their hand, and all their earrings which were in their ears; and Jacob hid them under the oak which was by Shechem' (Genesis 35.4). Another significant oak grew at Bethel where Rebecca's nurse, Deborah, was buried. At Beer-sheba, Abraham planted a *terebinth* where he called on the everlasting god.

By the time of the later prophets, however, trees were taking the full force of invective. Ezekiel had a particular aversion to them. 'Then shall ye know that I am the Lord, when their slain men shall be among their idols round about their altars upon every high hill, in all the tops of the mountains, and under every green tree, and under every thick oak . . .' (Ezekiel 6.13).

There is a curious prophecy in Ezekiel 20 which refers to the burning of trees, a possible cryptic implication of which will be uncovered later: 'And say to the forest of the south, Hear the

word of the Lord. Thus saith the Lord God; Behold I will kindle
a fire in thee, and it shall devour every green tree in thee, and
every dry tree: the flaming flame shall not be quenched, and all
the faces from the south to the north shall be burned therein'
(Ezekiel 20.47).

At some time, arguably in the reign of Ahaz, an *ašerah* of a
different mould entered the Temple. State religion was affected
by pagan influence no less thoroughly than it was at grass-roots
level, but in quite distinct ways. From the establishment of David's
kingship to the Babylonian exile, the Israelites only partially and
intermittently commanded their own culture. State religion was
deeply influenced by strategic and political events outside the
borders of the two kingdoms.

In 2 Kings it is implied that the majority of heirs to the
Davidic throne were 'backsliders' who fell prey to alien gods,
but this is grossly misleading. Unless they chose active revolt
against Assyria, they were as bound to set up Assyrian gods
beside Yhwh in the Temple as they were to meet Assyria's tax
demands.

The northern nation, Israel, lost sovereignty in 722 BC and
became the Assyrian province of Samaria, having made an unholy
alliance with Syria with whom she had jointly threatened Ahaz's
rule in Jerusalem. Ahaz turned for help to Tiglathpileser III who
obligingly marched the Assyrian army into Israel but, as forfeit,
reduced Jerusalem to little more than the capital of a vassal state.

Assyrian influence in the south is first mentioned in 2 Kings:
'And king Ahaz went to Damascus to meet Tiglathpileser, king
of Assyria, and saw an altar that was at Damascus; and king
Ahaz sent to Urijah the priest the fashion of the altar, and the
pattern of it, according to all the workmanship thereof' (2 Kings
16.10). Freeing this piece of narrative from Judaean propoganda,
Ahaz had been summoned to Damascus and Tiglathpileser had
presented him with settlement conditions, one of which was to
install the trappings of Assyrian religion in the Temple.

The Temple was steeped in pagan tradition from the outset.
Solomon did not design the building, nor did he call on local
architects. He approached his ally, Hiram, ruler of the Phoenician
city of Tyre which was one of the most notable cult centres for
the worship of the goddess Astarte, the Phoenician counterpart
of Ištar. Hiram provided his own architects and builders, none of
which activity could have taken place had Solomon been opposed
by a consensus of orthodox opinion. Predictably, the Phoenicians
wove many features of their culture into the design.

Today, we have little idea of what the finished building looked
like although we have measurements and details of ornamentation. The famous cedar wood was worked with motifs of cherubim
facing inward to palm trees interlaced with lotus blossoms and
pomegranates. The brasswork seems to have followed the tradition of furnishings in other pagan temples excavated along the
Mediterranean coast. The craftsmen also erected the two great
door pillars – cedar trunks bound massively with brass and similar
to the gateposts of Assyrian and Hittite cities.

Solomon named the pillars Jachin and Boaz. They too
were ornamented with pomegranates and lotus blossoms, motifs
strongly reminiscent of alien cults. The sense gained is one of
syncretization, brought into the very fabric of the holiest place
of Israelite worship, between two conflicting faiths over which
Solomon expressed considerable ambiguity.

Evidence suggests that Assyria was destined to bring pressure
on Judah to set up the trappings of state religion alongside those
of Yhwh and, beyond very much doubt, theirs was the model for
the *ašerah* which, in the course of time, entered the Temple.
Jeremiah 10 describes it in detail: 'For the customs of the people
are vain: for one cutteth a tree out of the forest, the work of the
hands of the workman, with the axe. They deck it with silver
and with gold; they fasten it with nails and with hammers, that
it move not. They are upright as the palm tree, but speak not: they
must needs be borne because they cannot go . . .' (Jeremiah 10.3
ff). There is suggestion here that the design was of the stylized
and ornamented Assyrian model, and that it was transported as
a standard. The texts do not overtly concede the presence of the
ašerah in the Temple until the reign of Manasseh. 'And he set a
graven image of the grove that he had made in the house, of
which the Lord said to David, and to Solomon his son, In this
house, and in Jerusalem, which I have chosen out of all the
tribes of Israel, will I put my name for ever' (2 Kings 21.7).

The biblical account brands Manasseh as a wicked and idolatrous man who elected to reverse the good orthodoxy of his
predecessor. Contemporary records from elsewhere in western
Asia reveal a more objective picture. After the death of Sargon,
Sennacherib was faced with various anti-Assyrian risings which
temporarily distracted him from the goings-on in Jerusalem.
Hezekiah siezed this temporary respite to throw off the suzerainty
of Assyria, create a tentative alliance with Egypt, and abandon
Assyrian state religion. Sennacherib extracted his toll four years

later. Having put his Mesopotamian house in order, his legions marched on Palestine. They wiped out the Egyptian expeditionary force, and placed Jerusalem under siege. Hezekiah was massively defeated and on his death was succeeded by his son Manasseh, known to be a 'safe' Assyrian loyalist. He restored Assyrian religion and took Judah into a fifty-year spell of prosperity.

After Manasseh's death, Josiah returned to Yhwhism but again biblical and contemporary accounts differ in their inferences. According to 2 Kings: '. . . the king commanded Hilkiah the high priest, and the priests of the second order and the keepers of the door, to bring forth out of the temple of the Lord, all the vessels that were made for Baal, and for the grove, and for all the hosts of heaven; and he burned them without Jerusalem . . .' (2 Kings 23.4). Assyrian records account that at this time Aššurbanipal was approaching the end of his last fraught years of reign in Nineveh. In about 620 BC Josiah took advantage of another spell of weak empire, and not only threw out the Assyrian cult but also attempted to restore Samaria to Israelite sovereignty. He is known to have destroyed the famous shrine at Bethel which, with Dan, was one of the key rallying points of cult in the north.

Bethel had long been a thorn in the flesh of the prophets. Amos, commenting in the previous century, had railed: 'Come to Bethel and transgress; at Gilgal multiply transgression; and bring your sacrifices every morning, and your tithes after three years' (Amos 4.4). The future, however, was doomed. The days of Assyria were numbered and a new force was poised to wreak havoc on Jerusalem: Nebuchadnezzar of Babylon.

It is difficult to imagine that the destruction of the *ašerahs* and the other trappings of pagan practice was seen as anything less than an evil omen of disaster. A small insight into the love for the fertility goddess, held by ordinary folk, emerges in 2 Kings. There is an admission that beside the Temple were houses where women spent their time weaving hangings for the decoration of the *ašerah*, following an old Assyrian vogue of decorating the Sacred Tree with strips of decorated cloth (2 Kings 23.7).

Jeremiah, with derogatory sentiment, uses the old Mesopotamian title of the goddess: 'The children gather wood, and the fathers kindle the fire, and the women knead their dough, to make cakes to the queen of heaven . . .' (Jeremiah 7.18). If the goddess of fertility was this well established in Israelite faith, and following a Canaanite or Assyrian model, there had to be also a Sacred Marriage, a situation which, assuming that it existed, must have presented some dilemma for the writers.

Solomon's ambivalent attitude to orthodoxy and his leaning towards cultic prostitutes is implied in 1 Kings: 'But king Solomon loved many strange women, together with the daughter of Pharaoh, women of the Moabites, Ammonites, Edomites, Zidonians, and Hittites (1 Kings 11.1). Some have argued that the women were the benefits from various trade deals, but the implication is that Solomon practised the Sacred Marriage with priestesses of a number of different cults, all of which were well represented in Jerusalem. His general inclinations towards idolatrous practices are observed again in 2 Kings: 'And the high places that were before Jerusalem, which were on the right hand of the mount of corruption, which Solomon the king of Israel had builded for Ashtoreth the abomination of the Zidonians, and for Chemosh the abomination of the Moabites, and for Milcom the abomination of the children of Ammon, did the king defile' (2 Kings 23.13). The 'mount of corruption' is, incidentally, the Mount of Olives on which had been built pagan shrines, and Ashtoreth must be seen as a Sidonian manifestation of the goddess known further north as *Ašerah*.

Hints of Sacred Marriage ritual emerge all through the prophetic texts in a scattering of veiled scenes.[10] The strongest comes in the Book of Hosea, whose marriage to Gomer the daughter of Diblaim was clearly not made in heaven. Gomer seems to have been a cultic prostitute who bore Hosea three children, and the opening chapters are an unremitting condemnation of Israel because it supported Gomer's conduct. 'For their mother hath played the harlot: she that conceived them hath done shamefully: for she said, I will go after my lovers, that give me my bread and my water, my wool and my flax, mine oil and my drink' (Hosea 2.5).

Ezekiel is also loud and long in his condemnations. He talks of the Holy City, unfaithful to her husband Yhwh, with certain chagrin: 'But thou didst trust in thine own beauty, and playedst the harlot because of thy renown, and pouredst out thy fornications on every one that passed by ... And of thy garments thou didst take and deckedst thy high places with divers colours, and playedst the harlot thereupon ... Thou hast built thy high place at every head of the way, and hast made thy beauty to be abhorred, and hast opened thy feet to every one that passed by, and multiplied thy whoredoms' (Ezekiel 16.15ff). What Ezekiel describes, fairly graphically, is a Sacred Marriage reduced to a free-for-all trade amongst the sacred prostitutes of the city. There emerges a growing ambivalence, which is part of the fascination of reading between the lines of the Testaments. Jerusalem, the Holy City, was simultaneously taking on a symbolic role which was acceptable to the orthodox leaders, that of 'the Bride'.

The most tantalizing observation of the Sacred Marriage rests in a single, slim masterpiece that fits, ever uneasily, among the books of the Old Testament, the Canticus canticarum or Song of Solomon. In its present form, the Song is recited in the synagogue on the eighth day of the Feast of Unleavened Bread. The sense though, is confused, the ordering of the verses wrong. We are looking at a collection of poems, their elements jumbled by time and pieced together haphazardly by the editor. At face value he has rendered an exquisite, lyrical evocation of love, yet it is far from being the innocent story of human passion that some orthodox readers insist upon. Even in the opening lines there is imagery which carries distant echoes from another time.

The initiative in this haunting duet lies with the bride, unthinkable in Semitic society were this an ordinary woman or even a royal princess with her king. The Song is of the fertility goddess, the Earth Mother. It tells of the coming of spring when at first her consort is sleeping: 'I charge you, O ye daughters of Jerusalem, by the roes, and by the hinds of the field, that ye stir not up, nor awake my love, till he please' (Song of Solomon 3.5).

When the god wakes he goes to greet his goddess: 'The voice of my beloved! behold, he cometh leaping upon the mountains, skipping upon the hills.' (Song of Solomon 2.8). Finally, he reaches her green bower, as he has for millennia past throughout the ancient world: 'Behold thou art fair my beloved, yea pleasant: also our bed is green. The beams of our house are cedar, and our rafters of fir' (Song of Solomon 1.16ff).

The Song continues: 'My beloved is like a roe or a young hart: behold, he standeth behind our wall, he looketh forth at the windows, shewing himself through the lattice. My beloved spake, and said unto me, Rise up, my love, my fair one, and come away. For, lo, the winter is past, the rain is over and gone' (Song of Solomon 2.9ff). In this stanza may also lie another tiny piece of the jigsaw. It may provide the words to match the imagery of such small fragments of fretted ivory as that which Mallowan found among the ruins of the Burned Palace of Ešarhaddon, at Kalakh. The deer on the Assyrian carving stands before a latticed tracery of branches.

In the third part of the Song, the bride wanders the city streets at night searching for her lover, in a passage that is strongly reminiscent of Hannahannas sending out a bee in search of Telepinu, the Hittite god. It is a particularly telling passage since it reveals the presence of the priestess as the bride leading the king to the gipar-house of the goddess: 'It was but a little that I passed from them, but I found him whom my soul loveth: I held him, and would not let him go, until I had brought him into my mother's house, and into the chamber of her that conceived me' (Song of Solomon 3.4).

The Song of Solomon reveals a yearning for the union of goddess and sacred king, the Sacred Marriage, which had sustained life amongst the peoples of Mesopotamia and other regions surrounding the Israelites. Ironically, the old Yhwhist war-horse, Ezekiel, lets slip another sharp 'cameo' insight: 'Then he brought me to the door of the gate of the Lord's house, which was towards the north; and behold, there sat women weeping for Tammuz' (the Hebrew rendering of Dumuzi) (Ezekiel 8.14).

Even the very trappings of pure Yhwhism were not without pagan mementoes. The Ark of the Covenant has much in its description that is familiar. The famous reference comes from Exodus 25: 'And thou shalt make a mercy seat of pure gold: two cubits and a half shall be the length thereof, and a cubit and a half the breadth thereof. And thou shalt make two cherubim of gold, of beaten work shalt thou make them, in the two ends of the mercy seat . . . And the cherubim shall stretch forth their wings on high, covering the Mercy Seat with their wings, and their faces shall look one to another . . . And thou shalt put the mercy seat above upon the ark; and in the ark shalt thou put the testimony that I shall give thee. And there I will meet with thee . . .'

Time has not dulled these eloquent lines, the details they relate seem to suggest North Syrian, Assyrian or Hittite design. Furthermore the name *cherubim* may not have been in general circulation amongst Hebrews in Egypt, since it is probably of Akkadian origin. In Akkadian and Babylonian texts, the winged human figures which face the Tree of Life and extend their protecting wings over it are usually named as *šedu* or *lamassu* according to gender. But they are called by another name, *kuribu*. It is possible that the Sinai Israelites had a box containing the Covenant but that the Ark described was fashioned in the north, its details introduced retrospectively by the writers of Exodus and Numbers. In 1 Samuel 4 the Ark was in Shiloh first, and when not being held by Philistines it was stationed at other northern cities before going south to Jerusalem with David.

Ezekiel's apocalyptic visions further reinforce imagery that bears uncanny resemblance to that of the beasts, the *aladlammu* and *apsasu*, depicted on Hittite and Assyrian sculpture: 'And every one had four faces, and every one had four wings. And their feet were straight feet; and the sole of their feet was like the sole of a calf's foot; and they sparkled like the colour of burnished brass. And they had the hands of a man under their wings on their four sides . . .' (Ezekiel 1.6 ff). Ezekiel goes on, in his vision of Jerusalem's new Temple: 'And it was made with cherubim and palm trees, so that a palm tree was between a cherub and a cherub; and every cherub had two faces; so that the face of a man was towards the palm tree on the one side, and the face of a young lion was towards the palm tree on the other side . . .'

It is arguable that eclecticism won the day to include almost all aspects of popular pagan belief and practice.[11] Cherubim found their way into the synagogues of the Christian era. So too did the Tree of Life in the form of the menorah. At Tell-Hum, the first century AD ruin of Capernaum, the lintel above the synagogue doorway bears a frieze of six winged figures carrying garlands, a rosette in the centre of each. The images have been hacked away, and now only a faint trace of wings bear witness that something once hovered over the ancient portal. A similar fate overtook figures on two other first-century synagogues, at Kafr Bir'm, and Er-Ramah. We do not know the exact appearance of these figures, or why they were removed, but by the third century AD the prohibition of cherubim depicted in their old Mesopotamian guise became incorporated in Jewish law and future artists were obliged to disguise the old 'hybrid beasts'.[12]

The later cherubim of frescoes have thus undergone obligatory changes to both personality and sex. They appear as full-faced figures of women from which all trace of the beast have been eliminated except for their gauzy wings. At the ruins of Beth Alpha, north of the Gilboa Mountains, a fine mosaic floor features a large zodiac bordered by four cherubim signifying the seasons, and these are clearly under Coptic influence.[13] Did they survive because they were 'cleansed' of fertility connotations?

The menorah provides some intriguing speculation. The Mercy Seat and the Ark of the Covenant perished with the old Temple, never to be restored to Judaism. The new Ark was more of a rabbinical cupboard. Only the design of the menorah was sustained. Exodus describes the original: 'And thou shalt make

a candlestick of pure gold; of beaten work shall the candlestick
be made: His shaft, and his branches, his bowls, his knops, and
his flowers, shall be of the same. And six branches shall come
out of the sides of it; three branches of the candlestick out of
the one side, and three branches of the candlestick out of the
other side' (Exodus 25.31 ff). In reality, the original design of
the menorah was less that of a candlestick than a lampholder,
but this description almost exactly matches pictures of some of
the Sacred Tree standards engraved on cylinder seals at Nuzi.

In 1921, the Jewish Exploration Society of Jerusalem excavated the ruins of a first-century synagogue at Hammath by
Tiberias.[14] They unearthed a massive block of limestone. On
its upper surface are seven grooves, designed to hold the clay
lamps of the menorah, and the branch tips are engraved to cor-
respond with the ends of the grooves. The artist seems to have
begged a certain interpretation to his work. On the face side he
has worked pomegranates and flowers and although, ostensibly,
he has followed the instructions of the ancient text, his menorah
begins to take on the appearance of a tree.

The most dramatic evidence though, was found at Al-Buqai,
close to the Lebanese border.[15] Under a layer of plaster in the
modern synagogue was found an aged stone in the centre of
which there persists the clear outline of a menorah with its
ritual objects. Here, though, there is no mistake about the real
meaning of the carving. It *is* a tree.

Other isolated hints emerge in support of the suspicion that
the menorah is no less than a disguised Sacred Tree. The monastery of Dormition, in Jerusalem, possesses a collection of ancient
reliefs.[16] On one, a menorah is flanked by two gabled structures,
and on either side of these are two large birds. These creatures
may be decorative but their posture, confronting the menorah,
is that of the winged beasts of old ministering to the Tree, and
it is equally possible that they are cherubim forced into a more
acceptable guise.

The Tree, the central tenacious symbol of the journey, was too
strong a force to eliminate, so writers allegorized it, beginning
in Genesis. The parallels between the scenario of the Garden of
Eden, and Gilgameš's quest for eternal life through the powers of
a magic plant, are unmistakable. Although the Tree of Knowledge
received the most overt attention from the Genesis writer, it was
the Tree of Life which ultimately centred at the climax of the
story: 'And the Lord God said, Behold, the man is become as
one of us, to know good and evil: and now, lest he put forth

his hand, and take also of the tree of life, and eat, and live for ever: Therefore the Lord God sent him forth from the garden of Eden, to till the ground from whence he was taken' (Genesis 3.22).

Like Gilgameš, Adam was thwarted in his desire for the elixir of life, its secret locked in the tissues of a magic plant and commanded only by the ever-youthful serpent. There are scattered references in the texts which suggest that the rod or sceptre represented branches of the Tree, as an emblem of life-giving power. The book of Numbers recounts that Moses was instructed to have the tribal leaders take twelve rods, one for each tribe, and to lay them before the Ark: '... Moses went into the tabernacle of witness; and, behold, the rod of Aaron for the house of Levi was budded, and brought forth buds, and bloomed blossoms, and yielded almonds' (Numbers 17.8).

Ezekiel alludes to rods in similar vein: 'Thy mother is like a vine in thy blood, planted by the waters; she was fruitful and full of branches by reason of many waters. And she had strong rods for the sceptres of them that bare rule ...' (Ezekiel 19.10ff). Arguably, his oblique reference to the mother goddess is confirmed by the comment: '... what is thy mother? A lioness: she lay down among lions, she nourished her whelps among young lions.' Both Ištar and Ninhursaĝa were strongly associated with lions, and Ninhursaĝa is described, more than once, as 'the great lion'.

The texts constantly attempt to water down the popularity of paganism amongst the Israelites and to avoid laying bare that which was obvious compromise. They provide an idealized picture of a situation in which, partly under pressure from outside, partly as a result of popularity amongst their own people, paganism played a very considerable part. They cast much of the blame on practices north of the Judaean border, and they also misrepresent the root causes for ebb and flow of Yhwhism at state level.

Stand back from the associations and conventions of Sunday School, church lessons, and cinema epics. The writings of the Old Testament become a beguiling insight, not only into the practical reality of a belief that was trumpeted as the great bastion against paganism, but into the mind and matter of a nation who, in practice, held ambiguous views about their gods. It is important to distinguish Judaism, the social, political, legal and religious way of a race of people, from Yhwhism, the observance of a faith. It is also important to appreciate that the Israelite story covers a long and turbulent period, and that its writers were incarcerated by an alien and hated regime and were writing anachronistically.

The Israelites had suffered the shock of realizing that the world, in terms of Jewish culture and destiny, did not end at their national borders. Yet even when it became clear that the twelve tribes were caught up, inextricably, in the tide of world politics they still clung naïvely to the belief that Yhwh was not merely the god of the Israelites but of the entire world. Any fate which befell them was no more than divine retribution. The dogged persistence of Israel in taking this view is summed up in the Prologue to the apocryphal Book of Jubilees, arguably written in the first or second century BC: 'And they will make hill shrines and sacred poles and carved images, and each one will worship his own carved image and go astray; and they will sacrifice their children to demons and to all the idols they have made in the error of their hearts . . . and I will hide my face from them and hand them over to the Gentiles to be taken captive and to be preyed upon and to be devoured; and I will drive them out of the land and scatter them among the Gentiles.'

Passionate Yhwhists like Ezekiel and Jeremiah must have taken it as a bitter blow that the great mass of the people would not accept the pure religion of Moses without attaching and infusing the old traditions. A considerable portion of blame attaches to the religious hierarchy itself. The reforms of Josiah were extremely unpopular. He restricted the use of hill shrines, and banned the local priests of the cultic high places, the priests of the 'second order', from making sacrifice. This was a catastrophic infringement on the traditions of worship and may well have been perceived to be forcibly removing the protection of the old gods from Israel. Ironically, the actual political reasons for the changing fortunes of Judah and Israel almost certainly eluded the man in the street.

The Achilles' Heel of Yhwhism though, may well have been the absence of two figureheads, the Mother Goddess and the Sacred King. They had steered the destinies of some of the most successful nations of the earth, in an era when limits of education and understanding demanded super-heroes. The prophets of the Old Testament tried hard to resolve the omission, in part, in their promise of a messiah who would arise out of the 'Stem of Jesse'.

10

The Empires of the West

More paper, ink and earnest Christian thought has gone into dissection of the Bible, in particular the words of the New Testament, than into any other single piece of literature. In the main, though, there has been a dogged refusal to allow common purpose between Christianity and the old cults which preceded and surrounded it.

One of the most well-publicized exceptions of recent times came in a thesis which was destined to stand briefly in the limelight of fame. In 1970 John Allegro's *The Sacred Mushroom and the Cross* was received with critical acclaim, described variously in the press as: 'something of a religious H-bomb', 'a dazzling foray into the obscure hinterlands of comparative philology' and, more economically, as: 'a remarkable feat of scholarship'.[1] The object of this ubiquitous applause was indeed a startling proposal – that Jesus Christ was little more than a figment of the Testament writers' imaginations, that the Apostles spread a message accountably different from that advertised, and that Christianity and Judaism were, in reality, manifestations of an ancient fertility cult whose focal point of worship was a mushroom with hallucinogenic powers. Allegro based his argument on philology. He selected key words from the Testaments and traced them back to Sumerian elements which, he asserted, gave them sexual or fertility connotations. Thus he alleged that Yhwh translates as spermatozoa, Sabaoth a penis, and so on.

On the face of it, Allegro offered impeccable qualifications including a first class honours degree in Semitic Studies. Yet within a short space of time, his 'dazzling foray' was dismissed by his academic peers as: 'an essay in fantasy'. They criticized his arbitrary use of a specialized knowledge of comparative philology – rightly described by Dennis Potter, writing for *The Times*, as an 'obscure hinterland'. Specific meanings of Sumerian word elements are often highly ambiguous and Allegro stood accused of cutting his cloth in a manner which the 'reader in the street' had no way of evaluating. He also stood full square to the path of a daunting avalanche of clerical analysis. Yet some of what Allegro argued may not be far from the truth, and had he not blinkered himself with the obsession of turning his case on points of philology, he might have unearthed more convincing support.

So wherein lies the truth? What really became of the fertility goddess? Did she and her eternal lover perish in the onslaught of the new order, consigned, as many would claim, to the fires of heresy, or did the immortal partnership survive the dawn of Christianity? Equally important, did they find a door into the new religious phenomenon? The search has to spread beyond Allegro's limited horizon. One strand of evaluation is not enough. The answers lie more in the nature of the stage and its historical context, and with the social and cultural moods of the day.

Although within a very short time it was to become an essentially European experience, Christianity began as a Palestinian vogue. Jesus Christ was born into a Jewish community with an ancient and somewhat outmoded culture which, though battered, was still firmly entrenched in the hearts of its conservative citizens. So Jewish tradition must feature heavily in the search for solutions. But, by the time the Christian era was opening, the scenario of cause and effect had become deeply convoluted. That astonishing chapter in the progress of mankind also coincided, by chance, with a political shift of momentous importance. Not only were the world and its needs evolving more rapidly then ever before, but they were going through a cataclysmic re-ordering.

For ten thousand years, the heartspring of civilization had rested in the near east, fashioned by the fabulous civilizations of Mesopotamia, Anatolia and Egypt; but their time was drawing to a close. The world with which Jesus was familiar would soon be shattered with the coming of a fresh order, vigorous and dynamic. There had arisen new stars, new seats of power and intellect. They were generating new laws, new language and art, new roads of communication and trade. Their centre of orbit lay not in Asia but Europe. They were stars of the occident. First Greece, then Rome.

Hence, ingredients from at least three separate but deeply influential sources – Judaic roots, Greek and Roman culture, and the great driving forces of ancient near eastern tradition – all interact in the writing of a remarkable, but infinitely subtle, plot.

At the alleged time of Jesus' birth, Judaism had seen a long period of active decline, probably since the period of exile, and throughout that traumatic era the ground into which the seeds of Christianity would be sown was being prepared.[2] It is worth taking a brief journey down those years.

In 539 BC Babylon fell to Cyrus the Persian who brought with him an unfamiliar cult of Ahura Mazda, the god of truth and light, and his prophet Zoroaster. Cyrus had achieved a reputation for tolerance and the city gates were opened to him voluntarily by the Marduk priesthood. Not only did he endorse the Babylonian cult, he also demonstrated remarkable open-mindedness towards the Jewish exiles. The Book of Ezra recalls that he authorized all religious trappings of Yhwhism to be returned, and the exiles despatched to Jerusalem with the funds and the approval to raise a new temple.

Cyrus' magnanimity effectively reinforced the arguments of a monotheistic lobby who could now claim that the god of Israel had effectively released his children from the oppressions of Marduk. Among the later chapters of Isaiah, written during Cyrus' reign, in the passage which begins: 'Comfort ye, comfort ye my people, saith your God', the prophet describes Yhwh as '. . . the everlasting God, the Lord, the Creator of the ends of the earth . . .' Such sentiments were the first tangible expressions of Jewish monotheism, as distinct from henotheism.

Under one of Cyrus' heirs, Darius, Persia succumbed finally to the Macedonian armies of Alexander, and with the dawn of the Hellenistic period the legacy of Sumer became distilled and scattered into the saddlebags of Europeans. Cultural focus was now poised to shift across the Mediterranean to the West. When Alexander died of malaria in 323 BC the stage was set for war which extended more than two hundred and fifty years. Syria and Palestine found themselves once again in the hard frontline of battle. The old Empire was carved up by a powerful clique of ex-Alexandrian generals, resulting in three dominant hierarchies

– the Ptolemies in Egypt, the Seleucids in Syrio-Palestine, and the Antigonids controlling the old European colonies. During the third century BC these super-powers clashed repeatedly on Syrio-Palestinian territory with a final outcome in the shape of victory for the Seleucid general, Antiochus III. His successor, Antiochus IV, instigated a reign of suppression and injustice which triggered the Jewish 'Maccabean' (the nickname of its leader, meaning 'hammer') revolt of 168 BC.

The uprising paved the way for the period of weak and much-criticized rule by the Hasmonaean dynasty of priests. They took on the mantle of kings which went very much against the grain with the more orthodox elements of the religious community. The apocryphal second-century-BC collection of the *Psalms of Solomon* contains an unremitting tirade against sexual profanities carried on in the Temple, including harlotry, unnatural intercourse and other wickedness, all of which implies continuing ritualistic activity between temple prostitutes and the priesthood.[3]

In what the Jews believed to be divine retribution for Hasmonaean misbehaviour, Pompey marched his Roman legions into Syria in 65 BC and annexed Palestine the following year. From that moment in history, Rome and her culture were to play a leading role in the shaping of Western ideas which must never be underestimated. With the new order was also coming a change of needs and aspirations no less radical than those which accompanied the evolution from hunting to farming. The European world into which Christianity would enter for its childhood and adolescence was a sophisticated place. This modern sphere enjoyed a chemistry of knowledge and ideas, and a literature, infinitely more complex than those of ancient Mesopotamia.

The Queen of Heaven was not to be thwarted. She moved with time and tide. She hitched up her skirts and prepared to meet the new demands of the classical empires. In the West she was dealing with a civilization whose focus of attention had shifted from that over which she had previously presided. Rome possessed lands which stretched from the River Tyne to the Nile and whilst nature's caprices in the form of earthquake, flood and famine, were anxieties that had not left people's minds, no more did her people find quite such peril in the changing of the seasons. The wealth and diversity of empire held at bay the yearly cycle of hunger and death, for the most part with admirable efficiency. Thus her peoples began to lose their feeling for the land and its sacred strength, although ancient tradition was still of great importance in the lives of men and women under the classical empires. Artists and writers living in the modern cities took delight in romanticizing the gods of nature, and the old cults were fiercely defended by large numbers of followers. Culture became the property of city dwellers cocooned from the vagaries of nature in a way that the peoples of the ancient world had never been. Rome alone probably enjoyed a population in excess of one million. The time had come to put new flesh on old bones.

The Egyptians were the real pioneers in the stage of religious adventuring which explored beyond the frontiers of the agricultural cults, but Greece, deeply influenced as she was by Egypt's discoveries, furnished the first Western interest in this new landscape. In turn, she exerted a powerful influence on Roman thinking.

Though local tongues and dialects always rubbed shoulders with those of empire, Latin and Greek were the passports of communication.[4] The two giants of the classical world provided the great languages of culture. In the East, Greek held far greater sway whilst Latin was a tongue generally more familiar to the West, spread primarily by the legions and by the development of new Roman towns in far-flung places. Greece led the field as the innovator of the style and the art through which the fresh horizons were described, and Greek was the more universal language. You could 'get by' with a little Greek almost anywhere in the civilized world. Greece delivered the kind of cultural impact to civilization that Sumer had given so many millennia earlier through the gift of her cuneiform script. Rome was the great organizer, the civil engineer who built the material roads along which the new dreams might travel. The effect of these cultures into which Christians migrated as they established themselves in Europe was enormous. On the shaping of their beliefs, it was as significant as the influence of Canaan and Assyria on infant Israel.

What were the origins of the traditions of Greece and Rome, the so-called classical cultures? Whence did the ingredients come? It is easy to overlook the fact that the Mediterranean region had seen its own prehistoric development, one not unlike that of the near east, though without quite the same rigours of climate.

Ice-Age travellers seem to have found Italy but missed the turning for Greece.[5] The peninsula does not reveal any of the palaeolithic images comparable with those found at sites in northern Italy. Although Greece acquired her culture through a number of prehistoric routes, all of them are comparatively recent. The earliest known people arrived in the peninsula about 3500 BC, from western Asia. They came across the Mediterranean and brought with them a culture that seems instantly familiar.

Though their settlements have been found mainly on the plains of Thessaly, the remnants abound with small fat female figurines not unlike those unearthed from Anatolia and northern Mesopotamia. Greece claimed a prehistoric reverence for the earth and its fecundity much like that which had been nurtured right across the Ice-Age 'axis'. There was no single incursion, rather waves of immigrants and warriors. A thousand years later there was an infusion of culture from the north. These Aryan peoples brought with them another familiar object – the emblem of the phallus. Thus the region had begun to build a culture, in part with roots remarkably close to those of the 'mystery' fertility religions further east, but mingled with a more patriarchal style of hunting religion from the north.

The Greeks themselves believed their earliest ancestors were the Achaeans, and they romanced the legends of Mycenae and Agammemnon and Homeric Troy.[6] The archaeological truth is that hundreds of years before the fall of Troy, a dynastic culture had arisen from yet another wave of Indo-European immigrants who had descended either from the north or the east. They were the Mycenaeans whose Age began in the sixteenth century BC and survived for more than four hundred years until it disintegrated in shambles. Its people left imprecise records and no king list, although in common with their contemporaries, the Minoans based in Crete, they developed a functional script which they incised into soft clay tablets. It has become known as Linear B.

Minoan and Mycenaean religion are very closely coupled and there is suggestion that one of the routes travelled by the mother goddess down to the classical era was through Minoan Crete. Crete may have made a strong impact on her mainland neighbour to the north. From about 2500 BC onwards she was a major trading nation with contacts in the Asiatic Levant, particularly with Phrygia, and her own culture became rapidly steeped in traditions that had spread west from Mesopotamia. It is, however, impossible to detect the exact extent of Minoan influence on Mycenae because there is so little written account of either religion.

One is left in no doubt though, that the mother goddess in all her complexity: queen of the mountains, mistress and mother of life, protectress of vegetation, stands paramount beside the son

and lover destined endlessly to die with the ending of the old
year. With the pair one also finds tree worship, pillar cults, and
other instantly familiar signs of ancient Mesopotamia.

Both the Mycenaeans and the Minoans absorbed the architecture of deities in triads or trinities, though these suggest complicated and sometimes paradoxical implications. In the Greek
pantheon, Artemis may well be a translation of the Cretan mother
goddess in her various forms. She is also one of the oldest of deities
with strong links to Asia Minor. Aphrodite is clearly modelled on
the old Mesopotamian Ištar, whilst Demeter, the personification
of the earth mother or corn mother, seems closer to Ninhursaĝa.
From Demeter also stems Persephone, her daughter yet her other
dark self too, who descends yearly to reign with the underworld
god whilst nature sleeps. The story is, of course, derived indirectly
from the legend of Inana, Ereškigal and Dumuzi.

The contrasting aspects of the mother goddess provide a strong
ongoing theme. From Linear B scripts found at Knossos and made
between the fourteenth and twelfth centuries BC, there comes
mention of Two Queens and the God Poseidon.[7] Such combina-
tions were surely based on models such as Ištar, Dumuzi and
Ereškigal, or Anat, Baal and Athirat. Poseidon, the sea god, was
the son and lover of the goddess. This same trio turns up on the
Greek mainland at Pylos, where inscriptions describe gifts to the
fertility goddess from Poseidon.

A delightfully worked plaque from Mycenae depicts a pair of
goddesses, with a god-child stretched across their laps. Its style
resembles such family groups of deities as those discovered at
Alaca Hüyük in Anatolia. In Greek mythology the trio become
the tragedy of Demeter, Persephone and Triptolemos their foster
child, the perhaps real, perhaps imagined boy-king of the golden
age whose most famous 'mysteries' were revealed through drama
at the town of Eleusis. Each year Triptolemos presented humanity
with Demeter's gift of the corn but came, in his tragic fate as a
fertility god, to be lost to the underworld where he joined for a
season with the infernal family.

A particularly fascinating series of terracotta figures have also
been unearthed from the same ruins, in which the two goddesses
are joined like Siamese twins with the young god seated on the
junction of their shoulders. Is there, at last, a light dawning on
the mystery of the strange Anatolian Siamese-twin figurines?

Other, more conventional, evidence of links with western
Asia is to be found in Crete.[8] From the Palace of Knossos, that
of minotaur and labyrinth fame in Greek legend, has come a seal

dated to about 1500 BC. A mother goddess stands on her mountain flanked by two rampant lions. In her outstretched hand is a spear and behind her is a temple decorated with the curiously distinctive 'horns of consecration' which were incorporated in all Cretan shrines. Facing the goddess is a naked male figure standing in a posture of worship, her eternal spouse of spring. One wonders inevitably whether the 'horns' are perhaps derivative of the Mesopotamian 'omega' uterus design.

Minoans probably copied and handed on to the Mycenaeans the cult of the Anatolian goddess Kybele and her consort Attis, since this was the version of the seasonal fertility story which developed in Phrygia. The Phrygian cult, as a vehicle by which god and goddess came to Europe, demonstrates precedents that are too important to brush aside. Attis, the Phrygian version of Dumuzi was said, like the Mesopotamian god, to have been a shepherd of the heroic age. Kybele, the Phrygian Ištar, was in some versions of the legend, his incestuous mother. In others he was conceived immaculately by the demi-goddess Nana when she placed a ripe almond in her bosom and Attis was thus cast as her half-godly, half-mortal lover.

Attis, inevitably, had to die to be reborn.⁹ Some stories told of his death, the cruel victim of a wild boar. Others rendered a more terrible account. This was no longer a symbolic descent to the underworld but a specific demise. Attis had castrated himself beneath the sacred tree of the goddess and bled to death. His corpse became a pine tree until the time of his resurrection. Here rests a mix of Mesopotamian imagery firmly recognizing the need for self-abasement of the god, and Egyptian tradition through which colours of Osiris and the incarceration of his corpse into a tamarisk trunk gently infuse the picture.

In the time-honoured way of re-enacting the circumstances of the legend to bring new life to the earth, it seems that the Greek priests of Kybele actually copied Attis' death in a supreme and dreadful act of self-denial, not evident from the Mesopotamian accounts of an annual but largely symbolic humiliation and chastisement. The Kybelene priests castrated themselves and presented their testicles to the goddess by burying them in the earth. Here was a far more savage version of Aššur-nasir-apli's presentation of a symbolic phallus to the Sacred Tree at Kalakh.

The priests who rendered the sacrifice of their manhood were the Galli. Once emasculated, they were destined to wear women's clothes and ornaments for the rest of their lives. Each year in the great rite they would draw fresh blood from their arms and offer it as sacrifice to the goddess in continuation of their devotion and the giving of their life strength.

The original introduction of the cult to the classical empires is uncertain, but in 204 BC, it arrived in Rome in a very tangible fashion. The legions were bogged down in a wearisome and drawn out war of attrition with Hannibal. Oracles suggested that if the icon of the great mother goddess of Phrygia was obtained, the war would be settled in Rome's favour, and so ambassadors were sent to the sacred city of Pessinus. They were entrusted with the jagged black stone which symbolized the presence of Kybele and they returned with it to Rome, to install it in the Temple of Victory on the Palatine Hill. Hannibal went his way unfulfilled.

Romans honoured Attis in death on the Day of Blood, 22 March. They similarly commemorated the Syrian god Adonis, the consort of Astarte (Aphrodite in Greece and Venus in Rome). Though the symbolism differs from the Mesopotamian style, there is much that reminds of the true birthright whence this grotesque version of the god's atonement began its journey.

The Attis rite was heralded by a pine tree carried into the Temple of Kybele, the honour entrusted to a Guild of Tree Bearers. They had swathed it in woollen bands and decked it with violets. A model of Attis was hung from its boughs. Here again seems to be a more solid explanation of a familiar but shrouded Mesopotamian imagery: the decoration of the trees symbolizing goddess and lover.

The new priests of Kybele no doubt considered that they were honouring the sacred traditions of a great and venerable rite. One cannot imagine that they dismembered themselves so grotesquely on a whim. But here was a thing of arcane purpose, its first piquant meaning lost and now become largely pointless. One wonders at the level of brain-washing induction its young initiates were put through. The scenes of the Day of Blood must have been like the worst nightmare of Hieronymus Bosch. Along the festival way all were dressed in the white of purity and innocence, yet more than a casual look would reveal grim portents. Sharpened swords were placed strategically in scabbards beside the road. Slowly, everywhere in the sunny streets began a macabre metamorphosis as the wings of the butterflies took colour. Scarlet frenzy spattered and spread across the pure white linen of living altars.

The priests in their curiously oriental and androgynous costumes with small images suspended on their breasts processed, chanting their hypnotic music to the thump of drums and the squeal of pipes, and all the while added their own shrill notes as they gashed themselves repeatedly with knives. The novice initiates caught the blood fever and horribly injured themselves with swords, broken pieces of pot, whatever instrument of self-abuse they could lay their hands on. They presented their opened flesh to the goddess' altar amidst the pervading stench of blood.

Bystanders too were driven to an obscene madness as the masochism spread. Besotted by the imagery and the lust for blood, youth after youth hacked off his manhood. High, it is difficult to believe on anything less than drugs and mind-bending fervour, the youthful pride of Rome, blood cascading down its adolescent white thighs, ran through the streets waving its balls aloft to dash them against the bloody black icon. There was in this, no doubt, some tragic determination to make a statement of deep and significant import, but their achievement produced little more than a cruel amputation. That no doubt struck home with fearsome thoroughness when the emasculated revellers awoke to greet the dawn of the god's impending resurrection. Fanatics had transformed a once deeply meaningful gesture of faith into an obscene excuse for violence and raucous blood-letting that no longer bore serious regard to meaning or purpose.

On the 25th, three days after the Day of Blood, there began a great celebration, the Hilaria Festival, preceded by an all-night vigil with candles. The whole event has clear similarities with the Good Friday and Easter rites, a comparison that was not lost on critics of later ecclesiatical claims that the events of Easter were without precedent. In the fourth century AD there were a number of verbal attacks on the Christian Movement suggesting, tartly, that Easter was little more than a blatant plagiarization of the Attis festival.

One paramount question for the quest after Christian origins has been whether there is any palpable precedent for the actual slaughter of the god king in the spring months. Did regicide ever become a reality? Certain hints come from Minoan sources again, and from a separate though related ritual, that of the 'gardening' of the goddess' Tree of Life.

The Tree arrived from the east in a variety of contexts.[10] From about the same period as the seal showing the goddess and her consort, there has come a massive but exquisitely wrought gold ring, allegedly that of King Nestor of Iliad fame. Found by a peasant farmer in a tomb at Pylos, one of the Mycenaean palace sites on the Greek mainland, on its face is carved a gnarled and aged trunk whose spreading branches seem to separate the underworld from that of life and genesis. Goddess and consort rest in the branches accompanied by her symbolic lion. Here may exist one of the earliest representations of the Tree in a cruciform shape, representing either the four quarters of the earth or four spiritual realms of her influence and adversity.

There were also sacred groves in Crete and on the mainland. Areas of land known as *temenos* were given over to the gods, and ancient shrines were often sited beside caves and springs high up in the hills. They became a part of the classical landscape to which people from the towns made regular pilgrimages. These rustic venues provided the loudest echo of the holiness with which the earth had once been so richly seeded. Even in the towns and cities shrines rested amidst their sacred groves of greenery. There existed a holy and famous olive tree in a sanctuary on the Athenian acropolis.[11] Such trees still possessed great spiritual powers. They were carefully tended, usually by slaves and eunuchs under the watchful eye of the cult priests, and they reached great age. Those which died were replaced diligently.

At the festivals in honour of the mother goddess a tree was often hewn down and carried in to the shadow of the temple where animals were tied to it in sacrifice, sometimes still alive, and it was dressed with gold and silver and pieces of fine cloth. The priest of the grove took a vow of marriage to his goddess. Part of his service was, literally, to perform intercourse with her earthly symbol. At the appointed time he approached the Tree, kissed and embraced it, ejaculating his life essence against its vaginal trunk.

The sacred groves nurtured their own mythology and superstition though inevitably it had become far removed from the original logic. There was a famous grove of the Roman Astarte, Diana Nemorensis, at Aricia in the Alban Hills which probably existed from a time deep in history.[12] According to legend, the god-king, priest of Diana's sacred wood, only achieved his office by slaying his predecessor. Thus the hapless servant of the goddess prowled the confines of the grove endlessly, sword in hand, awaiting his inevitable doom. The slightest lapse in vigilance would signal his end.

Such tales perhaps provide more alerting signals. In many parts of the world there is firm evidence of god-kings being put to death either when they suffered the first physical blemishes of age, or after a fixed period and presumably before they started to demonstrate signs of wear and tear which paid the lie to godhead. Did some of the cults which learned their ideology from Mesopotamia

run to the same extreme measures, though with altered principles in mind? Did they offer the bodily sacrifice of the young
god-king of the seasons to the goddess of life? There is no evidence that the sacred king was ritually slain in 'cold blood' in
any of the Mesopotamian cults. We have to wonder though, at
the possibility in at least some versions of the cults of Attis
and Kybele, Adonis and Astarte. There is a curious observation
to be made on Cretan artwork.[13] Nowhere is the king drawn in
his maturity. Always he is represented as a youth. To suggest
morbid meaning could be very tenuous conjecture but it needs
to be set alongside other evidence.

The dying and rising god was represented in Crete, as he was
in so many other cultures, by the bull, the symbol of strength
and virility. There are traces of secret initiation ceremonies during which novices to the priesthoods of Attis and of Adonis stood
in baptismal pits above which young bulls had their throats cut.[14]
The initiates emerged drenched with the blood of the animal and
some would argue that ritual slaying of the sacred bulls conveniently got the king 'off the hook' of following the difficult path to
regicide. There exist, however, hints from Minoan texts which
lend credence to the implication resting in the absence of a
mature kingly figure in art. They provide insistent details about
ritual killings, which may have taken place at the end of a carefully defined period, after each eight-year solar cycle of the planet
Venus. The period is a difficult one to account for, but seems to
have been arrived at because only once in eight years do the
lunar and solar cycles reach harmony and the coincidence was
regarded as the most propitious moment for atonement.

If the god-kings of Crete were slain in a ritual of regenesis,
then the knowledge of the tradition must have come to Greece
and to Rome and been familiar during the centuries leading up
to the time of Christ. Even if no longer enacted, it provided
another significant precedent to the Passion story.

To present criticism of paganism only within terms of the
Greek and Roman experience is to do the ancient religions a
profound disservice. Paganism is a term that was first coined at the
time when Christianity was poised to emerge on to the European
stage and much of the criticism of pagan religions stemmed from
Christian writers. Even within the limited classical orbits there
have grown genuine misconceptions. It has been claimed that
Greek and Roman religions were epitomized by cults of wild
orgies and debauchery and creeds of lowly horizons. Not so. In
spite of such corrupted rituals as those associated with Attis and

Kybele, Adonis and Aphrodite and, separately though sometimes linked, Dionysos and Artemis, the culture was often marked with great sensibility and even austerity.

What has fuelled the misconception is that with such a proliferation of minor cults, it was inevitable that some on the fringes developed fairly wild reputations. It is these, the excesses rather than the moderations, which have gone down in the annals of notoriety.

The festivals were on the whole jolly affairs, full of music and good humour, and no doubt a degree of over-indulgence on the part of the devotees.[15] They were also good for the commercial interests of the town and for its status. Large crowds drew money. The festivals provided an excuse for public holidays in the round of imperial life. Yet just as the happy-go-lucky flavour of some Easter traditions stands beside more serious principles, there was also profound purpose to many. It was deemed a great honour to carry the sacred objects and the symbols of the deities were taken in procession to the shrine by pillars of the community who had worked diligently and piously for their privilege.

Rome placed vast store on tradition and her logic said that each man was entitled to his god and that every deity imbued something to its follower. Thus the more gods Rome embraced, the greater her glory and the better her store in heaven and earth. In a sense, she collected deities and faiths as an insurance policy and this, in no small measure, gave classical religion the appearance of being a confused hotchpotch, particularly at the dawn of the Christian era which witnessed, ironically, a surge of interest in paganism because of imperial anxieties abroad. There was, however, no sense of jostling for position amongst the plethora, and no denunciations made the headlines. Heresy, in the Christian sense, was an unknown concept to followers of paganism; it implied only recognition of a school of thought.

The polytheism which had sustained the human breast for so long and so valiantly, was beginning to lose ground though. That logical development of the ancient and inspired ideas of animism where every object in nature had its spirit identity was effectively a redundant concept to the new radical intelligentsia of empire. The deities of woodlands and fields, sky and water, pots and pans had served countless millions in their passage. Most would shortly return to the heavens. But in the meanwhile, as Christianity struggled into the light, they basked in their glorious Indian summer. Classical scholar Robin Lane Fox describes the great precinct of Apollo at Didyma in the first century AD, as being so crowded that a visitor referred to its 'encirclement with altars of every god'.

Everywhere polytheism triumphed. But it was perhaps a case of too many sweets making you sick, and people began to find the logic naïve and faintly vulgar. Egypt had flirted with the idea, perhaps before its time, of the pantheon being obsolete, now other minds were taking up the challenge.

There was a logic which argued that all the various deities of everything from the bath house to the boletarium were perhaps no more than manifestations of the one. Syncretism, hardly a new phenomenon, began to gather its supporters, and by the end of the first century AD it is possible to see an increasing drift towards multiples of deities with similar roles merging into one. This sort of notion was not unattractive to its converts. To honour one 'high god' to whom a host of lesser lights were subordinate had its merits. Thus novel terms of address began to circulate: 'Zeus Helios Serapis'; 'Isis – the one who is all'; 'one Artemis' and so on. The god Zeus was a notorious philanderer, but under Cretan influence, all his mistress goddesses – an embarrassment as they stood in their multiplicity – became shades of the one. So in all parts of the Greek and Roman empires there was the Mother Goddess under one title or another, whom Zeus seduced with unrelenting vigour though accountably more fidelity. This was no monotheism. Worshippers acknowledged the lesser orders of divinity but the principle of a great god superintending minor deities paralleled that hinted at in the Old Testament distinction between El and *elim*. It suggests that broad patterns of religious thought were changing in ways that did not respect international boundaries.

The drift towards henotheism was preceded by another radical development. Some authors have argued that paganism was a matter of cult acts rather than creed or doctrine. Whilst such argument is not true for the faiths from which classical paganism was drawn, it does hold water for the almost redundant ritual of Greece and Rome.[16] The first signs of the abstraction of religion were beginning to advertise themselves. The ritual generally became distanced from the mythology. What had once been the enactment of a rite designed to safeguard some fundamental activity, now became a detached play. Ritual, by the same token became, to an extent, a cult act for its own sake. There had to be new and more updated avenues along which the mind could explore the changing uncertainties of life.

In the old order of things, the questions had been: 'What is the meaning of the world around me? How may I communicate with the forces which control it? How do I survive its rigours and its uncertainties?' The traditional styles of religion had applied themselves to answering these problems. But now there were new examinations, which asked not so much: 'How may I survive?' but, 'Why am I here? What is my purpose? Where am I going?' Some of the older cults had made conscious attempts to resolve the 'Where am I going?' debate, the Osirian creed being the best conceived example, but in an effort to answer their uncertainties more satisfactorily, men had begun to probe a new dimension of intellect. They had applied themselves to philosophy.

It was the Greeks who first framed the notion of a principle of pure knowledge existing in the primeval cosmos, Sophia. Thus the pursuit of wisdom began to rival the honouring of the gods in the old religions.

Early Greek philosophers like Xenophanes of Colophon and Antisthenes in the fifth and fourth centuries BC had already found much that was attractive in exploring the character and parameters of a single creator god. Xenophanes wrote: 'There is one God, greatest among gods and men, neither in shape nor in thought like unto mortals . . . He is all sight, all mind, all ear . . . He abides ever in the same place motionless, and it befits him not to wander hither and thither.' Antisthenes penned the sentiment: 'God is not like anything; hence one cannot understand him by means of an image.'

The main architects of Greek philosophy dealing with the infinite were Socrates and Plato and by the third century BC, pagan intellectuals had rationalized and directed themselves into a personal understanding of God based largely on their writings. The Platonists saw the route through self-knowledge. Others found it by looking beyond themselves into the beauty and orderly structure of the world.

Both strove to put mortal man on a plane of realization which removed him from the destiny of fate, something which hitherto had always been regarded as humanity's inevitable lot. To the new radical followers of philosophy, old-style religion was definitely passé. At one extreme, the Epicureans turned their noses up at any such decadent nonsense, deriding it as a sop to the terrors of the unknown after death. Others were more open-minded.

Anxiety about life after death was probably the single most compelling preoccupation of the inner man and no doubt determined the course of a lot of after-dinner discussion. The idea of bodily resurrection was not an innovation of Christians. Men were debating, rejecting, and accepting the notion centuries before the death of Christ. Many found the idea repulsive and ridiculous. There was after all the stark evidence of bones in the grave and such practical niceties as which wife or mistress would share the celestial love nest, and with what earthly possessions.

The immortality of the soul was something people took much more seriously though any surviving notion of a grey limbo into which the soul was destined to return after its brief sojourn on temporal earth tended to be viewed as a quaint anachronism. The idea of heaven and hell was, however, firmly established. It was not a Christian prerogative. Plato, in his *Republic*, gives a clear indication of the stark options open to mortal man prior to his demise.[17] It was felt that whatever was left after death was destined for one or the other. There was a preoccupation with the perils of Hades – terrifying tales abounded and people took them seriously.

Justifiably, Christians were to be attacked by their pagan critics for dressing up established philosophy in new clothes and claiming it as their own. Lane Fox describes the comments of the neo-Platonist Celsus towards the end of the second century AD. Celsus pointed out to the Christian Movement that their ideas of 'eternal damnation' were hardly original since, to mention but one precedent, they formed an integral part of the Greek Mystery plays of Dionysos whose followers' interest was also strongly directed towards the probability of life after death.

The Isis cult took on philosophical dimensions, particularly with its appeal to the notion of the female anima, one of the strongest features being the image of the mother nursing her holy child, the son of the dead Osiris, sensitively portrayed in the final book of Apuleius' *The Golden Ass*.[18] In Isis, one might infer, lies an immediate precedent for the Madonna imagery.

Even the cult of Mithraism, perhaps that most popularly associated with the Roman empire but, in reality, a late-comer almost unsponsored outside of the exclusive officer class of the legions, claimed that it could point out the way for the soul to rise through the spiritual spheres of the seven planets and so gain the paradise of the Milky Way.[19] Mithraism also indulged in sacred meals. To some this too overtly pre-empted the Christian experience. Here was the eucharist in different clothes.

Some of the new philosophies took on extremely austere clothing. The Stoics, amongst whom the emperor Marcus Aurelius was probably the most notable and gloomy follower, tended to the view that God is achieved by a kind of monastic self-denial and an emotional sterility. Once again, however, the Christians – ever with an eye open for useful ideas – saw great attraction in certain Stoic ethics and readily took them on board.

In spite of the probing of new frontiers, Rome was essentially a follower of traditional religious values. The casual observer might wonder at Rome's old-fashioned supplications but Rome continued to regard tolerance and the embrace of the many beliefs that came to her as an expression of all-round piety, an openness which saw its reward in the continuing success of empire. So, each deity on its day was wheeled out, washed, fed, paraded through the streets with much *joie de vivre* and returned to its stable for another year in guarantee of its goodwill. The one proviso was that none of these sects and movements incited subversion or any other kind of treasonable activity against the state.

The vital necessity to honour the gods and, ideally, to honour the many rather than the few eventually became a touchy subject in the Romans' attitude to professed Jews and later Christians who refused to bend the knee to any but their own essentially foreign deity. Their god had not seen Rome through her battles on the road to glory. Their god had not placed the good things of life on the groaning tables of her citizens. Their god had no record in protecting the eternal city from hail and tempest, earthquake, fire and flood.

The religions of the classical empires thus were distilled from three main sources: from their own traditions reaching back into pre-history, from those of the ancient near east, which came to them through Asia Minor and the Cretan civilization, the so-called 'mystery' cults; and from the Aryans in the distant, rumbling north. Within the span of the classical period, however, from Homer's Greece of 500 BC, to the reign of the Roman emperor Constantine nearly a thousand years later, faith and the pursuit of reason did not stand still. Philosophy was developing and adding its own not insignificant voice. It is in the context of all this that the beginnings of Christian religion have to be evaluated.

The curtain rose on the Christian era in the reign of the emperor Octavian, who became Caesar following Anthony's suicide pact with Cleopatra. He expanded the empire massively, and in recognition of his services to Rome the senate passed on him the rare and honoured title 'Caesar Augustus'. In the final years of his reign his ambition was to consolidate the far-flung reaches of Roman colonial rule. To oversee the 'stabilization' of Palestine he appointed Herod the Great.

The title was ill-fitting, since Herod governed neither with magnanimity, nor particular greatness.[20] His weapon of control was blunt oppression, and it was his tyrannical cruelty to the Judaeans which marked the years immediately before the appearance of Jesus. Whilst he showed some curious ambivalence – he purchased Egyptian grain to alleviate the great famine of 25 BC, and extended a degree of tolerance towards Yhwhism – Herod the Great stripped the Sanhedrin of any accountable self-government, made extortionate tax demands on the peasant, and treated him with great inhumanity.

Through typical insensitivity, Herod triggered one of the major catastrophes of the immediate pre-Christian era. He placed the Roman imperial eagle over the portico of the Temple, an act of blasphemy which enraged priest and commoner together. It persuaded activists to commit blatent insurrection shortly after Herod's death, and tear it down. The ringleaders were summarily executed, which in turn triggered a peasant revolt. On this occasion, the insurrection was doomed. A new Roman governor Varius, sensitive to the lessons of recent history, crucified two thousand rebel Jews in an exemplary demonstration of the penalties for revolution. It was an horrific climax to yet another attempt to rid the Judaeans of their yoke of endless subjugation. It lead only to a political and social climate in which their lot was even harder.

In the peculiar context of an exceptionally unhappy slice of their history, the children of Israel began to seek more and more earnestly for realization of the Messianic prophecy.

11

Ecce Homo

I have in front of me a copy of the New Testament. Exquisitely folded in its leather and gilt binding, it is the tiniest book I have ever seen. It stands less than 10 centimetres by a mere 2.5 centimetres in breadth and unless you are very keenly sighted or choose to peer at it through a magnifying glass, the print is too small to read. It is a 'finger bible', to be carried like a talisman of old in a lady's reticule. It is inscribed to my great grandmother, Lucy May Malabar, Christmas 1897.

My grandfather was vicar of the parish of Westhead in Lancashire and, as an orthodox Christian clergyman, he wore the New Testament and its more ancient preface like a suit of armour. He knew great tracts by heart. It was for him the divine word of God and of Jesus Christ and in its infinite wisdom and truth it protected him from doubt and from the devil. It was his irrefutable mandate as a priest.

People have carried and quoted from the 'good book' down almost all the generations of Christendom. It is the substance of their faith. Grandfather believed in the Bible for no single reason. He responded to it because generations of my family before him had followed the same path through its pages and therefore he revered that which his ancestors had lived by. He responded because, in the partnership of Old and New Testaments, the Bible alone amongst all the countless millions of books generated at the hand of humankind embraced the accumulated knowledge of his God back to the days of Abraham. He responded in veneration of its great age and because its teaching appeared to him to be reasonable and true.

The truth? Do we have proof positive or is it all down to blind faith? The question is a very trenchant one in the case of the life and times of Jesus because he is one of the most problematic figures in all of history. There is no contemporary record of him. His origins are wreathed in mystery and legend. His vocation is at best open to conjecture. The circumstance of his death is incomprehensible. Nothing in his life can reasonably account for the subsequent rise of the Christian Movement. All of this suggests, at once, that there is something amiss, that aspects of the story have been lost, or concealed, or changed.

A great limitation to disentangling reality from the legends which surround the origins of Christianity is that nowhere among the volumes making up the New Testament does anything emerge which can be properly described as an historical account.[1] Although theologians now take academic note of material once considered heretical, the Bible narratives are all that the Christian Church will accept officially as observation of Jesus' life and times. Yet the canonical gospels, those ancient manuscripts written in Greek on scrolls of papyrus and incorporated for whatever reason into the Bible, may have been compiled from little more than lists of quotations noted down by followers and later padded out into the familiar stories marking the brief public life of the man. The synoptic works – the narratives attributed to Matthew, Mark and Luke – are so-called because they disclose undeniable similarities when read in their original tongue.

Certain words and common phraseology suggest that all were derived from an earlier but lost written source.[2] Today we have other 'heretical' material which at least corroborates parts of the official biographies, but in reality it is almost impossible to verify if any of the sayings and parables attributed to Jesus are accurate, or to confirm or deny his activities, and in many respects his life remains enigmatic.

Even the Jewish historian, Josephus, writing in the first century AD, never mentions Jesus directly, referring once to: 'Jesus, the so-called Christ', and then only in passing when commenting on the early Christian community in Jerusalem.[3] It was not until Jesus' followers had emerged as an historically defined movement that authors such as Suetonius, the historian of the imperial court writing a *Life of Claudius* at the turn of the first century AD, and his contemporary, Tacitus, describing the great fire of Rome in his Annals, began to mention the Christians specifically but, again, only in the most fleeting terms.[4] Both men, it has to be said, were highly contemptuous of the Christians but, considering the intimate detail of home and colonial life which they often reported, the omission of serious comment can only suggest that Jesus and his followers occupied a far less prominent position in the life of the Roman province than the Gospels would have us believe.

The American author Ramsey MacMullen makes a very succinct observation on early historians like Jerome.[5] 'History is spread out before their eyes, but they see only events and persons floating loose in a timeless past, without caused links between them – a gallery of isolated portraits and anecdotes made classical by remoteness'. The remoteness of the four Gospels, aside from the texts which the early fathers failed to get their polemical hands on, offers precisely the experience of viewing pictures at an exhibition, the distinction being that the isolated portraits are all of the same subject. They range from the briefest of sketches to more detailed canvases, but if the main characters are in sharp focus, the general context is so vaguely drawn as to be close to an abstract. There is a sense of events being described almost at random to cover the final years of Jesus' life. The glimpses we are provided with are really little more than picture-book illustrations around which a narrative is embroidered.

Much of the material must be seen as being apologetic – written to a specific readership to vindicate the harassed membership of the early Church.[6] It was not intended, in the political climate in which it was written and circulated, to provide either a detailed record for posterity, or necessarily a true account of Christian expectations. One aspect which is massively lacking because of this shyness is any attempt to explain cause and effect. The biblical material merely takes Jesus into a series of very limited contexts and implies, probably truthfully, that the man was really quite harmless and well-meaning towards everybody but came in for very unjust treatment from his own people. The Gospels must have been edited very circumspectly.[7] They could not, for example, have pointed the finger of blame at the Romans – that would really have put the imperial cat amongst the kosher pigeons.

There are also heavy questions over authorship and dating of the New Testament writings.[8] The earliest work is that ascribed to Mark, followed ten years later by Matthew and Luke. Yet Mark is

thought to have been written, at the earliest, between AD 60 and
AD 70, in other words thirty or forty years after the crucifixion.
That is comparable with, let us say, the first surviving account of
Winston Churchill's wartime role being dated from the 1980s. The
book attributed to John the Divine is considered by most modern
analysts to have been penned not by him but by a group of his
students in Rome, thus completing a quartet of works all with
very dubious authorship.

The writers of the early Christian manuscripts which we
have to work with were hardly less detached from the cultural
and political stage on to which Jesus stepped, than are most of
the modern authors who attempt to analyse them. These writers
by and large fall into two camps. There are the Christian theologians who range from Bible thumpers to those who have made
a conscious effort to shake loose from dogma, but all of whom
are bound up ultimately within the perimeters of what is dog-
matically acceptable. At the opposite end of the spectrum are the
ideologists who would see Jesus repackaged as the Che Guevara
of his time.

The questions which arise about Jesus are highly sensitive,
yet there is an inevitability about them. They are questions
which many Christian theologians are reluctant to address, but
which, for anyone with an open mind, are impossible to evade
or ignore in light of what has transpired thus far. Was Jesus Christ
the embodiment of the dying and rising god, a perpetuation of
the ancient traditions applied at last to the Children of Israel in
their desperate need for national salvation, or was he truly the
apostasy of paganism, a unique and entirely novel incarnation
of the godhead? Was there a uniqueness about Jesus' death and
resurrection? Who was this remarkable man?

The weakness in any attempted investigation remains that we
have so little material to work with. That in itself, in an age of
Roman literacy, should raise alerting suspicions, but the effect is
to deny any positive and direct conclusions. All we can do is to
examine the circumstantial evidence and to search critically for
what may be wrong with the limited documentation that exists.

The Christian experience began as a Jewish experience.[9] This
much is certain. Whatever we do not know about it, we can at
least be sure that it arose in response to a very particular and
peculiar national problem. Jesus was a Jew. He was brought up
in Jewish traditions, suffered the penalties of being a citizen of
a country under the yoke of foreign domination, and by all
accounts was quite orthodox in many of his views and habits.

An immediate uncertainty is the nature of Jesus' relationship to other Jews, and yet it is an important question, since something about the man and his destiny provoked an irrevocable and anguished rift between Jews and Christians. The enquiry needs to start in the political and social arena, with what the Jews were looking for, and with whether they were all seeking the same thing.

Jesus would be born into a climate of belief which was dominated by thoughts of death and judgement – eschatology. Principles which the old Osirian faith had introduced were now deeply entrenched in Jewish minds, though many would of course argue that Egyptian wisdom had nothing to do with it. Certainly the Jews envisaged a different promise at the end of the journey. They believed, in their world of desperate oppression, that the end of all things was near and that out of the ashes of the old would arise the new kingdom promised by the prophets in which the God of Israel would rule the world. They had also come to expect realization of the Messianic prophecy of a redeeming leader.

The Jews were neither socially nor spiritually a united body though. They were already plagued by sectarianism, and the short answer to whether each sect was looking for the same thing is probably, no. The serious effort during the Maccabean period to introduce elements of Hellenic and Egyptian reasoning into Judaism, coupled with a strong resistance to Roman domination, was the catalyst for the founding of a group which became known as the Pharisees, the so-called 'Separated'. Whilst they did make religious advances and undoubtedly were a bastion of Mosaic Law, they rapidly descended to the realms of fanaticism insisting on extreme formality in religious theory and practice.

The Sadducees, the aristocracy from whom the priesthood was drawn, also held Mosaic Law as sacrosanct but they rejected some of the more adventuresome theology of the Pharisees.[10] It also needs to be remembered that they had, for generations, experienced close contact with the belief and practice of the old Mesopotamian religions at official level.

There also existed a number of sects about whom little is known but which generally become lumped as 'Essenes'. Those reported most fully, lived as a separatist organization on the shores of the Dead Sea. They formed a tightly knit, rather frugal community which in some respects pre-empted the early Christian Church. They rejected marriage, sacrifice, and the general officialdom of Jerusalem, preferring a life of quiet contemplation. They were

the 'hippies' of Jewish society and, technically, were more likely
voters for the Christian ideal. Various quasi-political parties in
addition to these religious factions worked within Judaism, on
the extremes of which were the acquiescent Herodians, and the
intensely nationalistic and patriotic Zealots.

What united all of the various factions seems to have been
their belief that the restoration of Israel would happen sooner
or later. John the Baptist, who paved the way for Jesus, and
with whom Jesus arguably began his vocation, hammered home
the message that judgement day was round the corner, and
that urgent repentance was needed to ensure acquittal. Jewish
literature repeatedly emphasized the dream of the day when the
twelve tribes would rise triumphant under their new leader. From
the Psalms of Solomon in the Apocryphal Old Testament comes
typical sentiment in Psalm XVII (21–26):

> Behold, O Lord, and raise up for them their king, the son
>   of David,
> For the time which thou didst foresee, O God, that he may
>   reign over
> Israel thy servant.
> And gird him with strength, that he may shatter unrighteous
>   rulers;
> And purify Jerusalem of the nations which trample her down
>   in destruction . . .
> And he shall gather together a holy people, whom he shall
>   lead in righteousness,
> And he shall judge the tribes of the people which has been
>   sanctified by the Lord his God.

The question over which the various sects and communities
may have been less united concerned the nature of the Messiah.[11]
Where would he come from? What would be the role of the man?

One point, on which there can have been little doubt, is
that the traditional Jewish picture of a warrior, the son of
David, wielding rods of iron and words of steel, was unrealistic.
The Zealots might have fantasized about some form of militarist
solution, but most people must have realized that it was a naïve
dream. Israel could not beat down the might of Rome by force of
arms. There had to be some other means of liberation and it could
only be with the assistance of a divine hand. God would provide;
thus the 'armoury' was drawn with weapons of righteousness not
belligerence.

The Sanhedrin and other élite circles in Jerusalem probably envisaged a Messiah arising from their own ranks, a strongly orthodox personality who would bring about the new Jerusalem through strict observance of traditional law and ritual: a man who would bring God's punishment on the transgressors with the Torah in his hands. The apocryphal book of Jubilees is strong on this point. It warns that in the time of retribution, the children of Israel will begin to study the laws and the commandments and return to the 'path of righteousness'.

The peasant community doubtless wished, in principle, for the same outcome. The means by which they envisaged achieving it, however, may have differed. One essential, but unknown, factor is the nature of their traditional beliefs at that time. As in any society, a considerable social and cultural gulf existed between, on the one hand, the religious intellectuals and socialites of Jerusalem who were obsessed with the precise execution of ritual and law and, on the other, the common people who had little time or sympathy for this approach. Some will argue that the establishment of synagogues in the period after the Babylonian exile brought the peasant community 'into line' on religious matters, but it cannot be assumed that synagogue worship supervised by local rabbis necessarily imposed orthodoxy any more effectively than did the Christian ecclesiatical establishment on the 'old' beliefs and traditions of local European communities. In fact, if the medieval Christian experience is any measure, the chances are that 'grass roots' Jewish religion may have followed different paths. The peasant communities found themselves shouldering ever more painful burdens of punitive taxation, high unemployment, and a slave status that had sunk to an all-time low. Additionally, they may well have nursed deep religious grievances. They were not allowed to enter the Temple sanctuary, nor were they officially permitted to sacrifice.

The official records of the Jewish establishment, the books of Chronicles and Kings, recorded a history which reveals a perversity: periods of prosperity tended to coincide with the reigns of kings who pandered to Assyria, and lean times accompanied rulers who sought to go it alone, worshipping their own Israelite god. Orthodox explanation of this apparent anomaly was one of crime and punishment. The disaster periods were interpreted as divine retribution for prior indulgences in paganism. Virtually every text hammered home the point that the wicked transgressions of the fathers had brought terrible retribution on the sons.

It cannot be assumed, however, that the peasant community regarded history in the same way.[12] Notwithstanding the teachings of the new synagogues, their sense of the past was preserved through an oral tradition kept alive round village fires. They had no access to written records and probably could not read anyway. Their stories may have offered a conflicting explanation about prosperity and hardship.

In the mind of the superstitious and conservative peasant, when Hezekiah had begun his rule in Jerusalem and thrown out the gods of the earth, he and not his pagan predecessor may have been seen to be sowing the seeds of destruction. Tales may have recalled that shortly afterwards, Sennacherib, the Assyrian overlord, had obliterated all the fortified cities of Judah with great loss of life. Another story may well have interpreted the peaceful and prosperous fifty years of government under the pagan Menasseh as being attributable to the return to the Temple of the Queen of Heaven and her ašera. Oral tradition may well have explained the downfall of Jerusalem with a different slant to that of orthodox history recounting how, after Menasseh's death, Josiah reversed religious practice yet again, and introduced highly unpopular reforms. These may have seemed to bear the mark of Cain, because Josiah was killed at Megiddo, and his ill-conceived alliance with the Egyptians marked the beginning of the end. In less than twelve years Jerusalem had fallen to the armies of Nebuchadnezzar.

In other words, history could have been interpreted in no less rational ways, but dictated by the influences of separate religious traditions. In response to those who claim that too great a gulf exists between the Babyonian exiles surrounded by the Mesopotamian fertility religion, and their descendants some five hundred years later at the time of Jesus' birth, it must be pointed out that five centuries is a very short period for the preservation of oral traditions. More significantly, it must be reiterated, the most important festivals of the old cults were still clearly in evidence as recently as two centuries before Christ.

The non-literate peasant level of society may have looked forward to a deliverer in the mould of an essentially pagan tradition. It would not have been illogical for it to put its faith in the coming to Israel of a mortal representation of the deity who had protected so well the destinies of the great cultures which overshadowed Israel. Her people were dominated by the supremely successful Roman empire whose pluralist faith included the cult of Attis and perhaps ritual regicide. Proud as they undoubtedly were of their Jewish nationality, Jesus' generation also held the memory of powerful nations – Babylonian, Assyrian, Hittite and Egyptian – whose traditions centred on the humiliation or death, and subsequent restoration, of a sacred king in the spring quarter so that their peoples might prosper. Names such as Tammuz, Baal, Marduk and Osiris were, one can believe, the stuff of much popular legend.

On to this troubled stage came Jesus. It is not the concern of this book to tread a very detailed path into the teachings and work of the man, although to an extent they are relevant since they contain clues which suggest a distinction between the purpose of Jesus, and the movement which took up his name. The questions which need to be addressed concern whether some of the traditions about Christ the redeemer, which constitute the core of Christian belief and upon which the doctrine and canon are structured, actually hold water.

It is the final chapters of the Gospel narratives which stand least scrutiny if they purport to relate a spontaneous chain of events with its own peculiar originality and integrity. From the outset, however, the biographical accounts are plagued by inconsistencies and anomalies.

The first major problem comes in the opening chapter of the Matthew Gospel. Both the Matthew and Luke writers – Luke's nativity account being the most detailed – were at pains to stress that Jesus' lineage descended from David – and both include enormously detailed though strongly differing genealogies terminating with Joseph. But if, as the Gospels assert, Joseph was not the father of Jesus, it is difficult to see how the Old Testament prophecy of Isaiah 7 can be reconciled:

> ... Hear ye now, O house of David; Is it a small thing for you to weary men, but will ye weary my God also?
>   Therefore the Lord himself shall give you a sign; Behold, a virgin shall conceive, and bear a son, and shall call his name Immanuel.

It is important to appreciate that neither the Mark nor the John Gospels discuss the nativity – and it is now widely accepted among theologians that the nativity accounts are late embellishments of Matthew and Luke, added not less than eighty years after Jesus' death. In fact, there is virtually nothing of substance in them beyond a regurgitation of prophetic Old Testament material. Only in

the Luke tale is there the romantic story of the Christ child born
in a stable behind the fully booked local hotel. Many of the picturesque additions, including the oxen and ass which people tend
to assume are a part of the original narrative, did not find their
way into the apocryphal account until several centuries later.

The gospel explanation of divine parentage is facile, and it
shrouds the familiar prerequisite which determined the lineage
of such role models as Dumuzi and Osiris. In many of the fertility traditions, the Sacred King has been the demi-god offspring
of a mortal and a divine parent. Thus Dumuzi was the heir of
the heroic Sumerian king, Lugalbanda, but he was also the son
(as well as the lover) of Inana. In a patriarchal society where
God was officially masculine, there had to be a virgin birth and
absence of a human father. The contradiction between prophetic
and nativity accounts was defended by the early Christian fathers
with the doubtful claim that Mary was also of the House of David
and was, in fact, Joseph's cousin. They argued that the Matthew
and Luke genealogies had to be patrilineal because a child could
not be enrolled in the name of its mother. There is, however,
nothing in any of the New Testament writings to support this
claim of Mary's hereditary right. In fact rather the opposite is
true. There is the jarring and inexplicable incident recorded in
Luke which involves Jesus in a humiliating rebuff of Mary when
she and Joseph find him in the temple. By contrast the same
chapter identifies Mary and Joseph as Jesus' parents. Although
Mary's origins will be detailed in another chapter, it is worth
noting here that, in the main, the Gospel accounts either ignore
her, or treat her in a fashion that is close to being derogatory. The
John Gospel, narrating the marriage at Cana, also shows Jesus
behaving in a manner which is hostile towards his mother to
the point of rudeness: 'Woman, what have I to do with thee?'
In almost all the instances when Jesus relates to his mother in
the Gospels, his attitude seems uncompromisingly harsh.

The surroundings of Jesus' childhood may be of significance.
He grew up in Galilee and, amongst Jews, the Galileans were
something of a special case.[13] At the time of Jesus' birth, one
of Herod the Great's sons, Herod Antipas, governed the province
where Jesus was to spend much of his childhood and adult life.

Galileans faced problems in some ways typical of the rest
of Palestine yet in others peculiar. Authors have argued that
they were the 'People of the Land', an inter-marriage between
those who had stayed behind in Jerusalem when the cream of
Jewish society had been bundled off into exile, and northerners

of an essentially pagan disposition. Ezra has some terse comments about them. He describes them as 'adversaries of Judah' who approached the fathers-in-exile on their return and offered assistance with building the new Cyrus temple. They were however sent away with a 'flea in the ear' and the admonition: 'Ye have nothing to do with us to build an house unto our God'.

Thus the Galileans, if they were representative of the 'people of the land', were already a distinctly non-orthodox culture perhaps more naturally in sympathy with pagan rather than Jewish traditions.[14] Within this environment, Jesus gained a local following as a miracle worker who removed demons, and who taught a kind of benign socialism. Miracle working was not a particularly unique phenomenon. The magician, Apollonius of Tyana, to name one of many, was a much-publicized contemporary of Jesus; magic is reported widely from the ancient world, where it enjoyed a high degree of respectability, and it appears to have been practised over many hundreds of years. It is worthy of note that the Greek Magical Papyri share many parallels with the style of miracles cited in the Gospels.

Jesus' following around Galilee is likely to have been gained more through his reputation as a miracle worker than as an orator and ideologist. His personal message, of course, involved a radical reform of social principles, a complete reversal of many more conservative ideas, and he was undoubtedly a visionary of unusual calibre and courage. He championed certain moral considerations which had been singularly lacking in his local Galilean experience, and he made a point of befriending social outcasts. He delivered his message through sayings and parables, often obscure, but generally in the context of the current vogue of interest about death and judgement. That these messages were charismatic is unquestionable, although with the reservation that they are unlikely to have come to us chapter and verse, even assuming that they were told and retold, and we have to accept that the strength and resonance of the Gospel prose rests, to a degree, in the imaginative polishing of later scholars.

Jesus believed passionately in the imminent arrival of the new kingdom.[15] His viewpoint was strongly apocalyptic. The existing order would end, and in its place would come a new heaven on earth. In fact, there were those in the movement who came to find these statements vaguely embarrassing, and once the 'End of the World' scenario had lost serious credibility the more urgent anticipation of an apocalypse was quietly dropped. Jesus followed a fixed and unshakeable vision, though he seems not to have been advocating the official line of repentance and return to strict observance of Jewish law which was being promoted by stalwarts like John the Baptist. On the contrary he took a dim view of some of the rigorous adherence to ritual and outmoded rules, and it was perhaps this which was exploited to bring about his death.

Jesus worked around Lake Gennesaret in what had been the old Assyrian province of Samaria, one of the bastions of paganism among the Israelites. Most of his time was spent on the north-western shores of the tetrarchy where there was only a limited Roman presence. Customs officers and frontier guards would barely have noticed him. He avoided the royal city of Tiberias and concentrated his work on small villages like Capernaum and Chorazin. Occasionally, he ventured further afield into Caesarea Philippi, or across towards Tyre and Sidon.

It was not until Jesus rode into Jerusalem on a donkey demonstrating the peacefulness of his mission – judges rode donkeys and soldiers came on horseback – that he attracted the attention of authority.[16] Even then events that are recognized as momentous in the Christian experience passed with hardly a ripple. The claim that he entered the city 'in triumph' is probably wishful embroidery. His arrival is more likely to have been accompanied by only a small following, and in the shadow of the great Passover celebrations his subsequent arrest, trial and execution would have been classed as a minor incident. Those were turbulent times and Jews were being despatched in summary fashion as an almost daily occurrence.

The lack of notoriety is not altogether surprising. The Gospels tend towards the impression that in the years prior to his death he became a national hero. In reality, he seems to have been a fringe radical who, for a brief period, earned popularity and affection from country people living in remote districts on the northern fringe of Palestine. The message which comes out of the Gospels is not that he was trying to gather the whole of Israel behind him but that he was appealing to a select band with a message that was for universal hearing and benefit.[17] There is a romantic notion that Judaism was rocked on its heels by the arrival of Jesus, whereas if the absence of contemporary reporting is any measure, it probably barely noticed him.

Yet the effect of a seemingly insignificant figure being led inexorably to his end in Jerusalem, in that fateful spring of his thirty-second or thirty-third year, was to change the course of a nation and was to have a radical impact on Western civilization.

Few would argue that whilst the life and teachings of Jesus are integral to the faith, it is his death and regeneration at Easter as the Christ which are central and which in the early years of the Christian Movement lured so many converts. The real magnet was, and always has been, the persuasion that through Jesus, and Jesus alone, comes bodily restoration beyond the grave.[18] In fact many would argue that the Movement would never have existed were it not for the dramatic accounts of the resurrection relayed by the disciples to the ears of a receptive world. But it is the sequence of narrated events surrounding the death and its inseparable companion of resurrection which is least convincing. The scepticism does not arise in reservations about whether death and resurrection took place – these things *are* a matter of faith – but in whether the events, as reported, possess the uniqueness and integrity of purpose on which the Christian Church rests much of its persuasive argument. It is this superior conviction, wielded in the hands of an influential élite, which has allowed the Church to grind down and scatter other faiths with such formidable effect.

A limited number of possibilities exist. We may have 'Gospel truth' in which case events took place spontaneously and as reported, or the narrative may have been coloured, innocently, through the shortcomings of oral communication. On the other hand there may have been a conspiracy to orchestrate the sequence of incidents in a particular way, and the Gospel narratives may have been deliberately 'doctored' for ulterior motives. In other words, was it the man, or those around him and who came in his wake, that produced the results?

If the events which colour the final chapters in the Gospels are purely circumstantial and accurately reported, they are phenomenal in their sheer weight of coincidence. The entire episode of Jesus' journey to Jerusalem and its aftermath is so shot with familiar colours that, were it true, it would be miraculous for that reason alone.

An obvious concomitance lies in the timing of events. Suddenly, in the spring month of Nisan, Jesus elected to travel halfway across the country to Jerusalem on what, according to the Gospel accounts, he knew to be a suicidal mission. Why Nisan? Why did the trip coincide exactly with the age-old anniversary of the death of the sacred king?

Taking the chronicle of events in Jerusalem during the Passover period, the Luke account of what took place immediately prior to crucifixion is sketchy and can be put to one side. Matthew and Mark, however, agree moderately well, and although John is based on other literary sources and contains differing details, all three concur over some interesting points.

The Franciscan friars introduced the 'Seven Stations of the Cross' to fifteenth-century Europe.[19] It is thought that they copied a custom which had come from Jerusalem, based on incidents alleged to have taken place between sentencing and execution. Although the John account lists some items which differ from those noted by Matthew and Mark, all finish up with seven. Matthew and Mark include: scourging; delivery for crucifixion; stripping and clothing in robe, crown and reed sceptre; spitting and beating; removal of the robe; Simon bearing the cross; and the giving of myrrh and vinegar. The John list adds presentation to the people and demands for Jesus' explanation, but omits removal of the robe and mention of Simon. Traditional explanation has it that seven had become a universal and well-established mystical number and therefore not unusual. True, but it should be remembered from where the number had come!

According to Mesopotamian legend of Inana's Descent, when the goddess of life descended to the underworld to confront evil with good, the seven doors of the stations on her journey were bolted, to be opened one by one.[20] Beyond each the goddess was to be subjugated and stripped of the seven emblems of power, and on passing the seventh gate the judges of the underworld pronounced her fate. The goddess, it should be remembered, was seated naked on a throne in bizarre parody of power. That small detail draws inescapable comparisons with the incident in which Jesus is reported to have been dressed in mock emblems of kingship. Strong parallels are also to be found in Babylonian records which describe commoners being substituted for the king, being given all the rights of royalty, access to concubines, finery, lavish food and drink, only to suffer eventual execution. Roman soldiers were not averse to dressing up victims either, but this particular incident seems an improbable subtlety on the part of conscripts, and none of the disciples are likely to have witnessed it. Why therefore, do all three Gospels make a point of narrating it?

The choice of crucifixion as an instrument of death is another curiosity. Outside of orthodox and apocryphal Christian references, there are only two known comments on the death of Jesus. The Roman historian Tacitus, discussing Christian persecution in the reign of Nero, notes: 'Christus, the founder of the name [Christians], had undergone the death penalty in the reign of

Tiberius, by sentence of the procurator Pontius Pilate . . .' The second is contained in Josephus' *Antiquities of the Jews*, a passing reference that: 'Pilate, having heard him accused by men of the highest standing among us . . . condemned him to be crucified.'

The Jews were not allowed officially to implement their own death penalties.[21] They therefore required the Romans to carry out appropriate punishment for what was perceived as blasphemy against Judaism. The accepted way of disposing of such offenders under Judaic law was by stoning, yet this option is never mentioned and whilst the demand for death came from the high priest, the specific call for crucifixion came from within the crowd. If the people wanted a spectacle, and the narratives imply as much, crucifixion was a poor choice.

The Acts describe crucifixion, more accurately, as hanging.[22] The shape of structure familiar in crucifixes of today may not, incidentally, reflect the actual historical object of execution. There is a considerable body of opinion among Christian historians that the 'crucifix' may have been a simple upright stake. The design of the Cross varies between the Greek and Celtic $+$, the Latin $+$, the Egyptian $\top$, and various other permutations which are now accepted to represent arms stretching out to the four corners of the world. It is perhaps more symbolic than structurally accurate. The procedure involved suspending the victim on a wooden frame with nails driven through the wrists and ankles. Unless the person was very weak there was no rapid outcome, and the condemned hung for hours and frequently days until they died from pain, exposure and exhaustion. In fact, to liven things up, Nero took to the practice of setting fire to crucified victims to provide illumination for his soirées.

In near-eastern tradition the goddess of life, and by implication her consort, died hanging from a hook or nail. It was part of the legendary and tapestried foundation upon which the sacred kings abased themselves in the month of Nisan, some suffering humiliation, some symbolically dying, and being reborn.

A final coincidence emerges. The resurrection of the Christ is alleged to have taken place on the morning of the third day after crucifixion. The description of the legendary Mesopotamian resurrection is also very specific. On the third day the Galla sprinkled the corpse with the water and food of life, and restored the goddess to her immortality.

It is difficult for an objective watcher to take these things as mere coincidence and therefore, profound as the alternatives may be, there are other scenarios for consideration – those of orchestration and fabrication.

One of the key points is whether the aspirations of Jesus, and the objectives of the people who surrounded him and whose successors were responsible for narrating his biography, were one and the same. The conservative view holds that the two are inseparable, yet there is virtually nothing which Jesus is said to have done or uttered that would have directed his followers to form a radical sect within Judaism, or which would have caused the Christian 'explosion'.

The eminent theologian Robert Morgan has commented that: 'The phenomenon of Christianity necessarily demands more than a liberal protestant Jesus to explain it.'[23] This might raise a third question, whether Jesus' work and ambitions were even relevant to his death.[24] Beyond reasonable doubt his disciples formed a non-political group which claimed him as the Messiah, but did any of his arguments or behaviour bear more than a circumstantial link with his crucifixion? Did he, as an innocent victim, become drawn into a more devious ploy than the narratives of the New Testament would have us believe?

The biblical explanation of Jesus' death is the most irrational part of the whole biography. Simply, it does not hold water. The suggestion of a death conspiracy by people close to him is not idle supposition. The Matthew and Mark narratives concur that a plot against his life was hatched as early as the occasion when he cured the man with the withered hand (Matthew 12.14, Mark 3.6). But by whom and why? The narratives are deceptive in that they offer the Pharisees as scapegoats: Matthew 12.14, 'Then the Pharisees went out, and held a council against him, how they might destroy him.'

Unless Jesus' followers had a fifth column operating deep inside Pharisaic circles, they could not have been party to a secret conspiracy of the kind described. It is more likely that the plot was hatched closer to home. All the Gospels agree that when Jesus arrived in Jerusalem he was betrayed to the Jewish authorities by one of his *own* followers.

Even the grounds on which Jesus was betrayed are fudged.[25] Some authors suggest Judas Iscariot provided confirmation that he had become a self-styled 'king', and whilst there is no direct evidence for this, the accusation formed a large thrust of the Roman questioning. There is no doubt that he was crucified under the title: 'King of the Jews', but did *he* see himself as a king? Matthew and John are the only Gospels to cite him as having made a specific claim to kingship, but according to all four he was reticent on the subject during his trial. He answered the Procurator's question 'Art thou the King of the Jews?' with an ambiguous response that implied more or less – you are saying it, not me. According to the John narrative, he qualified the comment by saying, 'My kingdom is not of this world', which implies again that he did not see himself in the role of an old-fashioned Sacred King. He identified himself as an apolitical, spiritual, second-in-command to his God in the world to come.

There has to exist, therefore, a possibility that another shadowy group connived at Jesus' death, but that their identity and objective was too contentious to be revealed.

It is worth disposing of any Roman interest in executing him. A Roman sentenced him and Roman soldiers carried out the edict, but it is a naïve belief that the Romans were truly responsible. A brief dip into the biography of Pontius Pilate, the Roman procurator who signed the death warrant, reveals that he was regarded as a highly suspect official by his own people in Rome. Shortly after the crucifixion of Jesus he was sent home in disgrace, but at the time he was clearly anxious to be all things to all men and to avoid anything which would draw further attention to his own ineptitude.

Roman law provided the death penalty for a variety of crimes, yet nothing in what Jesus is reported to have said or done would have constituted a capital offence. The penalty of crucifixion was reserved for non-Roman citizens found guilty of insurrection against the state.[26] It has been argued that Jesus must have attracted sufficient backing to be capable of mounting a rebellion, but again there is not a shred of evidence to support this. The man professed no aspirations to political or military leadership, nor did his followers, and at no time did he advocate rebellion against the Roman presence in Palestine. The only reasonable conclusion must be that the *Jewish* authorities passed on spurious information at the time of his trial which led the Pilate to consider crucifixion.

Miracle workers tended to attract crowds and a degree of excitement which might be construed as a threat to public order, but at worst this would have merited a public flogging and a prison sentence. Prophets were occasionally disposed of if the authorities sensed a stirring of dreams that threatened revolt, but insurrection was hardly a part of Jesus' message. If he ever claimed to be a Messiah, which is doubtful, it might just have

stimulated a reaction.[27] Had the Romans perceived in him any
serious threat to law and order they would have jumped on him
very rapidly, yet they sat back and waited for several days after
he entered Jerusalem. Inexplicably, he was left free to come and
go, and none of his disciples was touched. In fact, all the Gospel
narratives concur that the Roman authorities were mystified why
Jesus had been brought before them. The procurator summed
up the attitude of the ruling authority saying: 'What evil has he
done?'

Jesus was executed, to all intent and purpose, by Jews. His
violent and bloody end stained his fellow countrymen's hands,
not those of Romans. Jesus and the Jewish religious hierarchy
did not see eye-to-eye. He found them out of touch with ordinary
people, and hidebound by convention. From their point of view
he was preaching abrogation of the law and was proposing the
unthinkable, a restored Israel in which the existing *social* order
would be turned on its head; he was promoting doctrines which
in some respects threatened the institution of the priesthood. His
last act before being charged was to cause a near-riot in the temple
and to prophesy its destruction thus, it is implied, paving the way
for his new kingdom.

Some authors have suggested that Jesus preached of a new
kingdom which would open its arms to the gentile world.[28]
There is, however, nothing concrete in his quoted utterances to
suggest that he had any more than a passing interest in gentiles.
He had dealings with very few of them, and incidents like that in
Matthew 15 would seem to clarify where Jesus' sentiments lay.
He was reluctant to help a gentile Canaanite woman, claiming
that he was sent only to the lost sheep of the House of Israel and
commenting: 'It is not meet to take the children's bread, and
cast it to dogs.' This quoted utterance seems less likely to be
a case of literary tampering than such blandly universalist statements as in Matthew 24: 'And this gospel of the kingdom shall
be preached in all the world . . .'

It would seem therefore, that Jesus was not advocating a
dilution of Jewish religious integrity, a stance which could reasonably have inflamed the passions of the establishment. That was
to come later with the mission of Paul.[29] In fact, none of these
things offered the Jews any more convincing reason for wanting
him executed than the Romans. He was a local but fairly harmless
rabble-rouser from a distant province – less a serious threat than
an eccentric itch in the shirts of the establishment. The strangest
anomaly is that the one charge which could have been brought

legitimately, that of threats against the establishment, evaporated. The charges were dropped. Inexplicably, witnesses who testified against his activities 'could not agree', or 'were false'. The priests' main indictment seems to have been one of blasphemy, though it is difficult to see how that charge was levelled.

The entire reporting of the interrogation by the chief priests and elders has to be taken very cautiously. It took place in the middle of the night first (according to the John account) at the private house of Annas, and continuing at the high priest Caiaphas' palace. John was a member of the high priest's household, but in his gospel narrative any detail of the session before Caiaphas goes unreported, and although some members of the Sanhedrin may have become Christian converts, it seems improbable that any disciples or subsequent narrators were present at either inquisition.

Even if the principal charge that Jesus identified himself as the Christ the son of God is accurate, however, neither term is actually a blasphemy.[30] Separately or together they fall short of being a claim to divinity. There are in fact only two instances, both doubtful historically, when Jesus seems to have accepted the title of Christ or Messiah. In Mark 8, a claim was put indirectly on his behalf by Peter, and in Mark 14 the claim was allegedly made during the interrogation by the priests. Several other would-be Messiahs though, had not been executed and all Israelites believed themselves 'children of God'. Even in the Mark text the claim goes no further than that the Christ will sit with God after his death. That could have been interpreted as impertinent presumption, but hardly blasphemy. Yet, by morning, Jesus' Jewish jury had agreed on the death penalty and bundled him off to Pilate. Anxious, it must be assumed, to keep the peace during the period of a sensitive festival, Pilate acceded to the demands of the high priest that 'one man should die for the people', and what is reported as an almost fanatical desire for his crucifixion from among his peers.

What does all this mean? The short answer is that we do not know; we can only speculate. What it seems to be adding up to though, is that Jesus, the man, was a figure whose work and behaviour in all the respects which have been reported did not warrant the results of his visit to Jerusalem. There was no obvious causal link between Jesus' behaviour or teaching and his death. On the other hand, the nature of his death and the miraculous events which were subsequently reported undoubtedly triggered

the spread of a movement which came to recognize him as the
Christ, the sacred Messianic king.

Jesus talked continually about the kingdom and quite clearly
his disciples believed he would return in the restored world in
some position of authority.[31] The makings of the Sacred King
were thus already in place within the framework of a broad
Jewish belief. The question is did Jesus know, at any time short
of the final day of his life, that his premature and violent death
was inevitable, and if so did he see himself as a martyr resolving
his work, or did he place himself within the traditions of the
old-fashioned sacred kingship?

Some Christian authors, including Albert Schweitzer, have
suggested that Jesus did plot his own death to bring on the
apocalypse.[32] He could equally have martyred himself with
thoughts of an older faith: allegedly he predicted death and
resurrection in three days following the lines of the ancient
fertility traditions. It seems very doubtful though, that had he
been aware of the possible inferences he would have condoned
them. The Akitu festival of atonement possessed many elements
which would surely have struck a personal chord with him, but
the political infrastructure of the old-style kingship would have
been anathema. There is also a demonstrable lack of calculation
about Jesus' style which points to innocence.

If anything, and discounting the predictions of his own demise,
Jesus himself probably went to Jerusalem with the idea of working to promote his message rather than dying for it. A conspiracy
which he was not party to, or at least not in the way it was
intended, to have him slaughtered in a very public manner in the
Nisan month, seems likely. He was lured into making the journey
to Jerusalem where, because of his implacable loathing of temple
hierarchy and practice, there was a calculated likelihood that he
would pre-empt some kind of incident and in doing so seal his
fate. In fact, he rose to the occasion with considerable vigour.

Much has been made of the combined effects of Jesus' violent
behaviour and prophecy of doom in the sacred precincts of the
temple, and it may well be true that his actions inflamed large
numbers of people who, whilst they had little sympathy for the
administration, still regarded the temple as the most sacred house
in Israel.

The significant point is that the potential outcome, starting
with the goading of the chief priests who acted as the essential
intermediaries between the Jewish population and the Roman
authorities in matters of discipline, must have been clear to a

number of people within Jesus' immediate circle. His ministry would have been recognized by all the disciples as a key step in the restoration process, but from there it would have needed only a small mental jump to reach the conclusion that his death would generate infinitely greater effect.

The resurrection, above and beyond any other single phenomenon associated with Jesus, was the key to the huge success of the Christian Movement, but there are more inconsistencies to be reckoned with. The confession of the Nicene Creed affirms that Jesus Christ, 'Was crucified, dead, and buried, He descended into hell; The third day he rose again from the dead, He ascended into heaven . . .' Those who make this observation may take it for granted, yet exactly how and in what form the Christ arose constituted the crux of one of the great cankers that plagued the early years of the Movement.

Matthew makes no reference to any appearance by the resurrected Christ. Mark notes that he appeared first to Mary Magdalene, though no detail is given about this apparition, and then was seen by two unnamed disciples.[33] The point of interest lies in the kind of apparition which Mark described as being 'in another form'. This clearly implies that the visitation was ghostly and not of normal human dimensions. It is the Luke account, predictably, which provides the graphic account and in doing so offers the really 'explosive' material, for Luke describes not an apparition, a ghost, but the resurrection of the actual body. Luke alone, among the synoptic gospels, offers the concept of the Osirian bodily restoration, which the Christian movement took on board as one of the bastions of its faith. As if anxious to prove credibility, the Luke writer provides minute detail:

> Behold my hands and my feet . . . handle me and
> see; for a spirit hath not flesh and bones, as ye see me
> have.
> And when he had thus spoken, he shewed them his
> hands and his feet.
> And they gave him a piece of a broiled fish and of
> an honeycomb.
> And he took it, and did eat before them.[34]

Paul was a staunch supporter of the literal view of bodily resurrection. Towards the close of his first letter to the Christian community at Corinth, he devoted much space to emphasizing the significance of the resurrection, but he was careful to qualify the interpretation of the term 'bodily'. In his own words: 'There is a natural body and there is a spiritual body.' Later in the same letter: '. . . flesh and blood cannot inherit the kingdom of God . . . behold, I shew you a mystery; we shall not all sleep, but we shall all be changed.' There are also interesting contradictions about the nature of Paul's own experience of the resurrected Christ. The narrative account of his conversion in Acts 9 states that he saw a light and heard a voice, and that those with him also heard a voice. Yet in the 'first-hand' account related in Acts 22, those accompanying him 'heard not the voice of him that spake . . .'

The John account raises pithy issues of a different kind. Mary Magdalene was the first witness, yet she, like the disciples in the Matthew version did not recognize Jesus – she assumed that the figure was that of a gardener – nor was she allowed bodily contact. The enigmatic verse includes the comment: 'Touch me not; for I am not yet ascended to my Father.'[35] Yet shortly after this event, the Christ encouraged Thomas, the sceptic, to do the reverse: 'Then saith he to Thomas, reach hither thy finger, and behold my hands; and reach hither thy hand, and thrust it into my side.' The implication, and it takes on increasing importance, is that Mary, being a woman, even though accepted into the band of apostles, was not allowed direct contact with the risen Christ, but that the male disciples were so privileged. Here was good Jewish propaganda, male élitism rearing its head, a principle which later was to have a substantial bearing on the make-up of the Christian hierarchy.

We come back to John Allegro's ill-starred proposal, the questions over which Christian scholars are coy and which Allegro gallantly believed he had answered.[36] Was the Christian Movement, in its original mould, a vehicle for a religion of radical newness – that which has been described as the most successful Jewish heresy – or was it based on those ancient creeds suitably reformed to meet the changed needs of the Jews? Were the converts of the first century reaching for the same timeless clouds of glory and bowing to the same indestructible altars? Is that the reality of the Christian faith today?

That there was a conspiracy to kill Jesus is beyond argument, though when it started and between whom is an open question. Is the 'official' biblical inference of a priestly plot in which Judas Iscariot was a greed-driven pawn sufficiently realistic, or was there an unpublicized and more profound design at large, perhaps generated much closer to home?[37] It is worth realizing that we do not even know for certain the names of all the disciples or how many there were. Twelve is more of a symbolic number reflecting the tribes destined to be restored in the new kingdom than a firm tally.

One ingredient alone does not make a plot to turn Jesus Christ into an old-style Sacred King, but add them all together – the spring setting, the seven stations of the route to death, the choice of crucifixion, the three-day interval between execution and restoration – and biblical credibility becomes harder to swallow. The parallels are far from absolute proof that the writers embellished the account of Jesus' last days, nor that any aspects of his death were orchestrated, but they cannot be ignored. As it stands, the biblical story contains elements which can only be accepted through faith, not through an intelligent and rational view of history.

A problem with this kind of speculation is that, unless Jesus emerges bathed in uniqueness and spiritual eminence, it falls foul of those who espouse the Christian faith and tradition. Yet very recently, an eminent theologian, E.P. Sanders, Dean Ireland Professor of Exegesis at Oxford, asserted that not a single one of the things known about Jesus is unique; that his teachings, his visions of death and judgement, his miraculous healings, his championing of the poor and oppressed, all had their precedents within the history of Judaism.[38] Sanders also agreed with a statement by John Knox that critical history will not produce a figure of sufficient moral greatness to satisfy those who have felt their lives to be ennobled and uplifted by him.[39]

The assertions take on a fresh dimension when one steps beyond the historical parameter of Judaism and establishes that the story of Jesus' death and resurrection is not unique. It is to be found, with idiosyncracies, in the sagas of the Mesopotamian Dumuzi, of the Canaanite Baal, and of the Egyptian Osiris.

It is tempting to think that there is a uniqueness about the scenario in the effect it created, and yet this claim would be doubtful. Christianity has, thus far, survived a far smaller time span than many of its predecessors and, as will be seen, its spread was determined less by spiritual than political forces.

What seems beyond dispute is that the Christian Movement promoted Christ as something distinct from that which he claimed during his lifetime as Jesus the Nazarene. The disciples claimed him to be a divinity, the revelation of the living God who had been resurrected from the grave, and they believed emphatically that he was a king who would take his throne in the

new Jerusalem, and who would judge all souls. They placed
on him, in other words, an amalgam of the pretensions laid
upon the sacred kings of western Asia, and mortuary god of
Egypt.

If there were indeed radical elements who found in Jesus
a vehicle for the dying and rising god to take his place in
a new kind of Judaism, then the historical accuracy of the
Gospels becomes secondary to the way in which the writers
chose to elaborate the truth. It would have been impossible for
any Christian pen to come clean over such a plan. The Romans
would have perceived a major potential threat to security and
would have taken steps to wipe it out. One suspects, though,
that the Jewish priesthood was aware of the intention. They
must have found themselves in the worst catch-22. If they
allowed Jesus to continue his work, they risked a growing loss
of allegiance to what they saw as the necessity to prepare for
restoration through repentance and stricter adherence to the law.
If they killed him, they played into the hands of the conspirators.
It was that dilemma which brought the Jewish authorities, not
the Romans, to instigate an onslaught against the members of
the Movement.

A conundrum for which no Christian author has yet provided
a rational answer is that of the before-and-after response by Jewish rank and file. We have been provided with vividly depicted
accounts of 'multitudes' of people eagerly following Jesus through
Galilee. What happened to them? Where did they go? Why did
they not produce a groundswell of backing for the infant Christian Movement? Here was a man dedicated to the problems of the
hard-pressed Jewish masses, and yet Christianity failed utterly
with his own people. One possibility must be that they hoped
indeed for a sacred king who, as in days of old, would bring
new life to the promised land. Jesus offered them a message of
hope. His death and resurrection at Nisan raised their expectations still further. But nothing happened. New life was not
restored to the promised land. Liberty never marched for them.
Events disproved the promise.

The irony is that the dying and rising god appealed to the
more sophisticated Europeans with a message quite foreign to
that of old western Asia. They saw in Jesus' death and bodily
assumption the promise, not of a restored kingdom, but of a
renewal of personal existence in eternity. For as long as the cycle
of nature remained paramount in the lives of ordinary people,
the god-king met his annual death to restore cattle and grain. As

society progressed to a new level of chic in which dependence
on nature receded a little, the king died to purge the world of its
ills and he became the gateway of souls into the world beyond
death.

The story of Jesus also provides an immediacy and warmth
which are lacking in the old traditions of Mesopotamia and
Egypt. His personality was developed by the Gospel writers in very
human terms. Here was a man whose existence was not shrouded
in the mists of time, but whose experience people could recognize
as something which had taken place within the span of recorded
history. Both he and his so-called pagan counterparts were cast as
shepherds of flocks; both were attributed with royal parentage on
the one hand, divinity on the other; both died in their freshness
of youth and in the spring of the year. Jesus Christ was part of a
uniquely Jewish situation and his part in the drama was amended
accordingly, but in other respects his story is essentially a familiar
one.

Thus far the case has rested on evidence contained within
the orthodox books of the Testaments; evidence which must, if
viewed dispassionately, raise considerable doubt in the mind of
anyone whose reasoning is not dictated by arguments of pure
blind faith and by the infallibility of the documents which now
make up the official scriptures. Knowing whether the Gospels
relate precisely what took place before the chief priests, and in
the confrontation with the Roman procurator – questions which
Christian scholars have laboured over but now concede increasingly to be impossible – is pointless. Answers lie in the timing of
events, the method, and a myriad of other fine details.

Were it not for the curious hand of fate, the slim works of
the New Testament and apocryphal and pseudepigraphical books
might be all that we have to go on. The reasons for the paucity
of material are a great fascination in themselves. They stem from
human traits which Jesus the man could hardly have approved
– persecution, bigotry, self-seeking, jealousy. Yet these criticisms
cannot by and large be laid at pagan doors. They were marks of
Cain that scarred Christian pioneers.

Christianity began as a phenomenon intended to stand ready
for the new Israel and to open its arms to universal membership,
but the first shades of holocaust were rising over the horizon.
Jesus envisaged the end of the world within immediate lifetimes
followed by a restored kingdom. In a sense the first holocaust
came to Israel, but the new Jerusalem did not rise. Christianity put
down its first solid roots far away from the world of the ancient

near east, and the cathartic years which led to the establishment
of a Catholic Church, centred in Europe yet spreading its net into
western Asia and North Africa, reveal an infinitely complex and
devious story, barely hinted at in the orthodox Bible which my
grandmother guarded so closely.

12

Aftermath

The essential personality thus far denied an appearance in the Christian drama is the mother goddess. If the official scriptures are any measure, for the first two hundred years of Christendom she must have retired from view, yet her extraordinary rise to eminence, under another guise, which took place subsequently suggests an altogether different scenario. It implies a dominant personality hovering in the wings whose stardom for many of the faithful came to eclipse that of Jesus Christ. Before looking into the nickelodeon tale of the intricate and highly paradoxical re-packaging of the goddess though, the immediate behaviour of the Christian Movement as well as the context, mood and circumstances need to be explored.

The five hundred years which followed the death of Jesus represent the most confusing and convoluted part of this journey. In many senses the thread passes through a period as misty and imprecise as any from pre-history, not because the written word had, at the time, still to be achieved but because it was subject to a level of abuse and manipulation, ironically for objectives which were remarkably lacking in good Christian ethics.

The first question to resolve is whether the Movement was united in dogma, or whether there is evidence of separate elements each manoeuvring to win the doctrinal battle. We look around Christendom today and believe that its dissenting factions are a comparatively modern plague. We assume that the early Church was united in its belief and purpose. Not so. In fact during its first two hundred years the hierarchy was ridden with more rampant dissent and disagreement than at any time in its subsequent passage.

The complex relationship between Christianity and the world in which it grew, and the tortuous wranglings and internal struggles of the Movement itself all help to cloud the waters. Christian belief continued to be affected by established Greek, Roman and Egyptian philosophies which provided attractive, well-rounded arguments about origins, *raisons d'être* and destinies. Its fate was also subject to the constantly vacillating attitudes of imperial government. From within, its charter emerged as a compromise between factions which were indeed deeply divided on fundamentals of dogma and canon, yet each professing, with passionate conviction, to be following the true and only acceptable path. All these turbulent streams flowed into and jostled with one another before they settled as the defined, but decidedly muddy, river, which was the Christian establishment, the catholic and apostolic Church.

The fact that the Movement found itself so uncertain about policy and direction adds support to the suspicion that the aims of Jesus Christ and those of the Jews who founded the Christian Movement were, at least in some important respects, at odds.[1] A radical weakness with which the Movement found itself saddled was lack of clear mandate as to how it should proceed. At least, that is the way it seems now, although there has to be a cautionary note – no precise constitution has survived. If such a thing existed, it has been conveniently lost. The likelihood remains that Jesus the Nazarene did not, in his lifetime, envisage founding a society, and this lack of apparent pragmatism continually reinforces the argument that he was an innocent in the hands of schemers who were bent on creating a particular style of Jewish restoration movement that had little in common with the aims of the man.

The Sermon on the Mount, though sometimes imagined to be so, did not amount to a constitution. It was an exhortation to adopt Jesus' new social charter, poignantly relevant to a downtrodden nation and to a depressed minority living in northern Palestine in the province of Galilee. Only in the most casual way did Jesus address himself to the practical and political dilemmas which would face his legatees. His message and his personal expectation were clear, but what of his nature – divine or mortal? What was his filial relationship with God, the identity of his parentage, the mechanism for selecting his successors, the canon under which his followers would continue?

The Greek Christian historian Eusebius, when quantifying the Christ, referred constantly to Old Testament prophecies and to ambiguous utterances cited in the Gospels.[2] He was typical in his loss to define intent in any other way. Such questions bedevilled Christianity. But the problems went much deeper and Jesus became the subject of a battle royal between factions that were poles apart in ideology, yet each of whom wanted to set him as a figurehead to promote their cause and faith. In other words everyone was keen to mould Jesus' image so that it best reflected their personal views and predilections. As Albert Schweitzer puts it: 'The historical investigation of the life of Jesus did not take its rise from a purely historical interest; it turned to the Jesus of history as an ally in the struggle against the tyranny of dogma . . . It was not only each epoch that found its reflection in Jesus; each individual created him in accordance with its own true character'.[3]

Several factors influenced the outcome and decided which faction would eventually win the day and become the official spokesman.[4] Christianity reached its critical moments of crystallization in an area of the world where not only social and political conditions but also human aspirations had changed. Some of the architects suffered the disillusionment of seeing a torch which had been held up to light the way of Jews, attracting instead the moths of the gentile world. Followers lived in a very different 'ball park' to that of northern Palestine with its arid landscape and abject poverty. Many were affluent citizens, frequently members of government and their families, and for particularly convoluted social reasons, we know also that the Movement proved attractive to women – a turn for which some of its male activists were less than prepared.

It was the power play between factions whose views on fundamental principles were heavily at odds, that generated much of the discord which marked the first centuries of Christendom. Unfortunately the passionate argument was subject to strong disapproval and, eventually, censorship on a scale which raises the most disturbing questions about the credibility of the Christian faith as it thunders from its pulpits as the irrefutable and absolute word of God.

To begin with, there was probably a euphoric common purpose amongst the first Christians, those who had known Jesus intimately or who were invited to join the small and select band. They were too busy picking up the pieces and expending energy in the pioneering fervour of their vocation to worry about disagreeing with each other over doctrinal matters. Their mission to reveal to the world the shattering revelation which they alone felt they had witnessed was enough.

History confirms an important point though. Once the euphoria had worn off, the Christians expended more energy in-fighting and fending off their fellow Jews, than combating Roman persecution. On the death of their leader in Jerusalem, the first disciples, supposedly seventy of them, led by the original twelve apostles (less one admitted traitor who was replaced by Matthias) anticipated an immediate attack against themselves, but they anticipated it coming from amongst their own people. They were looking over their shoulders towards a Jewish purge.

Romans regarded the Christians merely as another odd-ball club in an already sect-ridden society, strengthening the view that any rumours about Jesus being heralded as a king were not taken seriously, at least by Rome. Roman persecution of Jews tends to have been far harsher, although it was recorded by Jewish historians who perhaps over-emphasized the treatment received at the hands of empire.[5] In times when they behaved in civilized fashion though, Roman rule had by and large given the Jews an untroubled ride. Rome was more than capable of dealing out extremely vicious punishment, but only when necessary to curb insurrections against empire. The Jews came in for more retribution than other annexed nations because they were constantly inciting rebellion. They were, in Rome's eyes, the most notoriously ill-behaved rabble in the empire, largely through the obsessive guerrilla tactics of the Zealots.

Insurrection was nonetheless a crime of which the Christians had not thus far been accused. It was, ironically, the provincial Roman government that tended to play referee and to haul offended Jews off the backs of the Christians. The authorities in Rome viewed the sect as being secretive, which undoubtedly it was; as practising perversions including incest and other kinds of nameless immorality – which some of its members may well have been doing – but as being essentially harmless.

Arguments are still presented that Christianity made a strong and early impact on the Jewish people, but they have no factual foundation. In the main, orthodox Jews rejected Christianity with the same repugnance as they extended to gentile traditions, and the supreme irony remains that, whatever the message of the Movement, it succeeded with the gentile world, not with Jewry. The apostles and disciples, however, still saw themselves not as a separate faction but very much as a Jewish group, and in many respects they were quite orthodox citizens. They subscribed closely to Jewish habits and customs: they circumcized their male infants, and refused to eat pork and any other meat which had been put to sacrifice.

Generally they observed the Pentateuchal teachings and codes, but for whatever reasons, these founding fathers were considered to be out-of-step. The Jewish priesthood referred stubbornly to the followers of the Movement as 'Nazarenes', a title which effectively distanced any link with the Messianic prophecies.[6] It was left to the generosity of the pagan population to introduce the identity tag 'Christian'. When Jerusalem fell, Christianity became a gentile or non-Jewish phenomenon wholly emancipated from its Jewish roots. Any Jews who persisted as Christians experienced a rough ride at the hands of their compatriots and in about 85 AD they were formally excommunicated from all involvement in the synagogues. The fateful condemnation read: 'May the Nazarenes and the heretics be suddenly destroyed and removed from the Book of Life.'

Jewish Jerusalem was, nonetheless, the first headquarters of the Movement and in the very early years its influence spread out into the surrounding countryside of Judaea, slowly encroaching northwards into Syria and Cilicia. Judaism, as it had existed for two thousand years, was doomed though.[7] In 66 AD, a new procurator of Judaea, Gessius Florus, slaughtered three thousand Jews as an object lesson in toeing the imperial line. Not surprisingly the frustrated and embittered Judaeans rose up once more. The revolt was quelled after a war of bloody attrition which ended when Titus laid siege to Jerusalem for seven long months in 70 AD. The holy city was literally pounded to pieces stone by stone, and within seventy years even its name had been wiped from the map. Jews were barred from Judaea. In this respect the end of the Israelite world really had come to pass.

Forewarned, the Jewish Christian community in Jerusalem had prudently gathered its possessions and taken off to the north where it settled for a while in comparative safety. New stepping-off points for missionary activity were established at Antioch in Asia Minor and later at Alexandria in North Africa. Slowly but surely though, the Christians were focusing their main ambitions on Rome. There lay the centre of the world's orbit and

Romans needed persuading of the superiority of the Word. Rome was the catalyst; she had become the new Babylon, and it was to Rome that infant Christianity, in the formidable shape of Peter, took itself.

Rome, on the whole, treated Christians with considerable tolerance. Occasional violent persecutions and lesser difficulties stemmed from government, depending upon the predilections of the emperor, but these were the exception. Christianity could hardly be frowned upon since a great deal that was in its book was borrowed from authorities whom Rome saw no reason to censure and in fact heartily endorsed. The first real external problems came in the unwelcome form of Nero, who abused the Christians by marking them as scapegoats to accept blame for the great fire of Rome in 64 AD for which, it was rumoured, he had quietly struck the match.[8] Nero's summary execution of both Peter and Paul marked the first occasion on which the death penalty was extended to confessed Christians. It set as important a precedent as Stephen's martyrdom had at the hands of fellow Jews.

The next decidedly difficult period for Christianity came towards the end of the first century under the emperor Domitian.[9] He was a firm believer in his own divinity, styled himself 'Master and God', and expected proper veneration from all his subjects regardless of religious persuasion. Knowing that the Jews and Christians were likely to sidestep this imposition, he applied a new tax on the Jewish community with instructions that Jews were to be hunted down and, if necessary, to be inspected physically for signs of their faith. This edict was far from popular either with Jews or Christians because many Christians bore personal evidence marks of being ex-Jews. They had the stark alternative of professing Judaism and paying up, or admitting Christianity and being dragged off to the arena.

The crisis was short-lived. Though Christianity was by now an established capital offence, Domitian's successor, Trajan, found its followers fairly harmless. An awkward technicality now existed on the statute books but by a formality of swearing loyalty to the gods of Rome, or to the emperor's genius, anyone could 'get off the hook'. Only if Christians repeatedly refused this simple patriotic test were they thrown to the bears in the arena or otherwise despatched. Trajan issued a much-quoted instruction advising that: 'The Christians are not to be hunted down . . .'

Nonetheless, persecution was a yoke which the Christians

saw particularly as their own, and many observers, both contemporary and modern, would argue that it was more the threat
of persecution that sustained the Movement as a coherent and
tight structure, than the strength of its ideals. Martyrdom became
a rallying point. Many fanatical Christians saw death in profession
of their faith as a guarantee of Paradise and as the ultimate expression of solidarity.

Thus whilst the popular view may have it that early Christians
were united to the man, and suffered constant and unspeakable
miseries at the hand of Rome, the reality is that the Christians
were primarily persecuted by fellow Jews and by each other.
Most of Christianity's problems came from within itself. Given
that the Movement was riddled with factions, some promoting
traditions and ideologies quite distinct from that which is now
considered to be 'true', the sources we work from take on considerable significance. Whoever was most vociferous and most
persuasive was destined to win the day, but did not necessarily
speak for all, or even the majority. The biggest problem is that
the trustees of Jesus Christ, his devoted court, a group of men
amongst whom some were literate, who should have committed
some evidence of their inheritance to posterity, seem to have left
almost nothing on record. The explanation we are offered is that
they anticipated the end of the world and therefore saw no point
in writing a biographical account.

James, the so-called brother of Jesus, became leader of the
Jerusalem Church where he stayed despite growing antagonism
from the local Jewish community until the Judaean administra-
tor, Agrippa I, instigated persecution of Jewish Christians. It was
a conciliatory move to keep the mainstream population happy. He
executed James in 62 AD either by beheading or by having him
thrown from a parapet and clubbed.[10] The record is ambiguous.
But James died with little more than romantic legend to support
the record of his existence. We have fragments purporting to be
part of a letter written by him to an unknown recipient and
containing certain secret instructions, but no more. The so-called
Epistle of James is highly suspect as an authentic document. Peter,
to whom most Christians attribute supreme authority handed
down from Jesus, went to Rome. We believe he was there in
the sixties and died at the hands of Nero, though what he did
or how long he stayed is a mystery. Odd notes are attributed
to him, but he too left nothing tangible. The Epistle in the New
Testament was written by an unknown hand. John, the son of
Zebedee, is said to have settled in Ephesus, the city of Asia Minor

in which the great mother goddess Artemis reigned. According to Ephesian tradition, the Virgin Mary went there and lived under the same roof. In his dotage, John gathered a group of devotees who later allegedly put pen to paper and recorded, in memoriam, his apocalyptic visions. We also have passing mention that Philip the Evangelist first worked in Syria then moved to Phrygia, the home of the goddess Kybele.

Aside from Philip, the chosen trio that accompanied Christ to the mountain to witness his transfiguration and to receive, according to the Testament, secret instructions, are the only members of the group of twelve who are detailed beyond being names on a page. The vital message of Jesus Christ seems to have passed down the decades following his death through a risky oral tradition, which seems, at the very least, odd. The suggestion that the Christians did not bother to write because they anticipated the end of the world is a tenuous one not born out by other crises in history.

Disturbingly, it was the élite but well-nigh anonymous group of apostles that possessed so many keys. They held the immediate message of Christ but, of greater significance, some of them were perhaps members of the circle which organized and orchestrated the Christian Movement. There has to be the likelihood that these men and the enigmatic, curiously maligned, Mary Magdalene who joined them, these trusted inheritors of the faith, wrote down their thoughts, their beliefs, their intentions, but that these documents, which by all logic should have been treasured and protected to the ends of the earth, were for some reason destroyed.

The apostles remain enigmatic, but not only in the lack of personal writing. What we know of them is contained all too briefly in the opening paragraphs of Acts and, as an objective study, Acts is not to be trusted. The main biblical brochure of the Movement, Acts was written later than the Pauline letters. It is attributed to Luke, Paul's personal physician but the authorship is doubtful.

There exists a vital key to understanding Acts and to placing it in proper perspective. That key rests in the first lines: 'The former treatise have I made, O Theophilus, of all that Jesus began both to do and teach.' As in the opening to the Luke gospel, Acts is not an open commentary – it is addressed to an individual, though the name may have been a pseudonym since it means 'lover of god'. We have no clue to his identity but we can make an educated guess. In the opening to Luke, he is addressed as 'most excellent Theophilus', and elsewhere in the books of the New Testament, this particular title is given only at the level of provincial governor. Theophilus was an influential member of the ruling circle, and the writer of Acts addressed to him what is in effect a defence of the Movement and its crucified leader, a vindication of their existence within the jurisprudence of empire. Apart from the slants in some of Paul's correspondence, Acts is thus the first of the Christian apologies and it is written as such. It implies constantly: 'We are the good characters. Don't blame us. We have done nothing wrong.' To hope for a balanced document with that subjective brief is expecting too much. Acts reveals only that which the writer wishes to reveal to one whose sympathy he seeks to achieve.

Acts contains discreet, perhaps unintentional, signposts though. The first chapter confirms that which was foremost in the minds of the apostles in a question to the risen Christ: 'When they therefore were come together, they asked of him, saying, Lord, wilt thou at this time restore again the kingdom to Israel?'[11] They received the enigmatic reply: '. . . it is not for you to know the times or the seasons which the Father hath put in his own power.'

Acts makes considerable mileage out of the utterances of the minor prophet, Amos, who foresaw restoration of the kingship of David: 'In that day will I raise up the tabernacle of David that is fallen, and close up the breaches thereof; and I will raise up his ruins, and I will build it as in the days of old: that they may possess the remnant of Edom, and of all the heathen, which are called by my name, saith the Lord that doeth this.'[12] Acts cites this prophecy no less than three times. Acts leaves no doubt that the restoration of Israel in a new world was still the paramount ambition and expectation of most early Christians. Unfortunately the first hundred years of Christendom, the so-called Apostolic Age when the pioneers were disseminating the Word, has been subject to such massive censorship by the Christian group who emerged as dominant that we do not know exactly what was being preached. We have but a single slant, the ideology which eventually became the 'orthodox' party line.

More of the truth has perhaps been destroyed than retained in the narrow band of edited material which has survived – the Acts, the letters, the four canonical Gospels, and the apocryphal texts like the Gospel of James which were neither admitted nor wholly proscribed. Until very recently, the only clues to the nature of the lost libraries of Christian thought lay in the polemical writings of anti-heretical bishops who spent much of their lives in the second century AD putting pen to paper in condemnation of fellow Christians. There existed tiny fragments of proscribed works, the offering of authors who did not fall into line with these powerful members of the establishment, but nothing from which to glean meaningful information.

A breakthrough came in December 1945.[13] Near the site of an ancient monastery in Upper Egypt, a set of twelve leather-bound codices was unearthed, written on papyrus and composed in Coptic – the Egyptian language using the Greek alphabet. These books were found to be translations of older, sometimes much older, papyrus scrolls written in Greek.

The writings they contain include some of the loveliest and most sensitive of poetry. They are also amongst the most disturbing documents to emerge throughout the history of Christendom, offering a wholly new attitude to many funda-mentals of creation philosophy and to Jesus himself. These will be explored more fully in the next chapter; let it suffice here to say that they suggest we may have got it all radically wrong and that the pages of the New Testament do not, as Christians have grown up to believe, reflect the immutable word of God. They are known as the Nag Hammadi Library, erroneously tagged the 'Gnostic Gospels' because they include tracts written by followers of *gnosis*.[14] These were Christians who essentially held a common view that the world had been produced in a flawed state and that the only way to rise above its fate and to find God was through knowledge generated within oneself, as opposed to the orthodox Christian perspective that humanity needs a divine hand outside and beyond itself. The codices reveal a plethora of Christian thought, which suggests that we are looking, within the pages of the Bible, not at conscientious redaction, but at the result of stringent censorship. The gritty problem, therefore, is one of doctrinal balance and the key figure in this respect, the promoter of 'orthodox' ideology, was Paul.

It is valuable, at this juncture, to reiterate some essentials in the scenario surrounding the historical Jesus:

1. There was a plot to kill him – officially attributed to the Pharisees but one for which they seem to have lacked sufficient motive.

2. The reported events before and after Jesus' death bear disturbing, though veiled, similarity to old near-eastern traditions.

3. Nothing stemming directly from those who knew him on an intimate basis has ever appeared in the official Christian doctrine

and narrative. To these must be added the 'Pauline component':

4. There were bitter, but largely undisclosed, doctrinal differences between various factions including the founders of the Movement, the Jerusalem apostles, in western Asia, and the Pauline followers who were selling a brand of Christianity to a comparatively sophisticated *urban* audience in Europe.

5. The ideologies of all other factions were ruthlessly suppressed.

Saul of Tarsus had been a tub-thumping firebrand of orthodox Jewry from Cilicia, a hard-line Pharisee and a rampant persecutor of Christians. Conversion had come suddenly and dramatically on the road to Damascus, perhaps through a sense of remorse at his involvement in the death of Stephen. Paul's attention was focused on the gentile world for whom near-eastern Semitic yearnings would have little meaning. He used the death and resurrection, not to promote the old vision of renewal of nature, but to feed a hungry audience with the vision of life beyond death.

Paul's vision of a universal Church which included both Jews and gentiles produced immediate and well-publicized conflict.[15] Christ had said nothing about *how* non-Jews should come into the faith. Should Jewish law apply to them? What about circumcision? Should gentile Christians avoid food with idolatrous taint? The debate was cooled when Paul and Barnabas were ordered before a sitting of the Jerusalem elders, resulting in a muted victory for the universalists. But Christendom was set on the rocky way to the division between western and eastern Churches whose differences were to become a running sore in the second century. It is also to no small extent attributable to the Jerusalem victory that Paul's writing largely dominates the biblical view of the Apostolic Age up to about AD 60. Paul met his death in Rome, with Peter, sometime between AD 60 and AD 70 and is reckoned to have written the letters between AD 40 and AD 60, although differences in style make it almost beyond doubt that not all are from the same hand. Pauline or not, the dating makes them the earliest written observations of which we have reputedly authentic copy, from a Christian pen.

Paul clearly had no time for anything other than what he regarded to be the message of his mentor in heaven, adapted to make attractive listening to gentile ears. Within the scattered Jewish diaspora it was inevitable that some Jews would welcome the radical alternative offered by Christianity, but they were not Paul's main concern. Paul possessed a particular and personal evangelical vision, and Paul was a superb orator. 'Alternative doctrines' clearly existed but they did not benefit from champions with the same eloquence and persuasive capabilities. So, the rest of what at the time was equally legitimate Christian thought succumbed to a superior campaign. Paul demonstrated the best qualities of a politician on the hustings! Yet Paul clearly had very different notions, not only to those of the Jerusalem headquarters but to an unspecified assortment of Christian splinter movements growing up within the Dispersal. That they constituted a force of some magnitude is beyond question, because of the vehemence of opposition raised against them.

There are scattered clues to the nature and extent of a controversy that went far deeper than the issue of gentiles and Jews. In his second letter to the fledgling Christian community at Corinth, Paul made an impassioned plea to the effect that he and his entourage were delivering the true message and purpose of the Christ, whilst others were postulating all kinds of doctrinal slants to which he could not subscribe. Elsewhere he talked of being 'jealous over you with godly jealousy' and of his fear that 'minds should be corrupted from the simplicity that is in Christ.'[16] 2 Corinthians renews the concern: 'For if he that cometh preacheth another Jesus, whom we have not preached, or if ye receive another spirit, which ye have not received, or another gospel which ye have not accepted, ye might well bear with him.'

One of these preachers was Simon the Magus, who gained a substantial following in Samaria because of his reported powers.[17] Acts implies that he was regarded as something close to a divinity, worshipped as 'The Great Power of God' and was thus perhaps seen as a Samaritan equal of the Judaean Christ. Simon Magus was, allegedly, won over by Philip the Evangelist but his beliefs were so alien to the later Christian establishment that the historian, Eusebius, was driven to comment of his disciples: 'Following their progenitor's footsteps they slip into the Church like a pestilential and scabby disease, and do the utmost damage to all whom they succeed in smearing with the horrible deadly poison concealed on them.'[18] Paul repeatedly stressed similar concerns. He was particularly outspoken to the Galatians about a Jerusalem-based lobby which had persuaded them to recant the Pauline doctrine: 'But though we, or an angel from heaven, preach any other gospel unto you than that which we have preached unto you, let him be accursed.'[19]

What is particularly interesting is that Paul had strong differences with the disciples headed by James in Jerusalem and Peter

in Rome. His cynicism emerges in the Corinth correspondence:
'For I suppose I was not a whit behind the very chiefest apostles.[20]
But though I be rude in speech, yet not in my knowledge; but we
have been thoroughly made manifest among you in all things.
Have I committed an offence in abasing myself that ye might
be exalted, because I have preached to you the gospel of God
freely?'

The rift between Paul and the Jerusalem group persisted
a long time, officially over the promotion of universality –
Paul's letter to the Galatians reveals that fourteen years after
the initial brush, Paul and Peter met again in Antioch and the
meeting was one of bitter acrimony. Yet this was the full nature
of the argument.

Acts raises the trenchant observation that whilst some gentiles
had become willing to abstain from heathen practice, other Christians had not. Judging by the volume of attacks on them, these
groups counted as a powerful force. The writer of Acts underlines
Paul's concern: 'Wherefore my sentence is, that we trouble not
them from among the gentiles that are turned to God: but that we
write unto them, that they abstain from pollutions of idols, and
from fornication, and from things strangled, and from blood.'[21]

One argument is that the criticism provides a revealing insight
into social behaviour, that it is directed at the domestic sins
of those first-century Christians who found themselves living
in Europe.[22] Many converts were married to pagan spouses.
Christianity was a religion that appealed, in a very two-edged
manner – partly masochistic, partly emancipating – to women.
Thus a practising Platonist might well find his bed vacated in the
small hours of the morning by a wife who had tip-toed off to early
prayers. Conversely the wife would be in close proximity to her
husband's pagan ritual including the blood sacrifice of animals
to his gods. Naturally in such a close environment, the Christian
partner would eat sacrificed meat imbued with the spirit of pagan
deities. By no means all that bled for Zeus or Aphrodite, Kybele or
Mithras climbed to the heavens in smoke and ash. Much ended
up on the dinner plate. There also existed an interesting fashion
for using pagan temples as venues for dinner parties. The god
played host. No one was unduly bothered by this intimacy at
street level. There pervaded a goodly principle of live and let
live. At the time, and for several centuries to follow, it has to
be remembered that Christians represented a very small fish in
a very large social pool and that they were swimming intimately
and constantly with practising pagans. On the whole these non-

Christians took to them warmly and openly and it is hardly surprising that many Christians preferred the prospect of a faith which fused the old and the new.

Yet there is nothing to imply that these goings-on were exclusive to the domestic front. Paul's antagonism may have been directed far more towards ritualistic behaviour amongst Christians who remained loyal to older traditions. The difficulty is that we have lost, or all but lost, any trace of such thoughts and practices.

On what authority were whole generations of human reasoning obliterated, the legacies of excellent minds condemned to extinction in the flames of pedantry and self-preservation? It was a slaughter of human endeavour, carried out in the name of a religion, on a scale which the world had barely witnessed. Even the legions which had stormed so destructively through the great libraries of Nineveh and Ras Šamra had not sought deliberately to extinguish knowledge and understanding. Who were the arbiters? Who decided that Paul was to be upheld whilst others were condemned to ignominy?

Justin the Martyr, born of Greek parentage in Samaria early in the second century, may have begun the censorship process.[23] Justin studied philosophy in Ephesus, wandering from Stoic to Aristotelian, Pythagorean and Platonic schools of thought before turning to Christianity. He maintained a deep commitment to the priciples laid down by Plato and applied many of them in his new-found faith. He liked Plato's idea of a transcendent God and he fell in with the Platonic notion of an intermediary between creator and created, the Logos. He wrote several apologies for Christianity and a polemic against Gnostics which has since been lost. Predictably, he was strongly against traditional paganism which he described as grossly evil and superstitious. Executed in one of Marcus Aurelius' purges against the Christian community in Rome in AD 163, he passed the anti-heresy banner on to his pupil, Tatian, born in Assyria in the early second century, of pagan parentage, and converted in about AD 150.

Tatian was markedly more rabid in his condemnations and was also violently opposed to Greek philosophical debate. He was bitterly anti-marriage and encouraged total chastity from all Christians — not exactly a supporter of the second-century women's movement. He was in other words, a hard-line fundamentalist taking the Pauline view to extremes. Yet this man was also responsible for a book, the *Diatesseron* which, whilst proscribing any others, effectively secured the future of four

Gospel accounts, and at one time even threatened to replace them. Tatian, the arbiter of the New Testament, eventually left the Church and founded an extreme ascetic splinter sect, the Encratites.

Another pupil of Justin the Martyr was Irenaeus, born of Greek parents in western Asia in about AD 120. Irenaeus became Bishop of Lyon, where he had fled to escape the purges of Marcus Aurelius, and was the most influential of the early writers. In about 180 AD, he completed a five-volume polemic which he titled: *The Refutation and Overthrow of the Knowledge Falsely So Called*.[24] Though it includes a damning indictment of the Gnostic teachings of Valentinius and Marcion, Irenaeus' vitriol was addressed to any who did not follow the 'orthodox' line. He admitted to the widespread existence of non-conformist elements in the Church of the late second century, writing of: 'Those who are believed by many to be presbyters but whose conduct is unworthy. From such it is right to hold apart but to adhere to those who keep the apostles' teaching and, together with their presbyterial order, display sound speech and a blameless manner of life for the instruction and correction of others.' Irenaeus also set the stamp on Tatian's proscribed list and defined an inflexible reading material for the Christian canon. *Refutations* was the edict through which he and his priests ordered the wholesale destruction of that which did not 'conform'. Yet he made his sweeping condemnation of all other Christian material on a near meaningless argument. He claimed that the only valid tradition was that which had been handed down from the original twelve, and guarded through the apostolic succession. In his criticism of the Gnostic spokesmen, Irenaeus wrote: 'We can enumerate those who were appointed bishops in the Churches by the apostles and their successors up to our own day. They neither taught nor knew anything resembling the ravings of these folk.'

Irenaeus was scathing about the oral traditions which Gnostics followed, without conceding that the intimate followers of Jesus had been notable in their lack of written commentary and that it was probably an oral legacy which was received by the bishops from the twelve. The four Gospels, on which Irenaeus placed so much store, written down long after Jesus' death, three of them from a common source, and all probably orchestrated, were then manipulated still further by those who used them. It is bizarre to discover that Tatian himself had made additions and alterations to several of the Gospel texts so that they lent themselves more forcefully to his narrow ascetic views. Jesus offered the conditional, 'if thou would be perfect'. Tatian considered it appropriate to insert 'take up your cross and follow me'.

There are a number of instances where suspicious doctoring appears to have taken place in the canonical narratives of the New Testament. Yet Irenaeus described these same works as having: 'come down to us, kept safe and sound without any forgery of scriptures, a complete statement, without addition or subtraction.' This is a nonsense.

Fifty years after the first appearance of Irenaeus' anti-heretical books, one of his acolytes, Hippolytus, produced a massive *Refutation of All Heresies* which is lost in all but fragments though it seems to have followed similar lines of attack.[25] Hippolytus died in obscurity in Sardinian salt mines.

One other figure worthy of mention, a prominent manipulator of second-century Christian doctrine, was Tertullian, Bishop of Carthage.[26] Tertullian was, by all acounts, a brilliant orator. He also became deeply impressed by the Montanists who believed implicitly in the literal resurrection of the flesh – blood, bones and all – and who expected the second coming to take place 'shortly'. He was, therefore, something of a fundamentalist who bitterly opposed anything which smacked of Gnosticism or non-orthodoxy. Yet he, like so many, ended his life on the fringes of Christianity, ranting against the establishment for its excessive reliance on the bishops rather than the more apostolic preachers.

Justin and his successors were the main arbiters of that which became 'suitable Christian reading'. Yet they arrived at their selections through highly subjective processing and the people who cherished the so-called heretical works regarded the orthodox establishment and its spokesmen as being equally heretical. They too had solid claim to be Christian. The Nag Hammadi texts have been analysed in terms of Christian and non-Christian, Gnostic, Jewish and philosophical authorship. It is an unrealistic measure of identity and value, and is based on the yardstick of what is now taken to be 'orthodox'. The texts may, in fact, all have been written by Christian pens and Christian minds. They reflect a desire to place not just the Christ, but many elements of progressive spiritual belief within the remit of Christendom.

The question arises, were there oral traditions which preserved uncensored truth but which have long since been forgotten? Eminent authors have worried over the inconsistencies. It has been considered that the account of Jesus' fateful visit to Jerusalem is so adulterated as to be almost meaningless. Schweitzer commented on the work of the eminent nineteenth-century German theologian, Wilhelm Wrede: 'If according to the original tradition, of which Wrede admits existence, Jesus went to Jerusalem not to die, but to work there, the dogmatic view, according to which he went to Jerusalem to die, must have struck out the whole account of his sojourn in Jerusalem and his death, in order to put something else in its place.'[27]

Wrede based much of his case on a whole string of inadequacies and irrationalities in the Mark Gospel which suggest the possibility that a tradition existed about Jesus' time in Jerusalem quite different to that which appears in the synoptic accounts. He argued that if Jesus was not condemned and crucified as Messiah, a version must have existed which preserved the real circumstances and reasons.

Nag Hammadi, undiscovered in Wrede's or Schweitzer's day, reveals inconsistencies of another kind. The Luke Gospel includes, in Chapter 14, a puzzling saying attributed to Jesus: 'If any man come to me, and hate not his father, and mother . . . he cannot be my disciple.'[28]

The banned Gospel of Thomas, the 'brother' of Jesus who founded churches in the East, and of which fragments exist dating prior to the second century, amplifies the Luke quotation in a revealing fashion. The words in brackets are assumed in deciphering damaged parts of the text: 'Whoever does not hate his [father] and his mother as I do cannot become a [disciple] to me. And whoever does not love his [father and] his mother as I do cannot become a [disciple to] me. For my mother [on earth gave me death] but [my] true [mother] gave me life.'

It seems less likely that the writer of Thomas embellished, than that the writer of Luke excised. He would have been unable, for reasons which will become apparent, to include the reference to a distinction between Jesus' earthly mother and his mother in the heavens, his 'true mother'.

The permitted works quoted by the Church were regularly subjected to its own propagandist manipulation. The letters ascribed to Paul, time after time, were abused to foster individual ends. Authors would take remarks out of context to place distorted emphasis on a point they wished to pursue. If words could be tampered with after official acceptance, they could be tampered with before. There is an irony, in that when Irenaeus' massive tract was translated into Latin, his own work was not spared from censorship. Irenaeus' references to the millennium, the second coming, were cut. They no longer conformed with current thinking. It seems doubtful, therefore, whether the four canonical Gospels, Acts, the letters and Revelation had any more right to claim authenticity than any others.

Irenaeus also took considerable strength from the fact that the official Church followed an institutionalized set of rules, whilst the so-called heretical branches of Christianity had no rule book. Gnostics played down the value of the Old Testament canon and narrative, and therefore appeared to some to preach a vacillating and novel theme. Tertullian, who was incidentally the first great Christian writer in Latin, took a similar line. He stated, with a certain degree of illogic, that: 'every one of them, just as it suits his own temperament, modifies the traditions he has received, just as the one who handed them down modified them, when he shaped them, according to his own will.'[29]

To argue that we possess a balanced picture of Christian origins and belief in the Bible is wrong. 'Balance' was arrived at by men who adopted, in some instances, a highly bigoted view; who were often misogynists; who themselves vacillated through all kinds of fringe beliefs; and who frequently finished their lives as outcasts from mainstream Christian society. In their time of glory, these were powerful men whose minds had become excessively moralistic and whose vision had become narrowed by self-interest – an unsound combination. Yet these same men determined the content of that which is handed to each and every child brought up in the Christian tradition, the Book which is described as the 'irrefutable and immutable' truth.

The broad truth died under censorship. The thoughts and the wrested conclusions of tens of thousands of believers searching for their God were expunged from the Book. For nearly two thousand years, it has been as if they only spoke through the minds of those who wished to purge Christianity into a precise and conforming model.

If truth perished, however, certain tendencies remained. One of the clearest was to treat the earthly life of Jesus with complete indifference. Early Christianity had virtually no interest in Jesus, the historical man. His earthly ministry only came under the microscope when the orientation of Christianity changed. In the meanwhile, focus of attention rested almost wholly on the death and subsequent exaltation.

The first century and the beginning of the second saw the spread of the apostolic missions, largely through the efforts of the much-travelled, letter-writing Paul and his group. But the passing of these mighty fathers of Christendom had left a vacuum, and the huge question marks about the direction and purpose of the Movement were set to bubble for a while even more fiercely.

The second century was an age marked in Christian terms by persecution of faith both from without and within. That which followed involved a consolidation and rationalization of ideas. It was the age devoted to formalizing doctrine and to establishing the canonical rule book. Christian strategists had already resigned themselves to the inevitable. The end of the world was not coming, and the desire, if indeed it existed, to revamp principles of the old cults for a Jewish Asian scenario was obsolete in the changed circumstances, certainly of western Europe. Those who may have wished for a religion based on the gods of the earth and the revival of the promised land were gone. Such may have been the original purpose of the Movement, but wiser heads saw that such a renaissance would not work. The vision of a new Jewish kingdom had been left far behind. Jewry had become irrevocably scattered and its orthodox core remained ideologically immovable.

The romance with the notion of a new sacred king was therefore not a strong enough selling point; it posed no attraction to the influential society of much of the Roman empire although in the eastern wing sentiments may, for a time, have been somewhat ambivalent. There had to be more to attract converts from the new and potentially vast market of gentile souls. Yet the men of the early Christian think-tank were nothing if not pragmatists. They were aware that the essence of a mother goddess bonded in sacred union to a super-hero was still an innate force to be reckoned with — a power deep in the human subconscious that would neither go away, nor be hemmed in by political or theological borders. They had the stark option of resisting or joining. They chose the latter. The promise of an afterlife in the new Israel faded in quiet embarrassment, and in its place the best features of the old near-eastern faiths, the so-called mystery cults, were merged with those of the current European philosophies. The new planners offered the security of the old traditions but with the immediacy of an historical event almost within living memory, and they coupled these attractions with the principles of the new intellectual adventure which was exploring the very reasons for existence.

Within the frame of these skeletal certainties, through the deceits and the inconsistencies, and sometimes the spilled blood that make up early Christianity, the chrysalis began to move and once again the Queen of Heaven prepared to unfold her wings and to continue her holy union. Traces of her coronation will not always be obvious; we are not necessarily intended to recognize them. Sometimes anomalies and inconsistencies may, once again, be the only indicators that all is not as it seems. The mother goddess was, and still is, the great crux of the Christian faith, but the tortured debate into which she was drawn can only really be appreciated in light of the context and conditions and moods of the Apostolic Age. We are searching for a thing which, in the strangest of paradoxes, was placed at the core of faith and at the same time excised with terrible exactitude. Therein lies the conundrum of the Whore and the Holy One.

13

Whore and Holy One

In the high summer of AD 431, letters were carried to episcopal sees throughout the eastern Byzantine wing of the Roman empire summoning their bishops to attend a special council. The invitations had come directly from the emperor Theodosius II in Constantinople for a meeting that was to open on 7 June in the city of Ephesus three hundred miles to the south. The diary of the early Church is peppered with such councils, but this was to be no ordinary convention.

Ephesus, on the shores of the Aegean was, ostensibly, a convenient place in which to assemble two hundred hot and dusty bishops for a debate which was bound to elevate tempers and temperatures still further. The town enjoyed the benefit of cooling breezes off the sea and it was also a politically attractive venue. In a Christendom that had become deeply divided, Ephesus lay well within the sphere of influence of the eastern Church.

The reign of Diocletian, which began in AD 284, had seen the Roman dominion rebuilt into two wings.[1] Empire was governed from seats in Rome which represented the west and, prior to the establishment of Constantinople, from Nicomedia whence all to the east of the Aegean was controlled. Each wing was ruled by an Augustus and a Caesar. The Christian Church had tended to separate along similar lines. It became established in the Greek East and in North Africa, spread along the coast by Greek-speaking travellers commuting to and from Alexandria and the old Phoenician port of Carthage, well before it made any significant inroads in the West. The West was comparatively slow to Christianize, and we know virtually nothing about early Christianity in Italy, Gaul, Spain and Britain. The main nucleus outside Rome developed at Lyon and is thought to have been promoted by missionaries from the Rome Church.

East and West tended to separate culturally and to speak different languages, and there arose, eventually, strong rivalry for moral and ethical supremacy between Eastern and Western Churches. Western faith was essentially a gentile experience delivered by Paul and his followers, but the Eastern wing maintained loyalty, more strongly and for longer, with some of the old Judaic traditions. It also, arguably, kept faith more seriously, though not always in an overt fashion, with some of the more esoteric aspirations which the Movement had cherished in its early days. Ephesus was a safe city in which to promote and win 'eastern' arguments.

Aside from its political desirability Ephesus was brushed with more subtle colours and the choice was in some respects a piquant one.[2] For centuries Ephesus had stood as the cult centre for worship of the great goddess Artemis. One of the most exalted Greek descendants of Ištar, Artemis was the embodiment of nature. Mistress of the trees, she commanded the beasts of the forest, and it was her ancient and sacred blessing that was sought before the hunt and the kill. In senses that had moved not a great deal from the days of the prehistoric hunters, she was the goddess of the chase. More than this though, Artemis was a bringer of boundless fertility and fecundity. Her images at Ephesus were sculpted in remarkable and provocative fashion which could have come straight from pre-history: a myriad of ripe breasts festoon a body that blossoms with an exuberant riot of life-giving essence.

True to vogue, the Romans renamed her Diana of the Ephesians but they kept faith with her old identity. For them she was a goddess of life and birth and only as an afterthought was she a huntress. She walked her sacred groves, and in Rome they copied her many-breasted image. They provided her with a magnificent sanctuary on the Aventine, and each year they held a great festival in her honour. A vast and splendid procession carried the votary priestess to the shrine riding in a car pulled by deer. A sacrificial pyre on which animals and harvest of all kinds were laid was built on her sacred altar, and a barrier of 'wet' green logs was raised around about to stop the fire from spreading.

There is, quite incidentally, in the passing detail of this ancient rite, a biological echo; perhaps it is another tiny fragment of colour to set into the greyness of an old puzzle. Is there some connection with the enigmatic prophecy of doom made by Ezekiel in his rantings over pagan practice in which he described the devouring of 'every green tree in thee and every dry tree'?

The goddess was loved enormously in Ephesus. Her temple dominated the city. A philanthropic donor had raised a superb marble colonnade from city to temple, a full mile in length, so that pilgrims could walk there comfortably in all weathers. When they arrived he provided a banqueting hall, lavishly constructed out of rare and exorbitantly expensive Phrygian marble.

Yet Ephesus enjoyed more modern traditions. Ephesians believed that another bringer of life, Mary the Virgin, had hallowed their streets with her footsteps. It was said that Mary had come there to live with John the Divine, and so she, as much as Artemis, had become a part of Ephesus. The citizens built a shrine for her to equal that of the ancient goddess, and it was in this church that the bishops assembled on the fateful June day, almost four hundred years after the events which catapulted Mary from near total obscurity into the public eye and controversy. It was from the Ephesus meeting that the mother goddess of life stepped out on the last part of her journey from the Ice Age to the twentieth century.

Mary, the wife of Joseph's unconsummated marriage, is one of the most shadowy and enigmatic figures of the Bible. As far as the canonical sources go we do not know who she was, beyond the fact that she married into the house of David, although, according to some reckonings, she was herself of the royal lineage. We do not know where she came from, what she looked like, anything of her personality, or of her role in the upbringing of the young Jesus. We are merely invited to believe that her marriage to Joseph remained unsullied, her hymen was physically intact and that, according to some fundamentalists, in this permanent state of grace and virginity she gave birth to one whose identity, god or mortal, became the subject of agonizing debate.

By the fifth century AD this woman had the popular title of *Theotokos*, the Mother of God. She was being pushed inexorably on to heights beyond the reach of mortality, and towards the extraordinary events of AD 431. The Council of Ephesus was a moment in the process of putting flesh on the infant bones of the

Christian Movement which, more than any other, demonstrated the deep and intransigent desire to bring most ancient principles of faith and primal need into the modern embrace. The Council of Ephesus assembled to settle, once and for all, the question of Mary the Virgin.

In light of the journey through the delicate tracery of religious belief, it seems quite inevitable that the mother goddess should take her place in the Christian dogma and canon. The innate and profound wish to set the quintessence of life and love at the pinnacle of worship is too tenacious to fade away. It will be with us for always. Yet the decades of build-up to Ephesus did not address this need publicly. The Christian establishment was faced with a very real catch-22 option over the mother goddess and its attention to her was buried deep within a tortuous debate about the nature of Christ and of God.

To pinpoint the beginnings of the discord, we have to turn back the clock perhaps a thousand years or more to the traditions of Genesis and its explanation of creation — traditions born of an Israelite society whose identity was being threatened by religions that cast a paramount goddess in radiant light, and which was, even by the standards of other patriarchal cultures, immersed in a strongly derogatory view of womanhood. There are anomalies in the attitude. Strong female personalities took their place in Israelite history: Esther was one of the outstanding rulers: and there were Judith and Deborah. But some would suggest that Esther was a late entry to the offical scriptures after heated wrangling for and against, and generally Israel treated its women as second-class citizens.

The Genesis myth, a yoke with which Christianity doggedly saddled itself, is the grossly over-simplified product of a campfire philosophy. The Jewish tale of beginnings gave sanction to rhetoric which constantly hammered home the fact that, in Jewish Palestine, the legitimate body of the community was male. It was virtually unparalleled in that it attempted to turn the natural process of genesis on its head. It suggested that, whilst Adam was clearly a man, he possessed some kind of androgynous virility which took over the female function and 'gave birth' to Eve. It also provided a creator god who possessed unmistakably male attributes and who ranked alone in the heavens, whilst the ancient world more often than not placed a creator goddess at least on equal plane with her male counterpart. Yet the shock and horror of such an alternative was enormous. It still is. One can imagine the stimulating conversation which must have sped around clerical breakfast circles when the Sunday tabloids came up with the infamous banner headline: 'Is God a Woman?!'

Israelite antagonism went much deeper though. The 'Sin of Eve' was, and still is, a formidable weapon against womanhood. In the Genesis story Eve, in her womanly weakness, is lured to bring about the Fall. It is she who is tempted to taste the flesh of the forbidden fruit, and who brings down the curtain on Paradise and on the state of grace in which the God has created human life. Eve it is who attracts mortality, hence the linking of sin and death in Jewish and Christian faiths.

Christian tradition has it that Eve picked and ate fruit from the Tree of Knowledge, but a different interpretation may have been understood by those who originally told and listened to the story. Genesis 3 states: 'And the eyes of them both were opened, and they knew that they were naked; and they sewed fig leaves together, and made themselves aprons.'

We are looking at probably the oldest musical-hall joke in the business, but do we miss a vital point? In her brilliant and sensitive survey of Marianism, Marina Warner notes that the once-happy pair did not cover their eyes or their mouths.[3] Their genitals were the focus of embarrassment. As it stands the Genesis myth may well provide a complete distortion and, in doing so, remove the significance of the transgression. Logically, eating the fruit of the Tree of Knowledge could hardly be the major catastrophe which is elaborated, and one has to ask if, once again, we are being misled by subtleties that people once recognized, but which now escape us. The Genesis account virtually admits the truth: 'Unto the woman he said, I will greatly multiply thy sorrow and thy conception; in sorrow thou shalt bring forth children; and thy desire shall be to thy husband, and he shall rule over thee.'

Eve was castigated for desire; not the urge to take a quick snack from the apple tree, but surely for her desire to gain 'knowledge' of her partner. She had intercourse with Adam, and sex reared its head in Paradise! That was the unforgivable 'sin', the anathema which many Jewish fundamentalists felt so abhorrent and which had to be condemned in the Genesis legend. The coupling of sex and sin was a hardline, essentially Yhwhist, reaction against the religions from which they had wished endlessly to distance themselves. Sex and sexual desire epitomized all that they feared in the popularity of the mother goddess.

At first appraisal it has always seemed quite irrational to label

one of humankind's most fundamental urges as 'sinful', yet set
in context the labelling makes sense. It was arrived at by Jewish
orthodoxy as much for political as spiritual motives. It was akin
to a modern conservative voter being discouraged from singing
the 'Internationale'. Sex in any mythological or religious context
undermined Israelite national identity.

Missionaries such as Paul, with his strong Pharisaic background,
carried the philosophy through into Christianity. As time went on
the reasoning changed, but the fact remains that a single verse
from Genesis composed by a political and misogynistic orator as
a piece of pure Jewish propaganda has been wielded to demean
and castigate women, and particularly pregnant women, virtually down to the present day. It is remarkable that the modern
Christian Church has never managed wholly to disentangle itself
from this bigotry, and that powerful Church factions still manage
to reconcile the ludicrous statements of Genesis with the notion
of a gentle and merciful God.

The continuance of antagonism towards women and the desires
of the flesh in the early Christian period can, nonetheless, only
evidence the probability that a major threat still persisted. Paul
was a liberal. He had parted with conventional Judaism, convinced that Christianity held the universal message promoted by
his Christ, yet he felt obliged to take a rigid, almost draconian,
stance supporting a tradition that one might think should have
become outmoded. Paul stopped short of supporting the extreme
ascetics in Corinth who argued that marriage and sexual intercourse were totally abhorrent: '. . . it is good for a man not to
touch a woman.[4] Nevertheless to avoid fornication, let every man
have his own wife, and let every woman have her own husband.'
The first letter to Timothy, one of the proselytes working in
Phrygia, laid the same cautionary note: '. . . some shall depart
from the faith, giving heed to seducing spirits, and doctrines of
devils; speaking lies in hypocrisy; having their conscience seared
with a hot iron; forbidding to marry, and commanding to abstain
from meats, which God hath created to be received . . .'[5]

Paul, though, maintained a dour view even of marriage, a poor
second best for those who could not accept celibacy. The Pauline
writer left little doubt that women were 'the flesh' and were
inherently evil. The point was pressed in the letters to Timothy:
'In like manner also, that women adorn themselves in modest
apparel, with shamefacedness and sobriety; not with broidered
hair, or gold, or pearls, or costly array . . . let the woman learn
in silence with all subjection . . . for Adam was first formed, then

Eve. And Adam was not deceived, but the woman being deceived was in the transgression.'[6]

Time after time, whether addressed to groups at Corinth and Ephesus, or to individuals like Timothy, the canker nagged away and it is through the correspondence that some of the real truth may emerge. The Pauline letters might leave the impression that the world of the first and second centuries, gentile and Jewish Christian alike, spent most of its waking hours indulging in domestic romping, and that this sporting but remonstrable conduct as often as not involved non-marital partners. But the analysis is facile and extremely deceptive.

The correspondence with the nucleus of Christian activists at Corinth contains fascinating insights: 'It is reported commonly that there is fornication among you, and such fornication as is not so much as named among the gentiles, that one should have his father's wife.'[7] This terse attack presents extraordinary implications. It identifies Christian Jews – it particularly distinguishes the group to whom the lecture is addressed from gentiles who would not even consider the practice under discussion – to be fornicating with their mothers. Are we really to believe this of a society which took a far tougher stance over sexual impropriety than did the gentiles, or is the implication disguised?

At one point the letter links various categories of sin: 'Know ye not that the unrighteous shall not inherit the kingdom of God?[8] Be not deceived: neither fornicators, nor idolators, nor adulterers, nor effeminate, nor abusers of themselves with mankind.' The last two are, at face value, curious inclusions, since Jesus made no particular criticism of homosexuals, fetishists, or any other deviants.

The answer may be that Paul was remonstrating, not at private adultery and bath-house parties, but about a deeper religious principle which clearly he felt to be at stake. Each and every time standard phrases like 'fornicators and idolators' are wheeled out, they do not refer to domestic misbehaviour, but to the Jewish abhorrence of sex in the setting of cultic ritual. Expressions such as 'effeminate' and 'abusers' address eunuch priests, and 'father's wife' is a euphemism for the mother goddess, the priestess of the Sacred Marriage. Almost every letter warns that there are groups claiming Christianity and yet practising 'immorality and idolatry', which can only imply that a sizeable force within the Christian Movement was devoted to worship based on less than good Jewish principles. The Pauline correspondence would seem to send clear announcements that the mother goddess was alive and well in early Christianity.

The picture is not a simple one though, because it is also touched by a modern world whose philosophy had advanced out of all recognition from that with which the founding fathers of Judaism had wrestled. Genesis did not relate to classical European society, and it took no account of the deep and trenchant probing of origins that had occupied minds, intellects of giant perception and vision, from the time of Socrates. The opening chapters of the Pentateuch stood beside excellent but, in terms of Jewish tradition, controversial explorations of man's beliefs about the origin of the world and of his God.

There were many intelligent Christians who found great inadequacies in the biblical creation story. The philosophy of one of the foremost Gnostic Christian teachers, Valentinus, who had come to Rome qualified in the Platonist tradition, was sophisticated and genuinely threatening to the Christian establishment.[9] His arguments were sufficiently subtle and well presented that he was identified by many as an orthodox Christian. Valentinus proposed that the supreme creator was an indivisible unit. 'He dwells alone in silence . . . since, after all, he was a Monad, and no one was before him . . .' So far so good, but Valentinus offended in his assertion that the creator god of Israel was only a lesser derivative, a demi-urge, of an original celestial principle.

More radical was Marcion, another Christian teacher who came to Rome from Asia Minor.[10] Marcion claimed that the god of Israel, and the god who had generated the Christ, were quite separate. The official term for this heresy was dualism: the ambiguities of mortal existence explained through two independent powers, one imperfect, the other perfect. The Israelite god was palpably flawed and had brought into being a world filled with disease, pain and suffering. This, Marcion argued, was incompatible with a god proclaimed by Jesus to be one of love and redemption.

A third and probably more threatening 'heretical' sect was the Manichaeans, an extreme ascetic group which gained a very widespread popularity and which remained a force to be reckoned with until well into the Middle Ages.[11] Manichaeans followed the teaching of the Persian-born philosopher, Mani. He also had promoted dualism as the most realistic explanation of the cosmos – a spiritual world of light, and a material world of darkness.

The common substance of these 'heretics' arguments which really rocked the establishment lay partly in dualism which effectively denied Jesus as anything other than a spiritual presence, since he was clearly a product of the non-physical world

of light, but no less in the sexual identity of the original principle. They had moved away from the mainstream belief that the
creator god was *strictly male*. They perceived a masculine dark
creator of the temporal world, the so-called demi-urge, but they
had discovered a higher level in the cosmos, the archons or
aeons, amongst whom walked an immensely powerful female
presence, the source of knowledge, the 'mind that has wisdom',
in other words the Greek philosophical notion of *sophia*.

Some of the Nag Hammadi documents, which to a degree find
common ground with the teachings of Gnostics like Valentinus,
Marcion and Mani, reflect the dramatically altered emphasis and
illustrate the growing acceptance of Greek thinking. Within the
second codex is a profound and detailed work that has been
given the title: *On the Origin of the World*. Its source is unknown
though it was probably compiled early in the fourth century AD
and its author has called on various traditions, some ancient,
some more contemporary. Its lines bear some tribal mythology
and Jewish influence but they are dominated by strong Gnostic
and European philosophical threads.

On the Origin of the World offers an overtly intelligent and well
thought out exploration of man's spiritual beginning. It would
undoubtedly win many arguments over the orthodox account
which opens the Bible. One of its fatal 'flaws' lies in that it
destroys the masculine superiority in the works of the Ancient
of Days and recognizes quite distinct features of the primordial
force – male and female.

'Origin' begins with the concept of the Infinite from whose
boundless power and presence stemmed the immortal beings,
the archons. From out of one, Faith, came a likeness, Sophia, the
eternal wisdom – both unquestionably female in nature. Sophia,
wholly missing from the Genesis story, manifested herself as light,
the veil dividing mankind from the immortals. But the light cast
a shadow, the 'limitless chaos', and from it emerged all the gods
of creation, the Authorities. The shadow sensed that there was
something mightier than itself and, in its anguish, it became
pregnant of its own accord and produced a formless offspring,
Envy, which lacked spirit. Wisdom erred but once. She caused this
nothing to take form as the demi-urge and to rule over the matter
of Chaos. She called him Yaltabaoth, though in ignorance of her
Yaltabaoth presumed he was alone in creation. At this juncture,
we have that which in Gnostic eyes was the flawed creator god
of Israel.

To reign over the matter of Chaos, Yaltabaoth created seven

androgynous children. He became very arrogant of his own power and this impiety greatly angered Wisdom. She chided him, calling him Samael, the 'blind god'. But in one of the seven archangels of Chaos, Wisdom also gained a champion, Sabaoth. He recognized the terrible flaw in his father and, because of his perception, Wisdom made him the great ruler against the Forces of Chaos and she empowered him with her daughter Zoe, life. The Authorities created their likeness in Adam but, although they had created the material being, it had no spirit. It was in a desperate struggle to prevent the Authorities from creating endless clones of Yaltabaoth, and in distress about her own mistake, that Wisdom commanded her daughter to breathe life into Adam.

Origin differs again, in fundamental detail, from Genesis. Eve did not spring from Adam's rib, everlastingly to live either in gratitude to man for her birthright, or in desolation for her sins. Wisdom and Zoe, their outlines blurring into one, placed Adam into a deep sleep and secretly left their likeness with him before Wisdom entered and became the Tree of Acquaintance with its symbol of eternal knowledge, the serpent, and Zoe mingled into the Tree of Life. When he awoke, Adam was deceived because he met, unwittingly, not some fission of himself but the mortal image of the goddess.

It was the deep chagrin and envy of the Authorities which brought about the Fall: 'Behold Adam! He has come to be like one of us, so that he knows the difference between the light and the darkness.[12] Now perhaps he will be deceived as in the case of the tree of acquaintance and also will come to the tree of life and eat from it and become immortal and become lord and despise us and disdain us and all our glory. Then he will denounce us along with our universe. Come let us expel him from Paradise down to the land from which he was taken . . .'

A wholly different emphasis is placed on the Fall. Eve is not held responsible. On the contrary Eve is the earthly manifestation of Wisdom, and it is the realization of good and evil gained by Adam, the understanding that there exist two conflicting dimensions in the cosmos, and the burgeoning vulnerability of the authorities now that he owns this knowledge that brings expulsion from Paradise.

On the Origin of the World is one of several detailed attempts in the Nag Hammadi codices, to answer the mystery of creation. Explanation is also met in the accountably more Christianized *Hypostasis of the Archons*, and in works such as *Trimorphic Protennoia*. In each case, nonetheless, it is the superior female force of

Sophia in the primordial heavens which controls and motivates and which ultimately castigates the lesser creator god for his arrogance and impiety.

Trimorphic Protennoia is an unfortunate title which translates badly but which means approximately *The First Thought, in Three Forms*. The primordial Thought, the original cosmic femaleness, came to exist as a triality moving everywhere and for all time, not the Trinity of the Bible but one of Father, Mother and Son, in which the Voice of the Thought comes as the ineffable one, the Christ: 'I am Protennoia, the Thought that dwells in the Light.[13] I am the movement that dwells in the All, she in whom the All takes its stand, the first-born among those who came to be, she who exists before All. She is called by three names, although she dwells alone, since she is perfect. I am invisible within the Thought of the Invisible One. I am revealed in the immeasurable, ineffable. I am incomprehensible, dwelling in the incomprehensible. I move in every creature.'

In several of the Nag Hammadi works, Sophia is also perceived as representing the human soul. *The Exegesis on the Soul* from Codex II describes how Sophia, virginal and inseparable from the male of an androgynous creative force, fell to earth and was polluted with many lovers who treated the soul as a whore. Her redemption came when the maleness of the creator sent her brother to unite with her in a Sacred Marriage and she was restored to her former state of purity.

'*Exegesis*' reflects a Valentinian concept: a divine being leaving the bright world above and then regaining the power of wisdom in the frame of the physical universe before returning to the light. It is a picture-book tale of the human soul born imprisoned in an earthly frame and searching for heaven but the same unquenchable femaleness shouts from its lines.

Apart from all the problems of duality, this bombshell of early Christian feminism battered at the very core of the old Jewish Genesis tradition and it explains why many of the more profound alternatives could not be accepted by the apostolic fathers. The story of creation in Genesis survived into Christianity, to no small degree because it is almost comically misogynistic. It was foisted on to Christendom more because it suited the purpose of the hierarchy than because of the political message it addressed to the Jews in Palestine. It feathered the right nests. Only once in the Old Testament does the veil slip. What seems a strangely misplaced passage lies in the eighth chapter of the Book of

Proverbs. Through lines which possess a unique and incandescent loveliness, Sophia speaks:

> I was set up from everlasting, from the beginning, or ever
>   the earth was.
> When there were no depths, I was brought forth; when
>   there were no fountains abounding with water.
> Before the mountains were settled, before the hills was I
>   brought forth:
> While as yet he had not made the earth, nor the fields,
>   nor the highest part of the dust of the world.
> When he prepared the heavens I was there: when he set
>   a compass upon the face of the depth:
> When he established the clouds above: when he strengthened
>   the fountains of the deep:
> When he gave to the sea his decree, that the waters should not
>   pass his commandment: when he appointed the foundations
>   of the earth:
> Then I was by him, as one brought up with him: and I
>   was daily his delight, rejoicing always before him;
> Rejoicing in the habitable part of the earth; and my delights
>   were with the sons of men.[14]

Sophia's appearance in an Old Testament manuscript is not particularly unusual, but in the way described here it is startling. Christians will argue that the poet refers only to a part of God's personality, an interpretation of the Holy Ghost, but although autobiographical, this Proverbs text implies a separate being, another identity in the heavens. Yet, according to Genesis, these are supposed to be staffed by the creator god alone. Why, if she announces herself here in such unmistakable terms, is Sophia not also present in the official creation story? For reasons unknown the editors have let slip something decidedly unusual in terms of Jewish thought.

Christendom found it impossible to abandon the mother goddess, though her recognition presented a great dilemma. Whether one describes it as Jungian anima-searching, or reluctance to discard that which had been at the centre of faith for millennia past, she was indispensable. The editors of the New Testament contrived to introduce her in various allegorical guises. By recalling Zechariah, Matthew announced her presence on the occasion when Jesus called for an ass on which to ride into the Holy City: 'Rejoice greatly, O daughter of Zion: behold thy king cometh unto thee!'[15] Jerusalem, the bride of Christ, became at least one acceptable Christian allegory for the Earth Mother.

The Johannine school in Antioch set themselves an interesting challenge in putting together the Book of the Revelation. This apocalyptic vision is the only vehicle in which, officially, the conflicting views of the goddess are brought together. How were the authors to place both aspects on the same page and yet seemingly discuss two distinct and separate personalities? The Book of the Revelation is scattered with reminders of this dilemma, though the Johannine writers were directing their spleen more towards Nero's Rome than old Babylon with its fertility cult that assaulted the sensitivities of the exiles like a licensed state brothel:

> . . . come hither; I will shew unto thee the judgement of the great whore that sitteth upon many waters: and with whom the kings of the earth have committed fornication and the inhabitants of the earth have been made drunk with the wine of her fornication.
>
> So he carried me away in the spirit into the wilderness: and I saw a woman sit upon a scarlet coloured beast, full of names and blasphemy having seven heads and ten horns . . . and upon her forehead was a name written, Mystery, Babylon the Great, the Mother of Harlots and Abominations of the Earth. . .
>
> And here is the mind which hath wisdom. The seven heads are seven mountains on which the woman sitteth. And there are seven kings; five are fallen and one is and the other is not yet come; and when he cometh he must continue a short space.[16]

The phrase 'mind that hath wisdom' is a clear hint that the Johannine school recognized and perhaps sympathized with Greek philosophical debate about the *sophia*. It is, significantly, one of the few occasions when the notion of the *sophia* is allowed to penetrate the purged and sanitized pages of the New Testament. Pure judgement-day tradition, Greek philosophy and fertility religion lie as bedfellows in a hopeless moral tangle. Sophia, the goddess, the wisdom of creation, the Queen of the Mountain, with her seven symbolic progeny is part Anti-Christ, part creative essence. Her branches become seven rulers, the sixth being the Christ himself, and the seventh, he of the second coming. A few chapters on, the writers promoted her in her other mantle as the new Jerusalem:

> . . . and there came unto me one of seven angels which
> had seven vials full of the seven last plagues, and talked
> with me saying, Come hither, I will shew thee the bride,
> the Lamb's wife.[17]

Coy euphemisms and discreet passing comments were all
that the officially accepted texts were permitted; any more was
purged from the eyes of history. Thus it might have remained
were it not for the bookish monk at Nag Hammadi who, perhaps
at risk to his own life, gathered together heirlooms of Christian
thought that would otherwise have perished. He sealed them in
a clay urn and left a testimonial for some future generation,
who, in another time and another place, would read and value
their beauty and their depth of vision.

The Nag Hammadi texts are full of references which must
raise all sorts of questions about the real feelings and beliefs
of early Christians. Buried in the banned Gospel of Philip is one
of many small glimmers, each of which cry out with such far-
reaching implications: 'Since Christ came the world had been
created, the cities adorned, the dead carried out. When we were
Hebrews we were orphans and had only our mother, but when
we became Christian we had both father and mother.' Why
does this document describe Israelite forebears as possessing a
heavenly mother, but no heavenly father?

A more unfettered truth rests in Codex VI of Nag Hammadi.
Enclosed within its shroud of dried and faded papyrus is a
fragile, poignant reality. This is a book which the Christian
hierarchy would have tried desperately to suppress. They would
have burned it on sight and condemned its writer. Yet it is one
of the loveliest and most candid of writings.

'The Thunder, Perfect Mind' is a song.[18] It has the hallmarks of having been an ancient hymn, to be chanted rather
than read. The word 'Thunder' in the Greek is in the feminine
and throughout Hebrew and Greek literature this same word
has been used to convey the sound of the creator's presence
on earth. 'Perfect mind' reflects the same source, the *sophia*. In
his introduction, the translator from the coptic, George MacRae,
describes the book as being virtually unique in the Nag Hammadi
library. How true! This noble work bears no debt to Gnosticism or
any other philosophy. It stands alone, yet it speaks for countless
stilled voices.

... For I am the first and the last.
I am the honoured one and the scorned one.
I am the whore and the holy one.
I am the wife and the virgin.
I am the mother and the daughter.
I am the members of my mother.
I am the barren one and many are her sons ...
... Why have you hated me in your counsels?
For I shall be silent among those who are silent,
and I shall appear and speak.
Why then have you hated me, you Greeks?
Because I am a barbarian among the barbarians?
For I am the wisdom of the Greeks
and the knowledge of the barbarians.
I am the judgement of the Greeks and of the barbarians.
I am the one whose image is great in Egypt
and the one who has no image among the barbarians.
I am the one who has been hated everywhere
and who has been loved everywhere.
I am the one whom they call Life,
and you have called Death ...

An inescapable truth that rests at the heart of Christianity is described in words so striking and so dangerously lucid that no 'orthodox' Christian could or would dare to acknowledge 'The Thunder, Perfect Mind' as a part of their creed.

The mauling ambivalence over the role and morality of 'woman' in Christianity has always threatened to pull the Church apart, yet it is a debate which was triggered by the Movement, not the man. There is reasonable evidence within the Gospels that Jesus adopted a liberal and congenial attitude to women. The biblical narratives tend to play them down, as do some of the Nag Hammadi texts. The Gospel of Thomas, a collection of sayings attributed to Jesus, concludes with a typical sentiment: 'Simon Peter said to them: "let Mary leave us, for women are not worthy of life".[19] Jesus said: "I shall lead her, in order to make her male, so that she too may become a living spirit, resembling you males. For every woman who will make herself male will enter the Kingdom of Heaven".' This is pure Jewish rhetoric. Women can participate in society provided they identify themselves with men.

Nag Hammadi, though, has some surprises in store. Bound into the same volume as the Gospel of Thomas, is the Gospel

of Philip and this reveals a more intriguing face of Jesus. Similar
to the previous work, it is essentially a compilation of statements
rather than a narrative. Parts of the texts have been damaged
beyond repair, but in spite of gaps which the translator has filled
in brackets*, the sense of one striking passage is clear:

> And the companion of the [Saviour was] Mary Mag-
> dalene. [Jesus loved] her more than [all] the disciples
> [and used to] kiss her [often] on her [mouth]. The rest
> of [the disciples complained]. They said to him, 'Why do
> you love her more than all of us?' The saviour answered
> and said to them, 'Why do I not love you like her? When
> a blind man and one who sees are both together in dark-
> ness, they are no different from one another. When the
> light comes, then he who sees will see the light, and he
> who is blind will remain in darkness.[20]

Paul acknowledged women to be his 'equals in Christ' only
because he had little option unless he was to appear to contra-
dict the views of his leader. In practice he found it very difficult
to throw off his traditional Jewish view of the subservience of
women, and it stimulated frequent rhetorical outbursts such as
that in the first letter to the Corinthians: 'Let your women keep
silence in the churches: for it is not permitted unto them to
speak; but they are commanded to be under obedience, as also
saith the law.'[21]

There was by now a powerful voting lobby within the Movement which stood behind the Pauline approach towards wom-
en.[22] Its attitude stemmed from sentiments on two levels. On
the old theological and political stance this lobby was determined to distance the Christian Movement from any notion of
a female power in the matter of creation but the antagonism
also reflected something of a current power play. To invite any
suggestion that the feminine had played a fundamental role in
the order of things would be to weaken the power base of the
apostolic bishops, ordained by God to carry the reins of power
first handed to Peter.

The Pauline bishops argued their case by pointing out that
Jesus was a man, that his disciples were men, and that the
Father was masculine in nature. All this, they claimed, proved
that men and men alone should administer the rites of the

*See Reference section

Church. Yet such dated sexist views were out-of-step with the modern Roman world. Christianity was appealing increasingly to women in a society which, compared with that known by traditional Jews, was facing a new mood of feminism and was fast becoming emancipated. This did not suit the Christian hierarchy who wished for nothing less than a preserved all-male club on the lines of the old Jewish priesthood. Women might join the congregation but they certainly were not eligible for membership of the committee or to conduct sacred rituals. It was on this account that the refusal to acknowledge Mary Magdalene among the official ranks of apostles was necessary, even though she had unusual rights to be considered a favourite amongst the twelve. Mere mention of special attention paid to her by Christ was enough to have the Gospel of Philip condemned, irrespective of any other 'heresy' the writing might contain.

Thus the stage was set for the agonized debate over the other Mary, the mother of Jesus, and in light of what has transpired it is very clear why she was accompanied by such interest. Jesus, after his death, was promoted as an aspect of the perfect divinity through whose beneficence he had been created in the flesh, so he required divine parentage on one side or the other. Yet that immediately placed the matter of his birth back into the Sacred Marriage arena and elevated his mother to a special position. Mary was someone different!

The New Testament writers had been very wary. They avoided significant comment about Mary. Outside of the nativity story she is mentioned only twice in the gospels, and those instances are limited to the writings attributed to Mark and John. Paul refers to her but once in his letter to the Galatians. Matthew and Luke provide virtually all the information, and most of that is highly suspect. The apocryphal Book of James is more forthcoming. Mary was born, we are told, of a previously barren mother, Anna, and of a wealthy father, Joachim, who at the time of her conception was absent working out forty days of penance in the desert for his childlessness. Mary was at once a prodigy, dedicated to the temple, and then married to an elderly widower, Joseph, chosen because he was too aged or infirm to destroy her virginity.

In her perpetual purity, the virgin conceived a child through the power of the Holy Spirit. Thus she escaped the curse of Eve, remained untainted by human desires and, alone amongst all other mortal women, gave birth in a state of grace. The argument that her hymen remained unbroken even after childbirth has lost much of its credibility among Christians, but there has remained a steadfast and unwavering belief that she was undamaged physically until that moment.

The 'conventional' birth of Jesus bothered many Christians nevertheless. Some discounted the whole affair: all the dualists claimed that the story of the virgin birth was clearly ridiculous since the true Redeemer, the manifestation of the spiritual god of light, could never have been born through the messy and strictly material process of pregnancy. Human birth, they argued, was a failing of the Israelite god, and to make earthly business as difficult as possible for the Old Testament creator, the more ascetic dualists, including Marcionites, forbade marriage within their sect. In spite of this fanatical stance, however, Marcion also horrified the orthodox Church by ordaining women as priests and even bishops.

A hundred years before the Council of Ephesus assembled to settle the questions surrounding Mary, the debate took a subtle turn in the Greek city of Alexandria, through a priest named Arius. The argument which erupted there concerned the nature of the Trinity which may seem at first to bear little relationship to the discussion of Mary, but which nonetheless was deeply relevant.

Alexandria became a meeting place between East and West, and between religion and philosophy. She watched as ancient Judaism swayed before the new Hellenic ideas. She hosted the transcription of the Septuagint translation of the Old Testament. Many schools of thought flourished within her walls. In that ancient city on the Egyptian coast traditional pagans rubbed shoulders with orthodox Christians, Gnostics, neo-Platonists, Stoics, and many more, resolving the secrets of the universe with the enthusiasm and freedom of academics at an ancient Sorbonne. Some of the greatest names in the early Church worked and evolved their thoughts in Alexandria. Clement and Origen, mighty men among the early Christian theorists, were both Alexandrians. But it was one of their descendants, a presbyter working around the many churches of the city, who set a course which was to wrench the Movement apart.

Arius began to air pulpit rhetoric which undermined further that most sacred and entrenched of 'orthodox' Christian principles – the singularity and peculiarity of a God whose relevance to Christianity was seen through the imagery of the Trinity.[23] The Son was envisaged, by some, as the perfect replication of the original, and the Spirit was a questing amorphous facet of the godhead. The orthodox notion was reflected by the sexless Greek noun *pneuma*, but was nothing short of a copy of *sophia*, the Greek and positively female principal. The Gospel of Philip uses this, incidentally, as argument against the virgin birth: 'Some said, "Mary conceived by the holy spirit."[24] They are in error. They do not know what they are saying. When did a woman ever conceive by a woman? Mary is the virgin whom no power defiled. She is a great anathema to the Hebrews who are the apostles and the apostolic men.'

The accepted concept was that the Son and the Spirit were indistinguishable from the Father. Arius, however, was talking in such a way as to imply three separate entities. He headlined the damaging question that if Jesus was a man, made in the flesh, born of mortal woman, how was he also of one and the same substance with the ineffable Christian God? This seemingly innocent enquiry over technicalities threatened to open a whole Pandora's box of issues which the Christian establishment was most reluctant to see aired because it provided ammunition for the dualists.

Arius' bishop, Alexander, added fuel to the flames by issuing guidelines to an understanding of the Trinity as *homoousios* – a Greek word, difficult to render accurately, but meaning 'of the same substance'. In Alexander's ideal, Father, Son and Spirit were equal facets of the one. The inconsistency of views on such basics, within the Church, is underlined by the fact that this pronouncement immediately ran Alexander up against the not-unpopular explanations of his predecessor as bishop of Alexandria, Origen, who argued 'oneness' but that the balance of the Trinity was subservient to the supreme Father.

It was an irony that in Arius' view, there was one God and the term meant what it said. For him the Christian tradition of the Trinity was unacceptable unless seen as one Supreme Creator God and two inferior deities. The Creator was indivisible and beyond contact with the temporal world. Arius argued in favour not of an imperfect creator of the material earth but of an intermediary, Logos, 'the Word'. Christ, the son, was the incarnation of Logos, the mortal image of the Being. The Spirit, the third corner of the triangle, was an intangible, invisible, offspring of Logos.

So great was the breach which Arius' arguments raised, that the emperor, Constantine the Great, was driven to bring together a vast assembly of bishops who met on 20 May AD 325 at the famous Council of Nicaea.[25] When it ended, at a small Bithynian town within striking distance of the imperial palace at

Nicomedia, two hundred and seventy bishops put their signature to a document which effectively outlawed Arianism and restored the principle of *homoousios*. They made the statement:

> We believe in one God, the Father almighty, maker of all things both visible and invisible;
> And in one Lord, Jesus Christ, the Son of God, only begotten of the Father, that is of the substance of the Father, God of God, Light of Light, very God of very God, Begotten not made, of one substance with the Father; Through whom all things were made, both the things in heaven and the things on earth;
> Who for us men and for our salvation came down, and was made flesh, and was made man,
> He suffered, and rose again the third day,
> Ascended into heaven, is coming to judge quick and dead;
> And in the holy ghost.

There was, however, sufficient antagonism within the Council that the successful lobby insisted on a series of imprecations being added to the document finally presented for signature: 'But those who say, There was once when He was not, or He was not before He was begotten, or He was made out of nothing, or affirm that the Son of God is of different hypostasis or substance, or is a creature, or is subject to change or alteration, these the catholic and apostolic Church of God anathematizes.'

The term 'anathematizing' amounted frequently to exile and death for Christians who, overnight, became labelled as heretics. It might seem, on the face of it, to have been an extraordinary outlay of energy and emotion over little more than technicalities on words. Arius' argument, however, was one which must have touched a chord in many members of the Church. His arguments presented dangers on various levels. To more conservative Christians, he fell only slightly short of admitting, if not outright dualism, a sense of pluralism that was far too pronounced to be healthy. On that count alone he came perilously close to heresy. He was opening the box not just to release arguments over the Trinity. Indirectly he was inviting debate both on the nature and sexual identity of God described in that unassailable myth of Genesis, on a world whose salvation lay in the hands of a benign and 'good' father, and on the precise filial relationship of Jesus with his parents.

Arius died, lonely and sick, in about AD 336, but his theosophy was to rumble on in a bitter struggle which brings the story back to Ephesus. In the fifth century AD the hands of a one-time monk from Antioch, Nestorius, effectively picked up on the identity debate where Arius had been forced to let go. Nestorius had no time for paganism or heresy. He was in most respects a thoroughly orthodox Christian and was considered a 'safe bet'. Certainly he did not approve in any way of Arianism. He was also a fine orator, and with these credits in mind the Roman government made him archbishop of Constantinople.

In spite of his agreement with the 'of one substance' argument, Nestorius supported the view that Christ existed on two levels, divine and human, and he was particularly bothered by the direction in which Mary the Virgin was going.[26] That title, incidentally, is slightly misleading. 'Virgin' in today's etymology describes a woman who has not experienced full sexual intercourse, but it was not always so. Once, the word in its Semitic equivalent implied a woman of independent spirit, one who was not subservient to men. Thus in Canaanite tradition, we have a thoroughly sexy and 'much travelled' lady described as Anat the Virgin! Virginity in the Jewish Christian sense, by contrast, bore a much narrower definition evidenced by nothing less than the unbroken hymen.

Mary had been quietly gaining a following and an aura which took her above and beyond the purely mortal frame. Rumours were well-circulated that Mary might not actually have died a mortal death, and that Christ was not alone in bodily assumption into heaven. His mother, it was being suggested, had risen the same way.

Visions of Mary had been noted from as early as the third century when Gregory, Bishop of Neocaesarea had received 'revelations' both from her and from John the Evangelist, and in this growing fervour an increasing number of orthodox Church leaders began to perceive in Mary a powerful weapon against the threat of the Gnostic dualists. Visionaries like Gregory saw considerable value in promoting Mary, if not as a divinity, then certainly as a focal female element in worship. At this stage, there was probably no thought of her in the vacant role of mother goddess. The consideration was taken purely in the light of dualism and Arianism. In Mary was a perfect answer to the Gnostic concept of 'two worlds, one good, one bad, and never the twain shall meet.' The third century had also seen the rise of several other elements which were to become closely linked with Marianism

– the veneration of relics and the adoration of images, and the
development of a monastic way of life which placed celibacy as a
benchmark of godliness.

The facts were plain. Mary had been born a mortal woman.
She had abstained from earthly desires. She had provided living
proof that the physical body could overcome the 'Sin of Eve' –
assuming that Eve was guilty more of an appetite for sex than
apple scrumping – and in doing so had reached paradise 'in the
flesh'. She therefore provided the perfect role model. Nestorius'
concern though, lay with what he saw as a trend towards clothing
Mary in the aura of a goddess, and his concern was not without
foundation. An increasingly influential lobby, spearheaded by
Cyril, Bishop of Alexandria, was promoting the title *Theotokos*,
'Mother of God'.

Nestorius believed the implication was wrong, and he argued
for the lesser title *Christotokos*, 'Mother of Christ'. He fought very
shy of dragging extra relatives into the celestial family. In his
terms, Mary was Joseph's mortal wife and that was the way
she should remain. How could God have had a mother, or a
maternal counterpart, even in his earthly form? Yet in this he
was inadvertently fuelling the duallists' argument. Whilst they
recognized a major female element in creation, they rejected the
notion of Christ being human, and so ignored the question of his
earthly mother.

Cyril backed the *Theotokos* notion heavily and was instantly
offended when reports filtered through to him of Nestorius'
criticism. It led to a protracted and public row between Cyril
and Nestorius and their respective parties, and it was this constant
bickering that goaded Theodosius into convening the Council of
Ephesus. Ephesus turned out to be an unlucky choice of venue for
Nestorius. The local bishop, Memnon, suspecting that his bread
was likely to be more generously buttered one side than the
other, backed Cyril. Memnon's monkish henchmen were raised
to such a state of belligerence that Nestorius had to be given an
armed military guard whilst in the city.

When it came to the ballot, which Nestorius declined to
attend in person, his fate was determined finally by the vagaries
of nature. Severe weather prevented his own backers, mainly
from Antioch and Syria, from reaching Ephesus in time to vote.
Without the missing 'humanists' of the Antioch school, the 'divinity' lobby supported by the Alexandrians were thus in total
control of the proceedings and claimed a 'landslide' victory. In
his earlier summing up Nestorius is alleged to have made the

momentous plea: 'Do not make the virgin a goddess!' All was in vain. In a pagan city, within the shadow of the huge shrine of Artemis, the bishops of the Alexandrian school solemnly decreed that the enigmatic Mary should become that which Nestorius and others had fought so hard to suppress. Through the strokes of 158 devout Christian pens, Madonna Maria was set officially in the footsteps of the Queen of Heaven.

Cyril's stance became ratified as catholic policy when, in spite of the very dubious proceedings at Ephesus, the Pope backed him and the *Theotokos* concept was thus effectively formalized in both East and West. Meanwhile the Syrian group had arrived in town and each lobby promptly excommunicated the other, supporting their respective expressions of distaste with some ripe theological curses fired off at opposing camps. Patience finally exhausted, Theodosius had the three architects of the row, Cyril, Memnon and Nestorius, put in gaol to cool off.

Thus Mary, increasingly forgotten as the earthly wife of Joseph, and ever more revered as the semi-divine *Theotokos* began the climb into a cult of goddess worship that by the thirteenth century would equal any in the ancient world. The great problem lay in that her aura was constantly shadowed by the paradox between the whore and the holy one. Through discreet analogy, the mother goddess was also instilled into the image of 'Jerusalem the Bride', and of the Mother Church. Minds that accepted her thus, sanitized and aloof from the slightest stain of sexuality, still rejected her vehemently when it came to her supreme part in the creation story.

The elevation of Mary would always sit as an uncomfortable compromise. It resulted in a figure who was dressed in very ambiguous uniform and who became peculiar to Christianity. The Christian propaganda machine rose to the occasion as best it could. It left Mary conveniently chaste, from the moment of her birth free from any sexual connotations, and thus the apostasy of the old mother goddess, that overtly carnal lady who enjoyed her matrimonial duties to the full. In Mary was a personality who would least offend, and who would best safeguard the male supremacy in the Church. She was the spotless and sexless maternal figure to whom men vowed to a life of abstinence could look for comfort without intimidation. In a movement for which, *in extremis*, even thoughts of sexuality brought the 'stench of corruption' to saintly nostrils this was not unimportant, though in practice Mariolatry was to be beset by hypocrisy and double standards.

Beside Mary the Virgin has been placed, quite clearly by design, that other Mary, Mary Magdalene, the so-called penitent whore. With her as a role model, less fortunate Christian womanhood was condemned to a life of second-class citizenship, the endless and unenviable inheritance of the 'Curse of Eve'. The effects, on medieval wives and twentieth-century convent-educated school-girls alike, was severe and at times catastrophic.

14

The Barbarians

Thus far the journey has followed a single broad road tracing signposts to the south. It has stepped over the graves of people who stemmed from the European axis of nomadic hunter gatherers and who chased the sun. They had come across or around the Alps, into Italy and the Balkans, and from there they had gone either by way of the Dardanelles or the Caucasus into the fertile crescent of western Asia before eventually crossing to Mediterranean Europe. The instincts and sentiments which we in twentieth-century Europe have inherited distantly from the hunting stock did not, however, come to us wholly from the south, and it is when the journey turns to the north that the links and the parallels begin to suggest a 'grand design'.

'Grand design' has to be a euphemism. It would be naïve to expect 'carbon copy' religious activities and experiences. There have been, however, and will continue to be astonishing similarities: common perceptions of animistic spirits; trees and water revered universally as sources of spiritual power; pantheons; sacred kings united in fate across continents; and mother goddesses fashioned in ways so similar as to be beyond rational explanation. These may be explained, in part, by obscure channels of communication forged through cultural exchange, trade and force of arms; environments affecting peoples in like manner have also generated similar responses. Yet other bonds of faith and practice seem inexplicable, and about those we can do no more than wonder.

The coronation of an Irish ruler may seem a far cry from the traditions of god-kings who arose and fell in the heat and dust of Mesopotamian summers and who reached their ultimate expression with the son of a Galilean carpenter. Yet connections are to be made. The halls of Tara, which clutch at the world's heart strings regrettably more through the romancing of Margaret Mitchell and Vivien Leigh than by the fame of the ancient capital of Ireland, provided the backcloth against which the Celtic kings of the remote island which Greek travellers knew as Ierne were married in sacred and splendid ceremony. The occasion was striking, not least because the sovereign wed two women. The first provided him with earthly company, the other was a priestess taking the part of a fertility goddess, the beautiful and mythical queen of Connaght, Medb or Maeve. On distant horizons there was also a tinge of menace for this happy moment because few Irish rulers were destined for long life. In the immaculate health and virility of kings, descended by repute from the tribal god, lay the prosperity of the people. The wrinkles and blemishes of mortality were seen as auguries of their doom, but so too was any blighting of the land over which they ruled. Thus, not only was it inappropriate that if the king managed to elude death in battle, he should continue as a scarred veteran, or that he should slide into old age and infirmity, he was also barred from presiding over an earth which had become barren. As physical human decay made its first untimely appearance, or crops failed, the goddess queen became symbolically transposed by a hag, the signal for the man to begin his lonely walk towards abdication or slaughter.

We have returned to the territory that was once roamed by the Ice-Age hunters and in the strict sense of a Mesopotamian model we are not about to discover a mother goddess or a dying-and-rising god amongst the Celts although many authors have tried to find them amongst the personalities of Irish legend. Both are present in principle but they have undergone shifts in identity and purpose to meet a fresh environment and altered circumstances.

The Celts and their immediate predecessors provide another bridgehead between south and north; they are the first civilization of northern Europe known to history by name, and Ireland takes a unique place in the Celtic story because its traditional literature, though of questionable accuracy, is one of the main storehouses of Celtic belief.

Much of the popular confusion over Celtic religion is attributable, unfortunately, to the fact that they have been victims of an almost unparalleled level of romance and distortion. During the centuries since the Renaissance a reawakening of interest, based on a great deal of imagination and little hard fact, has led to some wild notions that are only now being laid to rest. In the British Isles we tend to imagine the Celts as the 'ancient Britons' whose Druid priests waved golden sickles and bits of mistletoe and stamped round Stonehenge in white nighties. We imagine fondly that a surviving Celtic legacy has clung on through witchcraft, and folksy groups with long hair and open sandals, who practise 'earth religions'. Most is worth less than a second thought.

The truth about Celtic origins possesses its own fascination and is stronger than the fiction.[1] The Celtic star arose somewhere along the upper reaches of the Danube, perhaps in Switzerland or southern Germany, in about the seventh century BC with a central European people who came to the British islands only late in their time, and the word 'Celt' reflects less a tight ethnic character than an Indo-European language group.

Until the Roman Empire swallowed them up they were the masters of Europe above a line which began roughly at the Pyrenees, and followed the Alps and the river Danube to the shores of the Black Sea, the northern Europe which classical writers identified as 'transalpina'. At the peak of their power they also controlled large parts of the Iberian peninsula, the Balkans, Anatolia, and even Italy itself but by the first century BC the only independent Celtic region on the continent was Gaul.

As far as the British Isles are concerned, there is no evidence to suggest that the Celts ever made obeisance on the hallowed turf of Stonehenge, a monument to more arcane Bronze Age gods; and it is highly improbable that twentieth-century 'nature religions' have inherited an oral tradition faithfully passed down from distant Celtic ancestors.

If there is one over-riding weakness in the Celtic 'case' it is that they were the guardians of a complex and sophisticated religion which they themselves were unable to preserve other than by word of mouth. The journey has for some time been in company with the written word. Now, in part, it has to return to less well-defined sources of evidence. It comes perhaps as something of a surprise that, not only across the overall span of intelligent man's time on earth, but even over the last five thousand 'modern' years, only a tiny fraction of culture has benefited from writing. Progress has been reliant far more on the spoken word and on the immense skills of memory necessary to preserve an oral tradition. These skills may have been reliable whilst oral traditions were the norm, but as literacy gained ground the art of memorizing and reciting was lost.

The search for themes lies once again in the fallible arms of archaeology but, as with Christian beginnings, the pitfalls are compounded by the written word itself. Around the Celts were literate cultures with whom the recording of the Celtic heritage was placed, yet who invariably understood little and sympathized less. It was a case of incomplete knowledge being a dangerous thing, particularly when that scant understanding was also coloured by prejudice. The missing element which would have guaranteed a basis of truth, is a record in the Celtic language, or indeed anything in Greek or Latin written by Celts. Their legacy found itself instead in the cavalier hands of authors like Julius Caesar and Strabo (who themselves were observing indirectly from the now lost diaries of Posidonius), and worse, in the positively mischievious safe-keeping of Christian clerics and monks.[2] Deciphering the Celts, therefore, lies in meshing archaeological evidence with questionable written material and seeking to produce a realistic composite.

Until descendants of the pioneering farmers in the Fertile Crescent began, about six thousand years ago, to head north and west from the near east lured by the rich glacier-pounded soils of the virginal Danube and Rhine valleys, cultural change in Europe beyond the Alpine barrier had been extremely slow, hampered by the permafrost which was retiring, little by little, northwards. Civilization was still represented by bands of hunter gatherers existing at subsistence level. Then, over two thousand years, waves of immigrants mingled with the more primitive European tribes and developed a farming economy — cereal crops along the river valleys, cattle, sheep and pig breeding on the uplands.

The discovery and exploitation of sources of metal, principally copper, triggered Europe's metamorphosis from the Stone to the Bronze Age. Furthermore, in the second millennium, a drier and warmer European climate had an adverse effect on cereal growing encouraging a further swing towards pastoral farming. In about 1300 BC, in the valley of the upper Danube, a new and more sophisticated people, the Urnfield Culture (so-called because they cremated their dead and buried the remains in urns in vast flat cemetery fields) began the efficient mixed farming which has persisted to the present day.[3] They, like their predecessors, carried on a booming metal trade with western Asia allowing important cultural links with the south to persist.

The Urnfielders were followed in about 700 BC first by the Hallstatt and then La Tène cultures which extracted and worked iron, and it was with them that the Celtic identity probably took form.[4] The Celts cannot have been invaders or foreign newcomers, and even the Urnfielders may well have spoken a form of Celtic. There was probably some influx of blood from the Steppelands, because horse bits and other equestrian trappings suddenly appear in considerable quantity amongst grave goods, and there may have been further waves of immigrants from south of the Black Sea, but the Celts represent more of an evolution than a take-over. They kicked the European Iron Age into play.

In both Hallstatt and La Tène periods, funeral arrangements copied those of the Etruscans in northern Italy.[5] The Hallstatt dead, of both sexes, were laid on bronze biers under four-wheeled carts and accompanied by other equestrian gear, though by the later period the vehicles had changed to fast two-wheeled chariots drawn by pairs of horses. Both burials seem to speak of the beginning of a journey as well as an abiding spiritual and material concern with horses in a culture to which the horse represented prosperity and abundance, but the change to chariots underlines an increasing emphasis on warfare. The graves also provide the basis of some important distinctions. Not only does all the surviving evidence relate to an upper ruling echelon, it also confirms that women achieved considerable power and rank in a strongly class-organized society. We can guess that the 'huddled masses' followed their own religion – conducted localized rites, followed their seasonal festivals, worshipped regional spirits – but if the style and content differed markedly from that of the aristocracy, it has been lost irretrievably.

From 500 BC onwards archaeology traces the Celts pushing further westwards. We do not know exactly when or from where they reached Ireland, though they could have arrived as early as the sixth century BC, directly from the Continent or through mainland Britain. Alas, some less than competent digs in Ireland have destroyed a good deal of vital information on that count but certainly by 450 BC, traces are found in south-eastern England.

The discovery of icons and inscriptions has revealed a good deal about the religion of the Celts and we have an outline picture extending from Ireland to eastern Europe and down to the Iberian peninsula. Most of the material, it has to be said, comes from the Romano-Celtic period in Gaul and the British Isles, but earlier sometimes pre-Celtic evidence has emerged which may be significant. It includes many Bronze and Iron Age ritual shafts, found to be filled with bones of domesticated farm stock, sometimes human remains, iron implements and layers of grain.[6] Among the most productive in Britain, at Findon in West Sussex, a shaft some 2 metres across and 76 metres deep yielded huge quantities of deer bones and pottery fragments. This, like so many others, could have been a rubbish tip but it probably bears a strong message linking fertility, the earth and death.[7] The tradition of digging ritual pits, into which votive offerings and perhaps sacrifices were placed, extends back to the Middle Bronze Age in Europe and probably satisfied the same need to communicate with chthonic or earth gods that the deep caverns met for the Ice-Age hunters. A Bronze-Age shaft at Swanwick, dating to the late second millennium BC, was found to have a wooden pole at the bottom smeared with traces of human or animal flesh which may represent victims tied to it in sacrifice, and a shaft with similar evidence exists in Bavaria.

Individual trees or tree trunks certainly seem to have been held sacred. The sites of pre-Roman wooden sanctuaries often reveal massive post-holes and at Libeniče in Czechoslovakia the remains of a pair of burnt upright posts were found with ritual neck torques around them.[8]

Relics are abundant although often their message is vague. Rough wooden statues, invariably worked in oak, were abandoned in many places. An extraordinary hoard of 190 anonymous figures was unearthed from the temple of Sequana at the source of the Seine, and both France and the British islands sometimes turn up distinctive images of gods with three heads or faces.[9] Such things may be unearthed with little to identify them but in other works, by contrast, the intimations are clear. An impressively male figure holding a club, cut into the chalk hillside at Cerne Abbas in Dorset, offers little clue to identity but confirms strong Celtic interest in the male libido. Though of uncertain date and anonymous, the chalk relief of the 'Long Man of Wilmington' in the East Sussex Downs, like its counterpart, is no less obviously a fertility deity with striking phallic emphasis.

The strongest message is of the mother goddess for whom an almost uninterrupted cult has been traced from the Ice Age. There is unmistakable evidence that she was paramount in neolithic Europe and her descendants were scarcely less dominant.[10] But trends were emerging and in the late neolithic period of France one finds mother goddess images in tombs and on the walls of caves associated with inhumation as she became more clearly identified not only with fertility but also with war and with death. These are familiar patterns which persisted into the European Iron Age.

The powerful status suggested by the archaeology is perhaps a reflection of the role of Celtic women. Whilst there is no proof that the Celts were matriarchal, we have the evidence of the Hallstatt and La Tène graves, that two of the most outstanding and feared rulers of Britain were the queens Cartimandua and Boudicca and, furthermore, some of the Irish mythology implies a matrilinear succession in that the *Tuatha De Danann*, are the 'people of the goddess Danu'.

The Romano-Celtic period produced a welter of goddess names in inscriptions all over Europe and the British Isles which perhaps define variations of the one, titled after regions or tribes or even landmarks. There is little evidence of a pantheon based on division of labour and deities seem to be identified more by territory. Thus Medb was worshipped in Ireland's Connaght, Nehalennia at the mouth of the Rhine, Rosmerta in parts of Britain, Nantosuelta on other European rivers and so on. The goddess went with, and was inseparable from, the parcel of land which she protected in peace and war.

Her images come in several forms.[11] Singly they are often anonymous carvings, generally in relief on stone but also fashioned as individual votive offerings in pipe-clay. They carry the symbols of fertility and prosperity: apples, bread, *cornuacopiae* and children, and are also often accompanied by dogs which hold particular fertility connotations. Other figures of uncertain role, such as the hooded dwarfish *genii cucullati*, may appear with them, and the pipe-clay goddesses are frequently sculpted as nursing mothers with children at the breast.

Predictably, in a horse-breeding society, the equestrian goddess Epona is widely represented although more on the Continent than in the British Isles. A number of her dedications are from cavalrymen but she was more generally worshipped in a domestic context. Iconography usually reveals her riding side-saddle, often accompanied by foals, and she may carry the familiar attributes of bread, fruit and *cornuacopiae*. In Britain, the beautifully wrought horse in the limestone near Westbury in Wiltshire is probably a representation of the goddess.

Mother goddesses may appear in partnership with a god,

thus Nantosuelta is linked with the Gaulish deity, Sucellos, and Rosmerta with an anonymous Celtic god disguised as the Roman Mercury. In each case the male deity has both territorial and fertility significance.

Of all the archaeological depictions, the most familiar comes in the form of the *Deae Matres*, the three Mothers who, like the single goddess, are frequently linked with localities. Such threesomes emerge all over Europe and again many of the dedicants were soldiers; in the British Isles the Corinium Museum in Cirencester holds some of the finest examples of relief carvings.[12]

The grouping of similar deities in trinities apparently reflects an almost universal desire and, although in Celtic religion the significance seems superficially different to that in western Asia, it may still subscribe to an awareness of the young and old, light and dark, bountiful and destructive aspects of the divine female personality. Some *Matres*, such as the *Britannicae*, embraced wide areas whilst others, including the *Treverae* and *Nemausicae* from the regions of Trier and Nîmes respectively, had a very localized following.

The Celtic authority Miranda Green points out that topographical surnames are not found in Britain, suggesting that the *Matres* were an import from Gaul.

The three figures are typically seated in a row, staring out at the viewer, each accompanied by the familiar symbolism of bread, fruit, *cornuacopiae*, children and dogs. The goddesses may be identical but, significantly perhaps, some of the icons are worked with variations in respect of age; thus one youthful image may have long flowing hair, whilst her more mature companions wear bonnets.

Archaeology points to a Celtic religion which invaded all corners of civil and military life, and which was strongly influenced by a dependence on pastoral farming and the successful breeding of animals. The latter ties in with an emphasis on clan warfare. Those who grow crops tend to stay put and live comparatively peaceably, breed stock and there is a strong yen to rustle! Celtic life was an endless round of skirmish and raiding against neighbours because acquisition of herds meant power and it is not without significance that the great legendary saga of Ireland, the *Tain Bo Cuailnge*, is based on a cattle raid.

As far as Britain and Ireland were concerned it is true that the Belgic peoples from north-eastern Gaul, the last of the Celtic tribes to settle in these islands, introduced the plough and triggered the real growth of mixed farming in Britain.[13] But prior to that, in the sensitive period of Celtic religious development when seasonal festivals were being established and deities were taking on roles and personalities, life was dependent on the fertility of stock.

Were the archaeological evidence all that we had, we should probably be as lacking in the more intimate detail of Celtic religion as we are in that of the Urnfielders and their immediate successors. But there are two other major sources of information. Unfortunately both must be treated very warily.

Five hundred years before the rise of Christianity, Greek society was on the wane, but in the south Rome was flexing muscles with which to launch herself out of the Appennine peninsula. The Celtic and Roman cultures which were about to face each other presented almost diametric opposites. The Celtic realm was a loose federation of feuding clans, fiercely independent, non-literate, but with an eloquence and an intellect that were in a class of their own. The empire conversely functioned along the lines of a monolithic international corporation. Its western arm communicated through a language which, though not particularly articulate as a spoken tongue, was a vehicle of great literary strength. Latin, like Greek, had become established as a universal *lingua franca* and had allowed for the pooling and enrichment of ideas across national European boundaries.

Thus the Celts in history became the responsibility of contemporary commentators from Greece and Rome. Their accounts enter the formula and add colour, though not always objective insight, to the bare bones of the archaeological evidence. The Celts were no strangers to classical writers.[14] The Greeks had experienced both trading links and military skirmishes with them, to the extent that Greek authors of the fifth and sixth centuries BC considered people sufficiently *au fait*, that the *keltoi* were offered up to the readership without detailed introduction. The Romans had experienced an early and uncomfortable taste of northern military capability when the Celts swarmed down through the Alpine passes into Italy and briefly overran Rome itself late in the fourth century BC.

The Romans called the Celtic tribes beyond the Alps both Galli and Celtae – the name by which the continental Celts referred to themselves. Outside the European theatre the Celts were never described as such by the classical writers. In Anatolia the Romans knew them as the Galatae, the Galatians of the New Testament. On the other extremity of their range, in the islands referred to as Albion and Ierne, always fringe stamping grounds and finally the refuge of a culture in retreat, there is no evidence that they even called *themselves* Celts.

Before official Christianization of the Roman Empire under Constantine, Rome was prepared to open its arms to deities from wherever. But at the same time she was none too keen on promoting religious practices which she regarded as inferior and barbaric, and if the classical manuscripts are anything to go by, the Celts headed the league of barbarism; hence the danger in reliance on classical sources. The Druidic priesthood reportedly possessed a notoriously brutal streak, indulging in such niceties as ritual drowning, decapitation, and incineration of men and women in hideous wickerwork colossi. Some of this is borne out by archaeology but classical writers added fuel with a welter of lurid and perhaps malicious reporting.

Julius Caesar wrote, not unreasonably: 'The whole Gallic people is exceedingly given to religious superstition.' Relating Caesar's campaigns in Europe in the first century BC, however, the Roman author, Lucan, applied a generous measure of poetic licence to a Celtic sanctuary destroyed near Marseilles:

> A grove there was, untouched by men's hands from
> ancient times whose interlacing boughs enclosed a space
> of darkness and cold shade, and banished the sunlight
> from above. No rural Pan dwelt there, nor Silvanus, rul-
> er of the woods, no nymphs; but gods were worshipped
> there with savage rites, the altars were heaped with
> hideous offerings, and every tree was sprinkled with
> human gore. On these boughs, if antiquity, reverential
> of the gods, deserves any credit, birds feared to perch; in
> those coverts wild beasts would not lie down; no wind
> ever bore down upon that wood, nor thunderbolt hurled
> from black clouds; the trees, even when they spread
> their leaves to no breeze, rustled among themselves.
> Water also fell there in abundance from dark springs.
> The images of the gods, grim and rude, were uncouth
> blocks formed of felled tree-trunks.[15]

Lucan's description hardly breeds confidence as objective commentary, although it reveals a portrait which endorses archaeological evidence that the Celts worshipped in sanctuaries deep in the forests where they carried out sacrifice, some of it perhaps human, before barely defined wooden statues of their gods.

A number of classical writers touch on the importance of

heads. The Roman geographer and author, Strabo, comments: '. . . when they depart from the battle they hang the heads of their enemies from the necks of their horses, and when they have brought them home, nail the spectacle to the entrance of their houses.'[16]

Several Gaulish shrines offer confirmation.[17] The limestone walls of a sanctuary at Roquepertuse in Bouches-du-Rhône are punctured with niches that can only have held human heads, and in another sanctuary at Entremont a stone carver has left his personal memento. A pillar containing fifteen human skulls in niches, some still holding iron nails which had been used to skewer them to a doorway or a tree trunk, has been intricately engraved with decapitated heads.

The Celts were head-hunters, but their obsession with such gory trophies did not equate with mindless butchery.[18] They believed the brain was immortal, the place of the soul and so they attached great religious significance to the human skull. Forces contained within the severed head would protect its owner, and deter evil. Decapitation was carried out through precise ritual, the heads were sometimes decorated and embalmed, and the skulls were even used as talismanic drinking cups. Archaeology has suggested that the bond between fertility and death was as strong in the north as it was in the ancient near east, and for the Celts they walked in each other's shadow. But the gruesome evidence of the skulls points to a third connection, that of wisdom, a link whose significance was realized by the cultures of the south. Evidence also exists that the head and its wisdom may have been further linked with the other corner of the triangle, fertility, in that a number of peculiar Celtic icons have been discovered which depict the human head in the shape of a phallus.

Effectively the whole of their natural world was sacred to the Celts; woods, rivers, lakes and other features of the landscape all held religious significance and at one time Celtic sanctuaries, as Lucan's description suggests, probably existed only as groves or clearings in the forest set aside for religious purposes, not unlike the Greek *temenos*. Today there is hard evidence from archaeology that the Celts developed these simple sanctuaries and built temples, usually of wood and circular in outline. Whether they were open to the sky or roofed in thatch is uncertain. Although few authentically Celtic shrines have been found in mainland Britain, the majority being from the Romano-Celtic period, one superb site was uncovered at Heathrow Airport when the runways were being extended. Dating from the fourth century BC,

it follows less typical a rectangular outline surrounded with an
earth bank ditched on the inside (which distinguishes it from forts
ditched outside the defensive rampart) and enclosing a wooden
building.[19]

In Ireland, untouched by Roman occupation, sites are more
plentiful. On the hill of Emain Macha, just to the west of Armagh
town, lies what is left of the old religious centre of Ulster.[20] There,
a sanctuary has been discovered which was raised over the site of
an ancient royal house but destroyed in antiquity and covered
over with a mound of rocks and turf. Excavation has revealed
post-holes which trace a vast circular structure about 38 metres
across, made up of five rings of oak pillars perhaps supporting a
thatched roof, with an entrance way in the form of a long corridor
leading to the centre.

There is a tingling familiarity to this description; it rings
with the same womb and vagina connotations as do the earlier
Stone-Age passage graves of northern Europe. In the centre of
the excavated circle was found a packed earth slope beside a
huge post-hole. The ramp was built to erect a mighty 11-metre
oak trunk, from its remains calculated to have been hewn from
a tree at least two hundred years old, and probably one of the
earliest examples of the holy 'bile' trees of Ireland which seem to
equate very closely with the *terebinths* of the biblical Genesis. It
is, incidentally, from 'bile' that the 'bally' pre-fix on place names
comes.[21]

Such sacred places as Emain Macha saw the great pagan
festivals of Ireland. They possessed their dark side: some provide
evidence of sacrifice, but they also watched over happy affairs
where prodigious quantities of food and drink were consumed.
Games were played, bets won, paramours bedded, and a goodly
amount of market trade indulged, some of the profits no doubt
swelling the coffers of the priesthood.

Although the Roman occupation forces commandeered shrines
in places where they built forts or dug iron, converting them into
Romano-Celtic temples, most of the Celtic people away from the
big conurbations got on with their lives and their worship much
as they had always done. There was very little social contact with
the occupying military or domestic administration, and Romans
and their imperial gods kept themselves to the civilized confines of
city streets and country villas. Amongst the best of the sanctuaries
showing a Roman architectural hand is the temple on the banks
of the river Severn at Lydney in the Gloucestershire Forest of
Dean.[22] During the Iron Age, Lydney was a woodland shrine

belonging to a camp of Irish Celtic emigrés. Here the Romans showed their typical willingness to adopt foreign deities. Lydney was first dedicated to a god Nuadu Argatlam, 'Nuada of the Silver Hand', whose story comes later. When the Romans dug an iron mine there in the fourth century AD and built their own temple on the site, they dedicated it to Nodens, a Romanized version of Nuadu.

Several authors including Strabo and Diodorus Siculus, one of his contemporaries, distinguished influential classes of Celts: Druids who studied the science of nature and dispensed moral philosophy; Bards who 'chanted eulogies and satires' and compiled the great epic songs of Celtic heroes; and Vates or Manteis who were called upon to interpret the sacrifices and 'read the entrails'. Virtually nothing more of the conduct of these guardians of ritual and tradition is known though.

There was something of a renaissance of Roman interest in things Celtic during the fourth century AD when most of the Romano-Celtic temples were built. The Romans inscribed monuments and altars with names of Celtic gods and linked them to Roman counterparts. Often they included a shallow relief of the deity with the inscription. But enthusiasm was comparatively short-lived as the Roman world contracted before the onslaught of new northern powers.

The Celtic star waned everywhere but in Ireland, which leads to a final but very disparate source of information. It is the product of one century, and one country. Ireland gains its importance because it was the single sanctuary throughout the length and breadth of the Celtic lands on to which the Roman legionary, for strategic reasons, never placed his boot. Unlike the traditions of the Gaulish Celts, those in Ireland thus escaped Roman cultural influence. This unique repository was destined to fall into the hands of the Christian monks. Thus whilst in Gaul there is some evidence of Celtic religion but no mythology to explain it, in Ireland there exists a wealth of mythology though largely divorced from its religious authenticity and purpose. There must, in any event, be reservations about the Irish material because there is no definite proof that Celtic creed in Ireland and continental Europe were one and the same. The Celts, it has to be remembered, were not a single nation but a very loose federation of tribes, married only through similar Indo-European dialects. Ireland and continental Europe were separated, however, by two different forms of speech. 'Modern' Welsh and Gaelic are survivors of the Goidelic dialect, which is distinct from the Britonic continental form. There existed a degree of cultural separation between the two.

Quite apart from geographical and dialectic distinctions, Christianity has been at work and, in all probability, we have not received a faithful portrait through the Christian literary route. Two factors will have had a major down-grading effect. One can assume that the scholarly monks did not, on meeting the Irish Celts, immediately sit and put quill to parchment. They would have recorded the mythology related to them only after an amount of goodly Christian influence had been brought to bear on the story tellers, and it will become apparent in another chapter that Christianization, even in its early stages, had a particularly deleterious effect on oral traditions.

Antipathy also stood in the way of accurate preservation. The monks, whilst having some didactic interest in writing down quaint heathen fairy stories, would have belittled the mythology. It would have been quite illogical and out of character for the Christian evangelists to offer encouragement and assistance in perpetuating that which they regarded as inferior and dangerous heathenism. In their view all pagan practice and thought evidenced the devil at work. Stories all too frequently appear distanced from serious meaning, with their personalities cast in boorish and profane light. It is difficult to believe that a people with the eloquence and pride of the Celts would have worshipped the clownish caricatures which emerge, and one senses ever more strongly as one reads the ancient prose that the monks manipulated the authentic stories in such a way as to excise the dignity of Celtic gods.

It is also questionable whether the Celts actually wished some of the more intimate aspects of their tradition brandished on the written page. Occultism played no less important part in the power base of their priesthood than it has for other cultures. If the Druids were unwilling to divulge intimate details to their own people, how much less likely would they have been to commit such secrets to the hands of foreigners who had shown themselves eager to swamp Celtic faith? The Celtic priesthood may well have felt inclined to offer parodies as a mark of the disdain they felt towards the promoters of Christendom's roadshow.

Nevertheless, Irish literature provides the most extensive window that we possess on to Celtic religion. Although it bears boorish overtones, and much is crafted in settings of adventure and romance, the underlying messages are often discernible. The quality of life in the north was measured by good health of men

and animals alike, by success in battle, and by the fecundity of
herds. The frown of the Other World was reflected in disease
and wounds, in impotence and the barren womb, and the king,
as both the father of the tribe and the gods' elect, was a weather
vane of less-than-predictable celestial favour. If the gods looked
badly on him, he was no longer their chosen one, and the auguries for the prosperity of the tribe were bad.

By many accounts the Celts were mighty men with startling
blue eyes, trimmed red or golden beards and moustaches. To
the smaller and darker Mediterranean races they must have
presented formidable and apocalyptic images as they strode out
of the northern mists swinging their massive weapons of war.
But inevitably time and tide came to steal manly perfection.

There exists a bizarre tale which underlines the necessity for
the sacred kings of Ireland to retain perfect physical appearance.[23]
Nuadu Argatlam, 'Nuada of the Silver Hand', the legendary god-
king of Ireland allegedly lost his right hand in the famous Battle
of Moytura. So, the physician god, Dian Cecht, crafted a silver
hand as a gift to the king – perfect in every respect. Even with
this immaculate prosthesis, however, Nuadu was blemished. It
was impossible to disguise his mortality and the disfavour of the
Other World, and he could no longer remain as king.

The Irish kings, as has been said, were vulnerable not only
if their own physical state became flawed but also if the land
became blighted and the Irish sagas recount that King Bres was
deposed, partly due to his lack of charity but chiefly because the
land he ruled had become barren.

The analogy between the fitness and suitability of the sacred
king, and the health of Celtic affairs was also provided with a
graphic 'barometer' in the way the goddess queen was represented.

Her fruitfulness was, logically and very much as it had been in
the south, dependent on the virility of her partner, he chosen by
the gods to take the Irish crown and to be her mate.[24] In several
legends the mother goddess plays her casting hand whilst in the
disguise of the hag who made her appearance at the beginning
of the chapter, the symbol of sickly and withered nature. In one
such tale a prince and his brothers made a chance meeting with
this decrepit and repulsive shade. She requested each man to have
sexual intercourse with her. All but one declined. The single bold
individual who took her was, of course, the rightful and chosen
heir, and as they coupled so the hag shed her hideous mantle and
revealed herself to be the beautiful transfigured goddess queen,

the 'Sovereignty of Ireland'.

The king's intercourse with the mother goddess was no less vital to the future of his people than the embrace between the fertility goddess and the god-kings of Mesopotamia. But as he shed his virile and unblemished visage, so the mantle of the hag returned and the goddess awaited rejuvenation by a younger and fitter suitor. Life and death, sexuality and barrenness, wove their timeless and tangled skein.

In legend, Medb's original consort was Ailill though, beside her, he is drawn as a diminutive figure and generally in Irish mythology female deities are more prominent than their male counterparts. There is little doubt of a sexual 'pecking order'. Ailill was perhaps no more than the first king of Tara in the mythical heroic age to join with the goddess in the *banais rigi*, the royal wedding. Nine other kings are listed with Medb. The fact that in secular life the Celtic female exercised this dominance is noted, with homely candour, by the fourth century AD writer Ammianus Marcellinus:

> A whole troop of foreigners would not be able to withstand a single Gaul if he called his wife to his assistance, who is usually very strong, and with blue eyes, especially when, swelling her neck, gnashing her teeth, and brandishing her sallow arms of enormous size she begins to strike blows mingled with kicks, as if they were so many missiles sent from the string of a catapult.[25]

Bede sheds further light on the sexual supremacy, commenting on matrilinear preferences amongst the canny Celtic Scots:

> So the Picts crossed into Britain, and began to settle in the north of the island, since the Britons were in possession of the south. Having no women with them, these Picts asked wives of the Scots, who consented on condition that, when any dispute arose, they should choose a king from the female royal line rather than the male.[26]

The local territorial identity of the mother goddess accounts for the fact that in northern Britain she was known as Coventina, with a great Romano-Celtic centre at Carrawburgh, whilst she was Macha in Ulster, but Etain, or Maeve, or Medb in various parts of Eire, and in Wales she was Rhiannon, the 'Great Queen'. In

Irish literature the triple aspect of the goddess was known as the Morrigne, whose separate components included Medb or Maeve in aspects of fertility, and Morrigan, the 'Queen of Demons', as ruler of the underworld. In her third role, as arbiter of battle and destruction, she was known by the name Badb Catha, 'Raven of Battle', always a bringer of omens in northern traditions. Badb Catha is said to have appeared to Cu Chulainn, one of the great heroes of Irish legend, and confronted him with oracular portents before battle.

Like the deities of other early religions, those of the Celts possessed powers to transform into animals. A spiritual reverence for the animal world seems to have persisted, more or less continuously, since the Ice Age and many of the Celtic deities became identified with particular creatures. Thus the god Artio was associated with bears in Europe, the god Lugh was believed to prowl the Irish woods as a lynx, and the Gaulish deity Cernunnos, the 'Horned God', roamed as a huge phantom stag. There also exist various depictions in Europe of the Tarvos Trigarnos, the three-horned bull, though which deity it represents is unknown. A tradition of sacred bulls runs through the Irish sagas including the Great Bull of Cooley which was undoubtedly an animistic cloak for a god since it possessed human wisdom and understanding. The mother goddess was no exception, nor was her transmutation limited to birds since, as Epona, she also took the semblance of a white mare.

In this respect, the twelfth-century commentator, Giraldus Cambrensis, described a rite performed by the Ulster tribes at Emain Macha:

> He who is to be inaugurated not as a prince but as a brute, not as a king but as an outlaw, comes before the people on all fours, confessing himself a beast with no less impudence than imprudence. The mare being immediately killed and cut in pieces and boiled, a bath is prepared for him from the broth. Sitting in this he eats the flesh which is brought to him, the people standing round and partaking of it also. He is also required to drink of the broth in which he is bathed, not drawing it in any vessel, nor even in his hand, but lapping it with his mouth. These unrighteous things being duly accomplished, his royal authority and dominion are ratified.[27]

The description, from where we stand, seems a nonsense of depravity, and if any tribe did perform such a parody (there is no guarantee that the description is anything more than a defamatory invention of Christendom), it was perhaps some sad alternative gesture by a cult that had lost its way. Yet from where and what had it originated? For a mother goddess whose people enjoyed a robust and unrestrained sexuality, icons made of 'rude and uncouth blocks of wood' made poor partners, priests in Arician groves masturbating against sacred tree trunks notwithstanding. There are hints that the king's coronation celebrations once included intercourse with a white mare. In the context of an understanding that the king was mating with his mother goddess in her animal guise this was perhaps not the bestial obscenity we would perceive today, but it was perhaps such a rite which had been devalued into the spectacle witnessed by Giraldus Cambrensis.

Though the Celtic gods, Irish native and Gaulish alike, are gathered collectively in the later texts as the *Tuatha de Danann*, the 'Peoples of the goddess Danu' they do not reflect a true pantheon.[28] The deities, identified as they were according to territory, tended to be all things to all people. Some sense of hierarchy is, nevertheless, discernible. The elder statesman was the Dagda, general factotum and father of the Celtic nations, he who first consorted with the mother goddess. 'Dagda' means 'good god', not in the sense of morally good, but adept in practicalities. That which was needed, the Dagda was competent to provide. The buffoonish images are no more than poor character assassinations at the hands of uncompromising writers. The Dagda can only have been a manly and courageous god to whom mortal Celtic heroes could look for strength and wisdom, above the kind of crude grossness with which he is portrayed. In battle, he heft a massive club, sometimes exchanging it for a hammer, and a ceremonial club was hauled on the equivalent of a wheeled gun-carriage. In Celtic tradition, the Dagda is also known as Ruad Ro-Fhessa, 'Lord of Great Knowledge'.

Myles Dillon, one of the great modern authorities on Celtic culture commented that Christian clerks: '. . . have deprived them [the gods] of their original prestige as objects of cult and relegated them to an artificial setting fitting them to a scheme of pseudo-history which was quite foreign to their origin.'[29]

There has to be the second reservation that grossness to us may not have been grossness to the Celts. Social habits, values and aesthetic norms change with the years, and we should not judge automatically by what is sacred or profane, beautiful or grotesque, in our modern eyes. In eating habits, a northern god worth his salt could get his mouth round awesome quantities of food and ale, and the Dagda was no exception. He owned a magic cauldron the content of which was inexhaustible, a great fount of virility and plenty. In this vast tureen the god Gobniu, perhaps the Dagda in another form, brewed the ale of immortality, the youthful elixir.

Such a vessel has survived.[30] In the National Museum of Copenhagen rests one of the loveliest and most exquisitely crafted heirlooms of pre-Christian art in Europe, the Bowl of Gundestrup. Fashioned from pure silver, it was unearthed in 1891 from the small Raevemosen bog, near Borremose in Denmark. One wonders what thoughts must have touched the peat digger whose spade first struck its rim. The bowl had lain undisturbed since the turn of the Christian era, perhaps made in the Danube heartland, perhaps in Gaul, but brought to Denmark as a peace offering or loot. It had come into the possession of a tribe known as the Cimbrians and, whether in adoration or appeasement of some arcane war god, they consigned it to its boggy sanctuary. Nearly 75 centimetres across its rim, the upper section is built from two layers of moulded plates bearing mythical scenes. Gods and goddesses, sacrifices, ritual drowning, processions of horsemen, and fabulous beasts rest in enigmatic repose.

The Dagda was the father of the Celtic gods.[31] Other male deities existed but not in quite the distinct sense that has become familiar in the south. The Dagda had a son, Oengus, the offspring of a union, according to certain legends, with the fertility goddess, Boinn, after whom the River Boyne takes its name. A more youthful and possibly more accessible god existed in Lugh, also called Lamfota, the 'long-armed one' who reached out to rule the day and night. Amongst the most beautiful of Irish legends, several involve Lugh in tales of rebirth suggesting that he may also have been a fertility god, but he was a late-comer to the list of Celtic deities and his true origin is unknown. Some authors see Lugh as a more youthful manifestation of the Dagda himself. There is a sense that the many other names which emerge from inscriptions and texts all perhaps reflect aspects of the Dagda and the mother goddess.

The goddess, by whatever name, was the ultimate prize which urged the Celts into warfare. In the far reaches of Celtic antiquity there was need for a primordial conflict between good and evil, and the war was supplied in the shape of the two legendary

Battles of Moytura. Wreathed in magical mists created by the
Druids, and led by their king, Nuadu, the *Tuatha de Danann* first
came to Ireland to win it from the old inhabitants, the Fir Bolg.
But they found a mighty adversary in the form of the Fomoiri
– half-human monsters, terrible to behold, each with one hand,
one leg, and three rows of teeth. The Fomoiri were led by Balor,
Lugh's grandfather, a dark and fearsome warrior with a single
Cyclopean eye staring from his forehead.

Balor was to suffer defeat in the face of Lugh. Balor's eyelid
was so huge and so heavy that it took five men to lift it with a
ladle, and it was only opened in battle. As Balor confronted Lugh
and the eye revealed itself, Lugh took aim and let fly a stone from
his sling with such force that the eye was driven to the back of
Balor's skull so that all he could see was his own army. Thinking
that they were the enemy, he slew many of them, and thus evil
was vanquished by its own hand.

The Celts' lifestyle and the environment around them dictated
their religious diary.[32] The gods were celebrated in festivals at key
moments, not in the agricultural calendar, but in the pastoral
year. In the Irish texts the year was split, with a neat economy,
into two seasons – warm and cold. Samain, on 1 November, was
a night when the spirit forces were at large, and the invisible
barriers between temporal and other worlds were dissolved. On
Samain night the mother goddess and the Dagda met and coupled
and all thoughts were on fertilty and death. As the last days of
October ebbed away marking the fading breath of the old year
and the first infant cry of the new, the slaughter of stock, and the
selection of breeding rams and ewes, bulls and heifers, horses and
mares, boars and sows began. Amidst the falling leaves and the
mists, blood and semen flowed together. The blood of sacrifice
re-invigorated the damp cool earth; the semen of life pumped
vigorously in its heady quest to bring the magic of germination.

Imbolc, of which virtually nothing is known, took place on
1 February. It may have had strong fertility connotations at the
season when expectant ewes effectively come into milk.

Beltane was celebrated on 1 May, the most vigorous of the
fertility festivals. The spring had burst on to the countryside,
the land pulsated with life, and the warm time of the year was
beginning. It was the time of lighting huge fires in honour of the
god Belenus, a deity worshipped throughout much of Europe,
perhaps one of the most ancient Celtic gods, and one who is
equally arcane but who was apparently strongly linked with
fertility. Cattle were driven between the fires to protect them

from disease.

The last of the festivals, Lugnasadh, on 1 August, is better known today as Lammas, and it is the one date which can be associated with a time of agricultural importance, the gathering of the harvest.

The rites were presided over by Druidic priests, of whom so much arrant nonsense has been written because in reality so little is known. We are limited to a very small number of contemporary reports, none of which offers more than a 'trailer' to the story. Pliny commented:

> They call the mistletoe by a name meaning the all-healing. Having made preparation for sacrifice and a banquet beneath the trees, they bring thither two white bulls, whose horns are bound then for the first time. Clad in a white robe, the priest ascends the tree and cuts the mistletoe with a golden sickle, and it is received by others in a white cloak. They then kill the victims, praying that God will render this gift of his propitions to those to whom he has granted it. They believe that the mistletoe, taken in drink, imparts fertility to barren animals, and that it is an antidote for all poisons.[33]

On this skeletal observation, virtually all the seventeenth- and eighteenth-century romance was built. Portraits of benign-looking figures in long white robes, sporting snowy bushy beards, waving blood-stained golden sickles and bits of mistletoe, are based on no more substantial evidence than Pliny's account. In reality the Druids seem to have kept faith with other priesthoods, and been highly secretive and wary of divulging details, particularly to unsympathetic outsiders. Presumably they conducted the main festivals, performed the royal marriages, and sacrificed animal and occasionally human victims. There are also strong hints that the Druidic order included women. That is about the extent of it.

Nothing of the Druids in Ireland was written until after Christianization, and Christian writers were thoroughly unsympathetic. There seems little doubt that they distorted their accounts to place the pagan priesthood in as unattractive a light as the gods it served. How often sacrifice took place, how many human heads and bodies parted company on Druidic altars, is in the realm of fiction. Julius Caesar's earlier, though second-hand, observation of huge and horrifying wicker figures that were filled with living

victims and burned is probably too vivid and specific to be imagined, but when and why it happened is again open to speculation.

Modern authors have tended to shade their commentaries
towards the view that the Celts possessed no proper religion;
that their secret practices were little more than exhortations to
crude magic; and that Celtic mythology comprised simple entertaining fairy tales with no bearing on ritual. Yet if any lesson has
been learned, it is to treat such sweeping assumptions with great
care. Celtic religion was born out of hills and forests, lakes and
bogs; it was forged in spectral mists and nurtured around village
fires, delivered to an audience in whose hearts rested a poetic
eloquence and a rumbustuous 'anything goes' fighting spirit. But
this 'heart and soul' was never committed to paper and what is
left for analysis is less even than a synopsis.

That which has been uncovered speaks of a religion with very
ancient foundations and although some aspects were adopted
through cultural contacts with the south, the older strata are
probably peculiar to northern Europe. Reverence for the head,
the sacredness of rivers and lakes and notions of springs as seats
of wisdom, pastoral festivals, shape-changing – these are concepts
which pre-date the Romans or even the coming of agriculture.
Religion to the Celts was an integral part of their daily lives. It
infused everything they said and thought and did. Those who
belittle it are victims of their own cloistered perceptions.

If, as has been suggested, the sovereign power lay ultimately
with the priesthood, it was also the Achilles' heel which eventually
destroyed the Celtic dominance of Europe. No government in
history with an administration based on clerical in preference to
secular logic has survived the test of time. Such regimes invariably are fuelled by fanaticism and intolerance of worldly realities,
and are unable to withstand the pressures of the outside. In this
respect the Celts may have joined a celebrated club which still
draws new membership today.

A strange and unique beauty shines through the survivals
of Celtic faith. No Christian pen has been able to destroy the
sparkling freshness of the poetry. To use the words of Nora
Chadwick in her gentle and penetrating study of the Celts, it
is only by contrast with other mythologies that we realize Celtic
religion contains little that is ugly.

15

Gods of Asgard

In an island of the ocean is a holy grove, and in it a consecrated chariot, covered with a robe: a single priest is permitted to touch it: he feels the presence of the goddess in her shrine, and follows with deep reverence as she rides away drawn by cows: then come days of rejoicing, and all places keep holiday, as many as she thinks worthy to receive and entertain her. They make no war, take no arms: every weapon is put away; peace and quiet are then, and then alone, known and loved, until the same priest returns the goddess to her sacred precinct, when she has had her fill of the society of mortals.[1]

One could be forgiven for imagining that the account related to some Babylonian or Egyptian rite being enacted in the first or second millennium BC, but it is a portrait of a ceremony which may owe nothing to Mesopotamia or Egypt. Its author, the Roman historian, Tacitus, witnessed the event in the first century AD, but that may also be the extent of any association with the classical empires of Greece and Rome.

Tacitus completed the text of *Germania* in AD 98 with the intention of informing educated Romans about the life and style of the barbarians in northern Europe. These people were no longer Celts but the product of a new wave of European migration which had filled the vacuum left as the Celts retreated. It was from amongst these peoples that the Angles and Saxons who moved into the Low Countries and eventually crossed to England would emerge.

Tacitus did not recognize ethnic distinctions. He lumped together a motley of tribes inhabiting north European lands beyond the manageable imperial frontier as 'Germani'. Originally the name may have identified a single dominant clan, but it became misused when it was applied collectively to marauders who invaded Gaulish territory in the west in about 250 BC. Tacitus' 'Germani' were more accurately Cimbri, Suebi, Teutoni, Chauci, and others, all of whom shared the Teutonic form of the Indo-European group of languages. The 'Teutonic' territory was properly the area of Europe lying between the Jura and Vosges mountains and the river Rhine in the west, and the Carpathian mountains and the margins of the ancient Hercynian Forest in the east. In Tacitus' view, however, Germania not only spread up the Rhine but extended far north to the Baltic and Scandinavian lands.

Prior to the imperial campaigns the 'new' northern tribes had been virtually unknown but, increasingly, they cast a lowering shadow over Rome itself. 'War', Tacitus observed drily, 'has lifted the curtain'. In the first century AD Rome was still confidently expansionist, but by the fifth century the tide had turned and Rome's power and influence in the west began to diminish.[2] The Greek-speaking Byzantine empire was secure for another thousand years, but in Europe the legions fell back and, faced with serious loss of policing, the Roman infrastructure began its collapse before the vigour and exuberance of peoples determined to own regions over which they claimed stronger territorial rights than did the foreigners from the south.

By comparison with the Celts there is much more hard information to be gleaned about the Germanic and Nordic culture. There was no organization comparable with that in the south, yet neither was government on any arbitrary or whimsical basis, nor was there uncontrolled despotism. Rule was by example. The tag 'barbarian' has been well indulged but it underlines a false sentiment.[3] 'Barbarian' was used freely and in a derogatory sense by the Romans, and it was willingly adopted by Christendom. Yet even Tacitus, whilst belabouring a distance between himself and the barbarians, was forced into grudging admiration with an implicit admission that the northerners probably stood in equal, if not superior, light to many of those who castigated them as backward and idolatrous demon-worshippers.

Northern society showed a high moral fibre. Punishment was less a penalty dictated by men than an implementation of justice from the heavens. Tribal and family loyalty, and the rule of 'one wife apiece' stood high in these peoples' book of values. Women and children usually accompanied their men on campaigns, and courtesy and hospitality were strictly followed. People lived in small villages and kept fierce independence, not only one tribe from another, but between individuals. Even houses were physically separated by private land. The independent streak came through in their style of warfare. Warriors possessed fanatical bravery as individuals but they lacked any proper cohesion when it came to fighting as a disciplined force; thus the hordes which swept outwards from Scandinavia after the Roman retreat, dramatically successful at the time, had no staying power.

The Nordic and Germanic races are epitomized as nations of rampant fighting men whose zenith was reached with the Viking invasions. Revenue and power lay in the spoils of armed foray against neighbours and more distant adversaries. In battle, death walked hand-in-hand with glory and honour, and the quality of a man's moment of nemesis dictated the quality of his eternity. Frith, a difficult notion to grasp, was a key to life. It implies that the whole tribe shared a single spirit, all its members inviolate against each other and one defended one's kinsmen to the death.

Tacitus, with his usual finesse, caught a general attitude to life: 'You will not so readily persuade them to plough the land and wait for the year's returns as to challenge the enemy and earn wounds: besides, it seems limp and slack to get with the sweating of your brow what you can gain with the shedding of your blood'.[4] These are perhaps peculiarly northern sentiments, but the net result was a cavalier approach to the land and its fertility. Farming could charitably be described as lacklustre. Small herds of cattle and a few cereal crops marked the extent of enthusiasm. There was heavy reliance on obtaining the meat and the hides needed by hunting, and anything else was taken likewise by force of arms. None of which is to suggest that the seasons did not matter. Nordic mythology never shrugs off the shadow of eternal dark, ice and cold. But the attitude to these adversities, in fact to death itself, was superbly defiant. The spectre of death was not allowed to get in the way of the sheer gutsy, devil-may-care vibrance of living.

In their religion many of the tribes were not destined to

embrace Christianity for nearly a thousand years.[5] It may come as a surprise to some that the Christian conversion of Europe was such a drawn-out and reluctant process, but if Spain, France and parts of the British islands saw established Churches well before the fifth century, that experience should not be taken to reflect the timetable of the rest of the continent.

Sweden became Christian only during the twelfth century, and parts of central Europe were still officially flying pagan colours as little as six hundred years ago towards the end of the fourteenth. Few converted willingly and Christianity also remained predominantly a religion of the towns and cities. In the countryside the raw backbone of faith arguably remained staunchly traditional across much of the continent until the dawn of the Industrial Revolution.

To read the ancient poetry of the north is to open a door on a culture for which one is quite unprepared. The verses shine with a crisp, clear radiance; they scan with a striking and unfamiliar beauty which bears the aroma of woodlands, mists and hoar-coated sunrises. Northern 'paganism' encompasses the immortality of the soul, judgement, life in eternity, the quest for excellent human values, the struggle for a good that surmounts evil. These are hardly barbaric principles.

Macho chivalry invades ethics and mythology, and it is perversely a major stumbling block to getting beneath the skin of northern faith. Legends through which strands of belief might be discerned are obscured in their deeper meaning by swords and steeds, blood and fire, ogres and maidens. It is understandable – one does not send the troops into battle equipped with Mills and Boon, or Snow White – but the authors' reluctance to be anything more than objective and heroically stiff-lipped denies a twentieth-century reader any insight into personal attitudes and feelings. We know the stories, but the needs which they may reflect are buried deeply.

The same damaging obstacle that obscured the truth of Celtic 'philosophy' also stands in the way here. Prior to Christianization the northern tribes were effectively illiterate; until Roman incursion they had not developed a script suitable for committing long tracts to paper. Writing was limited to runic symbols carved on wood and metal. Tacitus provided, in *Germania*, one of the very few commentaries on the pre-Christian north from a contemporary pen. Julius Caesar offered another. But both reporters were Romans and both were influenced by the urge to superimpose familiar Olympian tradition on what they found.

So Tacitus observed: 'Of the gods, they give a special worship to Mercury to whom on certain days they count even the sacrifice of human life lawful.[6] Hercules and Mars they appease with such animal life as is permissible. A section of the Suebi sacrifices also to Isis . . .'

The description is revealing but everything is conveniently 'Olympianized'. Mercury is in fact Óthin of Scandinavia, and his German and Anglo-Saxon counterpart Woden. Hercules is Thor or Donar, the thunder god. Mars is Tyr, or Tiwaz, a god of war. As for Isis, she slipped through under her rightful name. (Tacitus confirmed her worship as being imported. She was symbolized in the shape of a galley, and it is well known that by the time she had settled in the heartland of Greek classical culture Isis, among other duties, was the guardian goddess of seafarers.)

After Julius Caesar and Tacitus there followed, in terms of literary offering, a huge time-gap during which we have nothing more than inscriptions. The literary dearth is compounded by the lack of surviving art, an omission largely down to the choice of wood as a building material. Buildings in which might have reposed carvings and paintings have long since provided luncheon baskets for dry rot and wood beetles.

Northern literature relating supposedly authentic tradition was penned from no earlier than the tenth century, and the bulk of it – if 'bulk' is an appropriate term – was written down by scholars living between the tenth and fourteenth centuries. By the earliest of those dates though, three of the five Nordic 'swans' – Norway, Iceland and Denmark – had been converted to Christianity, Sweden succumbing shortly after. Much as the 'heretical' literature of the early Church was erased from memory, so 'pagan' belief in the north was well and truly raped in its bed. The traditions and faiths of Europe did not benefit from the pragmatism and tolerance even of some of the more despotic governments of the ancient near east. Tolerance is a quality for which Christian missionaries in the Middle Ages were not renowned. In most parts of Europe the new faith was extended more through the language of the sword and the bonfire than the tongue. Only Iceland escaped the full impact of Christian laundering, and we have to thank the physical and political remoteness of that single outpost nudging the Arctic Circle for preserving the pathetically few and fragile pages of our own ethnic heritage.

Iceland's literary adventure is a romantic one.[7] During the ninth century a group of Norwegian aristocrats and their families fled Scandinavia precisely because they objected to centralization and the suppression of traditions. They founded an Icelandic colony, and whilst the rest of the Nordic countries were obliged, under the Christian advance, to make a fairly radical break with tradition, Iceland kept the faith. As so often happens, her expatriate families were far more jealous of their ancestry than were the people back home. Thus when the Christian missionaries brought the art of writing to Iceland, they were unable to stifle an entrenched determination to sustain the old word-of-mouth legacy. Gradually the emigré Norwegian landowners wrote and assembled great books relating the traditions of their forefathers. Their passion for preserving cultural history continued down to the fifteenth century by which time Iceland was politically a part of Denmark.

If there was one pivotal twist in the destiny of the ancient books, it was a decision in the seventeenth century by Frederic III of Denmark to instruct his bishop in Iceland, Brynjølfur Sveinsson, to collect together all the old codices he could lay his hands on and send them to the Royal Library. That archive now rests in Copenhagen.

The collection is all we have, and amongst its faded heirlooms the best surviving evidence of the ancient religion and mythology of the north rests with a slim volume known as Codex Regius No. 2365 containing forty-five handwritten sheets of parchment, all from the same pen, and dated to the second half of the thirteenth century. It begins with the *Voluspa*, the solemn apocalyptic prophecy of the seeress as she is raised from her eternal sleep to commune with the assembled gods:

Hear me, all ye hallowed beings,
both high and low of Heimdall's children:
thou wilt, Valfather, that I well set forth
the fates of the world which as first I recall.
I call to mind the kin of giants
which long ago did give me life.
Nine worlds I know, the nine abodes
of the glorious world-tree the ground beneath.[8]

The collection of mythological and heroic lays in the Codex Regius constitutes the Poetic *Edda*, so called to distinguish it from the Prose *Edda*, a brilliant and entertaining 'textbook' of northern tradition, pieced together and composed largely in the form of a dialogue, by an Icelandic scholar Snorri Sturluson.[9] Snorri, born in 1179 into one of the Icelandic-Norwegian families, was an intellectual politician who took it upon himself to assemble the only comprehensive creation-to-conflagration précis of northern mythology to come out of the Middle Ages. His is a genuine effort to explore the faiths of his ancestors through surviving oral tradition and through the poetry which he found in the codices. But Snorri's is a Christian pen, like that of Brynjølfur, and his own boundaries of faith have inevitably shaded the truth. The process by which Christianity was set to obliterate old memories was well on its way, the lights were dimming and traditions and legends were being outlawed ever more stringently. How much adulteration the Prose *Edda* and the small number of writings in the other ancient codices contain therefore is an open question.

A telling comment on Snorri's delicate position emerges from the way he constructed the first part of the Prose *Edda*. It is not a direct observation, but a coy arrangement wherein a fictitious king of Sweden, Gylfi, enters into dialogue with an equally imaginary trio of deities: High, Just-as-High and Third. They answer Gylfi, not Snorri, about everything from the creation of the world to its final apocalypse. There was good reason for this off-beat approach. Snorri could not risk being accused of endorsing pagan 'philosophy', and by writing obtusely he was able to inject subtle Christian interpretations of the 'place' of heathen deities whilst avoiding the necessity to condemn openly traditions for which undoubtedly he felt great sympathy.

Subtlety was a key word because, whilst the Christian view held that all pagan gods were demons to be consigned to the same hellish dustbin as Lucifer, trolls, elves, Hades, Persephone, and any other figures of which the Church disapproved sufficiently, Nordic and Germanic kings were by tradition descended from the gods!

The pedigree placed Christian argument in something of a dilemma, because to press it on a member of the Danish or any other Nordic royal court was to risk urgent contact with an axe blade. The compromise solution cast Nordic deities as human heroes, outstanding men and women all, on whom godliness had been laid mistakenly and foolishly by others. This characterization placed Othin and the rest of the pantheon neatly inside the Christian ball-park since, according to the telescoped chronology which formed the backbone of their medieval religious tradition, everyone was descended from Noah and his boating crew.

Thus there exist in the Anglo-Saxon Chronicles such genealogies as that of the sixth-century king of Wessex, Ceowulf:

'. . . he was the son of Cutha, the son of Cynric, the son of
Cerdic, the son of Elesa, the son of Esla, the son of Gewis,
the son of Wig, the son of Freawine, the son of Frithugar, the
son of Brand, the son of Baeldaeg, the son of Woden.'[10] The
Chronicles account Aethelwulf, who died in AD 858, as being
descended, through an even more tedious list of ancestors, from
Woden whose pedigree is then traced back a further thirteen
generations to Noah.

A second major source from the early medieval period is
the pen of the Danish historian Saxo Grammaticus, born in
1150, who wrote a massive treatise, the *Gesta Danorum*, the
first nine books of which contain a great deal of mythological
material based on folk traditions of western Norway.[11] Saxo's
main drawback is that he is openly hostile and therefore may be
even less trustworthy than Snorri. He writes of the gods as being
little more than devious humans who had deluded their fellow
countrymen: '. . . it is not surprising that barbarians yielded to
their weird hocus-pocus and were led into the rites of a debased
religion.' Such morality is hardly to be relied on as a source of
unbiased reference. Saxo wrote badly, in overbearing and bom-
bastic Latin, with none of Snorri's charm and sympathy, but he
does provide observations to complement the Prose *Edda*.

How much do the Royal Danish codices and Snorri's work
reveal of the gods of the earth? Was there a mother goddess
who walked the tracks of the Nordic north, and did some ill-
starred consort accompany her? In short the answer must be
that neither of these personalities is clearly defined, which is not
to say that they are missing, only that they are drawn in pictures
which at first seem unfamiliar.

The mythology is frustrating in that it offers tempting parallels
with the one hand, but then tends to wave them away with the
other, and always in the back of the mind the question lurks
over what is authentic, what is pre-Christian borrowing, and
what is involuntary Christian adulteration.

Through Snorri's systematic account of world beginning and
ending, *Gylfaginning*, one learns something of the northern view
of the cosmos.[12] A creator god, a primal being sharing the vague
and remote personality of an El or an An, made heaven and earth,
and has given man an immortal soul.

Before the earth was fashioned there existed a realm of
brooding cold, Niflheim, in the midst of which a spring arose to
feed the great rivers. To the south lay a realm of heat and fire,
Muspell, from whose flames its giant keeper, Surt, took sparks

hurling them into the firmament to become the stars. Between Niflheim and Muspell existed the mighty void, Ginnungagap, and in the void, out of the waters of the melting ice, there formed an androgynous being, Ymir, from whose two feet sprang a race of frost giants. Ymir was fed by milk from a cow, Audhumla, but where the cow licked the salty rime-stones there grew another being, Buri, from whose progeny the great gods descended, ever to wrestle in mortal combat with the giants. The first-born was Óthin, the father of the gods. These sons of Buri slaughtered Ymir, and from his blood they made the sea; his skull became the dome of the sky; his flesh the earth; his bones the rocks. The world of men was protected from the giants by a great wall, Midgard, built from Ymir's eyebrows, and in the ocean a giant serpent, the Midgard Worm, girdled the earth biting its own tail in endless writhings.

In *Gylfaginning*'s prologue, based largely on the *Voluspa*, familiar patterns stir, though in a matrix which is quite foreign. The cosmic cow which nourished the primal beings before the world was made is present in the earliest Egyptian belief. A strong flavour of animism goes with the picture of a tangible earth created from the parts of a being, but in Ymir there is also some resemblance to Yaltabaoth, the 'blind god' of the Nag Hammadi texts which provide that somewhere in the cosmic mists there existed an imperfect and culpable being, directly involved in the world's creation. Ymir, the 'ancient giant', was that being.

Ground rules need to be kept in mind when reading Nordic mythology – rules which may not always leap up from the page. Nordic religion is obsessively apocalyptic. It is wrapped up in the mystery of creation, and above all in Ragnarok – the ending, and the beginning of the new. The terrible enemy of gods and men alike is the darkness and cold of winter epitomized by the frost giants. The gods themselves possess almost all human traits, reflecting human strengths and weaknesses. They are born, they marry, they demonstrate rapacious appetites for adventure, food and sex, though not necessarily in that order. They show great courage but they are also vulnerable: they can die.

Óthin, the father of the gods, lord of hosts and god of battle, rules in Asgard; his purpose: the dogged pursuit of wisdom about the final apocalypse and the desperate collection of dead heroes destined to join him in the last fateful battle.[13] The Valkyries ride each day across the rainbow bridge between earth and heaven carrying the noble slain. A deep and complex character, Óthin is married to Frigg, a goddess of great wisdom and

inward strength beside whom Óthin, generally drawn finely and
showing great polish, can seem childishly naïve. Their children,
including some of questionable parentage, make up the twelve
gods of the Aesir, the eldest and probably best-loved of whom
is Thor, born of Óthin's liaison with the primal earth mother,
Iord. God of thunder, he swings the mighty hammer Mjollnir
in his mailed fist splitting clouds and skulls with equal jubilation. Thor is a rollicking, roaring, hard-drinking, red-bearded
trencherman, full of Nordic spunk, and though unquestionably
a child of the heavens not the earth, he bears something of the
style of Gilgameš.

Óthin's second son, one who needs to be studied with some
caution, is Balder, the beautiful ill-fated god destined to die violently in the flush of his youth. In terms of legendary popularity,
Tyr, a god of battle whose physical peculiarity lay in the possession
of an amputated wrist, ranks a close third amongst Óthin's brood.

The names are Nordic, but it seems that the 'Germanic' tribes
effectively looked to the same cosmic family with only minor
variations of title. Thus Óthin equates with Woden or Wotan,
Thor changes to Donar, Tyr to Ti or Tiwaz, Frigg to Frija or
Fricka, and so on. It was these Germanic variations which perme-
ated through to Anglo-Saxon religion, and which have been
immortalized in more recent times through Wagner's epic cycle:
Der Ring des Nibelungen.

The twelve Aesir, most of whom appear on stage only in
passing, were sky gods. But there existed another race in Asgard,
the Vanir, born of the god of wind and sea, Njord. Though a Vanir
himself, he had been hostage to the Aesir at a time when the
two races were at war, and had effectively become one of them.
The Vanir, including Freyr and his sister Freyja, were earth gods
concerned with fertility and abundance.

Inevitably, the northern heaven drew battle lines of sunshine
and cloud, good and evil, and there existed a mischievous
Machiavellian character, Loki, who bears some of the attributes
of a Nordic Enki; born of a giant, he lived amongst the gods almost
as a devil's advocate. He was, in the words of Snorri: '. . . pleasing
and handsome in appearance, evil in character, very capricious in
behaviour. He possessed to a greater degree than others the kind
of learning that is called cunning, and tricks for every purpose.
He was always getting the Aesir into a complete fix and often got
them out of it by trickery.' Since Loki was fathered by a giant he
could be seen to have an unhealthy amount of 'bad blood' running in his veins, and in him emerged three great adversaries of

the created world which, according to the ancient runes, would be instrumental in its downfall. Through a giantess wife, Loki fathered the darklings: the wolf Fenrir, the world serpent and Hel.

Ranking firmly on the side of giants, there lurked a pack of phantom wolves, the greatest and most terrifying of which, Fenrir, was bound by a magical thread. One day it would break free to chase the sun and the moon round the sky. When it caught the sun and swallowed it, the doom of the world would begin, Ragnarok. The world serpent was destined to increase its mad writhings and cause the sea to rise in flood, and on the day of Rangarok the waters would quench the flames of Surt's all-consuming fire. Hel was mistress of the dark and misted realm of Niflheim, whence rode all the battalions of the dead who had perished of old age or disease and not been taken by Óthin and Freyja as heroes of Valhall.

Inevitably paradoxes appear which are hard to penetrate. They range from the small detail in Snorri's tale describing the first two human beings springing from Ymir's left armpit, but almost in the same stroke of the pen, created by the gods from two trees on the sea-shore. One takes one's pick! On a more far-reaching scale, why did the gods invariably wed giantesses? The god Njord married a giantess called Skadi. Óthin consorted on occasions with giantesses. Freyr at one time took a bride Gerd from the giant world. There may be a logical answer following the maxim: 'if you can't beat them, join them'. The gods perhaps were given to seek such marriages in an effort to stave off the inevitable finality through the 'frith' of a marital bond.

We have thus not a little information about the dramatic scenario of the gods of the north, but we have little of the sense in which men worshipped them, perhaps because of the Christian editing of the surviving material. The ancient texts, as they have come to us, provide only a cartoon and they do little to answer the real questions. Did the gods of the earth as we have come to understand them from the south exist in the Nordic heaven? Did a dying and rising god take his place in the order of things, or did the Celtic experience set a new precedent? Was Freyja the goddess of life and fertility, or was it some other personality? How were these beings worshipped? Were there seasonal festivals and a Sacred Marriage?

Snorri and fellow medieval writers were interested in preserving legendary sagas, not details of heathen 'philosophy'. Yet many of the answers are staring at us. They need only

unravelling. In the prologue to the Prose *Edda*, Snorri sheds a
small chink of light which may add to our fragmentary apprecia-
tion of the mentality: 'They pondered and were amazed at what
it could mean that the earth and animals and birds had common
characteristics in some things, though there was a difference
of quality. One of the earth's characteristics was that when it
was dug into on high mountain tops, water sprang up there and
there was no need to dig further for water there than in the
deep valleys. It is the same with animals and birds, that it is
just as far to blood in the head as in the feet ... rocks and
stones they thought of as equivalent to teeth and bones of living
creatures. From this they reasoned that the earth was alive and
had life after a certain fashion, and they realized that it was
enormously old in count of years and mighty in nature. It fed all
creatures and took possession of everything that died.'

The world of the Eddaic lays had moved forward but it is worth
remembering from whence some of the foundations came. The
description shows real old-fashioned animism at work, the kind
of belief that might have produced the fabulous animal carvings
from the Scandinavian Bronze Age. It is something which, in
another chapter, is to be explored more intimately and from a
much more recent time.

How do we dig down to the wisdom that had matured by
the time of the Vikings? Tacitus' is not a contemporary account.
It relates to a time long before the Viking era, but it may be
relevant. He provides a single vivid insight when he describes
a goddess of the grove who he calls Nerthus, 'Terra Mater'.[14]
His 'island of the ocean' points to a cult centre in one of the
Danish off-shore territories like Sjaelland. He also indicates that
Nerthus was revered down through mainland Denmark and
across much of Europe north of the Danube.

Tacitus observes that Nerthus is associated with cows; she is
linked firmly to a sacred grove; she is carried concealed in a wagon
through 'the cities of men'; and her intimate companion is a male
figure identified as a 'priest'. Tacitus also describes apparently the
same 'mother of gods' symbolized, around the Baltic coasts, by
wild boars. Tribal warriors, he notes, wore the figure of a boar
as a protective talisman.

Compare Tacitus' description with something not dissimilar
contained in the huge Codex 1005 folio of the Royal Library.[15]
This book was written some time in the eleventh century or after,
and preserved by a farmer on the small island of Flatey, hence it
is called the *Flatey-yarbók*. The Codex covers the saga of King Olaf

Tryggvason and includes a sketch involving a hero called Gunnar
Helming, a young Norwegian living in Sweden. According to the
story Gunnar was attracted to the cult of Freyr and, more particularly, to the young priestesses who served the god in his temple.
Gunnar got himself invited to travel round the country with the
Freyr entourage on an annual procession in which the image of
the god, accompanied by a special priestess known as his 'wife',
was carried in a wagon pulled by oxen.

We know a little to back up the story. Out of at least three
major religious festivals – one in autumn, one at mid-winter, and
one in the spring – the Freyr tours were definitely winter events.
The Gunnar Helming tale has the wagon stuck in snowdrifts.[16]
The most dramatic confirmation of the tours came to light
in 1881 when some labourers at Dejbjerg in western
Jutland struck some solid objects whilst digging for peat – the
famous Dejbjerg wagons. In about AD 200 these two magnificent ceremonial carts from the Celtic period of Danish history
were consigned, in a deliberate ritual it would seem, to what
was then a sacred lake.

Slowly over the centuries the lake became a peat bog which,
by chance, preserved the wooden vehicles. One is larger than the
other and they are decorated differently, but they are so ornate
as to be practical only in ritual and, furthermore, in each rested
a low four-legged box and a wickerwork seat designed to carry
some person or object. Thus we appear to have the kind of vehicle
described by Tacitus.

The tale of Gunnar Helming degenerates into little more than
a trivial comedy plot, but it includes striking similarities with
Tacitus' account even though the two descriptions are separated
by a thousand years. Do the stories in some way duplicate each
other? The first and most obvious riddle is that Tacitus refers
to a female deity whom he calls Nerthus, but nobody of that
name appears in the Icelandic codices. How, if at all, did this
Germanic goddess relate to a Viking Vanir god, Freyr, who nonetheless seems to have been involved in similar rites?

There are a number of possibilities. Roman writers were notorious in changing names to suit themselves, so the title 'Nerthus'
may be a red herring. Nerthus is similar to the Celtic equivalent
of Njord, the name of the old Vanir god of the sea and its riches
who fathered Freyr and Freyja. There is also an Irish Celtic word
'nert' meaning strength and fertility of the earth. Thus Tacitus
may have coined a word to imply a fertility deity whose real
Germanic name he did not know. The rites of this goddess were

bound up in considerable secrecy.

It is also worth bearing in mind that the tribes adopted many names for their deities. Snorri lists no less than fifty-four attributed to Óthin, commenting rightly that 'each nation finds it necessary to adapt his name to their language'.[17] Freyja, the Viking goddess who might most closely equate to Nerthus, is not in fact a proper name but a title. It means little more than 'Lady of Freyr'.

We are still left with the major problem of a change of sex. The deity in the wagon was concealed. Another mention of the tour in the *Flatey-yarbók* suggests that the presence of the god was indicated when the wagon 'became heavy'. Tacitus states that the priest of Nerthus was permitted to touch the wagon, and 'felt' the presence of the goddess in her shrine. Since there is a cynical but not entirely inaccurate view that the Romans' study of their neighbours tends to have possessed the in-depth approach of an American coach tour, one simple possibility is that Tacitus got the sex of the deity in the wagon wrong. 'She' could thus have been the equal of Njord or his son, Freyr. The suggestion has also been raised that the sex of the deity was ambiguous. Not impossible – some classical deities were drawn as startlingly bisexual, and early northern legends reveal that, when it suited them, gods and goddess were not beyond occasional change of gender.

The most obvious conclusion is that a northern cult existed, a significant ritual of which was described both by Tacitus and in the Gunnar Helming story, and that the emphasis shifted over a millennium from goddess to god. Thus, by whatever name, the deity in Tacitus' wagon was the equal of Freyja, in the sense that she was the 'wife' of the fertility god. It is perhaps relevant to note that incestuous relationships between brother and sister are common in Nordic mythology. The question which remains is why the change?

Tacitus may, inadvertently, have thrown in at least one clue.[18] He refers to the priests among the Naharvali presiding over the rites of the grove 'in female dress'. It is worthy of note that our modern priests wear vestments that seem more appropriate to a woman, but there are mentions elsewhere in medieval literature that fertility rites were accompanied by 'unmanly clatter of bells and effeminate gestures'. These phrases have a distinctly familiar ring to them and there comes a suspicion that the rites which they describe must have been borrowed. They seem to echo the emasculated priesthood of such Mediterranean cults as Attis and

Kybele. If correct, such 'sissy' behaviour would hardly cut a great
deal of ice with the thoroughly virile and warring Vikings. Freyr
is described as a god of peace and tranquillity and it is a practical
consideration that you cannot farm land which is being fought
over; nonetheless he is also a macho fighting deity and his devotees would presumably find a fully equipped sexual relationship
between fertility god and partner, with the male element in the
ascendancy, rather more appealing. A number of Nordic chief-
tains held the title 'Priest of Freyr', but it is difficult to imagine
Harald Wartooth or Eric the Red dressing up in skirts!

The worship of the phallus was of great importance in northern
religion. The much-travelled medieval writer, Adam of Bremen,
reported in some detail on a magnificent temple, said to have
been totally adorned with gold, which he visited in AD 1070
at Uppsala, last bastion of paganism in Scandinavia.[19] It was
dedicated to three deities, Óthin, Thor and Freyr. For centuries
past, however, the temple was the main centre for a Freyr cult
for whom every nine years a great festival took place that slaughtered in sacrifice nine head of every male beast. Adam also notes
that the temple housed a statue of Freyr equipped with a gigantic
rampant phallus. A small male figurine, once obviously someone's
personal talisman, has been unearthed at Rallinge in Sweden and
its striking proportions fit the description of the Uppsala statue
suggesting that the temple figure may have provided spectacular
viewing.

We have already seen graphic illustration of the significance
of the phallus in the Osirian cult, and there is reason to believe
that the classical priests of the grove enjoyed physical sex with
sacred trees. It is not impossible that the pointedly single priestess
of Freyr indulged in sexual fetishism of a similar kind. Some of
the scattered comments on the Vanir cult are reminiscent of Celtic
accounts. As with the Celtic Epona, horses were sacred to Freyr,
and there are scattered anecdotes which suggest that the horse
phallus was revered as a sacred relic. The author Turville-Petre
describes how a farmer's wife was given the dismembered phallus
of a horse, and she dried and preserved it in a cloth packed with
herbs. The object was kept in her linen chest, but was brought
out each evening for a family ritual which involved prayers and
perhaps other unspecified ritual.

A number of modern place names refer to Freyr and Freyja,
probably marking the sites of ancient cult centres, or stops on the
tour.[20] A Freyr temple once stood near Thvera in the Eyjafjord
and beside it is known to have existed an ancient cornfield. Many

fields in Norway and Sweden have been called Freysakr, or Freyr's cornfield, and they perhaps witnessed seasonal rites. Although Freyr travelled overland in a wagon, he may well have been shipped around the coast, because there are hints that Viking ship graves were linked to a Freyr cult. Beneath some of the graves, the faint marks of ritual ploughing have been discerned. More strands thus bind fertility and death.

There is also a possible inference in that the name Gerd, Freyr's giantess liaison, derives from the word 'garder' meaning field and, in view of the fact that the giants symbolize the cold and darkness, Gerd may have symbolized the ice-clad acres of winter. A notion has even been put forward that the legend of *Skírnismál* from which the story of Gerd comes may hint at a Sacred Marriage, and that Nerthus is really Gerd.[21] Far-fetched as this proposal probably is, it is not without logic because Nordic gods frequently married into the families of giants.

As a Vanir deity who lived 'on the right side of the tracks' in Asgard, Freyja has considerable claim to involvement, though her role is far from clear-cut.[22] She was, like Inana of old, a goddess of war and death as well as the patroness of plenty – to her went half of all victims of battle. Like her more ancient counterpart, Freyja was also a highly sexed lady, and in company with her brother she was symbolized by an assortment of animals, none of which are renowned for their sexual restraint. Freyr took the boar as his sacred animal, and Freyja adopted pigs, which ties in conveniently with Tacitus and his 'mother of the gods'. She carried the nickname 'Syr' meaning 'sow'. Her chariot was frequently drawn by cats, and she was said to chase her lovers at night in the form of a goat. This raw level of sexuality in a religious context may seem offensive to modern ears but it needs placing in context. The men to whom Freyr and Freyja stood holy regarded fighting and gratuitous fornication as reasonable expectations of a working day. They had little time for the more delicate aspects of love-making.

In separate legends Freyja, and the goddess Idunn, the keeper of the thirteen apples of eternal youth, who are in many senses synonymous with each other, were threatened with abduction by the giants. According to the opening of Snorri's *Skáldskaparmál* Idunn was lost temporarily to the giant Thiassi and the gods were obliged to go to complicated lengths to retrieve her.[23] At another time, the mason who built the defences of Asgard stipulated that his wages must include the sun, moon and Freyja. The gods, with Loki's ambiguous assistance, once more had to rally to the rescue. Giants displayed a high degree of energy and art lusting after the goddesses of Asgard, but since both Freyja and Idunn epitomize fertility and genesis, and the giants stand for eternal winter, some deeper message lurks in these rather comic-strip dramas. The cameo of the wages demanded by the mason giant is, in itself, a chosen pointer towards the ultimate cataclysm.

We have an eternal partnership whose sexuality stands in defiance of the final winter. But what of a more frequent death and resurrection? There is no overt drama in which a god dies to be reborn with the changing of the seasons. Which brings us to the puzzling story of Balder.

Whatever logic lies in his tragic veneer, it is unquestionably the slaying of Balder which presages the end of everything.[24] Snorri's tale indicates that Balder, Óthin's favourite and the god of light and sunshine, experienced premonitions of his own death, and that after consultation between the gods, Balder's mother Frigg took insurance to prevent danger from touching her son. Whether from fire and water, from iron and stone, trees, animals, disease, she took oaths from all things that they would not harm Balder. It became an entertainment that the Aesir gods should throw things at Balder knowing he would stand unharmed. Yet life, as the northern poets understood well, is not so utopian. Loki was not amused. Disguised as a crone he probed Frigg to discover if anything had escaped her, and he learned that one plant, the mistletoe, too frail to cause any damage, had not taken the oath of fealty. The die was cast. On the next occasion that the gods were using Balder for target practice, Loki handed the blind god, Hod, a piece of mistletoe and directed him to hurl it. The sprig became a lethal missile and Balder fell dead.

There was no prominent cult of Balder in the north. One sanctuary has been found in western Norway where, although several deities were worshipped, Balder seems to have held sway, but it is an exception, and Balder is something of an enigma, not least because there are conflicting accounts of both his personality and his death. Snorri, probably the more inclined to attempt marrying him closer to Christian tradition, describes Balder as the personification of good and of suffering, a Christlike figure slaughtered by the seemingly innocuous mistletoe stick which is turned by magic into a spear.

Saxo Grammaticus has him down as a lustful tyrant, a demi-god warrior 'sprung from celestial seed' and watched over by a team of Valkyries, but who is killed by a rival possessing a magic sword! Which is the more accurate, which is the character

(Above) **Demeter. Marble. Classical Greek.** *Courtesy of the Trustees of the British Museum.*

(Left) **Persephone. Marble. Classical Greek.** *Courtesy of the Trustees of the British Museum.*

(Below) **Lake Gennesaret, Israel.** *Britain/Israel Public Affairs Centre.*

(Right) The Via Dolorosa, Jerusalem. *Britain/Israel Public Affairs Centre.*

(Below) 'Crucifixion' (Studio of Quentin Massys, fifteenth century). The three Marys at the foot of the cross. The Virgin Mary kneels wearing a blue sash, Mary of Bethany stands to the left in blue and Mary of Magdala kneels to the right of the picture wearing red with a green cloak.
Reproduced by courtesy of the Trustees, The National Gallery, London.

(Above) The collected codices discovered at Nag Hammadi. The papyrus sheets of the thirteen 'books' are bound in leather. *Institute for Antiquity and Christianity, California.*

(Right) The title page of the Gospel of Philip, Codex II, Tractate 2, Nag Hammadi. *Institute for Antiquity and Christianity, California.*

(Left) The site of discovery in 1945 of early Christian codices including the Papyrus Berolinensis, at Nag Hammadi in Upper Egypt. *Institute for Antiquity and Christianity, California.*

(Right) 'Adam and Eve'
(Jan Gossaert, died 1532).
*Reproduced by courtesy of the
Trustees, The National Gallery,
London.*

(Below) 'Two Trinities'
(Bartolomé Esteban
Murillo, 1617–82).
*Reproduced by courtesy of the
Trustees, The National Gallery,
London.*

*(Opposite: Top left and
right)* Wooden votive
figurines from among a
large collection
deposited in a pre-
Roman and Romano-
Celtic sanctuary at the
Source des Roches de
Chamalières (Puy-de-
Dome), France. *By kind
permission of the Musée
Archéologique de Dijon.*

(Below) Figure of a male deity bearing a club. Incised into chalk. Celtic. Cerne Abbas, Dorset. (Photo: Michael Jordan.)

(Right) Unnamed mother goddess holding three apples. Romano-Celtic, Cirencester. *By permission of the Corinium Museum, Gloucester.*

(Below left) Epona seated on a horse. Limestone. Romano-Celtic. Allerey, France. *By kind permission of the Musée Archéologique de Dijon.*

(Below right) The triple mothers or *matres*. Limestone plaque. Romano-Celtic, Cirencester. *By permission of the Corinium Museum, Gloucester.*

(Top left) Full-sized replica of the Celtic wicker image in which human and other victims were sacrificed by burning. Based on a description by Julius Caesar in *Gallic Wars*. *By kind permission of Weintraub Film Distributors for British Lion Films.*

(Bottom left) Silver ritual cauldron embellished with mythological scenes. Cimbrian period. From the Raevemøsen bog, Gundestrup, Himmerland. *By kind permission of the Nationalmuseet, Copenhagen.*

(Near right) Kneeling fertility goddess with large staring eyes and wearing a neck ring or torque. Bronze Age. Grevensvaenge, Denmark. *By kind permission of the Nationalmuseet, Copenhagen.*

(Centre) One of a restored pair of ornate ceremonial wagons, possibly used to carry the image of a deity on a tour. Late Celtic Period. Dejbjerg, West Jutland. *By kind permission of the Nationalmuseet, Copenhagen.*

(Bottom right) Replicas of the gold horns of Gallehus, based on old drawings of the originals discovered near Tonder, Denmark, in 1639, but destroyed in 1802. They were probably employed in seasonal fertility rites and are embossed with mythical scenes. Viking period. *By kind permission of the Nationalmuseet, Copenhagen.*

(Above right) Fertility god, the 'twin' of the kneeling fertility goddess wearing a horned helmet of a ceremonial type of which actual examples have been found. Bronze Age. Grevensvaenge, Denmark. *By kind permission of the Nationalmuseet, Copenhagen.*

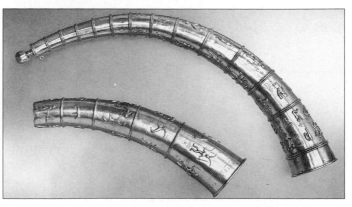

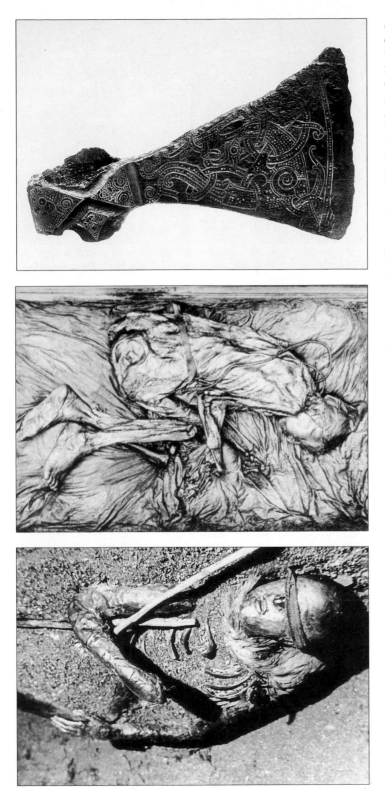

(Top left) The ceremonial 'Mammen' axe from a chieftain's grave in Jutland. Inlaid in silver with abstract and animal motifs, and with a bearded mask at the haft. Viking period. *By kind permission of the Nationalmuseet, Copenhagen.*

(Centre) Human sacrifice wearing only a leather belt and pointed cap, and with a rope around the neck. Probably a fertility offering. Iron Age preserved in a peat bog at Tφllund, Jutland. *By kind permission of the Nationalmuseet, Copenhagen.*

(Bottom left) The preserved corpse of a young woman driven through by a stake in a ritual sacrifice. Windeby, Denmark. *By kind permission of the Nationalmuseet, Copenhagen.*

(Right) Tree coffin hollowed from a split oak trunk. Egvted, Denmark. *By kind permission of the Nationalmuseet, Copenhagen.*

((Bottom left) Siberian couple in traditional costume. Yukaghir. *By permission of the American Museum of Natural History.*

(Bottom right) The guardian goddess of hunters, Asa D'ulin. Nanai tribe. Siberia. *By permission of the American Museum of Natural History.*

(Above) Dog sacrifice performed by the Koryak tribe. *By permission of the American Museum of Natural History.*

(Left) A black shaman in full working regalia beating a sacred drum. *By permission of the American Museum of Natural History.*

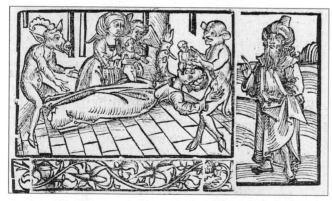

(Top left) The celebrated seventeenth-century English witch hunter, Matthew Hopkins. *Courtesy of the Trustees of the British Museum.*

(Middle left) The diabolical perils of childbirth, from a seventeenth-century woodcut. *Courtesy of the Trustees of the British Museum.*

(Bottom left) A seventeenth-century woodcut graphically associating women, sexuality and sin. *Courtesy of the Trustees of the British Museum.*

(Below) The execution of an English witch, Elizabeth Sawyer, at the Tyburn stake in 1621. *Courtesy of the Trustees of the British Museum.*

(Above) 'The Coronation of the Virgin' (Lorenzo Monaco, d. 1422).
The centre panel of a monastic altarpiece showing Christ crowning
his mother Queen of Heaven. Florence. *Reproduced by courtesy of the
Trustees, The National Gallery, London.*

(Right) 'The Annunciation' (Diego Velasquez 1609–60). Mary stands on the globe of the world arising from a dark sea, framed by the stars of heaven and the fiery clouds of creation. Beneath her are a ship and a fountain with the water of life.
Reproduced by courtesy of the Trustees, The National Gallery, London.

(Below) 'Madonna della Rondine' (Carlo Crivelli). *Reproduced by courtesy of the Trustees, The National Gallery, London.*

(Above) 'The Assumption' (Botticini). *Reproduced by courtesy of the Trustees, The National Gallery, London.*

(Below) Members of the Catholic student movement, wearing the cross of St George, in a Good Friday peace procession to the shrine of the Virgin Mary at Walsingham, England. *Eastern Counties Newspapers.*

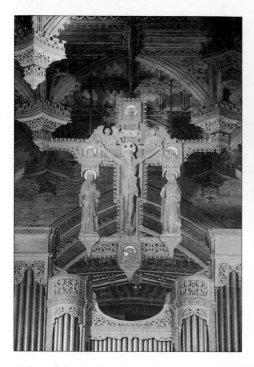

(Above left) Ornate hanging rood with the Christ in glory supported by Mary and John the Apostle and decorated by the heads of the winged beasts described in Isaiah and Revelation. St David's Cathedral, Wales. *By kind permission of the Dean of St David's Cathedral (photo: Ray Tarr).*

(Above right) A hobby horse parading through Padstow, Devon in re-enaction of an ancient spring ritual. *By permission of John Lyne.*

(Right) The traditional English Maypole, 20 metres in height and bearing garlands of flowers. Barwick-in-Elmet, Yorkshire, England. *Yorkshire Post Newspapers.*

assassination, and why such gross contradiction? Like virtually all other mythology, the Eddaic poetry which came to be written down by the Icelanders is a composite of many individual tribal strands, some of which inevitably were assimilated from foreign sources, and it seems more likely that in Balder several strands run together making up a complex and at times ambiguous character.

Balder symbolizes goodness, and justice, and peace. He is the bright one destined to rise from his burial ship when the new earth emerges from fire and ocean. Almost invariably in the lays he is described as 'good' or 'blessed' or 'the bright', but if he is cast in some respects as a Christ-like figure, an image arguably encouraged by Snorri, Balder is no Christian copy. If there is Christian embroidery on Balder, his birthright and his heart are rooted immutably in the pine forests of the north.

According to the lay of *Grímnismál*, a poem of ancient origin, Balder lived in the seventh hall of Asgard:

> Breithablik (the far shining) the seventh; there Balder the good
> hath reared him in his bright abode:
> in that land that it lies where least I know
> Falsehood and faithlessness.[25]

There are also parallels between the fate of Balder and that of the hero Sigurd of the *Volsung Saga*, better known to Wagnerian devotees as Siegfried.[26] If this connection is allowed, Saxo Grammaticus' portrait of Balder makes better sense. The story of the Rhine gold and the ring of power, although set amongst gods, is a morality play on human greed. Sigurd dies because he is unwilling to return nature's benign strength, the 'radiant gold of the earth' to its rightful place, and it is this short-sightedness which unleashes the forces of malignancy and triggers the end.

Some suggestions place altogether different motives, arguing that Balder's death may be unrelated to any fertility issue, and that he was killed at the instigation of his father so that both could stand side-by-side in Valhall to await Ragnarok. A tragically romantic scenario which seems short on reason.

Notwithstanding the strong position of Freyr and Freyja, other authors suggest that Balder is a contender for the role of the ill-fated consort of the fertility goddess, and that Balder and Freyr became interwoven in mythology. The argument might have its logic, except that Balder is not generally depicted as a fertility

god. Yet in certain less obvious respects Balder *is* drawn thus.
'Fertility' is a term of comparatively modern usage and it tends
to be applied all too freely. It has connotations of impregnation,
and in fairness many of the fertility deities are represented with
an ability to rut or be rutted firmly in the artist's or the poet's
mind. There are, unfortunately, very few words in ancient languages with which 'fertility' can be equated. Usually the nearest
offers a sense of abundance and plenty, of generous and pulsating
life. If the expression is applied to Balder in this context then,
by implication, he is indeed a fertility god because his death sets
the wheels irrevocably in motion to destroy the life-force of the
earth.

The absence of a clear-cut figure who died in the autumn
and revived in spring time in those dark limitless woods of
the north is not perhaps so hard to explain. Winter's apocalyptic horseman never rides unchallenged past the margins of
a forest. Its undergrowth and its lush evergreen citizens possess
a unquenchable spirit, a vital pulse, even in the coldest depths.
The yearly spectre of death which visits the icy tundra and the
sun-baked desert shuns the forest.

The most obvious preoccupation in Nordic religion lies with
Ragnarok, particularly the belief that the seeress, perhaps the
primal earth mother herself, is summoned from her eternal
sleep to speak words of wisdom to the assembled gods. Many
people have argued that the northern people did not possess the
intellectual sophistication to generate a masterly ethical concept
of doom and rebirth, and that the legends have been Christianized.
They will point to such obvious intrusion as that which infiltrates
a small prophetic manuscript, the *Voluspá hin skamma*. The poem
picks up from the death of Balder, but it ends with the verses:

Was a mighty one born, matchless in strength,
he was nursed and grew on the sap of the ground;
most high-minded he 'mongst the hallowed gods,
in sib with all sires and sons of earth.
A god will come then, an e'en greater one:
I dare not speak his dreaded name.
Farther forward few can see now
than Óthin fighting the Fenris-wolf.[27]

Yet it is a hasty temptation to assume all the deeper traditions
of the north to be misted with Christian or other alien belief.
There is, too often, no valid substance to the pro-Christian

argument. A story is to be found in northern mythology which contains several strong similarities with that of Balder.[28] The Finnish hero Lemminkainen undertook to catch a swan from the underground river of Tuonela in payment for a maiden whose affection he had won. But on reaching the river, a blind herdsman shot him with a magic reed, chopped him in pieces, and hurled his remains into the water. After a long search for her missing son, Lemminkainen's mother fished the scattered pieces out with a magic rake and restored him to life.

This story bears similarity to the Balder legend in that the hero is killed with a plant which is other than it seems, and the slayer is blind, but it is also so like the Isis and Osiris drama that conventional argument will maintain it to be a blatant plagiarization of the Egyptian theme. Lemminkainen, cut up and scattered piecemeal, meets a similar fate to his illustrious fellow-in-suffering Osiris, cleaved and winnowed by Seth. North Syrian legend also adopted the theme, albeit in a slightly con-fused state in the story of Baal and Mot. In both instances, the scattering of the fragments assumedly symbolize the scattering of seed. The core of the Lemminkainen saga, say the pundits, was theology obviously borrowed from travellers coming north from the Byzantine lands. But why? What would have been the point? The theme lacked sufficient interest in the north. A far more likely but perhaps less publicized source arises in pure northern sham-anism. As will be discovered shortly, a practice existed in which the corpses of dead shamans were dismembered and shared out around the tribe. In that case the story of Lemminkainen becomes a corruption of an ancient but local tradition peculiar, not to a southern origin, but to the circum-polar tribes.

The *Voluspa*, the radiant poetry of creation and apocalypse, lies at the heart of the Icelandic *Eddas*. It is confused, jumbled, intermittent, but it is probably as close to the untarnished truth of northern religion as we will get. In spite of proposals from time to time that the ending of the prophecy represents borrowed material, it looks safe to say that little or no Christian morality has invaded its verses. Joseph Campbell has suggested that the canvas of world beginning and rebeginning which it paints with such majestic brushstrokes was of an essentially physical, not moral, conflict or interaction.[29] But this reflects a curious reading of the material. On the contrary songs such as the *Voluspa* possess profound morality.

The men and women who told and retold the words of the *Voluspa*, the *Hávamál*, the *Skírnismál* and other such poems lived in a fearsome environment. They had little interest in the changing of seasons in the sense that the people of Mesopotamia awaited the coming of the floodwaters each year. They kept some herds, but in most areas they could not have tilled and sown the ground even had they wished to. They did, on the other hand, fear the elements mightily; they kept a deep unquenchable dread of the powers of endless cold and darkness, of mighty seas thundering against the coastal ramparts and frequently engulfing large parts of the land, of the awesome forces of fire (Iceland, it should be remembered, is strongly and actively volcanic). They perceived that one day, these forces would win through bringing the final cataclysm upon humanity and its gods alike. At this level Campbell's comment is fair, but the *Voluspa* is built on deeper foundations.

The seeress recalls an age of innocence broken by the first terrible war, not between the forces of light and destruction, but between gods and gods. On this battleground, in the first breaking of frith, were sown the seeds of doom, soon to be watered by broken treaties and fertilized by depravity. The side of light and good in nature was thus weakened, and bolts could no longer hold the door against the forces of evil. With the death of Balder, who symbolized all that was good in the world, the perdition was ready to be loosed. The bonds of the monstrous wolf were to be broken, and the day of wrath would come.

The eternal darkness and cold, the destroyers of life, would descend on the earth as Fenrir engulfed the sun. Gods and monsters would annihilate each other in a combat, not of greed and self-interest, but of life against death, light against darkness. Only the pure, the sons of the gods, would remain. Their fathers would have paid the price for foolish iniquity, and out of the wreckage of the old, in a world cleansed of its weakness and undoing, Óthin's slain child would be restored to lead a new generation of mankind in truth, loyalty, peace and honour.

Then in the grass the golden figures,
the far-famed ones, will be found again,
which they had owned in olden days.

On unsown acres the ears will grow,
all ill grow better; will Balder come then.
Both he and Hoth will in Óthin's hall dwell,
the war god's fane: do ye wit more or how?

Then will Hoenir handle the blood-wands,

and Ygg's brother's sons will forever dwell
in wide Wind-home: do ye wit more, or how?

I see a hall than the sun more fair,
thatched with red gold, which is Gimlé hight.
There will the gods all guiltless throne,
and live forever in ease and bliss.[30]

These are no words of a Christian mind or pen. Their vision
touches the reader out of dark forests, out of rain-washed skies,
out of sudden shafts of light cutting through lowering clouds.
They are possessed of a special kind of dignity and wonderment
that sets Icelandic poetry alone. Yet the *Voluspa* bears a message
that is also universal. Within its lines can be discovered a deep
and reasoned understanding, set against a vista of massive and
transcendental natural forces, of the innermost realities which
humankind recognizes of itself.

16

Trees, Pools and Ships of Death

The search for religion in the north has found elements of mother goddesses, fertility rites and sacred kings, but as yet it is incomplete. There exists another phenomenon, peculiarly northern and yet with uncanny similarity to counterparts in the south. Patterns have emerged in which special kinds of trees are bound up and imbued with powers of life, death and knowledge. In the Germanic and Nordic religions it is the Yggdrasil, the curiously named 'horse of Óthin', which is the focal point of this complex liaison.

A year or so back I happened to listen to a midsummer service addressed to a young congregation at an English boarding school by an Anglican bishop. Something in what he said struck me: 'Pick out the biggest, oldest, most gnarled tree you can find and throw your arms round it. If you feel this is too much, just stand with your back pressed to the tree, and shut your eyes, and wait. There will be a change. You will feel something remarkable. Something will flow out of the tree into you. It will be like energy charging a battery.'

From whence comes the mystical engine power of trees – that which draws us to them, and enmeshes us with a certain inexorability in their aura? It is a question which only a foolish man would attempt to answer, yet each of us touched in our own private ways by the huge spiritual strength of trees. To walk into a great forest is to walk into a living thing filled with immensity and mystery and with depths unfathomed.

Animism has probably held out for longer in respect of trees than for any other sentinel of nature. It lives still. Rare is the twentieth-century cynic who does not occasionally feel that spine-pricking tug as he walks a lonely woodland path through the gathering evening shadows. For peoples of the north who, in their experience of life and death, hacked out the frame of our ancestral traditions, trees have been possessed of the same vast power which they exerted upon the dwellers of the sun-baked plains of the near east, though perhaps not for entirely similar reasons. In Mesopotamia and Egypt, the tree stood out as a resilient and indomitable spirit in a world of nature that seemed so often to have perished. In the north, though, the trees *commanded* life! They were the *force majeur* that confronted every step.

Look up through the clear eyes of yesterday, and you have a glimpse of their immanence. Trunks surge from the earth out of roots that run deep in its womb. They raise their timeless gnarlings towards the clouds – tangled, immutable, stretching – spectral with the leaden rime of winter, but then with a kiss from fresh and fluttery lips of green. An ash tree extends its old and twisted limbs in grey embrace, a fir surges with cathedral-like serenity into the clouds, a birch trembles in its virginal shyness.

To begin to understand the significance of trees in European religion, one has first to appreciate the landscape of Europe as once it was. The classical writers touched often on the great woodlands of Italy and Greece, but north of the Danube in Roman times, if a person stood on a high vantage point in the Jura or Vosges mountains and looked eastwards across the Rhine, a vast and endless sea of trees rolled to the distant horizons.[1] It was the immeasurable and virtually impenetrable Hercynian forest. To the west of the Rhine wooded areas covered mile upon mile of country until they thinned into the marshes towards the western seaboard. Similar virgin forests covered a large part of the British Isles and Scandinavia.

Tacitus wrote of his Germania as 'a land of bristling forests and unhealthy marshes' and the description was probably true of much of Europe.[2] That which remains today is a scant vestige of a pre-eminent vegetation, torn down century by century to make way for the ever-increasing demands of agriculture.

Beyond any reasonable question, trees possessed a spirituality for the tribes of the north independent of influence which travelled up through such messengers as the Battle Axe traders and migrants from the Byzantine empire. It is not difficult to believe that the holy groves of Europe were 'creatures of their own invention'. They grew in a peculiarly northern seed bed, unlike anything described in the ancient near east. The spirituality stirred probably from the same principles that were carried down from the Fertile Crescent into the plains of Mesopotamia, but these principles trace back a great distance in time, to the common stock of hunters who perceived a particular kind of vitality in a rock, a cloud, a freshet of water, or a tree.

Everything in nature was seen to be a cloak for a being in human form.[3] In Scandinavia this hidden person was called a *landvaettir*, and so strong and so persistent was the conviction that as late as the thirteenth century laws were in force which expressly forbade belief that *landvaettir* lived in hills and waterfalls and groves. Notwithstanding the inroads of Christianity, staunch local tradition still persuaded women to carry presents of food to cairns and lay them before the spirits that lived within the stones.

Trees were more than tangible living things. They possessed a cryptic power which, for whatever less than conscious reasons, singled them out over all other objects in nature for a special kind of holiness. The great woods were sanctified, their own living cathedrals. Tacitus, with his sweeping mastery of words, abstracts a sharp portrait: 'They deem it incompatible with the majesty of the heavenly host to confine the gods within walls, or to mould them into any likeness of the human face: they consecrate groves and coppices, and they give the divine names to that mysterious something which is visible only to the eyes of faith.'

All across the north, priests bowed before their gods in hallowed groves: the dancing floors within the secret embrace of the forest that were more accurately clearings or glades perhaps marked by little more than a ring of small boulders or a rope. The one-time location of these groves is often revealed in place names. In Denmark the word for 'grove' is *lund*, most frequently linked with the gods Thor and Tyr, and in Sweden the same word is found associated with several deities including Óthin, Thor and Njord.

In Norway, however, *lund* is virtually never associated with the name of a god which leads to the conclusion that sacred groves did not hold the same significance there.[4] The Gallic name *nemeton* given to a sacred grove seems to stem from the same root as the Latin word *nemus* which spreads through classical literature. In

France, where there are many *nemeton* place names, the modern
Nanterre, to name but one, was called Nemetodurum. English
records include mention of Vernemeton, a Roman centre which
existed somewhere between Lincoln and Leicester.

Holiness turned the felling of trees into a matter of great
seriousness.[5] A spirituality was being destroyed. The Vikings
had it that the quality of the weapon which felled a man
measured the quality of his death. To die with honour was a
must, and to die before a fine weapon bode well. From the
Bronze Age the axe bore a sacred dimension as a holy weapon
of war. But the axe was not conceived thus. It began its existence far back in pre-history as a working tool, the instrument
of bringing down the great trees. The axe played its part in that
paradoxical liaison between genesis and death which also made
it a symbol of fertility. Thor, his earth link in the north similar in
sentiment to that of Adad, the north Mesopotamian storm god,
is generally pictured with his skull-crushing hammer, Mjollnir,
the thunderbolt of heaven in his iron-clad fist, but sometimes
he too swings the axe. The hammer summons dark clouds riven
with lightning and bearing rain, and in a distinct analogy the axe
blade also brings regenesis from the hewn corpse of the tree, out
of whose dark worms arise saplings of the new. Long before the
Vikind era, huge ritual axes, too mighty ever to be hefted by
human arms, were forged in the Scandinavian neolithic and
bronze ages, and carvings of a sexually virile god bearing such
massive symbolic weapons decorate rocks.

There are to be found other telling remnants of the sacred
strength of the axe: an ancient custom existed in Denmark of
burying an axe, blade-side upwards, beneath the footings of a
house to ensure the prosperity and progeny of those who lived
there, and there is a famous carving from Hitvlycke in which a
man and a woman stand beneath a giant who lifts the holy axe
over their heads, perhaps to bless their marriage.[6]

In an ancient peat bog from the passage-grave period of
Danish pre-history, a flint axe with a curiously shortened handle
was thrust upright in the earth, supposedly rammed into a split
trunk which has since disappeared. Similar symbolism perhaps
accounts for the imagery of the axe-head cleaving a rock, either
to represent the penetration of the phallus of the god into the
vagina of his mother, or to describe the nativity of life wresting
its way from the womb.

The sensitivity towards felling of trees only really faded under
the technological onslaught of the twentieth century. Until then

in many parts of Europe there existed a deep belief amongst woodcutters that the tree felt pain and should be asked forgiveness.

Frazer provides a starker insight on the degree of respect with which trees were clothed in at least one part of medieval Europe.[7] Old German laws rewarded anyone who dared to peel the bark of a standing tree. The offender's navel was cut out and nailed to the part of the trunk which had been stripped of bark, after which the victim was driven round and round the trunk as his guts dragged out and covered the wound. The dead bark was thus replaced by a living substitute.

That which the groves contained is to be gained only through fleeting glimpses. They were shrouded in mystery. Few ventured on to their sacred turf, and most of those who did were not destined to live. Tacitus mentions that tribal totems and emblems were fetched from the groves to be carried into battle, and that sacred animals were kept there for the purpose of divination: 'In the same groves and coppices are fed certain white horses never soiled by mortal use: these are yoked to a sacred chariot and accompanied by the priest and king, or the chief of state, who then observe their neighing and snorting.'[8]

Much of the detail is backed up by other sources. The totems are confirmed by Lucan, who writes of 'grim and rude blocks', and Tacitus describes the pinning of human skulls to the trees.[9] Yet the carnage was neither mindless nor purposeless. The northern groves were places of a more diffuse worship than their counterparts in the ancient near east. At least in Mesopotamia there is a reasonable certainty that the trees were outward clothing of the goddess of life and her consort, but in the north the groves were sacred not only to the Vanir earth divinities, Freyr and Freyja. In these places walked Óthin and other gods, and the purpose of sacrifice was not always the simple currying of favour for peace and prosperity.

Much of the slaughter was, undoubtedly, to keep the fertility god in a fair frame of mind. Describing the temple in the old Swedish spiritual centre at Uppsala, Adam of Bremen pointed out that every tree associated with the grove was sacred.[10] The place must at times have reeked of death. Adam mentions talking to an old man who claimed to have seen human corpses hung in the trees, as well as horses and dogs, and to have counted as many as seventy-two carcasses. Adam described the temple building standing on level ground surrounded by mounds and there is some argument that the present church at Uppsala is built over the ancient site. In recent times there have been a number of ash trees just to the west of the church, which are perhaps distantly related successors of the grove which Adam visited.

Quite probably Swedish kings were sacrificed as the priests of Freyr, and there is suggestion that the ill-fated royals may have been hung in the sacred grove at Uppsala, possibly at the end of a nine-year-term of office rather as the priest kings of the sacred groves in the south murdered their predecessors only to await a similar violent destiny. The Swedish victims were, evidence suggests, stabbed to death before hanging and their blood was spilt on the hallowed ground so that the earth might be reinvigorated.

There was, though, another very special element of the sacred grove, the tree which stood separate from and above all the rest. It provided a different reason for killing, one which needs to be distinguished from sacrifice to the fertility gods. In the margin of Adam of Bremen's description is a note: 'Beside this temple stands an enormous tree, spreading its branches far and wide; it is evergreen in winter and summer. No one knows what kind of tree it is . . .'

The Tree which Adam could not name, though by its description a conifer, probably reflected something which lies within the heart of Nordic creed. Evergreen yews which grow in today's churchyards, and Christmas spruces alike probably all owe their origin, at least in part, to the World Ash Tree, the Yggdrasil. Human sacrifice associated with it bore a complex significance. In Snorri Sturluson's tale of Gylfi's quest for answers to the riddle of the cosmos, the three mystic kings also describe the Yggdrasil: 'The ash is of all trees the biggest and best.[11] Its branches spread out over all the world and extend across the sky. Three of the tree's roots support it and extend very, very far. One is among the Aesir, the second among the frost-giants, where Ginnungagap once was. The third extends over Niflheim, and under that root is Hvergelmir, and Nithogg gnaws the bottom of the root.'

The origin of the Tree is missing both from the Nordic poems and from Snorri's evaluation. Its significance is elaborated, but we are denied explanation of how it came to be. In its topmost branches rests an eagle, whilst the much-travelled snake, here the dragon Nithogg, gnaws at its roots in company with a wriggling host of lesser serpents. The poetry also offers the homely detail of a squirrel, Ratatosk, who runs up and down the trunk as a go-between.

Some of the picture, one might think, is borrowed straight from the banks of the Euphrates. Can that be taken for granted though? Birds perch and serpents nest just as willingly in European ash trees as in near eastern willows, and there are other cautionary warnings in the words. The eagle seems at face value to equate to the Imdugud bird, yet the creature perched in the crown of the Mesopotamian tree is a symbol of death and desolation in nature whilst the northern poems imply that the eagle rests as the antagonist of the snake rather than its partner in crime. It is described as being the vanguard watchman against the terrible fire from the south.

The poets draw their Tree suffering the onslaught of predation much as the Mesoptamian *halub*. The World Ash abides misfortune 'more than to men is known' with the deer browsing on its foliage, and its trunk rotting away from the depredations of the serpent. This is a familiar picture of animals tearing away the foliage, but deer, goats and dragons are time-honoured part-players in the northern drama, and their presence is insufficient proof of copying. It may be that the old truth – that of similar interactions with environment producing similar religious beliefs – is working.

There are hints that the Yggdrasil is a tree with life-giving properties. In the Poetic *Edda*, the *Fjǫlsvinnsmál* includes a slightly obscure observation:

Tell me, Fjǫlsvith, for I fain would know;
answer thou as I ask:
of the fruit what becomes of that far spreading tree,
since nor fire nor iron will fell it?
Of its berries thou shalt bear on fire,
for ailing women to eat:
then out will come what within was held –
such strength is bestowed on that tree.[12]

These enigmatic verses interpret in at least two ways a crux which returns the question of how much or how little 'Christianizing' went into the *Edda* collection in its final form? They imply either that, as in the Genesis saga of Adam and Eve, the secret property of the Yggdrasil is a forbidden strength only to be revealed at the end of the existing order, or that the Tree is drawn on the more ancient style of a fertility symbol with fruit possessing generative powers, perhaps for women in pregnancy or labour.

In Snorri Sturluson's account a goat by name of Heidrun

stands on the roof of Valhall munching on the foliage of the
Tree, and the goat produces milk which Óthin's slain warriors
drink each day. The life-giving property is re-inforced in the *Edda*.
When, in the Eddaic *Sigrdrífumál* saga, the hero Sigurth awakes
his Valkyrie maiden and begs to learn her secrets, she tells him
of similar powers:

> Limb runes learn thou, if a leech would'st be,
> and wishest wounds to heal:
> on the bark scratch them of bole in the woods
> whose boughs bend to the east.[13]

The radiant world of the gods is to come crashing down in
the final battle with the frost giants, and in a manner that is not
immediately understood the World Tree, destined to be swept up
in the all-consuming immolation, is integral to the drama. At the
prelude the Tree will signal the 'engulfing doom of the mighty
gods and men alike':

> Mimir's sons dance; the downfall bodes
> when blares the gleaming old Gjallarhorn;
> loud blows Heimdall, with horn aloft;
> In Hel's dark hall horror spreadeth,
> once more Óthin with Mim's head speaketh
> ere Surt's sib swallows him.
> Trembles the towering tree Yggdrasil,
> its leaves sough loudly: unleashed is the giant.[14]

In reality, Yggdrasil is poles apart from the Mesopotamian
tree. It is part of the scaffolding of creation, a universal thing
whose branches spread over earth and heaven and whose roots
build a ladder between worlds. It is the guardian of the ordered
world and the channel of communication between three realms
of the cosmos. Its doom and that of the gods whose destiny it watches over are inseparably linked. These things are
very Nordic considerations which probably owe little to outside
influence. A key to Yggdrasil's special significance lies in its
curious name. Ygg is one of the many synonyms for Óthin,
whilst *drasill* translates as horse — thus 'Óthin's horse'. The
name is, however, obtuse because 'horse' is also an old col-
loquialism for a gallows. Yggdrasil is not, as Robert Graves
suggests in *The White Goddess*, a name for Óthin's flying phantom
steed, well-documented and called Sleipnir.[15] The name arose

because Óthin elected to hang himself from the World Ash Tree.

To understand the euphemism necessitates a return to the *Edda*. The issue is a keen one because Óthin's self-sacrifice is among the incidents most frequently trumpeted to justify the argument that much of the Nordic mythology is little more than a distortion of Christian traditions. The so-called 'Rune Poem' of the Eddaic *Hávamál* describes Óthin's suffering:

> I wot that I hung on the wind-tossed tree
> of all nights nine,
> wounded by spear, bespoken to Óthin
> bespoken myself to myself,
> upon that tree of which none telleth
> from what roots it doth rise.
>
> Neither horn they upheld nor handed me bread;
> I looked below me –
> aloud I cried –
> caught up the runes, caught them up wailing,
> thence to the ground fell again.
> From the son of Bolthorn, Bestla's father,
> I mastered mighty songs nine,
> and a drink I had of the dearest mead,
> got from out of Óthroerir.
>
> Then began I to grow and gain in insight,
> to wax eke in wisdom:
> one verse led on to another verse,
> one poem led on to the other poem.
>
> Runes wilt thou find, and rightly read,
> of wondrous weight,
> of mighty magic,
> which that dyed the dread god,
> which that made the holy hosts,
> and were etched by Óthin.[16]

Once aware of the march of his world towards an apparently inescapable destiny, Óthin became obsessed with the pursuit of knowledge; less in any vain hope that he could stem the current that was carrying all towards the day of Ragnarok, but more that he might understand the ancient runes amongst which were decreed the fates. And for this insight he turned to the Tree.

In northern religious belief, the World Ash is not only the bastion of life and of order in the universe, it is also the source of ultimate knowledge, an occult power which is explained in Snorri's tale of *Gylfaginning*:

> But under the root that reaches towards the frost-giants, there is where Mimir's well is, which has wisdom and intelligence contained in it, and the master of the well is called Mimir. He is full of learning because he drinks of the well from the horn Gjallarhorn.[17]

The Tree is fed by three springs, all perhaps arising from one. Mimir's Well, surging up to feed the roots in the land of the frost giants, is the source of eternal and infinite wisdom. Óthin once plucked out his right eye and threw it into Mimir's Well as forfeit in his quest for knowledge. In Asgard, the land of the Aesir gods, rises the Well of Destiny beside which live the three eternal seeresses, the norns – Fate, Being and Necessity. The norns water the tree each day from the spring and spin the rope of destiny, and the roots which rest in Asgard are the daily meeting place for the gods where they mete out judgement in the light of Óthin's knowledge. Ultimately though, Óthin was to learn the fullness of his own destiny by paying an extreme price – hanging himself from the Tree's branches and spearing his own body with the sacred weapon which he had first fashioned from its wood.

Óthin's ritual does not, at face value, make a great deal of sense, and to get to the implications of his sacrifice one has to side-step and spread out the gleanings of information we possess about death and its associations in the northern latitudes. That which comes out of the Viking age has, predictably, many features which appear familiar, but it bears its own peculiar brushstrokes. Nor is it a simple picture. The canvas relates as much to the earth gods as to Óthin, but all are somehow delicately interwoven.

There are many paradoxes, but universally across the north the ending of life was considered not to be a final extinction. This much must already be obvious from the elaborate style of prehistoric burials in Stone Age and Bronze Age Scandinavia.[18] Nemesis marked the beginning of a journey into an uncertain future. Although burial was practised, there was a strong leaning towards cremation with the logic that the spirit passed instantly to the next world. Men and women were accompanied in death by weapons, furniture, jewellery, food, horses, cattle, although

there is an oddity in that many of the grave goods which have
been excavated show signs of deliberate damage. It suggests that,
just as the dead move on in an unfamilar state, so the items they
take with them have to be 'changed'.

In some contexts the dead did not 'go away'. The northerner
told and re-told the romantic heroic sagas through which the
noble slain ended up trenchering and drinking mead in Valhall,
but the family dead also stayed within or close by the places of
their rest, content with each other's company in less illustrious
surroundings.[19] Burial mounds and the sites of cremation stood
alongside the homes of the living, so that a man's ancestors were
beside him from the time of his birth to the time of his own
departing. Proximity with the dead was deeply significant and
the spirits of ancestors played a crucial role in the well-being of
a man's family, his crops and his cattle.

In parts of the north where inhumation was preferred, there
are fascinating parallels of logic and 'philosophy' with those of
the Egyptians. In the desert the body was embalmed and mummified against decomposition. In the frozen ground of Scandinavia,
where a corpse could stay remarkably well preserved for a long
time and the dead, as in Egypt, were not wholly departed, the
sentiments generated were similar. The retention of the physical
body was necessary to the well-being of the dead. In fact there
existed a widespread belief that the dead walked and could, if
they felt so inclined, plague and terrorize the living. Hence those
that had left the temporal earth were treated with unswerving
respect. There took place very precise rituals – the eyes were
closed, the mouth and nostrils stuffed, and sometimes the body
was washed.

The contrary idea that the dead also embarked on a mysterious voyage is emphasized, from well before Viking times, by the
number of ship burials which took place in Scandinavia. Often,
as in the famous Suffolk ship funeral at Sutton Hoo the vessel
was dragged inland, but yet again there were reservations about
letting loose the occult powers that lay beyond.[20] The death ships
which have been uncovered have often been 'moored' to a large
boulder lying close by.

Only in death was the eternal knowledge to be fully revealed.
The dead took on the wisdom of the ages by communing with
those who had gone before, and it was this occult access which
Óthin sought by symbolically taking his life on the World Tree.
Frequently he had sat beneath the Yggdrasil to communicate
with the slain and to learn their wisdom, but ultimately he had

needed to experience the 'other side' at first hand. This is the element which has been likened to the Christian passion, but the argument falls in that motives were quite distinct. Christ, it is claimed, anticipated a redeeming sacrifice, whilst Óthin, more in the true style of a shaman, strove for occult knowledge.

There becomes discernible a deep and complex wisdom behind which lay the purpose of hanging heroes in the tree sacred to Óthin. Yet the ropes which bound together death and fertility also intertwine within the picture. Viking ship burials seem usually to have been dedicated to Freyr and although we have little of the precise ritual of Viking funerals, there exists a detailed account which may offer close parallels. It was written down by a travelling Arab observer, Ibn Fadlan, when he watched a funeral ceremony by the Volga River, in Russia in AD 922.[21]

Ibn Fadlan was invited to attend the cremation of a warrior chieftain, one of whose slave women, as was the custom, would accompany him in death. The man had been laid in a temporary grave whilst his funeral was prepared, and already the girl destined for sacrifice was being fêted with special honour. Special attendants washed her, followed her, and provided all that she needed. She was, Ibn Fadlan suggested, happy in the knowledge of her impending execution.

On the day of the funeral, the chieftain's burial ship had been dragged on to the river bank, propped up with wooden posts, and banked around with a huge pyre of logs. In the ship stood a bed covered with rich brocaded fabrics and cushions, placed there by an aged woman, described as a strongly built and grim figure – the 'Angel of Death'. Ibn Fadlan noted that when the corpse was removed from its temporary mortuary, it had turned black in the frost but did not smell unpleasant. It was carefully and respectfully clothed and placed on the bier surrounded by bread, meat, herbs, onions, two slaughtered horses and two cows.

In the meanwhile, the girl set out on a farewell tour around the village, and in each tent the man of the household had intercourse with her. She was ceremonially lifted three times so that she could see over a door frame, symbolizing a preview into the world of her ancestors. Then she was provided with a drugged drink and taken by the Angel of Death into the ship where another half-dozen men performed sex with the girl. Her final moment came by strangulation and stabbing – a rope around her neck pulled taut between two men, whilst the Angel of Death thrust a knife repeatedly in her chest. The bodies were placed side by side to await their immolation. A naked man held a torch to the piled

logs, and master and slave became ashes. Earth was piled over
the spot, and a birch post inscribed with the man's name was
fixed in the ground, in memoriam.

Through this provocative and moving account, the seemingly unavoidable fusion of genesis and death is perhaps more
graphically drawn than in any instance thus far. Although it
included some unusual features, the Russian ceremony com-
mended man and servant into the hands of a fertility god, in
a death ritual that was followed, albeit with small variations,
very closely throughout much of the north.

The rarer link lies between the Tree and wisdom, and one
has to ask from where the idea of the Tree of Knowledge came.
Was the theme put into such picturesque words by the writer of
the biblical Genesis a purely Israelite concept, or was it dredged
from deeper and more ancient levels of creed? Did some traveller
in a distant time carry it on the long journey from the south, or is
the Tree's possession of wisdom an innate thing that has grown
quite independently in the north too?

To the pattern must be added a fourth detail, water, and the
mystical bond of tree and water builds another tantilizing bridge
between north and south, although it is again hard to accept
that the link came necessarily through the ancient near east,
or through any biblical imagery. Water, like trees, has born
its own peculiar sanctity in the northern latitudes. Water and
sacrifice were drawn together in a way which is not found further
south. The ancient carvings of animals, for example, which so
often are found on heights near water would seem to be attested,
though not necessarily explained, by the urge to throw sacrificial
victims, human and animal alike, over cliffs into lakes, torrents,
or the sea.

Bog corpses, recently enjoying much popular attention, were
placed in water and they too may reflect its bond with fertility
and death. Often nude other than for a cape and perhaps a
bonnet, most seem to have been victims of deliberate sacrificial
killings. Invariably they were strangled or had their throats cut,
and sometimes the skull and limbs were crushed, mangled and
even partially dismembered.

Tollund Man, who came to light during peat digging in 1950,
arguably is the most famous of the bog corpses.[22] His face is striking, hauntingly so. The expression preserves an uncanny serenity,
and one wonders, notwithstanding the violence with which his
end came if, in a drugged euphoria, he had come to accept that
his death might provoke a greater good for the rest of his clan.

He was killed with a plaited leather halter constricting his neck and was then placed in water, apparently with some care, in a mode of sleep, on his side with his knees drawn up. He lay in much the same familiar foetal position of the dead of Sinai and Alaca Hüyük. But if he did not fall victim to a clannish dispute, and was some sacrificial offering, for whom was he slaughtered? Did he hang from a tree, fodder for Óthin's indomitable quest for occult wisdom, destined even to join the spectral band in Valhall awaiting the final battle? Or was his sacrifice to Freyr or Thor in the depths of winter and in face of harsh deprivation? We can only muse. If there is any object lesson to be found in Tollund Man's serene countenance, it is to avoid drawing heavy conclusions.

Some of Tollund Man's contemporaries suffered more gruesome departure. The body of a man found a few miles away from Tollund at Grauballe was finished off with the throat slashed from ear to ear. Other corpses like that of the young woman sacrificed at Windeby in Denmark, blindfolded and skewered by a stake were, beyond very much doubt, victims of fertility rites.

Much excitement and a goodly degree of wild speculation has been made from the microscopic analysis of the last meals eaten by such victims. Stomach contents, found to contain large quantities of seeds from a variety of wild plants, have been seized on as evidence of ritual fare including all the potential bounty of a natural world currently suffering under the rigours of winter. Such quaint explanations are probably more romantic than realistic. If Tollund Man was a chieftain, slain in winter and consigned to a watery grave to appease the fertility god, perhaps in the hope that he would rise again in the spring, any significance attributed to his stomach content is probably down to the hard fact that the man lived on a simple fare. There was no 'screening' of grain prior to harvesting, and winter porridge probably included, quite innocently, large amounts of rogue material in addition to odds and ends of edible seeds and nuts that happened to be available. Most of his contemporaries were, incidentally, riddled with worms and no doubt other diseases largely the result of poor diet and hygiene.

Against this argument, there is the curious evidence of Lindow Man, the Iron Age chieftain found at Lindow Moss in Cheshire, England.[23] His was beyond doubt a ritual sacrifice, he had been hung after his throat had been cut and then consigned to a pool. In his gut, however, in addition to the 'mixed bag' of seeds which had been used to prepare his last mortal meal, there was charred bread. Its inclusion could have been down to no more sinister cause than his wife's distraction from the kitchen. On the other hand we already have it from separate Celtic sources, that charcoal, or charred grain took a significant place in ritual. Lindow Man's stomach also included traces of mistletoe pollen which had long been accepted as imparting fertility, but which was unlikely to have intruded into the dish accidentally.

Adam of Bremen describes a sacred pool beside the World Ash Tree at Uppsala: 'There is also a well there, where heathen sacrifices are commonly performed, and a living man is plunged into it.[24] If he is not found again, it is deemed that the will of the people will be fulfilled.' He implies, however, that the sacrificial person was drowned, so whether Adam's account can be tied to the evidence of Tollund and other bogs remains uncertain.

Tacitus also shed what may be useful light from earlier centuries on the use of such sinister places in his account of the procession of Nerthus' wagon: '. . . the chariot and the robe, and, if you are willing to credit it, the deity in person, are washed in a sequestered lake: slaves are the ministrants and are straightway swallowed by the same lake: hence a mysterious terror and an ignorance full of piety as to what that may be which men only behold to die.'[25] In Tacitus' description comes, incidentally, a timely reminder of the importance of the occult in early religion. The image of the deity was, by all accounts, hidden from the eyes of the world at large thus clothing it with mystery and esoterism. Those who performed its more intimate bodily needs could not be left to tell the tale.

In the northern tree, the World Tree, elements of life, death and knowledge are entangled in a complicated skein. There is little point in trying to unravel it because it was not designed so. The norns are the seeresses of destiny, but they are also closely involved in the birth of children. The enigmatic verses of the *Svipdagsmál* speak of fruits 'burned in the fire' and given to women in labour.[26] Óthin communes with the dead beneath the tree. Finally, within its trunk, shelter the two human beings who will begin the new earth after the Ragnarok. Likewise Óthin himself presents a character that is far from straightforward. There exist several intriguing hints that he was less than entirely trustworthy. He is drawn as a sophisticated and yet at times heavily flawed personality. Some of the later medieval poetry underlines the message. The Eddaic *Hrolfs Saga Kraka* announces the suspicion: '. . . that it is Óthin who comes against us here, the foul and untrue . . .' *Ketils Saga Hoengs* makes a similar accusation: 'Balder's father has broken faith – it is unsafe to trust him . . .' Like the gods of Mesopotamian legend, he is capricious.

We have, in Viking culture, an intricate and imprecise cat's cradle of threads amidst which the Tree represents the unshakable and the immutable surrounded by chaos and confusion; it will give shelter against the ravages of fire and flood in the final holocaust.

Guardian trees have long been associated with houses in Europe and their oracular powers revered as deeply as any described by the classical authors of Greece and Italy. There has existed an ancient tradition of sacred oaks in Europe, trees which host the mistletoe with which legend has it that Balder was slain, and which are particularly linked to Thor and to the Celtic Druids in Gaul. The yew, the robust evergreen rampart against winter in the north, has also been imbued with great holiness still not entirely forgotten. It may be linked with old churchyards, but there is nothing Christian in its presence.

The living tree standing in the Germanic or Nordic grove was subject to its own pagan abstraction. From the early Bronze Age in Scandinavia coffins were hollowed out, with great labour, from large oak trunks.[27] The body was laid inside on cow hide and surrounded by flowers and the two halves of the trunk were tightly sealed before burial. Amongst the best preserved is the coffin from Egvted in Denmark.

In Icelandic literature there are mentions of 'high-seat pillars' which settlers carried with them from Norway, and some reports tell of boards or posts carved with intricate designs and vaguely human features. Ibn Fadlan, describing his journey of AD 922, mentions a Russian trading post on the Volga.[28] When the merchants went ashore they approached 'tall wooden pillars with human faces' each of which stood surrounded by smaller figures, by implication the wives and children of the gods symbolized in the taller posts. The large figures were greeted as 'lord' and the merchants offered them gifts of food apparently to bring fortune in their forthcoming business. If the trading was successful another gift of gratitude was laid at the foot of the totem.

Notwithstanding the 'escape' of the yew, the reverence for trees made sacred through their primal powers attracted the attention and indignation of the Christian camp. The shrines had to go! Any grove which bore the faintest whiff of holiness was put to the axe with righteous missionary zeal and its timber purified in flames.

The argument has been put that the Tree of Life which

began in Mesopotamia gave way to and was replaced by the cross in early Christian Europe. The World Tree, associated with Óthin's sacrifice, may have been similarly transmuted as the pagan earth was converted to Christianity.

One small argument standing against the suggestion that the World Tree and Óthin's self-sacrifice are linked with Christian traditions lies in an omission. Snorri Sturluson, in his frequent mentions of the Yggdrasil, comes out with no such implication. Had the link existed, it would be more in character with his narrative to make some allusion to Christian principles. All that can be said with certainty is that Trees were as central to the old faiths of Europe as they had been in the ancient near east and, as far as Christmastime goes, they provided a focus of evergreen hope under the icy and leaden skies of the north, in the festivals which originally marked the midwinter solstice.

17

Echoes

Truly satisfactory conclusions have not come from the works of Ice-Age artists or from the later pre-literate cults which have filled so many of the pages of this book. It is one thing to dig up a perforated bronze axehead and to reason how a warrior used the product of his labours. It is quite another to unscramble some faded expression on the wall of a cavern, or to assess why a Bronze-Age chieftain was buried within a ship, hauled with laborious dedication across miles of dry land, or to evaluate the true meaning behind the dispassionate and disinterested commentary of a classical author. To hope to understand such faded and, all too often, distorted reflections now, when the core of the original sentiment has long been burned from our memories, may be impossible. The ashes are cold and their meaning has gone.

Analogy with the customs and beliefs of primitive people living today sends a collective shudder through the academic fraternity. There is no argument to be won that because a primitive twentieth-century clan fashions axeheads in a way similar to that of its prehistoric ancestors, it shares a similar outlook on life. The passage of time is too great but also, no less importantly, those early tribesmen were part of a progressive society possessing great curiosity and energy, exploring and fighting to master a new and unfamiliar world. Modern hunting societies, by contrast, are generally in a state of active decline. Their outlook has to be totally different. So all that analogy proves is that it can generate metaphors; it cannot shed light on the original mystery.

Were any credible analogy to be introduced it would need, at least, to be with people whose surroundings generated similar priorities to those in prehistoric Europe. Meeting the necessary criteria would require a culture sufficiently untouched by the outside world. No Roman or Christian influence could be allowed since, as is by now apparent, these things exert a massive effect.

Nothing of the kind survives today. Probably the nearest approximation would be with some of the more remote tribes of Lapps or Esquimaux, but all of these have by now experienced the touch of twentieth-century culture, and that which they have to offer probably has no more or less value than the Celtic traditions of the Irish. At the turn of this century though, a culture did exist, its tradition not inviolate but as pure as we are likely to see. It found itself not in Europe but in eastern Asia and its people lived just under the Arctic Circle, on and around the Kamchatka Peninsula, in what is still one of the remotest parts of the northern hemisphere.

In the nineteenth century, even in Russia, hardly anyone knew of the existence of the Kamchatka culture. The geography of Siberia is built on mind-stretching distances. Kamchatka alone would just about swallow up the British Isles, and in the days before the advent of the aeroplane convenience of a neighbourly visit in that region of the world would have been judged on how many days or weeks it took to get there.

Three ethnically distinct and very primitive Iron-Age tribes roamed the wilderness. On the peninsula the Koryaks rubbed shoulders with the Kemchadal whilst to the north, spread through the mountains and steppes where the land-mass of eastern Siberia faces Alaska, were the Chukchee. Stringing out along the coast of Kamchatka small bands of Koryak hunted the seal and the great white whale for their livelihood. But inland, where the peninsula becomes mountainous with sparsely wooded lower slopes running down close to the sea, there were other Koryaks, and they hunted reindeer.

In 1900, as part of the Jesup North Pacific Survey, an American-Swedish ethnologist, Waldemar Jochelson, was sponsored by the American Society for Natural History to go to Kamchatka and to live with the Koryaks for a year. When he reached there he found an extremely primitive society which, although already in the early stages of decay, still possessed remarkable integrity. To an extent the Kamchatka clans had been protected by their sheer isolation; they were geographically the furthest distant from Russian and Greek orthodox influence and so their culture was least affected. The American Museum of Natural History later funded Jochelson to spend time with the Yakut and Yukaghir tribes living further to the west, but by the time he reached them it was difficult to tell where ancient culture left off and Russianization began. Many of the traditional spirits had changed names and identities, and had become partly Christianized compromises of their old personalities.

Even in the Kamchatka wilderness a people of simple and pristine culture was defending itself against the opening assault of the twentieth century. Their heritage was about to be raped by Russian ways of life and by the interests of the Orthodox Church. The virgin religion which the Koryaks had defended and nurtured was poised for adulteration by Christian doctrine and mythology, and was already dwindling, in some areas, to no more than lip-service for ancient rites and beliefs. Myths and legends were beginning the tragic descent into confused tales and fables, often incomplete or remembered in barely more than name. Story tellers were becoming muddled about narrative and meaning. The Koryak shamans, once venerated intercessors with the spirits, were fewer and were being replaced by young men of ambivalent loyalties, often little respected and on the fringes of society.

The industry of the Koryaks was very simple; they took their needs from the reindeer and the whale, and from nuts and berries for which they foraged in times of need. They eked a cold and harsh existence in an uncompromising land. It seems, on evidence, that they lived in conditions of climate and surroundings very much like those of the prehistoric clans that ranged through the northern Europe of millennia past. The Koryak had persisted as a nomadic population in part because there are no lakes in their territory, and in hunter-gatherer societies it is often water that provides a focal point to encourage settlements. Kamchatka is a cruel environment where the average temperature rests between $-5°C$ and $-8°C$ making farming impossible. The Kamchatka way of life may therefore have shared many similarities with that even of the Ice Age and its cavern painters, and Siberian art sounds its own uncanny echoes. Because the tribes lived on the move, the strength of their culture did not lie in the raising of statues or great buildings. Their art expressed itself in things which they could carry: simple carvings on wood and bone, and quaint stick-like drawings. It expressed itself above all in wonderful flights of imagination into the world of the spirits and the unseen. Without written language all that their culture aspired to was translated into art, rituals and legends. The latter they handed, as treasured gifts, from one generation to the next by word of mouth.

The traditions of Kamchatka take on a unique importance in the search for answers to early wisdom not just because they were to a large extent untrammelled by outsiders. Their huge value lies in the fact that they were recorded by a man whose interest lay only in accurate and scientific ethnology and the legacy which, in their dying years, the Koryaks entrusted to Jochelson, innocent of its implications and potential value to the world, has become something beyond price. To turn the pages of Jochelson's massive faded diaries, and to discover the deeds and adventures of the spirits and folk heroes who rest there, is to step through a unique doorway into the past and into the authentic life and love of a pre-literate culture.

There are no startling parallels to be found and the material creates as many conundrums as it resolves. We will not find sacred kings, nor even mother goddesses – at least not in the sense which has become familiar. The world we are entering is one driven by concepts of animism and elemental forces as yet largely undirected by any clearly defined pantheon.

The story is best begun with Koryak art. In common with almost all simple cultures the Siberians demonstrated a great and instant pleasure in their artistry. Jochelson summed up their fondness: 'I believe that the aesthetic taste is a strong and spontaneous longing of primitive man, as are his beliefs. Whoever has lived among primitive people knows well how strong is their passion for all kinds of ornaments.'

Some of the artistry was directed into creating personal gods or guardians. The most important object in the house was the sacred drum made from hide stretched over a wattle frame. It stood on the hearthstone of every family and the noise of its banging kept at bay the forces of evil. Each household also owned a sacred fire board, another protector of hearth, herd and home.

The plant world features hardly at all in Siberian art, and in this there is common experience with the Ice-Age epitaphs. Jochelson saw some fantastic ornamental engraving which seemed part plant, part geometric design, but nobody he talked to could offer any explanation. In their creation of human and animal figures though, the artists were talented and prolific. When they wished, their carving and sculpture was lovely and lifelike, and every household had its treasured collection, its own 'mantelpiece knick-knacks'. Siberian toys were crude and rudimentary: the wooden dolls the Koryaks made for their children were often roughly carved with flat faces and bodies. There was, however, crudeness of a different vein, one of purpose and not economy, when it came to religious works as, with uncanny echoes from earlier times, the sculptors shunned the experience of eyes and hands and relied on some different inner motivation to generate parodies of human form. Images of personal guardians often verged on the totally abstract. Some of the sacred fire boards had vestigial similarity to human form, in others the connection was almost impossible to grasp though each wore a sacred collar made of dried grass, no doubt a primitive form of the type of metal torque commonly worn by Scandinavian and other European images.

The seafaring Koryaks cut forked alder twigs into the vague outline of a man who sat in the bows of their newly built skin and wattle boats, and these crude images bear comparison with fertility figures found at Viborg and Rebild in Denmark. The obvious desire for stylization was echoed across the Siberian plain. Further west the Yukaghir tribe had a twin-headed spirit of the tent, the Nganasan, its body reduced to a peg and head and arms entirely rudimentary in a style reminiscent of the Ice-Age figurines.

Although there has been reticence about explaining precisely the maxims on which distinction between real and surreal art were founded, the inference was that generating images of the spirits was a risky business and the less chance such models were given of 'coming to life' the better. It was acceptable for the spirit world to maintain its discreet invisibility but to have it walking abroad in the shape of animated wooden figures was a fearful thought. There was also, incidentally, a mortal terror of the dead walking – bodies were tied up and squeezed into the smallest of wooden coffins. As always at such a stage of understanding people wanted the comfort of seeing the supernatural in human form, yet too much realism was clearly a danger.

Art worked for religious purpose was not only very schematized but usually two-dimensional. Until very recent times it was possible to find strange wooden figures of great age hanging in trees on mountain paths in Yukaghir territory, generally overlooking the old hunting grounds. These figures were called Can-coro'mo, the 'wooden men'. The Can-coro'mo was made from a flat board often more than a metre long. Crudely designed, the board was

split along part of its length to represent legs. The artist cut a
notch for the neck and a deep scar for the mouth but, otherwise,
the image bore few recognizable features.

The 'guardians', whilst by no means constituting a pantheon
of gods with individual duties, did nonetheless serve particular
needs. The whaling clans set up wooden posts on the seashore
called *kamaks*, whose resident spirits would attract new whales.
These *kamaks* may shed better light on the 'high seat pillar'
which the Norwegian emigrés took to Iceland. It is also worth
remembering the carved wooden posts which Ibn Fadlan came
across on his travels up the river Volga, and the information put
together begins to suggest a mix of household god and sacred
tree. Small versions of the *kamak* called *kalaks* were carved for
children in answer to a quaint but charming piece of lore. The
kalak bore a face, the 'searching face', and threaded on a piece
of string it was worn on a small child's *back*. If the child became
sick and its soul wandered away, the 'searching face' would catch
the soul and put it back.

Jochelson became aware that the Koryaks extended an intense
reverence to dead animals. A slaughtered beast was treated as a
dear and honoured friend. Its face was covered and the hunter
did everything to disguise premeditated murder. When hunters
met, their conversation did not include phrases like: 'How many
animals did you kill?' but: 'How many animals did you *meet*
today?' These hunters believed also that if the bones of a dead
animal were placed on a platform, away from the ravages of
other wild animals, they would be reassembled and returned to
life. There was always a sense that the killing of an animal was
carried out after formal agreement between the hunter and the
animal's guardian spirit and correct relationship with the animal
world was fundamental to the Siberian hunter's way of life.

In the hunters' world where the spiritual power of animals
is a highly significant factor, the hunting and killing of prey
becomes greatly complicated. The kill may bring down the
wrath of the animal's spirit guardian, and there is an additional
risk of slaughtering something else disguised as the prey! Thus
providing the next meal involves more than a physical interplay
between hunter and hunted, a strong spiritual chemistry exists.
Were this form of belief to have held true for the more ancient
hunters, it could begin to explain some aspects of the reverence
they demonstrated so powerfully for the animal world. It may
shed light on why they included in their art so many animals
that were not normally relied on as a source of food. All of the

animal kingdom would have been part of the powerful magic which bound the hunters' world to that of the spirits.

The Koryaks held a bear festival each year, involving wooden models of bears tantalizingly similar to the Ice-Age sculptures found at Wogelherd. If the Koryak wisdom is good for earlier prehistoric cultures, then some possible explanation begins to emerge. The object was in part to placate the spirit of a dead bear but also to equip it for its journey home. In a ceremony watched by Jochelson, women danced with firebrands, the animal's skin was taken off, complete with the head, and one of the women danced wearing the skin and begging the bear not to be angry but to be kind to the clan. There was a strong concern that, without the proper ritual, the bear in its next life would seek revenge. Wolves also took a sensitive place in Siberian cult. A wolf was considered to be a powerful and evil shaman in animal disguise, hostile to the reindeer, and particularly vengeful on those who hunted it. Other festivals took place reflecting the main needs of people whose livelihoods depended on the vagaries of animals. Where reindeer were hunted, the return of the herd from the northern summer pastures was celebrated, and in the spring there was a second festival of the birth of the fawns.

Animals were sacrificed, not as an excuse for raucous blood-letting but, in part, in a sincere effort to appease the spirits with offerings of meat or life. The act of ritual slaughter was, as it may have been for the Ice-Age hunters, the formal enactment of the real hunt's climax so as to minimize its potential dangers. The northern tribes occasionally sacrificed reindeer but usually they resorted to the camp dogs as victims. Dog meat was only considered palatable as mortal fare in dire emergency, and this form of offering also conveniently regulated the swelling canine population of the encampments. In contrast with popular images of sacrifice, considerable humanity was shown to these dogs in their final moments of life. According to Jochelson the slaughter was carefully staged. Dogs would be rounded up and gently hog-tied, then, still on their feet and apparently undistressed, the attention of each was distracted whilst it was run through with a ceremonial spear. The bodies were offered to the spirits having been hung by their chins from tall stakes outside the camp.

A primitive tribesman, one realizes, sees his world as having both earthly and spirit form. It is as if, once the human mind has recognized the two-fold nature of its own being, it has applied the same principle to all of nature. Every living thing possesses its personal psyche capable of overcoming the hurdle of death. Has this spirit been innate in the human mind for always? It lived in the Neanderthal cave dwellers. It lived in the *ka* of the Egyptian pharaohs. It instilled into the minds of Socrates and Plato. Now, 60,000 years on from that first flower burial, it persists undaunted in the space age as we reach for our gods in the distant stars.

The principle extends beyond that which is biologically alive. There is often a vagueness and even contradiction about tribal wisdom, but there is also a remarkably universal level of understanding. Before the human brain can grasp the essential fact that our individual personalities separate each of us, irreversibly, from the rest of the world, it first recognizes everything as part of a huge and constantly varying chain. Every object, living or inanimate, is a link but the links are fluid and can drift one into another. It is not merely possible, but sometimes necessary, for a man to become a bird, animal to become rock, bird to metamorphose into cloud. The power to generate these changes comes from the spirit world. A spirit can turn in an instant into objects of daily life and into everything in nature. It can become a log of wood, a stone, a reindeer, a tree, or the morning mist rolling in from the sea. In the Koryak mind, things could never be presumed from appearances. Everything, at the whim of its spirit guardian, could take on another self.

A touchstone of shamanism is the premiss that if a spirit is offended it must be placated; if it is likely to be irritated by some future action, insurance must be paid to guard against its wrath. In other words, if any activity in the day-to-day life of a hunter incurs the risk of annoying the spirit world, it is important to do whatever is necessary to render that activity legitimate. It must be acceptable in the eyes of the 'guardians' and thus freed from possible supernatural repercussion.

Legitimizing the action involves effectively 'passing the buck' on to the spirits concerned. In twentieth-century terms the logic is hard to follow, but the transfer of responsibility constitutes a very basic necessity for the security and comfort of a hunter. Unless appeased, the offended spirit can bring illness, failure in the hunt, accidental death. The agency to provide release from impending misfortune, or illness, is the shaman's ritual and trance-like intercession with the powers of the spirit world. Therein lies the power base of the oldest form of priest and witch.

Shamans go by many names but their purpose is always to be honest brokers between the world of the supernatural and temporal earth. They are the men and women of particular intelligence and dexterity who mediate with the spirit world, and with the birds, animals and trees. The shaman sees that which ordinary people are unable to see, at a level of intelligence and expertise which means that he or she is often the artist of the tribe; it is someone who has the mental agility and discipline to turn the images of the mind into tangible pictures and objects.

The shaman's role is as complex as that of a modern-day priest, changing with circumstances and local tradition. The black shaman, the archetypal 'black witch', who performs ritual with full and sacred regalia, dispenses rough justice for the spirits of the underworld and it is partly out of fear of the black shaman that each family employs its own private insurance against malevolent spirits, its household guardians. The white shaman, dispensing no harm and without ritual trappings, intercedes with the more benign spirits. Generally speaking though, a comfortable balance is maintained between the powers of good and bad, and the roles of black and white shaman may even merge.

Detail of genuine ritual has been consistently missing from the story. For a hunting culture the art of shamanism is at the core of ritual, but it is by its nature a very secret thing. In 1918 the Russian anthropologist Vitashevsky managed to gain access to a shaman of the Yakut tribe expelling evil spirits from a sick person, but the report was very inconclusive. It was almost dark in the hut where the ritual took place and, despite having an almost flawless understanding of the Yakut dialect, Vitashevsky could not understand many of the words used. He was left with the impression that the rite had been compromised by his presence and would be unlikely to benefit the recipient. The shaman, in full regalia, first puffed on a ceremonial pipe and then began to sing and beat on his drum. At the climax he imitated the neighing of a horse, a creature sacred to the Yakuts, and the shrill cry of a bird, before drawing from the sick man's breath four evil spirits and spitting them out of the hut.

In recent times some of the paucity of evidence can be attributed to a monumental lack of enthusiasm for ethnology. When, for example, between 1884 and 1886, a Tsarist regional governor visited the Kamchatka Peninsula, his memoirs included a small but piquant observation. He was invited to enter the hut of an elderly shaman to talk but, since the hut was partly underground and the entrance was very low, he refused the offer on the grounds that it would have seriously marred his dignity.

The shaman was a person of enormous power and influence,

and his death brought a strange practice which offers new possibilities for the ritual dismembering and scattering familiar in
Osirian and other cults. Yukaghir consigned their rank-and-file
dead to the next world via raised wooden platforms, but for
their shamans there was a more profound rite. On death the
shaman's body was dismembered. His bones were cleaned and
kept as sacred ancestor relics within the clan, but the flesh and
organs were cut up and distributed. Each member of the hunting group took away a piece of the body and, with great care
and reverence, dried it and tied it to his personal Can-coro'mo.
If the 'wooden man' was small it might be worn by the owner
as a protective talisman. If large it was hung in a tree and, once
decked with the flesh of the shaman, became the dead man's
spiritual house. We have thus a kind of sacred tree.

Wherever there is evidence of shamanism, its rituals very
often set out to emulate the behaviour of animals. Rarely is
this authentic behaviour, but rather that which might occur if
human logic were applied to the animal. As in the Koryak bear
festival, the shaman dresses in skins and takes on a creature's
instincts as *he* imagines them within the scope of human emotions – elation, fear, rage, sorrow. If such an impersonation is the
subject of the anthropomorphic 'dancing' figures of the Ice Age,
then it is possible that a similar logic existed for the palaeolithic
hunters.

The climactic moment of the shaman's rites often came during a state of hallucinogenic trance which relied on a magical
plant, revered amongst the northern hunting tribes, the sacred
mushroom. In the 1900s the Fly Agaric grew all over Kamchatka
though it seems to have been particularly dense in Koryak territory along the edges of the river Varkhalam. The Koryaks carried
on a thriving trade exporting to their neighbours, and in one village visited by Jochelson he found a group of shamans making
judicious if bizarre use of the limited material available. Jochelson
was always meticulous in his attention to detail which on this
occasion provided his account with its lighter moment. Each man
chewed on the fungus, keeping it in his mouth for a long time
without swallowing. He sat motionless as the hallucinogen took
effect then rocked gently from side to side, and without warning
began to gesticulate convulsively, pupils widely dilated. He sang,
danced and talked with someone he imagined was with him,
but then, as the experience subsided, he urinated solemnly into
an empty can labelled 'California Peaches'. The liquid was then
shared out and drunk.

Dried in the sun to make it less noxious, the effect of the fungus's principal drug, mycoatropine, on the central nervous system is dramatic. Once in the bloodstream this complex alkaloid first causes giddiness and nervous excitation, and then a state of trance heightened by vivid hallucination. The narcotic is rapidly passed out of the body in urine, but how the shamans learned of this is difficult to imagine. Necessity must have become the mother of invention. Among Koryaks the fungus was only eaten by men but in other cultures shamankas used it too. It is not difficult to imagine the logic which this strange plant must have generated. Its shape, at least when young, is reminiscent of a phallus that has pushed erect through the earth. Garishly coloured, it is like little else in nature and although it is reluctant to emerge during drought, it appears with astonishing speed after rain with all the significance which that relationship suggests.

For a shaman though, the strongest endorsement of the mushroom's powers was that to consume it unlocked the door to the heavens. These special plants possessed a latent energy which, in context, was as enormous as the power of the atomic bomb. Ownership could place men of intelligence and vision infinitely higher than their peers, a strength which dictated that it should be used only by the right people and at the proper time, accompanied by the correct ritual and with the knowledge that a legend has been created to account for its beginnings. Ownership and use were regulated through strict social taboos.

The reverence attached to plants made sacred by an accident of their chemistry is not restricted to Siberian tribes. It happens the world over and involves many other plants than Fly Agaric. Yet in spite of their influence, note of them rarely finds its way into the records of shamanistic practices. The magic fungus was a basic element of Koryak culture but there is no evidence that it ever appeared in the art of the Koryaks. For all its importance, had it not been for men like Waldemar Jochelson, all trace of its use would have vanished.

Such plants, or species like them, were evolved in Europe soon after the last Ice Age, and it seems unlikely that objects of such striking appearance would go unchallenged by curiosity. It must therefore be a probability that the hunters of the upper palaeolithic found their own doors to the spirit world through the power of magic plants, but that they too chose not to describe such things in their art, even in the secret depths of the earth.

There exists a clear framework for Koryak religion. It involves a folk hero, sometimes with a pedigree of pure ether, sometimes part real part imagined, who has carried out the potentially hazardous activity. This tribal ancestor, who lived in the 'dream time', has carried out all the important tasks of day-to-day living, from house building, to fashioning weapons, to making fire, to hunting food. These are seen as exemplary deeds that the folk hero has undertaken. Sometimes he has run the gauntlet of the deities with his impudence but, at the end of the day, he has always come away unscathed. For each adventure a legend has grown to perpetuate the account, often fashioned as a tale of confrontation and acquittal where good wins through.

Whether in origin legend precedes ritual is an egg and chicken dilemma. What is beyond question is that the legend preserves, in a precise and established manner, the procedure of ritual. It allows a sequence of events to be memorized through the medium of a story which is passed from one generation to the next. Mythology is one of the foundation stones of primitive religion. It provides not so much an understanding of the mysteries of life as a mechanism for placing them in a familar and structured framework, working much as theorems and formulae that provide abstract containment for the problems of science. The ritual which accompanies mythology provides the means of control. Primitive religion and science both seek answers to the awesome forces of nature but mythology offers another dimension, that of entertainment. Koryak stories involve the raw ingredients of faith yet they are drawn in such a way that its articles merge indefinably with pure vicarious *divertissement*.

The mythology recorded by Jochelson provides its own idiosyncracies, but some principles are almost universal throughout the time and spatial span of mankind. For virtually all faiths, Christianity notwithstanding, the spirit world exists on three distinct levels. For the Siberian tribes, rising above everything was a creator spirit, the ultimate force in the heavens. The tribes of Kamchatka called him Tenanto'mwan, Master on High, Existence, Universe. He was the Urun Ajy Toyon, the White Creator Lord, of the neighbouring Yakuts. In Esquimau belief he was the Tornarssuk. Perhaps the most apt name for this sublime deity was that known to the Yukaghir; they called him Pon, the 'Something'. The Yukaghir came the closest to summarizing a vague, remote and shadowy figure. No cult was ever addressed to him. He brooked no icons. The head of the archetypal pantheon, he controlled all that is visible in nature occasionally lending a hand to tip the scales of destiny, but distant and out of reach.

Ranking somewhere below this illustrious being, there existed a number of other spirits, some friendly, some malevolent, yet all watching over their own principalities of nature. These were spirits of fire and light, wind and rain, sun and moon. They were the keepers. They, like the creator spirits, seem to have stemmed from very ancient times. Down the spiritual pecking order – a descent in altitude as well as on the social ladder – stood a vast group of more animate and essentially earthbound entities, the 'masters' or 'owners', the beings who controlled the various domains of visible nature. Every mountain and forest, meadow and lake, river and sea, had its own deity answering to the keepers.

The third group of spirits lived somewhere beneath the world, vagrant beings, often essentially evil but not associated with any objects. They represented the forces of darkness, often sky spirits that had lost grace, the so-called 'fallen angels' of which Lucifer is a part. It seems that every society, no matter how ancient, follows the innate notion that good is only good if balanced against evil. The Koryaks perceived spirits they called the Kalau, the cohorts of the underworld. For the Yakuts, the same spirits were manifest in the single, ghastly figure of the Arsan Duolai, the 'Terrible Dweller of the Underground World'.

The existence of these levels in the spirit cosmos did not mean that the hunting tribes necessarily imagined a heaven and a hell. In fact for most there has been a complete absence of such a notion and its implication of blessing or punishment dependent on the quality of worldly behaviour has not occurred. For a hunter, an offended spirit must be placated or it will bring calamity through illness, failure in the hunt or, in extremis, death. Rarely is there any consideration of nirvana as a natural progression of old age. It is always an event of circumstance brought through the direct intervention of the spirit world.

Into the mystic array of supernatural beings entered a special figure, less a god but more an immortalized super-hero. Some primitive societies dispense with the single being and rely on the collective powers of ancestral spirits, but the imagery is essentially the same. In Koryak mythology, Quikinnaqu, 'Big Raven', was such a hero. He and his wife Miti are singled out as the two truly humanized figures and, whilst there is no clear-cut earth mother in Siberian legend, this couple and their contemporaries provide a time-honoured sexual chemistry. As with the Celts, the Siberian tribes were at heart probably often matriarchal. Miti was a much cleverer personality than her husband, and there seems to be an obscure snippet of legend about her origins which bears scrutiny beside some of the Adam and Eve creation stories. Miti was said to have been thrown from heaven by her father, Universe, but Big Raven was ignorant whence she had come.

Big Raven was, nonetheless, regarded as the first all-powerful shaman of the tribe, technically the founder of the temporal world. Everything existed before Big Raven but it was through his shamanistic powers that trees, animals, rocks and humankind took substance − a gelling of the ether that has been a common early explanation of creation out of chaos.

Big Raven was also a major-domo, a one-man celestial navvy gang, responsible for overseeing the immediate temporal world and sorting out its practical wants. His equals can be found far and wide in such characters as Arnakuagsak, the 'old woman of the sea', who supplied all of the physical needs of the Esquimaux. Big Raven was half-man and half-bird. He donned a cloak of feathers to carry him to the skies, giving him direct access to the ear of his 'Number One'. The dream of flight to the heavens may just provide a clue to the significance of the bird-like heads on many of the hybrid figures drawn by the Ice-Age artists, but the ability of such beings as Big Raven to fly is one which he shares with counterparts from many cultures and many eras. Amongst the Irish tales is the Siege of Druim Damhghaire in which the Druid wears an *enchennach* − a bird cloak: 'Mog Ruith's skin of the hornless, dun-coloured bull was brought to him then, and his speckled bird-dress with its winged flying, and his druidic gear besides. And he rose up, in company with the fire, into the air and the heavens.'

Big Raven and his contemporaries were embodied to a greater or lesser extent by the shaman of the tribe, and if it has appeared at times that the roles of sacred god-king and high priest blur into one another, the cause lies here. The shaman was the earliest king and priest. There is also a familiarity about the characterizations: each legendary figure was once mortal but had perished and achieved immortality: and each possessed the powers of intercession, transcendence, prophecy and miraculous deed. The super-hero of the hunters was thus the blueprint for the god-king of the ancient near east, for the Pharaoh, for the rulers of Tara and Uppsala, and one might argue, for the last of the great Jewish prophets, Jesus Christ.

Most of the traditions of the Koryaks were centred around the exploits of Big Raven, and to read the legends confirms the great emphasis on sexuality and fecundity that cries out from the non-secular art of other pre-literate and ancient cultures. The preoccupation may seem, for some, to distance the Siberian tribesman from credible religious belief, but it is hazardous to judge others by our own social values. One of the less admirable 'cuts' which Christianity has laid upon mankind is that sex equals sin equals death. In other cultures, where sensibility better takes precedence over ill-conceived dogma, sex equals life. We judge from the standpoint of twentieth-century Christian Europe at our peril.

The Siberian clans relied totally on the ability of the reindeer herds and the whales to produce offspring. They were also painfully aware of the importance of renewing their own human stock. In Kemchadal legend Big Raven's counterpart, Kutq, seems to have concentrated most of his energies towards attempting sexual dalliance with anybody or anything he met along the way. This would not have been seen as blatant prurience but as a vital and sacred activity necessary for life.

Siberian folklore, like that of many primitive societies, is thus littered with what we would label as 'prurient' material. The legends are full of sexual humour, occasionally savage but on the whole gentle. There is a general focus on bodily emission of one sort or another. Emanating from spirits, these have an omnipotent power of genesis.

Root Man had a daughter grass woman. She had many suitors, but refused to marry any of them. Finally Big Kamak came and said to Root Man, 'I will marry your daughter.' He took his chamber vessel into Root Man's hut and said, 'I am going to urinate. Let Grass Woman carry the chamber vessel out.' Then Grass Woman took the vessel to carry it outside. Then Big Kamak put her and the vessel on a shovel and carried them into Big Raven's house. There Big Kamak urinated again, but Big Raven took him and the chamber vessel, put them on a shovel and threw them out.

Grass Woman remained in the house, and Ememqut married her. Soon she was delivered of a son. After a while Ememqut went with his wife on a visit to Root Man, who however did not recognize his daughter. He said, 'This is not Grass Woman. It was Big Kamak who married my daughter.'

After spending some time with his father-in-law, Ememqut prepared to return home with his wife.

Grass Woman's brother, Tree Trunk Man went with them. Tree Trunk Man married Canainant, the daughter of Big Raven at her father's house. They got along very well, and Ememqut and Tree Trunk Man with their wives often went to visit both Root Man and Big Raven. That's all.

(after Jochelson)[1]

The tale of Big Kamak seems, in a somewhat confused manner, to be recounting a ritual marriage in which distinction between urine and semen becomes blurred. Almost all cultures in the first flush of their belief perceive the rain falling from the sky as the product of some colossal transcendental urination or ejaculation. The conviction spans ages and continents. Rain is the semen of the gods. It is the great procreative agency in the heavens that permits germination amongst life on earth. Often breath and saliva are visualized in a similar role. So if legend describes a mythical hero or heroine spitting, masturbating or urinating, they are invariably delivering life-giving sap.

The religious view is, of course, always a subjective one, and in the wet chilly conditions of Siberia, rain is received with sentiments rather at odds with those in a hot and arid desert. If the people of Mesopotamia awaited the dispensation of rains with feverish expectation, the Siberians sometimes could not persuade their spirits to remove them fast enough!

In the spring of 1901, Jochelson's wanderings led him along the Chaibuga River at the northernmost extremity of the Koryaks' hunting range. He came across a small temporary encampment where he met an aged lady called Kucanin. She was a shamanka, a female shaman. Across the smoke of her fire, as the evening sun set behind the rim of the tundra, she told him a strong and grotesque story accounting for the making of rain.

Big Raven and his son Ememqut flew to Universe. They went out, put on their raven coats, and flew up. They came to Universe. While still outside, they heard the sound of a drum. They entered the house, and found Universe beating the drum, and his wife Rain-Woman sitting next to him. In order to produce rain, he cut off his wife's vulva, and hung it to the drum; then he cut off his penis and beat with it, instead of an ordinary drumstick. When he beat the drum, the water squirted out of the vulva, which caused rain on earth.

When Universe saw Big Raven and his son enter, he stopped beating the drum and put it away. The rain stopped at once.

Big Raven and Ememqut pretended to leave the house, and made it appear that they went through the entrance, but they both turned into reindeer hair, and lay down on the floor. Thereupon Universe said to his wife, 'Hand me the drum; I will beat it again.' She gave him the drum and he began to beat it with his penis, and the rain poured down out of the vulva upon the earth.

Big Raven said to his son, 'I will make them fall asleep. You must watch where Universe puts the drum and the stick.' Suddenly Universe and Rain-Woman became very sleepy. He put the drum aside, and both fell sound asleep. Big Raven took the drum, and noticed that Rain-Woman's vulva was attached to it then he took the stick, and found that it was Universe's penis.

Big Raven took the drum and stick, and roasted them over the fire until they were dry and crisp. Then he put them in their former places, and broke the sleeping-spell of Universe and his wife. They arose, and Universe began to beat the drum; but the more he beat it, the finer the weather became. Finally there was not a single cloud left, and the sky cleared up entirely.

Big Raven and his son flew away home. Clear weather set in, and fine days followed one after another; but they had no luck in their hunt. They could not procure anything, either sea animals or reindeer.

They were starving because Universe was sleeping. Finally Big Raven said, 'I will go back to Universe, and see what he is doing.'

He came to Universe and said to him, 'We are having good weather now; but we are famine-stricken, we cannot procure any food.' — 'It happens so because I don't look after my children,' said Universe. 'Go back home. From now on you shall have success in your hunt: I will take care of you now.' Big Raven left. After his return, when his sons went hunting, they caught sea animals and wild reindeer.

Then Big Raven pulled out from the ground the post to which the dogs are tied, and reindeer came out of the hole in the ground. A whole herd came out. Big Raven

sacrificed many reindeer to Universe, and after that he
had good luck on his hunt. That's all.

(after Jochelson)[2]

This is a classic confrontation and acquittal myth, and it underlines the message that only through Big Raven and his shaman
successors can the caprices of the spirits be controlled. The drum,
to which is attached the vulva of the Creator's wife and is beaten
by Universe's equally dismembered penis, appears as one of the
universal symbols of spiritual power. If rain is celestial semen,
the logical progression is that the earth on which the rain falls
is a womb. It is the receptive female element of the natural
world; a patient, resilient, unchanging place of genesis which,
in the fullness of time and with the proper magic, achieves its
germination. Here lies the quintessence of the earth mother who,
in many primitive cultures, is drawn as a ripe-bodied woman,
full-breasted, with the mouth of her womb, her vulva, in great
prominence. Yet amongst the tribes with whom Jochelson met,
he was shown no icons of an earth mother.

It was the understanding of the origin of rain which perhaps
lay at the heart of the Siberian tribes' less overt regard for the
plant world. Their security lay in the hunt. Their lifestyle was
not suited to agriculture and the climate would have rendered
it impossible. Their view of the plants from which they gleaned
their nuts and berries was probably, for the most part, a casual
one. Imagine, however, walking through a green world having
no understanding of science, no technology and no microscopes.
The birth of a plant may be a thing of great wonderment. The
act of procreation does not happen visibly. The minute grains of
pollen plunging deep into the ovary to ejaculate their life-giving
germs are innocent flecks of dust on the breeze. Yet, with each
spring, new generations emerge from the once dead and frozen
earth. By what secret and magical means are they inseminated
to grow and take substance in the womb of the soil? The answer
can only be by the seminal rain that falls from the sky when the
heavens have darkened with the presence of the creator god.
Since the gods are the inseminators of the earth, then every
plant is of their creation. This sacredness of the plant world,
coupled with its spirit *alter ego*, accounts equally for the blueprint
of the Tree of Life, and for the curiosity and experiment which
has attached to such growths as the sacred mushroom.

The Koryaks who travelled the edges of Penzhinskaya Bay
hunted the white whale. One of their shamankas told Jochelson

the intriguing Legend of the Whale's Carrying Bag which involves
the powers of the Fly Agaric, but which, more importantly, reflects
the importance of returning a dead animal to its spiritual home.
Each slaughtered beast was provided with a bag made of grass in
which was placed provisions for its journey.

> Big Raven caught a whale, but could not send it to
> its home in the sea. He was unable to lift the grass bag
> containing travelling provisions for the whale. Big Raven
> called to Existence to help. Existence said, 'Go to a level
> place near the sea; there you wilt find soft white stalks
> with spotted hats. These are spirits, the Wapag. Eat some
> and they will help thee.' Big Raven went to the place that
> Existence had told him of and meanwhile Existence spat
> on the Earth. Out of his saliva at the place where it fell,
> fungus appeared which Big Raven found and ate, and
> began to feel gay. He started to dance and the Wapag
> spirits of the fungus said to him, 'How is it that though
> being such a strong man, thou can'st not lift the bag?'
> – 'That is right,' said Big Raven. 'I am a strong man. I
> shall go and lift the travelling bag.' He went and lifted
> the bag and sent the whale home. The Wapag showed
> him the whale going out to sea and how it returned to
> its brothers and sisters. Big Raven said, 'Let the fungus
> remain on earth and let my children see what it will
> show them.
>
> (after Jochelson)[3]

Many of the legends possess a strongly animistic theme.
Jochelson was told a tale in the village of Tilliran on the
Bering Sea coast. It is the legend of the Stone Pine Girl.

> Big Raven went to the woods and finding a stone-pine
> cone, pounded it with a stone. Out of the stone-pine
> cone came a girl with a head like a copper tea-pot. Big
> Raven said, 'Oh. What a pretty little girl.' – 'Do you say
> that I am pretty? Mama says, come into the house.' The
> house was a twisted stone-pine and the sleeping room
> was in the hollow of the bough. He entered the house.
> 'I am very hungry – open the old woman's abdomen.'
> He opened it and looked in. Behold! it was full of the
> meat of a mountain sheep, all nice and fat. He fell to
> eating, choked himself and died. That's all.
>
> (after Jochelson)[4]

In its adulterated version the storyline has become almost a nonsense. Its confusion, its lost logic, are typical of many. The story though provides another, quite distinct, concept of a spirit being who has taken over and resides in a tree. It is clearly built around a ritual to which many primitive societies are devoted. It is a moment of sacrifice in which the tree is decorated and hung or filled with meat and other offerings to its spirit. There also emerges in this and other stories the same intriguing transmutation of young girl and hag which was so much a part of Celtic tradition, and it begs the question of how old and how widespread that notion is. The legend also offers one of the many accounts of Big Raven's death. The Koryaks accepted that he had died in some far distant time, and here he meets his end punished for taking the sacrifice due to the spirit of the tree.

Rarely is any attempt made to describe the guardians beyond their titles. Thus there is Rain Man, Grass Woman, Root Man and so on, but they enjoy a lack of detail which falls in with the general pattern of vagueness attached to the spirits of animism.

It would be highly misleading to suggests that Jochelson's contacts at the turn of the century provided the sole observation of primitive tribes by objective researchers. But Jochelson has provided a unique commentary on a pre-literate Iron-Age culture within the catchment area and climatic range of the hunters and gatherers with whom, in part, this quest is concerned. Tempting analogies are to be drawn between the 'modern' northern tribes, the pre-literate Celts and Germans and others, and the Ice-Age hunters, and perhaps some are justifiable. Here and there it seems that in spite of such a mighty time chasm, there may have been genuine common experience. In each instance wild animals represented a large slice of sustenance in an uncompromising world. Life revolved around following the herds, were they reindeer and horse, sheep and cattle, pig and goat, or at sea the whale and seal. Meat was food, skins were clothing and shelter, fat was an insulation and a source of light, bones were the raw fabric of much utility.

Many of the tribes knew little more than a landscape of semi-frozen tundra and forest. As far as we can tell, lifestyles were not dissimilar to those of their distant counterparts, and both ancient and modern cultures found an all-encompassing spiritual dimension in the environment which surrounded them and on which every day they were utterly dependent. Cult grew in response to the problems and pressures of environment. But, were these various factors close enough, or sufficiently relevant, to provide criteria on which to argue common understanding and creed?

There is a small but tacit object lesson in the pitfalls, on the unlikely subject of calendars. The Yakuts made calendar 'clocks'. Wooden circles, drilled through with holes that represented days of the week and the month, were plugged with pegs to indicate the date. This alleged invention of the Siberian tribesmen has been used by some pre-historians, including Marshack, to support the argument that Ice-Age hunters were capable of similar advances. There are two drawbacks. The Yakut device contained an obvious cursor which the so-called calendars of prehistoric hunters did not. There is, however, a less well-defined inconsistency. The Yakuts seem to have divided their year into lunar months, but their time count is extremely confused. They regarded one year in our calendar as two, but if asked the number of months in a year they would invariably answer twelve. When asked to list these more than twelve names emerged, and, in general, theory did not reconcile with actual method of reckoning. This, Jochelson found, was based less on lunar cycles than on actual events taking place in the world – ice breaking, fish spawning, ripening of hay, autumn rutting.

The suspicion is that use of calendars was not part of the Yakuts' ancestral culture. It was an innovation picked up, though not fully understood, from Russian travellers, and though each family owned a calendar it was less a working instrument than an ornament. It is significant that throughout Jochelson's field notes from other Siberian expeditions he makes no further mention of calendars. He was thorough in his attention to detail and if any of the Kamchatka tribes had possessed calendar clocks he would probably have reported it. Once more it has to be remembered that the Koryaks and their neighbours were much less affected by Russian influence than the more westerly located tribes like the Yakuts.

There exists a reasonable likelihood that Celtic and Icelandic religions owe their origin to simple faiths like those of the Siberian tribes, and Jochelson's reports arguably represent one of the great landmarks in the search for truths about the early religion of the north. Some will argue that the kind of cult followed by the Koryaks and their neighbours demonstrated little that can be called religion but a great deal to do with magic. They will find objection to the use of such terms as 'religion' and 'creed' when applied to prehistoric cultures. T. G. E. Powell in his book *The Celts* says of their beliefs: 'It is well to stress the word magic, for of religion, except in the modern anthropological sense of primitive religion, it cannot be said that the Celts were at all conscious.'

Piggott relies on a definition of religion which states that it must be evidenced by a clear-cut and consistent body of belief, and he implies that religion in that sense is not to be found amongst primitive cultures. The trouble with such assertions is that they rely on the doubtful assumption that we know enough about beliefs of such prehistoric cultures as the Celts to be able to evaluate them. Yet to assume that the Irish monks provided a diligent record of the deeper aspects of Celtic wisdom is no less naïve than the assumption that Jochelson managed to preserve the innermost thoughts and wisdom of the Koryaks. It may be a fairer observation that if one were to judge solely on the evidence of the Bible, one would obtain a very limited view of the deeper aspects of Christianity even though the biblical texts are the polished offerings of Christian minds and pens. Piggott allies the great religions to the historical period, without recognizing that it may only be the wealth and depth of sympathetic and often propagandist historical record that makes them seem superior.

It may be argued that religion has adopted a remarkably consistent attitude down the ages, only adjusting to environmental conditions, and to the political and social demands of the day. Magic is not a primitive alternative to religion and the two cannot be separated. All that can be said is that magic may have played a more prominent part than it does today, but magic has been, and continues to be, part of the integral structure of religion. We intercede with the twentieth-century supernatural in much the same ways as the most primitive worshippers, and our intercession includes the use of magic. We pray, we make incantations, we eat and drink the symbolic equal of sacrificial meals, we insist on statues that bleed, madonnas that weep, relics that possess magical properties. Schoolgirls enjoy miraculous visions, and some Christians make public claim to powers of conjuration. Vicars exorcize, and priests remove the stain of sins at a stroke in the confessional. Many of these things demonstrate nothing more or less than reliance on magic.

The argument that primitive religions rely largely on prescribed cultic activities to achieve their ends, without having advanced to properly measured creeds, and that their mythologies only serve to move the spirit world to acquiescence is difficult to justify when one examines some of the material. The stories may not appear, in our sophisticated view, to reflect a broad religious message, neither may characters such as Big Raven seem to exemplify a doctrine, but to such people as the Koryaks beliefs may have been incorporated in their mythology, and observed in their rites, no less profound in context than any we profess today. It is possible to discern deep strands of awareness in such legends as Universe and the Making of the Rain, and by labelling them only as vehicles to constrain the magical powers we may do them a great disservice.

Intellectually our approach to our gods, and our beliefs about existence, may have modified somewhat since 'stone-age' days, but on an emotional level religion meets needs to which it has always responded. It asks that powers beyond our full understanding provide the necessities of life, and that they pay heed to human welfare. 'Give us this day our daily bread' and 'deliver us from evil'. Probably the only major distinction is that today we are not merely concerned about the ups and downs of earthly life, we are equally interested in the prospects of a celestial welfare state beyond the pearly gates.

18

The Pagan Christians

It would make a neat conclusion to the story if the new broom of Christianity had swept the old orders of belief cleanly out of the door. In reality it only consigned them under the carpet, from whence they have had a habit of reappearing. It is therefore necessary to turn the clock back, though now with the focus on Christian rather than pagan Europe, to the point of schism with Roman civil and military ascendancy. The story takes on its own peculiar and often devious complexity because for many centuries a major battle for hearts and minds was to be waged between the ecclesiastical establishment and the non-Christian traditionalists. Its 'theatre of operations' exists on various levels, constantly entangling with and affecting one another.

Much within the ancient roots of the Church, as has already been established, owes itself to pre-Christian origins, but further 'pagan' elements have been allowed to infiltrate at various times since the Council of Nicaea established the indelible 'charter'. There is also the openly 'pagan' profession of faith which has continued, with varying degrees of repression and tolerance, and which, today, is subjected to a goodly amount of romantic nonsense.

A picture of the true balance during the first thousand years and into the early medieval centuries is virtually impossible to

achieve because, although it may have discovered a new freedom of expression, post-Roman Europe took a giant cultural
step backwards. The 'Dark Ages' were aptly named. At their
close, with the Carolingian renaissance of the ninth century,
spoken Latin had disappeared in large areas of the continent and
very few people could read or translate it. Writing in any other
vernacular was a hesitant and exploratory adventure. The *Anglo
Saxon Chronicle* gains much of its prominence because it was one
of the very few annals of life in Europe between the time of the
great tribal migrations and the Norman conquest. Bede's *History
of the English Church and People* is similarly a unique document.

What is certain is that European Christianity gained an irre-
versible position under Constantine, crowned in AD 311.[1] The
'heretical' elements within the Christian camp had, by then,
fallen foul of a highly organized core of men who insisted that
the only valid passport to paradise was to be applied for through
the Church, and that one's visa into eternity must be stamped by
none other than the apostolic succession of priests. Constantine
had, notwithstanding his Christian zeal, tolerated paganism, but
his successor Theodosius outlawed all non-Christian religious
cults.

In the new atmosphere of religious prejudice and persecution
Rome's political eagle was also losing its feathers, a decline in
which many believed Rome had been instrumental because she
had abandoned her gods to a new and unconcerned deity. In
western Asia, Christendom was to enjoy two more centuries
of comparative tranquillity until the spread of the new and
pervading Arabic faith of Islam born out of revelations to the
Prophet Muhammad, but in AD 410 Rome fell with great bloodshed to the Visigoth army of Alaric. Through the turmoil, the
Church expanded out from Rome and the other great apostolic
centres around the Mediterranean like an advancing spring. It
left pockets of paganism to be thawed as time permitted, and in
the more remote hinterlands of the far north it failed to make an
impact until modern times, but outwardly the Catholic Church
was set on a firm path of spiritual and political supremacy until
the Protestant upheavals of the sixteenth century. Away from
public scrutiny though, its success was far from clear. It had
found a solid adversary in the older religions and against these it
was not the self-assured and relentless tide that popular history
assumes.

It is important not to lose sight of the fact that the Church
came to wield enormous political as well as spiritual muscle.

Areas of population had become divided into dioceses ruled by urban bishops, carrying on the apostolic succession and answering to metropolitan archbishops. They, in turn, responded to the Pope in Rome, who claimed his patriarchal succession from St Peter. But the credentials on which the temporal power of the Papacy was based were actually fraudulent.[2] The eighth-century Pope, Stephen II, claimed political control of former Byzantine lands, under the aegis of the infamous *Donation of Constantine*. The document, a letter dated 3 March 315, ceded imperial power in Italy and all Western territories to the papacy of Silvester I, but it was a forgery, generated in the papal chancery in the late eighth century. For some three hundred years the power was little used but it formed the basis on which, for example, Pope Leo III crowned Charlemagne emperor of the West in AD 800. In the tenth century, control of the Church passed briefly into the hands of kings and nobility until, under Pope Gregory VII, it was wrested back from the lay establishment and papal influence began to dominate European politics in earnest. One of its most effective tools was the anti-semitism stirred up against Islam and the Jews which resulted in large armies effectively coming under papal control to fight the crusades.

The ecclesiastical establishment made believe that the majority embraced the new faith willingly and with joy in their hearts. Resistance came only from those who, in today's parlance, would be identified as the 'hooligan element'. But beneath its veneer of confident complacency, and despite its awesome powers, the Church came to realize that conversion was no easy matter and in practice it was often to be achieved more through secular 'carrots' than theological persuasion. Whilst publicly full of spirit and zeal and with no time for compromise on principles, the Church was resigned to a private tolerance dictated by the acceptance that in practical terms it could not stamp out old traditions and beliefs without risk of a catastrophic backlash particularly amongst the great mass of people who lived and worked the rural ecomony. A not-inconsiderable problem was a sheer lack of available priests. Churches were expensive commodities and took a long time to build and to become established as an efficient network of parishes in which the priest, as the bishop's delegate, had the 'cure' of souls.

To avoid driving too strong a wedge between people and their 'grassroots' traditions, churches were built on the sites of non-Christian temples,[3] sacred springs became holy wells imbued with the sanctity of saintly patronage, and trees and cairns which

had overseen pagan rites became properly Christianized. When
the Anglo-Saxon priests were faced with the popularist religions
of earth and altar, they elected for compromise not confrontation,
and this meant that ordinary people continued to make offerings
of food at shrines dedicated to Frigg and Woden, Diana and
Apollo, though ostensibly they were now making their offerings
in the name of Christ. Tree shrines in particular experienced a
splendid change of clothing. Bile trees in Ireland, remnants of
Celtic symbolism, became integrated into the more modern faith.
Old ceremonies, such as those enacted around maypoles which
once marked a decidedly pagan worship, suddenly became part
of rural Christian practice and the old reasons were conveniently
forgotten. In many villages the trees were still decked with bits
of cloth to honour the most ancient of deities whilst assuming
quasi-Christian colours. All, from Easter eggs to 'holly and ivy',
were derived from pagan ceremonies and trappings.

Virtually all the old festivals which marked the seasons and
encouraged fertility of crops were blandly taken on board as
part of the Christian year and, in the course of time, were
given altered words and new names such as Whitsun, Rogation
Sunday and Hallowe'en. Thus important Christian dates fell on
days which perennially had been sacred. Frequently the devotion
of the common man had become a jumble of pagan and Christian
themes.

Bede shed a degree of light on the situation in Saxon England.
Born in AD 673 he spent his adult life serving in the monastery
of St Paul in Jarrow, and much of his anecdotal material was
gathered from like-minded Christian clerics and travellers. His
writing is valuable because he was unusually willing to preserve a
mix of history and tradition. He drew attention to material which
was recognizably suspect in Christian terms, and his *laissez-faire*
attitude has provided a reasonably accurate if limited picture of
the day and its people's sentiments.

Bede's records reveal that as late as the seventh century the
south-east of England was still firmly in the grip of paganism.[4]
In the year 640 the Kentish king, Earconbert, issued an edict
ordering the abandonment and destruction of idols throughout
his realm – according to Bede the first English king to do so.
Only a few years before in 633, the successors of a Christian
king, Edwin, are recorded as having taken their kingdoms back
into the old ways: 'As soon as they had obtained control of their
earthly kingdoms, however, both these kings apostatized from
the faith of the kingdom of heaven which they had accepted,

and reverted to the corruption and damnation of their former idolatry.'[5]

Bede grew up in an age of miracles and he drew numerous cameo portraits of happenings which can have been little different from the mysteries of a thousand or ten thousand years earlier. Where Oswald, king of Northumbria, died, the earth was regarded as being so potent that people mixed it with water and drank it. They took it away until a large pit formed. Animism played a major part in superstition and the elemental forces were no less revered. Chad, Bishop of Mercia, may have been a devout and not unsophisticated man but he obeyed instincts of a most ancient origin: 'For god stirs the air and raises the winds; he makes lightning flash and thunders out of heaven, to move the inhabitants of the earth to fear him.'[6]

Liberalism bore its limits, even for Bede, and when narrating Christian conversion he often adroitly masked the more sordid circumstances with tales of miraculous persuasion. In the context of a protracted quarrel which had gone on for decades, a seventh-century king of the Middle Angles, Peada, was anxious to secure a marriage contract with the daughter of the Christian-convert Northumbrian king, Oswiu. Peada's acceptance of Christian faith and baptism was a condition of the deal: 'So when Peada had received instructions in the true Faith, and had learned of the promises of the kingdom of heaven and of man's hope of resurrection and eternal life to come, he said he would gladly become a Christian, even if he were refused the princess.'[7] Much of the early process of Christianization was conducted, one suspects, through similar schemes.

Ecclesiastical strategy was often to persuade the leader assuming that the rest would follow and churchmen in positions of power were not above pecuniary sanctions and 'back-handers' in order to loosen key figures from their pagan loyalties. Bede described the conversion of an influential pagan priest named as Coifi: '. . . the religion that we have hitherto professed', the convert admitted piquantly to Paulinus, Bishop of York, 'seems valueless and powerless.[8] None of your subjects has been more devoted to the service of our gods than myself; yet there are many to whom you show great favour, who receive greater honours, and who are more successful in all their undertakings . . . if on examination you perceive that these new teachings are better and more effectual, let us not hesitate to accept them.'

Apart from the writing of such observers as Bede, the early evidence is scarce. Printed books did not begin to circulate until

the fifteenth century and, prior to that time, sources are largely
diocesan records and the limited number of surviving private
manuscripts. The bulk of meaningful accounts did not come into
being until the seventeenth century. Yet, in spite of the dearth
of literary material, some familiar snippets emerge which reveal
that during the medieval period, far from securing a universal
devotion to orthodox Christianity, the Church found itself continuing to rub uneasy shoulders with paganism and experienced
a widespread disaffection with its dogma and rituals.

At an intellectual level, there seems to have been little voice
in support of pagan sentiments before the fifteenth century.[9] The
comparative flowering of thought which followed the Dark Ages
had produced a broader theological speculation and a renaissance
of interest in philosophy amongst such scholars as Thomas
Aquinas, Duns Scotus and William of Ockham with arguments
about the relationship between reason and faith, philosophy and
religion. Analyses of the natural world and the cosmos postulated
by Aristotle and the more radical Plato began to find a receptive
ear. Platonism, effectively the last of constructive thinking prior
to Christianity, captured imaginations and was hotly argued and
reformulated. At the same time there was a desire to discover the
underlying influences which governed the magic of the village
wizard, and the root of principles on which practices further
down the social scale were founded.

For a long time, however, intellectuals were unwilling to
risk speaking out in defence of strictly heretical notions. Born in
Einsiedeln in 1493, Phillipus Aureolus Theophrastus Bombastus
von Hohenheim, better known as Paracelsus, was variously considered as the darling of neo-Platonic revival in northern Europe,
or the Swiss 'mad hatter' of his age, or a most dangerous heretic.[10]
Either way he was a courageous man and history reveals him
to have been a brilliant philosopher and alchemist. He dared to
meld and unite Platonic theories on the mysticism of nature with
Christian dogma in a manner which argued a hierarchical ladder
of creation ascending from base matter to God. He also defended
the need to pull down barriers between ritual practised in and
out of the Church. He considered that all should be regarded
as manifestations of faith in the same God. 'Holy scriptures', he
argued, 'call sorcerers – without distinction – all those who were
versed in supernatural things and were not at the same time holy.
But this matter must be given some consideration . . . we must
not regard as sorcerers all those who are so-called in the Holy
Scriptures . . . magic is an art which reveals its highest power

and strength through faith . . . for there are holy men in God
who serve the beatific life; they are called saints. But there are
also holy men in God who serve the forces of nature and they
are called magi. God shows his miracles through his holy men,
both those of the beatific life and through those of nature: what
others are incapable of doing they can do, because it has been
conferred on them as a special gift.'

One of Paracelsus' preoccupations was with the matrices.
He envisaged the whole cosmos as the *Diva Matrix*, the divine
womb of the earth mother. It was hardly a new concept. Irenaeus
had lambasted heretical groups who argued for the womb as
'maker of heaven and earth', and his protegé Hippolytus also
provided an elaborate account of the 'cosmic womb' notion. But
Paracelsus enlarged the idea into medieval philosophy, and in
this there remains a specific unexplained aspect. From whence
did Paracelsus' philosophy arise? It is a curious fact of history
that he could not have gained access to Hippolytus' polemic
on the matrices, because that particular section of his writing
was only discovered in the nineteenth century. None of the
original philosophies on which Hippolytus commented were
available either.

Paracelsus argued for the elements to be perceived as wombs
in which all natural objects dwell and from which they receive
their identity and purpose. All ultimately descend from what he
described as: 'the Mysterium Magnum which is the one mother
of all things and of all elements and a grandmother of all stars,
trees and creatures of the flesh . . . earth is the "mother" of man
who shares "mother earth" with the plants, minerals and certain
spiritual emanations.'

Mortal womanhood became a carnate analogy for the whole
cosmic structure, and into this vision Paracelsus also drew the
Tree: 'Woman is like the earth and all the elements, and in this
sense she must be considered a matrix; she is the tree which grows
from the earth, and the child is like the fruit that is born of the
tree. Just as a tree stands in the earth and belongs not only to
the earth but also to the air and the water and the fire, so all
the four elements are in woman – for the Great Field, the lower
and the upper sphere of the world consists of these – and in the
middle of it stands the tree; woman is the image of the tree. Just
as the earth, its fruits, and the elements are created for the sake
of the tree and in order to sustain it, so the members of woman,
all her qualities, and her whole nature exist for the sake of her
matrix, her womb.'

The focus of the fertility religions, the mother goddess, arguably took her place in medieval Christianity in no uncertain manner and her biography comes later. But in many peripheral respects old traditions survived with equal tenacity and paganism flourished in the parishes for many hundreds of years. At a more humble level than that of Paracelsus few pagan practitioners were in a position to commit their beliefs and activities to the record, and much of the comment and terminology was therefore supplied from a Christian viewpoint.

Educational ignorance was an adverse element which also confronted the Church, but much of the apathy it faced was attributable to other circumstances. Environment and social conditions were, as much as ever, a weather vane of religious attitudes. Though the climate had changed dramatically, the physical quality of life in medieval Europe had progressed very little from prehistoric times for most of the population. Industry was still a thing of the future. The economy was rural, concerned almost wholly with subsistence food production, and manufacturing operated on a localized cottage industry footing.

The earliest population surveys reveal that life expectancy was still limited to twenty-five or thirty years.[11] Infant mortality was rampant, and for most people adult life was yoked to disease and infirmity of one form or another. Pandemic infections were less the exception than the norm. Diet was poor and unbalanced. The rich turned their noses up at fresh vegetables and ate meat and more meat, improperly cooked and often worm-infected. The poor were chronically malnourished and resigned to a life-long fare of cereals frequently laced with pathogenic fungi like 'ergot'. Medicine had no comfort to offer. It still stagnated in the age of Hippocrates and Galen, and physicians, for what they were worth, were few and far between. Surgery was crude, terrifying in prospect, agonizing in application, and rarely effective other than for lancing boils and amputating limbs. Dentistry was an unremitting horror.

Christianity was not designed to flower any more readily in European conditions of backwardness, poverty and disease, than in those of biblical Palestine. 'Love thy neighbour' is a fine sentiment if you are in a better state than the fellow next door. Whilst Christianity held out a long-term prospect of paradise, it offered little immediate solace when one was cold, hungry, and suffering from scrofula, constipation and rampant toothache. Day-to-day life sought relief in alcohol, herbal medicine and spiritual powers which applied themselves more to remedying current problems than to preparation for the here-after.

Humanity wanted cures for its ailments and its sick animals, fortunes prophesied, charms to help recover lost possessions, potions to bring love. Because of the lack of medical help, people turned to the local cures which were dispensed through the occult authority of the wise women and wizards. Some of the potions and powders were indeed possessed of sound thera-peutic properties, but all were regarded as being effective more by spiritual or magical than by physical attributes. The time of day and the astrological situation also bore strong influence on the effect. In medieval times herbs were gathered to the accom-paniment of prayers, and at prescribed moments, and the belief was promulgated that, unless the precise ritual was followed, the value of the herbs, as simples, would be negated.

These things, identified as magic and witchcraft, were a part of the pagan vestige against which the Catholic and, in its time, Protestant Church fought and arguably lost. Magic was the opium of the Middle Ages and beyond and faith was its carrier, and it is the interaction between the wizard, the witch and the Church which now becomes the focus of attention.

Witchcraft, the 'Wiccan' way, has become a popular vogue in the British Isles since legal relaxation in the 1950s. Unfor-tunately it has also become the subject of a great deal of silly claptrap including the wishful but wholly unsubstantiated notion that modern witches descend from an unbroken line of priestesses reaching back to the Celts and their mother goddess. It is impor-tant, therefore, to appreciate what witches actually were during, and after, medieval times and in terms of this journey.

A witch could be of either sex though was more frequently a woman, and a legal treatise of 1594 defines witchery thus:

> A witch or hag is she who being eluded by a league
> made with the devil through his persuasion, inspiration
> and indulging, thinketh she can design what manner
> of evil things soever, either by thought or implication
> as to shake the air with lightnings and thunder, to
> cause hail and tempest, to remove green corn or trees
> to another place, to be carried of her familiar which
> hath taken upon him the deceitful shape of a goat,
> swine or calf . . . and to spend all the night after
> with her sweet heart in playing, sporting, banqueting,
> dancing, daliance and diverse other devilish lusts and

lewd desports, and to show a thousand such monstrous mockeries.[12]

In effect, although any such distinction was disclaimed by the Church, witches in Christendom fell into two categories, according to whether they used their occult arts for benefit or harm.[13] Those who practised for the common good were the wise or 'cunning' persons who were relied on to cure ailments and whose magic was employed for such purposes as locating lost property. Such people could, in modern terms, be described as 'white' witches. The 'black' witch was an individual who used magic arts to generate harm, the so-called *maleficium*. Thus, in many respects, the witch was the equal of the local shaman. What distinguishes witches who practised in Christendom from their equals in all other religious cultures is that they were regarded by the Church, irrespective of intent, to have made a pact with that peculiarly Christian character, the devil. As the sixteenth-century authority Reginald Scot wrote in his *Discoverie of Witchcraft*: 'it is indifferent to say in the English tongue, "she is a witch" or "she is a wise woman".'

On the beneficial side, the magic of the peasant population was a very immediate thing, applied to produce practical results. One of the worst hazards for woman, prior to the advent of scientifically based medicine, was bearing children. Since she was guilty of original sin, and the infant she carried was similarly tainted before it received the cleansing of baptism, the mother-to-be was vulnerable to all kinds of diabolical influences.[14] Midwives were thus required to ensure that doors were opened and closed to relieve labour pains, and charms were recited over the child bed. But often the midwife, better versed in magic arts than obstetric skills, caused more harm than good and it was possible for her to be banned from the bedroom when the time came for delivery. Coupled with the immediate worries of pregnancy and birth, lack of hygiene meant that women constantly suffered from infections of the vagina and the womb and afflictions from venereal disease to prolapse were common. Not surprisingly women looked to any kind of spiritual strength to protect them.

Formulae were extensively adopted, and not just in child-birth.[15] It has been argued that prayer is a form of supplication the outcome of which is uncertain, but incantation associated with charms and spells results in effects which are a foregone conclusion. Yet, in practice, it has come down to a nicety of *words*. Whilst the Church condemned magical incantations it was not averse to adopting them when they suited its purpose. The medieval Cantries were designed to assist the dead, through the mechanical repetition of prayers; the more times recited, the stronger was the possibility of the prayer being effective.[16] The rosary works on a somewhat similar principle. The Church thus did much to foster belief in the magical power of words in day-to-day situations. An expectant mother would mutter repetitive Church-inspired doggerel. Plague might be kept at bay with the right incantation. Farmers would recite rhymes to ensure a good harvest. A bric-à-brac of Christian liturgy found its way out of churches and frequently played a key part in resolving secular problems through incorporation with charms and spells. Some of this reliance was, needless to say, an insurance policy, since reciting prayers to gain a result could never be termed a punishable offence. Customers of local magicians and wizards probably believed most practitioners to be carrying out Christian deeds and many of the rituals bore religious tones:

> Haile be thou holie heerbe
> growing in the ground
> All in the mount of Calverie
> first wert thou found,
> Thou art good for manie a sore.[17]

Some relied on biblical authority:

> In the bloud of Adam death was taken
> In the bloud of Christ it was all to shaken
> And by the same bloud I doo thee charge
> That thou doo runne no longer at large.[18]

Other charms amounted to debased and adulterated versions of orthodox prayer:

> I conjure thee O serpent in this houre, by the five holie wounds of our Lord, that thou remove not out of this place, but here staie, as certeinlie as God was borne of a pure virgine. Otherwise I conjure thee serpent *In nomine patris & filii & spiritus sancti*: I command thee serpent by our ladie *S. Marie*, that thou obeie as wax obeieth the fier, and as fier obeieth water: as thou neither hurt me, nor anie other christian, as certeinlie as God was borne of an immaculate virgine, in which respect I take thee

up *In nomine patris & filii & spiritus sancti: Ely lash eiter,
ely lash eiter, ely lash eiter.* Otherwise O vermine, thou
must come as God came unto the Jews.[19]

As the eminent social historian Keith Thomas puts it: 'The
rural magicians of Tudor England did not invent their own
charms: they inherited them from the medieval Church, and
their formulae and rituals were largely derivative products of
centuries of Catholic teaching.'[20]

The Church was no less responsible for aiding and abetting
in respect to fetishism. Talismans and amulets represented a
source of animistic power for thousands of years, and such
belief was strong in the Middle Ages.[21] Cowry shells and other
bivalves became popular because of the physical similarity of the
underside to the vulva. It was the thinking which prompted such
masterpieces as Botticelli's *Birth of Venus* in which the fertility
goddess rises from a sea-shell. One of the more ancient concepts
brought into vogue by the Egyptians and copied by the European
classical cultures was the winged uterus, a curious motif stimulated originally by the association of a bird, the vulture, with
the fertility goddesses of lower Egypt. By the time it came into
Europe, the original SA design had changed and instead of the
neck of the uterus being tied, engravers preferred the addition
of a key barring the way across the entrance of the womb. It
was a charm to ensure safe childbirth and to protect the wearer
from innumerable clinical problems.

Until the seventeenth century there was a flourishing trade
in talismans to protect the wearer from a host of gynaecological
and other complaints. In general though, the origin of a particular charm or formula can rarely be traced because classical
traditions and those from northern Europe became thoroughly
fragmented and syncretized. Very often the reciting of formulae
included debased words that had long since disappeared from
circulation, and the magician was as ignorant of the meaning as
was his client.

The Church, for its part, encouraged the belief that sacred
artefacts carried mystical auras and breathed supernatural powers.
The whole Catholic establishment took on an animistic éclat and
its trappings became charged with magical currents. The relics of
saints, a friar's cloak, a sash from holy orders, a consecrated vessel all bore mystique and powers which, from a more detached
viewpoint, was distinctly un-Christian and difficult to distinguish
from some of the principles of local magic.[22] It was, in part, a

critical response to Catholic ambivalence, coupled with the corruption resulting from such things as the sale of indulgences, that stimulated Protestant rebels like Martin Luther, Hugh Latimer and John Knox to speak out.

The Church also knowingly permitted ceremonial including Baptism, Confirmation, Marriage and Churching of Women after childbirth, to be viewed in a deeply superstitious light by congregations.

In its public ideology the Church has accepted no compromise or middle ground with the magic arts. Supernatural forces have emanated either from saints and angels dispensing the omnipotence of the Christian God, or they have been of diabolical origin, and a large gulf has existed between the two. Off the record though, such distinction has been much less polarized and has been the subject of much hypocrisy. The Church resorted to magic as whole-heartedly as any local wizard and whilst, officially, it judged according to a shifting view of the formulation of the natural world, the evaluation of God's handiwork at any one time was open to interpretation. The result was that those who sat in ecclesiastical judgement of whether a ritual, a talisman or an incantation were appropriate or otherwise, arbitrated according to what suited their personal interests and the designs of the Church at any one time.

The ordinary people who took comfort from the magic arts probably did not consciously regard themselves as anything less than good Christians, and certainly to admit more was to curry the wrath of the local priest and ultimately the bishop's court. The Church, for its part, played with words, substituted pagan charms and spells with Christian rhymes, and adopted small rituals whose roots it simultaneously castigated.

The Church also shifted its stance periodically in its attitude towards cunning persons and witches though continuing to profess, in principle, that such distinctions did not exist. Before the thirteenth century it fell short of condemning magicians working towards healing and such other obvious benefits as knowingly being in the devil's pay. Attitudes hardened after a pronouncement in 1398, by the theology faculty of the Paris University, that all magic amounted to conscious heresy and diabolism, a most serious implication because to be a heretic was to renounce the Christian God and to stand behind the Anti-Christ.[23]

There is a popular misunderstanding about the role of ecclesiastical courts.[24] They did not actively seek out witches and it was only those who invited the disaffection of their fellow parishioners that reached the record books. In practice it was often difficult to bring prosecutions through the Assizes because of lack of evidence, and parishes resorted to employing professional witch finders who were supposed to have better experience than the local 'vigilantes'. Even the Inquisition, an institution which never reached England, was not the source of terror that popular history assumes.[25] Set up by Pope Gregory IX in about 1233, and then reformed by Pope Paul III in 1542, it was not a court of jurisdiction. As its name implies, the Inquisition was a commission of inquiry installed as an autonomous body with a brief to detect and obtain depositions from heretics. It used torture at times but rarely called on its ultimate sanction even during the infamous heresy trials of the thirteenth century.

Although the continental Catholic Church took a more rigid stance towards magical practices than its counterpart in England, the courts were generally disposed towards leniency. Penances, pillorying, and at worst, excommunication were the more routine sentences.

The Assize Records in England indicate that the medieval, sixteenth- and seventeenth-century witches who were brought to trial generally stood accused of using the *maleficium* to the detriment of others, either to bring misfortune on animals or crops, or to commit murder.[26] Those found culpable in the first category were usually sentenced to a year's imprisonment. A 1593 entry for the Home Circuit details: 'Alice Alberte of Felsted, spinster on 25 July bewitched to death 22 sheep valued at £5; 1 cow valued at 40 shillings; 1 calf valued at 8 shillings; and 1 pig valued at 8 shillings of the goods and chattels of Roger Wood.' In the later English Tudor and Stuart times those convicted of murder were hanged. On the Continent the stake and burning were more common. An English case entry of 1593 which resulted in hanging records that: 'Agnes Haven of Boreham, spinster on 10 April bewitched John Brett, who languished in divers parts of his body for a long time.'

The records only show end results and day-to-day reality might, if we could but establish it, produce a less draconian picture of witchcraft. In their own debased and fragmented knowledge, and in the heat of Christian invective, witches may often have been ignorant of the true elements of their devotion. Some turned to witchcraft believing that it would save them from a Christian hell, a sentence promised for their past sins by some industrious parish priests. Devotees came from all social classes, though belief that the devil would provide food, clothing and money in return for discipleship was a lure which drew in the destitute, and the lower orders had the misfortune of being most often reported. Trial records suggest that the profession predominantly attracted women, a statistic in which, arguably, the Church revelled.

A witch was supposed to bear certain marks on the body, and often warts or pappilli would be enough to hang someone.[27] Trial by water was one of the most grotesque processes of ecclesiatical law. The accused was stripped naked and was bound, left thumb to right foot, and right thumb to left foot. He or she was then thrown into a river or village pond to discover if they would sink or swim. Sinkers generally drowned but in doing so were confirmed to be innocent. Swimmers were guilty and were hauled out to be hanged or burned. But a confession was the ultimate disclosure of guilt and frequently it was extracted under severe duress.

There is little doubt that witchcraft included sexual rites whose origins go back into antiquity and, in this respect, there is a link to the old fertility traditions. The ninth-century so-called Bishop's Canon describes that which was to be popularly known as the Wild Hunt or Sabbath.[28] 'Some wicked women . . . seduced by illusions and phantoms of demons, believe and profess themselves in the hours of the night to ride upon certain beasts with Diana, the goddess of the pagans and in the silence of the night to traverse great spaces of earth, and to obey her commands as of their mistress, and to be summoned to her service on certain nights.' The event seems to have been a festive invocation of the mother goddess much as she had been worshipped through Europe for centuries, though the reference to Diana is probably a vestige of Roman influence.

Accounts of witches performing sexual intercourse in the secrecy of nocturnal woodlands bore a strong basis of fact. Women were brought before Church courts following claims that they had slept with demonic spirits, the *incubi*.[29] Male witches were said to have indulged with the female couterparts, *succubi*, and in both we are probably looking at the faint remnant of a Sacred Marriage. Trials for the offence and for partaking generally in Sabbath gatherings were again more commonplace in Europe but such covens undoubtedly took place in England.

Succubi and *incubi*, having no flesh-and-blood substance, were believed to remove semen from sleeping men and use it to spawn witches. Many women convicted of the felony of witchcraft were sent to the gallows or the stake pregnant, victims of a myth that was open to abuse from all quarters. Husbands were reported to have: 'actually seen Incubus devils swiving their wives, although they have thought that they were not devils but men.' Nor was the Church free from taint. Reginald Scot cites a case where: '. . . in the night time Incubus came to a ladies bedside and made hot loove unto hir; whereat she being offended, cried out so lowd, that companie came and found him under hir bed in the likenesse of the holie bishop . . .'

Whilst few would subscribe to the argument that medieval witchcraft linked back to Celtic fertility religion there is much, both in the folklore and what we know of the practice, which argues that witchcraft was primarily a devotion to and reliance on the spirituality and fecundity of the natural world, perpetuating the bond first forged by the shamans of hunting societies.

Witches in England were said to own 'familiars' such as the black cat, dogs, rats, frogs and toads.[30] A record of 1671 identifies that: 'one Katherine Barrett of Woolwich, widow on 23 July did consult, covenant with, entertain, employ, feed and reward a certain evil spirit in the likeness of a rat.' In 1579 at Windsor it was reported that: 'one Mother Dutton dwellyng in Cleworthe Parishe keepeth a Spirite and Feende in the likenesse of a Toade, and feedeth the same Feende lying in a border of greene Hearbes, within her garden, with blood which she causeth to issue from her owne flancke.' Witches also made occasional claims that they could change into the shape of their familiars and equally were accused of changing their victims into beasts, another vestige of shamanism, as was the notion that witches could fly.

The Church built a formidable library of information about diabolism, and formulated a style of prosecution for witches which resulted in a Papal Bull, issued in 1484 in Germany where witchcraft was particularly strong. Under the seal of Pope Innocent VIII, it was known as the *Summis Desiderantes Affectibus*. This edict was followed about two years later by a manual, the *Malleus Maleficarum*, compiled by two Dominican inquisitors, Heinrich Kramer and James Sprenger which set out the circumstances of and response to witchcraft.[31] A considerable part of this long and not overly erudite manuscript is devoted to the particular problem of *succubi* and *incubi* which indicates that ritualized sexual activity was regarded very seriously by the Church. The *Malleus* failed to gain an English language translation until modern times, though it was printed in repeated editions on the Continent.

In England, *maleficium* first entered the statute books in 1542

as a felonious crime technically attracting the death penalty. The
Act, with various modifications, remained in force until 1736
when the capital offence was dropped from the statute books. The
last person to be hanged in England was, according to available
records, Alice Molland, tried at the Exeter Lent Assizes in 1684,
though in Europe the death penalty was in force until the end
of the eighteenth century.[32] How many magicians and wizards
existed at any one time is unknown because they rarely left any
record of their activities. They were only exposed to the curious
gaze of history if they fell foul of their local community. Reginald
Scot confirmed that during the sixteenth century a magician
lived in every English parish, but that some enjoyed seventeen
or eighteen. The last known trial and judicial execution was in
Poland in 1793 when two women Satanists were burned at
the stake.

The Church harangued its parishioners about the evils of
the devil and the security of Christ, yet in some respects it
did little to attract devotion from its flock. Despite efforts to
enforce attendance, a sizeable proportion of the population never
went to church, nor did they understand the most elementary
principles of the Christian dogma. This was particularly true of
the poorer classes and of those living in remote and isolated
situations. Ignorance played a part. Records from Tudor times
reveal that large numbers of the laity could recite neither any
parts of the Creed, nor even the Lord's Prayer.[33] What is even
more striking is that ignorance of doctrine and dogma extended
to a sizeable percentage of the diocesan clergy. In 1551 a Bishop
of Gloucester carried out a survey amongst 311 of his Protestant
parsons and discovered that more than half could not recite the
Ten Commandments! Among the guarantors of ignorance and
indifference was the fact that worship went on in churches that
were too small to include all the population, and in a foreign
language, Latin. Services, contemporary commentators suggest,
were conducted in a congregational atmosphere of irreverence
with social in-fighting for pews amongst the upper classes, and a
lesser flock which thought nothing of frequent hawking, spitting,
belching and general insolence during services.

The Church also did much to foster the belief that its priesthood was concerned less with leading popular devotion than
conducting esoteric and private performances. Sermons were
pitched far above the head of the average illiterate churchgoer,
more often than not composed to satisfy the egos of wealthy
patrons. The lure towards ageless occultism had been put on a

firm path as early as the fifth century when the Greek Church
started to veil the altar from view and the stone or wood screen
across the transept of medieval churches substantiated the gulf.
Since for most of the congregation the Latin recitations would
have been incomprehensible – perhaps one of the foremost
reasons why the services continued in Latin – this physical
deprivation turned Church dogma into virtually meaningless
mumbo-jumbo. But even this level of esoterism was not enough
and some time prior to the ninth century, the officiators of the
Latin mass adopted the practice of lowering their voices to a
mutter, so that the congregation were unable even to hear the
words.

Nowhere was the gulf between priest and laity wider than
in the cult which grew around the Eucharist. Henry Chadwick,
Regius Professor Emeritus of Divinity at Cambridge has commented: 'the part of the people in the sacraments began to
become less important than the acts of the priest in the mystery:
and the priest became rather more remote'. Esoterism actually
backfired. In the *Historie of Witchcraft* Reginald Scot laid out the
common Protestant view of such acts of popery, confirming that
many saw the sacrament as little less than indulgence in canni-
balism:

> ... with their carnall hands they teare his humane
> substance breaking it into small gobbets; and with their
> externall teeth chew his flesh and bones, contrarie to
> divine or human nature, and contrarie to the prophesie
> which saith: There shall not a bone of him be broken.
> Finallie, in the end of their sacrifice (as they say) they
> eate him up rawe, and swallo downe into their guts
> everie member and parcell of him ...

Because the 'host' took on a tremendous occult significance,
partaking of it became less a means of communion with the risen
Christ than a magical source of benefit. The *Malleus Maleficarum*
cites a number of cases: 'When a certain witch received the Body
of our Lord, she suddenly lowered her head, as is the detestable
habit of women, placing her garment near her mouth, and taking
the Body of the Lord out of her mouth, wrapped it in a handker-
chief, and afterwards, at the suggestion of the devil, placed it in
a pot in which there was a toad, and hid it in the ground near
her house by the storehouse, together with several other things
by means of which she had to work her witchcraft.'[34]

Certainty about the sacrament was so strong that in 1215, the Lateran Council decreed that the eucharistic vessels, communion bread, holy oil and water should be locked away to prevent theft and use for magical purposes.

The Catholic Church, sometimes consciously, sometimes perhaps inadvertently, moved to satisfy omissions with which it found itself saddled and through all its persecution of older non-Christian traditions – that which it labelled as diabolism and heresy – it stood guilty of hypocrisy. It indulged its congregations in magic and other pagan ritual dressed up in Christian colours. The inherent weakness remained that its figureheads were remote and the social and moral message of Jesus bore little immediate relevance to a poverty-stricken peasant stock whose clerical élite continued to amass ever more wealth and power. People still needed tangible evidence of their gods at work and, against the distance of the establishment and the abstraction of dogma, unofficial religion, represented by wise men and women going about their business in the parishes, bore a much greater relevance. People found greater assurance in placing their faith with a local wise person who would promise results than with a distant god whose clergy delivered words of wisdom they could neither relate to nor understand.

19

Madonna

At this juncture the quest for the mother goddess might also seem to be over. One might also argue that the search for her has run out of energy and that the only remaining interest lies in a scattering of twentieth-century oddities, the echoes of footsteps which have passed by and are gone. Within the borders of the canvas the patriarchal Christian god has won the day, and the lady who captured countless millions of heartbeats with her vibrance, her lust for life, and her driving personality, is vanquished. Nine hundred million Catholics might agree.[1]

Yet another chapter insistently demands its place to complete the biography of the Queen of Heaven – a chapter in the peculiar faiths of mankind that is, in some respects, as bizarre as it is remarkable. If a single phenomenon takes the candidacy for carrying mother goddess worship from the early Christian era to the twentieth century through what, at times, have been the decidedly hair-raising religious currents of two thousand years of European history, it is the cult of Marianism.

There is enough literature on the subject of Mary, the mother of Jesus – earnest and trivial, hallowed and profane, academically sound and lunatic trash – to fill several libraries. To distil and balance the essence therefore, and to give it objective place presents a task scarcely less formidable than the probing of the early Christian period itself. Nine hundred million devotees will profess, literally to the death, that the cult which has grown to surround Mary the Virgin is a purely Christian matter, free in the heat of its forging from pagan taint.

Mary is the Catholics' bastion against heresy and subversion by non-orthodox persuasions; yet Marianism has been a divisive and contentious power, labelled in some quarters as a heresy. Not least among the causes of friction has been an apparent love affair with principles that, to some, have seemed barely to distinguish Roman Catholicism from the spectre of paganism. The cult of Mary was instrumental in the schism between the Greek Church in the east, and the Latin faith in the west.[2] It wrenched European Christendom apart with fearsome violence when the Protestant movements rebelled against what they saw as deeply suspect excesses. They were concerned about the credentials, in respect of biblical texts and the evangelism of the apostles, of beliefs and practices which came to be associated with the 'packaging' of Mary.

The one source which, ironically, will not yield judgement on the appropriateness of Marianism is the Bible. The Old Testament, whilst proposing a virgin birth, is largely silent on the subject of Mary. In the search for reasons and role models some authors have tried to draw an analogy between her and Miriam, the Hebrew protector and saviour of Moses in his bulrush baby carriage, but the link is infinitely tenuous. Nor does the New Testament offer much more encouragement. As we have seen, Mary hardly features there.

One thing is beyond argument. Much as it requires more than the protest movement of a liberal Jesus to explain Christianity, so it demands more than the miraculous experiences of a Jewish housewife to account for the cult of Marianism. An uncomfortable truth lies in that the causes can claim little from hard fact, and perceptions of Mary do not stem from any written-down historical portrait. Whatever personality the real woman had, it evaporated, and once the focus expanded, as it did during the early medieval period, from the Nativity into the Annunciation, Dormition, Assumption, and idealization as Maria Regina, perceptions became ever more fictional. Mary's personality and circumstance have evolved, and are still evolving, in the minds of people who never knew her and she is now as much a product of fervent but imaginative interpretation as was Inana, or Isis, or Kybele. She is the star of an apocryphal 'mystery play' whose character has transcended anything which she may have claimed in life. If Mary had been living today, her image would be the product of media packaging as effective as any which catapults a modern screen heroine into the realms of legend. But it is a packaging which has been geared as much to political as to religious demands. Religion did not cease to be the prostitute of politics when it took the Christian label and, if anything, the liaison became more mutually dependent than ever.

The fabric of the packaging takes a great deal of explaining. It is largely irreconcilable with any Biblical criteria, and an enquiry might well ask how much of what has been effected is owed to Christianity and how much to paganism? But the borders between Christianity and other older religions have already been blurred beyond clear separation, and the more accurate question must be to what extent do the traditions which have grown up around Mary, and how many of the practices conducted in her name, owe loyalty to origins remote from and more ancient than Christianity?

It was from the tenth and eleventh centuries that Marianism gained its awesome proportions, but it was growing steadily in the early centuries of Christianity. It is fairly certain that some time before the momentous AD 431 meeting at Ephesus which officially conferred on Mary the *Theotokos* title, something decidedly peculiar had developed in Christian thinking. Perhaps Epiphanius, the fourth-century bishop of Salamis, was right when he wrote in his *Medicine Chest for the Cure of all Heresies* that the '79th heresy' lay in the existence an heretical feminist sect that can be traced back to a time before the Christian era, in sympathy with the restoration of ancient traditions and the Queen of Heaven.

The promotion of Mary was, from an orthodox viewpoint, supposed to offer a counterblast to dualism since it provided a human mother. The move possessed its weaknesses though. It created a two-edged weapon because it was linked inseparably with the idea of Anna's Immaculate Conception and so the Marianists argued Mary had been born free from original sin and the curse of Eve. But it was also tantamount to an admission that Mary had never been mortal in the full sense of the word. Conveniently separating her from the rest of womankind thus, perversely, scored an own goal to the benefit of the dualists.

Marianism took shape in a climate of faith that was fearful of death perhaps more than at any other stage of civilization, triggered by the terrors of the apocalypse and the fiery torments introduced by the biblical writings. Christians lacked, by their own decrees, the kind of warm and sympathetic household gods who would intercede with the great power above. Jesus was pictured less as the meek and mild redeemer than as the judge prepared to toss souls into the scales at the sound of the last trumpet. Christians sought assurance in Mary the Virgin to steer them safely through the terrors of death. But in the fervour to find a buffer between earthly life and the potential damnation beyond, Marianism became synonymous with many practices which never gained a seal of biblical approval.

From the fifth century a fervour of devotion to images was sweeping through Christendom.[3] Saints took shape amongst the intricate delicacy of mosaics. Jesus, Mary, the godhead, and a host of biblical characters gazed from huge icons that must have impressed themselves on the minds of worshippers as thoroughly as any statue hewn in the temples of Assyria and Egypt.

The trend did not, however, meet with wholehearted approval, and to appreciate the reasons involves a brief dip into the strategic positions of Church and Empire. The last accountable emperor in the western arm of the Roman dominions, Linerius Severus, witnessed the sack of Rome in AD 455.[4] Thereafter the Lombard kings established themselves in northern Italy, and the seat of secular Roman power moved to the eastern capital, Constantinople, the old Greek city of Byzantium. But the established order was under threat from another quarter: suddenly the Moorish hordes from north Africa invaded Spain with terrifying success, and many Europeans must have feared that within weeks or months the civilized world would be in Moslem hands. In hindsight there was little to worry about in lands north of the Pyrenees, but at the time, Moslem take-over of Latin and Greek culture was a very real threat.

The Arabs, openly contemptuous of iconolatry and saint worship, were ardently monotheistic and they saw the practice falling little short of crude paganism. Byzantine emperors,[5] already anxious to curb the wealth of the monasteries which relied greatly on iconolatry, became sensitive to jibes so close to home, and in 726 Leo the Isaurian issued an edict declaring open season on icons and the rest of the trappings which he saw linked to the rise of Marianism. Church property was confiscated, and icons burned, smashed, and hurled into the sea.

The Church's vulnerability was exacerbated because people were increasingly convinced that the icons emanated a certain ethos, the spiritual power of the persons represented in the imagery. Taking place – and in reality it has never ceased – was in part an acknowledgement of Platonic principles wherein supernatural forces can imprint in material things. But it was also a clear reversion to totemism – the worship of images with magical properties.

There is little doubt also that the seat of secular power in Constantinople considered the Church far too rich for its own good, and saw an excuse for clipping its ever-more gilded wings. The papal authority in Rome renounced Leo's edict, but it had no sound defence against the paganist label and it responded with muddled arguments such as that preserved in a letter from Pope Gregory II to the Emperor: 'In forbidding the worship of images you are worthy of praise; in destroying them worthy of blame.[6] It is one thing to worship images; it is another thing to learn, from the images, whom we should worship.' Leo was unimpressed by this posturing and sent a fleet to quell the papal resistance. It sank in a well-timed Adriatic storm, but had it sailed on Christian history and theology books might have been written very differently.

Matters came to a more convulsive head with Leo's son Constantine V who took a rabid stance against the whole direction of the Church.[7] Every icon in lands under Byzantine control was to be destroyed, monasteries sacked, prayer to saints forbidden. This latest edict triggered a virulent purge, Christians attacking Christians. Inevitably large numbers of the faithful rebelled and many ended their days displaying fanatical devotion to the iconographic fashion.

The Empress Irene offered a brief respite from iconoclasm after some seventy years of persecution, but it was short-lived, and under Leo the Armenian iconophiles lost eyes, tongues, limbs and lives. The reform was finally quelled through the so-called Festival of Orthodoxy of 843 ordered by another empress, Theodora, which ended a hundred years of icon-bashing. The century had not been without enormous cost in life and limb, and it fuelled the schism between Greek and Latin churches in a way that was to prove irreparable.

Meanwhile, large numbers of devotees had fled to Europe, and in the Latin West the net effect of the purges was to stiffen resistance. The papacy in Rome seized the occasion to make long-desired political gains, anticipating advantage in an open stand of defiance against the authority of Constantinople, and knowing that it had the solid backing of a public who, by and large, did not share the eastern mood. Pope Gregory III cocked a deliberate snook at the imperial court by decking out icons in Rome with the most luxuriant trappings that mind and matter could offer. He commissioned an icon of Mary the Virgin for his personal chapel, the Grotte Vaticane, which was to be crowned with a gold encrusted diadem and necklace, and with earrings smothered in precious stones.

Disquiet showed itself even in Rome where, for some, the decking-out of images in ever increasing opulence was a nonsense. Arguably these were the first rumblings of that which would explode into the religious fireball of sixteenth-century Protestantism, but the reformers' time had not yet come and successive Popes rewarded their temerity by having them flogged and bundled off to ignominious exile.

The race was on for the political and moral upper hand over Constantinople, with the Church fighting to establish itself in Rome, not only as mother of hearts and souls in its western sphere of influence, but as an unassailable political authority. It used the power of icons and relics in much the same way as an advertising agency will use a page of a newspaper or air time on a television screen to promote a product, and Mary was fast becoming the most glittering announcer. Inevitably she was destined to be manipulated as a political and psychological brickbat, a fate which she shared in common with many of the deities who preceded her.

Was Mary made a goddess through the machinery of her cult, a Queen of Heaven like Ištar and Isis, or did she remain a mortal saint? Does her cult differ in the make-up of its 'book', or distinguish itself apart, from any of the accountable criteria that announce the mother goddess? The universal Church is, and always has been, in a catch-22 because it seems not to be able to do without an apocryphal cult which lays it open to the accusation of mother goddess worship. The weakness provoked such desperate and sensitive cries as that of St Anselm at the end of the eleventh century: 'All nature is the work of God, and God was born of Mary! God created all things, and Mary gave birth to God!'[8]

The Church falls short of providing intelligent conclusions. It argues doggedly that there is no case to answer since the mere act of adoption by the Church absolves its devices, however blatantly pagan they may seem, of all previous connotations and associations. Followers of Mary will argue passionately that she and the mother goddess are clothed in wholly different auras and that the two can never be compared.

Perhaps the first step in this all too fleeting exploration should be to quantify that which announces a mother goddess; not necessarily straightforward because if one is to draw a word portrait it will need to be varied according to the time in history, and the kind of environment over which she has reigned. Nonetheless, on the strength of the goddess' biography thus far, some predictable features will write themselves into the fabric and govern the overall impression.

The mother goddess frequently emerges as a complex personality showing several contrasting faces. She is goddess of life, yet in another aspect she commands the nether world of death. She rules in matters of love, yet she wields weapons of war and she champions the warrior. Her hands are white and alluring at one moment, plunged in gore the next. She tends to take precedence over others when it comes to establishing her place in the pantheon, but often she wears the mantle of an intercessor to whom men can turn with their earthbound problems. She is linked incestuously in marriage with a semi-divine son, a sacred king who suffers death, and in whose restoration she is strongly instrumental. She is identified as the Queen of Heaven or some such title, she wears a crown and other vestments of royalty, and she carries emblems of power. Her earthly presence is signified, in common with other deities, through images drawn both realistically and in abstract, and which often possess magical powers. Frequently she is associated with astral symbols of stars and moon.

How many of these things apply to Marianism? For some it will be a provocative suggestion that, in one measure or another, virtually all have been applied in the 'making' of Mary. Yet the conclusion is inescapable and confirmation that so many apocryphal and pagan strands went into the cult of Mary must add fuel to the argument that pagan mythology also contributed not a little to what is preserved as the incontrovertible Gospel biography of Jesus Christ.

It may be a mistake to assume finding all the strands of the goddess within a single personality. She shows faces and performs roles which outwardly conflict. Should the search be confined to just one Mary, or are there other players in the New Testament texts who should ring alerting bells? Mary, the mother of Jesus, was linked with more than one namesake, who for some obscure but perhaps significant reason have been the subject of almost as much rich and imaginative embroidery.

The Matthew and Mark texts relate an incident in Bethany immediately before the Last Supper, when an unidentified woman poured ointment over Jesus' head as he sat eating a meal.[9] The Luke account draws a similar cameo but identifies the incident as having taken place on an earlier occasion in the city of Nain.[10] A woman, again unidentified, washed Jesus' feet as he dined, dried them with her hair, and anointed them. Jesus' Pharisee host described the woman, without further qualification, as 'a sinner'. The John gospel identifies a woman who wiped and anointed the feet of Jesus as one Mary of Bethany, describing her as the sister of Lazarus.[11] Thus we have Mary number two, arriving on the scene in a confused and inconsistent story, with the Matthew and Mark versions at odds with the Luke account, and the later John narrative making a pointed attempt to reconcile the discrepancies.

Mary the mother of Jesus and Mary of Bethany are to be linked with a third and more widely proclaimed mystery woman, Mary of Magdala, the so-called Mary Magdalene. She does not appear by name in any of the canonical Gospels prior to the crucifixion. Her first mention is as one of the women who attended Jesus' corpse, taking part in the customary annointing, but there is a bombshell attached to this Mary. According to Mark she was uniquely privileged, the *first person* to see the risen Christ! The Gospel of Philip has already singled her out as receiving intimate physical attention from Jesus and as being someone he regarded as special: 'There were three who always walked with the Lord: Mary his mother and her sister and Magdalene, the one who was called his companion. His sister and his mother and his companion were each a Mary.'[12]

A profusion of artists have been tempted to create scenes bringing the three Marys together. A fine fifteenth-century crucifixion study from the studio of Quinten Massys is typical, having the Virgin in white adorned by her famous blue sash, accompanied by Mary of Bethany in blue and the red-haired Mary of Magdala in red with a green cloak. Yet the context has been virtually effaced from legend, and Mary of Magdala is only the penitent whore. The medieval Church fabricated distortions casting her as a reformed city prostitute, but the texts never identify the unnamed woman, or Mary of Bethany, or Mary of Magdala as courtesans. The allegation is based wholly on the 'sinner' tag applied to the anonymous woman of Nain, and a note that Jesus had cast out 'seven devils' from the Mary at the crucifixion. The woman could have been a thief, an embezzler, a child beater, or a lunatic! The link between the three women is in fact based on the so-called prophetic remark in the Matthew and Mark accounts that Mary of Bethany 'did it for my burial', and that Mary of Magdala took part in the annointing of Jesus' corpse.

Why have the anomalies appeared? Once more, we may be missing reasoning which evolved in the occult privacy of the early Christian 'think tanks'. The Church vigorously distances Mary, mother of Jesus and epitome of purity, from Mary of Magdala the paradigm of carnal weakness. They are poles apart. Yet how confident can we be of that assertion? We have the extraordinary omission whereby Mary the Virgin was the one person of real note who did not see the risen Christ. Mary of Magdala effectively took her place in being the first to witness him. There is, surely, a message locked into that anomaly. The words of *Thunder, Perfect Mind*, the hymn of self-proclamation from Nag Hammadi, knock insistently at the Marys' door:

I am the abiding and I am the dissolution.
I am the one below and they come up to me.
I am the judgement and the acquittal.
I am sinless and the root of sin derives from me.
I am lust in appearance and self-control exists within me.[13]

Does the real truth lie here? The mother goddess presents a complex personality. She can appear as bride, as matron and as hag. In Florence there is a striking sculpture of *La Maddalena* by the fifteenth-century artist Donatello in which she appears as a hideous, withered crone, long hair covering her emaciated limbs. This Mary is frequently portrayed in medieval literature as having chastised herself with fasting and self-denial. Yet nothing in the biblical texts, in the words of her leader and confidante, point her to such a fate. We need to remember, in the topsy-turvy world of Christian logic, that sexuality is rewarded by desolation and despair, whilst abstinence guarantees a life of spiritual ecstasy for body and soul. Mary Magdalene becomes a strong candidate for the hag aspect of the goddess. She should, by rights, reflect the withered aspect of nature denied the impregnation of the god-king, but in Christian terms she is the fate of the natural body that has tasted earthly fulfilment. There is a logical argument that as good is meaningless without evil, the Madonna is only half a personality without the Magdalene. The one is the mutually exclusive mirror of the other.

It was from the twelfth century that the Marianists' propaganda machine really swung into action and it is through painting and sculpture, prose and song, that the full flavour of her cult becomes clear. In Florence, in the Duomo, that most glorious marble-hewn monument to Catholic faith, is one of Michelangelo's many *pietàs*, made curiously memorable by remaining unfinished. The broken body of the Christ is lifted by Joseph of Arimathaea and, bent under the weight, by Mary his mother. Here is the *Mater Dolorosa*, one of the few accountable aspects of Mary, but it is less than typical.

In the church of S. Maria in Trastavere, Rome, rests the massive eighth-century Byzantine icon, commissioned by Pope John VII. It is similar to many in which fact has moved aside for faith. The years have been stripped away and Mary has risen to become the triumphant Queen. If she is weighed down, it is not by the body of Jesus, but by the sheer weight of opulence lavished upon her. The Byzantine refugees have made up for opportunity lost elsewhere, and Mary wears a massive jewel-studded crown and an ornate gown. The Pope prostrates himself at his queen's feet, and there is an inscription, badly damaged, which reads: 'As God himself made himself from thy womb, the princes among the angels stand by and marvel at thee, who carried in thy womb the child that is born.'

Regal status was constantly emphasized until the end of the medieval period. In the first-known portrait of Mary the queen, in the sixth-century Roman church of S. Maria Antiqua, she is painted as a conventional monarch – resplendent in pearls and other jewellery – seated on a throne. From the fifteenth century, the *Madonna della Rondine* of Carlo Crivelli is lavishly described as a queen, clothed in a heavily gilded blue cloak, who cradles the naked Christ. The swallow which gives the picture its name perches on a balustrade above her head. Her dominant position is reinforced in nativity scenes such as a fine twelfth-century wall painting in the church at Lagoudera in Cyprus which depicts the Christ child wholly eclipsed by Mary, a central and dominant figure reposing on a mountain. Often the Magi are drawn, very deliberately, less as 'wise men' than visiting kings bringing the symbols of sovereignty. In the basilica of S. Appolinare Nuovo at Ravenna, it is thus Mary and not the infant who is the royal recipient.

The regal image has as much to do with politics as with faith. With the papacy fighting for political supremacy, there was an increasing question about whether the authority of God should rest with the Emperor in Constantinople or the Pope in Rome? Each side now sought divine patronage, promoting Mary with the paraphernalia of queenship and in doing so providing itself with she who, in effect, was a tutelary deity, a royal personality who would give authority to her agents on earth.[14] It was a question of which could outdo the other in gaining her favours. The desire for Mary's tutelary favours can be discovered elsewhere. A superb twelfth-century mosaic in the abbey church of Monreale outside Palermo has King William II offering the building to the enthroned Virgin, and for much of the medieval period the royal courts of Europe were barely distinguishable from outposts of heaven on earth, sometimes with bizarre consequences. The twelfth-century artist, Abbé Suger, influenced many works depicting the Virgin and was probably responsible for a fashion of merging royalty with divinity.[15] In a Bible prepared for Blanche of Castile, the queen is illuminated sitting to the right of her son, Louis IX, in precisely the pose of intercession found in contemporary portraits of the Virgin and Christ which bedeck French cathedrals. The Virgin, conversely, found herself modelled with features that bore uncanny resemblance to Queen Blanche.

Mary the Virgin has always been regarded as approachable, more so than the Christ. She possesses a feminine compassion, arguably the same maternal 'anima' attraction that has drawn suffering humanity down the ages from the eras of Willendorf and Dolní Veštonice. Eminences, like John VII and the ninth-century Pope Paschal I, had themselves drawn stretched beneath her throne so as to emphasize Mary's accessibility. She was there, listening intimately and ready, like a transcendental bridge, to intercede with heaven. There is implicit in the picture the prospect of holding on to Mary for comfort, for safety and for wisdom.

In the conch of S. Maria in Trastavere is a twelfth-century mosaic, created under the commission of Pope Innocent II, in which Mary and Christ, mother and son, sit gazing down with the doe-eyed, expressionless, yet utterly compelling stare that is a hallmark of Byzantine art. Here, there emerges a marked distinction between the style of the figures. The Christ is clothed in a robe lifted only by a modest patterning round its borders but, by contrast, Mary wears a massive jewel-studded crown and a lavish golden gown. There are other provocative elements in the mosaic. Mary has the paraphernalia of a queen but appears in one of the earliest Roman portraits in which she is seen to be crowned by her son, a vogue which may also have started in France. Innocent II spent time there and probably was familiar with a stained glass window in the old medieval Notre Dame. The same window was presented to the new cathedral, begun in 1163, by Suger again, where it remained until destroyed in the eighteenth century. It depicted the Christ placing a crown

on his mother's head and was probably the innovator of the
'Triumph of the Virgin' theme repeated throughout the medieval
cathedrals and churches of Europe.

There is, however, a marked peculiarity about the Trastavere
mosaic. The couple are depicted in a style which is distinctly
marital. The Christ's right hand does not hold the crown but rests
on his mother's shoulder, and on his knee an open book reads
as a phylactery, a device popular in medieval art for conveying
words uttered by the subject: 'Come my chosen one I shall place
thee on my throne.' Mary also holds a phylactery in the form of
a scroll which reads: 'His left hand should be under my head,
and his right hand should embrace me.'

The significance of the remark lies in its context. Mary utters a
quotation from the *Canticus Canticorum*. The extraordinary collection of ancient poetry will not let go, and it is worth for a moment
returning to its credentials, because more cant and hypocrisy has
been delivered in its name than any other book of the Testaments.
Christian and Jewish commentators alike have made desperate
and laboured attempts to sanitize the evocations of the *Canticus
Canticorum*, to free it from its physical connotations.

Typical of the clerical hectoring is a comment of the fourth-
century spokesman, Gregory of Nyssa: 'Some there may be
who . . . try to drag down the pure words of the Bride and
Bridegroom to the level of irrational animal pleasure, and thus
become absorbed in shameful images. Such as these must be cast
out of the community who joyfully participate in the marriage
and be assigned to the weeping and gnashing of teeth instead of
the happiness of the marriage chamber.'[16]

The liaison between Solomon, highly suspect in his loyalty to
Yhwhism, and the Shulamite woman, we are urged to believe,
transcended carnal pursuit. Yet immediately preceding the quotation attributed to Mary, the Song includes such provocative
material as:

> O that thou wert as my brother, that sucked the breasts
> of my mother! When I should find thee without, I
> would kiss thee; yea, I should not be despised. I would
> lead thee, and bring thee into my mother's house, who
> would instruct me: I would cause thee to drink of spiced
> wine of the juice of my pomegranate.[17]

One also finds:

> My beloved put in his hand by the hole of the door,
> and my bowels were moved for him.
> I rose up to open to my beloved; and my hands dropped
> with myrrh, and my fingers with sweet smelling myrrh,
> upon the handles of the lock.[18]

Such visual analogy of closed and open rooms, locked and unlocked doors, enclosed gardens, and sealed fountains, was frequently called on to convey the condition of a hymen.

Nevertheless the Marianists were determined to expunge all fleshy thoughts from the words which, thus cleansed, were claimed to anticipate Mary's spiritual wedding to her Christ and son.

It is questionable why the Church, like the Jewish religious establishment before it, has laboured to include this blatantly pagan description of the Sacred Marriage in its canon and, in doing so, opened itself to criticism. The effort to maintain the old Jewish analogy of Yhwh wedded to a recalcitrant Israel, through the imagery of Jerusalem the bride, is difficult to justify, but marriage between Christ and his mother has no logical explanation and certainly no biblical endorsement. The exercise is as incongruous as that of a Western democracy which elects to fly the 'Hammer and Sickle', claiming to have found in the symbolism a perfect analogy for the free-market economy. To what purpose though, given the predictable rumours which will fall?

For a Church that had been spearheaded by the misogynistic Paul, and that had fought tooth and nail to cleanse itself of any taint of sexuality, acknowledgement of a Sacred Marriage smacks either of reckless determination to prove that the spirit in which the words are received is greater than the spirit in which they are composed, or of a more esoteric undercurrent which has run counter to the public face of Christian belief.

The counterblast was the image of Mary the *Theotokos*, the Mother of God and product of Immaculate Conception, which marched in parallel with that of Queen and Bride. Mary's perpetual virginity was given a further stamp of approval, beyond that of Ephesus, at the Council of Chalcedon in 451.[19] Then in 649, at the First Lateran Council in Rome, Pope Martin I incorporated the *Aeiparthenosis* (eternal virginity) as a Church dogma that was placed beyond debate. Feast Days were laid down in Mary's honour: the Feast of the Annunciation on 25 March. The Dormition, the Falling Asleep of the Virgin, was celebrated on 15 August, with the Feast of the Nativity on 8 September, and the

Purification on 2 February. In the old Byzantine calendar this
was the Feast of the Presentation in the Temple, held on 21
November. The Purification celebration is a moving and memorable event, taking place at night, when columns of young girls
dressed in white and holding lighted candles join in procession
to demonstrate Mary's powers over darkness and despair. The
origin of the Purification motif is Judaic, coming from a society
in which childbirth was the product of carnality and therefore
the mother was impure. That connotation could not apply to
Mary so the festival was turned around to promote the triumph
of purity over sin. Yet the origins of the candlelit procession are
probably pagan, tracing back to a time when the mother goddess
searched the darkened streets for her missing god, and coming
to be associated with the end of dearth, pestilence and famine.
Such festivals were celebrated as far apart as Egypt and probably
Canaan and Babylonia.

Icons of Mary as *Theotokos* were painted from the fifth century
at least, but some of the most striking emerge from the period
when Catholicism was recovering from the Protestant onslaught.
A revealing portrait hangs in the Marnel Collection of the Museo
del Prado, Madrid – Diego Velasquez's *The Coronation of the Virgin*.
Immersed in counter-reformation fervour of the seventeenth
century, Velasquez painted a Mary who is far removed from
the mortal and sorrowing mother of the *Pietà*. Assumed bodily
to the supreme heights, Mary is poised to take the title Maria
Regina, but the impression of the *Theotokos* is paramount. She sits,
awaiting her accolade, as Christ and the Ancient of Days hold over
her head the crown of triumph which will equate and unite her
with the godhead. The dove, wings outstretched, hovers above
within a sunburst which reminds so strongly of the winged disc
that protected the sacred kings and mother goddesses of earlier
eras.

There are many ultimate expressions of the *Theotokos* to be
found in art, but one Velasquez study is surely unequalled. In
the *Immaculate Conception*, the apotheosis is complete. Neither God
nor the Christ enter the picture. Mary stands alone and supreme
in the cosmos, as one who has been since the beginning of time,
who was 'set up from everlasting, from the beginning, or ever
the earth was'. She has achieved the final elusive, illogical, paradoxical accolade. Painted as if she were a child, she is immersed
in the ancient symbols of the Queen of Heaven. Her feet rest on
the globe of the world, the fiery chaotic clouds of creation swirl
around her, and the twelve stars of the apocalypse frame her

head. The fountain of the water of life plays beneath her feet, and the Stella Maris, the ship of Isis, sails a tranquil sea. One could transpose the image and find Ištar or Isis. In her plain dark dress Mary stands as provocative as she is beautiful.

That Mary existed as an integral part of the godhead for many of the great painters of Catholic Christian Europe seems beyond argument. In Bartolome Murillo's huge and spellbinding *Two Trinities*, God rests at the apex and beneath him, in vertical column, one finds the dove of the spirit and the Christ child. The second Trinity is overtly composed as a triangle of Christ with Mary holding his right hand and Joseph his left. But there exists a more subtle triad. Of the four faces contained in Murillo's study, the cast of light draws the eye to Mary and Christ more or less evenly whilst the figure of God dominates in soft focus. Joseph is only partially lit and seems redundant looking out of the picture. Mary looks to Christ, who in turn stares upward as God returns his gaze.

Such masterpieces of medieval and counter-reformation art sum up a perplexing, contradictory experience that is Mary and her relationship with God and with her son. It is a relationship which fights the rules that should be dictums of Christianity, and yet somehow emerges free from taint in the hearts of millions of devotees. Many artists fell back on themes which were clearly of pagan inspiration, particularly those working under Byzantine influence. The Berlin Ehemals Staatliche Museen possesses a fine sixth-century ivory diptych from Constantinople which depicts Mary and Christ enthroned. Above their heads on carved panels are palmettes which had become firmly established devices of classical art but, more fascinatingly, Mary is drawn with a hairstyle that faithfully copies the Hathor 'omega' wig, and with an encircling hood the drape of which restates the emphasis by offering another classical uterus design.

Two aspects of the Mother Goddess emerging in the contrived personality of Mary remain thus far unexplored; those which involve her with war and with death. There is some justification for the argument raised by Marina Warner in her excellent study of Marianism, and by others, that Mary has represented the Queen of Hell.[20] Until 1900, in the Forum at the foot of the Roman Palatine hill, there existed a church known as St Maria Liberatrice. Its more ancient name of St Maria de Inferno recalled a legend that the entrance to the underworld was close by and that Mary was stationed there to intercede for sinners at the hour of their death.

The Catholic world has possessed an unremitting terror of hell with its flames, the devil and his predatory shop stewards equipped with red eyes, curly tails and toasting forks. But the road to this ultimate sanction has an 'escape lane', the very medieval concept of purgatory.

In the Catholic mythology, purgatory is a place where earthly sins can be expiated during the interval of time before the *Dies Irae*, the day of doom when all souls will be judged and returned in the flesh. Hence a soul can be posted to purgatory and still manage to catch the ascending elevator to paradise. Mary's intercession on behalf of the soul undergoing purging demands particular devotion to her during life, and it has stimulated the practice of indulgence – an insurance premium on sin, the paying of which can offer forgiveness. In the Catholic faith, with the Osirian figure of Jesus judging the dead in a questionable mood of attrition, the fate of many a soul lies in the clemency of Mary and her ability to tip the scales. Herein lies much of the strength of the Rosary, and it is no coincidence that the Hail Mary, one of the oldest and most oft-recited prayers of Catholics worldwide, ends with the cry: 'pray for us sinners, now and at the hour of our death.'

It may seem incongruous that a figure of mercy and compassion should also preside over war, yet it has been a familiar paradoxical feature of the mother goddess, and Mary wreathed in the aura of an avenging Christian valkyrie is well documented. Several of the Roman emperors in Byzantium set the precedent by erasing the image of their pagan war goddess from seals and replacing it with Mary and child.

In the seventeenth century, as Spanish imperial power was beginning to wane, morale was boosted when Philip IV proclaimed Our Lady of Victories Patroness of the Royal Arms, and instructed the strict celebration of her feast days throughout the Spanish dominions.[21] In the Thirty Years' War between the Catholic armies of Ferdinand of Austria and the Protestant reformers, an icon of the Madonna was thought sufficiently instrumental in securing a crucial victory near Prague that a church in Rome, already heavily associated with visions of the Virgin, was renamed S. Maria della Vittoria. Mary found herself cast on amulets as late as the Crimean War when nurses surreptitiously inserted talismanic medals bearing her image between the bandages of the wounded. These were considered to possess miraculous properties.

Mary retained her huge following in spite of such challenges as medieval Catharism and the onslaught of Calvin and Luther. Her role as the intercessor and protectress has been one of the most powerful attractions for her millions of worshippers. It proved particularly effective in the armoury of the Catholic missions to South America which used Mary's protective powers against natural disaster to draw the colonial peasant communities away from their local gods, though the methods used were sometimes less than open.[22]

According to popular mythology, in 1531 a converted Mexican Indian, Juan Diego, experienced a vision of the Madonna and her miraculous image appeared on his cloak, which also produced a shower of roses in the presence of the local bishop.[23] In consequence, and encouraged by a disastrous outbreak of plague, a basilica was built as the shrine of Mary of Guadelupe. It presaged a cult in which Mary became patroness, first of Mexico, and then of the Americas in the capacity of a protectress against plague, flood, and other pestilential mishaps. What has been less well reported is that the local community was loyal, not to Mary the Virgin, but to their own mother goddess, Tonantzin of Tepeyac, whose shrine they regarded the basilica to be. A Franciscan chronicler, Bernadino de Sahagun commented: 'It is clear that in their hearts the common people who go there on pilgrimages are moved only by their ancient religion.' Eventually, by combination of subtle infusion and then coercion and instilling of the terrors of natural disaster which would befall if the object of devotion were anything other than Mary, the Mexican devotees of Tonantzin were 'won over' by the Church hierarchy. The Virgin of Guadelupe was, however, a syncretization with an existing mother goddess.

Mary became the object of visions as no other religious figure. These very often are of a premonitory kind, and she has come to be relied on increasingly to warn of wars and other disasters. The visionaries have regularly been young, either children or girls at around the time of puberty, very often coming from impoverished backgrounds, though their numbers are swelled by more mature women in holy orders and by eccentrics and recluses. Frequently their tales have met with disbelief and it has only been when they have revealed some detail of their experience that cannot be explained away by normal criteria that their stories have been accepted. They belong to the band of seers who experience communication with the spirit world through a state of trance. Christianity prefers terms such as 'visions' and 'ecstasies', but such people possessed of unusual powers are no different perhaps to hundreds and thousands of shamankas and prophets whose psychical abilities have been feared and revered down the ages. The fine dividing line beyond which lies sorcery and witchcraft has already been discussed, and it is probably only the subject of their visionary experiences which has kept many of such people away from the flames and the gibbet.

Over the centuries, and in spite of the aversion to casting Mary in a sexual role, she has become identified in a number of instances with fertility. The black Madonna of Monserrat, which dates from the twelfth century, rests in the Benedictine monastery atop a drought-ridden Catalonian hill.[24] The place defies probability by remaining green and luxuriant, and it is regarded as a fount of the Virgin's fertility to which newly married couples make pilgrimage currying the boon of children.

Other icons and relics of Mary have become empowered with fertility but none more so than the sash which she wore round her hips and, allegedly, she dropped at the moment of her Assumption into heaven.[25] The location of the magical cloth is hotly contested. One claimant rests in the Italian cathedral of Prato, and has been the subject of several quaint legends, all of them relying on the slightly erotic connotation of such a garment. Chartres cathedral, on the other hand, has housed the chemise which Mary wore at the moment of Jesus' conception, and again this object is a devotional magnet for would-be parents.

Notwithstanding the popularity of such uneasy fetishes, Mary the abstainer crushing Eve's serpent of desire beneath her heel has been the paragon which the millions have tried to emulate in hope of gaining the boon of intercession. Mary's chosen rejection of the desires of the flesh was the justification for imposing strict celibacy on the priesthood. As early as AD 387 Siricius, the first Bishop of Rome actually to take the title 'Pope', and the first to claim primacy over the universal Church, made celibacy a prerequisite of joining holy orders.[26] The edict was received with less than wholehearted enthusiasm, one or two opponents pointing out that the gospels actually fall short of claiming Mary's sexual abstinence or her perpetual virginity. Siricius rubber-stamped the process, and left it to his contemporary and henchman, Ambrose, Bishop of Milan, the effective founder member of the Western cult of Mary, to hound the so-called heretics.

Once again politics was to intrude on the picture. By the eighth century the imperial court in Constantinople correctly perceived that Marianism, celibacy and iconolatry were inseparable. Constantine V not only banned icons and saint worship, he also demanded that monks and nuns should be married off, forcibly if necessary, and this persecution in the Greek East persisted until the empress Theodora restored the full trappings and conduct of the cult under the Festival of Orthodoxy.[27]

Thereafter two powerful institutions ensured that the cult of Mary flowered and continued to blossom energetically – the monasteries and the religious orders of military knights. The monasteries had begun early in the fourth century in Egypt as places of contemplative retreat and renunciation of worldly ties. The monastic way of life spread to the West at the end of the century and for a while followed the same extreme asceticism. But with the coming of St Benedict of Nursia in the sixth century there began a process of liberalization in Europe which slowly gained momentum.

By the eleventh century monastic orders had gone significantly beyond a routine of prayer and bodily mortification, and in the twelfth the Order of St John was founded to care for the sick in a Jerusalem newly liberated from the infidel by the crusaders.[28] It was this which gave rise to the celebrated military order of Knights Templar, officially licensed by Pope Honorius I in 1128.

The monastic institutions were the bedrock on which the whole apparatus of papacy was supported. All professed abandoning themselves to celibacy and to a life spent in contemplation and adoration of the Virgin. They gained colossal wealth from the simple but effective philosophy that the larger the cash premium paid to the Church the greater the insurance dividend guaranteed in Mary's pre-judgement office. Out of their bottomless coffers they promoted the art and architecture which gave vent to their fervour. The veritable barrage of painting, music and prayer had the effect of elevating Mary above and beyond anything which the councillors of Ephesus might have anticipated, and of course fame bred fame. It is sobering to realize that in France alone eighty cathedrals, largely devoted to honouring the Madonna, were constructed in the twelfth and thirteenth centuries.

Things were, however, not quite so sanctimonious beneath the public image. Christianity had saddled itself with a flaw as deep and as ill-conceived as that which attempted to remove Israelites from mother goddess worship in the old Jewish scenario. It failed to recognize one essential fact of life, and it chose to fly precariously in the face of all that history told it: religion and sex are bonded in an inseparable embrace. The crux lies once more in the superb crystallization of the Christian paradox that is *Thunder, Perfect Mind*: 'I am the one whom they call Life, and you have called Death . . .'

The outcome of equating sexuality with moral and physical decay was predictable – an outward show of purity and ascetic behaviour, and behind the scenes conduct as robust as any that the old cults could have mustered. It is not to say that the Catholic priesthood and the religious knights disregarded the perils of thwarting the sexual prohibition, but like that of the 'Roaring Twenties', it was a ban that human nature was not prepared to endorse. The prospect of abstinence drawing Mary's favour may have been laudable in theory, but it was often unworkable in practice. It ran in the face of the biological certainty that sexuality is an inherent and inescapable facet of human psyche, and rebutted the possibility of a God-given thing to be taken not denied. The ancient cultures had all recognized the illogic of distancing sexuality and spirituality. They had acknowledged sexuality as the great material and spiritual life force which sustains humanity's very existence, and which for them became a rightful and natural part of their relationship with their gods.

They had treated intercourse as a celebration, candid and joyous, not as something tainted and shut away, an embarrassing stigma of human weakness. It is the conviction that abstinence and self-denial will expiate the body from the stink of corruption, and leave it pure and whole to clothe the soul in blissful but sexless eternity, that has put at least one aspect of Christian devotion at risk of diminishing, at times, into a level of hypocrisy that makes it the butt of jokes.

Ironically the difficulty for all but very few of choosing between natural instincts and unnatural dogma was brought into sharp focus and notoriety by those who most ardently professed the latter course. Amorous misbehaviour of monks, nuns and saintly knights was a constant source of medieval scandal.[29] Monks luxuriated in concubines that were only barely concealed from their critics, and celibacy amongst the military orders was something of a standing joke. Sexual impropriety amongst the priesthood reached such embarrassing proportions that late in the twelfth century Pope Alexander III attempted to introduce a saner situation in which monks and other clerics could marry. The move was quashed by the orthodox Marianist voice and liberal romping behind cloister walls was set to continue more or less unabashed and unabated through the Middle Ages.

Christian propaganda has done its best to foster the belief that the orders of monastics and saintly knights were bastions of chaste and spiritual desire who looked to emulate the example of their patron lady. Not exactly so, and the songs of the troubadours illustrate the kind of hypocrisy that was rife. The vogue of 'courtly love' captured the romantic medieval imagination between the eleventh and thirteenth centuries and it was popularized through the songs of the Provence and Languedoc regions of southern France.

By the latter part of the troubadour era these songs spoke of ardour that had risen beyond carnal lust, and in such admirable guise they became enmeshed conveniently with love for Mary.[30] It would be quite wrong to imagine that one sprang from the other – each began quite independently and in distinct social currents – but in its way each fed off the other. The songs added fuel to the popularity of Marianism, and by such religious colouration the troubadours gained respectability. The pious sentiments were, however, based on something of a sham.

The troubadour songs began as outpourings of less ascetic sentiments. Far from being declarations of spiritual love elevated above and beyond fleshy passions, they were the amorous pantings of healthy sexual appetites which found food in the frustrating but thoroughly down-to-earth embrace of other men's wives.

Courtly love probably took root in a climate of arranged and all too often loveless marriages. A troubadour sought the attentions of a lady, preferably one above his own social level, his songs playing on her beauty and her inaccessibility, but falling short of implying that the lusty singer failed to gain his paramour's bed. Chastity was not a part of the troubadour code, nor was adultery seen to be immoral. In several chansons, Jesus is actually invoked to help the adulterer in and out of the casement window. The spirit of longing came not from abstinence or unrequited desire but from the frustrations of extra-marital sex. It lay in the mistress's legal ties to another, and in the practical limitations of arranging lovers' trysts with any measure of regularity.

Thus whilst outward expressions of pious devotion were directed to Mary the Virgin, behind the scenes some of the supposed upholders of her honour were indulging in an ongoing sexual free-for-all which paid service less to the Madonna than the Magdalene.

Nor was the realization of human sexuality limited to troubadours, knights and monks. One of the most poignant admissions of the difficulty experienced, even by the most devout apostates, in juxtaposing spiritual idealism and biological reality is the revelation of St Teresa of Avila.[31] In her own biographical account she wrote of dreamlike experiences with an angel: 'In his hands I saw a great golden spear, and at the iron tip there appeared to

be a point of fire. This he plunged into my heart several times
so that it penetrated to my entrails. When he pulled it out, I felt
that he took them with it, and left me utterly consumed by the
great love of God. The pain was so severe that it made me utter
several moans. The sweetness caused by this intense pain is so
extreme that one cannot possibly wish it to cease . . .'

In his celebrated sculpture of the dream, *The Ecstasy*, Bernini
depicted Teresa leaning back on a cloud-like swirl of marble, her
eyes closed, her mouth open as she gasps for breath. Her hand
grips the rock and her foot hangs limply whilst over her stands
an angelic figure with a spear.

Aside from the sexual and moral ambiguity in the lives of some
of her devotees though, the cult of Mary as a true diva developed
rapidly and with quite remarkable fervour. It was from the outset
part of the ordnance of the ecclesiastical establishment and it was
destined to become the 'big gun' in the armoury of the papacy.
This, in effect, meant that challenges to the Pope and his court,
from whatever source, also set out to undermine Marianism and
its trappings, aside from such specifics as the Cathar heresy. Revolt
against the official doctrine of the Church would invariably target
priestly celibacy, iconolatry, veneration of relics and so on.

Some certainties are pressed time after time in the cult of
Mary. She was herself the product of Immaculate Conception,
the beloved daughter and mother of God alone from the moment
of her birth and thus of the same exclusive spiritual club as Father
and Son. She was totally without sin or the desire to sin, and
thus escaped from the Fall which burdened all other women. In
accordance with these unique qualities she was removed bodily
into heaven where she reigned as queen on an equal plateau of
excellence to the rest of the godhead.

There is no overt suggestion that the cachet which envelops
Mary can be compared directly with that surrounding such figures
as Ištar and Isis, but, perversely, the secular Christian art world
has done its level best to create and sustain such an aura. In the
face of this popular approbation the Catholic Church has not, it
seems, been able to avoid, or to resist, providing Mary with the
trappings and the kudos of a paramount goddess. The question
remains: has it been more a case of the tail wagging the dog,
or has the Catholic Church done its share of the promotion?
Whether inadvertent or not, the Church embraced many principles of cult which, in any other context, would have been
condemned as demonstrations of pagan worship. The spasmodic
revolts against Marianism, which culminated in the full-blown

Reformation movement, were to no small extent reactions against what was perceived to be mother goddess worship and idolatry. The outstanding oddity of the entire Marian affair is that little which has developed in the cult can be traced to hard biblical sources, nor can any part of it really lay claim to be the message of Jesus. It is almost the exclusive product of Catholic Christendom's demands and imagination.

20

A Thoroughly Modern Mother

The beginning of the twentieth century marked a watershed in society's attitude to its environment. Moral sensibility to the world in which we live has been declining almost since the first chapter of human endeavour, but what makes the recent decades particularly significant is the acceleration of change. The materialist northern hemisphere has systematically raped the Third World of its resources, and its consumer-oriented society has treated the natural environment with contempt. Two World Wars have catalysed technological advance, steering European modernism down a road which has subjugated nature to predacious demands for economic progress irrespective of consequences. Western Europe has begun to respond to the danger, but in the old 'iron curtain' countries, economies occupying a vastly greater land mass have lagged behind in technical progress towards an environmentally conscious economy, and sizeable areas are virtually uninhabitable. Exploitation of the planet has replaced reverence for nature on a scale never before witnessed, and now we face the first signs of global catastrophe.

Not surprisingly spiritual attitudes have also seen momentous change. Magic has declined in popularity in the last two centuries. Day-to-day magic away from the auspices of the Church has lost much of its credibility, replaced by the assurances of technology, although the change has not always been a matter of substituting the one for the other. It may be argued that it is less the actual emergence of technical and medical solutions to problems previously addressed by magicians as the confident anticipation of solutions which has brought a shift in loyalties.

Mankind *believes* in the empirical ability of science to resolve its problems. Faith in supernatural powers has not died, but the priorities have changed and magic and religion are no longer the first recourse in worldly matters. They are only called upon when science fails or appears incapable of rendering a solution. When war threatens, when medical science cannot provide remedies for cancer and other life-threatening diseases, when crops fail, when police forces are unable to trace a missing person, there are still 'last resort' moves towards faith healing, psychics and other remedies far removed from technology. Great strides in communication, the invasion of everyone's living room by media technology, and a contraction of the world through advances in travel have given us a more confident view. All has been part of the undoing of magic.

Decline is far from universal, however. Orthodox religion is still driven by some seemingly illogical counter-currents. Nowhere can this be more true than in the continuing and burgeoning 'star treatment' of Mary the Virgin. In June 1987, space-age technology and the modern mother goddess joined forces in an astonishing, some even suggested quasi-miraculous, global television 'road show'.[1] Eighteen satellites beamed simultaneous pictures from shrines around the world to celebrate a Marian jubilee on a scale which would have left the councillors of Ephesus dumbstruck. In an event staged more on the lines of an Olympian spectacular, Pope John Paul II torched a sacred flame which was carried to the world's faithful in recognition of Mary's universal acclaim.

The Marian jubilee is the latest demonstration of a new kind of romantic militancy which began to take over Catholicism in Europe from the mid-nineteenth century. In 1854 and in the face of growing modernism, communism, socialism, and other sects not kindly disposed towards the Church, all of which were drawing the faithful away in droves, Pius IX 'rubber stamped' the doctrine of the Immaculate Conception.[2] It was therefore official that Mary Mother of God had never been tainted with original sin. Pius IX's declaration, made on the strength of his own papal infallibility, was seen by many to be a measure of Vatican ostentation and short-sightedness. But, against all logic, it turned the tide of Catholic disaffection and heralded an era of

Marianism which appears more than ever to be placing Mary, not Christ, as the focus of Christian faith.

On 1 November 1950, in the basilica of S. Maria Maggiore, Rome, Pius XII stripped away any remaining ambivalence over Mary's qualifications.[3] His deed was no less controversial than that of his nineteenth-century predecessor. The psychologist Carl Jung, it is said, was delighted and intrigued by the news since it added considerable fuel to his theories of a towering subconscious need to worship the female principle. Anglican and other more conservative theologians reacted to the announcement with disquiet. Pius XII appeared on the balcony of St Peter's and announced to a rapturous congregation of a million, many of whom verged on emotional hysteria more familiar at a pop concert, that Mary had been carried bodily into heaven. Immaculate Conception and *Theotokos* were finally joined by official recognition of carnal Assumption, a matter long accepted by most Catholics as beyond dispute.

The Church of Rome regards Mary as a 'special case' in devotional practice. Catholic worship falls into prescribed categories, the adoration of God being the *latria* and that of the saints the *dulia*.[4] Already the Virgin receives what is described as *hyperdulia*, and it seems predictable that the Church will progress eventually towards full *latria*.

The 1950 announcement blurs still further the edges of Catholic ideology. That Mary was mortal has encouraged millions in the promise of a fleshly resurrection, but the dogma which Pius XII endorsed implied that she was uniquely honoured among the created because of her supreme state of holiness. The way was being pointed ever more stridently towards recognition of Mary, no less than Jesus, as an indivisible part of the godhead from before the moment of her incarnation. The Catholic Church now seems perilously close to admitting Mary as one whose existence predates the Christian experience.

The fervour to elevate Mary with still greater honours continues. Through another remarkable pronouncement it is now confirmed that her motherly embrace encircles the world irrespective of religions and divisions. On 24 March 1984, Pope John Paul II used the medium of television to reach a worldwide audience measured in millions.[5] In St Peter's Square, a place well used to such revelations, the supreme pontiff knelt before the figure of Our Lady of Fatima and dedicated the entire planet to the Immaculate Heart of Mary. It was a consecration which, he stated: 'lasts for all time and embraces all individuals, peoples and nations.'

The idea of Mary's eternal presence in the cosmos invades many corners of Catholic devotion. She is the *Stella Maris*, star of the primal water across which the force moved at the advent of the world. For the Feast of the Immaculate Conception, the epistle of the proper Mass is taken from the evocative and splendid imagery of Proverbs 8.22–3 drawing the forceful parallel between Mary and Sophia wrenching order from chaos:

> The Lord possessed me in the beginning of his way,
> before his works of old.
>   I was set up from everlasting, from the beginning,
> for ever the earth was.

The Queen of Heaven title has been railed over, but today's Catholics embrace it with an enthusiasm that would probably have brought despair to the prophets of Israel. The final antiphon of the Compline Mass includes a hymn of praise:

> Hail, Queen of Heaven,
> Hail, Lady of the Angels.
> Salutation to thee, root and portal,
> Whence the light of the world has arisen.

Marian impact on the twentieth century has been boosted from the decisions of the early Catholic Church to create a personality for Mary which owes nothing to biblical sources and a great deal to legend. The apocryphal conviction about her rise to heaven in the flesh has given credence to the numerous mystical but decidedly bodily returns she has made to greet the faithful.

The cult of apparitions and miraculous events has become an integral part of modern Catholic religion and has been the main inducement for millions to join and maintain the Catholic ranks. Since gaining the papacy in 1978, John Paul has done much to invigorate the miraculous aspects. Committed to the notion of intervention in earthly affairs by Our Lady, and to the positive nature of her appearances, the pontiff delivers regular lectures on the apparitions which have descended on popular shrines.[6] The Anglican Church, its dogma based on Bible content rather than ecclesiatical notion, distances itself from what it has always regarded as deeply inappropriate. The endorsement coming out of Rome, however, tends to deny the argument voiced by many theologians that the magical and the miraculous in Christianity are for its less educated flock. The hyperbole has been generated by the Church hierarchy, not the common lay people. The magic power of relics and sacred objects, the visions, the voices from the ether, may have been revealed first to children and illiterate peasants but they are endorsed at the highest level.

The wave of apparitions which has created so much romantic fervour in modern times began in 1830 in Paris. In that year of revolt Catharine Labouré saw the heart of St Vincent 'Father of the Poor' hovering in the mother house of the Sisters of Charity.[7] She was visited subsequently by the Virgin who delivered warnings of the impending collapse of France and the monarchy, and instructed Catharine in the striking of a Miraculous Medal which was to protect those who wore it.

In September 1846 two teenage girls at La Salette in the French Alps received a message, part secret, part for public consumption, from a weeping and luminous Virgin who also showed them a sacred spring.[8] As with the Paris visions, the region was poised on the edge of revolt and famine. Crowds flocked to La Salette where they drank the water, told their rosaries and prayed for deliverance. By 1852, the foundations of a basilica had been laid and La Salette entered Roman Catholic history whilst triggering a plethora of shrine building to the 'Virgin of the Alps'.

The most celebrated spate of French appearances began in 1858, in a riverside grotto at Lourdes in the Pyrenees.[9] Marie-Bernarde Soubirous, the sickly fourteen-year-old daughter of a convicted father and a drunken mother witnessed eighteen visitations which included warnings and the discovery of a spring, and crowds watched as she told her rosary with Mary, scampered up and down the hillside at astonishing speed, ate grass penintentially on the command of her unseen mentor, and drank the waters.

Cynical argument suggests that the rash of phenomena, which saw no respite in the early part of this century, was carefully orchestrated. It points to a repeating pattern in which the Virgin delivered her warning messages dressed in white with a blue sash, wearing a scapular, and carrying a rosary. Her words would carry a secret component and the beautiful, sometimes sorrowful and weeping, apparition pointed out a curative spring and requested a sanctuary. The recipients, too, became fairly typecast – young girls, frequently illiterate and from impoverished homes, at or around the age of puberty.

In the present century, the Iberian peninsula has taken over the focus of European and probably world attention. Strangely enough Italy has come in for very little Marian experience. In a Portuguese village of Fatima north of Lisbon in 1915, Lucia, the illiterate eight-year-old daughter of an alcoholic herdsman witnessed an angelic figure floating in the air.[10] On 13 May 1917 in a woodland near the village, the Virgin announced herself, hovering in a small holmoak tree. She was, they reported, 'more brilliant than the sun', and she instructed them to recite the rosary daily so that the world and Portugal, fighting as an ally of the British, could return to peace. On 13 October, the excitement of Fatima having spread, 100,000 people gathered and, it is said, experienced a miracle when the sun 'spun in the sky like a Catherine wheel throwing off great arcs of fiery light'. Portugal, as in other cases, experienced relief from a political crisis shortly thereafter and the Catholic Salazar dictatorship endorsed a protracted romance with Marianism.

In the 1920s, when Lucia has become a Dorothean novitiate, communism was perceived as the main threat to the Catholic Church, and in 1925 and 1928 she was given a 'secret' message concerning the future role of Russia. The message was received in three parts, two of which Lucia delivered: '. . . I shall come to ask for the consecration of Russia to my Immaculate Heart . . . if my requests are heeded, Russia will be converted and there will be peace; if not, she will spread her errors throughout the world, causing wars and persecutions of the Church . . . various nations will be annihilated . . .' She doggedly refused to disclose the final part until 1943 when she wrote it down and it was deposited in the Vatican's secret archives. It was allegedly examined in 1960 by Pope John XXIII but its content has never been made public.

The aura of Fatima was preserved throughout Franco's long term of Spanish power when Catholicism stood behind conservatism, and against Freemasonry, Protestantism and Communism.[11] Such was the approbation that, at the end of the Spanish Civil War, which Portugal perceived as a communist threat rumbling perilously close to her borders, the nation's bishops led a pilgrimage of half a million people to the shrine to give thanks for protection against the 'Red danger'. It was a period that saw the growth also of such extreme and ascetic right-wing religious movements as the Opus Dei, of which Mary was 'founder and patroness'.

Opus Dei is to be compared with similar societies all over the Catholic world.[12] In America a flurry of quasi-militant and secretive Marianist clubs such as the Knights of Columbus emerged. The Militia Immaculatae thrived in the 1920s and 30s in Poland, claiming nearly a million subscribers by the outbreak of war, again principally designed to counter Masonic and Semitic activity. Movements of a similar model spread worldwide and included the Legion of Mary, the Knights of St Columbanus in Ireland, the Knights of the Southern Cross in Australasia, and many more.

All over the Catholic dominions, the Queen of Heaven gained troops through the fame of her appearances. The Catholic Action movement initiated and continues to recruit millions of converts with the so-called 'Marian oath' through which they swear defence of the Immaculata 'to the death'.[13] She emerged to a welter of 'coronations'. She became Queen of the Hispanic peoples. Her shrines were bedecked with even more extravagance, but at the same time the magical paraphernalia of her cult took on new shades of colour which reflected changing political conditions.

At no time has Mary worn the uniform of goddess of war more blatantly than in this century. Within Spanish frontiers the famed Nuestra Señora del Pilar, the virgin of Saragossa who, according to legend, had sought refuge in Aragon 'in the flesh', and who had planted a stone pillar to mark her safe arrival, was closely allied to the army both at home and in the Latin American colonies.[14] The sash of a captain-general frequently found its way to her waist, and military honours were constantly showered on her, often to the accompaniment of martial music and artillery salutes.

Saragossa was the focal point of Nationalist fervour during the Spanish Civil War. On 26 August 1936, the newspaper *Heraldo de Aragon* printed an account of a triumphal entry to the Saragossa shrine by a Falangist general and his troops. With cries of 'Long Live Death! Long Live the Virgin of the Pillar' ringing in his ears, he offered his cap to her in salute. In a 1939 victory speech at Saragossa, Franco conceded that if the Virgin of the Pillar: 'had not given us all energy, bravery, the spirit of sacrifice, living conscience of the past and blind faith in our future, all our armed guards would have kept vigil in vain.' Her militarist colours were taken into the Second World War theatre when the 'Blue Division', committed to defence of Mary fought on the Russian front armed with a rifle and a photograph of the Virgin of Saragossa.

Elsewhere in Europe, Poland's national security had been entrusted to Mary as early as the seventeenth century when she was proclaimed 'Queen of the Polish crown'.[15] In August 1920, when Poland was at odds with Soviet Russia, the so-called

'Miracle of the Vistula' enabled inferior Polish forces to rout the
Russians and take a sizeable bite of Russian territory. It was
attributed to direct intervention by Our Lady.

Political warnings were playing an increasing part in the
Virgin's visitations. Apparitions came to be examined in the
context of Nazi Germany, and since Hiroshima the Fatima message in particular has been linked to the nuclear danger. Visions
of Mary 'more brilliant than the sun' have been taken to be the
premonition of an atomic holocaust, suggesting that the third part
of Lucia's message reveals details of a catastrophic war. Nowhere
has this been taken more seriously than in the United States, the
scene of the most remarkable fundamentalist Catholic awakening.

In the 1950s and 60s, Marianism was behind much of the
anti-communist fervour of the Un-American Activities Committee and the McCarthyite 'witch' hunts.[16] The Blue Army
of Our Lady was founded with the specific brief of crushing
the Red Army under Mary's foot through the militant power
of the rosary. That visionaries had reported Mary to be wearing
a blue sash was politically convenient. It implied that she stood
solidly behind monarchy or right of centre politics, and against
socialism and communism. Blue Army members recognized each
other by a blue ribbon or string.

The attitude of many prominent and influential Americans
in the 1980s and 90s, echoing the view of the Blue Army,
may give cause for concern. Some of the hawkish posturing
of the Reagan era is said to have stemmed from an implicit
belief amongst born-again fundamentalists that détente has been
a waste of time because only Mary controls the options. Ex-
President Reagan is known to support many fundamentalist
views. He expressed close spiritual links with Pope John Paul II
during his term of office and allegedly he subscribes to the view
that at the moment of Armageddon, in the seconds before outbreak of nuclear war, Mary's righteous millions will be lifted
into the air and saved.[17]

Considering its two-edged effect, Mariolatry is an extraordinary
tool. It has served to draw millions, yet the peculiar sexual inhibi-
tions which the modern Church continues to foist on the mother
goddess have done little for the cause of universal suffrage. It has
been impossible to part with the obsessive linking of women and
sin.

The term 'a scarlet woman' should never have been taken
into a temporal context. It stems from the apocalyptic vision
of the goddess sitting upon her scarlet coloured beast, full of

names and blasphemy: 'And the woman was arrayed in purple
and scarlet colour, and decked with gold and precious stones and
pearls, having a golden cup in her hand full of abominations and
filthiness of her fornication . . .' Yet the Church, Anglican and
Catholic alike, has continued to play on the theme and one finds
such comments as:

> I have officiated in churches where the separation of
> the sexes was very striking from all of the men wearing
> the rustic costume of white smocks, and all the women
> red cloaks and black bonnets. The nave of my father's
> very large church at Saffron Walden was always filled
> with red cloaks, the wearers each bringing a stool from
> the bottom of the church for her own use, and taking it
> back again after the service.[18] (Revd A. N. Bull of
> Woolavington in the 1880s)

The imagery – white, a sign of purity, and scarlet the colour
of the 'Mother of Harlots and abominations of the earth' – is
pithy, yet the nineteenth-century attitude to women continued
to be derogatory and widespread. Thus a male child, about to be
carried to church on his christening day, might be met on the
doorstep by a small boy, employed in payment of a traditional
cake and cheese wrapped in paper because for an unbaptized
child to encounter a woman as its first stranger was to brand
it with the mark of Cain.[19] A mother carrying her baby to its
Christening often carried a small gift of bread and cheese which
she gave to the first person she met on the way, to protect the
child from the evils of witchcraft.

The division of the sexes in church, enforced by early Apostolic
decree, was alive and well in many parts of Europe in the nineteenth century. The Vicar of Thaxted in Essex wrote to a colleague
in 1873: 'The separation of sexes is almost universal amongst the
poorer classes.[20] I remember at Little Easton Church, before its
restoration, Lord and Lady Maynard each had a large pew on
opposite sides of the church and they always used each to occupy
his or her own pew.' Division was officially abolished in England
during the second half of the nineteenth century, but old habits
died hard; thus at Christ Church in Birmingham in 1860 it was
still very much the form. One Oxfordshire writer recalled a young
couple coming into his parish church one Sunday afternoon and
sitting together on the women's side of the nave until the aged
verger removed the man with the terse rebuke: 'We don't have

no sweethearting here!' In many churches men and women took the sacrament separately up until the early 1900s.

Antagonism was particularly directed towards pregnancy.[21] The stigma persisted that a woman who had conceived and was bearing a child was no longer in a state of grace; she was unclean and unfit to attend church or receive the sacrament. There was a widespread fear that should a pregnant woman act as godmother to an infant, the child for which she stood at catechism would die. In many parts of England, the neighbours of a new mother would not permit her into their houses until she had been 'churched' and, in fact, before this ceremony had taken place there was a distinct disapproval of the woman venturing beyond her front gate.

Ironically it was often among women themselves that the most passionate convictions over the necessity for confinement and churching were stimulated. A vicar of Legbourne in Lincolnshire made a succinct observation about his first contact with the parish, in 1860: 'I at once tried to knock on the head the custom of having baptisms after the (churching) service, and on one occasion when I told a woman who came to be baptised, that the baptism would take place after the second lesson, she replied, "That is impossible, for I cannot walk down the church until I have been churched." The churching service used to be read just before the general thanksgiving, so I overcame the scruple by having the churching service before the general service began.'[22]

The service required the woman to attend church at the appointed time, in English custom a full month after delivery, and wearing appropriate dress including a veil which was often included on the church inventory. In the past arriving at church without this attire had been an excommunicable offence. The old Book of Common Prayer underlined the Church's patronizing attitude in its service for Churching: 'The Lord preserveth the simple: I was in misery and he helped me. Turn again then unto thy rest, O my soul: for the Lord hath rewarded thee. And why? Thou hast delivered my soul from death: mine eyes from tears, and my feet from falling . . . I will receive the cup of salvation: and call upon the name of the Lord. I will pay my vows now in the presence of all his people.'

Churching still goes on. A number of vicars will admit conducting voluntary thanksgiving services and the modified rite in the revised prayer book is a remnant of the obligatory and derogatory ceremony of the last century.

In the 1990s little has changed. It has been argued that, in
contrast to their taboo of mortal woman, the adoration of the
Virgin has allowed the celibate Catholic priesthood a degree of
warmth and of gentleness in what was historically often a very
harsh existence. It has been maintained that marriage for the
Catholic priesthood would constitute a distraction from the cause
of godliness and would sway a man called into religious service
from his true vocation. At the heart of the ban though, is the
anguish that the hands which touch the Eucharist could also be
defiled by contact with woman. The ordination of the first woman
bishop in Boston, Massachusetts engendered a savage outcry
among orthodox Catholics and threatened to split the Church
irrevocably. It stems from an undiminished horror of women
handling the sacrament.

Anything which can effectively enhance or stimulate Mariolatry continues to be manipulated, much as it was in medieval
times, to strengthen the Catholic Church's popularity. The relics
of her visionaries, Bernadette, Catharine Labouré, and others,
most of whom the Church persuaded to spend the remainder
of their lives closeted away from public view and enquiry,
take on magical powers particularly when they have resisted
corruption. Merely to stand in the proximity of these bodily
remnants immured behind hermetically sealed glass is enough
to gain benefit from their supernatural auras.

The almost fanatical desire for a tangible presence is never
more strongly demonstrated than in the 'Mary House' in
Ephesus. In 1876 details of a vision revealed to an Augustinian
nun and mystic, Anne Catherine Emmerich were published.[23]
She claimed, at a time when her Westphalian Catholic Church
was under great pressure, to have seen the house where the
Virgin had lived under John's protection. A team of Catholic
archaeologists subsequently uncovered the ruins of a tiny first-
century building which was 'restored', and to certain chagrin in
Jerusalem, which also claims the honour of sheltering Mary's last
residence, Ephesus is now the centre of a re-invigorated Marian
devotion.

There is a constant excitement about each and every miraculous phenomenon associated with Catholic shrines. Statues weep,
nod their heads, glow in the dark, bleed, and crowds follow
burning with new found ardour. But Mariolatry has taken on
a number of other connotations and visible trappings, including
trees and water.

In too many instances to be coincidental the Virgin's appearances have been witnessed in or close by trees and in the vicinity of springs. Leaves and branches can play strange tricks with sunlight, but the continuing spiritual link with trees is more solid. The proper Mass for the Feast of the Immaculate Conception includes words drawn from the Book of Ecclesiasticus which possess familiar imagery:

> I was exalted like a cedar in Libanus, and as a cypress tree in Mount Sion. I was exalted like a palm tree in Cades, and as a rose plant in Jericho; as a fair olive-tree in the plains and as a plane tree by the water in the streets was I exalted. I gave a sweet perfume like cinnamon and aromatic balm. I yielded a sweet odour like the best myrrh.

The symbolism of the Tree of Life was being incorporated into Christian religious art from the time of Constantine. The mosaic of the Great Cross of Lateran, an exquisite work by an unknown hand, is based on the Tree, and it has been the model for many later studies of the Crucifixion. In about 1830, there appeared from the hands of a Rennes woodcarver a striking and provocative work in which the outline of the cross has become perfunctory. The tree has a bird, now the dove of the Holy Spirit, perched in its branches. The snake, persistent symbol of knowledge and evil, coils at its roots. The winged cherubim look on in their familiar inward-facing protective pose. The tree is ringed by rosettes whose meaning extends back to the time of Ištar. The garden with its young sapling is drawn, so are the astral deities of sun and moon. Even the godhead bears remarkable resemblance to the winged disc so beloved by the ancient pagan world.

In the traditions of the Christian Church, one can sense that it is the wood not the apparatus, tree rather than crucifix, which bears the timeless message of life and death. The design of churches in the West, as distinct from the Byzantine style, appears to recognize the life-death significance of the Tree. Above the flight of steps conventionally separating choir from sanctuary in many Catholic and Anglo-Catholic churches is a Rood Beam, designed to carry the Holy Rood, or Rod, the stem of the Tree. Traditionally this crucifix is depicted as the instrument of death and suffering whilst on the altar stands the antithesis dressed as a vehicle of triumph and immortality. The Christ in robes of glory is suspended from the centre of a cross radiating a great auriole. The positions have been varied, thus in the Cathedral of St David in Wales the Rood carries the crucifix of triumph but its modern sculptor has, significantly, surrounded it with the old-style winged beasts of the apocalypse.

The Mass of the Pre-Sanctified, a service of great antiquity celebrated in the Catholic Church on Good Friday, closes its Reproaches with an antiphon which describes the transmutation of the cross from instrument of death to source of life. The antiphon is followed by a hymn of praise, the Adoration of the Wood of the Cross and one wonders how many Catholic adherents actually consider the implication of the words they sing. Translation can never do the words adequate justice:

> Crux fidelis, inter omnes arbor una nobilis:
> Nulla silva tamen profert fronde, flore, germine:
> De parentis protoplasti fraude factor condolens,
> Quando pomi noxialis in necem morsu ruit:
> Ipse lignum tunc notavit, damna ligni ut solveret.

(Faithful cross, the one tree noble above all: no forest affords the like of this in leaf, or flower, or seed . . .)

Many trees have links with the Virgin. There exists a tradition of decorating churches with boughs of birch on Whit Sunday, a tree which Coleridge described as 'The Lady of the Woods'. Frazer mentions a comparable tradition before Whitsun in Russia when villagers 'go out into the woods, sing songs, weave garlands, and cut down a young birch-tree, which they dress up in woman's clothes, or adorn with many coloured shreds and ribbons.'[24] The dressed tree was kept as a 'houseguest' until Whit Sunday.

Away from the traditions which are incorporated into Church lore, other lay customs persist around trees, and in almost all cases their roots are immersed in pagan tradition which derived from the cults of fertility and the earth. The maypole seems to be a fusion of themes from many sources. A small continental version still forms the focus of village festivities to usher in the spring, but a striking example of the tall traditional English maypoles stands at Barwick in Elmet in West Yorkshire. In London's Leadenhall Street the church of St Andrew Undershaft takes its name from an enormous pole, Chaucer's 'Great Shaft of Cornhill', which stood there until destroyed by Puritans during the Interregnum.[25] In most parts of Europe an equivalent tradition used trees, particularly young firs and birches, cut freshly for May Day and carried into the village with great celebration to be decked with ribbons and flowers.

Yew, maple and mistletoe were all hung inside churches or on steeples at Easter and Whitsun and left there until the following year, as were garlands of roses and other spring flowers. In almost all cases the practices have little in common with Christianity and a great deal to do with the sacredness of the living earth.

Rogation Sunday ostensibly gave blessing to the rising crops, but it included a ceremony known as 'Beating the Bounds' which can owe little to Christianity. This description comes from Burpham in Sussex: ' . . . procession included a stop at an old ash tree which they stripped on the east side and from this tree they go directly south to the Lady's Coppice and then by the maple stem in the hedge they throw up a heap of stones, and from the maple stem they go along the ditch between Lady's Coppice and Well Coppice to the corner of Blakehurst Field where they make a cross and a bound, and from thence they surround all the woods and the Burpham four acres to the corner of Candle Croft.[26] They end up at the Walnut Tree in Burpham Street where all free holders and copy holders bring a gallon of ale and a cake and cheese.'

Many holy wells and springs have seen customs that bear familiar signs of very early origin. Visitors to wells have been, and still are in parts of Derbyshire for example, encouraged to hang the bushes around the wells with strips of material, and the decking of Sacred Trees with rags of cloth has, almost certainly, been modernized into the Victorian ceremony of dressing the Christmas Tree with gifts, lights and baubles.

Direct links between the Yggdrasil, the World Ash Tree, and the modern Christmas tree are unproven and the habit of bringing a fir tree indoors and dressing it seems to have developed comparatively recently. Legend has it that the eighth-century missionary St Boniface cut down a sacred oak in Germany on Christmas Eve and as it fell a fir sapling emerged.[27] Boniface was inspired to adopt the fir as an emblem of Christian faith. Alternative Christmas mythology suggests that as Martin Luther was walking home under a starry sky he was moved to dig up a fir tree as a frame for candles to remind his children of the Christian heaven. In England George III's wife, Charlotte, had a seasonal Christmas tree erected at Windsor whilst in Victorian times the Prince Consort began the seasonal import of firs from his native Coburg.

Water has borne an equally deep significance for Christianity although, again, the power attributed to sacred water has unquestionable pagan precedents and it can be argued that its ancient mysticism as the semen of life has been the inspiration for continuing Christian use, rather than the comparatively recent and more abstract biblical connotations. Water is an integral feature of the modern Church and many Christians come into intimate contact with its sacred powers at Catechism. Water is considered in the very design of the church. The familiar layout resembles a figure spread-eagled in a cruciform. At the head is the altar, the gateway between mortality and eternity. At the foot is the baptismal font, always at the west end, 'the immaculate womb out of which man is born into life'.

In many parts of Europe springs and wells, for long the overseers of rites associated with the mother goddess, became re-dedicated as Christian oratories and baptistries. Yet people continued to treat them more as pagan than Christian shrines. They threw bent pins into the waters as a mark of luck following a quaint notion, its origins lost, that anything crooked was also charmed: hence the rhyme of the crooked man and his crooked sixpence. Women carried a talismanic bent coin in their apron pockets. Those of us who today cast pennies into wells and fountains follow an arcane tradition as we make our secret wishes.

The claim of appearances by Mary has always been enough to sanctify a well, and such holy places exist all over Europe, the waters gushing out beneath niches armed with statues of Our Lady. Near Kings Cross in London, St Chad's Well in an enclosure known locally as 'The Garden' was presided over by 'The Lady of the Well', a figure said to have worn a black bonnet, a cotton gown and a chequered apron.[28] For a subscription of one guinea a year, or sixpence a visit, one could drink as much of the water as one wished for its remedial properties. The well, like the trees around it, was decorated with flowers. According to Chambers *Book of Days*: 'It is scarcely possible to describe the vivid colouring and beautiful effect of these favourites of nature arranged in wreaths and garlands and devices of every hue, and then the pure sparkling water which pours down from the midst of them into the rustic moss-grown stones beneath completes the enchantment and makes this feast of the well-flowering one of the most beautiful of all the old customs that are in merrie England.'

Christian Europe also persists with the mother goddess in the shape of corn dollies which, although nowadays made as ornamental figures, were once created from the last sheaf of harvested corn and left in the field to quicken the seed for the coming year. In human guise she appears as the 'Queen of the May' whilst her consort is represented by such strange characters as the 'Green Man', 'Green George' and 'Jack-in-the-Green'.

The horse and its pagan fertility symbolism has also pervaded modern Europe. The tradition of the hobby-horse is celebrated in many places such as Padstow in Cornwall which draws huge crowds each May Day, but there has existed, until recent times, a more bizarre form of the rite known as 'hodening' which took place on Christmas Eve.[29] The head of a decapitated horse was animated by a cord attached to the lower jaw. Covered by a horse cloth tied around the neck someone would walk around with a party of carol singers, snapping the horse's jaw open and shut. In its principle this was pure animistic shamanism, yet hodening, with all the other quaint pagan traditions, has been tolerated and presumably quietly endorsed by the Church.

Much of the emphasis in this final stage of the quest for the gods of the earth has been on the Roman Catholic Church and it is, of course, no casual coincidence. Her devotion to the more mysterious and magical aspects of religion in general and to Mary the Virgin in particular seems largely responsible for the continuing dynamic interest — Roman Catholicism commands a flock of some 188 million north and middle Americans alone — whilst the Anglican Church worldwide faces decline.[30] The Protestant rejection of 'Church magic' — reliquaries, iconolatry, recitation of rosaries and the like — may, perversely, have made it vulnerable. Today some see the Church of England in its death throes, not through primary loss of faith amongst its congregation but by its own hand. It has abandoned whatever remaining mystery was written into its charter to a 'social security cosiness' and a 'crass newspeak liturgy' which curry popularity in a style that history would argue does not work. The Anglican response to dwindling attendance through the Seventies and Eighties was to promote God less as the mysterious Ancient of Days than a white bearded hippy strumming his electric guitar to banal rock beat and lyrics that package Jesus as a soap-opera star. Its newest leader continues that trend.

The Virgin has been the driving element in the worldwide success of Roman Catholicism, and in its basic ideology Christianity might be considered to have got its balances wrong. Uniquely amongst the religions we have travelled through, other than Judaism, it set out by placing the emphasis on a male figure and attempting to exclude the female essence of the godhead. Yet through the ever-evolving adulation of Mary, the figure of Christ has increasingly taken a backseat and the impression grows that for millions of Catholics he has become virtually obsolete in the machinery of communion with heaven. However contentious the thought, Christian religion might largely have been abandoned had it not been for Mary.

Christianity has also suffered from its obstinate and damaging ideology regarding sex. At virtually all levels the preaching does not find reward in practice. A religious doctrine which becomes the near-universal butt of jokes and scandal is open to criticism, particularly when it derives from apocryphal sources. In 1989 the Martin Scorcese film, *The Last Temptation of Christ* was condemned amidst considerable media commotion as a blasphemy, not because it dared to endow the Christ with human emotions but because those feelings included the sin of sexuality. Yet the gulf between the ideology and the bare Gospel facts of Jesus' own attitude, unfortunately, remains as wide as ever. Nowhere in the narratives is there any positive indication that the man who provides the source of Christian inspiration lacked normal sexual drives and attitudes. The Nag Hammadi revelations suggest quite the contrary. As one eminent Christian, Lord Soper, said in a television interview: 'There is a great deal of distinction between the practice of the Christian Church and adherence to the teaching of its founder'.

If Christianity has a persistent flaw when set beside so many other faiths, it lies in the failure of the Church to recognize that the style of religion reflects environmental pressures and social and economic conditions. The doctrine which the Church has to impress was peculiarly relevant to an historical situation and a specific social structure. Christian missionary activity has failed singularly to take account of this and, whilst it has undoubtedly provided some material comforts in its places of operation, it has been by and large an unmitigated spiritual disaster for those to whom it was aimed because it has destroyed religions which were far more relevant and appropriate.

What of other, unorthodox worship of the mother goddess within the Christian sphere? The right to heresy, though not blasphemy, has become an accepted part of our modern freedom of expression. The last execution of a witch in England took place in Bideford, Devon in 1684, and the most recent legislation against witchcraft was repealed in 1951. Many thousands of priests and priestesses practise what they perceive as the resumption of an ancient art. The wise women have returned to the countryside recognizing that the earth is a thing to be cherished.

The mother goddess has travelled a long way since she was perceived, or so we may believe, through the dumpy little figure of the Venus of Willendorf and one of the most important questions must be whether the various personae whose images human imagination has generated, and which we lump together as mother goddesses, indeed represent one and the same. Affirmation may lie less with religion than with psychology. We are back with Carl Jung. Religion has been fashioned and administered, its parameters determined, predominantly by men. It has opened its doors to priestesses but its creeds have been arrived at through male eyes and male rationale. The strongest and most pervading masculine emotions are directed towards the maternal figure which nurtures man through his formulative years, and towards the sexual drive which dominates his adult life. He has also assumed, not unreasonably, that the tangible natural world around him mirrors that which he perceives only through his inner senses. The dual urges of mother love and sexuality are reflected in the way he envisages the core, the heartbeat, of the supernatural.

Some authors maintain that a simple mother image coupled with a ritualized sex act made up the fundamental of early religion, and was replaced gradually by a more sophisticated awareness falling under the definition of a Jungian-type anima ideal. But is this not too neat a position? It tends to rely on the old humbug that mankind arose to spiritual fulfilment and a sense of ascetic values out of a primitive and lusty ignorance which subscribed purely to 'gut instincts'. Yet the first evidence of religion, the clear mental agility and refinement that generated the earliest art, the pointers to understanding of an afterlife, the profound and eloquent nature of much of the oldest writing suggests otherwise. One must doubt that ancient man was deprived of an anima, and those Ice-Age models seem, on appearances, to reflect his urge to translate the collective unconscious ideal into a spiritual principle. Jung after all did not invent the feminine element in man; it merely awaited his definition! If there has been change, it had been in translation of the ideal as outlook and vocabulary have been modified.

We still find our ideal in the living earth and in the trees and in the image of fertile womanhood, the sum of the parts of a motherly cosmic womb which Paracelsus married so succinctly. The sacredness of the earth is strong even today. The pontiff of the Church of Rome adopts the quaint habit of kneeling to kiss the earth at his feet each time he steps from an aeroplane.

What is he doing if not indulging his own personal obeisance to a goddess whose strength and durability is to be found not only in rosaries, visions and marble Madonnas?

Trees have embodied the spirit of the goddess. It is not hard to perceive in them a numinous quality. A great oak or ash may indeed have its roots planted in hell and it uppermost branches entering the ineffable realms. Some mighty span of trunk in a forest glade possesses all the accumulated experience of humanity for a hundred, maybe a thousand years. Ancient people knew well that trees are the heartspring of life on our planet. How many countless millions of fingers have reached out surreptitiously to the panacea? How many of us, even in our level-headed age of scientific enlightenment, can do without touching wood? Some will quest for its strength in strips of timber fashioned into a cruciform; some put a hand to a piece of furniture; others will take strength in the nearness of trees. It is a provocative thought that today mankind is destroying that same heartspring of life with a determination and a ferocity which seems unstoppable. With each passing year, we are obliterating about 100,000 square kilometres of the earth's forests. As we snuff out the temples of the goddess, it seems increasingly possible that we also seal our own doom.

The equation between female principle and life can only be complete by insertion of a male component. Again we are generating a mirror of our own experience, that which man perceives to 'make the world go round', but on to it we place the 'risk factor' in the chemistry. The male element is the feckless one, that which comes and goes. But it has also come to satisfy another quite separate need, that of atonement. The earliest shamanistic societies were dependent on 'passing the buck' – expiating human action which might be interpreted as misdemeanour by placing it on supernatural shoulders. They also accepted that an evil or damaging spirit could be drawn from one object to another. It is all part of the same comforting escape which still says that we can shift our ills, and misfortunes which derive from them, elsewhere.

In a shamanistic society removal of nail parings or hair from a sick person and feeding them to an animal will allow disease to be shed as will pinning a lock of hair to a tree and wrenching it loose. More sophisticated religions create a figure on to whom the collective ills of society can be passed. We also conclude that with the death of our scapegoat, the world is cleansed and renewed. Out of dismemberment comes genesis. But there can be scant distinction, other than in personal attitudes, between animistic transfer of problems, the annual humiliation of the Mesopotamian ruler, the winnowing of Osiris, or the death of the Christ who 'takes away the sins of the world'.

The quest has no ending. Today's innovation is tomorrow's history. In the fullness of time no doubt the names and the identities of the mother goddess and the dying and rising god will change again. Madonna Maria Virgine and Christ will become part of the catalogue of man's past creed. That which will remain, I suspect, is a deep and unquenchable need to reach out and feel the warmth and compassion, the sexuality and tenderness of the eternal mother. She is the womb of the world, and out of the womb we struggle into the world. She is the morning and the evening of our life. It was Hermann Hesse who said: 'without a mother we cannot die'.

Postscript

It is perhaps appropriate since I began this book on a personal note that I should end it in a similar fashion.

I recognize many influences which have played on my sentiments. I cannot deny that the strength of trees provided a great initial stimulus and it is one which I find is shared. When I was just five years old I remember being lost in a wood, and once in a while the terror of that passing childhood moment still tugs at my sleeve. Yet I have spent much of my working life tramping lonely forest paths and the years have engendered a great love in me which is stronger than my childhood anguish. The trees are my last refuge. I wonder, if the holocaust was approaching, would I not run to find some illogical shelter in the encircling arms of a green wood.

Wishful nonsense? The question may not appear important, yet what is the origin of these sentiments which so many of us share? Are they with us as innate things in the depth of human psyche, or have they been instilled? If so, are they a heritage from the classical south, or from an Anglo-Saxon or Teutonic or Nordic background, or do they represent a little of both?

Many writers have drawn on the esoterism of trees. John Steinbeck provided a haunting picture of their perceived strength amongst American farmers in his novel *To a God Unknown*: 'As he rode, Joseph became timid and yet eager, as a young man is who slips out to a rendezvous with a wise and beautiful woman. He was half-drugged and overwhelmed by the forest of Our Lady. There was a curious femaleness about the interlacing boughs and twigs, about the long green cavern cut by the river through the trees and the brilliant underbrush. The endless green halls and aisles and alcoves seemed to have a meaning as obscure and promising as the symbols of an ancient religion.'

The trend has been for modernism and humanism to shelter behind technology and to lose touch with the old values, but some of the catastrophes born out of the materialistic dash of the Sixties and Seventies now choose increasingly to haunt us. The environment of our modern world begins to pose a threat in a way that has not been witnessed since the days before the dawn of Christianity. That the problem is of our creation, makes it no less fearful than the terrors which ice and bitter cold presented to the hunters, and which drought and blistering sun created for the desert pioneers. Out of that fear is dawning, slowly, a renaissance of reverence and awareness for our natural world as we poison the air and the seas, and begin a metamorphosis that may turn our fertile, fragile earth into the bleakest of deserts.

We harbour, each of us, our own private covenant with the gods of the earth, our articles of faith. I set out to write this book with the sincere intention of maintaining a good editorial impartiality. I have, of course, failed. It is impossible to live with such a subject for so many years without becoming involved personally and developing one's own views. Some will read and find a personal odyssey, others a deliberate attempt to debunk Christianity. Perhaps that is what it is. I know that some kind of intelligently researched argument, altruistic towards the pre-Christian and pre-Jewish faiths, is long overdue. My only real apology is that I have, of necessity, been a pundit. The subject is too vast and crosses too many disciplinary boundaries to be anything else.

I cannot help but feel in awe of the evidence. Sixty thousand years of intelligent searching for the infinite have borne an adherence to principles of faith which seem to me to maintain an astonishing constancy. I do not believe that all those generations of humanity can have got it wrong. Nor do I underestimate the depth of their perception. It is not possible for me to look at the Ice-Age Venuses and accept that they reflect only maternal imagery and raw sexual proclivities. Deeper reasoning has prevailed to produce such extraordinary caricatures. It is impossible to read Sumerian poetry and find in

Inana and Ninhursağa only incestuous motherly hands steering affairs.

What is more whilst the religious establishment continues steadfastly to argue radical distinctions, the sheer volume of hard evidence contradicts any real schism between the 'old' and the 'new' in either faith or practice. It is exceedingly difficult to detach Mary the modern madonna from the mother goddesses of old, and Jesus from such legendary figures as Dumuzi and Osiris, when one ponders such revelations as the Nag Hammadi codices and the poetry of the ancient pagan world. Environment and social evolution may have changed the superficial dressing, but like the 'king's new clothes' it is an illusion fostered largely amongst those who wear it.

The sum of my learning has also made me appreciate the importance for human imagination, since its earliest awakening, to define the supernatural in some tangible manner and it has made me starkly conscious of the richness of that imagination. To stand in the presence of the great herds of Lascaux or the bison of Tuc d'Audoubert, to face the goddess of Dolní Veštonice, to cradle the tiny Vogelherd horse in the palm of one's hand, is to bridge a giant gulf, but it is also to be touched with humility.

We have really come a very short distance since those distant artists created their masterpieces of understanding and faith. Irrespective of credibility, or lack of it, I suspect we all need our Jesuses and our Marys. We need to be able to close our eyes and see God, in whatever form or gender, in those small threatening hours of the night.

REFERENCES

Chapter 1

1   H.L. Chakravarty *Medicinal Plants of Iraq*, Iraq Ministry of Agriculture, Directorate General of Agricultural Research and Projects, Baghdad 1964
   Ralph S. Solecki *Shanidar IV, a Neanderthal Flower Burial in Northern Iraq*, Science 190 1975
   Arlette Leroi-Gourhan *The Flowers Found with Shanidar IV, a Neanderthal Burial in Iraq*, Science 190 1975
   J.A. Tyldesley and P.G. Bahn *Use of Plants in the European Palaeolithic: A Review of the Evidence*, Quaternary Science Reviews 2 1983
2   G. Riek *Altsteinzeitkulturen am Vogelherd bei Stetten ob Lontal (Wurtemberg)*, Ipek 1933
3   A.M. Brodrick *Lascaux, a commentary*, London 1949
   F. Windels *Lascaux*, Montignac-sur-Vezère 1948
4   Henri Breuil *Bas-reliefs féminins de la Magdeleine près Montauban*, Quaternaria I 1954
5   E. Rivière *Les parois gravées et peintes de la grotte de la Mouthe*, L'Homme préhistorique I 1903
6   L. Capitan, H. Breuil, D. Peyrony *Les Combarelles aux Eyzies*, Paris 1924
7   L. Capitan, H. Breuil, D. Peyrony *La Caverne de Font-de-Gaume*, Monaco 1910
8   H. Begouen *Les statues d'argile de la Caverne du Tuc d'Audoubert*, L'Anthropologie XXIII 1912
9   G. Malvesin-Fabre, L.R. Nougier, R. Robert *Empreintes de pieds humains préhistoriques de la caverne de Niaux*, Bull. Soc. Préhist. de l'Ariège VII 1952
10   H. Breuil and H. Begouen *Nouvelle gravure d'homme masqué de la caverne des Trois Frères*, C.R. Académie des Inscriptions et Belles Lettres 1930
   P.J. Ucko *The Interpretation of Prehistoric Anthropomorphic Figurines*, Journal of the Royal Anthropological Institute of Great Britain and Ireland 92 1962
11   Mircea Eliade *Images and Symbols: Studies in Religious Symbolism* (Engl. transl. Philip Mairet), New York 1969
12   D.F. Thomson *The Seasonal Factor in Human Culture*, Proceedings of the Prehistoric Society V 1939
   J.G.D. Clark *Seasonal Settlement in Upper Palaeolithic Times*, Proceedings of the Prehistoric Society V 1939
13   H.G. Bandi and G. Maringer *Art in the Ice Age: Spanish Levant Art*, London and New York 1953
   M. and L. Dams *Prehistoric Rock Art of the Spanish Levant*, Illustrated London News March 1973

14 de Nadaillac *Le baton de commandement de Montgaudier*, Bull. Mem. Soc. Anthrop. de Paris 1887
15 M. Delcourt-Vlaeminck *Les Représentations Végétales dans L'Art du Palaeolithique Supérieur*, Bulletin de la Societé Tournaisienne de Geologie, Préhistoire et Archaeologie 31 1975

GENERAL

Henri Breuil (Abbé) *Four Hundred Centuries of Cave Art* (Engl. transl. Mary E. Boyle), Centre d'Études et de Documentation Préhistoriques, Montignac 1952
Margaret W. Conkey *Art and Design in the Old Stone Age*, San Francisco 1982
Paolo Graziosi *Palaeolithic Art*, London 1960
Annette Laming-Emperaire *La Signification de L'Art Rupestre Franco-Cantabrique*, Paris 1962
André Leroi-Gourhan *Les Religions de la Préhistoire*, Paris 1964
André Leroi-Gourhan *Treasures of Prehistoric Art*, New York 1967
Alexander Marshack *The Roots of Civilization*, New York 1972
John E. Pfeiffer *The Creative Explosion*, New York 1982
Nancy K. Sandars *Palaeolithic Art in Europe*, London 1968
Ann Sieveking *The Cave Artists*, London 1979
P.J. Ucko and A. Rosenfeld *Palaeolithic Cave Art*, London 1967
P.G. Bahn and J. Vertut *Images of the Ice Age*, London 1988

Chapter 2

1 D. Peyrony *La Ferrassie*, Préhistoire III 1934
2 E. Piette and J. de la Porterie *Fouilles à Brassempouy en 1896*, L'Anthropologie VIII 1897
3 K. Absolon *Représentations idéoplastiques anciennes et nouvelles de femmes du Paléolithique moravien*, XV Congrès Internat. d'Anthrop. et Arch. Préhist, Paris 1931
4 J. Szombathy *Die Aurignacienschichten in Löess von Willendorf*, Korrespondenzblatt der Deutschen Gesellschaft für Anthrop. Ethnol. und Urgeschichte XL 1909
5 R. de Saint-Périer *La statuette féminine de Léspugue*, Bull. Soc. Préhist. Française XXI 1924
6 E. Golomshtok *Trois gisements du Paléolithique supérieur russes et sibériens*, L'Anthropologie XLII 1933
    M.M. Gerasimov *Malta, paleoliticeskaià stojanka*, Irkurtsk 1931
    A. Salmony *Die Kunst der Aurignacien in Maltà (Siberien)*, Ipek 1931
7 H. Breuil, D. Peyrony *Statuette féminine aurignacienne de Sireuil*, Revue Anthropologique XL 1930
8 E. Peters *Die Kunst des Magdalenien von Petersfels*, Augsburg 1930
9 A. Lemozi *La grotte-temple du Peche-Merle*, Paris 1929
10 P. Darasse *Deux oeuvres d'art magdaléniennes de l'abri de Fontales*, Bull. Soc. Préhist. Française LII 1955
11 D. Peyrony *Sur quelques pièces intéressantes de la grotte de La*

Roche près de Lalinde, L'Anthropologie XL 1930
12 J. Marconi Bovio *Incisioni rupestri dell'Addaura*, Bull. di Palentologia Italiana VIII(V) 1953
13 K. Absolon op. cit.
14 L. Capitan, H. Breuil, P. Bourrinet, D. Peyrony *L'Abri Mège. Une station magdalénienne à Teyjat*, Revue de l'Ecole d'Anthrop. XIV 1906
15 C.G. Jung *The Concept of the Collective Unconscious* (1936), from the *Collected Works* (ed. G. Adler, M. Fordham, H. Read) 1959

C.G. Jung *Concerning the Archetypes, with special reference to the Anima Concept* (1936), ibid.

F. Fordham *An Introduction to Jung's Psychology*, London 1953
16 A. Marshack op. cit.

GENERAL

As for Chapter 1
Sir Edward B. Tylor *Primitive Culture*, London

Chapter 3

SCANDINAVIA

1 J. Brønsted *Danmarks Oldtid* (2nd edn), Copenhagen 1959
Grahame Clarke *The Earlier Stone Age Settlements of Scandinavia*, Cambridge 1975
2 A. Hagen *Rock Carvings in Norway*, Oslo 1965
P.V. Glob *Rock Carvings in Denmark*, Jnl. Arch. Soc. VII 1969
G. Mandt Larsen *Rock Pictures in Hordaland*, Acta Univ. Bergensis 2 1970
G. Burenhult *The Rock Carvings of Gotaland*, Acta Archaeological 8 1973
3 T. Mathiassen *Ravsmykker fra aeldre Stenalder*, Aarboger f. nord. Oldkyndighed 1959
4 Rock Art Symposium (Acts of) 1972 *The Relationship between Rock Art, Religion and Society*, Inst. for Comp. Res. in Human Cult. 1978
5 T. Mathiassen op. cit.
D. Liversage *Ornamental Mesolithic Artefacts from Denmark*, Acta Archaeologica. 37 1966
6 G. Hallstrom *Monumental Art of northern Europe from the Stone Age*, Stockholm 1938
7 B. Rying *Danish in the South and North Prehistory*, Vol.1 Royal Dan. Min. of Foreign Aff., Copenhagen 1988
14 A. Bagge *Die Funde aus Dolmen und Ganggrabern in Schönen, Schweden*, Stockholm 1950
L. Kaelas *Dolmen und Ganggraber in Schweden*, Offa XV 1955
G. Daniel *The Megalithic Builders of Western Europe*, London 1963
15 C.F. Fox *Life and Death in the Bronze Age*, London 1959
17 O.G.S. Crawford *The Eye Goddess*, London 1957
18 C.F. Fox op. cit.

CENTRAL EUROPE

8   V.G. Childe *Prehistoric Migrations in Europe*, Oslo 1950
    V.G. Childe *The Dawn of European Civilisation*, London 1957

ANATOLIA AND A.N.E

9   R.J. Braidwood *From Cave to Village (1948)*, Scientific American
1952
    R.J. and L. Braidwood *The Earliest Village Communities of southwestern
Asia*, Jnl of World Hist. 1 1953
    R.J. Braidwood *Near Eastern Pre-history*, Science 127 1958
    R.J. Braidwood *The Agricultural Revolution*, Scientific American 203
1960
    L.S. Braidwood *Prehistoric Village Archaeology in southeast Turkey*,
Oxford 1982
    Carleton S. Coon *Cave Exploration in Iran 1949*, Monograph of
the University Museum, Philadelphia 1951
10   N. Tzori *Munhata*
    Y. Aharoni *Archaeology of the Land of Israel* (Engl. transl. A.F.
Rainey), SCM Press 1982
11   Hamit Z. Kosay *A Great Discovery (excavations at Alaja Hüyük)*,
Ill. Lond. News 21 July 1945
12   W.F. Albright *From the Stone Age to Christianity*, Doubleday, New
York 1957
    W.F. Albright *The High Place in Ancient Palestine*, Suppl. to the
Vetus Testamentum IV 1957
13   G.E. Wright *Excavation of the Temple at Megiddo*, Jnl. Am. Or.
Soc. LXX 1950
16   T. Ozgüc *Kültepe Kazisi Raporu*, Ankara 1950
    T. Ozgüc *Excavations at Kültepe. Level 2 Finds*, Belleten XIX 1955

GENERAL

Carleton S. Coon *The Hunting Peoples*, London 1972
Hilda R. Ellis Davidson *Pagan Scandinavia*, London 1967
C. Laurin, E. Hannover, J. Thiis *Scandinavian Art*, New York 1922
Elisabeth Munksgaard *Denmark. An Archaeological Guide*, Copenhagen
1970
T.G.E. Powell *The Celts* (new edition), London 1980
H. Shetelig and H. Falk *Scandinavian Archaeology* (Engl. transl. E.V.
Gordon), Oxford 1937

Chapter 4

1   André Parrot *Les Fouilles de Mari. Troisième campagne (Hiver 1935–36)*,
Syria XVIII 1937
    André Parrot *Les Fouilles de Mari. Huitième campagne (Automne 1952)*,
Syria XXX 1953
2   Seton Lloyd *The Archaeology of Mesopotamia*, London 1978.

3   A. Sjøberg and E. Bergmann *Texts from Cuneiform Sources*, Augustin 1969
4   S.T. Kang *Irrigation of Ancient Mesopotamia*, American Water Resources Assoc. Bull. 8(3) 1972
    T. Jacobsen and R.M. Adams *Salt and Silt in Ancient Mesopotamian Agriculture*, Science 128 1958
5   S.N. Kramer *The Sacred Marriage Rite*, Indiana U.P., Bloomington 1969
6   S.T. Kang op. cit.
7   Rainer M. Boehmer *Die Entwicklung der Glyptik wahrend de Akkad-zeit*, Berlin 1965
    P. Amiet, N. Ozgüc, J. Boardman *Ancient Art in Seals*, Princeton U.P. 1980
    Dominique Collon *Western Asiatic Seals*, Catalogue of the British Museum Collection 1982
8   S.N. Kramer *Tablets of Sumer (from the)*, Indian Hills 1956
9   A. Sjøberg and E. Bergmann op. cit.
10 H. Rawlinson *Cuneiform Inscriptions of Western Asia* (5 vols), 1861–1891
    G. Barton *The Royal Inscriptions of Sumer and Akkad*, New Haven 1929
11 A. Sjøberg and E. Bergmann op. cit.
12 Ibid.
13 Henri Frankfort *A Note on the Lady of Birth*, Jnl. of Near Eastern Studies III 1944
14 Loris Premuda *Storia dell' Iconografia Anatomica*, Milan 1956
    W.J. Stewart McKay *A History of Ancient Gynaecology*, London 1961
15 T.H. Gaster *Thespis: Ritual, Myth and Drama in the ancient Near East* (2nd edn), New York 1961
    Samuel N. Kramer *The Sacred Marriage Rite*, Indiana U.P., Bloomington 1969
16 Ibid.
17 Thorkild Jacobsen *Sumerian King List*, Journal of Assyriological Studies 11 Chicago 1939
18 S.N. Kramer op. cit.
19 W.R. Sladek *Inanna's Descent and the Death of Dumuzi* (PhD Thesis paper), Baltimore 1974
    S.N. Kramer *Inanna's Descent to the Netherworld*, Journal of Cuneiform Studies 5 1951
20 W.R. Sladek op. cit.

GENERAL

Martin A. Beek *Atlas of Mesopotamia*, London 1962
L.W. King *A History of Sumer and Akkad*, London 1910
Thorkild Jacobsen *The Treasures of Darkness*, Yale U.P., New Haven 1976
Samuel N. Kramer *The Sumerians*, Chicago 1976
Samuel N. Kramer *Sumerian Mythology*, Philadelphia 1944
Seton Lloyd *The Archaeology of Mesopotamia*, London 1978
Diane Wolkstein and S.N. Kramer *Inanna, Queen of Heaven and Earth*, London 1983

Chapter 5

1   André Parrot *Les Fouilles de Mari*, op. cit. (note: the main surviving piece of the pot was discovered in the area of a neighbouring temple but it is possible that it was dislocated due to ground disturbance by the public at the time)
2   S.N. Kramer *The Myths of Sumer (from the)*, Philadelphia 1944
3   Thorkild Jacobsen *Sumerian King List*, Jnl of Assyriological Studies 11, Chicago, 1939.
4   S.N. Kramer *Gilgamesh and the Huluppu-tree*, Journal of Assyriological Studies 10 Chicago 1938
5   Aaron Schaffer *Sumerian sources of Tablet 12 – Epic of Gilgamesh*, Philadelphia 1963
6   J.B. Pritchard *Ancient near eastern texts relating to the Old Testament*, Princeton 1950
7   J.V. Kinnier Wilson *The Legend of Etana*, Warminster 1985
8   A. Sjøberg and E. Bergmann op. cit.
9   Rainer M. Boehmer op. cit.
    Dominique Collon op. cit.
10   Babylonian and Oriental Record IV, London 1889–90
    Paul Popenoe *The Date Palm* (ed. H. Field), Field Research Projects of Miami 1973
11   Texts from Cuneiform Sources in the British Museum (C.T.)
12   G. Widengren *The King and the Tree of Life*, Uppsala 1951
13   E.D. van Buren *The Flowing Vase and the God with the Streams*, Berlin 1933
14   H. Rawlinson op. cit.
    G. Barton op. cit.
15   P. Witzel *Analecta Orientalia* 10 (p.124), Rome, 1935
16   H. Zimmern *Sumerische-babylonische Tamuzlieder*, Leipzig 1907
17   M. Witzel *Ninhursag und Enki*, Analecta Orientalia 15 (pp239–285), Rome 1946

GENERAL

As for Chapter 4

Chapter 6

1   G. Waterfield *Layard of Nineveh*, London 1963
2   Edith Porada *Seal impressions of Nuzi*, AASOR 24 New Haven 1947
3   P. Amiet, N. Ozgüc, N. Boardman *Ancient art in seals*, Princeton U.P. 1980
    Rainer M. Boehmer *Die Entwicklung der Glyptik wahrend der Akkad-zeit*, Berlin 1965
    Dominique Collon *Western Asiatic Seals*, British Museum 1982
    H. Frankfort *Cylinder Seals*, London 1939

E. Porada *Corpus of ANE Seals in North American collections*, Washington 1948

W.H. Ward *The seal cylinders of western Asia*, Washington 1910

4   Michael Scotus *Liber Physiognomiae*, circa 1400 MS in Biblioteca Ambrosiana L.92 Sup., f.96v

Magnus Hundt *Anthropologium*, 1499

R. Keller *Das Problem der Geschlechtsdifferenzeirung und der Hermaphroditismus*, Ciba Zeitschrift 70 1939

L. Premuda *Storia dell' Iconografia Anatomica*, Milan 1956

R.M. Wynn and W.P. Jollie *Biology of the Uterus*, New York 1989

A.A. Barb *Diva Matrix*, London 1953

5   M.E.L. Mallowan *Nimrud and its Remains* (3 vols), London 1966

K.F. Muller *Das Assyrische Ritual*, Leipzig 1937.

G. Widengren *The King and the Tree of Life*, Uppsala 1951

7   R.F. Harper *Assyrian and Babylonian letters in the British Museum*, London 1914

8   H. Rawlinson *Cuneiform inscriptions of western Asia*, London 1875

9   R.F. Harper op. cit.

10   J.A. Black *The New Year Ceremonies in ancient Babylon*, Religion 11 1981

11   G. Waterfield op. cit.

GENERAL

S.H. Hook *Babylonian and Assyrian Religion*, Oklahoma U.P. 1975

Thorkild Jacobsen *Towards the Image of Tammuz*, History of Religion 1 Yale U.P. 1962

K.F. Muller *Das Assyrische Ritual*, Leipzig 1937

Sidney Smith *Early History of Assyria*, London 1928

F. Thureau-Dangin *Rituels Accadiens*, Paris 1921

Chapter 7

1   L.W. King *The Letters and Inscriptions of Hammurabi*, London 1898–1900

L.W. King *Chronicles concerning early Babylonian Kings*, London 1907

Anton Deimel *Codex Hammurabi* (3rd edn), 1953

Joan Oates *Babylon*, London 1979

2   Ursula Seidl *Die Babylonischen Kudurru-Reliefs*, Deutsches Archaeologisches Institut, Berlin 1968

3   Texts from Cuneiform Sources in the British Museum (C.T.)

4   S.A. Pallis *The Babylonian Akitu Festival*, Copenhagen 1926

J.G.P. MacEwan *Priest and Temple in Hellenistic Babylonia*, Wiesbaden 1981

S.H. Hooke *Babylonian and Assyrian Religion*, London 1953

Joan Oates op. cit.

5   Joseph Campbell *The Masks of God: Occidental Mythology*, New York 1964

6   John Garstang *The Hittite Empire*, London 1929

Oliver R. Gurney *The Hittites*, London 1975
7 C.G. Jung *The Structure of the Psyche* (1927), from the Collected Works (ed. G. Adler, M. Fordham, H. Read) 1960
8 S. Mowinckel *Han Som Kommer*, Copenhagen 1951
9 O. Puchstein *Boghazköi, Die Bauwerke*, Deutsche Orientgesellschaft, Wissenschaftliche Veröffentlichung 19, Leipzig 1912
   K. Bittel and R. Naumann *Bogazköy-Hattusa*, Deutsche Orient. Wissen. Veroff. 63, Stuttgart 1952
   T.M. Güterbock *Guide to the Ruins at Bogazkale (Bogazköy)*, Ankara 1966
10 G. Furlani *La Religione degli Hittiti*, Bologna 1936
   T. Gaster *Thespis*, New York 1950
   O.R. Gurney *Myth Ritual and Kingship – Hittite Kingship* ed. S.H. Hooke, Oxford 1958
11 H.M. Ransome *The Sacred Bee in Ancient Times and Folklore*, London 1937
12 J. Gray *The Canaanites*, London 1964
13 J.A. Montgomery and Z.S. Harris *The Ras Shamra Mythological Texts*, Philadelphia 1935
   J.A. Montgomery *A Myth of Spring*, Journal of African and Oriental Studies 56 1936
   A. Kapelrud *Baal in the Ras Shamra Texts*, Copenhagen 1952
   M. Pope *El in the Ugaritic Texts*, Suppl. to the Vetus Testamentum II 1955
14 C.H. Gordon *Ugaritic Literature*, Scripta Pontificii Instituti Biblici 98 Rome, 1949
   J. Gray *The Legacy of Canaan. The Ras Shamra Texts etc.*, 2nd edn Leiden 1965.
15 C.H. Gordon op. cit.
16 O.R. Gurney op. cit.
17 K. Bittel *Die Felsbilder von Yazilikaya*, Istanbul 1934
   E. Laroche *Le Pantheon de Yazilikaya*, Jnl of Cuneiform Studies VI 1952
18 K.A. Bernhardt *Asherah in Ugarit und im Alten Testament*, Mitteilungen des Instituts fur Orientforschung Geschichtforschung (MIO) 13 1967
   R. Patai *The Goddess Asherah*, Jnl of Near Eastern Studies 24 1965
19 S.R. Driver *International Critical Commentary*, 1895

GENERAL

A. Hultkrantz *Configurations of Religious Beliefs*, Ethnos 1956
S. Langdon *Semitic Mythology*, 1931
S.H. Hooke *Myth, Ritual and Kingship*, Oxford 1958

Chapter 8

1 Sir J.G. Frazer, *The Golden Bough*, London 1922.
2 Plutarch *De Iside et Osiride*
3 Ibid.
4 Normandi Ellis *Awakening Osiris – The Egyptian Book of the Dead*,

Grand Rapids 1988
5 R.O. Faulkner *The Book of the Dead*, extract derived from translation of the 26th spell of the Papyrus of Ani, New York 1972
6 R.O. Faulkner ibid., extract derived from translation of the 23rd spell of the Papyrus of Ani.
7 E. Ebeling *Tod und Leben nach den Vorstellungen der Babylonier*, 1, Berlin and Leipzig 1931

GENERAL

J.H. Breasted *Development of Religion and Thought in ancient Egypt*, London 1912
Alexander Moret *Kings and Gods of Egypt*, New York and London 1912
E.V. Baumgartel *Cultures of Prehistoric Egypt*, Leipzig 1947
Henri Frankfort *Ancient Egyptian Religion*, New York 1948
J.H. Breasted *History of Egypt* (2nd edn), London 1949
J. Cerny *Ancient Egyptian Religion*, London 1952
S.A.B. Mercer *The Pyramid Texts*, London 1952
G. Michailides *Contribution à l'étude de la grande Dées en Egypte*, Bull. de L'Institut d'Egypte XXXVI 1955
R.T. Clark *Myth and Symbol in Ancient Egypt*, New York 1960
Miriam Lichtheim *Ancient Egyptian Literature*, (3 vols) 1973–1980
Erik Hornung *Conceptions of God in ancient Egypt – the One and the Many*, London 1982

Chapter 9

1 S.A.B. Mercer *The Tell El-Amarna Tablets*, Toronto 1939
   The Dead Sea Scrolls in English (Engl. transl. G. Vermes 3rd edn), London 1987
2 Bleddyn J. Roberts *The Old Testament Text and Versions*, Univ. of Wales Press 1950
   A. Weiser *The Old Testament: Its Formation and Development* (Engl. transl. D.M. Barton), New York 1961
3 Martin Noth *The History of Israel* (Engl. transl. S. Godman and P.R. Ackroyd 2 edn), New York 1960.
   T.J. Meek *Hebrew Origins*, New York 1950
4 W.F. Albright *Archaeology and the Religion of Israel* (3rd edn), Baltimore 1953
   G.E. Wright *Biblical Archaeology*, Philadelphia 1957
   Yohanan Aharoni *Archaeology of the Land of Israel* (Engl. transl. A.F. Rainey), SCM Press 1982
5 George Hart *A Dictionary of Egyptian Gods and Godesses*, London and New York 1986
6 O. Eissfeldt *El and Jahweh*, Jnl of Semitic Studies 1 1956
7 E. Bickerman *The God of Maccabees*, Leiden 1979
8 W.F. Albright *The High Place in Ancient Palestine*, Suppl. to Vetus Testamentum IV 1957
9 M. Dahood *Ancient Semitic Divinities in Syria and Palestine* (ed.

S. Moscati), Rome 1958
   K.A. Bernhardt *Asherah in Ugarit und im Alten Testament*, MIO 13 1967
10   A.R. Johnson *Sacral Kingship in Ancient Israel*, Univ. of Wales 1955
   T.J. Meek *Commentary on the Song of Songs*, The Interpreters Bible
V 1956
11   T.L. Wiegand and M Schrader *Priene, Ergebnisse der Ausgrabungen*,
Berlin 1904
   E.L. Sukenik *Ancient Synagogues in Palestine and Greece*, London 1934
12   Rabbi Ishmael *The Mekhilta Yethro*, ed. Horowitz (Engl. transl.
J.S. Lauterbach)
13   E.L. Sukenik *The Ancient Synagogue of Beth Alpha*, Jerusalem 1932
14   E.L. Sukenik *Ancient Synagogues in Palestine and Greece*, London 1934
15   E.L. Sukenik *The Ancient Synagogue of Beth Alpha*, Jerusalem 1932
16   L.A. Mayer and A. Reifenberg *Three Ancient Jewish Reliefs*, Palestine
Exploration Quarterly 1937

GENERAL

The Old Testament (King James' version)
J. Bright *A History of Israel*, Philadelphia 1959
H. Jagersona *The History of Israel*, SCM Press 1985
Martin Noth *The History of Israel* (Engl. transl. S. Godman and P.R.
Ackroyd, 2nd edn), New York 1960
J. Pedersen *Israel, its Life and Culture*, Oxford 1959
Helmer Ringgren *Israelite Religion* (Engl. transl. D. Green), SPCK 1966
N. Scherman and M. Zlotowitz *History of the Jewish People*, Mesorah 1982

Chapter 10

1   John M. Allegro *The Sacred Mushroom and the Cross*, London 1970,
revised edn 1973
2   H. Jagersona *The History of Israel*, SCM Press 1985
3   *The Apocryphal Old Testament* (Engl. transl.), ed. H.F.D. Sparks,
Oxford 1984
4   Joseph Campbell *The Masks of God: Occidental Mythology*, New
York 1964
5   V.G. Childe *The Dawn of European Civilisation*, London 1957
   Joseph Campbell op. cit.
6   J. Chadwick *The Mycenaean World*, Cambridge 1976
   William Taylour *The Mycenaeans* (revised edn), London 1983
7   Sir Arthur J. Evans *Scripta Minoa I*, Oxford 1909
   Scripta Minoa II, ed. J.L. Myres Oxford 1952
8   M.P. Nilsson *The Minoan-Mycenaean Religion* (2nd edn), Lund 1950
9   Sir James G. Frazer *The Golden Bough*, London 1922
   M.J. Vermaseren *Cybele and Attis* (Engl. transl. A.H.H. Lemmers),
London 1977
10   Sir Arthur J. Evans *The Palace of Minos*, 4 Vols, London 1921–1935
   C.W. Blegen et al. *The Palace of Nestor*, Princeton 1973
11   I.T. Hill *The Ancient City of Athens* 1953

12   Sir James G. Frazer op. cit.
13   Joseph Campbell op. cit.
14   Sir James G. Frazer op. cit.
15   Robin Lane Fox *Pagans and Christians*, London and New York 1986
16   Ramsay MacMullen *Paganism in the Roman Empire*, New Haven 1981
17   Plato *Republic* (Engl. transl. Paul Shorey), Loeb Classical Library edn
18   Apuleius *The Golden Ass* (Engl. transl. W. Adlington 1566), London 1947
19   Franz Cumont *The Mysteries of Mithra* (Engl. transl. T.J. McCormack), London 1903
20   Stewart Perown *The Later Herods*, London 1958
     H. Jagersona op. cit.

Chapter 11

1   B.H. Streeter *The Four Gospels: a Study of Origins*, London 1927
    R. Bultmann *Die Geschichte der synoptischen Tradition* (Engl. transl.), Oxford and New York 1963
2   R. Bultmann ibid.
3   Josephus *Antiquities of the Jews*, 18.63. from *Collected Works* (transl. H. St J. Thackeray, R. Marcus and L. Feldman), Loeb Classical Library edn.
4   Suetonius *Life of Claudius*, Loeb Classical Library edn
    Tacitus *Annals*, 15.44. (transl. J. Jackson), Loeb Classical Library edn.
5   Ramsey MacMullen *Paganism in the Roman Empire*, New Haven 1981
6   Birger Gerhardsson *Tradition and Transmission in early Christianity*, Coniectanea Neotestamentica XX, Lund 1964
7   E.P. Sanders, *Jesus and Judaism*, London 1985 (p.298)
8   B.H. Streeter op. cit.
9   N. Scherman and M. Zlotowitz *History of the Jewish People*, 1982
    H. Jagersona *A History of Israel*, London 1985
    G.B. Caird *Jesus and the Jewish Nation*, London 1965
    G. Bornkamm *Jesus of Nazareth* (Engl. transl.), London and New York 1960
10   Emil Schurer *The History of the Jewish People in the Age of Jesus Christ* (Engl. transl.), Edinburgh 1973, 1979, 1987
    Henry Chadwick *The Early Church*, London 1967
11   G.W.E. Nickelsburg *Jewish Literature between the Bible and the Mishnah*, Philadelphia and London 1981
12   E. Nielsen *Oral Tradition*, Chicago 1954
13   Sean Freyne *Galilee from Alexander the Great to Hadrian*, Notre Dame 1980
14   Philostratus *Life of Apollonius* (Engl. transl. F.C. Conybeare), Loeb Classical Library edn
    Morton Smith *Jesus the Magician*, New York and London 1978
15   Johannes Weiss *Jesus' Proclamation of the Kingdom of God* (Engl. transl. R.H. Hiers and D.L. Holland), London 1971

N. Perrin *Jesus and the Language of the Kingdom*, London and Philadelphia 1976

16   E.P. Sanders op. cit. (p.304)

17   Martin Hengel *The Charismatic Leader and his Followers* (Engl. transl.), Edinburgh 1981

18   R.C. Bultmann *Theology of the New Testament I* (Engl. transl.), London 1965

H. Conzelmann *An Outline of the Theology of the New Testament* (Engl. transl.), London and New York 1969

19   Bernard Hamilton *Religion in the Medieval West*, London 1986

20   W.R. Sladek *Inanna's Descent and the Death of Dumuzi*, Baltimore 1974

21   M. Ari-Yonah *The Jews under Roman and Byzantine Rule*, Jerusalem 1984

22   Acts of the Apostles, 5.30 and 10.39

23   Robert Morgan *Non Angli sed Angeli*: Some Anglican Reactions to German Gospel Criticism, New Studies in Theology I (ed. S. Sykes and D. Holmes), London 1980

24   E.P. Sanders op. cit. (p.296)

25   Ibid. (p.309)

26   Ibid. (p.231)

27   Ibid. (p.306)

28   Ibid. (p.218)

29   J.W. Drane *Paul: Libertine or Legalist*, London 1975

E.P. Sanders *Paul and Palestinian Judaism*, London and Philadelphia 1977

30   E.P. Sanders *Jesus and Judaism* (p.297), London 1985

31   Martin Hengel op. cit.

32   Albert Schweitzer *The Quest for the Historical Jesus* (Engl. transl. W. Montgomery), London 1911.

33   Gospel according to St Mark 16.9.

34   Gospel according to St Luke 24.39

35   Gospel according to St John 20.17 and 20.27

36   John Allegro *The Sacred Mushroom and the Cross*, London 1970

37   E.P. Sanders op. cit. (p.101)

38   Ibid. (p.319)

39   John Knox *The Church and the Reality of Christ*, New York 1962

GENERAL

The Biblical Old and New Testaments (King James version), Oxford

The Apocrypha and Pseudepigraphia of the Old Testament (ed. R.H. Charles), Oxford 1913–1963

The Apocryphal New Testament (transl. M.R. James), Oxford

Josephus *Collected works* (transl. H. St J. Thackeray, R. Marcus and L. Feldman), Loeb Classical Library edn

Tacitus *The Annals* (transl. J. Jackson), Loeb Classical Library Edn

Albert Schweitzer *The Quest of the Historical Jesus* (Engl. transl. W. Montgomery), London 1911

J. Klausner *Jesus of Nazareth* (Engl. transl.) London and New York 1925
E.P. Sanders *Jesus and Judaism*, London 1985
C.H. Dodd *The Founder of Christianity*, New York 1970
A.E. Harvey *Jesus and the Constraints of History*, London and Philadelphia 1982

Chapter 12

1   Henry J. Cadbury *The Peril of Modernizing Jesus*, New York 1937 (reissued London 1962)
   Martin Hengel *The Charismatic Leader* (Engl. transl.), Edinburgh 1981
2   Eusebius *The History of the Church from Christ to Constantine* (Engl. transl. G. A. Williamson), London 1965.
3   Albert Schweitzer *The Quest of the Historical Jesus* (The Problem), London 1911
4   E.R. Dodds *Pagan and Christian in an Age of Anxiety*, Cambridge 1965
   Robin Lane Fox *Pagans and Christians*, London 1986
5   M. Ari-Yonah *The Jews under Roman and Byzantine Rule*, Jerusalem 1984
6   Henry Chadwick *The Early Church*, London 1967.
7   M. Ari-Yonah op. cit.
   J.W.C. Wand *A History of the Early Church to AD500*, London 1937.
8   H.B. Workman *Persecution in the Early Church*, London 1960
9   Eusebius op. cit.
   Robin Lane Fox op. cit.
10   Eusebius op. cit.
11   Acts 1.6
12   Amos 9.11; Acts 15.16
13   James M. Robinson *The Nag Hammadi Library* (N.H.L) (Engl. transl.), Leiden 1988
14   H. Jonas *The Gnostic Religion*, Boston 1958
   Elaine Pagels *The Gnostic Gospels*, New York 1979 and London 1980
15   E.P. Sanders *Paul, the Law and the Jewish People*, Philadelphia 1983
   L. Goppelt *Jesus, Paul and Judaism* (Engl. transl.), New York 1964
16   2 Corinthians 2.17; 11.2
17   Acts 8.9ff
18   2 Corinthians 11.2ff
19   Eusebius *The History of the Church* Book 2 (transl. G.A. Williamson), London 1965
20   2 Corinthians 11.5
21   Acts 15.19
22   Robin Lane Fox op. cit.
23   *The Ante-Nicene Fathers* (ed. Roberts, Donaldson and Crombie, 40 vols), London 1896
24   Irenaeus *Libros Quinque Adversus Haereses* (Engl. transl. A. Roberts), Ante-Nicene Christian Library 1867
25   Hippolytus *Refutationis Omnium Haeresium* (Engl. transl. J.H. Macmahon), A.N.C.L. 1867

26 Tertullian *De Praescriptione Haereticorum* (Engl. transl. J. Betty), Oxford 1722
27 Wilhelm Wrede *Das Messiasgeheimnis in den Evangelien*, Göttingen 1901
28 Luke 14.26
    Gospel of Thomas II.2 (101), Nag Hammadi Library
29 Tertullian op. cit.

GENERAL

Eusebius *The History of the Church from Christ to Constantine* (Engl. transl. G.A. Williamson), London 1965
Henry Chadwick *The Early Church*, London 1967
J. Daniélou and H.I. Marrou *The Christian Centuries, I The First Six Hundred Years* (Engl. transl.), 1964
John G. Davies *The Early Christian Church*, London 1965
L. Duchesne *Early History of the Christian Church* (Engl. transl.), London 1914–1924
J.W.C. Wand *A History of the Early Church to AD 500*, London 1937

Chapter 13

1 A.H.M. Jones *The Later Roman Empire*, London 1964
    J. Daniélou and H.I. Marrou *The Christian Centuries, I The First Six Hundred Years* (Engl. transl.), 1964
2 C. Foss *Ephesus after Antiquity*, Cambridge U.P. 1979
    R. Oster *A Bibliography of Ancient Ephesus*, London 1987
    Robin Lane Fox *Pagans and Christians*, London 1986
3 Marina Warner *Alone of all her Sex*, London 1976
4 1 Corinthians 7.1
5 1 Timothy 4.1
6 1 Timothy 2.9
7 1 Corinthians 5.1
8 1 Corinthians 6.9
9 *A Valentinian Exposition* XI 22, 1–39, Nag Hammadi Library
    Tertullian op. cit.
10 Ibid.
11 Robin Lane Fox op. cit.
12 *On the Origin of the World* II,5 (120)25, Nag Hammadi Library
13 *Trimorphic Protennoia* XIII 35 1–15, Nag Hammadi Library
14 Proverbs 8.23–31
15 Matthew 21.4
16 Revelation 17.1–10
17 Revelation 21.9
18 *The Thunder, Perfect Mind*, VI, 217ff, Nag Hammadi Library
19 *The Gospel of Thomas* II,2 (114), Nag Hammadi Library
20 *The Gospel of Philip*, II,3 (63)30, derived from the Nag Hammadi Library translation

21 1 Corinthians 14.34
22 J. Balsdon *Roman Women, Their History and Habits*, London 1962
S.A. Pomeroy *Goddesses, Whores, Wives and Slaves*, New York 1975
Elaine Pagels op. cit.
23 *St Athanasius* (Engl. transl. Cardinal Newman et al. ed. A. Robertson), Library of Nicene and Post-Nicene Fathers Vol. 4 1892
E.P. Meijering *Athanasius contra gentes* (Engl. transl.), Leiden 1984
24 The Gospel of Philip II,3 (55)20, Nag Hammadi Library
25 J.N.D. Kelly *Early Christian Creeds*, London 1950
Cyril C. Richardson *Early Christian Fathers*, London 1953
26 F. Loofs *Nestorius and his Place in the History of Christian Doctrine*, Cambridge U.P. 1914
Henry Chadwick op. cit.

Chapter 14

1 V.G. Childe *The Danube in Prehistory*, Oxford 1929
T.G.E. Powell *The Celts* (Rev. Edn), London 1980.
2 J. Zwicker *Fontes Historiae Religionis Celticae*, Bonn 1934–5
3 V.G. Childe op. cit.
4 E. von Sacken *Das Grabfeld von Hallstatt*, Vienna 1868
5 F. Morton *Hallstatt und die Hallstattzeit*, Hallstatt 1953
S. Schiek *Das Hallstattgrab von Vilsingen* (Festschrift für Peter Goessler), Stuttgart 1954
F. Hanč ar *Das Pferd in prähistorischer und früher historicher Zeit*, Vienna 1956
Anne Ross *The Pagan Celts*, London 1986.
6 Anne Ross *Pagan Celtic Britain*, London 1967
7 J.V.S. Megaw and D.D.A. Simpson *Introduction to British Prehistory*, Leicester U.P. 1979
8 Miranda J. Green *The Gods of the Celts*, Gloucester 1986.
9 E. Thevenot *Dieux et sanctuaires de la Gaule*, Paris 1968
10 M. Gimbutas *The Goddesses and Gods of Old Europe*, London 1982
11 Anne Ross *Pagan Celtic Britain*, London 1967
Miranda J. Green op. cit.
12 Miranda J. Green *A Corpus of Religious Material from the Civilian areas of Roman Britain*, British Archaeological Reports 24 1976
13 Anne Ross *The Pagan Celts*, London 1967
14 T.G.E. Powell op. cit.
15 Lucan *Pharsalia I* (Eng. transl. J.H. Duff), Loeb Classical Library edn
16 P. Lambrechts *L'Exaltation de la Tête dans la Pensée et dans l'Art des Celtes*, Bruges 1954
17 S.J. de Laet *Van Grafmonument tot Heiligdom*, Brussels 1966
18 *The Mabinogion*, (Engl. transl. G. Jones and T. Jones), 1949
19 Myles Dillon and Nora K. Chadwick *The Celtic Realms*, London 1967
20 Anne Ross *The Pagan Celts*, London 1967
21 George Henderson *Survivals in Belief among the Celts*, Glasgow 1911

22 R.E.M. Wheeler *Report on the Excavations. . .in Lydney Park, Gloucestershire*, Oxford 1932
23 T.W. Rolleston *Myths and Legends of the Celtic Race*, London 1985
24 Ibid.
25 Ammianus Marcellinus *Collected Works* (Engl. transl. J.C. Rolfe), Loeb Classical Library edn
26 Bede *A History of the English Church and People* (Engl. transl. Leo Sherley-Price), London 1955
27 Giraldus Cambrensis *Topographia Hiberniae* Vol iii (Engl. transl. Sir R.C. Hoare), London 1847
28 J.A. MacCulloch *Celtic and Scandinavian Religions*, London 1948
  Myles Dillon and Nora K. Chadwick op. cit.
29 Myles Dillon and Nora K. Chadwick op. cit.
30 Bent Rying *Danish in the South and North, Prehistory* (Vol. 1), Royal Danish Ministry of Foreign Affairs Copenhagen 1989
31 Myles Dillon and Nora K. Chadwick op. cit.
32 T.G.E. Powell op. cit.
33 Pliny *Natural History*, 10 vols, ed. D.E. Eichholz, Loeb Classical Library edn.

GENERAL

Nora Chadwick *The Celts* London 1971
T.G.E. Powell *The Celts* (revised ed.) London 1980
Stuart Piggott *The Druids* (revised edn.) London 1975
Miranda J. Green *The Gods of the Celts* Gloucester 1986
Anne Ross *The Pagan Celts* London 1986

Chapter 15

1 Tacitus *Germania* 40.2 (Engl. transl. M. Hutton, revised edn), Harvard 1970
2 A.H.M. Jones *The Later Roman Empire*, Oxford 1964
3 Tacitus op. cit. 1.7–27
  R.P. Robinson *The Germania of Tacitus*, Connecticut 1935
  Peter Foote and D.M. Wilson *Viking Achievement*, London 1970
4 Tacitus op. cit. 13.4
5 A.P. Vlasto *The Entry of the Slavs into Christendom*, Cambridge 1970
  H. Mayr-Harting *The Coming of Christianity to Anglo-Saxon England*, London 1972
  Monks, Bishops and Pagans. Christian Culture in Gaul and Italy 500–700, ed. E. Peters, Philadelphia 1975
  Bernard Hamilton *Religion in the Medieval West*, London 1986
6 Tacitus op. cit. 1.9
7 E.O.G. Turville-Petre *Origins of Icelandic Literature*, Oxford 1953
  Jon Helgason *Litteraturhistorie (in Nordisk Kultur)* Vol. VIII:B, Oslo, Stockholm, Copenhagen 1953
  Stefan Einarsson *A History of Icelandic Literature*, New York 1957

8 *The Poetic Edda* – *Vǫluspá* 1–2 (Engl. transl. L.M. Hollander), University of Texas Press 1962

9 Snorri Sturluson *Edda* (Engl. transl. A. Faulkes), London 1987

10 *The Anglo-Saxon Chronicle* (Engl. transl. G.N. Garmonsway, revised edn), London 1972

11 Saxo Grammaticus *Gesta Danorum* (Engl. transl. Lord Elton), London 1894

12 Snorri Sturluson op. cit.

13 Hilda R. Ellis Davidson *Gods and Myths of Northern Europe*, London 1964

14 Tacitus op. cit. 49.2

15 Stefan Einarsson op. cit.

16 O. Klindt-Jensen *Foreign Influences in Denmark's Early Iron Age*, Acta Archaeologica XX, Copenhagen 1949

17 Snorri Sturluson op. cit.

18 Tacitus op. cit. 43.12

19 Adam of Bremen *Gesta Hammaburgensis ecclesiae pontificum* (Engl. transl. F.J. Tschan), Columbia U.P. 1959

20 Peter Foote and D.M. Wilson *Viking Achievement*, London 1970

21 *The Poetic Edda* – Skírnismál

22 Hilda R. Ellis Davidson op. cit.

23 Snorri Sturluson op. cit.

24 Hilda R. Ellis Davidson op. cit.

25 *The Poetic Edda* – *Grímnismál* 12

26 *The Poetic Edda* – *Brot af Sigurbarkviou*

27 *The Poetic Edda* – *Vǫluspá hin skamma* 16–17

28 Hilda R. Ellis Davidson op. cit.

29 Joseph Campbell *The Masks of God* – *Occidental Mythology*, New York 1964

30 *The Poetic Edda* – *Vǫluspá* 60–63

GENERAL

V. Grönbech *The Culture of the Teutons*, Copenhagen 1931

H. Shetelig and H. Falk *Scandinavian Archaeology* (Engl. transl. E.V. Gordon), Oxford 1937

Hilda R. Ellis Davidson *The Road to Hel*, Cambridge U.P. 1943

Palle Lauring *The Land of Tollund Man*, London 1957

Hølger Arbman *The Vikings*, New York 1961

E.O.G. Turville-Petre *Myth and Religion of the North*, London 1964

Hilda R. Ellis Davidson *Pagan Scandinavia*, London 1967

J. Lindlow *Scandinavian Mythology* (bibliography only), Gorland 1988

Bent Rying *Danish in the South and the North. Prehistory* Vol. 1, Royal Danish Ministry of Foreign Affairs, Copenhagen 1988

Chapter 16

1 Dionysius of Halicarnassus *Roman Antiquities* (Engl. transl. Spelman), Loeb Classical Library edn

T.G.E. Powell *The Celts*, revised edn, London 1980
2   Tacitus *Germania* 1.5
3   E.O.G. Turville-Petre op. cit.
4   Peter Foote and D.M. Wilson op. cit.
    T.G.E. Powell op. cit.
5   P. Paulsen *Axt und Kreuz in Nord und Osteuropa*, Bonn 1956
    Hilda R. Ellis Davidson *Thor's Hammer*, Folklore LXXVI 1965
    Hilda R. Ellis Davidson *Pagan Scandinavia*, London 1967
6   Ibid.
7   Sir James G. Frazer *The Golden Bough*, London 1922
8   Tacitus op. cit. 10.5
9   Lucan *Pharsalia*
10 Adam of Bremen op. cit.
11 Snorri Sturluson op. cit.
12 *The Poetic Edda – Svipdagsmál (Fjǫlsvinnsmál)* 21
13 *The Poetic Edda – Sigrdrífumál* 12
14 *The Poetic Edda – Vǫluspá* 45
15 Robert Graves *The White Goddess*, London 1961
16 *The Poetic Edda – Hávamál* 138–142
17 Snorri Sturluson op. cit.
18 A. Bagge *Die Funde aus Dolmen und Ganggrabern in Schönen, Schweden*, Stockholm 1950
    C.F. Fox *Life and Death in the Bronze Age*, London 1959
    G. Daniel *The Megalith Builders of Western Europe*, London 1963
19 Peter Foote and D.M. Wilson op. cit.
20 C. Green *Sutton Hoo*, London 1963
21 Peter Foote and D.M. Wilson op. cit.
22 P.V. Glob *Mosefolket*, Copenhagen 1965
    Palle Lauring op. cit.
    Bent Rying op. cit.
23 G. Waite *Human Burial and Animal Sacrifice in the Iron Age* (Archaeology of Death), CBA 9 Annual Conference, Oxford 1985
24 Adam of Bremen op. cit.
25 Tacitus op. cit. 40.5
26 *The Poetic Edda – Svipdagsmál (Fjǫlsvinnsmál)* 16
27 Bent Rying op. cit.
28 Ibn Fadlan op. cit.

GENERAL

As for Chapter 15

Chapter 17

1   Waldemar Jochelson and W. Bogoras *Koryak. Jesup North Pacific Expedition*, Memoirs of American Museum of Natural History 10 1905
2   Ibid.
3   Ibid.
4   Ibid.

GENERAL

Waldemar Jochelson and W. Bogoras *Koryak. Jesup North Pacific Expedition*, Memoirs of American Museum of Natural History 10 1905
Waldemar Jochelson *The Yakut*, Anthropological Papers American Museum of Natural History 33 1933
W. Bogoras *The Chukchee*, M.A.M.N.H. 7 1902
N.P. Dyrenkova *Bear Worship among Turkish Tribes of Siberia*, Int. Congress of Americanists, New York 1928
M.G. Levin and L.P. Potapov (ed.) *The Peoples of Siberia* (Engl. transl. S. Dunn), University of Chicago Press 1964
W.M. Mikhailovsky *Shamanism* (Engl. transl.), Comparative Ethnographic Studies, Moscow 1892
H.J. Rink *Tales and Traditions of Eskimo*, London 1875
T.G.E. Powell *The Celts*, London 1958 (new edn 1980)

Chapter 18

1 J. Daniélou and H.I. Marrou *The Christian Centuries, I The First Six Hundred Years* (Engl. transl.), 1964
2 F. Laehr *Die Konstantinische Schenkung in der abendländischen Lit. des Mittelalters bis zur Mitte des XIV Jhts*, 1926
   R.W. Southern *Western Society and the Church in the Middle Ages* (Pelican History of the Church 2), London 1970
3 Bernard Hamilton *Religion in the Medieval West*, London 1986
4 Bede *A History of the English Church and People* (Engl. transl. Leo Sherley-Price), London 1955
5 Bede ibid. iii.1
6 Bede ibid. iv.3
7 Bede ibid. iii.21
8 Bede ibid. ii.13
9 May McKisack *The Fourteenth Century, 1307–1399* (Oxford History of England Vol.5), Oxford 1959
10 Walter Pagel *Paracelsus – an Introduction to Philosophical Medicine in the Era of the Renaissance* (Engl. transl.), London 1958
11 Keith Thomas *Religion and the decline of Magic*, London 1971.
12 C.L. Ewen *Witch Hunting and Witch Trials. The Indictments for Witchcraft from the Records of 1373 Assizes held for the Home Circuit AD 1559–1736*, London 1929
13 J.B. Russell *Witchcraft in the Middle Ages*, London 1972
   Keith Thomas op. cit.
14 G.L. Kittredge *Witchcraft in Old and New England*, 1929, reprinted London 1953.
15 Keith Thomas op. cit.
16 P. Aries *Western Attitudes to Death from the Middle Ages to the Present*, Baltimore 1974
17 Reginald Scot *The Discoverie of Witchcraft*, 1584, New York 1973
18 Ibid.
19 Ibid.

20   Keith Thomas op. cit.
21   Alfons Barb *Survival of Magic Arts*, Oxford U.P. 1963
22   Nicholas Perry and Loreto Echeverría *Under the Heel of Mary*, London and New York 1988
     Keith Thomas op. cit.
23   Bernard Hamilton op. cit.
24   E. Peters *The Magician, the Witch and the Law*, Hassocks 1978
     C.L. Ewen op. cit.
     J.B. Russell op. cit.
25   M. Lambert *Medieval Heresy. Popular Movements from Bogomil to Hus*, London 1977
     Bernard Hamilton op. cit.
26   C.L. Ewen op. cit.
27   Keith Thomas op. cit.
28   J.B. Russell op. cit.
29   Ibid.
     C.L. Ewen op. cit.
30   Ibid.
31   Heinrich Kramer and James Sprenger *Malleus Maleficarum (1486)* (Engl. transl. M. Summers), London 1928, reprinted 1971
32   Keith Thomas op. cit.
33   Ibid.
34   Heinrich Kramer and James Sprenger op. cit.

GENERAL

J.W.C. Wand *A History of the Early Church to AD 500*, London 1937
Henry Chadwick *The Early Church* (Pelican History of the Church 1), London 1967
R.W. Southern *Western Society and the Church in the Middle Ages* (Pelican History of the Church 2), London 1970
The Oxford Dictionary of the Christian Church, ed. F.L. Cross and E.A. Livingstone, 2nd edn 1974
Bernard Hamilton *Religion in the Medieval West*, London 1986
G.L. Kittredge *Witchcraft in Old and New England*, 1929, reprinted London 1953
Keith Thomas *Religion and the Decline of Magic*, London 1971

Chapter 19

1   The Catholic Media Office, London
2   Nicholas Perry and Loreto Echeverría op. cit.
    S. Runciman *The Eastern Schism. A study of the Papacy and the Eastern Churches in the XI and XII centuries*, Oxford 1955
3   André Grabar *Christian Iconography. A Study of its Origins*, London 1969
    Ernst Kitzinger *The Cult of Images before Iconoclasm*, Dumbarton Oaks Papers 8, Cambridge, Mass. 1954
4   A.H.M. Jones *The Later Roman Empire*, London 1964

5   André Grabar *L'Iconoclasme Byzantine. Dossier Archéologique*, Paris 1957
6   Ibid.
7   *The Prayers and Meditations of St Anselm* (Engl. transl. Sister Benedicta Ward), London 1973
8   Ibid.
9   Matthew 26.7 and Mark 14.3
10 Luke 7.37
11 John 12.3
12 Gospel of Philip ii.3.59, Nag Hammadi Library
13 *The Thunder: Perfect Mind* vi.2 19, Nag Hammadi Library
14 Marina Warner *Alone of All Her Sex*, London 1976.
15 Émile Mâle *L'Art Religieux du Douzième Siècle en France*, Paris 1966
16 Alfons Barb *Survival of Magic Arts*, Oxford U.P. 1963
17 Song of Solomon 8.1
18 Song of Solomon 5.4
19 R.V. Sellars *The Council of Chalcedon*, London 1953
20 Marina Warner op. cit.
21 Nicholas Perry and Loreto Echeverría op. cit.
22 Ibid.
23 J. Lafaye *Quetzalcóatl and Guadelupe, The Formation of Mexican National Consciousness 1531–1813* (Engl. transl. B. Keen), Chicago 1976
24 Marina Warner op. cit.
25 Marina Warner ibid.
26 H. Lea *An Historical Sketch of Sacerdotal Celibacy in the Christian Church*, Philadelphia 1867
27 G. Ostrogorsky *A History of the Byzantine State* (Engl. transl. J. Hussey), Oxford 1986
28 S. Runciman *A History of the Crusades* (Vol.1), Cambridge U.P. 1962
29 Nicholas Perry and Loreto Echeverría op. cit.
30 Marina Warner op. cit.
31 *The Life of St Teresa of Avila* (Engl. transl. J.M. Cohen), London 1957

GENERAL

Marina Warner *Alone of All Her Sex*, London 1976
Geoffrey Ashe *The Virgin*, London and New York 1976. Note: (consulted with reservations)
Nicholas Perry and Loreto Echeverría *Under the Heel of Mary*, London and New York 1988

Chapter 20

1   Nicholas Perry and Loreto Echeverría *Under the Heel of Mary*, London and New York 1988
2   Papal Bull *Inneffabilis Deus*, 8 December 1854
3   Papal Bull *Munificentissimus Deus*, 1 November 1950
4   Alan W. Watts *Myth and Ritual in Christianity*, London 1954
5   *Osservatore Romano*, 2 April 1984
6   Nicholas Perry and Loreto Echeverría op. cit.

7   René Laurentin *The Life of Catharine Labouré*, London 1983
8   W.J. Fortier *Our Lady of Salette*, London 1931
9   C.C. Martindale *Bernadette of Lourdes*, Catholic Truth Society, undated
10   Fr. L. Kondor *Fatima in Lucia's Own Words* (Engl. transl. Dominican Nuns of Perpetual Rosary), Fatima 1976
11   G. Hermet *Les Catholiques dans l'Espagne Franquiste*, Paris 1980
    Nicholas Perry and Loreto Echeverría op. cit.
12   D.M. Helming *Footprints in the Snow. A Pictorial Biography of Josemaría Escrivá, the Founder of Opus Dei*, New York and London 1986
13   Nicholas Perry and Loreto Echeverría op. cit.
14   Ibid.
15   M. Helm-Pirgo *Virgin Mary, Queen of Poland*, Polish Inst. of Arts and Sciences in America, New York 1957
16   D.F. Crosby *God, Church and Flag. Senator Joseph R. McCarthy and the Catholic Church 1950–1957*, North Carolina 1978
17   *National Catholic Reporter*, 2 November 1984
    H. Lindsey *The Countdown to Armageddon*, New York 1981
18   J. Edward Vaux *Church Folk Lore* London 1902
19   Ibid.
20   Ibid.
21   Ibid.
22   Ibid.
23   C.E. Schmöger *The Life of Anne Emmerich*, 1870
24   Sir James Frazer *The Golden Bough*, London 1922
25   J. Edward Vaux op. cit.
26   Ibid.
27   Ibid.
28   Ibid.
29   Ibid.
30   Catholic Media Office, London

GENERAL

John Chamber *Book of Days*, c.1604

Postscript

GENERAL

John Steinbeck *To a God Unknown*, London 1935

Index